Infants and Toddlers

CAREGIVING AND RESPONSIVE CURRICULUM DEVELOPMENT

Ninth Edition

Terri Jo Swim

Indiana University–Purdue University

CENGAGE
Learning·

Australia • Brazil • Mexico • Singapore • United Kingdom • United States

Infants and Toddlers: Caregiving and Responsive Curriculum Development, **Ninth Edition**

Terri Jo Swim

Product Director: Marta Lee-Perriard

Product Manager: Mark Kerr

Content Developer: Kassi Radomski

Marketing Manager: Christine Sosa

Managing Developer/Managing Editor: Megan Cotugno

Art and Cover Direction, Production Management, and Composition: MPS Limited

Manufacturing Planner: Doug Bertke

Intellectual Property Analyst: Jennifer Nonenmacher

Intellectual Property Project Manager: Sarah Shainwald

Cover Image Credit: © Crezalyn Nerona Uratsuji/Getty Images

For product information and technology assistance, contact us at **Cengage Learning Customer & Sales Support, 1-800-354-9706.**

For permission to use material from this text or product, submit all requests online at **www.cengage.com/permissions.** Further permissions questions can be e-mailed to **permissionrequest@cengage.com.**

Library of Congress Control Number: 2015945297

Student Edition:
ISBN: 978-1-305-50101-0

Loose-leaf Edition:
ISBN: 978-1-305-63960-7

Cengage Learning
20 Channel Center Street
Boston, MA 02210
USA

Cengage Learning is a leading provider of customized learning solutions with employees residing in nearly 40 different countries and sales in more than 125 countries around the world. Find your local representative at **www.cengage.com.**

Cengage Learning products are represented in Canada by Nelson Education, Ltd.

To learn more about Cengage Learning Solutions, visit **www.cengage.com.**

Purchase any of our products at your local college store or at our preferred online store **www.cengagebrain.com.**

Printed at CLDPC, USA, 04-21

Brief Contents

Contents

PART TWO Establishing a Positive Learning Environment   124

Preface

This revised, expanded, and updated edition was developed with the intention of guiding the reader through the acquisition of skills necessary to provide high-quality care for infants and toddlers in any educational setting. Information based on current theories and research, as well as standards for infant-toddler teacher preparation, is reflected throughout the book. The ninth edition's new subtitle, *Caregiving and Responsive Curriculum Development*, better reflects the book's goal of providing appropriate caregiving and educational techniques, along with curriculum ideas, for groups of very young children and for individual children within those groups. Early childhood educators, administrators, advocates, and parents will find practical information that can be put to immediate use to promote the highest quality care and education possible for all children, birth to age 3.

Major Revisions in the Ninth Edition

As with previous editions, *Infants and Toddlers: Caregiving and Responsive Curriculum Development*, Ninth Edition, strives to bridge the gap between theory and practice. As scholar-practitioners, teachers need to use theory to inform their practice and in turn use their practice to inform theoretical understanding. Building from the strong foundation of previous editions, the text has been updated and thoroughly revised. Although notable differences set this edition apart from the previous edition, points of continuity remain. For example, in this ninth edition, the child continues to be at the center of care and education. Defining infants and toddlers as engaging, decision-making forces within their environments sets a tone of excitement and enthusiasm. No longer can we afford to agree with the description of toddlerhood as the "terrible twos." Rather, we need to embrace the image of the child as capable, competent, and creative. Doing so opens a number of educational options that were unavailable previously.

Results of research on brain structures, functions, and development as well as social and emotional development have been expanded as foundations for this edition. For example, links among cortisol levels, parenting behaviors, and memory skills for very young children are investigated. In addition, incorporating key components of the high-quality infant-toddler and preschool programs in Reggio Emilia, Italy, has improved our understanding of what developmentally appropriate practice looks like in action. Respecting children; designing effective physical, social, and intellectual environments; building partnerships with families; and planning individually appropriate curricula are discussed throughout this edition.

Major content revisions in this edition also include the following:

- **NEW Chapter 10, Early Intervention.** This chapter takes an in-depth look at early intervention. It was created based on reviewer feedback that indicated a need for a clearer focus on the care of and interventions for infants and toddlers with special rights. Chapter 10 now highlights the importance of collaboration among family members, caregivers, and intervention specialists.

- **NEW Chapter 14, Developmentally Appropriate Content.** Given the national preoccupation with school readiness, a new chapter, Developmentally Appropriate Content (Chapter 14), is now available. Older toddlers are ready to explore and experience fine arts, science, mathematics, literacy, and social studies. However, much guidance is provided on how to do this in a way that complements and heightens young children's curiosity. In other words, these content areas must be taught through engaging, integrated projects, rather than in terms of isolated facts.

- **NEW combined chapters.** In response to reviewer feedback, the chapters that discuss infant and toddler development have been combined to eliminate repetition of content. So Chapters 10, 11, and 12 in the eighth edition, which spanned birth to 12 months, are now covered in Chapter 11, Teaching Children Birth to Twelve Months. The content in Chapters 13 and 14 in the eighth edition, which covered children from 12 to 24 months, now appears in the ninth edition's Chapter 12, Teaching Children Twelve to Twenty-Four Months. Finally, the eighth edition content in Chapters 15 and 16 now appears in Chapter 13, Teaching Children Twenty-Four to Thirty-Six Months, in the ninth edition.

- **NEW research results.** Results of new research and scholarly articles have been incorporated into each chapter. For example, new research on social and emotional development can be found in Chapter 3, Social and Emotional Development; current thoughts about how aggression may be normative behavior for toddlers is in Chapter 6, Building Relationships and Guiding Behaviors; and new information on compliance for supporting health and safety guidelines can be found in Chapter 8, The Indoor and Outdoor Learning Environments.

- **NEW concept coverage.** Chapter 3 has a new Spotlight on Research box that focuses on Effortful Control, a newer concept being investigated by researchers.

New Instructional Features

To help aid the student's comprehension and understanding of infant-toddler development and learning, several new instructional features have been created for the ninth edition.

- **A Lesson Plan** now appears at the end of each chapter and can be digitally downloaded. (They are called Professional Resource Downloads.) The goal of this feature is to provide examples of lesson plans that are grounded in observations of a young child and are respectful and engaging through the use of responsive strategies.

- **Learning Objectives and Standards Addressed** are now listed at the beginning of each chapter. The learning objectives correlate directly with major sections in the chapter, as well as with the Summary at the end of each chapter.

In each chapter, the list of Standards Addressed includes the related 2010 NAEYC Standards for Initial and Advanced Early Childhood Professional Preparation Programs, NAEYC's Developmentally Appropriate Practices, and the NAEYC standards specific to infant and toddler care.

- **Family and Community Connection** boxed feature, which is now included in every chapter, is intended to assist the readers in applying strategies for engaging family and community agencies in the care and education of young children. Each box contains a number of questions to spark thinking about important concepts.

Enduring Instructional Features

- **A focus on professional standards** with a Standards Correlation Chart on the book's inside front cover, which offers an at-a-glance view of where discussions related to NAEYC's Standards for Early Childhood Professional Preparation and Developmentally Appropriate Practice guidelines can be found. In addition, the DAP icon DAP focuses readers on principles of developmentally appropriate practice throughout the text.

- **Spotlight boxed feature** highlights key research topics, professional child care organizations, the personal experiences of child care professionals to enhance the book's real-world perspective.

- In **Spotlight on Practice** "Voices from the Field," found in Chapters 11–14, practicing teachers apply and reflect on concepts discussed in the chapter. For example, in Chapter 14, a teacher discusses how she incorporates literacy in her room by using local community resources, and she reflects on how a specific child reacted to her selection of books.

- **Reading Checkpoints** included throughout each chapter help to improve comprehension by asking students to pause and consider what they have just read.

- Revised **Case Studies** present real-life examples of the concepts and principles discussed. The content of those cases, such as diversity or special rights, is now highlighted in the title of the Case Study.

- Updated references can be found at the end of the text.

- A list of developmental milestones for children from birth to 36 months is provided in Appendix A for the four major areas of development, which assists caregivers in recording observations and assessing each child's current level of development.

- Appendices C and D have been updated to provide a current list of board and picture books that are appropriate to use with infants and toddlers.

- The text is current and comprehensive so that caregivers can acquire the skills necessary to function at nationally accepted standards of quality.

- The level of the language used is easy to follow and offers practical examples for self-study by caregivers-in-training.

Text Organization

Part I Understanding the Foundations of Professional Education

This section prepares the reader as a professional educator who possesses the knowledge, skills, and dispositions necessary to meet effectively the developmental and learning needs of infants and toddlers. An overview of the theories and research in the fields of child development and early childhood education, including new information on brain development and attachment, helps lay that foundation.

- **Chapter 1** highlights the importance of taking a developmental perspective when working with infants and toddlers as well as an overview of trends in education and development that influence learning environments for very young children.

- **Chapter 2** creates a framework for understanding the growth and development of physical and cognitive/language areas from birth to 36 months.

- **Chapter 3** focuses on growth and development in the emotional and social areas from birth to 36 months. In both Chapters 2 and 3, sections are devoted to expanding the readers' information on brain development.

- **Chapter 4** presents the master tools of caregiving—Attention, Approval, and Attunement—as a model of conscious caregiving, combining practical principles and techniques from current theories and research in the field.

- **Chapter 5** describes specific knowledge bases that professional educators acquire through informal and formal educational opportunities. One such knowledge base involves the appropriate assessment of children. This chapter, then, focuses on various observational tools for tracking development and learning, and how to use the data as the groundwork for other aspects of the caregiver's work.

Part 2 Establishing a Positive Learning Environment

Four chapters provide the reader with details about how to create appropriate environments for very young children. Learning environments include consciously building the physical, social, and intellectual elements of the classroom. No longer can professional educators attend to the physical arrangement and placement of equipment and materials to the exclusion of the socioemotional and intellectual climates created among adults and children.

- **Chapter 6** uses key components of educational philosophy found in the schools in Reggio Emilia, Italy, as the foundation for creating a caring community of learners. Respectful and effective communication and guidance strategies are outlined.

- **Chapter 7** is devoted to appropriate communication strategies to use when creating reciprocal relationships with family members and colleagues. Family situations that may require additional support from the caregiver, the program, or community agencies are presented.

- **Chapter 8** covers components of high-quality and developmentally appropriate indoor and outdoor learning environments from the teachers', children's, and society's perspectives and presents common health and safety issues for children.

- **Chapter 9** presents practical techniques for designing the intellectual environment. Curriculum—both routine care times and planned learning experiences—must be specially designed to enhance the development and learning of *each* child. Emphasis is placed on engaging in project work with infants and toddlers.

Part 3 Developing Responsive Curriculum

This part explores strategies for designing curriculum that reflects current levels of development and learning. Two new chapters have been added to this section, and the other three have been significantly reorganized.

- **Chapter 10**, a new chapter, covers early intervention for infants, toddlers, and families. It explores not only how we should approach early intervention from a strengths perspective but also common characteristics of children with special rights.

- **Chapters 11–13** explore tasks, materials, and specific learning experiences to enhance development for children from birth to thirty-six months. Now, each of these chapters focuses on working with children in a one-year age range. This practical section provides specific techniques, teaching strategies, and solutions to many of the common problems confronted when addressing the rapid growth and development of infants and toddlers.

- **Chapter 14**, which is also new, builds on information provided throughout the text as it investigates strategies for supporting content area learning for infants and toddlers. Central concepts for emergent literacy, mathematics, fine arts, social studies, and science are provided.

Supplements

MindTap™: The Personal Learning Experience

MindTap for Swim, *Infants and Toddlers: Caregiving and Responsive Curriculum Development*, Ninth Edition, represents a new approach to teaching and learning. A highly personalized, fully customizable learning platform with an integrated e-portfolio, MindTap helps students to elevate thinking by guiding them to do the following:

- Know, remember, and understand concepts critical to becoming a great teacher.

- Apply concepts, create curriculum and tools, and demonstrate performance and competency in key areas in the course, including national and state education standards.

- Prepare artifacts for the portfolio and eventual state licensure to launch a successful teaching career.

- Develop the habits to become a reflective practitioner.

As students move through each chapter's Learning Path, they engage in a scaffolded learning experience, designed to move them up Bloom's Taxonomy, from lower- to higher-order thinking skills. The Learning Path enables preservice students to develop these skills and gain confidence by:

- Engaging them with chapter topics and activating their prior knowledge by watching and answering questions about authentic videos of teachers teaching and children learning in real classrooms

- Checking their comprehension and understanding through Did You Get It? assessments, with varied question types that are autograded for instant feedback

- Applying concepts through mini-case studies—students analyze typical teaching and learning situations, and then create a reasoned response to the issue(s) presented in the scenario

- Reflecting about and justifying the choices they made within the teaching scenario problem

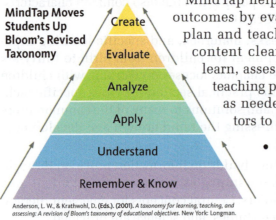

MindTap Moves Students Up Bloom's Revised Taxonomy

Anderson, L. W., & Krathwohl, D. (Eds.). (2001). *A taxonomy for learning, teaching, and assessing: A revision of Bloom's taxonomy of educational objectives.* New York: Longman.

MindTap helps instructors facilitate better outcomes by evaluating how future teachers plan and teach lessons in ways that make content clear and help diverse students learn, assessing the effectiveness of their teaching practice, and adjusting teaching as needed. MindTap enables instructors to facilitate better outcomes by:

- Making grades visible in real time through the Student Progress App so students and instructors always have access to current standings in the class

- Using the Outcome Library to embed national education standards and align them to student learning activities, and also allowing instructors to add their state's standards or any other desired outcome

- Allowing instructors to generate reports on students' performance with the click of a mouse against any standards or outcomes that are in their MindTap course

- Giving instructors the ability to assess students on state standards or other local outcomes by editing existing or creating their own MindTap activities, and then by aligning those activities to any state or other outcomes that the instructor has added to the MindTap Outcome Library

MindTap for Swim, *Infants and Toddlers: Caregiving and Responsive Curriculum Development*, Ninth Edition, helps instructors easily set their course because it integrates into the existing Learning Management System and saves instructors time by allowing them to fully customize any aspect of the Learning Path. Instructors can change the order of the student learning activities, hide activities they don't want for the course, and—most importantly—create custom assessments and add any standards, outcomes, or content they do want (e.g., YouTube videos, Google docs). Learn more at www.cengage.com/mindtap.

Online Instructor's Manual with Test Bank

An online Instructor's Manual accompanies this book. It contains information to assist the instructor in designing the course, including sample syllabi, discussion questions, teaching and learning activities, field experiences, learning objectives, and additional online resources. For assessment support, the updated test bank includes true/false, multiple-choice, matching, short-answer, and essay questions for each chapter.

PowerPoint Lecture Slides

These vibrant Microsoft PowerPoint lecture slides for each chapter assist you with your lecture by providing concept coverage using images, figures, and tables directly from the textbook.

Cognero

Cengage Learning Testing Powered by Cognero is a flexible online system that allows you to author, edit, and manage test bank content from multiple Cengage Learning solutions; create multiple test versions in an instant; and deliver tests from your Learning Management System (LMS), your classroom, or wherever you want.

About the Author

TERRI JO SWIM, PH.D., is a professor and Chair of the Department of Educational Studies at Indiana University–Purdue University in Fort Wayne, Indiana. She has taught in higher education institutions for almost 20 years. In addition, she has worked in private child care centers, university-based laboratory programs, and summer camps with children from birth to 13 years of age. Terri was a co-editor of *The Hope for Audacity: Recapturing Optimism and Civility in Education*. Her current research interests include infant–toddler and preschool curriculum, Reggio Emilia, documentation, and teacher education.

Questions or discussions on any topics covered in the book can be sent to her at the e-mail address below.

TERRI JO SWIM

swimt@ipfw.edu

Acknowledgments

This Ninth Edition of *Infants and Toddlers: Caregiving and Responsive Curriculum Development* would not have been possible without the influence, loyalty, and positive influence of the following very exceptional people.

Special thanks goes to my husband, Danny—without you, I would starve, both physically and emotionally! To the rest of my immediate and extended family members—each of you have taught me much about the importance of strong attachments. To all of my students, thanks for the feedback on earlier versions of the text—it is improved because of you! Thank you to Gina Wilson for her assistance with updating Appendix C.

To Mark Kerr, product development manager, Kassi Radomski, content developer, and other staff at Cengage Learning and MPS Limited for continued support and guidance during product development and production.

To the following reviewers of the eighth edition, whose feedback was used to help us make decisions about the revisions that were needed in this edition, we thank you for your candid feedback and support:

Laurel Anderson, *Palomar College*

Teresa Bridger, *Prince George Community College*

Margaret Dana-Conway, *Norwalk Community College*

Evia Davis, *Langston University*

Jennifer DeFrance, *Three Rivers Community College*

Marissa Happ, *Aurora University*

Jeannie Morgan-Campola, *Rowan Cabarrus Community College*

Bridget Murray, *Henderson Community College*

Sandra Own, *Cincinnati State*

Boyoung Park, *Radford University*

Stacey Pistorova, *Terra State Community College*

Wendy Ruiz, *College of the Canyons*

Pamela Sebura, *Saint Mary-of-the-Woods College*

Jacque Taylor, *Greenville Technical College*

Linda Taylor, *Ball State University*

Cheryl Williams-Jackson, *Modesto Junior College*

Eileen Yantz, *Gaston College*

1
CHAPTER

Taking a Developmental Perspective

Learning Objectives

After reading this chapter, you should be able to:

1-1 Determine how the four major developmental areas for assessment differ from one another.

1-2 Explain the theories of child development.

1-3 Justify how the use of Bronfenbrenner's ecological systems theory explains current trends in development and education.

1-4 Recognize the impact of each individual child's culture on classroom interactions and curriculum.

Standards Addressed in This Chapter

naeyc **NAEYC Standards for Early Childhood Professional Preparation**

1 Promoting Child Development and Learning

DAP **Developmentally Appropriate Practice Guidelines**

1 Creating a Caring Community of Learners

In addition, the NAEYC standards for developmentally appropriate practice are divided into six areas particularly important to infant/toddler care. The following areas are addressed in this chapter: *Relationship between Caregiver and Child*, and *Policies*.

© 2017 Cengage Learning

Never before in our history do we know so much about the importance of the infant and toddler years. New brain scan technologies allow us to unobtrusively peak into the developing brain to understand how very young children's brains are being wired. The results show us amazing rates and patterns of development in response to the type and amount of caregiving received, the nutrition provided, and the environmental factors such as exposure to trauma, violence, or maternal depression. The role of early childhood educators is more significant than ever. As a result, educators need to learn more theories, principles, and skills to keep pace with the demands of their profession.

Child care settings are powerful contexts for influencing the development and learning of very young children. High standards require that teachers learn to take good care of both themselves and the children, and to be aware of the interests, abilities, and desires of the child, family, community, and society as a whole. Part 1 provides current trends in caring for infants and toddlers, theories and principles of child development, and a structure for caregiving that helps prepare the caregiver for the challenging and rewarding profession of early childhood education.

This edition continues to emphasize science and new discoveries by researchers (e.g., on brain development and attachment) as well as the influences these findings have on caregiver behavior when working with very young children. By closely observing and recording the behaviors of children, the child care specialist will create a powerful framework to use in caring for and educating infants and toddlers.

When you finish Part 1 of this book, you'll have the knowledge and principles necessary to care for children effectively and enhance the development of each child through your direct, intentional interactions. Parts 2 and 3 build on this base of knowledge to give you all the specific skills, techniques, strategies, and activities needed to function confidently as a professional.

Even though your work is vital within your classroom and educational program, it can't stop there. Early childhood educators need to use the information gained from this text to advocate for collective responsibility and commitment to all children from birth to age 3. The next generations deserve nothing less from us.

What do people who work with young children need to know, and what do they need to be able to do? Early childhood educators* have long debated these questions. For almost a century, people from all areas of the field and all corners of the world have worked to answer these two key questions as well. Current research has helped early childhood specialists clearly define a core body of knowledge, as well as standards for quality in both teacher preparation and in programming for young children. Scholarly research has validated what early childhood professionals have always known intuitively: the quality of young children's experience in early care and education settings is directly related to the knowledge, skills, and dispositions of the adults caring for them.

Today's theories and philosophies regarding child development and learning have evolved over time and have been influenced by both

---

*In this book, the terms *early childhood educator, teacher, caregiver,* and *primary caregiver* will be used interchangeably to describe adults who care for and educate infants and toddlers. Other terms, such as early childhood specialist, educarer, practitioner, staff, child care teacher, head teacher, assistant teacher, or family child care provider, might also be familiar. The use of these four terms is not intended to narrow the focus of professionals discussed in this book or to minimize a particular title, rather the purpose is to provide some consistency in language.

ancient and modern society and thought. They are the direct result of early childhood professionals and scientists building on previous theories and research to better understand children today.

How teachers use and apply the developmental theories depends not only on their understanding of those theories and associated research but also on their personal beliefs and dispositions. Because we are unable to attend to every aspect of an interaction, our mind filters and categorizes information at astonishing speeds. Our beliefs impact not only how our brain does this work but also how we make sense of the information after it is available. Matusov, DePalma, and Drye (2007) suggest that adults' responses constantly and actively impact the trajectory of development of children. Thus, teachers participate in "… co-constructing the observed phenomenon of development" (p. 410) such that "development defines an observer no less than the observed" (p. 419). In other words, what we observe and what we think the observations mean are as much a reflection of us (our beliefs and knowledge bases) as it is a reflection of the child we observed. This is illustrated in conversations between two adults after observing the same event. They each describe the actions, behaviors, and implications of the phenomenon differently. Thus, recognizing how teachers shape the development of children must subsequently result in the opening of dialogue and communication.

These points are made so that you'll take an active role in reflecting on your own beliefs and how they are changing as you read this book and interact with infants and toddlers. Developing the "habit of mind" for careful professional and personal analysis will assist you in thinking about your role as an educator.

1-1 Developmental Areas

The structure of this book allows for the philosophy that the author believes is most helpful in child care settings. The major contributions of early childhood theorists are presented within this structure. This philosophy, which follows a *Developmental Perspective*, states that teachers and other adults must be consciously aware of how a child is progressing in each area to create environments that facilitate her ideal development. Unlike the tabula rasa theory of the past, which claimed that children are molded to parental or societal specifications, current research indicates that each child's genetic code engages in a complex interaction with environmental factors to result in the realization (or not) of her full potential.

A child born with a physical disability such as spina bifida may not realize as much potential in certain areas as a child born neurologically intact, and a child whose ancestry dictates adult height less than five feet will most likely not realize the potential to play professional basketball. However, within these limiting genetic and environmental factors, every child has the potential for a fulfilling and productive life, depending on how well his or her abilities are satisfied and challenged, and to what extent the skills necessary to become a happy and successful adult are fostered by family members and caregivers.

As you can see, from the moment of birth, the child and the people around the child affect each other. This dynamic interaction is sometimes deliberate and controlled and sometimes unconscious behavior. Caregivers working with infants and toddlers plan many experiences for children.

Simultaneous with these planned experiences are the thousands of actions that are spontaneous, that stimulate new actions and reactions, and that challenge both the child and the caregiver. Teachers must learn to be mindful in all of their interactions.

Magda Gerber (Gerber & Weaver, 1998) has established an approach and structure for child care that emphasizes mindful interaction between child and caregiver. This approach is illustrated through her "10 principles of caregiving."

1. Involve children in activities and things that concern them.
2. Invest in quality time with each child.
3. Learn the unique ways each child communicates with you and teach him or her the ways you communicate.
4. Invest the time and energy necessary with each child to build a total person.
5. Respect infants and toddlers as worthy people.
6. Model specific behaviors before you teach them.
7. Always be honest with children about your feelings.
8. View problems as learning opportunities and allow children to solve their own problems where possible.
9. Build security with children by teaching trust.
10. Be concerned about the quality of development each child has at each stage.

Interactions that reflect these principles focus on the development of the whole child; that is, attention to cognitive development is not at the expense of social or physical development. When teachers who are new to the profession are required to think about all of the areas of development at once, they can become overwhelmed. Child development knowledge, in this situation, can be divided into distinct, yet interrelated, areas for easy understanding. It is important to note that no area of development functions in isolation from another. This division is arbitrary and is done for the ease of the learner, you. For children, the areas of development come together and operate as a whole, producing an entirely unique individual. Table 1–1 lists the four developmental domains that will be used in this book. Coming to understand the four individual areas well is necessary for you to promote optimal development for each child in your care.

A major goal of this book is to help caregivers understand normal sequences and patterns of development and to become familiar with learning

TABLE 1–1 ▶ Developmental Domains

AREA I	**Physical:** height, weight, general motor coordination, brain development, and so on
AREA II	**Emotional:** feelings, self-perception, confidence, security, and so on
AREA III	**Social:** interactions with peers, elders, and youngsters, both one-on-one and in a group, social perspective-taking, and so on
AREA IV	**Cognitive/Language:** reasoning, problem solving, concept formation, verbal communication, and so on

© Cengage Learning

tools that enhance development in the four major developmental areas. After you understand the normative patterns or **milestones**, you can more easily recognize and honor the unique patterns that each child demonstrates. Throughout this book, you'll learn to evaluate the development of an individual child by comparing milestone behaviors with the larger group that was used to establish normative behavior for that age. Therefore, necessary aspects of preparing to be an infant/toddler teacher are learning to observe children carefully, record those observations, and analyze that data. After individual parts are understood, early childhood educators can apply the knowledge to care for the whole, constantly changing child in a competent manner.

milestones Specific behaviors common to an entire population that are used to track development and are observed when they are first or consistently manifested.

1-2 Theories of Child Development

Before the Reformation in sixteenth-century Europe, little importance was placed on children; they were considered little adults. With the Reformation and the Puritan belief in *original sin* came harsh, restrictive child-rearing practices and the belief that it was the "duty of the responsible adult to control the child's willfulness and stifle acting-out urges with stern, powerful, and consistent discipline" (Lally, 2006, p. 10).

The seventeenth-century Enlightenment brought new theories of human dignity and respect. Young children were viewed much more humanely. For example, John Locke, a British philosopher, advanced the theory that a child is a *tabula rasa*, or blank slate. According to his theory, children were not basically evil but were completely molded and formed by their early experiences with the adults around them (Locke, 1690/1892).

An important philosopher of the eighteenth century, Jean-Jacques Rousseau, viewed young children as *noble savages* who are naturally born with a sense of right and wrong and an innate ability for orderly, healthy growth (1762/1955). His theory, the first child-centered approach, advanced an important concept still accepted today: the idea of **stages** of child development.

stages Normal patterns of development that most people go through in maturation, first described by Jean-Jacques Rousseau.

During the late 1800s, Charles Darwin's theories of *natural selection* and *survival of the fittest* strongly influenced ideas on child development and care (1859/1936). Darwin's research on many animal species led him to hypothesize that all animals were descendants of a few common ancestors. Darwin's careful observations of child behaviors resulted in the birth of the science of child study.

At the turn of the twentieth century, G. Stanley Hall was inspired by Darwin. Hall worked with one of Darwin's students, Arnold Gesell, to advance the *maturational perspective* that child development is genetically determined and unfolds automatically—leading to universal characteristics or events during particular time periods (Gesell, 1928). Thus, Hall and Gesell are considered founders of the child study movement because of their **normative approach** of observing large numbers of children to establish average or normal expectations (Berk, 2012). At the same time, in France, Alfred Binet was establishing the first operational definition of intelligence by using the normative approach to standardize his intelligence test.

normative approach Observing large numbers of children to establish average or normal expectations of when a particular skill or ability is present.

psychosocial theory Erikson's stage theory of development, including trust, autonomy, identity, and intimacy.

Erik Erikson created the **psychosocial theory** of child development. Erikson's (1950) theory, which is still used in child care today, predicted several stages of development, including the development of trust, autonomy, identity, and intimacy. How these stages are dealt with by family members and teachers determines an individual's capacity to contribute to society and experience a happy, successful life.

behaviorism School of psychology that studies stimuli, responses, and rewards that influence behavior.

While Erikson greatly influenced the fields of child development and care, a parallel approach was being studied, called **behaviorism**. John Watson, the father of behaviorism, in a historic experiment, taught an 11-month-old named Albert to fear a neutral stimulus (a soft white rat) by presenting the rat several times accompanied by loud noises. Watson and his followers used experiments in *classical conditioning* to promote the idea that the environment is the primary factor determining the growth and development of children. Skinner and Belmont (1993) expanded Watson's theories of classical conditioning to demonstrate that child behaviors can be increased or decreased by applying *positive reinforcers* (rewards), such as praise, and *negative reinforcers* (punishment), such as criticism and withdrawal of attention.

social learning theories A body of theory that adds social influences to behaviorism to explain development.

During the 1950s, **social learning theories** became popular. Proponents of these theories, led by Albert Bandura, accepted the principles of behaviorism and enlarged on conditioning to include social influences such as *modeling, imitation,* and *observational learning* to explain how children develop (Grusec, 1992).

cognitive developmental theory Piaget's theory that children construct knowledge and awareness through manipulation and exploration of their environment.

Jean Piaget is one theorist who has influenced the modern fields of child development and care more than any other. **Cognitive developmental theory** predicts that children construct knowledge and awareness through manipulation and exploration of the environment, and that cognitive development occurs through observable stages (Beilin, 1992). Piaget's stages of cognitive development have stimulated a significant body of research on children, and his influences have helped teachers view young children as active participants in their own growth and development. Piaget's contributions have many practical applications for teachers.

attachment theory A theory that infants are born needing an emotional attachment to their primary caregiver.

Attachment theory was developed on the premise that infants need a strong emotional attachment to their primary caregiver. This theory examines how early care, especially relationships between adults and children, impacts later development. Bowlby (1969/2000), after observing children between the ages of one and four years in post–World War II hospitals and institutions who had been separated from their families, concluded that "the infant and young child should experience a warm and continuous relationship with his mother (or permanent mother substitute) in which both find satisfaction and enjoyment" to grow up mentally healthy (p. 13). Relying heavily on *ethological* concepts, he proposed that a baby's attachment behaviors (e.g., smiling, crying, clinging) are innate and that they mature at various times during the first two years of life (Bowlby, 1958). The ethological purpose of these behaviors is to keep the infant close to the mother, who keeps the child out of harm's way (Honig, 2002). However, the quality of attachment is not just determined by the infant's behavior. The caregiver's responses to the attachment behaviors serve to create a foundation for their relationship to develop (see Oppenheim & Koren-Karie, 2002). Attachment history has been associated with emotional, social, and learning outcomes later in life (see Copple, 2012) and has been very influential on classroom practices.

Over the past one to two decades, technologies, such as innovations in noninvasive neuroscience imaging techniques, have begun to significantly impact our understanding of brain development. It was once believed that nature, or the basic genetic makeup of a child, played a dominant role in determining both short- and long-term cognitive developmental outcomes. Newer technologies allow for close examination of nurture, or environmental impacts, on the same outcomes. Scientists have found that harmful, stressful, or neglectful behaviors early in life can affect the development of the brain, potentially leading to lifelong difficulties (Carlson, Hostinar, Mliner, & Gunnar, 2014; Center on the Developing Child at Harvard University, 2011; Nelson, Bos, Gunnar, & Sonuga-Barke, 2011). The quality and consistency of early care will affect how a child develops, learns, copes with, and handles life. The more quality interactions you have with the children in your care, the more opportunities you create for positive development.

Another theory of child development is the **ecological systems theory** developed by Urie Bronfenbrenner, an American psychologist. Bronfenbrenner (1995) expanded the view of influences on young children by hypothesizing four nested structures that affect development (see Figure 1–1).

ecological systems theory
Bronfenbrenner's theory of nested environmental systems that influence the development and behavior of people.

FIGURE 1–1 ▶ Model of Urie Bronfenbrenner's Ecological Systems Theory

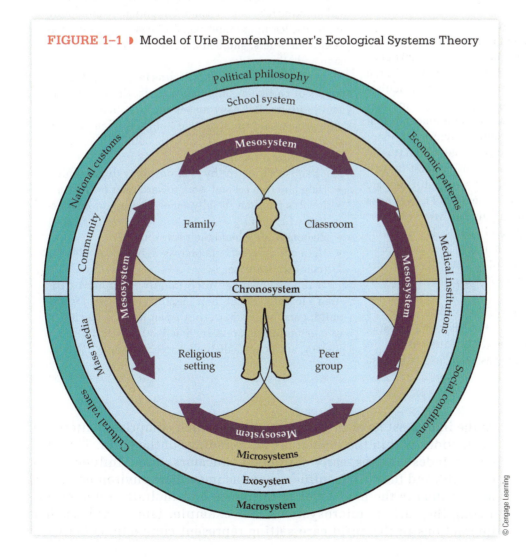

© Cengage Learning

Spotlight on Research

ESSENTIAL LIFE SKILLS FOR INFANTS

Ellen Galinsky outlines in her book, *Mind in the Making: The Seven Essential Life Skills Every Child Needs* (2010), what parents, educators, and community members must know to help children grow and develop optimally. She expertly weaves together research on brain development, social development, emotional development, and environmental influences on those processes to draw her conclusions. As the title indicates, there are seven essential life skills that must be developed for young children:

- Focus and controlling oneself
- Perspective taking
- Communicating
- Making connections
- Critical thinking
- Taking on challenges
- Self-directed, engaged learning

One overarching theme of this book is recognizing and building on the competencies of very young children. Research continues to illuminate how children have remarkable skills long before they can articulate what they are thinking. For example, infants and toddlers are capable of demonstrating brain functions that manage attention, emotions, and behaviors in pursuit of goals (i.e., executive functions) (p. 39); 18-month-old children can take the perspective of an adult (p. 81); infants can read adults' emotional cues to differentiate a range of emotions (p. 113); 6-month-old babies have number sense and can distinguish an array of 8 versus 16 dots (p. 169); and 6- and 10-month-old infants demonstrate people sense when they indicate a preference for the character in a play that helped another (rather than the character who hindered another; pp. 212–213).

A significant contribution of this book is Galinsky's description of the seven essential life skills as being "social-emotional-intellectual (SEI) skills" (p. 71). In other words, current research has elucidated how these essential life skills reflect the multifaceted interplay between those three areas of development. Parents, teachers, and community members can no longer continue to treat these complex skills in simplistic and isolated ways; we must recognize how each area of development works with other areas to result in complex understanding and behaviors.

This book not only blends data generated from rigorous research with interviews of those researchers but also provides practical suggestions that parents and teachers can use to promote brain development via these seven essential skills. For example, Chapter 1 provides 19 suggestions to promote the development of focus and self-control such as encouraging pretend play because it promotes the development of the working memory and playing sorting games with changing rules because they support cognitive flexibility. Critical thinking (Chapter 5) can be supported by promoting curiosity, learning from "experts," evaluating information from others, and being a critical viewer of television and other media.

The last essential skill (self-directed, engaged learning) is of particular importance for teachers of infants and toddlers. Galinsky makes the case that research supports seven principles that help "children unleash their passionate desire to learn" (p. 300). Following are some of those principles:

- Establish a trustworthy relationship with each child.
- Help children set and work toward their own goals.
- Involve children socially, emotionally, and intellectually in learning.
- Elaborate and extend their learning.
- Help children become increasingly accountable for their own learning.

When teachers act intentionally to support children's learning about their passions (e.g., cars for one child, cats for another), they open up new worlds of understanding in areas such as mathematics, history, literacy, and science that will serve them for a lifetime.

---

microsystem Bronfenbrenner's term for the innermost level of influence found in the immediate surroundings of the child, such as parents or an early childhood educator.

At the innermost level is the **microsystem**, which comprises patterns of interactions within the immediate surroundings of the child. This system includes families, early childhood educators, direct influences on the child, and the child's influence on the immediate environment. The **mesosystem** is the next level of influence and includes interactions among the various microsystems. For example, family and teacher interactions in the child care setting represent connections between home and school that impact the child's development. The **exosystem** includes influences with which the child is not directly involved that affect development and care, such as parent education, parent workplace, and the quality and availability of health and social services. The **macrosystem** consists of the values, laws, resources, and customs of the general culture in which a child is raised. This theory has wide applications in understanding and categorizing the factors that affect child care.

The final developmental theory to be discussed here is **sociocultural theory**. A Russian psychologist, Lev Semenovich Vygotsky, hypothesized that culture, meaning the values, beliefs, and customs of a social group, is passed on to the next generation through social interactions between children and their elders (1934/1986). Those social interactions must be at the appropriate level for learning to occur. Adults must observe and assess each child's individual levels of performance as well as her assisted levels of performance on a given task to judge what supports (also known as scaffolding) are necessary for promoting learning (Berk & Winsler, 1995; Bodrova & Leong, 2007), social or emotional development (Morcom, 2014), and play (Leong & Bodrova, 2012). Cross-cultural research has supported this theory through findings that young children from various cultures develop unique skills and abilities that are not present in other cultures (Berk, 2012).

mesosystem Bronfenbrenner's term for the second level of influence for the child that involves interactions among microsystems, such as a teacher in a child care center and family members.

exosystem Bronfenbrenner's term for the influences that are not a direct part of a child's experience but influence development, such as parent education.

macrosystem Bronfenbrenner's term for influences on development from the general culture, including laws and customs.

sociocultural theory Vygotsky's theory on development that predicts how cultural values, beliefs, and concepts are passed from one generation to the next.

1-2a Unique Patterns of Development

These theories differ in their view of various controversies in development (McDevitt & Ormrod, 2013). For the purposes of this chapter, the focus will be placed on the controversy of universal versus unique patterns of development. Theories on the universal end of the continuum (see Figure 1–2) state that development stages or accomplishments are common to all children. As you can tell from the preceding descriptions, some theorists such as Piaget and Gesell describe development as occurring in set patterns for all children. In other words, there are universal trends in cognitive reasoning and physical development. From these perspectives, if you know a child's age, you can predict with some degree of confidence how that child might think or act.

On the other end of the controversy, theories espousing a unique view of development suggest that patterns of development cannot be determined or predicted because environmental factors impact each child differently. Ecological systems and sociocultural theories are both examples on this end of the continuum. These theorists did not believe that teachers could predict a child's behaviors or abilities by knowing a child's age

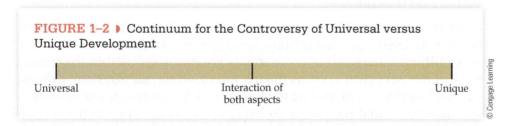

FIGURE 1–2 ▶ Continuum for the Controversy of Universal versus Unique Development

Universal   Interaction of   Unique
                             both aspects

© Cengage Learning

PHOTO 1–1 Toddlers share many characteristics, yet they are all developmentally unique.

or where stage of development. Each child is unique in his or her progression of skills, knowledge, and behaviors (Photo 1–1).

Some theories of development are at neither end of the continuum. Rather, they fall somewhere in the middle, suggesting that development is representative of both controversies. Attachment theory, for example, is based on the belief that all children experience similar phases; yet, the relationship each child has with her caregivers greatly impacts the type of attachment displayed.

It must be kept in mind that the United States is a world leader in the fields of child development and care, but we cannot assume that research findings on developmental skills and abilities from one group of children (e.g., Caucasian American) directly apply to other cultures or subcultures (Diaz Soto & Swadener, 2002; Fleer & Hedegaard, 2010; Lee & Johnson, 2007; Matusov et al., 2007). Only through taking a developmental perspective and paying close attention to universal and unique patterns of development as well as cultural influences will we be able to determine the practices to optimally enhance the growth and development of individual infants and toddlers.

READING CHECKPOINT

Before moving on with your reading, make sure that you can answer the following questions about the material discussed so far.

1. Justify why an infant-toddler teacher should employ a developmental perspective in his work.
2. Explain what the four developmental domains are and why it is useful, yet artificial, to divide development in this manner.
3. Select two developmental theories. Compare and contrast them; in other words, explain how they are alike and how they are different.

1-3 Current Trends in Development and Education

Current child care trends considered in this section reflect the research being completed concerning brain development, attachment theory, and sociocultural theory. All of these trends are discussed within the framework of the ecological systems theory: microsystem, mesosystem, exosystem, and macrosystem. In this theory, human relationships are described as bidirectional and reciprocal. *Relating* is the act of being with someone and sharing the same space and setting, expressing needs and accepting responsibility for interacting with each other. Interactions are respectful to all parties involved.

The recommendation to respect children is also expressed by the educational leaders of the infant and toddler centers of Reggio Emilia, Italy. These professionals believe that all children have rights, which include, among other things, the right to be held in high regard and treated respectfully. This book emphasizes that the teacher be mindful of positive intentions toward the child and engage in reflective, careful planning, resulting in good outcomes for both.

1-3a Microsystem Trends

Trends in the microsystem involve effects that adults and children have on each other. For example, an adult who consciously uses attention, approval, and attunement with children elicits a positive response from them. Any third party who is present may also be affected. How this person is affected is determined by whether or not the reciprocal relationship is positive or negative. If the people interacting are supportive, the quality of the relationship is enhanced.

The microsystem is the closest system to the child. It contains the child, the immediate nuclear family, and others directly related to the child. Development of the child is directly impacted by the contexts in which the child is being raised and the child directly impacts those same contexts. In other words, bidirectional influences are at play. Gabbard and Krebs (2012) theorized about the importance of considering physical development from Bronfenbrenner's perspective. They suggest that family members can constrain development (e.g., placing an infant in a crib for long periods of time), or they can support and enhance development (e.g., providing toys, materials, and space that encourage a variety of motoric activities). Yet, a child that craves movement can resist being placed in a crib for too long, resulting in an adult changing her location and providing new physical experiences.

Until the recent recession, the trend over the past 20 years has been for more and more children to have parents who work outside the home and to live in single-parent households. One direct consequence of these changes is that more children receive nonfamilial care in the United States than ever before. Child care settings, then, have become an important aspect of the microsystem. Approximately 60 percent of the infants, toddlers, and preschool children aged 5 or younger (not enrolled in kindergarten) in the United States are in at least one weekly nonparental child care arrangement (Mamedova & Redford, 2013). The most prevalent type of care children experience is center-based care, followed by relative care, and then nonrelative care. These children have widespread cultural differences in customs, family structure, and parenting styles. For example, children experience living with one parent, two parents, or grandparents. In addition, more and more children grow up experiencing poverty (see Table 1–2). Respectful, mindful teachers are necessary in all child care settings to promote interest, acceptance, and pride among children and families.

TABLE 1–2 ▶ Facts and Figures on Families in the United States with Infants and Toddlers

All Infants and Toddlers

More than 11 million infants and toddlers live in the United States. Every 1.5 minutes, a baby is born to a teen mother.[a]

Every 1.5 minutes, a baby is born at low birth weight. Black babies are about twice as likely as White or Hispanic babies to be born at low birth weight.

Every 22 minutes, a baby dies before his or her first birthday. When compared to other industrialized countries, the United States ranks 31st in infant mortality rates and 25th in low-birthweight rates. When comparing the Black child well-being in the United States to other nations, 72 nations have lower infant mortality rates.

Approximately 20 percent of 2-year-olds are not fully immunized. In 2013, 17 states had MMR (Measles, Mumps, and Rubella) coverage below 90.0 percent, and these states are at higher risk for measles outbreaks.

Among all infants and toddlers, 13 percent of infants and toddlers living in low-income or poor families in the United States do not have health insurance.

A child is abused or neglected every 47 seconds; infants are the most likely to suffer from maltreatment.

In 2011 (latest year data reported), the average cost of center-based care for infants was greater than the annual tuition and fees at an in-state college in 35 states and the District of Columbia.

Infants and Toddlers in Poverty

Every 32 seconds, a baby is born into poverty.[a] Of the infants and toddlers in the United States, 48 percent are in families living below or near the federal poverty line. Children under the age of 3 are more likely to live in poverty than older children. Poverty, however, is related to race and ethnicity, with African American, American Indian, and Hispanic infants and toddlers being more than twice as likely to live in poverty as young White children. In addition, 56 percent of infants and toddlers with immigrant parents live in low-income families.

Eighty-eight percent of infants and toddlers with parents who have less than a high school degree live in low-income families.

Most poor infants and toddlers live in families where at least one adult works. Seventy-six percent of low-income families have at least one parent who works part-time or part-year year-round. Thirty-two percent of low-income families have at least one parent who works full-time, year-round.

Of infants and toddlers living with a single mother, 74 percent are in low-income families.

Nationally, in 2013, 150,000 infants, toddlers, and pregnant women participated in Early Head Start programs. This represented only 4 percent of infants, toddlers, and pregnant women who were eligible to be served.

In 2010, nearly 9 million infants, children, and women participated in the WIC program.

[a]Based on calculations per school day (180 days of seven hours each).
Sources: National Center for Children in Poverty. (2014). Basic facts about low-income children: Children under 3 years, 2012, and Investing in young children: A factsheet on early care and education participation, access, and quality. Retrieved September 23, 2014, from http://www.nccp.org/; Children's Defense Fund. (2014). The state of America's children. Retrieved September 23, 2014, from http://childrensdefense.org; Centers for Disease Control and Prevention. (2014). Childhood immunization coverage infographic: Infant vaccination rates high, unvaccinated still vulnerable. Retrieved September 26, 2014, from http://www.cdc.gov/vaccines/imz-managers/coverage/nis/child/index.html

© Cengage Learning

In the past, it was thought that the immediate family had the greatest single impact on a child's life. However, with the increased need for parents of very young children to engage in the workforce, the need for child care is so great that this is no longer true. Attachment research (to be reviewed in the next section) explains that infants can form positive, secure relationships

© 2017 Cengage Learning

PHOTO 1–2 Close relationships between toddlers and teachers support and enhance parent-child relationships.

with both family members and early childhood educators. Child development experts now understand that close relationships between a toddler and a teacher are not a substitute for parent-child relationships; rather, they can support and enhance each other (Photo 1–2). Now such experts encourage important practices such as family grouping, continuity of care, primary caregiving, and creating partnerships with families to minimize the effects on children of long hours away from family members.

Family Grouping

When a small number of children of different ages (e.g., infants and toddlers) are cared for in the same room, it is called **family grouping**. Such arrangements reproduce relationships that children naturally have in a home setting. For example, families often have siblings who are two or fewer years apart in age. Organizing the program so that the six children who share the room vary in age from a very young infant (e.g., 6 weeks) to 3 years of age provides opportunities for interactions that are similar to those that may be found more naturally.

Continuity of Care

Attachment theory suggests that infants, toddlers, and adults need time to create positive emotional bonds with one another. Having the same teachers work with the same children for a three-year period is one way to promote strong attachments (Bernhardt, 2000; Honig, 2002). This type of arrangement is often referred to as **continuity of care** and should be viewed as a primary component of high-quality programming for very young children. As this term suggests, the emphasis is placed on maintaining

family grouping Method for grouping children where children are of different ages.

continuity of care Having the same teachers work with the same group of children and families for more than one year, ideally for three years.

relationships for long periods of time. With older children, this is often referred to as *looping*. Continuity of care can appear in several different forms in practice. For example, a teacher and her group of children could remain in one classroom for the infant and toddler years, changing furniture, instructional tools, and supplies as needed to respond to the developing capabilities of the children. In contrast, a teacher and her group of children could move each year into a new classroom, which already is equipped with age-appropriate furniture, supplies, and materials. In either case, emphasis is placed on building strong, stable, and secure attachments between the caregiver and child throughout the first three years of life. Unfortunately, when infants and toddlers experience too many changes in caregivers, they can become reluctant to form new relationships, and their optimal social and emotional development is impeded.

National statistics suggest that many infants and toddlers do not experience continuity of care. According to Mamedova and Redford (2013), the mean length of time that children had been in their primary care arrangement was longer for children in a relative care arrangement (18 months) compared to nonrelative care (15 months) or center-based care arrangement (13 months). In other words, children in center-based care had experienced more changes in who cared for them during their first years of life. Some reasons for a lack of continuity in child care centers are explored next.

Implementing continuity of care might seem simple, yet it requires a great deal of organizing and changing policies on the part of a program. For example, practices for hiring often have to change (e.g., hiring teachers of "children from birth to age 3," rather than an infant teacher), and communication with families has to include a rationale for this approach. The program also has to respond to changes in external policies that impact the program. In the state of Indiana, to illustrate, child care licensing regulations require that all programs make a "reasonable effort" toward implementing continuity of care for children up to 30 months of age. Recent research discovered that while many programs say that they are doing continuity of care, the majority of them did not keep infants or toddlers with their teacher when they moved to the next class (Ruprecht, 2011). The imprecision of the licensing regulations may be influencing how programs define and implement this concept.

Looking more broadly at policy issues can also demonstrate how regulations can impact the continuity of care a child receives. When the state of Oregon decided to develop more generous child care subsidy policies for how to use federally funded Child Care and Development Funds, the goal was to increase parent's child care options by allowing them access to care they believed was best for their child. The impact on the policy was found to be twofold (Weber, Grobe, & Davis, 2014). First, more families selected center-based care for their toddlers. Second, the children had more stable participation in the program selected by their family. Thus, while the state policies were not about continuity of care within any specific classroom, the increase in consistent funding led to more consistent participation in the child care programs. While changes in state licensing regulations and subsidy policies are often welcomed by many professionals, more work needs to be done to assist program directors and teachers in executing continuity of care in practice and to research the impact of such changes on child outcomes.

Primary Caregiving

Another way to help adults bond with infants is to divide the work using a **primary caregiving system** (Kovach & De Ros, 1998). In this method, one teacher in the room is primarily responsible for half of the children, and the other teacher is primarily responsible for the rest. While a teacher would never ignore the expressed needs of any infant or toddler, she is able to invest time and energy into coming to understand a smaller group of children and their families. Frequently, the primary caregiver is the person responsible for providing assistance during routine care times such as diapering, feeding, or napping. According to teachers, the primary caregiving system is valuable because it helps them maintain a balance between their routine work and their availability to be responsive to the children (Ebbeck & Yim, 2009). While this research suggests that teachers value the primary caregiving system, recent research from Indiana suggests they are still working to align behaviors that would support such a system. State licensing regulations require that each infant and toddler classroom use a primary caregiving system and that the assignments are posted for families. When asked what other behaviors the teachers engage in to support these relationships, teachers reported that they document daily activities, provide information on the child's development, and sit with the care group during meals (Ruprecht, 2011). They were less likely to report that they were responsible for changing diapers, soothing the child to sleep, interacting with the child, and talking to parents on a daily basis. It appears that teachers need support in defining and carrying out behaviors that would promote their role as a primary caregiver.

An important aspect of implementing a primary caregiving system is strong communication and collaboration between the adults in the classroom. When adults know children well, they can communicate with each other quickly about next steps or how to divide tasks. For example, if three children are still eating snacks, and four children are ready to go outside, the adults can determine who should stay inside to finish the snack and clean the tables for the next learning experience and who should go outside and support outdoor learning. In addition, the adults can be flexible in helping each other meet the children's needs. For example, when the primary caregiver is unavailable, the other adult can "fill in" and express his willingness to assist the child instead. Thus, the adults have modeled a sense of working together, communication, and everyone pitching in to finish all that needs to be accomplished.

primary caregiving system
Method of organizing work in which one teacher is primarily responsible for half of the children, and the other teacher is primarily responsible for the rest.

1-3b Mesosystem Trends

The mesosystem reflects the relationships between the various components of the microsystem. In other words, at the mesosystem level, we have to consider bidirectional influences between family, peers, school, and so on. Of particular importance for early childhood educators is the relationship that teachers have with families. The transition between home and school should be smooth and continuous. The only pathway for achieving this is through *partnering* with families. Families are experts on their children; recognizing and using this can improve your effectiveness as a caregiver. On the other hand, you are an expert on this time period—infancy and toddlerhood—given your experiences with numerous children of this age and your intentional study of child development. Help each family member bring her or his

Family and Community Connection

Think back to your experiences as a young child. Go as far back in your memory as possible. Feel free to ask a family member for assistance if necessary or desired. What were your experiences like? Where, for example, did you live, and with whom did you live? What did that person or those persons do to earn money? What type of community agencies did you participate in most often (e.g., public library, food banks, social service agencies)?

How do you think your experiences as a young child have shaped the person you are today? How do those experiences impact, both positively and negatively, your understanding of and interactions with very young children and their families? In addition, how might it impact your knowledge of the resources available in your community?

strengths to the relationship. Valuing each family's child-rearing practices while helping them to understand child development is not only respectful but also part of your ethical responsibility (NAEYC, 2005a).

Positive relationships within the mesosystem level have been shown to result in encouraging outcomes for children, families, teachers, and programs (Photo 1–3). Used in combination, the effects of each setting can be particularly strong. The reason for highlighting the relationships between the systems is to help you understand that the purpose of child care is not to replace familial influences on very young children but to enhance them.

1-3c Exosystem Trends

The exosystem refers to social settings that do not contain the child but still directly affect the child's development, such as parent workplace, community health services, and other public agencies. To illustrate, the impact of being a child in a military family depends on where the child is at developmentally because the timing of separations and reunifications in military families matters (Masten, 2013). Growing evidence suggests that stress in a pregnant mother can alter development in the fetus with lasting effects on health or brain development (Shonkoff et al., 2012). Very young children are sensitive to the effects of separations during the period when attachment bonds are forming. In addition, when toddlers lack the ability to understand information related to the deployment, it can result in a sense of abandonment, confusion, and emotional turmoil or anxiety. Thus, "different developmental stages bring different vulnerabilities and capacities that may affect how a child responds to deployment experiences" (Paley, Lester, & Mogil, 2013, p. 254).

© 2017 Cengage Learning

PHOTO 1–3 Infants, toddlers, and adults need time to create positive emotional bonds with one another.

Spotlight on Organizations

WESTED'S PROGRAM FOR INFANT/ TODDLER CARE

WestEd is a nonprofit agency whose mission is to work with education and other communities to promote excellence, achieve equity, and improve learning for children, youth, and adults. As one way to achieve this mission, WestEd has created a training series for infant and toddler teachers called Program for Infant/ Toddler Care (PITC). This program provides ongoing training and professional development opportunities which ensure that America's infants get a safe, healthy, emotionally secure, and intellectually rich

start in life. The PITC is based on current research that espouses the importance of responsive, respectful, and relationship-based care for infants and toddlers. Currently, this agency is conducting a research study to evaluate the implementation of PITC teachers' caregiving strategies. In other words, they are seeking to understand whether their intensive training has a positive impact on the way their graduates build relationships with and create meaningful environments for very young children. For more information on this agency, go to the Program for Infant/Toddler Care website.

The exosystem structure also manifests itself in the work of professional organizations that lobby and advocate for quality child care services. Many local, regional, and national organizations stress child care advocacy that sets higher standards of care, along with education that touches each child in the community. NAEYC, for example, has created standards defining high-quality early educational programs. The accreditation process, revised in 2014, is a way for programs to demonstrate they are providing exceptional care and educational experiences for young children. Hence, this organization, while a part of the exosystem, can directly impact the work of teachers in early education programs. Moreover, NAEYC works with other agencies to advocate for best practices. To illustrate, in April 2014, NAEYC endorsed the National Science Teachers Association (NSTA) Position Statement on Early Childhood Science Education to support appropriate science experiences from age 3 through preschool, and the NAEYC has an ongoing relationship with the Council for the Accreditation of Educator Preparation (CAEP) to recognize teacher-preparation programs that have achieved high standards for preparing future professionals.

Being an advocate yourself might seem like an overwhelming task. However, each time you interact with family members, colleagues, and community members, you are a teacher-leader. Your dedication to applying and sharing professional knowledge and practices makes you an advocate for young children, families, and the early childhood profession.

1-3d Macrosystem Trends

Next we turn to trends within the macrosystem, the most general level of Bronfenbrenner's ecological systems theory. The child is ultimately affected by decisions made at this level because the macrosystem consists of the laws, customs, and general policies of the social system (government). This is where the availability of resources (money in particular) is determined. The macrosystem structure of the United States has gone through remarkable changes over the past 10 to 20 years.

Early Head Start (EHS), which started in 1994, is a federally funded program for low-income pregnant women and families with infants and toddlers. This program evolved from the Head Start program and the clear need to provide early intervention for children and families. In 2003, the federal budget for EHS was $653.7 million for more than 700 programs serving more than 62,000 children under the age of 3 (Mann, Bogle, & Parlakian, 2004). By 2010, the number of programs expanded to more than 1,000 serving more than 133,000 children under the age of 3 in 50 states, the District of Columbia, Puerto Rico, and the US Virgin Islands (Early Head Start Program Facts, 2011). However, the funding increase was temporary (i.e., two years) as a result of the American Recovery and Reinvestment Act (ARRA), which appropriated $1.1 billion for EHS Programs in FY 2009. However, another law was passed in 2011 expanding partial funding for one more year (Early Head Start Programs Facts, 2011). Although those figures may sound impressive, EHS services continue to reach only 4 percent of the infants, toddlers, and pregnant women who are eligible for its services (Schmit, Matthews, Smith, & Robbins, 2013). Significantly more federal funding is warranted to address this community need.

Even though far too few children are served by this important program, the children who are enrolled have documented positive outcomes in all areas of development. For example, they have higher immunization rates, larger vocabularies, and better social-emotional development as indicated by lower rates of aggression with peers and were more attuned with objects when playing (National Head Start Association [NHSA], 2014). They had higher early reading and math scores than peers who were not enrolled in EHS (Lee, Zhai, Brooks-Gunn, Han, & Waldfogel, 2014). African American children who were in EHS programs had better cognitive outcomes (e.g., increased receptive vocabulary and sustained attention) and social outcomes (e.g., increased engagement with parents during play, and reduction in aggressive behaviors; Harden, Sandstrom, & Chazan-Cohen, 2012).

In addition, EHS has been found to have positive effects on parents such as decreased rates of depression, increased participation in educational or job training, and higher rates of employment (NHSA, 2014). They have been found to score higher on measures of parenting supportiveness (Harden et al., 2012), especially for mothers with less initial attachment avoidance or attachment anxiety (Berlin, Whiteside-Mansell, Roggman, Green, Robinson, & Spieker, 2011). NHSA (2014) research found that EHS parents were more likely to read to their child on a daily basis.

These positive outcomes fuel current concerns about the quality of nonfamilial care during the first three years of life for all of the *other* children in our communities. How can underfunded child care programs provide quality care and education, adequately compensate teachers and directors, and be responsive to family's changing needs? Professionals have been working diligently to improve the minimal educational requirements for child care teachers by demanding that their state and/or local governments raise training and care standards. NAEYC, for example, has raised standards for teacher qualifications while maintaining their high standards for teacher-child ratios (NAEYC, 2014). Taken together, these requirements demonstrate that good, affordable child care is not a luxury or fringe benefit for some families but essential brain food for each child in the next generation.

1-4 Valuing Cultural Diversity

As mentioned previously, child care settings are becoming increasingly diverse. We can't ignore these differences but rather need to respect, embrace, and value them. It is important for the early childhood educator to accept the challenge to develop a multicultural curriculum that involves both parents and children because many young families are beginning to explore their own cultural backgrounds.

Multicultural curriculum development fits into Vygotsky's theory of the dissemination of culture. He viewed cognitive development as a socially mediated process, dependent on the support and guidance that adults and more mature peers provide as children attempt new tasks (Berk, 2012). A culturally rich curriculum encourages the recognition of cultural differences and helps young families connect with the traditions of their own heritage and culture.

Each person employed in early childhood education draws upon his or her own cultural model for behavior that is both relevant and meaningful within his or her particular social and cultural group. The knowledge and understanding that caregivers use with families is drawn primarily from two sources: their educational knowledge base and their personal experiences as family members and educators. Therefore, we need to recognize and continually reexamine the way we put our knowledge into practice. We need to develop **scripts** that allow us to learn more about the families' cultural beliefs and values regarding the various aspects of child rearing. In other words, we must create a method or sequence of events for getting to know each family. That way, we can understand the family's actions, attitudes, and behavior, as well as their dreams and hopes for their child.

scripts A method or sequence of events to learn more about each family's cultural beliefs and values regarding the various aspects of child rearing.

Consideration of cultural models can help us bring coherence to the various pieces of information that we are gathering about families and organize our interpretation of that information. Organizing and ongoing reflection on what parents tell us about their strategies can help us discover their cultural model for caregiving, and then we can compare it with the cultural models that guide our own practice (Finn, 2003).

We caregivers must recognize the richness and opportunity available to us in our work with families of diverse ethnic, racial, and cultural groups (Photo 1–4). We can learn the different ways that families provide care for their children when they are all striving toward similar goals—happy and healthy children who can function successfully within the family culture and the greater community. We can use that knowledge to construct a cultural model of culturally responsive practice, designed to support families in their

© 2017 Cengage Learning

PHOTO 1–4 More children with a wide diversity of backgrounds are in early childhood education programs.

caregiving and assist them in meeting their goals for their children (Finn, 2003; Rothstein-Fisch, Trumbull, & Garcia, 2009).

Bronfenbrenner's ecological systems theory assumes the interconnectedness of each person to others and examines the ways in which one system affects another. It recognizes the importance of respecting each individual's uniqueness and considers carefully the decisions made at every level that affect us all. This theory helps us understand that children are not passive recipients of whatever happens in their environment but are very involved in influencing their environment and aiding their own development. It is important for the primary caregiver to understand that even newborns have a part in their own growth and development. Infants' wants, needs, and desires must be respected.

Take it as your individual responsibility to be aware of the power of your actions and their immediate and future impact on children. When you see that the early childhood educator also influences the family, community, and culture, you can truly understand the old African saying, "It takes a village to raise a child." This often-quoted saying is a simple way to understand that Bronfenbrenner's term *bidirectional* describes the relationships that influence a child—occurring between child and father, child and teacher, child and school—and explains that the influences go both ways.

READING CHECKPOINT

Before moving on with your reading, make sure that you can answer the following questions about the material discussed so far.

1. Explain at least four current trends in early care and development.
2. How does the diversity of families in today's society influence early education programs and teachers?

Summary

1-1 Determine how the four major developmental areas for assessment differ from one another.

Educators must come to understand how patterns of development within the four major areas, physical, emotional, social, and cognitive/language, are useful to their work with young children. When teachers working with infants and toddlers adopt a developmental perspective, they are more apt to address the capabilities of the children in their care. Teachers and other adults must be consciously aware of how a child is progressing in each area to create environments that facilitate her ideal development.

1-2 Explain the theories of child development.

This chapter also provided an overview of major developmental theorists and theories that impact teacher behaviors and classroom practices. Some theorists and theories were presented to provide a historical understanding of past reasoning about young children. Other theorists and theories were used to outline a more contemporary understanding of young children, their families, and contextual impacts on both.

1-3 Justify how the use of Bronfenbrenner's ecological systems theory explains current trends in development and education.

Bronfenbrenner's theory was used as a framework for understanding contextual variables that directly and indirectly impact children's development.

1-4 Recognize the impact of each individual child's culture on classroom interactions and curriculum.

Early childhood education programs serve children from a wide diversity of backgrounds. As a result, there is an increased need for teacher education regarding how to create culturally responsive practices and materials in child care curricula.

CASE STUDY   Trisha

Applying Bronfenbrenner's Theory

Trisha works at the Little Folks Child Care Center as an assistant teacher while she attends classes at a local community college to earn her associate degree in early childhood education. She was surprised to learn that her center was using family grouping with continuity of care. Although she always knew that she had the same children from the time they enrolled until they were around 3 years old, she did not know it was associated with a particular term or of such great educational value. Currently, she assists the head teacher with caring for eight children who range in age from 8 weeks to 17 months. Like those in the rest of the program, this group of children is culturally diverse. Trisha has worked with parents, staff, and the children on multicultural issues; she always attempts to learn more about each culture represented in her room. As part of a course, she organized a tool for gathering information about child-rearing practices and used the results to individualize routine care times.

As she has learned new ideas, such as the primary caregiving system, accreditation standards, and Bronfenbrenner's ecological systems theory, she has assumed a more active role in the microsystem. She has repeatedly discussed with her director and lead teacher the need to reduce the number of infants and toddlers per classroom to six and to adopt a primary caregiving system. Although they are enthusiastic about learning more about the primary caregiving system, they have not yet seriously considered cutting the class size by two children per room, due to financial concerns.

1. Provide two examples of how Trisha has, in her words, "assumed a more active role in the microsystem."
2. In what other systems does Trisha work? Provide examples for each system you identify.
3. What might be the added benefits of the center adopting a primary caregiving system even if it is not possible for them to reduce the number of children in each room?

Additional Resources

Edwards, S. (2009). *Early childhood education and care: A sociocultural approach.* Castle Hill, NSW, Australia: Pademelon.

Hanson, M. J., & Lynch, E. W. (2013). *Understanding families: Supportive approaches to diversity, disability, and risk* (2nd ed.). Baltimore, MD: Paul H. Brookes.

Howes, C. (2010). *Culture and child development in early childhood programs: Practices for quality education and care.* New York: Teachers College Press.

Lally, J. R. (2013). *For our babies: Ending the invisible neglect of America's infants.* New York: Teachers College Press.

Leach, P. (2009). *Child care today: Getting it right for everyone.* New York: Alfred A. Knopf.

Lynch, E. W., & Hanson, M. J. (Eds.) (2011). *Developing cross-cultural competence: A guide for working with children and their families* (4th ed.). Baltimore, MD: Paul H. Brookes.

Mooney, C. G. (2010). *Theories of attachment: An introduction to Bowlby, Ainsworth, Gerber, Brazelton, Kennell, and Klaus.* St. Paul, MN: Redleaf.

Raikes, H., & Edwards, C. P. (2009). *Extending the dance in infant and toddler caregiving: Enhancing attachment and relationships.* Baltimore, MD: Brookes.

Physical and Cognitive/Language Development

Learning Objectives

After reading this chapter, you should be able to:

2-1 Discuss the differences between development and learning.

2-2 Investigate typical patterns of physical development between birth and thirty-six months of age.

2-3 Deconstruct typical patterns of cognitive/language development between birth and thirty-six months of age.

Standards Addressed in This Chapter

naeyc **NAEYC Standards for Early Childhood Professional Preparation**

1 Promoting Child Development and Learning

DAP **Developmentally Appropriate Practice Guidelines**

2 Teaching to Enhance Development and Learning

In addition, the NAEYC standards for developmentally appropriate practice are divided into six areas particularly important to infant/toddler care. The following area is addressed in this chapter: *Policies.*

© Cengage Learning

2-1 Differences between Development and Learning

As mentioned in Chapter 1, developmental theories differ on a number of controversies. That chapter discussed universal versus unique patterns of development. In this chapter, we will investigate briefly the nature versus nurture controversy. Some theorists contend that child development is the result of heredity and natural biological processes, largely independent of learning and experience (nature), whereas others argue that development mostly depends on learning (nurture) (McDevitt & Ormrod, 2013). The best conclusion to date is that child development is a complex process occurring through natural sequences and patterns that depend on learning and experience, among other processes (McDevitt & Ormrod, 2013).

Based on the nature-nurture complexity, this book defines **development** as cumulative sequences and patterns that represent progressive, refined changes that move a child from simple to more complex physical, cognitive, language, social, and emotional growth and maturity. It is recognized that although children grow in the developmental areas in the same general sequences and patterns, each child is affected differently by social, cultural, and environmental influences. Children move through these developmental sequences at widely varying rates.

In contrast, **learning** is operationally defined as the acquisition of knowledge and skills through systematic study, instruction, practice, and/or experience. As such, learning requires action by a learner. According to a blog by Boller (2012), "learning implies 'I' am doing something. I am taking part and doing the work." This definition takes into consideration both overt behavioral changes in responses and more internal changes in perceptions resulting from practice or conscious awareness, or both. In other words, changes in a response to a stimulus either can be observable to another person (overt) or can occur internally without obvious change in observable behavior (internal). Both overt and internal learning occurs during the first three years of life. Therefore, caregivers must consistently observe the child very closely to understand how changes in responses create the perceptions, thoughts, beliefs, attitudes, feelings, and behaviors that constitute the young child's evolving map of the world. The biggest challenge for early childhood specialists is to understand each child's individual map for development and learning because no two individuals can have the same one.

Figure 2–1 represents three different ways to conceptualize the relationship between development and learning. Given the definitions provided for each, which representation do you think fits best and why?

development Operationally defined as general sequences and patterns of growth and maturity.

learning The acquisition of new information through experiences, investigation, or interactions with another.

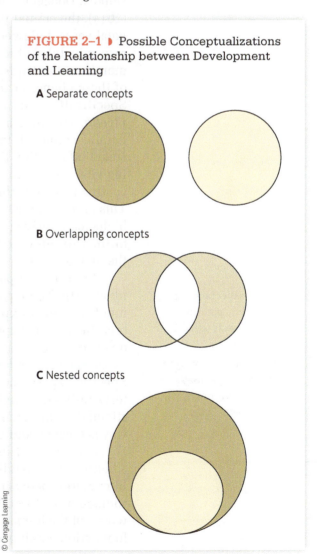

FIGURE 2–1 ▶ Possible Conceptualizations of the Relationship between Development and Learning

A Separate concepts

B Overlapping concepts

C Nested concepts

© Cengage Learning

2-2 Patterns of Physical Development

Physical development includes brain development, physical characteristics, sensory, and motor. Each of these is discussed next. Other aspects of physical development, such as teething, sleep patterns, and elimination control, will be discussed in future chapters.

2-2a Brain Development

The nervous system is responsible for communication among all body parts and ultimately with the environment. This section defines and familiarizes the reader with the major nervous system functions. Newborns are complex beings whose growth and development are closely related to the health and integrity of the nervous system, which is made up of the brain, the spinal cord, and nerve cells (neurons).

Brain development is particularly intense during the last weeks of gestation and the first years of life. This is evidenced by the nonlinear growth in the cranial perimeter and in the brain's weight. According to Dubois, Dehaene-Lambertz, Kulikova, Poupon, Huppi, and Hertz-Pannier (2014), the cranial perimeter grows about 14 cm during the two first postnatal years, followed by only 7 cm until adulthood (5.52 and 2.76 inches, respectively). At birth, the brain weighs 25 percent of an adult's, and by 24 months, it has tripled its weight, being about 80 percent of an adult's. Both of these changes can be attributed to growth in the brain's white matter. Specifically, brain cells called *glia* are coated in a fatty sheathing called *myelin*. Myelin is a substance that protects, coats, and insulates neurons, helping connect impulses from one neuron to another. These impulses are coded information lines that function like insulated electrical wires, carrying vital current to where it is needed in the body and brain. The myelin coating promotes the transfer of information from one neuron to another. This process, however, is not entirely under the control of genetic codes or biologically driven factors because the human brain is not fully formed at birth. This allows environmental stimuli to influence the development of the human brain.

experience-expectant Type of motor neuron pathway that apparently expects specific stimuli at birth.

experience-dependent Type of motor neuron pathway that waits for environmental experiences before being activated.

Motor neuron pathways, for example, apparently expect specific stimuli at birth. These pathways are called **experience-expectant**. The environment provides expected stimuli; for example, reflex sucking during breastfeeding is experience-expectant. Infant survival obviously depends on experience-expectant pathways. Another set of neuron pathways, called **experience-dependent**, seems to wait for new experience before activation. Specific experience-dependent cells form synapses for stable motor patterns only after environmental stimuli are repeated several times. When stimulation from the environment occurs in a consistent way, a stable pathway is created, and physical changes occur in the nervous system.

As mentioned in Chapter 1, technological advancements have led to a better understanding of how brain development results from complex interactions between nature (i.e., genetic makeup) and nurture (i.e., environmental factors). Whereas genes are initially responsible for the basic wiring of the human brain, by the end of the eighth week of pregnancy, the foundation for all body structures, including the brain and nervous system, is evident in the growing fetus. The electrical activity of brain cells while still in the womb changes the physical structure of the brain, just as it will facilitate learning after birth.

Using MRI technology, toddlers (18–22 months) who were born at a very low birth weight were compared to full-term babies and found to have differences in the volume of their brain structures (Figure 2–2). Some structures were larger, and other structures were smaller (i.e., cerebral and cerebellum white matter, thalamus, and hippocampus) (Lowe, Duvall, MacLean, Caprihan, Ohls, Qualls, et al., 2011). The important conclusion from this research is that both biological and environmental factors interact in complex ways, resulting in different developmental trajectories.

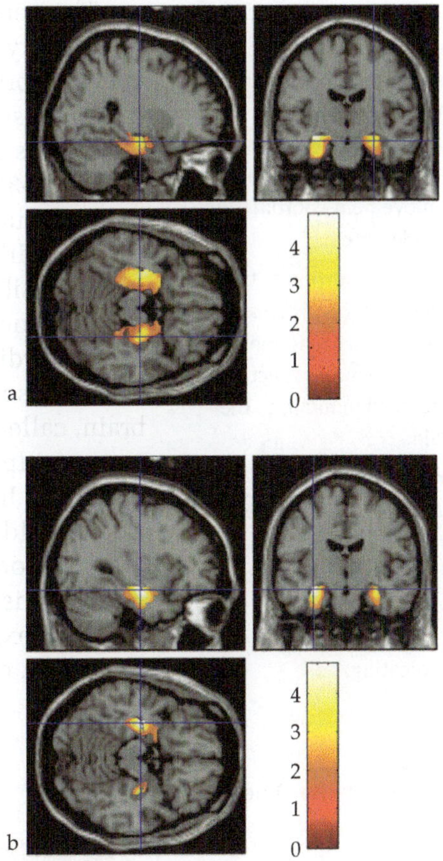

The human brain is organized into regions that are predetermined for specific functions. For example, all individuals have a language center and an emotion center. However, environmental stimuli affect how the language center and emotion center will develop due to which neurological circuits are activated and the number of times they are used (Fox, Levitt, & Nelson, 2010; Meyer, Wood, & Stanley, 2013). At birth, the brain is packed with an estimated 100 billion neurons whose job is to store and transmit information. The newborn's brain is constantly taking in information available in the environment, utilizing all existing senses. The brain records these pieces of information, whether they are emotional, physical (sensory), social, or cognitive in origin. This information influences the shape and circuitry of the neurons, or brain cells. The more data taken in, the stronger the neuron connections and pathways become. A repeated behavior or the consistency of a behavior increases the chance of the pathway becoming strong.

The brain has two specific yet different modes for responding to environmental inputs. First, the neural pathways that are not consistently used will be eliminated, or **pruned**. Many more neural pathways exist in the brain than are efficient. When there is not a consistent pattern of stimulation for some neural pathways, the brain's job is to cut off the circuitry to that area. This process streamlines children's neural processing, making the remaining circuits work more quickly and efficiently (Zero to Three, 2012). The second mode is called **brain plasticity**. This concept refers to the process of adaptation; when one part of the brain is damaged, another part of the brain takes over the functions of the damaged area. It also means that if a major change occurs in the environment, infants can form new neural pathways to adapt to the change. By gaining a deeper understanding of brain plasticity, better therapies can be developed to improve **hemiparesis** caused by cerebral palsy or childhood strokes (Johnston, 2009). Unfortunately, the human brain doesn't have infinite capacity to change; not all damage can be compensated for, and not all neural pathways can be replaced. What this means for us as caregivers is that infants

FIGURE 2–2 ▶ Structural MRI Comparing Hippocampal Volume

prune The elimination of neural pathways that are not consistently used.

brain plasticity When one part of the brain is damaged, other parts take over the functions of the damaged parts.

hemiparesis Slight paralysis or weakness affecting one side of the body.

and toddlers are in the process of forming nerve pathways, and by providing them with the proper nutrition and experiences, we can influence the quality of their brain development.

The nervous system is the "command center" for all the vital functions of the body. Pathways and networks of neurons must be organized to carry coded information from the brain to all body parts and vice versa. The brain is comprised of complex systems that interact with each other and with other parts of the body to create all thoughts, feelings, actions, and reactions (Figure 2–3). For ease of understanding, the brain is discussed here as being divided into three main parts; each part is further divided into specialized regions with specific functions (McDevitt & Ormrod, 2013). The **hindbrain** is responsible for regulating automatic functions, such as breathing, digestion, alertness, and balance. This part of the brain also controls motor movement coordination and muscle tone in an area referred to as the cerebellum. This is also the site for storing emotional knowledge. Another part of the brain, called the **midbrain**, controls visual system reflexes (e.g., eye movements, pupil dilation), auditory system functions, and voluntary motor functions. In addition, the midbrain connects the hindbrain to the forebrain. Like an old-time telephone operator's switchboard, this part of the brain tells the forebrain what messages from the hindbrain to respond to. The **forebrain** is what distinguishes our species as human; it contains the cerebral cortex, which produces all of our complex thoughts, emotional responses, decision-making, reasoning, and communicating.

hindbrain The portion of the brain responsible for regulating automatic functions and emotional knowledge; contains the cerebellum, which controls motor movement coordination and muscle tone.

midbrain The portion of the brain that controls visual system reflexes, auditory functions, and voluntary motor functions; connects the hindbrain to the forebrain.

forebrain The portion of the brain that contains the cerebral cortex, which produces all of our complex thoughts, emotional responses, decision-making, reasoning, and communicating.

FIGURE 2–3 ▶ The Human Brain

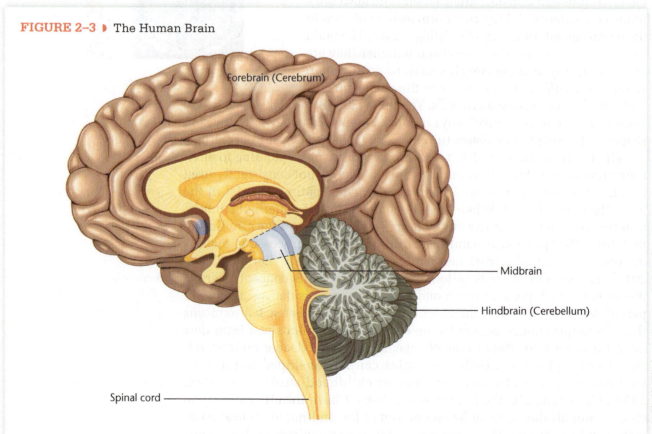

Forebrain (Cerebrum)

Midbrain

Hindbrain (Cerebellum)

Spinal cord

From BANICH/COMPTON, Cognitive Neuroscience, 3E. © 2011 Cengage Learning.

Family and Community Connection

As mentioned previously, most family members do not always recognize or understand the importance of brain development in the first three years of life. What could you do with the families you work most closely with to change that situation? Consider what information you would share and how you would share it.

Now think about how to share this information with your greater community. How would you go about setting up a brain development event? Who in the community would you expect to target? Do you want to focus, for example, on grandparents or business owners? What information would you share with this audience, and how would you share it? Find at least two local, state, or national organizations that you could partner with to bring this information to your community.

Considered the most important part of the brain, the cerebral cortex is the slowest growing and largest part. Around 12 months, the cerebral cortex begins to organize and specify functions for neuron activity. Other parts of the brain continue to grow rapidly only through the second year, whereas the cerebral cortex continues to grow until the fourth decade of life.

The cerebral cortex receives stimuli in the form of sensory information. Associations are formed between the thought processes and physical actions or experiences. Specific areas of the cerebral cortex control special functions, such as planning, problem solving, and decision making (frontal lobes), vision and color recognition (occipital lobes), receiving and processing sensory information (parietal lobes), and emotional responses, memory, and production of language (temporal lobes). Neurological development of these specialized areas follows predictable patterns as the overall development of the child progresses due to related brain development.

Brain development during infancy is best promoted when caregivers engage in developmentally appropriate practices, especially those associated with creating positive relationships with very young children. Responsive adults tend to provide infants proper nutrition; protect them from harm and excessive stress; soothe them when they are distressed; and talk about objects, patterns, or people who have attracted their attention (Prado & Dewey, 2012; Shore, 2003). Infants rely on adults to help them regulate their emotions, toddlers are exploring their new freedoms of mobility, and teachers provide a pivotal role in it all. Watch what they are trying to do, and find ways to support them without being intrusive. When they have mastered a task, challenge them to go to the next level. For example, when infants are able to push up, adults can lay them on their bellies with an interesting toy or mirror at their sight level. During such interactions, adults need to provide support and guidance that is nurturing, responsive, and reassuring. Thus, responsive caregiving by parents, teachers, and others is a major factor in brain development. Competent caregivers for infants and toddlers recognize the impact they have on the children's neurological growth; they initiate activities that reinforce the natural sequences of behaviors supporting healthy growth in all areas. The adult role is critical because early experiences significantly affect how each child's brain is wired (Patterson & Vakili, 2014; see also Fox et al., 2010, and Meyer et al., 2013, for reviews). Positive social, emotional, cognitive, language, and physical experiences all work together with the child's biological and genetic makeup to influence the development of a healthy

Spotlight on Shaken Baby Syndrome

CAUSES AND EFFECTS

Approximately 1,300 infants in the United States experience severe or fatal head trauma each year as the result of abuse (National Center on Shaken Baby Syndrome, nd). **Shaken baby syndrome** occurs when a baby or child is violently shaken by an adult or older child. Damage can occur if the shaking lasts for only a few seconds. According to the Centers for Disease Control and Prevention (CDC, nd), children under the age of 1 (especially babies ages 2 to 4 months) are at greatest risk of injury from shaking. Shaking them violently can trigger a "whiplash" effect that can lead to internal injuries. An infant's neck muscles aren't strong enough to provide sufficient support for the head; violent shaking "pitches the infant's brain back and forth within the skull, sometimes rupturing blood vessels and nerves throughout the brain and tearing the brain tissue. The brain may strike the inside of the skull, causing bruising and bleeding to the brain" (KidsHealth, 2014b, para. 7).

This syndrome can result in death or severe and irreparable damage. Some common outcomes include the following:

- Blindness
- Mental retardation or developmental delays (any significant lags in a child's physical, cognitive, behavioral, emotional, or social development, in comparison with norms) and learning disabilities
- Cerebral palsy
- Severe motor dysfunction (muscle weakness or paralysis)
- Spasticity (a condition in which certain muscles are continuously contracted—this contraction causes stiffness or tightness of the muscles and may interfere with movement, speech, and manner of walking)
- Seizures (CDC, nd)

Some researchers have begun to investigate hearing losses associated with shaken baby syndrome as some preliminary evidence suggests it could accompany these other outcomes (Alzahrani, Ratelle, Cavel, Laberge-Malo, & Saliba, 2014). The overall prevalence of hearing loss as the result of being shaken has not yet been established.

Shaken baby syndrome does not result from normal parent-child play interactions such as tossing a baby in the air or bouncing her on your knee (CDC, nd; Kids Health, 2014) or by accidental falls (Yamazaki, Yoshida, & Mizunuma, 2014). It is the result of at least one abusive event.

---

shaken baby syndrome
Damage that occurs when a baby or child is violently shaken by an adult or older child.

brain. In addition, as you will explore in more depth later, the prevention of developmental and learning issues through high-quality adult-child interactions and healthy environments is always preferred over providing intervention services later (Hyson & Biggar Tomlinson, 2014).

2-2b Physical Growth

Human babies are different from those of any other species because they can't stand immediately after birth and so can't get themselves out of harm's way. Physical growth in terms of body weight, however, occurs at an astounding rate during the first 12 months of life when infants are physically nurtured and active. Height usually parallels weight, so children who gain weight slowly in the first three years also tend to grow in height slowly. In general, a baby gains an average of 10 inches in height and triples his birth weight during his first year (KidsHealth, 2014a). Growth slows significantly during the toddler years, as often does the child's appetite. Caregivers should be aware that large variations occur in the rate of physical growth in children under 3 years of age. Growth spurts and plateaus are normal for development of height, weight, activity levels, and so on; therefore, the caregiver should keep careful records of observations of physical growth and share them with parents on a regular basis.

As you have no doubt observed, the newborn's head is the largest part of the body. Babies often look disproportional when comparing the size of the head to the rest of the body. Even though the head is large, it is not fully developed. At birth, the bones in the baby's head are not fused, but rather "soft spots" are found in the front and back of the head. The back soft spot closes after a few months, but the front spot stays soft for almost two years. These soft spots allow space for the growth of the brain (especially from the myelinization process) as described previously. Adults must protect the baby's head from bumps and during falls, and they must never shake a baby for any reason.

Almost all infants are born with well-defined **reflexes** or automatic responses. These responses are important when the infant is faced with particular environmental stimuli because they are not yet able to think through and coordinate a response. For example, if a bright light is shone in an infant's eyes, he will automatically close his eyes. Or, if a finger is placed in his mouth, he will begin to suck without thinking.

> **reflexes** Automatic responses that are present at birth.

Several reflexes form the beginnings of more complex behavior. In other words, they change from involuntary reactions to purposeful, intentional actions that support the growing child over time. For example, the rooting and sucking reflexes that are initially necessary for feeding can be combined with the ability to bring the hand to mouth so that the older infant can comfort herself.

The purposes of other reflexes are less well understood. The plantar grasp reflex, to illustrate, is evident when the sole of the foot is stroked causing the toes to flex. How this reflex assists the newborn is not well understood. However, an absent or weak reflex can be a sign of neurological problems.

2-2c Hearing and Vision Development

Newborns respond to a range of sounds. They startle easily with sudden loud noises and become agitated at high-pitched noises. They turn their heads to locate sound and show interest in their caregivers' voices (Photo 2–1). Infants explore their own utterings and use their bodies and toys to play with sound. Infants who are later discovered to be deaf or have impaired hearing coo and babble according to expected developmental patterns for the first few months. As hearing children increase their quantity and variability of babbling, deaf or hard-of-hearing children actually decrease (Marschark, 2007). This is why hearing problems can be difficult to detect until 7 or 8 months of age, even with universal newborn hearing screenings. For children who underwent routine screening (e.g., at the hospital after birth or at well-baby checkups), the diagnosis for severe to profound hearing loss was 6.8 months, while children who did not have such screening were not diagnosed, on average, until 20.5 months (Canale, Favero, Lacilla, Recchia, Schindler, Roggero, et al., 2006). While it might seem counterintuitive that early screening does not result in a diagnosis until six months later, it is important to consider that

© 2017 Cengage Learning

PHOTO 2–1 Talk with infants about what interests them, such as what they are looking at or what they are hearing.

Spotlight on Research

VISION IN INFANTS AND TODDLERS

Infants use their eyes from birth, although their vision develops relatively slowly. By the fourth month, coordination of both eyes can be observed. Four-month-old infants demonstrated looking preferences that were similar to adult preferences when given simple visual, black-and-white displays (Chien, Palmer, & Teller, 2005). They focus well with both eyes at a distance of 12 inches, which is the normal distance for breastfeeding. By age 2, vision is around 20/80; full 20/20 acuity is not expected until they reach school age.

In one of the most comprehensive studies to date, Hatton, Ivy, and Boyer (2013) investigated 5,931 children age 3 and younger with severe, uncorrectable visual impairments in the United States. They discovered that the three most prevalent diagnoses were cortical visual impairment, retinopathy of prematurity (ROP), and optic nerve hypoplasia. For those children whose legal blindness status was known, 60 percent were identified as legally blind. In addition, they found that a diagnosis of a vision impairment was made at the mean age of 4.9 months. As you may recall, this is approximately two months sooner than a hearing impairment diagnosis is typically made. However, similar to a hearing impairment, referrals did not result in entry into a specialized intervention program until, on average, six months later.

at least one follow-up evaluation must be conducted to determine the type and severity of the hearing impairment (Vos, Lagassea, & Levêquea, 2014). Late diagnosis has implications for the impact of early intervention strategies on improving speech, language, and cognitive development outcomes as well as the quality of parent and infant life (Canale et al., 2006; Lachowska, Surowiec, Morawski, Pierchała, & Niemczyk, 2014; Vos et al., 2014).

2-2d Motor Development

One theory of motor development, called the dynamic systems theory, predicts that individual behaviors and skills of the growing infant combine and work together to create a more efficient and effective system. Reaching, grabbing, and putting an object in the mouth are put together when eating with a spoon. Each new skill is acquired by practicing, revising, and combining earlier accomplishments to fit a new goal. Consequently, infants typically achieve motor milestones around the same time but in unique ways.

Physical development occurs in a predictable order, starting from the head and chest and moving to the trunk and lower extremities. This directional growth is readily observable as the infant gains control of head, chest, trunk, and then legs to turn over. To crawl, the infant gains control of lower back and leg muscles; to walk, the infant gains control of neck, shoulders, back, legs, feet, and toes. Infants develop control of their arm movements from erratic waving to accurate reaching. Hand control develops from accidentally bumping and hitting to purposefully touching. Reaching occurs first, with an open hand grip. Then the fingers develop, from reflexive pinching, grasping, and reflexive releasing to controlled opening and closing.

Physical development involves both large movements, or **gross motor control**, and small muscle activity, **fine motor control**. Gross motor development involves large movements through milestone achievements, such as crawling, standing, walking, and throwing. Fine motor development milestones involve smaller, more refined movements, such as grasping and pointing. Three areas of movement that develop over the first three years are (1) stability, (2) locomotion, and (3) manipulation. *Stability* refers to sitting and standing upright; *locomotion* refers to crawling, walking, and running; and *manipulation* includes reaching, grasping, releasing, and throwing.

Milestones of development are essential for teachers to know because although the progression of motor development is fairly uniform, individual children vary within and between cultures in the age at which they develop both gross and fine motor skills. Appendix A provides an overview of Developmental Milestones for motor skill for infants through 3 years of age. At around 6 weeks old, infants begin to hold their heads steady and erect. By 2 months, they lift their upper bodies by their arms and can roll from side to back. From 3 to 4 months, babies begin grasping palm-size objects and can roll from back to side. From 6 to 8 months, they can sit alone and begin to crawl. Between 8 and 10 months, babies pull up to stand and perhaps play patty cake. At this time they begin to stand alone, and then begin to walk. From 13 to 16 months, children can build a tower of two cubes, vigorously scribble with a large crayon, and begin to walk up stairs with help. At around 20 to 24 months, toddlers begin to jump in place and kick objects. By 26 to 30 months, children begin to climb, stand on one foot, and have some interest in toilet learning. Usually at around 36 months, the child can jump and independently use the toilet.

As this general outline indicates, motor development does support the dynamic systems theory described earlier. Children progress from one milestone behavior to the next, based on successful integration of the previous behaviors and neurological maturity resulting from environmental experiences. Children who develop within the average range do not necessarily proceed through all of the developmental milestones or move in the exact sequence because movement forward in skill development is interspersed with periods of regression (Gershkoff-Stowe & Thelen, 2004). It is hypothesized that those periods of regression occur because children are uniquely combining old and new skills together, which can result in behaviors appearing to be less developed in one context than in another (Gershkoff-Stowe & Thelen, 2004).

Moving away from dynamic systems theory momentarily, we will consider the impact of the environment on physical development. Humphrey and Olivier (2014) investigated the impact of having a teenager mentor work with a selected toddler or preschooler for 1.5 hours a week for 18 weeks on seven areas of development. They found that the young children who were paired with a mentor had significantly higher levels of physical development when compared to the control group. This research suggests that one-on-one mentoring can positively impact the acquisition of physical skills and promote physical development.

gross motor control The control of large muscles.

fine motor control The ability to control small muscles such as those in the hands and fingers.

© 2017 Cengage Learning

PHOTO 2–2 Walking is a milestone of physical development.

In a review of research, Cardon, Craemer, De Bourdeaudhuij, and Verloigne (2014) explored the impact of intervention projects with parents, teachers, and schools, especially those programs with a focus on creating environments that support healthy behaviors. When parents participated in intervention studies that provided information on the importance of physical activity, Belgian preschoolers engaged in more moderate to vigorous physical activity during after-school hours. When preschool and elementary schools modified their outdoor learning environments to increase play space, children's physical activity levels also increased. Minimal results were found for teachers who participated in research interventions regarding sedentary behavior. The authors hypothesized that teachers' personal beliefs and perceptions might be creating barriers to adopting new practices. Thus, it is clear from this research that the ecology (e.g., environments) young children experience can either positively or negatively impact their levels of physical development.

No matter whether a physical skill is the result of a system integration or environmental impacts, the challenge for early educators is to observe physical skills and milestones and determine where individual children fall on the general scale of motor development (Photo 2–2). By performing evaluations on a regular basis, caregivers can determine whether an area of motor development requires specific tasks and experiences to enhance development and whether there are areas in which the child shows advanced development in motor skills.

READING CHECKPOINT

Before moving on with your reading, make sure that you can answer the following prompts about the material discussed so far.

1. You have been asked to debate the relationship between development and learning. What position will you take and why?

2. Explain how the growth of the brain demonstrates the complex interaction between nature (i.e., genetics or biology) and nurture (i.e., environmental factors).

3. Describe how being born with a physical deformity such as cleft lip/palate influences not only physical development but also social and emotional development.

4. Identify the major milestones for motor development from birth to 3 years of age, and choose two examples (not already provided) that illustrate the dynamic systems theory.

2-3 Patterns of Cognitive and Language Development

As mentioned in Chapter 1, the most widely applied theories of higher cognition are Piaget's cognitive developmental theory and Vygotsky's sociocultural theory. Later chapters detail several applications of these theories in educational settings, but major principles from each theory are discussed here before we move into language development.

2-3a Cognitive Development: Piaget's Theory of Reasoning

Newborns use all their senses—listening, seeing, tasting, touching, and smelling—to learn about their world. This leads young children to think differently from adults. Adults are logical thinkers; they consider facts, analyze relationships, and draw conclusions. Young children are *prelogical* thinkers; their conclusions are based on their interactions with materials and people in their environment and perhaps on an incomplete or inaccurate understanding of their experiences. For example, 2 1/2-year-old Ivan has made a tilting stack of blocks. When he places a small car on top of the blocks, the stack tumbles down. Ivan tells Mrs. Young that the car broke the blocks. Ivan has constructed his understanding based on his interactions with the materials. He does not yet understand gravity, the need to stack blocks straight up rather than at a tilt, and the impact of the car's rolling wheels. The object Ivan put on the stack just before it fell was the car; as far as Ivan is concerned, the car broke the blocks.

Jean Piaget's research contributed significantly to the knowledge of cognitive development in young children. A brilliant young scientist, Piaget began his studies as a biologist. Later, listening to children respond to questions on an intelligence test, he became intrigued by their incorrect responses and the patterns of their verbal reasoning. Combining his scientific orientation, his knowledge of biology, and his experiences with the children's incorrect response patterns, Piaget began to study children's cognitive development. Piaget's clinical observation method included close observations of his own three young children as well as many other children in his extensive subsequent research. He observed what children did and wrote narrative descriptions. Later, analyzing these detailed observations, he developed his theories of cognitive development. Piaget's (1952) approach is central to the school of cognitive theory known as **cognitive constructivism** because young children actively construct knowledge about themselves and their world. They interact with materials in their environment and construct their own understanding and meaning of the events. Each of their actions and interpretations is unique to them. Young children's thinking organizes information about their experiences so they can construct their own understanding.

However, central to Piaget's theory is that there are stages of cognitive development; that is, 4-month-olds are cognitively different from 24-month-olds. Piaget contended that the sequence of development is the same for all

cognitive constructivism
Theory that describes learning as the active construction of knowledge. Humans organize information about their experiences and therefore construct understanding based on their interactions with materials and people in their environment. This is also referred to as individual constructivism.

© Cengage Learning

PHOTO 2–3 Hard rattles are good for chewing on! According to Piaget, this infant learned this through the processes of assimilation and accommodation while exploring the environment.

adaptation A change in behavior that helps the child survive in his or her environment; described by Piaget as a cognitive skill.

accommodation Piaget's process of changing or altering skills to better fit the requirements of a task.

assimilation Piaget's way of explaining how children refine cognitive structures into schemes.

equilibrium A state of homeostasis or balance that reflects how an infant's or toddler's current cognitive schemes work to explain his or her environment.

children. However, the age and rate at which it occurs differ from child to child. Children develop higher cognitive skills in a systematic manner through four stages: (1) sensorimotor, (2) preoperational, (3) concrete operational, and (4) formal operational. At each of these stages, similar structures of intelligence are used to learn: adaptation, organization, and schemas.

Adaptation involves using schemes that have direct interaction with the environment, for example, grasping and dropping an object over and over. **Accommodation** involves changing schemes to better fit the requirements of a task or new information. Thus, a child will change or alter his or her strategies to fit the requirements of a task. For example, banging on a hard toy will produce a noise. Yet, when faced with a soft toy, the child finds that banging is insufficient to produce a response. Squeezing might be tried instead. When children are in a familiar situation, they function by means of **assimilation**, which involves dealing with an object or event in a way that is consistent with their existing schemes (McDevitt & Ormrod, 2013) (Photo 2–3). When children are in such situations, they are considered to be in the internal state called **equilibrium**. Their current cognitive schemes work to explain their environment. However, when faced with information that is contrary to their current schemes and understanding or placed in an unfamiliar situation, they experience **disequilibrium**. This internal mental state provides a motivation for learning because the children are uncomfortable and seek to make sense of what they have observed or experienced. The movement from equilibrium to disequilibrium and back to equilibrium again is known as **equilibration**. Equilibration and children's intrinsic desire to achieve equilibrium move development toward greater complexity of thought and knowledge (McDevitt & Ormrod, 2013).

Another cognitive function through which schemes are changed is called organization, which takes place internally. **Organization** is a process of rearranging new patterns of actions and linking them with other patterns to form a cognitive system. For example, a baby will eventually relate the actions for sucking, dropping, and throwing with new, more complex ideas of near and far. As you can imagine, these more complex ideas are actual cognitive concepts or **schemas** used to organize the child's understanding of the world.

The schema of ball is constructed as Shane sees, touches, holds, and tastes a ball. When faced with new information, for example, when he sees the ball bounce for the first time, that does not fit into his schema of "ball-ness." He continues to construct his knowledge of ball-ness by reorganizing his schema so that now bouncing is included in ball-ness. Shane's schema of ball today is different from his schema yesterday, when he had not noticed a bouncing ball. Individual experiences and behavior bring about changes in schemas.

Although some of the hypotheses of Piaget's theory have come into question after the advent of research demonstrating that infants and toddlers have been seriously underestimated in their cognitive skills by Piaget (Bergin & Bergin, 2012; Newcombe, 2013), the interpretation of those results from a Piagetian perspective continues to be a controversy in the field (Bibace, 2012; Kagan, 2008). However, this author believes the principles and stages defined by Piaget have value for the caregiver in supporting very young children in their cognitive development. Thus, our discussion will turn next to his stages of cognitive development.

Piaget's first two stages of cognitive development involve children between birth and 3 years of age. These stages, the sensorimotor stage and the beginning of the preoperational stage, are the aspects of cognitive development relevant to an infant and toddler curriculum. The **sensorimotor stage** starts at birth, when the baby explores self and the environment. Sensorimotor development involves the infant understanding his or her body and how it relates to other things in the environment (Piaget & Inhelder, 1969). Yet, how infants explore objects and, therefore, think, changes over time.

A recent longitudinal study videotaped mother-infant interactions four times between 4 months and 12 months of age to investigate object exploration. They found that, at 4 months, infants focused all of their sensory modalities on objects introduced by the mother (de Barbaro, Johnson, & Deák, 2013). Later, between 6 and 12 months, infants began to separate their sensorimotor exploration so that their eyes and hands were doing different things. For example, infants may hold a toy in one hand, explore it with the other, and look at family members at the same time. This outcome is called triadic attention (baby, family member, and object). Triadic attention allows for increased conversation and interaction around the object. Previous researchers had concluded that triadic attention is a novel social-cognitive function that emerges around 12 months (see de Barbaro et al., 2013, for a review). However, this study clearly demonstrated that actions in each session built on those observed in earlier sessions. The authors concluded that triadic attention is based on "continuous changes in the activity of our participants rather than a simple shift in internal structures" (de Barbaro et al., 2013, p. 246). In other words, slowly, over time, increased infant skills elicited new behaviors from the mother, which provided novel opportunities for triadic attention.

As you can see, the earliest form of thinking occurs during the sensorimotor stage. Three key aspects of development occur during this early stage: (1) infants play an assertive role in their own development, (2) their knowledge base is acquired by means of their own actions in the environment, and (3) infants need moderate challenges provided by adults and materials to master the environment. For caregivers, tasks should be provided that challenge babies but are not beyond their ability to succeed.

disequilibrium An internal mental state that motivates learning because the child is uncomfortable and seeks to make sense of what he or she has observed or experienced.

equilibration The movement from equilibrium to disequilibrium and back to equilibrium again.

organization A process of rearranging new sets of information (schemes) and linking them to other established schemes, resulting in an expanded cognitive system.

schemas Piaget's concept to explain cognitive patterns of actions used to learn new information.

sensorimotor stage Piaget's first stage of cognitive development, which is focused on motor activity and coordination of movements.

Sensorimotor Stage

The sensorimotor stage of cognitive development occurs from birth to about age 2. Piaget identified six substages.

Substage 1 (birth to approximately 1 month)	**Reflex** Reflex actions become more organized. Directed behavior emerges.
Substage 2 (approximately 1–4 months)	**Differentiation** Repeats own actions. Begins to coordinate actions, such as hearing and looking.
Substage 3 (approximately 4–8 months)	**Reproduction** Intentionally repeats interesting actions.
Substage 4 (approximately 8–12 months)	**Coordination** Intentionally acts as a means to an end. Develops concept of object permanence (an object exists even when the infant cannot see it).
Substage 5 (approximately 12–18 months)	**Experimentation** Experiments through trial and error. Searches for new experiences.
Substage 6 (approximately 18–24 months)	**Representation** Carries out mental trial and error. Develops symbols.

Preoperational Stage

The early part of the preoperational stage is called the preconceptual substage and occurs from about 2 to 4 years of age. At this time, the child can now mentally sort events and objects. With the development of object permanence, the child is moving toward representing objects and actions in his or her thinking without having to have actual sensorimotor experiences. Development and structuring of these mental representations is the task undertaken during the preoperational stage of cognitive development. Cowan (1978) outlined the preoperational stage as follows:

Preconceptual substage
   Mentally sorts objects and actions.
   Mental symbols are partly detached from experience.

Nonverbal classification
   Organizes objects graphically.
   Focuses on figurative properties.
   Forms own interpretations.

Verbal preconcepts
   Meanings of words fluctuate and are not always the same for the
      child.
   Meanings of words are private, based on own experience.
   Word names and labels are tied to one class.
   Words focus on one attribute at a time.

Verbal reasoning

Reasons tranductively—from particular to particular.

If one action is in some way like another action, both actions are alike in all ways.

Generalizes one situation to all situations.

Reasoning is sometimes backward—from effects to causes.

Reasoning focuses on one dimension.

Quantity

How much?

Some, more, gone, big.

Number

How many?

More, less.

Space

Where?

Uses guess and visual comparison.

Up, down, behind, under, over.

Time

Remembers sequence of life events.

Now, soon, before, after.

Piaget identified, beyond his four stages, the importance of three types of knowledge and the positive impact of play on the constructing knowledge.

Types of Knowledge

Physical knowledge is knowledge children discover in the world around them. Twenty-five-month-old Tommy kicks a pine needle as he walks in the play yard. He picks up the pine needle, throws it, and picks it up again. He drops it in the water tray, picks it up, and pulls it through the water. Tommy has discovered something about pine needles from the needle itself. Tommy uses actions and observations of the effects of his actions on the pine needle to construct his physical knowledge of pine needles.

Kamii and DeVries (1978) have identified two kinds of activities involving physical knowledge: movement of objects and changes in objects. Actions to move objects include "pulling, pushing, rolling, kicking, jumping, blowing, sucking, throwing, swinging, twirling, balancing, and dropping" (p. 6). The child causes the object to move and observes it rolling, bouncing, cracking, and so on. Kamii and DeVries (1978) suggest four criteria for selecting activities to move objects.

1. The child must be able to produce the movement by his or her own action.
2. The child must be able to vary his or her action.
3. The reaction of the object must be observable.
4. The reaction of the object must be immediate (p. 9).

A second kind of activity involves changes in objects. Compared to a ball, which when kicked, will move but still remain a ball, some objects change. When Kool-Aid is put in water, it changes. Ann sees the dry Kool-Aid and observes that something happens when it is added to water. She can no longer see anything that looks like the dry Kool-Aid. She sees the water change color and can taste the difference between water without Kool-Aid and water with Kool-Aid in it. Her observation skills (seeing and tasting) are most important to provide her with feedback on the changes that occur.

Logico-mathematical knowledge is constructed by the child and involves identifying relationships between objects. Andrea is in the sandbox playing with two spoons: a teaspoon and a serving spoon. She notices the spoons are different. Although they fit into her schema of *spoon,* she notices some difference in size. Thus, in relationship to size, they are different. At some time, someone will label these differences for her as different or bigger or smaller than the other, but these words are not necessary for her to construct her concepts of sizes.

Social-arbitrary knowledge is knowledge a child cannot learn by himself or herself. It has been constructed and agreed upon by groups of people (Branscombe, Castle, Dorsey, Surbeck, & Taylor, 2003). This type of knowledge is passed on or transmitted from one person to another through social interaction. "Language, values, rules, morality, and symbol systems are examples of social-arbitrary knowledge" (Wadsworth, 1978, p. 52).

Chad is eating a banana. He bites it, sucks on it, swallows it, looks at the remaining banana, and squeezes it. All of these are concrete actions that help him construct his physical knowledge of this object. Then someone tells him this object is a banana. The name *banana* is social-arbitrary knowledge. It could have been called *ningina* or *lalisa,* but everyone using the English language uses *banana* to name that object.

In another example of social-arbitrary knowledge, Kurt follows Mrs. Wesley into the storage room. She sees him and says, "Kurt, go back into our room right now. You are not supposed to be in this room." Kurt did not make the decision that it is not permissible for him to be in the storage room; someone else decided and told him the rule.

PHOTO 2–4 Children begin enjoying pretend play between 18 and 24 months.

Play

Play is the child's laboratory for cognitive trial and error and rehearsal for real-life problem solving. Children begin active pretend play between 18 and 24 months (Photo 2–4). As they rapidly develop symbols and interpretations and start to reason verbally, complex sequences of play are executed. For example, 2-year-olds might play "cooking," using blocks and sticks for food and utensils. From basic themes, children develop more complex strategies, perhaps using water and sand to explore measurement while learning about textures, temperatures, smells, and liquidity. Table 2–1 presents levels of exploratory and pretend play. Play develops from simple mouthing and touching objects to extremely abstract activity, in which materials are

TABLE 2–1 ▶ Levels of Exploratory and Pretend Play

1. **Mouthing:** Indiscriminate mouthing of materials

2. **Simple manipulation:** Visually guided manipulation (excluding indiscriminate banging and shaking) at least 5 seconds in duration that cannot be coded in any other category (e.g., turn over an object, touch and look at an object)

3. **Functional:** Visually guided manipulation that is particularly appropriate for a certain object and involves the intentional extraction of some unique piece of information (e.g., turn dial on toy phone, squeeze piece of foam rubber, flip antenna of toy, spin wheels on cart, roll cart on wheels)

4. **Relational:** Bringing together and integrating two or more materials in an inappropriate manner, that is, in a manner not initially intended by the manufacturer (e.g., set cradle on phone, touch spoon to stick)

5. **Functional-relational:** Bringing together and integrating two objects in an appropriate manner, that is, in a manner intended by the manufacturer (e.g., set cup on saucer, place peg in hole of pegboard, mount spool on shaft of cart)

6. **Enactive naming:** Approximate pretense activity but without confirming evidence of actual pretense behavior (e.g., touch cup to lip without making talking sounds, touch brush to doll's hair without making combing motions)

7. **Pretend self:** Pretense behavior directed toward self in which pretense is apparent (e.g., raise cup to lip; tip cup, make drinking sounds, or tilt head; stroke own hair with miniature brush; raise phone receiver to ear and vocalize)

8. **Pretend other:** Pretense behavior directed away from child toward other (e.g., feed doll with spoon, bottle, or cup; brush doll's hair; push car on floor and make car noise)

9. **Substitution:** Using a "meaningless" object in a creative or imaginative manner (e.g., drink from seashell; feed baby with stick as "bottle") or using an object in a pretense act in a way that differs from how it has previously been used by the child (e.g., use hairbrush to brush teeth after already using it as a hairbrush on self or other)

10. **Sequence pretend:** Repetition of a single pretense act with minor variation (e.g., drink from bottle, give doll drink, pour into cup, pour into plate) or linking together different pretense schemes (e.g., stir in cup, then drink; put doll in cradle, then kiss good night)

11. **Sequence pretend substitution:** Same as sequence pretend except using an object substitution within sequence (e.g., put doll in cradle, cover with green felt piece as "blanket"; feed self with spoon, then with stick)

12. **Double substitution:** Pretend play in which two materials are transformed, within a single act, into something they are not in reality (e.g., treat peg as doll and a piece of green felt as a blanket and cover peg with felt and say "night-night"; treat stick as person and seashell as cup and give stick a drink)

Source: J. Belsky & R. K. Most. (1981). From exploration to play: A cross-sectional study of infant free play behavior. *Developmental psychology, 17,* 630–639.

substituted and transformed to make up a complete story with beginning, middle, and end.

2-3b Cognitive Development: Vygotsky's Sociocultural Theory

Vygotsky viewed cognitive development as an interaction between children and their social environment. For Vygotsky, knowledge is co-constructed through social interactions. When an adult engages the child in problems that are just above what his or her independent problem solving indicates, the adult supports properties of the child's intellectual functions that are emerging but not yet fully matured (Christy, 2013; Gredler, 2012). Cultural tools mediate and facilitate this co-construction of knowledge; the most important tool for humans is language because "Language is thought; language is culture; language is identity.... Denying language is denying access to thought" (Wink & Putney, 2002, p. 54). In Vygotsky's own words:

> Thought is not merely expressed in words; it comes into existence through them. Every thought tends to connect something with something else, to establish a relationship between things. Every thought moves, grows and develops, fulfills a function, solves a problem. (1934/1986, p. 218)

Speech is comprised of three distinct, yet interrelated, types: social, private, and inner. Although the continuum of speech internalization (i.e., from social to private to inner) is not clearly understood, it clearly represents "a chain of structural and functional transformations between the already evolved, the currently evolving, and the-about-to-evolve speech types" (Damianova & Sullivan, 2011, p. 346). Vygotsky believed that, after social language is developed, children develop **private speech**. The importance of private speech is that children use this talk as a means of self-guidance and direction (Vygotsky, 1934/1986), using words acquired during social speech as symbolic representations of the concepts (Damianova & Sullivan, 2011).

private speech Vygotsky's term for internal dialogue that children use for self-guidance and understanding.

Young children who use more private speech show more improvement on difficult tasks (Berk & Spuhl, 1995; Winsler, Naglieri, & Manfra, 2006) and were more creative (Daugherty & White, 2008) than children who do not use much private speech. In addition, children use more private speech as tasks become more difficult (Berk, 1994; Winsler, Abar, Feder, Schunn, & Rubio, 2007), and when children with learning/behavioral problems use private speech, they are more likely to complete the task successfully (Winsler, Abar, et al., 2007; Winsler, Manfra, & Diaz, 2007). Research with older children suggests that in some group problem-solving situations, private speech may actually serve a social function (e.g., influencing the thinking and behaviors of others), not just a cognitive function for the child engaging in the private speech (Zahner & Moschkovich, 2010).

zone of proximal development Vygotsky's term for a range of tasks that a child is developmentally ready to learn.

Vygotsky hypothesized that higher cognitive processes develop from verbal and nonverbal social interactions. This is accomplished when more mature individuals instruct less mature individuals within their **zone of proximal development** (Wink & Putney, 2002). This term refers to a range of tasks that a child is able to learn with the help of more knowledgeable others (e.g., peers or adults). The zone of proximal development is established by assessing the child's individual level of performance and the child's assisted level of performance. The gap between these two levels is considered the "zone" (Wink & Putney, 2002). As a child is able to accomplish skills at the assisted level independently, the zone shifts upward to the next skill to be addressed. However, the process does not always move in an upward direction. Tzur and Lambert (2011) found that children in their study demonstrated a temporary regression in counting skills when faced with different mathematical problems during one testing session; sometimes they used the more advanced counting strategy, and sometimes they used a less advanced strategy. The phenomenon was explained by the authors when they stated that within the zone of proximal development, one must consider the combined factors of task features, teacher-student interactions, and how the task fits with the student's present schemas (Tzur & Lambert, 2011). While children adopt the language and actions of dialogues and demonstrations of the more knowledgeable other into their private speech and then use those to guide and regulate their own actions, it is not always a straightforward process. We will explore two other aspects of this process in the next section: intersubjectivity and scaffolding.

Intersubjectivity refers to how children and adults come to understand each other by adjusting their views and perspectives to fit the other person. Adults must invest energy in figuring out how the child is approaching or thinking about a particular task to be most effective in helping the child to acquire a new skill or understanding. **Scaffolding** involves changing the support given a learner in the course of teaching a skill or concept (Berk & Winsler, 1995; Bodrova & Leong, 2007; Wink & Putney, 2002). The more knowledgeable other can use a number of instructional strategies to scaffold learning during a new, challenging, or complex task. Verbal encouragement; physical assistance; coaching; providing hints, clues, or cues; asking questions; and breaking the task into manageable steps (without losing the wholeness of the task) are all strategies to assist in accomplishing the given task. As the learner starts mastering the new skills, the more knowledgeable other withdraws instruction and encouragement in direct response to the learner's ability to perform successfully. Caregivers who effectively learn to use intersubjectivity and scaffolding help promote development because children learn to use positive private speech and succeed more easily (Behrend, Rosengran, & Perlmutter, 1992).

A final aspect of Vygotsky's theory involves the use of **make-believe play** in higher cognitive development. Vygotsky believed that children who engage in make-believe play use imagination to act out internal ideas about how the world operates and to set rules by which play is conducted, which helps them learn to think before they act (Berk & Winsler, 1995) (Photo 2–5). Language, therefore, becomes critical for the development of organized make-believe play because metacognitive self-control and self-monitoring behaviors are largely developed through language (Berk, Mann, & Ogan, 2006). The ability to organize or plan make-believe play at advanced levels appears to be dependent on a child's ability to use language for three distinct, yet interrelated, purposes: (1) to reflect on past experiences, (2) to predict future experiences, and (3) to reason about the relationships between past and future events (Westby & Wilson, 2007). Researchers have found that children with greater vocabularies are better able to understand the intentional states (e.g., their beliefs and desires) of other children (Jarrold, Mansergh, & Whiting, 2010), which in turn has been related to engaging in more developed pretend play (Peterson & Wellman, 2009). In contrast, the play of an infant or toddler who is abused would be expected to be at a lower level because of the critical

intersubjectivity Vygotsky's term to explain how children and adults come to understand each other by adjusting perceptions to fit the other person's map of the world.

scaffolding A term describing incremental steps in learning and development from simple to complex.

make-believe play Vygotsky's term for using imagination to act out internal concepts of how the world functions and how rules are formed.

© 2017 Cengage Learning

PHOTO 2–5 Make-believe play can occur in almost any learning area—inside and outside.

role parents have in influencing play that supports social behaviors. In a longitudinal study (children observed playing with the mother at 12- and 24-months of age) of low-income maltreated and nonmaltreated children, only 51 percent of the children demonstrated complex, pretend play (Valentino, Cicchetti, Toth, & Rogosch, 2011). That is significantly lower than previous research on play behaviors of low-income children (see, e.g., Belsky & Most, 1981). Given the importance of pretend play to other areas of development, this result might indicate that interventions to help abusive mothers learn to scaffold their child's pretend play are warranted.

2-3c Language Development

As is evident from the previous discussion, language plays a critical role in cognitive development from a Vygotskian perspective. Language is a tool for thinking (Bodrova & Leong, 2007; McDevitt & Ormrod, 2013). How do children come to acquire language skills for thinking and communicating? The easiest answer, of course, is through engaging in conversations with others.

When adults and children talk with infants and toddlers, they provide examples of the four basic components of language: **phonology**, the basic sounds of the language and how they are combined to make words; **semantics**, what words mean; **syntax**, how to combine words into understandable phrases and sentences; and **pragmatics**, how to engage in communication with others that is socially acceptable and effective (McDevitt & Ormrod, 2013). These conversations must be responsive, however, because responsiveness supports a growing understanding that language is a tool that allows interests, ideas, needs, and desires to be shared socially (Tamis-LeMonda, Kuchirko, & Song, 2014).

Yet, the easy answer is not always the best answer. Complex and somewhat controversial theories have been developed about language and word acquisition. Booth and Waxman (2008) theorize that "as infants and young children establish word meanings, they draw upon their linguistic, conceptual, and perceptual capacities and on the relations among these" (p. 189). Language acquisition from this perspective is not merely the adding on of new vocabulary words but involves the cognitive functions of organizing words by grammatical function (e.g., noun) or conceptual dimensions (e.g., shape, size, real, or pretend). In their study, toddlers extended the use of novel nouns systematically based on the conceptual information provided to them in vignettes (Booth & Waxman, 2008). Tamis-LeMonda et al. (2014) extend our understanding of the role responsive adults play in vocabulary development when they theorized that being responsive assists infants in mapping words to their referents.

Newman (2008), in contrast, suggests that language acquisition is about learning what information to store for later retrieval. She suggests that infants must store enough information so that new words can be distinguished from old words and that initially infants store too much information. Infants may store, for example, information on what words were spoken, who said them, and how they were spoken (e.g., tone).

To fully comprehend language, infants must learn to ignore perceptible but irrelevant information such as tone of voice and to recognize words spoken by a variety of talkers. Variability in the input helps infants recognize

phonology Understanding the basic sounds of the language and how they are combined to make words.

semantics The study of meaning in language, including concepts.

syntax How words combine into understandable phrases and sentences.

pragmatics An understanding of how to engage in communication with others that is socially acceptable and effective.

which acoustic properties are important and which can be ignored. When an infant is familiar with a word spoken by only a particular talker, or in a particular tone of voice, the word's representation is tied to that talker/tone of voice. However, if the infant hears the same word spoken by multiple talkers, in multiple tones of voice, the child learns that these other factors are irrelevant, and the representation becomes less tied to those details. Across a range of language domains, when exposure is more varied, infants focus less attention on the specific details of the input and instead begin to abstract across exemplars, focusing on areas of commonality (Newman, 2008, p. 231).

Thus, from this perspective, providing infants with a language-rich environment involves exposing infants to a number of different speakers so that commonalities can be uncovered. As you can see, learning to communicate is a complex task that involves several different, yet related skills.

Infants must learn strategies for sending verbal and nonverbal messages to others. Newborns initiate interaction by making eye contact, and by 4 months of age, they gaze in the same direction as the caregiver (Tomasello, 1999). Around the same time, they also begin to engage in verbal communication when they **coo** (or make repetitive vowel sounds). Babies are able to screen out many sounds that are not useful in understanding their native language by the age of 6 months (Polka & Werker, 1994). The way adults speak with infants influences language acquisition. For example, Singh, Nestor, Parikh, and Yull (2009) found that, as early as 7 months, infants demonstrated greater word recognition when a new word was introduced by an adult who spoke using **infant-directed speech** (sometimes called motherese). The characteristics of infant-directed speech, exaggerated intonation, reduced speech rate, and shorter utterance duration, seem to match how infants learn language. Furthermore, the use of infant-directed speech in one-on-one parent-child interactions at 11 months and 14 months was positively correlated with both concurrent speech utterances and word production at 24 months (Ramírez-Esparza, García-Sierra, & Kuhl, 2014). In a series of experiments, infants who heard infant-directed speech that was comprised of higher pitch, greater pitch variation, and longer durations acquired word labels and meanings more readily than when those words were presented using adult-directed speech (Estes & Hurley, 2013). These findings suggest that infants begin to discriminate, associate, and analyze the structure of words and sentences before 9 months of age. These skills are vital to acquiring productive language skills within their native language.

Around 6 or 7 months of age, infants begin to **babble** (or produce speech-like syllables such as *ba, ra*) using sounds from their native language. The first "real" word is typically spoken around the first birthday. For a while, toddlers will blend babble with a real word in what is called **jargon**. To illustrate, an infant says "tatata car bebe" while playing. The teacher might respond with elaboration by saying "You moved the car. You pushed it. It went bye-bye." In this case, the adult supplies words that help to explain what the child is experiencing, thus encouraging the acquisition of other new words and facilitating the linking of two or three "real" words into sentences or **telegraphic speech**. Just as a telegraphic message omits words, telegraphic speech includes only the words vital to the meaning the toddler is trying to convey. By 36 months, most toddlers are able to clearly and effectively communicate their wants, needs, and ideas.

coo A vocalization typically produced by infants from birth to 4 months old that resembles vowel-like sounds.

infant-directed speech Exaggerated intonation, reduced speech rate, and shorter utterance duration used when speaking to infants. In the past, other terms used to describe the same speech patterns were child-directed speech, motherese, or parentese.

babble Prelanguage speech with which the baby explores the variety of sounds.

jargon Language term that refers to the mixing of one real word with strings of babble.

telegraphic speech When infants and toddlers combine two or three words into a sentence including only key words (e.g., "go daddy").

Adults use a combination of gestures and words when communicating with infants. Research suggests that this is important to how children learn language (labels, categories), create meaning (symbolic understanding), and understand references. In an experimental study, Graham and Kilbreath (2007) found that infants possess a more generalized symbolic system at 14 months than at 22 months. Early in development, infants use both words and gestures to delineate object categories and guide their inductive inferences. At 22 months, they relied on just words. In another study, infants (13 months) were shown a video of an actress pointing to a location of a hidden object and naming it. When the object was revealed, the infants looked longer when the object was found in a location not indicated by the gesture (Gliga & Csibra, 2009). This indicates that very young infants expect that concurrently occurring words and gestures communicate the same message in reference to an object.

Just as adults do with them, infants use gestural communication to show what they want. Early on, infants combine behaviors from multiple modalities (language, gesture, and affect) to deliver a communicative message at levels greater than expected by chance (Parladé & Iverson, 2011). Using parental diaries, Carpendale and Carpendale (2010) concluded that the pointing gesture evolves from private fingertip exploration that parents responded to. Babies touch objects, the caregiver notices and gives attention, and they further direct the caregiver to do something by pointing or gesturing. The pointing behavior was transformed from one of personal exploration to social meaning between the adult and child. Gestures have also been found to change as the child develops and gains more language. For example, when experiencing a language explosion (rapid increase in number of words in vocabulary), the communicative system of language, gesture, and affect was disrupted (Parladé & Iverson, 2011), and the number of coordinated words decreased. Others have found that as children's brains develop, they process words and gestures differently. For example, at 18 months, evidence shows that infants attend to both gestures and words when noticing a mismatch in information, whereas at 26 months, they attend to just the words (Sheehan, Namy, & Mills, 2007). In addition, as a child's vocabulary increases and becomes more descriptive, the use of gestures tends to lessen. Taken together, these results suggest that children go through recognizable periods of communicative reorganization during the first three years of life.

While an adult must learn to understand the infant's gestures, the infant must learn to understand the adult's (Photo 2–6). This task might be more

© 2017 Cengage Learning

PHOTO 2–6 Adults need to learn to understand the gestures of infants, just as infants need to understand an adult's gestures.

challenging as the infant must understand what object her attention is being directed toward (e.g., referential intention) as well as why her attention is being directed there (e.g., social intention). Liebel, Behne, Carpenter, and Tomasello (2009) found that as early as 14 months of age, infants responded more to gestures that reflected a shared experience with the adult. In other words, the infants used the shared experience to identify referents and to infer the social intention, "thus showing a very flexible use of shared experience to interpret others' communicative acts" (p. 270).

Gestures and signs are not only important for children to communicate their desires, but they also help adults rethink young children's capabilities; by "listening" to their gestures, adults gain insight into individual infants' capabilities and respect for the capacities of preverbal children (Vallotton, 2011) as well as become more responsive to their nonverbal cues (Kirk, Howlett, Pine, & Fletcher, 2013). When adults take the children's preverbal vocalizations, gestures, and words seriously, as important forms of communication, they might be enhancing important aspects of children's language development.

Engaging in conversations about events as they happen supports and facilitates language development. Yet, that has been found to not be enough. As mentioned previously, infant-directed speech promotes language development because it captures and sustains the baby's focal attention when the adult adjusts her tone, volume, and speech patterns. In addition, caregivers should label and describe things to which the baby visually attends. Dominey and Dodane (2004) theorized that when adults use both infant-directed speech and joint attention (i.e., attend to what the child is looking at), infants are better able to use general learning mechanisms to acquire knowledge of grammatical constructions. To illustrate, when a caregiver copies or mimics the baby's vocalization, the child can attend to the sounds that the caregiver makes as well as engage in turn-taking: the baby vocalizes, the caregiver vocalizes in return and waits for a response, and the "conversation" continues. Games such as patty cake help babies interact actively and even initiate turn-taking interactions.

These interactions are indicative of the relationships between the caregiver and a specific infant. Infant-directed speech has been found to be different depending on whether the adult is speaking with a boy or a girl, yet those differences do not seem to appear in children's productions before the age of 3 (Foulkes, Docherty, & Watt, 2005). If one person within the relationship is not functioning optimally, the relationship and the developmental outcomes for the children can be drastically altered. For example, caregivers who interrupt or restrict the baby's focal attention and activities impede language development (Carpenter, Nagell, & Tomasello, 1998). In another example, babies who cry for long periods of time or who are frequently distressed may elicit fewer positive vocal interactions from the parent or caregiver, thus impeding the typical pattern of language development (Locke, 2006). The language relationship does not stay static over time but rather responds to the growing capabilities of the infant. Almost as soon as the baby starts to use "real" words, caregiver speech changes to more information, directions, and questions rather than infant-directed speech (Murray, Johnson, & Peters, 1990).

Baby signing is a technique that has been studied in relationship to preparing youngsters to conquer the challenges of communication and is considered by many to be a method that enhances learning. A follow-up study of children who learned Baby Sign demonstrated that those children outperformed their nonbaby signing peers by a very impressive margin on the WISC III, a universal test to measure language (Acredolo, Goodwyn, & Abrams, 2009). Yet, a more recent study calls into question the benefit of baby signing on language outcomes. Kirk et al. (2013) did not find any significant differences in five measures of receptive and productive language when a parent used gestures or gestures in combination with verbal communication. Interestingly, although the infants did acquire and use the gestures associated with the targeted words before the onset of speech, "this did not promote the acquisition of those target words, nor did it boost the infants' language abilities" (Kirk et al., 2013, p. 580). Thus, for this sample of very young children, encouraging the use of gestures did not result in higher scores on any of the measures of language.

As you now understand, learning to receive and produce verbal and nonverbal communication is a very complex process on which theorists and researchers do not always agree. It is beyond the scope of this text to fully investigate all aspects of language development. It must suffice to say that young children quickly learn the rules of speech governing their native language, and most are proficient language users by around 6 years of age. Teachers and parents enhance children's language development by labeling, describing, mirroring, and actively engaging the child in conversations.

READING CHECKPOINT

Before moving on with your reading, make sure that you can answer the following questions about the material discussed so far.

1. Discuss Piaget's stages of cognitive development in terms of learning experiences for 2-year-olds. Include concepts such as assimilation, accommodation, and disequilibrium in your answer.
2. Provide a specific example of each of Piaget's types of knowledge.
3. Use Vygotsky's theory to explain how you would scaffold a toddler with the skill of dressing, including the concept of private speech.
4. Explain the typical pattern of language development and the role adults play in the process.

Summary

2-1 Discuss the differences between development and learning.

Development and *learning* are not synonymous terms. They have precise definitions that need to be understood and applied to your observations of very young children.

2-2 Investigate typical patterns of physical development between birth and thirty-six months of age.

Typical patterns of physical development were investigated for children birth to age 3. Emphasis was placed on understanding brain development, patterns of physical growth, the impact of hearing and vision, and milestones for motor development.

2-3 Deconstruct typical patterns of cognitive/language development between birth and thirty-six months of age.

This chapter explored how very young children develop cognitively, using two theorists: Jean Piaget and Lev Vygotsky. Although these theorists have some aspects in common, they do differ on important points. Language development was investigated in terms of milestones for verbal and nonverbal communication. Additionally, the value of teaching Baby Signs was considered based on current research.

CASE STUDY Amanda

Family Stress Impacts Development

Amanda Hasha is a 9-month-old girl who has been in child care for the past three months. Lately, Sheila, her primary caregiver, notices that Amanda is not gaining weight, looks tired but does not sleep well, and cries often. Sheila meets with the director and the other caregivers in her classroom to share her concerns and listens as they all confirm her observations and suggest a family conference. Sheila then sets up a conference with Mrs. Hasha to discuss Amanda's problems.

Sheila starts the conference by describing her observations. She informs Mrs. Hasha that the other caregivers have observed the same behaviors and tells her the steps that have been taken to comfort Amanda. Sheila then asks Mrs. Hasha what she sees at home and listens to her.

Mrs. Hasha: "I've had a lot of problems lately that I'm sure have affected Amanda. Her father had an accident and is in the hospital, so I go to see him every chance I can."

Sheila: "My! It sounds like you have been under a lot of stress and worry lately."

Mrs. Hasha: "I just don't know what to do. No one else is around to help, so I sometimes have Amanda's sister watch her even though she's only eight."

Sheila: "So, you've had no help except for your older daughter. It sounds overwhelming."

Mrs. Hasha: "Yes, it certainly is! I wish I knew how to get the kids cared for so I could be at the hospital more often."

Sheila: "It sounds like you really need help with the children so you can help your husband more."

Mrs. Hasha: "That's right. Do you have any idea who might help me?"

Sheila: "I know there are many sources for help in the community. Have you thought to ask at the hospital, your church, or here at school?"

Mrs. Hasha: "That's a very good idea. Our church has a volunteer program, but I don't want to impose on our minister. She is very busy."

Sheila: "I'm sure your minister would help, if you just talk with her. Would you like me to ask around at some of the programs the county offers? I'm sure help is available for this kind of situation."

Mrs. Hasha: "Yes. Thank you so much. I will ask at church also. I know that Amanda will be better if she has an adult to care for her when I can't be there."

Within a week, Mrs. Hasha has volunteers from her church helping to care for the children. Amanda has changed from being stressed to calm and happy. She has begun to eat better at school, and minimal weight gain has been noted. Through the use of a family conference, Sheila was able to help Mrs. Hasha share her problems and arrive at solutions to improve Amanda's health and development.

1. Discuss what "warning signs" Sheila noted in Amanda's behavior. Would you have wanted to act on this information? Why or why not?
2. How did Sheila use her relationships (i.e., colleagues and child's family) to support and enhance her work with Amanda?
3. Imagine that Sheila said the following during her conversation with Mrs. Hasha: "You leave Amanda with your 8-year-old daughter. Do you know how dangerous that is?" How might the outcome of the conversation been affected? Why?

Lesson Plan

Title: *Who's Outside?*

Child Observation:

Ceren (14 months) toddled over to the window and began to hit his hand on it. The 3-year-old child in the outside learning environment turned to look at him. She ran over and put her nose on the window. Ceren leaned back and then began to giggle.

Child's Developmental Goal:

To develop receptive language skills.

To engage in turn-taking as part of a conversation.

Materials: *None*

Preparation: *None*

Learning Environment:

1. When you notice Ceren near the window, join him.
2. While looking out the window with him, discuss what you notice outside by using descriptive language. To illustrate, you could say:

    "The preschool children are enjoying being outside today. They are running in the grass. I think they might be playing chase. Sophia is laughing while she runs."

3. Invite the child to participate in a conversation by asking prompts or open-ended questions such as:
    a. I wonder why she is smiling so much.
    b. What do you think she will do next?
4. Accept and elaborate on the toddler's answers. For example, if the child says "sing," you might respond:

    "She is swinging. That must be making her happy. Do you want to swing when we go outside later?"

Guidance Consideration:

If Ceren becomes excited and hits the window, redirect him to tap the window gently. If he becomes too excited or rough, give him a choice of two other learning experiences. For example, you can offer drawing what he saw through the window or dancing with scarves to music (e.g., two of his favorite experiences).

Variations:

Make up a story about what you are watching outside. Invite the child to answer questions that could add details to the story.

⌄⌄ Professional Resource Download

Additional Resources

Gallahue, D. Ozmun, J., & Goodway, J. (2012). *Understanding motor development: Infants, children, adolescents, adults* (7th ed.). New York: McGraw-Hill Humanities/Social Sciences/Languages.

Justice, L. M., & Redle, E. E. (2014). *Communication sciences and disorders: A clinical evidence-based approach* (3rd ed.). Upper Saddle River, NJ: Pearson Prentice Hall.

Pica, R. (2014). *Toddlers moving and learning: A physical education curriculum.* Minneapolis, MN: Redleaf Press.

Stamm, J. (2008). *Bright from the start: The simple, science-backed way to nurture your child's developing mind from birth to age 3* (reprint). New York: Gotham.

3 Social and Emotional Development

CHAPTER

Learning Objectives

After reading this chapter, you should be able to:

3-1 Determine typical patterns of emotional development between birth and thirty-six months of age.

3-2 Sequence typical patterns of social development between birth and thirty-six months of age.

Standards Addressed in This Chapter

naeyc NAEYC Standards for Early Childhood Professional Preparation

1 Promoting Child Development and Learning

DAP Developmentally Appropriate Practice Guidelines

2 Teaching to Enhance Development and Learning

In addition, the NAEYC standards for developmentally appropriate practice are divided into six areas particularly important to infant/toddler care. The following area is addressed in this chapter: *Policies*.

© 2017 Cengage Learning

3-1 Patterns of Emotional Development

Unlike most other warm-blooded species, human infants are totally depen-dent on the environment to supply their most basic needs. For independent physical survival, children are born nine months too soon because they require assistance for that amount of time before they can crawl and move independently within the environment. Therefore, a caregiver needs to cre-ate a safe and secure space for the physical and emotional survival of the child. A child should be provided with conscious care; be kept warm, fed, and exposed to optimal levels of stress; and should have his needs responded to in a respectful manner. Very young children should be touched, kept close to the chest, talked to, exposed to soft music, and rocked. Babies should be provided with appropriate transportation to move from one place to another safely.

High-quality child care centers create positive learning atmospheres in which children feel secure in initiating responses to their environment based on interest and curiosity. Children should not be judged because they are learning socially acceptable emotional responses; this takes a great deal of time—many, many years to accomplish. When the child's emo-tional needs are met, he experiences a world that invites his participation.

The most basic feelings on a physical level are pleasure and pain. It was once thought that newborns experience only these two general feeling states. However, anyone who has cared for young infants extensively under-stands that they experience and express the full range of human emotion from ecstasy to deep sorrow. Through active experience with their envi-ronment, babies quickly learn to repeat behaviors that result in pleasurable experiences and avoid, as much as they can, those that result in pain. Yet, this desire to repeat or avoid outcomes goes far beyond a behavior-response pattern; it reflects how the brain is being wired (see Chapter 2). Repeated experiences as well as emotional deprivation early in life rewire the brain.

It is impossible to protect infants and toddlers from experiencing phys-ical and emotional pain, no matter how sensitive and caring we are. Pain is a natural and normal life experience and is extremely valuable for our ability to stay alive and learn from experience. Just as athletes understand the saying "No pain: no gain" because muscles don't grow stronger unless they are taxed, most changes that produce growth cause some pain along with pleasure. Adults should help children learn to cope during moments of pain. Caregivers who try to protect children from all pain and keep them in a state of pleasure establish unrealistic expectations for themselves and the children in their care.

However, it should be noted that infants and toddlers are especially vulnerable to painful experiences because of their lack of defenses. When young children cannot escape a situation of persistent emotional pain, such as consistent abandonment, rejection, or adult anger, or a situation of chronic physical pain, such as physical or sexual abuse, healthy emotional development is jeopardized. Under these conditions, children learn their own feelings or the feelings of others are not important, leading to a lack of self-awareness and insensitivity to others.

It may seem that infants are selfish because they attend only to their own needs, but that is not possible because infants are limited in their ability to understand the impact of their behaviors on others. For example, when a 3-month old baby wakes up hungry in the middle of the night, she does not have the awareness that her hunger is an inconvenience to her sleeping caregiver. However, when the child's basic needs are filled, she is able to be curious, sensitive, and aware of other people. From this basic level, children progress to balancing their own feelings and needs with the feelings and needs of other people and become capable of intimate relationships with equal give and take.

It sometimes appears that young children move through emotions rapidly. One minute a young toddler may scream, and the next moment jump into your arms and give you a hug. As cognitive and language skills develop with age, the child can use words better to specify and describe many different feeling states. By the age of 5 or 6, children who have experienced quality caregiving are capable of sophisticated, conscious discrimination of self from others in terms of thoughts, feelings, and behaviors.

During the first three years of life, the combination of traits present at birth, including physical size, health, and temperament, interact with pleasurable and painful experiences in the environment to form the growing child's identity (e.g., the child's perceptions of self, others, and the world). The next sections describe theories of identity development as they pertain to infants and toddlers. The theories discussed here show how children create models of the world through a complex process whereby the characteristics they bring with them impact and are shaped through interactions with adults and other children. These models of the world become the basis for the enduring reactions and patterns people have throughout life—what we call personality.

3-1a Erikson's Psychosocial Theory

Erikson's lifespan theory (1950) adds to our understanding of how children develop emotionally by responding to life's challenges. He labeled his theory psychosocial because the various challenges refer to simultaneous concerns about oneself (*psycho-*) and relationships with other people (*-social*) (McDevitt & Ormrod, 2013). He believed that children must resolve eight crises or stages as they progress from infancy through old age. Each crisis is seen as a turning point where development can move forward successfully or take a turn in a more negative direction. Although he believed that the resolution of prior stages impacts the outcomes of future stages, he also thought that people could revisit crises that were unresolved (or resolved toward a negative outcome) during later development. Of the eight stages, the first three are extremely important in the development of infants and toddlers.

1. **Basic trust versus mistrust.** Children learn to trust or mistrust themselves and the world during infancy depending on the warmth and sensitivity they are given. Trust is developed through consistent, responsive, and appropriate behavior from the caregiver. In those situations, infants learn that their needs are important and that they can trust others will respond to their signals with helpful solutions. When infants are required to wait too long for comfort, when they are handled harshly and insensitively, or when they are responded to in an inconsistent manner, they develop basic

mistrust of themselves and others. While the responsibility for appropriate response rests solely on the shoulders of the adult, the child also plays an active part in the interaction. When infants are difficult to soothe, it is discouraging, and frustration levels rise. Hence, even if the adult starts out calm and responsive, when the issue is not easily resolved, negative emotions may become part of the interaction.

2. Autonomy versus shame and doubt. After infants become mobile, a process of separation and individuation begins, eventually resulting in autonomy. Children need to choose and decide things for themselves. When caregivers permit reasonable free choices and do not force or shame children, autonomy and self-confidence are fostered. If caregivers place too many limits on behavior or constantly restrict choices, children learn dependency and lack confidence in their ability to make decisions. Thus, parents and teachers must balance support and encouragement with protection and guidance (Graves & Larkin, 2006).

3. Initiative versus guilt. When caregivers support a child's sense of purpose and direction, initiative in the form of ambition and responsibility is developed. When caregivers demand too much self-control or responsibilities that are not age appropriate, children respond by feeling overcontrolled, guilty, or both.

Erikson's stages reveal how children develop the qualities that result in a happy, meaningful life. As the first stage suggests, developing a sense of trust during the first year of life can result in positive, lasting personal assets that impact the resolutions of future stages. As caregivers, the impact of our day-in and day-out responses to children's basic needs cannot be overestimated. Moreover, recent research suggests that infants as young as 12 months demonstrate trust for an adult when the adult behaves as an expert (Stenberg, 2013). For example, when the expert adult used appropriate language to describe the toy (e.g., color, shape) and successfully used the toy, the infant looked more at the expert and played with the toy more (as compared to the nonexpert). The author concluded that "In terms of social referencing, these findings can be interpreted as infants showing more interest in seeking information from a reliable information source and more motivated to use information from a reliable source than from a less reliable source" (pp. 898–899). Thus, when trust is established with an infant (in this case based on expertise), the very young child uses that person as a source of information or as a model for behavior.

Developing Trust

Trust and security develop largely from adults' own trustworthy behavior. Consistently responding to the child's cues or behaviors within an atmosphere of acceptance and appreciation is important to building trust. Some ways to ensure consistent and appropriate caregiver behavior with children include establishing consistent routines and supplying generous amounts of the three *A*s of child care: Attention, Approval, and Attunement (see Chapter 4). Consistently responding to the needs of the child with warmth and respect will help her to develop security and trust. Reading the infant's or toddler's cues and being able to look at things from her perspective are necessary components in responsive caregiving

(Oppenheim & Koren-Karie, 2002). Responsive caregivers also provided sensitive guidance when discussing potentially emotionally distressing topics with children (Koren-Karie, Oppenheim, Yuval-Adler, & Mor, 2013). When child care policies that ensure a low infant-caregiver ratio are in place, early childhood educators are available to respond to the many emotional needs of each child (Photo 3–1).

Developing Autonomy

As mentioned previously, toddlers struggle with balancing autonomy with shame and doubt. Sakagami (2010) believes that defiance and compliance are both examples of autonomy, albeit in very different forms. When adults impose too much control, toddlers experience anger, resist being controlled, and can be viewed by adults as defiant. Thus, "defiant" behavior is a demonstration of autonomy. Toddlers also express autonomy when they eagerly commit to and comply with the parents' or adults' agenda.

Supporting Initiative

Thus, Sakagami (2010) concurs with Erikson's suggestion that children need reasonable freedom and expectations as they journey through toddlerhood

© 2017 Cengage Learning

PHOTO 3–1 Children need help from adults when learning to regulate their emotions.

to minimize defiance and maximize compliance. To provide such freedoms and expectations, you need to know (1) normal patterns of development, and (2) each child's individual pattern of development. Because the sequence of development is similar among children, you have some guidelines for your expectations. A caregiver needs to know where each child fits within the range of development. If you expect children to accomplish things that are below or above them developmentally, you produce undue stress. For example, you can expect 30-month-old Mark to want to feed himself lunch because he possesses the skills to hold a spoon in his hand, fill it with food, and usually get it up to his mouth. It is unreasonable to expect 9-month-old Naomi to have that level of muscular coordination or the desire to show such initiative. The Developmental Milestones in Appendix A can assist you in recording observations, evaluating developmental levels, and using that information to make informed decisions when interacting with very young children. Understanding developmental milestones helps to establish security and trust because the children engage in experiences that are met with success, mastery, and the three *A*s rather than stress, frustration, and rejection.

3-1b Separate and Together

Two competing theories attempt to explain the process by which infants develop a sense of self. The theories use many of the same ideas but examine the process from opposite directions. A pediatrician from Vienna named Margaret Mahler wrote extensively about the importance of bonding between parent and child and the process is called **separation-individuation** (Greenberg & Mitchell, 1983). Mahler argued that children begin life believing that they are fused or physically a part of their mother. Over the course of the first few months and years, they must separate to become an individual person. Between birth and 4 months of age, infants slowly come to show increased sensitivity to the external world and develop a beginning awareness that their primary caregiver is an external object. Mahler's four subphases of separation-individuation begin around 4 months of age and are as follows:

separation-individuation
The process of defining self as separate from others, which starts in infancy and continues throughout childhood.

Subphase	Age
1. differentiation	4 months to 10 months
2. practicing	10 months to 15 months
3. rapprochement	15 months to 36 months
4. libidinal object constancy	36 months throughout childhood

Differentiation

From 4 to 10 months of age, the *differentiation* subphase occurs, in which the baby begins to act in more self-determined ways and explores the caregiver (e.g., pulls hair, clothes). The baby also scans the world and checks back to the caregiver to discriminate "caregiver" from "other." The baby develops skill in discriminating external from internal sensations as well. This discrimination forms the basis for self-awareness (self-concept).

Practicing

After the baby becomes mobile, the *practicing* subphase begins. Because the baby can now move away from the caregiver, increased body discrimination and awareness of separateness from others are manifested. The child begins using the caregiver as an emotional and physical "refueling station"—moving short distances away and then returning for emotional nourishment. The child also concentrates on her own abilities separate from the caregiver and becomes **omnipotent** (not aware of any physical limitations). According to Mahler, Pine, and Bergman (1975), the caregiver must allow physical and psychological separation during this phase if the child is to establish a strong identity.

omnipotent The sense of being unaware of any physical limitations and feeling above physical laws.

Rapproachement

Between 15 and 18 months, the toddler enters the *rapprochement* subphase, where the sense of omnipotence (having no limits) is broken. What is wanted is not always immediately available, so the child experiences frustration, separation anxiety, and the realization that caregivers are separate people who don't always say "yes." Often, children will alternate between clinging neediness and intense battling with caregivers because of conflicting dependence and independence needs. Because of rapid language development during this period, the child struggles with gender identity, accepting "no," and the development of beliefs, attitudes, and values to add to the already formed self-concept.

Libidinal Object Constancy

Mahler's final subphase of *libidinal object constancy* starts around 36 months and involves developing a stable concept of the self (one that does not change) and a stable concept of other people, places, and things. Self-constancy and object constancy are required so that the toddler develops a coherent sense of self (e.g., identity). During this phase, it is crucial that the caregiver act as a buffer between the child and the world while supporting and respecting the competencies of the growing child to separate and individuate without anxiety or fear.

Stern's Theory

Daniel Stern, while using the same concepts of bonding and separation, theorized that the process worked in the opposite direction of Mahler. Stern reasoned that infants are born alone and must learn to be with others (Galinsky, 2010). Using videos of infant-parent interactions, Stern analyzed frame by frame how the adult and child responded to each other. He discovered that infants were in synchrony with their mothers, mirroring her actions (Stern, 1985). For example, when the mother lifted her arm, the infant lifted her arm. The infants' actions must take place in a temporal space that is minute given the child's memory capacities (Stern, 2000). In other words, they have limited capabilities to take in the visual information, store it, process it, and create a deliberate reaction. These results raise the question: How can infants be responsive in this manner, if they believe they are fused or a part of the mother? Stern (2008) believes that infants must be born with the "capacity for intersubjectivity in some primary fashion" (p. 181), or the ability "to participate in and, in some way, sense or know about the other person's experience" (p. 182). Intersubjectivity is present but not fully formed at birth and then develops further over time. Research (reviewed in Stern 2008) suggests that infants quickly learn to read the intentions of others, not just their behavior. The challenge for infants, from this perspective, is not separation from important adults but finding ways to join their intentions with these adults.

The three theoretical perspectives of Piaget, Mahler, and Stern demonstrate, albeit in different ways, the importance of adults in the formation of identity and personality during the first three years of life. Because of the significance of individual child characteristics in all of these theories, the discussion will now turn to three other factors integral to emotional development: temperament, emotional intelligence, and self-esteem.

3-1c Temperament

Temperament has been defined as "the basic style which characterizes a person's behavior" (Chess, Thomas, & Birch, 1976). All children are born with particular temperaments. Temperament will influence what they do, what they learn, what they feel about themselves and others, and what kinds of interactions they have with people and objects.

Early research suggested that temperament is stable and not very changeable by environmental influences (Caspi & Silva, 1995). More recent research supports the position of continuity in temperament from

temperament Physical, emotional, and social personality traits and characteristics.

infancy to toddlerhood to 3 (Losonczy-Marchall, 2014) or 4 (Carranza, González-Salinas, & Ato, 2013) years of age. However, a larger body of research provides evidence that child-rearing practices and other environmental factors can dramatically influence temperament during the first three years (Gunnar, 1998; Worobey & Islas-Lopez, 2009). More specifically, Jansen and colleagues found that infants in lower-income families were more likely to have been rated as having a difficult temperament and that the association was partially explained by level of family stress and maternal psychological well-being (Jansen, Raat, Mackenbach, Jaddoe, Hofman, Verhulst, et al., 2009). This raises the question of whether child temperament is a cause or a consequence of particular contextual impacts because other research discovered that as aspects of infant temperament become more negative, parenting becomes more negative (Bridgett, Gartstein, Putnam, McKay, Iddins, Robertson, et al., 2009; Davis, Schoppe-Sullivan, Mangelsdorf, & Brown, 2009) or mothers reported higher levels of parenting stress (Oddi, Murdock, Vadnais, Bridgett, & Gartstein, 2013; Siqveland, Olafsen, & Moe, 2013). These results suggest that infants play a significant role in shaping their own development and the context in which that development is occurring.

Chess et al. (1976) worked with hundreds of children and their parents to investigate how babies differ in their styles of behavior. The analysis of observations and interviews revealed nine patterns of behavior. Within each pattern, they found a range of behaviors. Table 3–1 lists the nine

TABLE 3–1 ▶ Behavioral Categories of Temperament

BEHAVIORAL CATEGORY	EXTREMES	
	MORE	LESS
(1) Activity Level	Hyperactive—can't sit still	Lethargic—sedate, passive
(2) Regularity	Rigid and inflexible patterns	Unpredictable and inconsistent patterns
(3) Response to New Situations	Outgoing, aggressive, approaching	Withdrawing, timid, highly cautious
(4) Adaptability	Likes surprises, fights routine, dislikes structure	Dislikes change, likes routine, needs structure
(5) Sensory Threshold	Unaware of changes in light, sound, smell	Highly sensitive to changes in light, sound, smell
(6) Positive or Negative Mood	Feels optimistic	Feels negative; denies positive
(7) Response Intensity	Highly loud and animated, high energy	Very quiet and soft; low energy
(8) Distractibility	Insensitive to visual and auditory stimuli outside self	Unable to focus attention, highly sensitive to visual and auditory stimuli
(9) Persistence	Persists until task completed	Gives up easily, doesn't try new things

© Cengage Learning

categories and extremes of behaviors observed in each category. The behavior of most infants falls somewhere between these extremes. Chess and her colleagues further collapsed the nine patterns into three basic types of temperament: flexible and easy, slow to warm up, and difficult.

More recent research suggests that it is helpful to consider how children react to new experiences, rather than attempt to classify them into patterns based on a variety of different behaviors. Some children react to novel or unfamiliar situations by expressing delight or excitement, or they easily engage in interactions with the object or person (i.e., exuberance); other children react to the same situations by being hypervigilant and using motor reactivity, crying, and other means to express negative affect (i.e., behavioral inhibition) (Fox, Henderson, Rubin, Calkins, & Schmidt, 2001; Hane, Fox, Henderson, & Marshall, 2008). Kagan and his colleagues discovered that crying at 4 months, not motor reactivity, was associated with behavioral inhibition during the second year of life (Moehler, Kagan, Oelkers-Ax, Brunner, Poustka, Haffner, et al., 2008). That result caused the researchers to wonder about the role motor reactivity plays early in development; this is important because behavioral inhibition has been associated with both short-term and long-term social adjustment issues. Preschoolers and adolescents who were higher on behavioral inhibition in infancy or toddlerhood were more socially withdrawn (Pérez-Edgar, Bar-Haim, McDermott, Chronis-Tuscano, Pine, & Fox, 2010; Pérez-Edgar, Reeb-Sutherland, McDermott, White, Henderson, Degnan, et al., 2011; Pérez-Edgar, Schmidt, Henderson, Schulkin, & Fox, 2008).

The following descriptions illustrate how you might notice temperament (exuberance or behavioral inhibition) in response to classroom situations.

> Jamol hides behind his mother as he enters the room each morning. He hides behind the caregiver whenever someone strange walks in the door. When others play with a new ball, he stands by the wall and watches. He leaves food he does not recognize on his plate, refusing to take a bite. Jamol needs time to get used to new situations. Jamol becomes distressed when he is pushed into new activities. Telling him that a new ball will not hurt him or that the strange food is good for him does not convince him. When he feels comfortable, he will play with the new ball. He needs time and space for himself while he becomes familiar with a situation. It may take several offerings before he eventually tries the new food.
>
> Paulo arrives in the morning with a big smile. She looks around the room and notices a new puzzle set out on the table. She rushes over to it, asking the caregiver about it and giggling at the picture. She takes the puzzle pieces out, puts some of the pieces back in, and then seeks assistance from the caregiver. Paulo is excited about new situations and eager to try new experiences.

Goodness-of-Fit Model

Thomas and Chess (1977) suggest that the type of temperament a child has is less important to her overall functioning than the temperamental match she has with her caregiver. The adult-child goodness-of-fit model has been supported by research with families (Karreman, de Haas, van Tuijl, van Aken, &

goodness-of-fit The temperamental match between very young children and their caregivers.

© Cengage Learning

PHOTO 3–2 This persistent baby may be thinking, "I can do it. I know I can reach that toy!"

Deković, 2010; Schoppe-Sullivan, Mangelsdorf, Brown, & Szewczyk Sokolowski, 2007; Van Aken, Junger, Verhoeven, Van Aken, & Deković, 2007) and early childhood educators (Churchill, 2003; De Schipper, Tavecchio, Van IJzendoorn, & Van Zeijl, 2004; LaBilloisa & Lagacé-Séguin, 2009; Rudasill, 2011).

Identifying each child's temperament as well as your own will help you better respond as an effective caregiver (Photo 3–2). Franyo and Hyson (1999) found that temperament workshops designed especially for early childhood teachers resulted in their gaining important knowledge about temperament concepts. However, there was no evidence that these workshops effectively increased the caregivers' acceptance of children's behaviors and feelings. Carefully reflecting about your own and the children's temperament can assist you with creating "goodness of fit" by identifying strategies to responsively and respectfully meet the needs of the children who are different from yourself.

Consider the following example.

> Olaf is playing with blocks. The tall stack he built falls over, one block hitting hard on his hand. He yells loudly. Ray is playing nearby and also is hit by a falling block. He looks up in surprise but does not say anything.

What will you as a caregiver do? What will you say? What is *loud* to you? What is acceptable to you? Why is a behavior acceptable or not to you? Do you think Ray is *better* than Olaf because he did not react loudly? What you do and say to Olaf reflects your acceptance or rejection of him as a person, reflects whether you are able to help him adapt to his environment, and reflects your ability to adapt to the child.

3-1d Emotional Intelligence and the Brain

Emotional competence is the demonstration of self-efficacy in emotion-provoking social interactions. In other words, infants and toddlers must learn to know, for example, not only when they need to regulate their emotions but also how they need to be regulated in a given situation. The application of emotional intelligence through the demonstration of emotional competence is a lifelong task that begins early in life and is influenced significantly by the development of particular regions of the brain.

limbic system The system responsible for emotional control, emotional responses, hormonal secretions, mood, motivation, and pain/pleasure sensations.

The **limbic system**, which cuts across and connects the three parts of the brain discussed in Chapter 2, is responsible for emotional control,

FIGURE 3–1 ▸ Limbic System

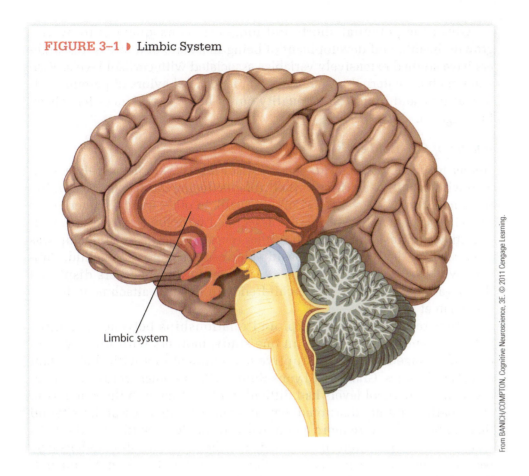

Limbic system

From BANICH/COMPTON, Cognitive Neuroscience, 3E. © 2011 Cengage Learning.

emotional responses, hormonal secretions, mood, motivation, and pain/ pleasure sensations (Figure 3–1). This system includes, but is not limited to, the following parts of the brain: amygdala, hippocampus, thalamus, and hypothalamus. These structures help infants generate basic emotions (e.g., fear, joy, anger), produce bodily responses to emotions such as facial expressions (e.g., frown) and physiological changes (e.g., increased heart rate), and with positive environmental input, assist children in learning to appropriately express and control their emotions.

The thalamus and amygdala play particularly important roles in emotional regulation. When a threat is perceived, the thalamus sends sensory signals to the cortex, which processes the information and, if necessary, sends a message to the amygdala to respond. The amygdala then signals the rest of the body to get ready for a response by releasing adrenaline and other stress hormones such as cortisol. These hormones increase heart and breathing rates and cause the person experiencing the threat to have more focused attention on "fight or flight." The release of these hormones results, then, in diverting the body away from functions unnecessary to survival such as growth, reproduction, and defending against germs or disease (e.g., immune system decreases functioning). When a person is "emotionally hijacked," however, this pathway is disrupted, and the message bypasses the cortex ("thinking" brain) and goes immediately to the amygdala, which can produce an intense and sometimes irrational or destructive response.

Given the potential short- and long-term consequences to overall growth, health, and development of being in a state of distress, researchers have studied extensively variables associated with cortisol levels. Variables such as maternal prenatal cortisol levels, behaviors of parents and/or teachers, and indicators of quality out-of-home experiences have been investigated.

Impact of Cortisol Levels

Higher levels of maternal prenatal cortisol levels were negatively associated with cognitive abilities of their infants during the second year of life (Bergman, Sarkar, Glover, & O'Connor, 2010). In other words, higher levels of maternal prenatal cortisol were associated with lower ratings of infant cognitive abilities. This research further revealed that the relationship was moderated by the type of relationship between the mother and child. Children who displayed an insecure attachment to their mothers displayed this negative association, while children with a secure attachment did not (Bergman et al., 2010).

Other researchers have explored relationships between parenting behaviors and cortisol levels. In one study, mothers with low levels of cortisol engaged in more disruptive communications with their infant (Crockett, Holmes, Granger, & Lyons-Ruth, 2013). In other words, the mothers with low cortisol levels had difficulty interacting with their infants in an empathic and nondisrupted way. In contrast, other researchers found that mothers who were more emotionally available at bedtime had infants who secreted lower levels of cortisol during the night than did mothers who were less emotionally available (Philbrook, Hozella, Kim, Jian, Shimizu, & Teti, 2014). Taken together, these results demonstrate that the quality of the parent-child relationship can be impacted by the adults' and the infants' production of cortisol.

Bugental, Schwartz, and Lynch (2010) explored relationships between cortisol levels, parenting behaviors, and memory skills for very young children. They found that children's cortisol levels were reduced when their mother participated in an intervention that focused on "constructive reinterpretation of caregiving challenges, along with their perceived capacity to resolve those challenges" (p. 161). However, when mothers engaged in avoidance/withdraw behaviors in response to conflict with their infant, the infant had elevated cortisol levels. The authors hypothesized that parental failure to respond to infant distress may lead to problems in emotional regulation for the children. Short-term memory functioning at age 3 was associated with cortisol levels when measured during the 1-year visit (Bugental et al., 2010), providing further evidence of the possible long-term impact of early experiences on later development.

Other research teams have investigated the impact of specific parenting behaviors on cortisol levels. Beijers, Riksen-Walraven, and de Weerth (2013) found that parents who co-sleep with their infant more (i.e., sleep with infant in the same bed or in the same bedroom) had infants who had lower cortisol reactivity in response to a stressful situation. In addition, infants whose mother breastfed them longer had a quicker recovery from increases in cortisol during the stressful situation.

The impact of other environments, especially out-of-home care, on cortisol levels has been studied extensively. Studies have found that the impact of child care differs for low-risk children and high-risk (including low-income) children. More specifically, for middle-class children, there was no significant change in children's levels of cortisol from midmorning to midafternoon when at home with their family, but they experienced a significant increase in levels when in a family child care center (Gunnar, Kryzer, Van Ryzin, & Phillips, 2010). In fact, for low-risk children, the more hours spent in child care were predictive of higher cortisol levels (Berry, Blair, Ursache, Willoughby, Garrett-Peters, Vernon-Feagans, et al., 2014). For a sample of children who were living in poverty or had multiple risk factors, their cortisol level decreased over the course of the morning at child care (Rappolt-Schlichtmann, Willette, Ayoub, Lindsley, Hulette, & Fischer, 2009) and with greater number of hours spent in a child care setting (Berry et al., 2014).

What variables have been associated with a rise or decrease in cortisol levels in children when in a child care program? Measures of quality have been found to relate to children's cortisol levels. For example, Sajaniemi, Suhonen, Kontu, Rantanen, Lindholm, Hyttinen, et al. (2011) found that scoring low on measures of quality indicators for classroom arrangement and team planning was associated with elevated cortisol levels as well as an increase in cortisol levels throughout the day. Regarding teacher-child relationships, Lisonbee, Mize, Payne, and Granger (2008) found that when teachers reported higher levels of conflict and overdependence in their relationships with the children, the children had higher cortisol levels. On the contrary, when children were in classrooms with teachers who provided more emotional support (Hatfield, Hestenes, Kintner-Duffy, & O'Brien, 2013) or when children had a more secure attachment relationship with their teacher (Badanes, Dmitrieva, & Watamura, 2012), they had a greater decline in levels of cortisol from morning to afternoon. Relatedly, when Rappolt-Schlichtmann et al. (2009) investigated the impact of teaching in large groups versus smaller groups, they found that children's cortisol levels decreased when moved from a large group environment to a small group context; children who experienced more conflict with their teachers (based on the teacher's report) experienced less decrease in cortisol during that change. Observations of teacher behavior have resulted in similar findings. Teachers who were rated as higher on intrusive/overcontrolling care were associated with children experiencing a rise in cortisol levels from midmorning to midafternoon (Gunnar et al., 2010).

As this research demonstrates, unresponsive, harmful, stressful, or neglectful caregiving behaviors affect the development of the brain negatively. Children who experience unresponsive and stressful conditions, either in a home or in a child care setting, were found to have elevated cortisol levels (see Gunnar & Cheatham, 2003, for a review). Monitoring cortisol levels in children may help in creating interventions and preventing negative outcomes associated with high levels of cortisol in adults, such as depression and anxiety (Engert, Efanov, Dedovic, Dagher, & Pruessner, 2011), posttraumatic stress disorder (Lopez & Seng, 2014), heart disease (Seldenrijk, Hamer,

Lahiri, Penninx, & Steptoe, 2012), and lower waking (Roisman, Susman, Barnett-Walker, Booth-LaForce, Owen, Belsky, et al., 2009) or higher waking (Nelemans, Hale, Branje, Lier, Jansen, Platje, et al., 2014) cortisol levels in adolescence.

Emotional Intelligence

Daniel Goleman has provided a concise and comprehensive view of how brain development links to the skills necessary for healthy social and emotional development in his books titled *Emotional Intelligence* (1996) and *Social Intelligence* (2006). In these books, Goleman reports that the usual way of looking at intelligence as consisting only of cognitive abilities is incomplete. Eighty percent of the skills necessary for success in life are determined by what he calls **emotional intelligence** (Goleman, 1996). Healthy emotional development involves helping young children recognize their feelings, experience security and trust in others, and establish healthy attachments as well as gaining specific skills and self-efficacy in "emotion-eliciting social transactions" (Saarni, Campos, Camras, & Witherington, 2006, p. 250). Goleman defined five *domains* that are learned early in life and are necessary for high emotional intelligence and healthy identity development (Figure 3–2).

emotional intelligence Skills learned early in life that are necessary for healthy emotional development, good relationships, and fulfillment in life experiences.

self-awareness Sensory-grounded information regarding one's existence; what a person sees, hears, and feels in the body related to self.

1. **Knowing one's emotions.** Recognizing a feeling as it happens, or **self-awareness**, is the keystone of emotional intelligence. The caregiver

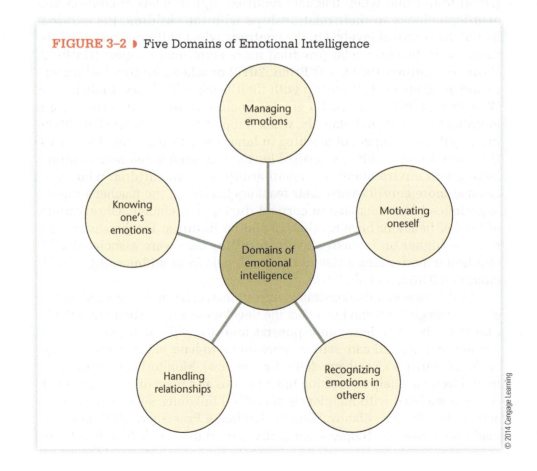

FIGURE 3–2 ▶ Five Domains of Emotional Intelligence

© 2014 Cengage Learning

should start helping children at birth to recognize, experience, label, and express their feelings in healthy ways. Research conducted on maternal emotion-related socialization behaviors (such as reported emotional expressivity, responses to her child's emotions, and observed emotion talk) found that such behaviors were predictive of children's emotion self-awareness skill one year later (Warren & Stifter, 2008). Specifically, they found that mothers who engaged in more supportive emotion-related socialization behaviors had preschoolers who had higher self-awareness of happiness, whereas less-supportive maternal emotion-related socialization behaviors were predictive of low self-awareness of sadness (Warren & Stifter, 2008).

Parents and early childhood educator can help young children develop the cognitive skills for understanding their own thoughts, feelings, and behaviors. Caregivers who describe what they are observing (e.g., "Your face is red, you must be angry."), give feedback about the emotion being experienced (e.g., "It is scary to be alone in the climbing structure."), and ask questions about children's thoughts, feelings, and behaviors (e.g., "Are you feeling sad or embarrassed?") help children develop cognition skills in relationship to emotions. From a Vygotskian perspective, these strategies may be particularly valuable during the toddler years when the young children use their budding language skills as a mental tool to control their own emotions and behaviors. Toddlers with greater breadth of spoken vocabulary were found to be better able to use language to self-regulate their behaviors (Vallotton & Ayoub, 2011).

2. Managing emotions. Handling feelings in a way that is appropriate to the situation is a skill that builds on self-awareness. Skills in soothing oneself and maintaining a balance among thoughts, feelings, and behavior are necessary to manage emotions. Caregivers need to help children with this process of **self-regulation** by providing a model of balance between rational behavior and expression of emotions. Toddlers, while not being expected to control their emotions all of the time, should be assisted in gaining "effortful control." According to Rueda, Posner, and Rothbart (2005), effortful control refers to a set of self-regulatory skills that includes attention modulation, response inhibition, persistence, and delay of gratification. Toddlers who demonstrated high levels of effortful control were lower in externalizing behaviors and higher in social competence (Spinrad, Eisenberg, Gaertner, Popp, Smith, Kupfer, et al., 2007). Thus, it appears that toddlers who can manage their emotions are better able to get along with other age-mates. See the Spotlight on Effortful Control box for more information.

self-regulation The skills necessary to direct and control one's own behavior in socially and culturally appropriate ways.

As caregivers help infants regulate their emotions, they contribute to the child's style of emotional self-regulation. For example, a parent who waits to intervene until an infant has become extremely agitated reinforces the baby's rapid rise to intense stress (Thompson, 1988) and makes it harder for the parent to soothe the baby in the future and for the baby to learn self-soothing. Parents who expressed negative emotionality when their toddler was completing a task were associated with toddlers who were less attentive to the task (Gaertner, Spinrad, & Eisenberg, 2008). Thus, adult negativity might actually decrease a child's ability to attend when

Spotlight on Effortful Control

WHAT IS IT AND WHY IS IMPORTANT?

Effortful control is a newer concept in the child development literature, receiving significant attention during the past five years. Because it is a newer concept, understanding effortful control and factors impacting its development have been of great interest to researchers. Researchers have investigated the stability of effortful control over the first three years of life and have found it to be stable. For example, measures of effortful control showed continuity from infancy (12 months) to toddlerhood (24 months; Li, Pawan, & Stansbury, 2014). Eisenberg, Edwards, Spinrad, Sallquist, Eggum, and Reiser (2013) took a different approach and wanted to know if effortful control, reactive undercontrol (impulsivity), and reactive overcontrol (inhibition to novelty) were three distinct constructs between 30 and 54 months of age. They found that at 30 months, effortful control was separate from reactive control (combination of impulsivity and inhibition) while at 42 and 54 months, all three were separate constructs. The authors concluded that this pattern demonstrates how effortful control and reactive control are two different aspects of temperament that "become increasingly differentiated with age as a function of brain development" (p. 2092).

Influences, such as parent and toddler characteristics, on the development of effortful control have been investigated. In one study, mothers who were higher on measures of extraversion had toddlers who demonstrated more effortful control, whereas mothers who reported higher levels of parenting stress were associated with toddlers with less effortful control (Gartstein, Bridgett, Young, Panksepp, & Power, 2013). For toddlers with an "exuberant" (e.g., active) temperament, a combination of parental behaviors and emotional tone was associated with effortful control. Specifically, mothers who used commands and prohibitive statements with a positive emotional tone in interactions with their toddlers predicted higher levels of effortful control when their children were preschoolers (Cipriano & Stifter, 2010).

Parental behaviors (e.g., support, sensitivity, and warmth) have also been found to impact the development of effortful control. In one study, the researchers wanted to know if skills in effortful control were associated with maternal sensitivity and recovery from a challenging task. They found that, as hypothesized, maternal sensitivity during infancy predicted better effortful control and, in turn, shorter periods of time to generate positive emotions following a challenging task at 33 months (Conway, McDonough, Mackenzie, Miller, Dayton, Rosenblum, et al., 2014). Relatedly, infants' effortful control at 12 months predicted mothers' comforting and cognitive assistance at 24 months (Li, Pawan, & Stansbury, 2014). In other words, mothers who were more sensitive took into account their prior knowledge of the children's regulatory capacities; demonstrating how the infants' characteristics impact mothers' emotion coaching behaviors. Eiden, Edwards, and Leonard (2007) investigated the role of parental warmth in alcoholic families. Mothers scoring lower on measures of warmth when their toddler was 24 months was associated with their children exhibiting less effortful control a year later (i.e., 36 months).

Why have researchers put some much time and energy into studying effortful control? As mentioned previously, higher levels of effortful control have been associated with exhibiting fewer externalizing behaviors and higher levels of social competence (Spinrad et al., 2007). Thus, children who are higher in effortful control are better able to engage in positive interactions with peers. In addition, there is a strong emphasis on school readiness skills in our society, and effortful control may play an important role. Specifically, the role of particular cognitive and social-emotional skills, including effortful control, to influence how young children acquire preacademic skills is a newer line of inquiry. Merz, Landry, Williams, Barnes, Eisenberg, Spinrad, et al. (2014) investigated whether effortful control is a developmental skill that could explain the association between contextual factors and preacademic knowledge for toddlers and preschoolers (e.g., 2- and 4-year-old children). They found that levels of effortful control did mediate the relationships among parental education, home environment, and early academic skills (e.g., early literacy and emergent math). For example, children who experienced a higher quality home environment had higher effortful control, and the level of effortful control mediated the relationship between home quality and early literacy skills (Merz et al., 2014). Because effortful control is a primary developmental task of early childhood, and these skills develop as a result of cumulative parent-child interactions in the home, these results may be particularly important to understand.

negative emotions are expressed. On the other hand, when caregivers validate children's wants and needs by supporting and helping the child fulfill the need expressed by a feeling, children internalize a positive approach to managing emotions, regulating negative behaviors, and interacting with others (Gaertner et al., 2008; Spinrad et al., 2007). In contrast, when fathers were high on both frightening (e.g., threatening physical and/or verbal behavior) and insensitive parenting behaviors, their children were rated higher in emotional underregulation at 24 months, compared to children whose fathers were frightening and sensitive (Hazen, McFarland, Jacobvitz, & Boyd-Soisson, 2010). These researchers concluded that frightening behaviors by themselves might not be problematic because "fathers who stay sensitive while keeping babies highly stimulated, on the fence between fear and fun, may actually be scaffolding their children's later development of the ability to regulate intense emotions [and] cope with overstimulation" (p. 64).

3. Motivating oneself. Channeling emotions in the service of a goal is essential for paying attention, mastery, and creativity. A basic attitude of optimism (the belief that success is possible) and self-responsibility underlie the skill of getting into the flow (Csikszentmihalyi, 1990). Caregivers of young children and infants can observe flow in infants and toddlers. For example, when an infant becomes totally engrossed in exploring her hand or the caregiver's face, you can see that her cognition, perceptions, emotions, and behaviors are all intensely focused and coordinated in her joyful exploration.

Many researchers of motivation consider curiosity the primary human motivator. Infants and toddlers are naturally brimming with curiosity and the desire to explore. When caregivers help fulfill basic needs at appropriate physical and safety levels and respect the children as separate individuals with the ability to take some responsibility for their own experiences, children feel secure and are able to get into the wonderful flow of exploring both internal and external worlds.

4. Recognizing emotions in others. A fundamental relationship skill is **empathy** (sensitivity to what others need or want). Research in infant development has demonstrated that newborns exhibit empathy within the first months of life. Recent research provides evidence that infants respond empathically to the distress of both their mother and a peer and that they become more empathic over the first two years of life (Geangu, Benga, Stahl, & Striano, 2011; Roth-Hanania, Davidov, & Zahn-Waxler, 2011). If it is true that empathy is present at birth, then insensitivity is learned from the environment. Styles of caregiving have a profound impact on emotional self-regulation and empathy as children grow; children who see adults' model empathy and frustration tolerance are more likely to develop those qualities themselves (Eisenberg, Fabes, & Spinrad, 2006). Similarly, when parents respond appropriately and sensitively to the toddler's emotional expressions, the toddler displayed more empathic behaviors (Emery, McElwain, Groh, Haydon, & Roisman, 2014; Tong, Shinohara, Sugisawa, Tanaka, Yato, Yamakawa, et al., 2012). On the other hand, when infants and toddlers receive care that is abusive, they have significantly lower scores on emotional regulation and exhibit more externalizing behaviors

empathy Sensitivity to what others feel, need, or want; the fundamental relationship skill present at birth.

(e.g., aggression) with peers (Kim & Cicchetti, 2010). In addition, it appears that a lack of appropriate care (i.e., neglect) during the early years negatively impacts emotional intelligence. Sullivan and colleagues found that 4-year-old children who were neglected were rated more poorly on measures of emotional knowledge than age-mates who were not neglected (Sullivan, Bennett, Carpenter, & Lewis, 2008). Teachers must take great care to create a positive learning environment that promotes stability and fosters compassion for children who have not had such experiences.

DAP

Implications of this research for caregivers of young children should be obvious: insensitivity, negativity, or aggression directed at infants and toddlers results in children exhibiting those qualities toward themselves and others. Child care that is sensitive, positive, and nurturing results in children who exhibit those qualities as they grow up. Although many skills need to be encouraged and modeled, teachers should intentionally implement an "emotion-centered curriculum" that facilitates the children's development of appropriate emotional responses, regulation, and styles of expression (Hyson, 2004).

5. Handling relationships. The last domain of emotional intelligence involves interacting smoothly and demonstrating skills necessary to get along well with others. It may seem odd at first to suggest that infants and toddlers manage their relationships with others, but research indicates that infants as young as 4 weeks old detect others' emotions through crying contagion; research provides strong evidence for a valenced response to crying (Saarni et al., 2006). When testing infants who were 1-, 3-, 6-, and 9-months-old, between 59 percent and 79 percent of the infants responded to a pain cry with increased vocal and facial expressions of distress (Geangu, Benga, Stahl, & Striano, 2010). Infants clearly respond to the crying of other newborns by crying. Goleman (2006) explains that through a process called **emotional contagion**, infants and other humans "catch" emotions from those they are around (c.f. Yong & Ruffman's [2014] study of the emotional contagion of dogs). "We 'catch' strong emotions much as we do a rhinovirus—and so can come down the emotional equivalent of a cold" (p. 22). This process of catching emotions is unconscious, occurring in the amygdala, an almond-shaped area in the midbrain that triggers responses to signs of danger.

Infants also imitate others' behaviors and expressions within the first three months. There is no question that the behavior of a baby elicits responses from caregivers. Many families even mark their child's first smile, step, word, and so forth with great celebration. Therefore, children learn very early in life that their behavior affects others, even though the conscious awareness that "When I do A, Mommy does B" doesn't come about until the end of the first year. Specific skills in working with others are spelled out later in this textbook, but it is important to understand here that development of these people skills occurs during the first years of life as a part of the relationships with primary caregivers.

emotional contagion The process through which infants and other humans "catch" emotions from those they are around.

Interactional Synchrony

Very little research has been reported on how young children develop skills to manage emotions in others. Studies of the baby's contributions to their primary relationships involve the temperament research discussed previously and studies on **interactional synchrony** (Isabella & Belsky, 1991). This term is best described as a sensitively tuned "emotional dance" in which interactions are mutually rewarding to the caregiver and the infant (Photo 3–3). The two share a positive emotional state, with the caregiver and infant switching the roles of "following" and "leading" as necessary during different points in the dance (Goldsmith, 2010). According to Feldman (2007), interactional synchrony "provides the foundation for the child's later capacity for intimacy, symbol use, empathy, and the ability to read the intentions of others" (p. 330). However, engaging in interactional synchrony is not only emotionally rewarding for infants but also is related to lower levels of physiological distress for them (Moore & Calkins, 2004). Although there are cultural-specific behaviors related to how adults interact with infants, research suggests that there are more commonalities than differences. For example, mother-infant dyads who had recently immigrated to the United States from France and India displayed similar types of interactional synchrony, yet at a lower frequency than did the nonimmigrant group (Gratier, 2003). Similarly, mothers and fathers do not differ in their ability to be in synch with their toddlers during play interactions (de Mendonça, Cossette, Strayer, & Gravel, 2011; Feldman, 2007). However, mothers of infants with profound hearing loss overlapped their utterances with their infant's vocalization more than mothers of hearing infants, demonstrating less interactional synchrony (Fagan, Bergeson, & Morris, 2014). Yet, within seven months after the infants received cochlear implants, interactional synchrony improved.

PHOTO 3–3 Interactional synchrony is the basis for healthy relationships.

interactional synchrony A sensitively tuned "emotional dance," in which interactions are mutually rewarding to caregiver and infant.

Taken together, this research demonstrates that caregivers need to learn how to establish rapport and develop interactional synchrony with infants and toddlers to enhance their emotional development and help them learn to manage their relationships. However, do not pressure yourself to always be in sync, which is an unrealistic expectation (Tronick & Cohn, 1989).

To summarize, healthy emotional development involves recognizing their feelings and those of other people, establishing trust and autonomy in relationship with caregivers, having temperament traits supported, and having a healthy balance between bonding and separation-individuation. In addition, caregivers should understand how brain development impacts emotional development, the five domains of emotional intelligence, and how to use strategies that enhance both of them. McLaughlin (2008) argues in her critical reflection of emotional intelligence that while skills reside within a particular individual, they must be taught through emphasizing specific relationships and community building. In other words, while emotional intelligence can be boiled down to a set of skills to be learned, to be meaningful and useful, these skills must be intentionally used and taught during authentic, face-to-face interactions.

READING CHECKPOINT

Before moving on with your reading, make sure that you can answer the following questions about the material discussed so far.

1. How do parent-child interactions impact healthy identity development according to Erikson, Mahler, and Stern?
2. What factors influence how teachers use the concept of goodness-of-fit with children in their care? Why is it important to realize this concept with each child?
3. How does a child's brain development and emotional IQ skills influence his or her relationships with others?
4. Explain why caregivers should establish interactional synchrony with children.

3-2 Patterns of Social Development

Normal patterns for social development are the result of our all-important relationships with our primary caregivers. The word *relationship* implies two entities: one person *relates* with another. During infancy and toddlerhood, respect for the child's physical and psychological boundaries is crucial to healthy social development. Because infants begin life unable to care for their physical being, it is necessary for caregivers to intrude on their physical boundaries to provide care. The term *intrude* was intentionally selected because the baby has no choice in how the caregiver handles his or her body. When the caregiver respects the baby's body, the baby feels secure and loved. However, when the caregiver doesn't respect the baby's body and is rough or insensitive, he or she causes feelings of insecurity and physical pain. Children who have their physical and psychological boundaries respected learn to respect other people's feelings as well. As a result of being able to value their own wants and needs while being sensitive to other people, these children are able to establish, manage, and maintain healthy relationships with other people.

3-2a Attachment Theory

The infant's first years of life are dedicated to the development of strong emotional ties to the caregiver (Bowlby, 1969/2000). While research on mother-child attachment preceded research on father-child attachment, the importance of developing strong, secure relationships with both parents cannot be denied (Bretherton, 2010). According to Bowlby's ethological theory of attachment, the infant's relationship to the parent starts as a set of innate signals that keep the caregiver close to the baby and proceeds through four phases, as follows:

1. *The preattachment phase* (birth to 6 weeks old) occurs when the baby grasps, cries, smiles, and gazes to keep the caregiver engaged.
2. *The "attachment-in-the-making" phase* (6 weeks to 8 months old) consists of the baby responding differently to familiar caregivers than to strangers. Face-to-face interactions relieve distress, and the baby expects that the caregiver will respond when signaled.
3. *The clear-cut attachment phase* (8 months to 2 years old) is when the baby exhibits separation anxiety, protests caregiver departure, and acts deliberately to maintain caregiver attention.

4. Formation of a *reciprocal relationship phase* (18 months old and onward) occurs when children negotiate with the caregiver and are willing to give and take in relationships.

Researchers measure attachment history for young toddlers using an experimental design called the Strange Situation. This experiment involves a series of separations and reunions. Four categories have been used to classify attachment patterns: secure, ambivalent/insecure, avoidant/insecure (Ainsworth, 1967, 1973), and disoriented/insecure (Hesse & Main, 2000; Main & Solomon, 1990) (see Chapter 4 for more information on each of these). These attachment patterns have been found to be influenced by the caregivers' behavior and beliefs and to result in different social outcomes for toddlers, preschoolers, and school-aged children (see next section).

Securely Attached Infants

Infants' attachment styles have been found to correlate to sets of caregivers' behaviors (Figure 3–3). Regarding secure attachments, infants and caregivers engage in finely tuned, synchronous dances where the adults carefully read the infants' cues, see events from the infants' perspectives, and respond accordingly (Isabella & Belsky, 1991; NICHD Early Child Care Research Network, 1997; Oppenheim & Koren-Karie, 2002) (Photo 3–4). More specifically, infants classified as securely attached tend to have caregivers who do the following:

- Consistently respond to infants' needs
- Interpret infants' emotional signals sensitively
- Regularly express affection
- Permit babies to influence the pace and direction of their mutual interactions (for reviews, see Honig, 2002; McDevitt & Ormrod, 2013)

Insecurely Attached Infants

In contrast, caregivers of insecurely attached infants tend to have difficulty caring for the infants (e.g., dislike physical contact, are inconsistent,

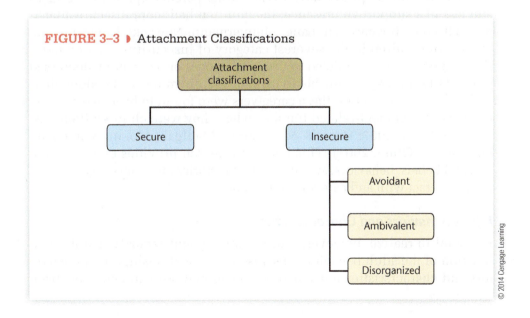

FIGURE 3–3 ▶ Attachment Classifications

© 2014 Cengage Learning

PHOTO 3–4 Healthy relationships develop from positive attention, approval, and attunement.

unpredictable, insensitive, and intrusive) or are unwilling to invest energy in the relationship (Belsky, Rovine, & Taylor, 1984; Isabella, 1993; Thompson, 1998). They might also struggle with interactive misattunement (i.e., a lack of the synchronous dance described earlier), especially with an adopted child (Honig, 2014). George, Cummings, and Davies (2010) found that father-child and mother-child attachments were predicted by paternal and maternal responsiveness to children's emotional distress, respectively. For both mothers and fathers, being less emotionally responsive was related to their child exhibiting more attachment insecurity. Similarly, mothers who were less supportive with their children reported greater personal levels of attachment avoidance behaviors (Berlin, Whiteside-Mansell, Roggman, Green, Robinson, & Spieker, 2011). When foster parents reported more stress and less of a supportive presence, the children had more insecure attachments (Gabler, Bovenschen, Lang, Zimmermann, Nowacki, Kliewer, et al., 2014). For children in the severest category of insecurity—disoriented—the caregivers can be addicted to drugs or alcohol or be severely depressed or mentally ill; they are unable to care for their own needs, let alone their child's. In several studies, these caregivers were found to have experienced their own attachment-related traumas when they were children (Behrens, Hesse, & Main, 2007; Hesse & Main, 2000; Madigan, Moran, Schuengel, Pederson, & Otten, 2007). This body of research provides evidence that parental beliefs, behaviors, and attachment histories are related to how caregivers interact with and care for their infants.

Infant Behaviors and Characteristics

It is vital to realize, however, that the attachment security is not just a function of the adult behaviors. Because it is a relationship, infant behaviors and characteristics must also be considered. Researchers have been interested in the impact of adoption on attachment security. In a study of adopted toddlers who experienced institutionalization as infants, toddlers with greater preadoption adversity took longer to form an attachment to their adoptive parents (Carlson, Hostinar, Mliner, & Gunnar, 2014). While it took longer, eventually 90 percent of the children achieved a high level on the attachment scale utilized, which was no different from the nonadopted children in the study. Yet, the toddlers who were rated as more insecure had a higher likelihood to be disorganized in their attachment patterns than the nonadopted children.

Teacher Relationships

Teachers of infants and toddlers also form ongoing relationships with young children. The primary caregiving system (discussed in Chapter 1) has been found to support secure teacher-child attachments (Ebbeck, Phoon, Tan-Chong, Tan, & Goh, 2014). Relatedly, when interviewing teachers, Ebbeck and Yim (2009) found that teachers felt "being responsive and emotionally available was the most important and direct approach to foster their relationship with infants/toddlers" (p. 902). To illustrate, 14-month-old Louise is walking in the yard carrying a small truck in her hand. She sees Randy, the caregiver, and squeals and giggles. She walks rapidly to Randy with arms up and a big smile on her face. Randy picks her up, snuggles, and greets her verbally.

The relationships families and caregivers form with very young children help to determine what relationships children will develop later in life. Strong, sensitive attachment can have a positive influence on a child's confidence, self-concept, and patterns of social interactions for the remainder of his or her life. While most research on caregiver-child relationships has examined infants with their parents, the findings from this research apply equally well to infant-caregiver relationships.

Being a responsive caregiver, however, goes beyond just examining your own behaviors and interactions with children. Teachers must also come to understand attachment relationships from the child's and the family members' perspectives. In both cases, experiences with others set the foundation for later relationships. Children use their relationships with their family members to guide how they interact with peers, whereas adults (teachers and parents) use their past relationships (with their own parents and/or romantic relationships) to influence how they interact with children. Berlin et al.'s (2011) findings suggest that some parents, given their attachment history, might be resistant to building a collaborative relationship with caregivers. Thus, early childhood educators might need to find additional avenues for building strong relationships with some family members. The following list explores avenues for affecting healthy development for young children.

1. **Infants need to establish emotional attachment with their caregivers.** This attachment develops through regular activities that address the infants' basic needs such as feeding and changing diapers. Yet caregivers should use sensitive physical contact such as cuddling and touching to comfort and stimulate interactions. When caregivers learn the child's needs, schedules, likes, dislikes, and temperament, and then respond to the child's preferences, they teach the infant that he or she is an important person.

As discussed in Chapter 1, when more than one caregiver is responsible for a group of children, a primary caregiving system can be used to divide the work and best meet the needs of the children. The primary caregiver works closely with family members to establish consistent routines and strategies for meeting the infant's needs. She can share her knowledge about the child's needs and preferences so that other caregivers can match their care to the child. Alternate caregivers should report observations about the child's behaviors to the primary caregiver. Thus, the primary caregiver has two main responsibilities: to establish a special attachment with the child, and to gather, coordinate, and share information about the child with other caregivers and the family.

Each child needs to have a caregiver respond sensitively and consistently to cries and cues of distress. The child then learns to trust the caregiver. When crying infants are left alone for several minutes before a caregiver responds, or when the caregiver responds quickly sometimes and leaves them alone sometimes, children are confused and have difficulty establishing a strong attachment because they cannot develop a strong sense of trust in the caregiver. Responding quickly to infant and toddler needs does not spoil children. It conveys that you hear their communication and that they are important enough for you to respond to it. Your response should be quick but not hurried.

Consider the following example. Nancy is rocking Alvero when Karola wakes from her nap. Nancy greets Karola by saying, "Look who is awake. I am rocking Alvero. He is almost asleep. I'll put him in his crib and then get you up." As this example shows, Nancy talked to Karola, the crying infant, in a soothing voice before she was able to physically address her need to get out of her crib. Although some readers may question the amount of language provided to Karola, they should recall that receptive language develops before productive language and that language serves not only as a communication function but also as a tool for regulating strong emotions. Remember, the most important task for an infant or toddler is to develop trust and a secure attachment to the caregiver. For this to occur, the caregiver must respond consistently and sensitively to the child's needs.

2. Each child and his or her primary caregiver need special time together. This "getting to know you" and "let's enjoy each other" time should be a calm, playful time to relax, look, touch, smile, giggle, cuddle, stroke, talk, whisper, sing, make faces, and establish the wonderful dance of interactional synchrony. Sometimes this can be active time, including holding an infant up in the air at arm's length while you talk and giggle and then bringing the infant up close for a hug. Other times, this can mean very quiet activities, such as rocking, cuddling, and softly stroking in a loving way.

3. The caregiver must treat each child as a special, important person. Infants and toddlers are not objects to be controlled but individuals of worth with whom you establish a respectful, positive emotional relationship while providing for their physical, cognitive, social, emotional, and learning needs. More information will be provided in Chapter 9 regarding how to build curriculum that is respectful, is responsive, and facilitates development.

Spotlight on Research

FATHER-CHILD INTERACTIONS AND DEVELOPMENTAL OUTCOMES

Much research has been conducted on the impact of mother-child interactions on developmental outcomes for young children. The amount and type of engagement fathers have with their children has long been assumed to be important to the development of young children. Yet, much was not understood about this topic until recently.

Drawing from a national sample of more than 5,000 fathers, Cabrera, Hofferth, and Chae (2011) investigated whether father involvement in three tasks (i.e., verbal stimulation, caregiving, and physical play) varied by race/ethnicity. When controlling for variables such as fathers' education, depression symptoms, and quality of family relationships, African American and Latino fathers engaged in more caregiving and physical play activities than did White fathers, whereas no differences were found between the three groups of fathers on verbal stimulation activities. Fathers who reported higher levels of conflict with their partner engaged in less caregiving and physical play activities with their infant.

While understanding the amount and type of father engagement is important, researchers have also focused on how fathers play an important and differential role in their child's developmental outcomes. A meta-analysis of 24 publications discovered that 22 of the publications showed father engagement (i.e., direct interaction with the child) to be associated with a range of positive outcomes, although no specific form of engagement was shown to yield better outcomes than another (Sarkadi, Kristiansson, Oberklaid, & Bremberg, 2008). For example, there was "evidence to indicate that father *engagement* positively affects the social, behavioral, psychological and cognitive outcomes of children" (Sarkadi et al., 2008, p. 155, emphasis in original).

Fathers seem to provide an important context as children are learning to regulate their emotions. The data suggest that fathers in low-income families are particularly important for helping very young children gain control over intense emotions. Children who live with their biological fathers or children who have involved nonresidential biological fathers had more optimal emotion-regulatory competencies (Bocknek, Brophy-Herb, Fitzgerald, Schiffman, & Vogel, 2014), fewer behavioral problems (Choi, Palmer, & Pyunas, 2014), as well as higher levels of self-regulation and lower levels of aggression when compared to children with unstable father connections (Vogel, Bradley, Raikes, Boller, & Shears, 2006). The researchers concluded that "to some degree, children living with their biological fathers seem developmentally better off, primarily in the self-regulatory and behavioral domains" (Vogel et al., 2006, p. 204) as such relationships provide more stability and predictability in father-child interactions (Bocknek et al., 2014). When children are better able to manage their emotions, they should engage in aggressive or harmful behaviors less frequently. The meta-analysis described earlier also found that father involvement was associated with decreased aggressive behaviors for boys (Sarkadi et al., 2008). While these positive behaviors are most important developmental outcomes, the origin of the pathway is still unclear. It is possible that the outcome of reduced aggression is linked to the increase in emotional regulation skills. More research is needed to discern the complex relationships between father involvement and child developmental trajectories.

Other research has shown the positive impact of father-child interactions on cognitive development. Feldman (2007) discovered that father-child synchrony at 5 months of age was related to complex symbol use and the sequences of symbolic play at 3 years of age. In addition, Bronte-Tinkew, Carano, Horowitz, and Kinukawa (2008) found that various aspects of father involvement (cognitively stimulating activities, physical care, paternal warmth, and caregiving activities) were associated with greater babbling and exploring objects with a purpose as well as a lower likelihood of infant cognitive delay. Fathers who read with their toddler more frequently had preschoolers who were better on assessments of reading, math, and social-emotional outcomes (Baker, 2013).

Another research study compared father-toddler social toy play for families involved in an Early Head Start (EHS) program to dads not involved in that program. These researchers found that fathers who had been in an EHS program showed more complexity in their play with their children (Roggman, Boyce, Cook, Christiansen, & Jones, 2004). For children, this complex play was associated with better cognitive and social outcomes; specifically, the children scored better on tests of cognitive competence, language acquisition, and emotional regulation.

DAP This body of research makes it clear that educators need to create policies and engage in practices

(continued)

that actively involve fathers in the care and education of their infants and toddlers because doing so is related to better developmental outcomes (i.e., cognitive, social, and emotional) for the children. We need to (1) help families understand the "the potential value of active father involvement in children's lives during these critical early years" (Roggman et al., 2004, p. 103); and (2) involve fathers in the daily care and educational decisions as much as we do mothers. Many educators, like the population in general, continue to view mothers as the primary caregiver. This means that we tend to direct more communication toward them rather than the fathers. As the expectations of fathers change, many are often unsure of how to carry out these new responsibilities. Educators can provide information to families about the important role fathers play in promoting child development and coach fathers as they acquire the skills necessary for positive engagement and/or complex play with toys.

In conclusion, caregivers should be very aware of factors that affect attachment security in young children. Sensitive caregiving that responds appropriately to the child's signals and needs is the most important factor in supporting children's development. The findings from many studies clearly reveal that securely attached infants have primary caregivers who respond quickly to signals, express positive feelings, and handle babies with tenderness and sensitivity. The best principle for infant and toddler social development is probably that adults cannot be too "in tune" or give too much approval and affection; young children can't be spoiled. Your sensitive caring sets the basis for future relationships that they will have throughout their lives.

3-2b Relationships with Peers

While relationships are being established with adults, the children generalize the knowledge gained in their relationships with peers (Bowlby, 1969/2000). Infants demonstrate an increased desire to interact socially with peers over the first year of life. Research reveals "that during the second year of life, toddlers do display social skills of modest complexity" as they develop friendships and begin to negotiate conflicts (Rubin, Bukowski, & Parker, 2006, p. 587). The complexity can be shown in the quality and depth of their relationships with peers as toddlers. For example, toddlers have been found to have reciprocal relationships based "not only on their mutual exchange of positive overtures, but also by agonistic interactions" (Rubin et al., 2006, p. 588). In other words, their relationships can be characterized by great warmth, aggression, and argumentative interactions as they learn to work closely with peers. Toddlers tend to respond to cries by a familiar peer more than an unfamiliar peer (Kato, Onishi, Kanazawa, Hmobayashi, & Minami, 2012) suggesting that even toddlers use relationship knowledge to guide social responses. As this research shows, there is rapid development in the acquisition of social skills during the first two years of life as infants move from initiating basic interactions to developing reciprocal relationships with others. Other developmental milestones facilitate peer interactions and relationships as well. For example, between 24 and 36 months of age, the rapid language development of the toddler provides the basis for understanding the feelings of other people, using more words to express feelings, and actively participating in managing relationships. As language increases, so does the toddler's more complete model of the social world. Pointing gestures, talkativeness, and vocabulary are "tools for both communication in and representation of the social-emotional world...[and] may actually help these young children build their concepts of the social-emotional world" (Vallotton & Ayoub, 2010, p. 620). In addition, active self-talk dialogues; make-believe play; and beliefs about the self, the world (including other people), and the self in relation to others are exhibited during this period. By the time children reach school age, they have established a model of the world that includes self-concept, beliefs about the world (including other people), and a style of communication that influences how they will manage relationships with others.

This model of the world, based on the child's attachment history with parents, has been shown to relate to the quality of relationships with peers. Securely attached children tend to be more independent, empathic, and socially competent preschoolers, especially in comparison to insecurely attached children (DeMulder, Denham, Schmidt, & Mitchell, 2000; Kim, 2010; Rydell, Bohlin, & Thorell, 2005). When toddlers had a secure attachment to their father, they were more likely to have a greater number of reciprocal friendships during preschool (Verissimo, Santos, Vaughn, Torres, Monteiro, & Santos, 2011). The impact of infant secure attachment classification has also been associated with various aspects of social competence for preschoolers (Veríssimo, Santos, Fernandes, Shin, & Vaughn, 2014) as well as school-aged children and adolescents (Abraham & Kerns, 2013; Booth-LaForce & Oxford, 2008; Chen, Liu, & Liu, 2013; Eceiza, Ortiz, & Apodaca, 2011; Feeney, Cassidy, & Ramos-Marcuse, 2008; Yoon, Ang, Fung, Wong, & Yiming, 2006), while an insecure attachment has been related to maladaptive behaviors such as bullying (Eliot & Cornell, 2009).

Social Learning Theories

Contributions by numerous social learning theorists help us understand how infants and toddlers develop relationships. The first relationships we have in the world with our parent(s) and caregivers result in the formation of the self, which forms the basis for future relationships. Through these relationships, very young children come to understand how they are separate from others (e.g., **self-recognition**) as well as how they produce reactions and react to other's behavior (e.g., sense of agency). Infants as young as 9 months old demonstrate the emergence of self-recognition; the majority of 18- to 24-month-olds have it (Nielsen, Suddendorf, & Slaughter, 2006).

Self-recognition is measured by putting a mark on an infant's face (typically the nose, but Nielsen et al., 2006, studied both legs and faces) and having him look in the mirror. If he demonstrates self-recognition, he wipes his nose to remove the mark; if he laughs at the reflection or touches the mirror to wipe away the mark, he has not yet demonstrated self-recognition. While it may seem like a simple concept to grasp, self-recognition is a

self-recognition Conscious awareness of self as different from others and the environment; occurs first usually between 9 and 15 months of age.

complex developmental task that represents not only social development but also the brain's ability to represent the concept symbolically and mentally (Bard, Todd, Bernier, Love, & Leavens, 2006; Sugiura, Sassa, Jeong, Horie, Sato, & Kawashima, 2008). In fact, visual self-recognition in a mirror emerged prior to the use of personal pronouns and photo identification, two other indices of self-recognition (Courage, Edison, & Howe, 2004). When 18-month-old children demonstrated self-recognition, they also imitated a behavior more completely (Zmyj, Prinz, & Daum, 2013). In other words, these toddlers were able to imitate both the action and the appropriate location for displaying the action. The authors concluded that precisely reproducing the observed behavior of others is related to the increased competence in relating one's own behavior to the corresponding visual feedback.

3-2c Self-Esteem

self-esteem Personal judgment of worthiness based on an evaluation of having, or not, particular valued characteristics or abilities.

Self-esteem can be defined as follows: the evaluation the individual makes and customarily maintains with regard to himself; it expresses an attitude of approval or disapproval, and indicates the extent to which the individual believes himself to be capable, significant, successful, and worthy. In short, self-esteem is a personal judgment of worthiness that is expressed in the attitudes the individual holds toward himself (Coopersmith, 1967, pp. 4–5). Information regarding one's self-esteem is acquired through relationships with others and interactions with materials.

Summarizing his data on childhood experiences that contribute to the development of self-esteem, Coopersmith wrote, "The most general statement about the antecedent of self-esteem can be given in terms of three conditions: total or near total acceptance of the children by their parents; clearly defined and enforced limits; and the respect and latitude for individual actions that exist within the defined limits" (1967, p. 236). Research with socially anxious preadolescents (10–13 years of age) who reported high levels of fear of negative evaluations found that positive peer feedback resulted in greater gains in self-esteem while negative peer feedback resulted in greater decreases in self-esteem (Reijntjes, Thomaes, Boelen, van der Schoot, de Castro, & Telch, 2011). Thus, socially anxious children seem to be highly reactive to feedback from others. Unfortunately, many adults believe that providing frequent praise will raise a child's self-esteem, regardless of other child characteristics (e.g., presence of social anxiety). Although it is important that children think they are worthy people, they must develop this from their experiences of mastery and competence that are often born out of struggle and discomfort (Pawl, 2012). The conditions for fostering self-esteem—acceptance, limits, respect—provide guidelines for caregivers and will be discussed in more depth in Chapter 6.

In general, research in the area of self-esteem has found that people who develop good self-esteem have learned and exhibit three specific skills: self-responsibility, enlightened self-interest, and a positive attitude.

self-responsibility Taking over responsibility for fulfilling some of one's own needs.

1. People with good self-esteem assume ownership of their own thoughts, feelings, and behaviors. **Self-responsibility** is the keystone to independence. It is accurate to state that the most important task of child care is to prepare children to function as healthy, autonomous individuals capable of providing for their needs in ways acceptable to society. Caregivers should help children take responsibility for their own wants and needs as is appropriate for their developmental level, while allowing dependency in areas in which they are not yet capable of providing for themselves. For example, learning to manage one's emotions and respond using nonaggressive strategies when a want cannot be immediately fulfilled is a developmental challenge that children face early in life (Fuller, 2001). Helping a child take as much responsibility as is age appropriate provides the child with a sense of mastery and overall successful emotional development (see Chapter 6).

2. People with good self-esteem are sensitive and kind toward other people while addressing their own desires. In a research study, toddlers were observed interacting with familiar peers in their own homes. The focus children in the study were found to respond more positively to distress they had caused in their playmate than to distress they merely witnessed (Demetriou & Hay, 2004). Hence, the toddlers were more sensitive and responsive when they were responsible for the source of their playmate's distress.

Learning to balance one's own needs with the needs of others is not a trivial task. It is interesting that a review of the English language reveals no single word that describes a healthy self-interest in having one's needs and desires fulfilled. On the other hand, many words are available to describe a lack of self-interest (e.g., *selfless*), too much self-interest (e.g., *selfish*), and a lack of interest in other people (e.g., *insensitive, egocentric, narcissistic, aloof*). Because the skills necessary for positive self-esteem and emotional intelligence require balance between awareness of one's own needs and sensitivity to the feelings of other people, a term is required that accurately denotes a healthy amount of self-interest. The term enlightened self-interest will be used to describe the skill of balancing awareness of one's own needs and feelings with the needs and feelings of other people.

enlightened self-interest The skill of balancing awareness of one's own needs and feelings with the needs and feelings of other people.

Although there are individual differences at birth, the sensitivity that children exhibit toward others later in life is clearly related to the quality of sensitivity, kindness, and respect they are shown by caregivers in the first few years of life (Lawrence, 2006; Farrant, Devine, Maybery, & Fletcher, 2012). Yet, accounting for the impact of contextual variables is not always straightforward. Demetrious and Hay (2004) found that toddlers who had older siblings were more likely than other target children to respond negatively to their playmate's distress. Thus, adults and siblings might provide conflicting models of how to respond sensitively to another person's distress and, therefore, impact the development of self-esteem in different ways.

3. People with good self-esteem have a positive attitude about themselves. In other words, they make conscious positive statements to themselves about their own value and self-worth (Kocovski & Endler, 2000). Infants and toddlers internalize the moral values, beliefs, and attitudes of the people in their environment. This becomes part of their personality.

positive attitude An aspect of self-esteem whereby children make conscious positive statements to themselves about their own value and self-worth.

© Cengage Learning

PHOTO 3–5 Providing choices of what to clean up helps to develop responsibility and an internal locus of control.

The infants and young toddlers adopt the attitudes, statements, and feelings that their caregivers direct toward them. When caregivers consistently direct affection, positive attention, approval, and respect toward young children, they feel valuable, worthy, and proud. However, when caregivers are critical, angry, demanding, or judgmental toward children, they learn guilt, anxiety, shame, and self-doubt.

3-2d Prosocial Behaviors

Children's displays of prosocial behaviors increase significantly during the second year of life (Brownell, 2013). Children who possess a healthy internal locus of control know that their actions impact those around them (Photo 3–5). Yet, that is not a sufficient condition for ensuring that young children use their personal power to benefit others. It has been found that when parents adopt particular guidance strategies (e.g., induction, which is a type of verbal discipline in which the adult gives explanations or reasons for why the child should change her behavior), they tend to have children who are more socially competent (Kwon, Jeon, & Elicker, 2013) and exhibit more prosocial behaviors (see Eisenberg et al., 2006, for a review). Likewise, when parents were taught to avoid more permissive parenting behaviors, their toddlers displayed more social competence with peers (i.e., less verbal aggression; Christopher, Saunders, Jacobvitz, Burton, & Hazen, 2013). Thus, adults who provide feedback about appropriate, helpful behaviors, emphasizing the impact of the child's actions on another person, tend to be associated with children who engage in more prosocial behavior.

Emotional Talk

To elaborate even more, Brownell, Svetlova, Anderson, Nichols, and Drummond (2013) investigated the impact of reading books that prompted emotional talk about others' feelings on toddlers' prosocial behavior. They discovered that parents who elicited more emotional talk by asking their toddler to label and explain emotions were associated with toddlers who helped and shared more quickly and more frequently. What is particularly important about this study is that it was the parent's elicitation of children's emotional talk, rather than their own emotional talk, that was most impactful on prosocial behaviors. Similarly, when parents engaged in practices that encouraged their preschooler to take another person's perspective, the children demonstrated more prosocial behaviors (Farrant et al., 2012). These authors concluded that although parent-child interactions in infancy play critical roles in the development of prosocial behaviors, parents must continue to facilitate the development of prosocial behaviors during the latter part of the early childhood period (3–8 years of age).

Family and Community Connection

Imagine that you are working in a continuity of care classroom, caring for eight infants and toddlers. Because they are of different ages, family members tend to notice that some children engage in different social behaviors than do others. A family member has asked you how to assist her child with being more "helpful" (i.e., prosocial) at home. What questions would you want to ask him before answering his question? Make a list of five resources in your community that could be of benefit to this family. Then, determine how you would share this information with him.

Intrinsic Motivation

According to Hepach, Vaish, and Tomasello (2013), very young children engage in prosocial behavior because they are intrinsically motivated rather than motivated by extrinsic rewards, and they are more inclined to help those for whom they feel sympathy. For example, when toddlers were given rewards (physical object) for engaging in a prosocial behavior, they were less likely to help an adult in need than children who were given a verbal reward (praise) or no reward at all (Hepach et al., 2013). The finding about the impact of praise differs from previous research. Others have found that the application of verbal praise for prosocial behaviors actually undermines children's development (Grusec, 1991). It appears that external rewards (verbal or concrete) decrease the internal drive to do a good deed because the adult places emphasis on getting something. In other words, such adult behaviors undo the child's natural tendencies toward prosocial behaviors by teaching him that he should engage in a prosocial behavior only if it benefits himself (Warneken & Tomasello, 2008).

Sympathy

As mentioned previously, toddlers engage in prosocial behaviors when they feel sympathy for the person in need. Two recent studies have found that toddlers accurately respond to displays of distress by demonstrating helpful or prosocial behaviors (Hepach et al., 2013; Williamson, Donohue, & Tully, 2013). One of those studies will be discussed in more depth to illustrate the importance of feeling sympathy for a victim. In an experimental situation, toddlers participated in one of two conditions. In the harm condition, the toddler was present when one adult took or destroyed the belongings of another adult (recipient), whereas in the control condition, the toddler was present when one adult took or destroyed the belongings that did not belong to the recipient present. Next, the recipient was given one balloon, and the toddler was given two balloons. The adult "accidently" lost her balloon, could not retrieve it, and displayed overt sadness. Toddlers showed significantly more prosocial behaviors in the harm condition than in the control condition (Hepach et al., 2013). In addition, the level of concern displayed by toddlers when viewing the harm condition was positively correlated to their exhibiting prosocial behaviors. In other words, toddlers who displayed more concern engaged in more prosocial behaviors. Thus, it appears that child characteristics (e.g., attention to another's needs) impact the development and demonstration of prosocial behaviors.

Temperament

Some children may be more inclined to engage in prosocial behaviors based on their temperament. As discussed previously, temperament reflects how a person typically behaves. One research team investigated the relationship between temperament and engaging in prosocial behaviors. They found that preschoolers who were rated as high to moderate on self-regulation and low to moderate on negative emotionality engaged in more prosocial behaviors during preschool, first grade, and third grade (Laible, Carlo, Murphy, Augustine, & Roesch, 2014). The opposite relationship was also true. Specifically, preschoolers who were low on self-regulation and high on negative emotionality, especially displays of anger, engaged in fewer prosocial behaviors during the same time period. The authors concluded that "temperamental dimensions work in complex ways to predict social behaviors" (p. 749).

In conclusion, it appears that healthy social development is related to secure attachment and trust in our primary caregivers, healthy identity development, and caregiver respect and sensitivity to children's physical and psychological boundaries. Healthy social development involves children being aware of their own needs and desires and those of other people, as well as communicating verbally and nonverbally in ways that establish interactional synchrony with others. Table 3–2 presents some of the major milestones for social development from birth through 36 months of age. However, when a child does not meet developmental milestones or otherwise displays unhealthy social development, issues regarding mental health can be raised. The issue of infant and early childhood mental health will be explored further in Chapter 10.

TABLE 3–2 ❱ Milestones for Social Development: Birth to 36 Months

AGE	ACTIVITIES
Birth to 6 months	Fusing with mother evolves into basic self-discriminations Matches feelings and tones of caregiver Demonstrates empathy Exhibits interactional synchrony Exhibits social smile Shows happiness at familiar faces Gains caregiver attention intentionally
7–12 months	Exhibits self-recognition and discrimination from others Seeks independence in actions Keeps family members or caregiver in sight Starts imitative play
12–24 months	Exhibits possessiveness Acts differently toward different people Commonly shows stranger anxiety Engages in parallel play Shows strong ownership
24–36 months	Shares, but not consistently Recognizes differences between *mine* and *yours* Understands perspective of other people Helps others Begins to play cooperatively

© Cengage Learning

Before moving on with your reading, make sure that you can answer the following questions about the material discussed so far.

1. What does it mean for a child to be securely attached? Insecurely attached? Why is it important for caregivers to establish secure relationships with the infants and toddlers in their care?
2. What role does having and enforcing limits have on the development of healthy self-esteem? Why?
3. Provide and explain an example of a teacher facilitating the development of prosocial behavior in a toddler.

Summary

3-1 Determine typical patterns of emotional development between birth and thirty-six months of age.

Four different concepts related to emotional development were discussed in this chapter: Erikson's psychosocial theory, separation and together, temperament, and emotional intelligence. Recent research, including studies of brain development, provides evidence that biological and environmental influences work in complex ways to result in children being emotionally competent (or not).

3-2 Sequence typical patterns of social development between birth and thirty-six months of age.

Adults must assume responsibility for supporting and facilitating very young children's social development. One of the primary vehicles through which such competencies develop is the adult-child relationship. Responsive, attuned care that is delivered in synchrony with the child provides a strong foundation for secure attachments, relationships with peers, self-esteem, and prosocial behaviors.

CASE STUDY   Marcus

Evaluating Development

You should now have a working knowledge of normal patterns of development in each of the four areas for children under the age of 36 months. To test your understanding of information in Chapters 2 and 3, decide if Marcus is advanced, behind, or at age level in the following evaluation summary.

Marcus, who is 24 months old, is in child care from 7:30 a.m. to 4:00 p.m., five days a week. He lives with his mother and grandfather in a three-bedroom duplex. An evaluation of his development in each of the four major areas revealed the following observations:

Physical Factors. Marcus is 34 inches tall, weighs 35 pounds, has 20/20 vision, and can focus and track across a line of letters fluidly. He has all 20 baby teeth, can stand on one foot and hop, and is interested in toilet learning. He can throw a ball with each hand and use a fork to eat.

Emotional Factors. Marcus clings to his caregiver during drop-off and shows anxiety at the presence of strangers. He is compliant and follows directions when he feels secure, but he can whine when he needs more individual attention. He has difficulty understanding his feelings or soothing himself. When not involved with his caregiver or other children, Marcus tends to wander around the room.

Social Factors. Marcus has some difficulty determining what things are his, and he cooperates with other children when he has the full attention of his caregiver. He is easily emotionally hurt by other children and does not defend himself when they take a toy he was playing with. He frequently focuses on his own needs and has difficulty reading the feelings of other children. Although his language skills are sufficient, Marcus often screams rather than uses words when his peers bother him.

Cognitive Factors. When he feels secure, Marcus is curious, explores his environment, and gains a lot of physical knowledge. Although he has some difficulty interacting with peers, he participates in active, creative pretend play and exhibits a logical sequence in the stories he makes up. He uses double substitution in play and understands four- and five-direction sequences.

1. Use the Developmental Milestones provided in Appendix A to determine if you think Marcus is advanced for his age level, at age level, or below age level for each area of development. Explain how you drew each conclusion.
2. What contextual factors should be considered when evaluating his development and why?
3. In which of the four areas is it most difficult for you to make an assessment of Marcus? What additional information do you need? Why?

Lesson Plan

Title: *It's a Mess*

Child Observation:

Jozie (22 months) toddled over to the art shelf. She grabbed a chunk of paper and carried it to the table. Then, she returned to the shelf and retrieved the markers. She made marks on the paper for 5 minutes. During the process, I noticed her looking at her hands; the pinky-edge of her left palm was turning colors due to the markers. She looked at me with concern, and I said "It's okay. You can wash it off when you are all done with your picture."

Child's Developmental Goal:

To respond to the emotional expression of others (especially distress).

To help clean up after a messy experience.

Materials: 2 colors of finger paint, shallow trays, a spoon for each tray, finger paint paper, paint smock, 2 wet sponges

Preparation: Clear a table for this experience. Create an individual work space for two or three children by putting a piece of finger paint paper in front of each chair. Then, transfer the finger paint to shallow trays, and place them on the table so that it is easily accessible for each child. Lay a smock on the back of each chair to cue children that they need to wear one. Wet the sponges and place them near you to help with cleaning up.

Learning Environment:

1. When you notice a child near the finger paint table, join her or him.
2. Encourage the child to invite a friend to paint with her or him or do it yourself.
3. While helping the children get their smocks on, discuss how this experience involves a new type of paint and that you don't use a paintbrush like at the easel. To illustrate, you could say:

   "This is called finger paint. You scoop it into the spoon and put it on your paper. Then, you use your fingers to move the paint around on the paper."

4. Observe and record the children's actions with the finger paint. Take pictures of them working as well.
5. If Jozie or another child becomes overly excited and paints on the table, use redirection to focus on "painting on the paper." If paint is dropped on the floor at any time, encourage the child to use the sponge to clean it up. Remind them that "the paint is slippery, and we don't want anyone to fall and get hurt."

6. Invite the children to participate in a conversation by asking prompts or open-ended questions such as:
   a. I hear lots of squeals of delight. What is so great about the finger paint?
   b. Anthony has a scared look on his face. I wonder what is wrong. How can we help him?

7. Accept and elaborate on the toddler's answers. For example, if the child says "Need hug," you might respond: *"You think a hug would help Anthony feel better? That might work because a hug helps you feel better. Do you want to give Anthony a hug?"*

8. When the child is done painting, encourage her or him to clean up the work area. Give one or two directions at a time to help with compliance. To illustrate, you can tell the child:
   "You have to clean up your work area. I'll help you put your painting on the rack. Then, we will use the sponges to wipe up the table." After that is completed, go to the sink with the child to assist with washing hands/arms/smock.

9. Thank the child for helping to clean up her or his work area. You could say:
   "Thank you for cleaning up your area. It is important to help keep the room clean."

Guidance Consideration:

Some children do not like to wear smocks. Offer them a choice of a smock or a recycled, button-down shirt worn backwards. If they refuse, discuss with their family members how to handle this situation so that the child does not miss out on this learning experience. Some families are okay with having their child change into another set of clothes after painting and washing the paint-covered clothes at the end of the day.

Variations:

Invite the children to stand up while finger painting at the table. This will provide a different perspective for their work. It will also challenge them to stay in the painting area, so be prepared with good guidance strategies such as limit setting and choices.

❯❯ Professional Resource Download

Additional Resources

Center on the Developing Child at Harvard University. (2011). *Building the brain's "air traffic control" system: How early experiences shape the development of executive function: Working Paper No. 11,* http://www.developingchild.harvard.edu.

Nelson, K. (2010). *Young minds in social worlds: Experience, meaning, and memory.* Cambridge, MA: Harvard University Press.

Odom, S. L., Pungello, E. P., & Gardner-Neblett, N. (Eds.) (2012). *Infants, toddlers, and families in poverty: Research implications for early child care.* New York: Guilford Press.

Schutt, R. K., Seidman, L. J., & Keshavan, M. S. (2015). *Social neuroscience: Brain, mind, and society.* Cambridge, MA: Harvard University Press.

Underwood, M. K., & Rosen, L. H. (Eds.) (2013). *Social development: relationships in infancy, childhood, and adolescence.* New York: Guilford Press.

Attachment and the Three *As*

Learning Objectives

After reading this chapter, you should be able to:

4-1 Explain the changing roles concerning attachment for early childhood educators.

4-2 Understand the three *As* and how to use them in interactions with very young children.

Standards Addressed in This Chapter

naeyc **NAEYC Standards for Early Childhood Professional Preparation**

1 Promoting Child Development and Learning
4 Using Developmentally Effective Approaches to Connect with Children and Families

DAP **Developmentally Appropriate Practice Guidelines**

2 Teaching to Enhance Development and Learning

In addition, the NAEYC standards for developmentally appropriate practice are divided into six areas particularly important to infant/toddler care. The following area is addressed in this chapter: *relationship between caregiver and child.*

© Cengage Learning

The lifelong effects of positive, consistent, and conscious infant and toddler care have been understood by child development and early childhood experts for a long time. A working premise of this book is that what you do with children matters. Positive intention coupled with responsiveness to developmental characteristics makes a profound difference in the lives of children. As previously discussed, the quality of your caring, including actions, verbal messages, voice tone and tempo, and secure handling, helps create the neural pathways that determine each child's perceptions and models of the world. Your interactions with young children help determine how each child will eventually perceive himself or herself—as worthy or unworthy, capable or incapable, hopeful or hopeless.

Caregivers have a mission that is monumental in nature. Your daily movements, efforts, and attitudes affect each and every child; no position in society is more important. The abilities to understand and fulfill academic requirements and to master specific skills, such as feeding babies and building appropriate curricula for toddlers, are necessary to your professional work with young children and may even extend into your personal life. These immensely important aspects of child care, however, are not enough.

Students studying child care must also integrate their *selves* into their work because in no other field is the professional in need of self-integration more than in this most humanistic endeavor. Taking charge of tomorrow's leaders on a daily basis demands human investment because it supports future human relationships. Just how valuable are these first relationships to future development? Look at what just a few experts have to say about the importance of human connections:

> "Every experience lives on in further experiences" (Dewey, 1938, p. 28).
>
> "It is in that context of loving, paying attention, and turn-taking that infants begin to feel more or less competent, good about themselves, and begin to make the most miraculous mutual adaptations with those caring for them" (Pawl, 2012, p. 22).
>
> As we acknowledge our responsibility as caregivers, we must also readily accept that involving "the child as an active, thinking participant" is the best way to support the developing brain (Thompson, 2006, p. 50). "More than any toy, CD, or video, a sensitive social partner can respond appropriately to what has captured the child's interest…[and] provoke new interests and exploration" (p. 49).

The importance of warm, loving, verbal interactions between parent or caregiver and child, particularly in the first two years, should not be underestimated. The three *As* are the master tools that ensure that your effect on children is positive and productive. There is no better way to provide quality care than a wonderfully soothing dose of consciously administered attention, approval, and attunement. Before the details of the three *As* are addressed, we will first return to the importance of attachment theory for teachers.

4-1 The Attachment Debate and the Roles of Caregivers

Discussion of the three *As* begins with the scientific fact that infants and toddlers require secure attachments or enduring emotional ties to their caregivers for normal, healthy development. An ongoing debate in the research literature concerns whether infants exhibit less secure attachment when they experience child care as opposed to being raised exclusive by family members. This debate cannot be discussed without considering the changing roles of mothers and fathers in the care of infants. One historical view was that *only* the mother could bond with the infant sufficiently to ensure healthy development. In contrast, current perspectives suggest that nonfamilial persons can meet the needs of infant equally well. Because a great number of infants and toddlers are spending the majority of their day in child care, the question of what quality of attachment to one consistent person the infant may require to develop security and trust is being studied more intensely.

As is discussed in Chapter 3, researchers have identified a pattern of secure attachment and three patterns of insecure attachment (Ainsworth, 1967, 1973; Ainsworth, Blehar, Waters, & Wall, 1978; Hesse & Main, 2000; Main & Solomon, 1990):

secure attachment A connection between infant and primary caregiver in which the infant feels safe and responds warmly to the caregiver.

avoidant attachment One of the types of attachment between infants and primary caregiver that is related to inconsistent and insensitive caregiver attention.

resistant attachment A form of connection between infant and primary caregiver in which the infant simultaneously seeks and resists emotionally and physically connecting with the caregiver. The term ambivalent can be used to describe the same types of attachment behaviors.

disoriented attachment A form of attachment between infant and primary caregiver in which the infant has usually been traumatized by severe or prolonged abandonment.

separation anxiety Fear exhibited at the loss of physical or emotional connection with the primary caregiver.

1. **Secure attachment.** The infant uses a parent or other family member as a secure base, strongly prefers the parent over a stranger, actively seeks contact with the parent, and is easily comforted by the parent after being absent. This type of attachment describes the majority of infant-parent relationships worldwide (Bergin & Bergin, 2012).

2. **Avoidant attachment.** The infant is usually not distressed by parental separation and may avoid the parent or prefer a stranger when the parent returns.

3. **Resistant attachment.** The infant seeks closeness to the parent and resists exploring the environment, usually displays angry behavior after the parent returns, and is difficult to comfort.

4. **Disoriented attachment.** The infant shows inconsistent attachment and reacts to the parent returning with confused or contradictory behavior (looking away when held or showing a dazed facial expression).

A phenomenon related to attachment is **separation anxiety**, which appears to be a normal developmental experience because children from every culture exhibit it. Infants from various cultures all over the world have been found to exhibit separation anxiety starting at around 9 months old and increasing in intensity until approximately 15 months old (Bergin & Bergin, 2012). Separation anxiety is exhibited by securely attached infants, as well as each type of insecurely attached infants.

A summary of the research on infant attachment suggests that infants are actively involved in the attachment relationship. Babies are normally capable of attaching securely to more than one adult or parent. Contemporary researchers have examined how children create attachments with caregivers, including fathers (Condon, Corkindale, Boyce, & Gamble, 2013; Feinberg & Kan, 2008; Figueiredo, Costa, Pacheco, & Pais, 2007), grandparents (Farmer, Selwyn, & Meakings, 2013; Poehlmann, 2003), brothers and sisters (Kennedy, Betts, & Underwood, 2014; Volling, Herrera, & Poris, 2004), adoptive and foster families (Dyer, 2004; Gabler et al., 2014; Oosterman & Schuengel, 2008; Stovall-McClough & Dozier, 2004), and professional early childhood educators (Buyse, Verschueren, & Doumen, 2011; Caldera & Hart, 2004; Commodari, 2013; O'Connor & McCartney, 2006).

While infants can form multiple attachments, the quality of those attachments is not static; they can change over time in response to changing environmental conditions. Booth-LaForce et al. (2014) report that changes in family structure (e.g., divorce or remarriage) or job status (e.g., job gain or loss) can result in either continuity or discontinuity of attachment. Some changes, such as entrance to foster care for an infant or toddler, have been assumed to be negative. However, Jacobsen, Ivarsson, Wentzel-Larsen, Smith, and Moe (2014) found that when toddlers entered foster care with a secure attachment, they were more likely to be rated as securely attached a year later. In addition, when children with disorganized attachments were placed in foster care, they were less likely to be rated as disorganized a year later. Taking these results together leads the author to conclude that stable, well-functioning foster homes can have a positive impact on children's attachment (Jacobsen et al., 2014).

© 2017 Cengage Learning

PHOTO 4–1 The type of attachments a child forms with her caregivers impacts how she relates to other adults and children.

Caregiving that is supportive and sensitive to the child's needs promotes secure attachment (Photo 4–1). For example, mothers who responded to their child's cues with insightfulness (e.g., seeing the problem from the child's perspective) had children who were significantly more likely to have secure attachment (Koren-Karie, Oppenheim, Dolev, & Sher, 2002). Secure infant attachment and continuity of caregiving are related to later cognitive, emotional, and social competence. The research on adoptive families, for example, illustrates two of these patterns. Infants adopted at younger ages showed higher levels of secure behavior and more coherent attachment strategies than those adopted when they were older (Stovall-McClough & Dozier, 2004), and these positive attachment relationships predicted later socioemotional and cognitive development (Stams, Juffer, & van IJzendoorn, 2002).

From these findings, we can draw several important implications for caregiving and changes in early childhood educators' roles. Research on attachment security of infants with full-time working mothers suggests that most infants of employed mothers are securely attached, and that this relationship is more influential on early social and emotional growth than the relationships a child has with other caregivers, both inside and outside the home (NICHD Early Child Care Research Network, 1997, 1998a, 1998b, 1999, 2005). However, when a child has an insecure relationship with her mother, early childhood educators can establish a secure relationship with the child, providing a buffer against some of the negative developmental outcomes (Buyse et al., 2011). Hence, with more mothers of infants in the workplace, the responsibility for forming secure attachments must be shared with fathers, other family members, and teachers. Everyone must work together to provide secure and consistent attachment and bonding with infants.

Forming reciprocal relationships or partnerships with families will assist in this process. Our responsibilities as teachers are twofold: we must not only help children develop trust and secure attachments with us but also assist family members to form strong, secure relationships with the infant. As discussed previously, employing particular strategies such as a primary caregiving system, family grouping, and continuity of care can ensure that each infant and toddler has as few caregivers as possible, each providing consistency and predictability over time. Pawl (2006) suggests that caregivers need to help the parent exist for the child and help the child know that she also exists for the parents when they are separated during the day. For example, reminding the child that his foster parent is "leaving work to come and get him because she misses him" is important both to providing quality care and supporting the development of strong relationships. The second prong of our approach must be to provide family support and education to help family members form and maintain secure attachments with their children. Family education should include the importance of mothers, fathers, and other family members providing direct care of the children so that they can experience consistent, loving, and healthy relationships. Working together, parents, family members, and teachers can create consistent, secure attachment with infants and toddlers.

READING CHECKPOINT

Before moving on with your reading, make sure that you can answer the following questions about the material discussed so far.

1. Why are early relationships important to later development?
2. How does knowing about and understanding the attachment relationships that the children in your care have with their family members help you as an early childhood educator?

4-2 The Three *As*: Attention, Approval, and Attunement

attention One of the three *As* of child care; focusing sensory modalities (e.g., visual, auditory) on a specific child.

approval One of the three *As* of child care; feedback that a person is accepted as he or she is.

attunement One of the three *As* of child care; feedback that is in tune with or responsive to the behaviors or moods being currently displayed by the child.

The three *As* of child care—**attention**, **approval**, and **attunement**—are the master tools for promoting a positive environment and maintaining a positive emotional connection between the young child and the caregiver. The three *As* are extremely powerful tools available to any person in just about any situation, yet they are *essential* in the care and education of very young children. The three *As* are called master tools because they apply to everything we do all day long. Attention, approval, and attunement are necessary for positive interactions, good self-esteem, and remaining at ease.

The concepts of attention, approval, and attunement are meant to empower you and help facilitate an attitude change toward yourself, which emphasizes that early childhood educators' feelings have a profound effect on children. The three *As* are derived directly from current perspectives on development and care (discussed in Chapter 1): brain research and ecological systems, sociocultural, and attachment theories. In addition, they are supported by our understanding of the guidelines for developmentally appropriate curriculum, which are addressed in more detail in Chapters 11, 12, and 13 (Copple & Bredekamp, 2009; Copple, Bredekamp, Koralek, & Charner, 2013). This theoretical knowledge helps a teacher appropriately care for and educate children; when that same caregiver uses this knowledge for personal development, he or she can enjoy benefits as well.

Spotlight on Research

INFANT PERSISTENCE

Infants are born curious about the world and their place in it. This curiosity results in a great deal of internal motivation. It should be no surprise then that infants spend a great deal of time exploring the people and objects in their environments. Is being persistent a stable, individual quality that varies among individuals, and, if so, how does more or less persistence impact later development?

Banerjee and Tamis-LeMonda (2007) set out to explore these questions with their sample of 65 low-income mother-infant dyads. These researchers videotaped infant-mother interactions in their home during a teaching task when the infants were 6 months and 14 months of age. The measure of infant persistence was coded from a three-minute interaction with a toy at 6 months of age. Infant cognition was measured after each session using the Mental Scale of the Bayley Scales of Infant Development.

The results showed that as early as 6 months of age, infants differ in their degree of persistence and that there was a significant correlation in persistence scores over the eight-month period. In other words, infants who were more persistent at 6 months old tended to be more persistent at 14 months old. Additionally, "infants who persisted early on also . . . had higher scores on the Bayley Mental Development Index" (Banerjee & Tamis-LeMonda, 2007, p. 487). Thus, persistence was associated with greater levels of cognitive development.

Next, the researchers investigated the impact of mothers' teaching on cognitive development. They found that "mothers' teaching at six but not fourteen months was associated with persistence at both ages and predicted cognitive development at fourteen months" (Banerjee & Tamis-LeMonda, 2007, p. 487). The researchers concluded from this result that mothers' early teaching had a dual function of helping infants to be persistent at a challenging task as well as promoting cognitive development.

Similarly, other researchers have found short- and long-term impacts of mother behaviors and characteristics on young children's persistent behaviors. Mothers' positive affective responses to their 18-month-old child during a semi-structured play session were associated with more persistence and competence during preschool, whereas dismissed affect exchanges had negative relationships with children's persistence and independent mastery (Wang, Morgan, & Biringen, 2014). Mothers who reported more stress when their infant was 6 months old tended to have children who showed lower mastery motivation at 18 months (i.e., less persistence during interactions with people and toys; Sparks, Hunter, Backman, Morgan, & Ross, 2012).

These research studies have implications for early intervention specialists as well as early childhood educators. If teachers and intervention specialists work with infants and their families to support the development of persistence, they would also be supporting important cognitive skills. Wheeler and Stultz (2008) suggest that music therapy can be used to assist young infants with regulating their attention to environmental stimuli, especially people. For example, therapists can use their voice, face, and hands as tools for gaining the attention of an infant. Then, they attempt to gain eye contact, even if infrequent, and to be attuned to the infant's cues while working to extend periods of interactions. It would seem reasonable to conclude that "extending periods of interactions" (Wheeler & Stultz, 2008) is another way to describe the infant's ability to persist in an interaction with another person. Gaining and maintaining this balance is not easy as infants frequently change states of arousal and often have difficulty regulating their reactions to new stimuli. Wheeler and Stultz (2008) conclude that therapists support moderate arousal by soothing and containing the agitated child, enticing the withdrawn child, and inviting the child's attention to the social environment.

4-2a Attention

You have likely heard the saying, "Smile and the whole world smiles with you." Can you remember a time when you were put at ease when greeted by a stranger's smile or felt instant rapport when someone returned your smile? So much is communicated without words; often the unspoken message conveys exactly how a person is feeling. When we realize that

70 percent of our total communication is nonverbal, it is easy to understand why a smile says so much.

In the simplest way, a smile is a way to attend to yourself and to someone else. When you bring attention to a behavior in another person, you are sending a message about the importance of that behavior. Using the words of Vygotsky, you are helping children construct an understanding of the meaning behind a smile. For example, the child may construct the notion that people smile when they are happy or see a behavior that they like. In this way, young children begin to associate a smile response with engaging in an appropriate behavior. Our responses can be overt and filled with emotion (e.g., "You did it!") or more neutral (e.g., sitting nearby and observing a child play; Copple et al., 2013). In either case, a neural pathway is then built to remember this association; in this way, what we attend to helps the brain to grow. The opposite is also true. If we attend to negative behaviors displayed by children, then children may construct an understanding that these behaviors are appropriate ways to interact with others.

Of course, attending is much more complicated than just producing a smile or reacting to a negative behavior. Attention, for early childhood educators, also involves higher mental functions (Bodrova & Leong, 2007) or "cognitive processes acquired through learning and teaching...[that]... are *deliberate, mediated, internalized* behaviors" (pp. 19, 20, emphasis in original). Teachers must learn to engage in focused attention to observe the behavior, skills, and needs of the children in their care. Observing closely, or attending, facilitates your analysis of the child's behaviors and appropriate responses to those behaviors. In other words, attending makes it possible to identify each child's **zone of proximal development (ZPD)**, which is "the distance between the actual developmental level as determined by independent problem solving and the level of potential development as determined through problem solving under adult guidance or in collaboration with more capable peers" (Vygotsky, 1978, p. 86).

zone of proximal development (ZPD) Vygotsky's term for a range of tasks that a child is developmentally ready to learn.

Classifying the ZPD is vital for teachers because it determines where to place educational emphasis. Scaffolding, or assistance from a more skilled other, facilitates learning at the "higher" end of the zone. In other words, behaviors by the more skilled partner contribute to acquiring skills that were outside of the child's independent level of functioning.

Another component of attending entails recognizing ecological factors from other systems that impact children's development and learning (Bronfenbrenner, 1979, 1989). As discussed previously, these factors both affect the child and are influenced by the child. Such bidirectional influences must continually be considered by early childhood educators to recognize the active role children play in their own development. For example, teachers must be culturally sensitive and responsive to the way families want to raise their children. Families hold particular beliefs that may or may not be shared by the caregiver; this should affect how you do your work. Altering your routines and behaviors to support family practices assists with more continuous care for very young children (Gonzalez-Mena, 2001).

In general, what we attend to matters. As early as 3 months of age, infants follow the head turn of an adult, disengaging from what they had been attending to and shifting their attention to what the adult is attending

Family and Community Connection

You have begun to notice that you leave your toddler classroom each day feeling stressed and tense. Upon reflection, you realize that you and your co-teacher spend a great deal of your day correcting and otherwise attending to the children's negative behaviors. You have also noticed that some parents consistently focus on their child's positive behaviors during the often-stressful drop-off and pick-up times. You really want to talk with the family members about how they decide what they choose to focus on at these times, but you are worried that you might send the message that you are not a "knowledgeable" professional. What questions could you ask that would help you learn from the families, build positive relationships with them, and maintain your sense of professionalism?

to (Perra & Gattis, 2010). Thus, adults can influence what an infant attends to in very subtle ways. What we attend to also communicates to us and others ideas regarding the meaning or value of particular behaviors while influencing the very behavior we are examining. Matusov, DePalma, and Drye (2007) suggest that, from a sociocultural perspective, the observer directly and indirectly influences the development of the observed by how the behavior is thought and talked about.

To illustrate, Kemit takes a while each morning to join the group. He likes to watch the fish before selecting an independent activity. After he has played alone for 10–12 minutes, he usually selects to work with one of his friends. When the caregiver, Trace, speaks with Kemit's grandmother at pick-up time, he often expresses concern about Kemit being "shy." Kemit's grandmother, who initially felt this behavior was acceptable and reflective of Kemit's way of doing things, becomes worried. So she works with Trace to create a plan for helping Kemit transition to school "more smoothly." In this example, Trace has altered Kemit's grandmother's view of Kemit and her expectations for his behavior. By setting up this transition plan, they are directly changing Kemit's development. They are communicating to Kemit that working alone is not acceptable and that he should be more interactive with peers. Although these are not detrimental outcomes by any means, it does seem to be disrespectful of who Kemit is as a person.

Thus, we must continually remember that what we attend to matters because it alters the course of development for children—positively or negatively.

4-2b Approval

Approval from others teaches us to approve of ourselves. The best type of attention is approval. Approval of another person is a clear message that you have respect and positive regard for that person. According to the *American Heritage Dictionary of the English Language* (2000), respect is all of the following:

- To feel or show differential regard for
- To avoid violation or interference with

respect A feeling of high regard for someone and a willingness to treat him or her accordingly.

- The state of being regarded with honor or esteem
- Willingness to show consideration or appreciation

How do early childhood educators translate this multifaceted definition into their daily practice? Swim (2003) suggests that both allowing children time to try or complete tasks and helping them to make choices reflect respect for the children because these behaviors demonstrate refraining from interfering with them. In addition, valuing individual children's ways of doing and being shows that they are held in high esteem by the caregiver.

Educational leaders in the municipal infant/toddler and preschool programs of Reggio Emilia, Italy, take the understanding of respect to another level. They have declared respect an educational value (Rinaldi, 2001a) and devised the concept of the **rights of children**. This concept reflects their image of the child as "rich in resources, strong, and competent. The emphasis is placed on seeing the children as unique individuals with rights rather than simply needs. They have potential, plasticity, openness, the desire to grow, curiosity, a sense of wonder, and the desire to relate to other people and to communicate" (Rinaldi, 1998, p. 114). Teachers use their image of the child to guide their instructional decisions, curricular planning, and interactions with children (see, e.g., Edwards, Gandini, & Forman, 2012).

To children, approval says they have done something right, and it helps them feel worthwhile. Approval builds trust and self-confidence, which in turn encourage children to try new things without fear. The most important concept a caregiver must learn is always to approve of the child as a person, even when you disapprove of his or her behavior. For example, it must be made clear to the child that you like who he is, but not what he is doing right now.

Appropriate and consistent approval develops trust in the child. Trust depends not only on the quantity (e.g., number of interactions) but also on the quality of the caregiver's interactions and relationships with children. Positive approval creates a sense of trust as a result of the sensitive way in which the caregiver takes time to care for the child's individual needs. Adults must convey to each child an honest concern for that child's welfare and a deep conviction that there is meaning in what he or she is doing. Trust based on consistent, positive caring allows children to grow up with a sense of meaningful belonging and trust.

Some caution should be exercised regarding when to give approval. Caregivers who approve of every little behavior and shower children with unconditional approval lose respect with them. Genuine approval for meaningful accomplishments serves to encourage children to try harder and helps them value their own efforts. Make sure the children have made a genuine effort or have accomplished something of value, and your approval will help them become the best that they can be.

4-2c Attunement

Attunement involves being aware of someone, along with her moods, needs, and interests, and responding to all of these. In other words, when

rights of children The belief that children do not just have needs for adults to deal with but rather rights to appropriate care and education.

you are "in tune," you are providing high-quality care and education that meet the individual needs, interests, and abilities of each child.

Attuned caregivers often look natural in their interactions with infants and toddlers. However, being attuned is not instinctual for all persons. Often, our beliefs about child rearing or parenting interfere with providing such care. For example, a strongly held belief by many parents, teachers, and physicians is that responding to the cries of infants too quickly will spoil them. Of course, as was stated previously, you cannot spoil a young child. All of the research on attachment reviewed in this chapter and in Chapters 1 and 3 discounts this belief. Responding sensitively to a child's communication strategies helps the child develop trust in his or her caregiver; form strong, secure attachments; and grow socially and emotionally.

Attuned caregivers devote a great deal of time to carefully observing and recording the infants' behaviors. In fact, the guidelines for developmentally appropriate practice state that the early educator should know each child well and learn each child's cues (Copple et al., 2013). Then, the adult should respond to the child's individual characteristics so that interactional, instructional, and caregiving strategies "... are *caring* and *specific* to each child ..." (Copple et al., 2013, p. 67, emphasis in original). For example, Nicole knows that Tiffany, 27 months old, has a very regular routine for eating and sleeping. Today, however, she was not hungry right after playing outdoors and had difficulty relaxing for a nap. Upon closer observation and questioning, Nicole came to understand that Tiffany's throat hurt. Nicole was able to use her knowledge of Tiffany to "tune into" this change of routine and uncover the beginning of an illness.

When caregivers engage in respectful and responsive interpersonal interactions with infants and toddlers, they are attuned in the way researchers use the word. They are in synchrony with the child (Isabella & Belsky, 1991). Reading and responding to the child's cues is crucial to engaging in this "interactional dance."

For example, picture caregiver Carlos feeding Judd his lunch. Judd is hungry and eating quickly. Carlos talks about how good the food must be for an empty stomach. He is smiling and laughing between bites. All of a sudden, Judd begins to slow the pace. Carlos reads this behavior and slows down his offering of food and pattern of speech. Judd smiles and turns his head away from Carlos. Carlos pauses and waits for Judd to turn back around. He does turn back and opens his mouth. Carlos provides another bite of vegetables.

Perceptions, however, can get in the way of a person's ability to be attuned. Ghera, Hane, Malesa, and Fox (2006) found that maternal perceptions of infant soothability influenced the degree of maternal sensitivity. When mothers viewed their infants as more soothable, they were able to provide sensitive care even when the baby was displaying negative reactivity. On the other hand, when mothers viewed their infants as less soothable, they provided less sensitive care when their infants were displaying negative reactivity. Similarly, foster mothers who perceived typically developing children as requiring easier care were more sensitive to them

© 2017 Cengage Learning

PHOTO 4–2 Children respond positively to caregivers who use attention, approval, and attunement in their interactions with them.

as compared with children who had developmental delays (Ponciano, 2012). Adopting mothers, however, were found to be more sensitive to children requiring complex care (Ponciano, 2012). As you can see from this research, perceptions of the adult can influence the quality of interactions. Therefore, early educators must reflect on their own views of children to ensure that they identify and remedy beliefs that could interfere with the ability to be attuned.

When early childhood educators combine attention, approval, and attunement, children cannot help but respond positively (Photo 4–2). That is why the three As are the master tools for child development and care. You might already use the three As without much thought about them. Consider how you approach an unknown infant. You get down to her level (floor, blanket, or chair). You act calmly, move slowly, make eye contact, enter her space, get even closer to her physically, smile, and gently begin soft speech to engage her. If you believe you have permission from her to stay close, you keep eye contact and slowly begin to inquire what she is doing, such as playing or eating. When she gestures, you follow the gesture with a similar response, this time making a sound that seems to identify her movement and keep pace. This usually elicits a smile or giggle. Once again, you smile and make noise. You may try gently touching a shoulder or finger, and before long, you are accepted into the child's space. This slow progression of building rapport is also the slow progression of the use of the three As. First you give attention, then approval, and then attunement. When this is done consciously, all involved feel worthy.

While many of these behaviors may come naturally to you, you should spend a great deal of time thinking about them, reflecting on how you use them, and analyzing their impact on children. How, for example, can you use them more intentionally and effectively? Only through conscious decision-making can you use these tools to help children develop to their fullest extent.

The three As are powerful and rejuvenating for you as well. They elicit responses in children that will sustain you in your vocation. One of the most positive assurances of worthiness a caregiver can receive is the full-body hug given unconditionally as a gift from a gleeful toddler who sweeps down upon you when you are playing on the floor. This hug, which is often accompanied by a loud and joyful sound, enters your space with such focused positive energy that each of you feels the impact. The result of this positive energy is felt by the two of you, and brings smiles to the faces of all who observe it.

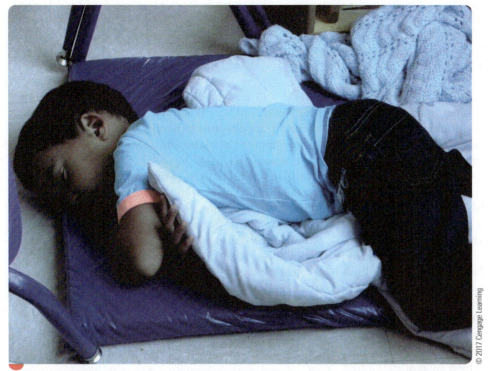

© 2017 Cengage Learning

PHOTO 4–3 Infants and toddlers who feel safe can relax and rest peacefully.

Before moving on with your reading, make sure that you can answer the following questions about the material discussed so far.

1. List, define, describe, and provide a specific example for each of the three *As* of child care.
2. How are the three *As* grounded in the theoretical perspectives described in Chapters 1, 2, and 3?
3. Why are the three *As* powerful tools to use when working with children?

READING CHECKPOINT

Summary

4-1 Explain the changing roles concerning attachment for early childhood educators.

Infants can form strong, positive attachments with a number of different people. All of these relationships evolve over time and form the foundation for how the infant thinks about and engages in relationships with others.

4-2 Understand the three *As* and how to use them in interactions with very young children.

When the three *As* are focused on children, they promote appropriate behaviors and enhance a positive learning environment for children. The caregiver structures an emotionally safe context in which the young child explores and masters all of his or her growing abilities by solving problems that naturally occur within the environment. A stable, positive environment promotes trust and confidence and allows the growing infant to express all of his or her needs.

CASE STUDY   Responding to Rangina's Diverse Needs

Rangina has been in Abebi's class for seven months now. Rangina's family immigrated from Afghanistan right before she was born. She started coming to the child care center when she was 1 year old. The transition was difficult at first, but Rangina quickly settled into a routine. Nap time was a particular challenge as Rangina cried herself to sleep nearly every afternoon. After many conversations between Abebi and Rangina's father, they decided that his wife would tape record her nightly singing and playing of the Waj instrument. When Abebi played this during nap time, the music and singing were so soothing that they helped not only Rangina to fall asleep but also some of the other children.

This particular morning, Rangina came dressed in a new embroidered kuchi-style dress with a matching chador (head scarf). Her mother explained that they were observing Eid al-Fitr, which celebrates the first day after the Ramadan fast. Rangina was clearly excited about her new clothing. Abebi commented, "Your new dress must be soft. Can I feel it?" Rangina exclaimed,

"Yes!" and hugged her. Then, Rangina danced to another area of the classroom. Abebi noticed that she danced from one area to another during the first half of free choice time, and she seemed to have trouble finding experiences to engage her. For example, she declined to paint at the easel or draw with markers, some of her favorite things to do. When Abebi asked about these decisions, she would only say "No dirty." Abebi moved to her eye level and asked if she was afraid to get her new clothes messy. When Rangina replied yes, Abebi found other attractive, nonmessy art materials for her to use. When it was story time, Rangina began to run around the room. Abebi decided that a game of follow the leader might be best, and she invited Rangina to be the first leader.

1. From the case study, what do you think is the most important tool Abebi used with Rangina? Why?
2. How did Abebi's relationship with Rangina's parents help her to be more responsive to Rangina?
3. How does interactional synchrony apply to this case study?

Lesson Plan

Title: *What do you need?*

Child Observation:

Noor is 4 months old and just started in your classroom. She and her family finished the *inserimento* period (see Chapter 6), and she started full-time last week. Her father told you that she typically takes a 2-hour morning nap. So far, she hasn't slept more than 20 minutes at a time.

Child's Developmental Goal:

To develop positive attachment to the caregiver

To be soothed by another

Materials: Child's favorite "lovie" (e.g., blanket, stuffed animal)

Preparation: *None.*

Learning Environment:

1. When you notice Noor getting tired, gather her favorite animal blanket and pacifier. Talk with her about what you are doing and why. For example, you could say:

    "You are getting tired. I think you would like your bear blanket. Isn't that soft?"
2. Take her to a comfortable spot in the classroom where you can still supervise and interact with the other children, if necessary.
3. While getting situated, respond to her behaviors. To illustrate, if she yawns, you could say:

    "You are really tired. It is nap time. Do you want your pacifier?" Judge her response to the question and respond accordingly.
4. Using information her parents provided, sing her favorite song while holding her in her preferred way (i.e., with her head on your shoulder).

5. Because she is having trouble staying asleep, hold her as long as possible before putting her in her crib.

Guidance Consideration:

If Noor does not respond to your caregiving by relaxing and falling asleep, you might need to consider other aspects of the environment that need to be altered. For example, could the comfortable spot be located to a part of the room that can be darkened? Or, would soothing music be more comforting than your singing?

Variations:

Be responsive to Noor's needs when she is hungry or wants to play.

Professional Resource Download

Additional Resources

Gray, D. D. (2014). *Attaching through love, hugs and play: Simple strategies to help build connections with your child.* London, England: Jessica Kingsley Publishing.

Hughes, D. A. (2009). *Attachment-focused parenting: Effective strategies to care for children.* New York: W.W. Norton & Co.

Krechevsky, M., Mardell, B., Rivard, M., & Wilson, D. (2013). *Visible learners: Promoting Reggio-inspired approaches in all schools.* Hoboken, NJ: Jossey-Bass.

Newton, R. P. (2008). *The attachment connection: Parenting a secure & confident child using the science of attachment theory.* Oakland, CA: New Harbinger Publications.

Raikes, H. H., & Edwards, C. P. (2009). *Extending the dance in infant and toddler caregiving.* Baltimore, MD: Paul H. Brookes Publishing Co.

5

CHAPTER

Effective Preparation and Tools

Learning Objectives

After reading this chapter, you should be able to:

5-1 Describe the characteristics necessary to become a competent caregiver.

5-2 Specify the various types of knowledge, skills, and dispositions professional educators should possess.

5-3 Defend the importance of formal educational experiences for teachers on child outcomes.

5-4 Justify how to match observational tools with your data needs.

Standards Addressed in This Chapter

naeyc **NAEYC Standards for Early Childhood Professional Preparation**

3 Observing, Documenting, and Assessing to Support Young Children and Families

6 Becoming a Professional

DAP **Developmentally Appropriate Practice Guidelines**

4 Assessing Children's Development and Learning

In addition, the NAEYC standards for developmentally appropriate practice are divided into six areas particularly important to infant/toddler care. The following area is addressed in this chapter: *policies.*

The heart and soul of excellent care and education are people and the tools they use in supporting the development of young children. This chapter provides specific, effective tools that enhance development. The early childhood educator should practice using each of the tools in this chapter from the developmental perspective that was described previously. Careful assessment of infants and toddlers is an essential starting point for professional child care. Recording specific, descriptive observations on an ongoing basis and then using that information to inform educational decisions ensures optimal growth and development for the infants and toddlers in your care.

5-1 Characteristics of a Competent Early Childhood Educator

As you learned in Chapter 4, it is essential for caregivers to take good care of young children's physical and mental health. They also need to take care of their own needs. Therefore, the first tools we will examine are those related to your professional preparation as a caregiver.

5-1a Physically and Mentally Healthy

Physical health is necessary to provide the high energy level needed in caregiving. Good health is also necessary to resist the variety of illnesses to which you are exposed. The importance of a healthy staff is reflected in state child care regulations. From Alabama to Indiana to Delaware to Wyoming, prospective teachers must provide evidence of being in good physical health and free from active tuberculosis to gain and remain employed in a child care setting. These policies were created to protect adults as well as the children.

In your daily relationships, you must provide physical closeness and nurturing for an extended time, give emotionally more than you receive, be patient and resolve conflicts caused by someone else, and calm one child right after you have been frustrated with another. Emotionally stable teachers have learned how to handle a variety of emotional demands in their daily experiences and how to encourage greater mental health in others.

5-1b Positive Self-Image

Your feelings of self-confidence and positive self-worth show that you believe in yourself. This gives you the strength to take risks, solve problems, consider alternatives, and make decisions in situations where there may be no obvious correct answer. Your observations, perceptions, and knowledge base are all sources of information you can use in evaluating situations and making decisions. Awareness of your expectations and those of children help you remain open minded. Your decisions may not always be accurate or appropriate because they are based on incomplete information. Admit this, reevaluate the data or gather more information, and make a new decision. Doing so helps you continue to grow professionally and enhances your self-image as a competent caregiver.

© 2017 Cengage Learning

PHOTO 5–1 The caregiver develops skill in working with children and gains satisfaction from interacting with them.

professional capital Assets that add to the long-term worth of each professional and the education profession; comprised of human, social, and decisional capital.

5-1c Caring and Respectful

There is pleasure, enjoyment, and satisfaction in providing effective, high-quality care (Photo 5–1). Although some tasks may be difficult, unpleasant, or repetitious, your accepting behavior and considerate treatment shows that you value meeting the children's needs. They are worthy of your time and effort because they are important people. When early childhood educators reflect caring feelings to the children, families, and other staff members, they can build better partnerships, but it is more than that. According to Noddings (2002, 2005), human-to-human caring relationships for self, others, and community are the core that can bring social justice and caring together for world survival.

Professionals

Caregiving is an essential profession that should receive more respect. You provide a very important service to children, families, and the community. The care you provide directly affects children at critical times in their lives. You have great influence and importance in the child's life and must be rational and objective in your decisions and actions.

Striving to do your best is essential for high-quality caregiving. Read, study, visit, observe, and talk with other early childhood educators. Hargreaves and Fullen (2012) suggest that **professional capital** is built when teachers work together to analyze episodes of teaching and learning. In turn, teachers' increased professional capital maximizes program effectiveness. Ongoing learning is vital because professional knowledge is not static; you will never finish learning everything you need to know to be an effective caregiver. New information and experiences lead to new insights, understanding, and skills. Openness to learning helps you seek new ideas and take advantage of new opportunities to expand your knowledge and skills. Professional educators value and therefore set aside time for frequent and systematic reflection on their work. What plans do you have to learn more about yourself, children, teaching, and your program?

5-2 Acquiring Professional Knowledge, Skills, and Dispositions

Before you start learning about children, families, and the field of early childhood education, you need to understand more about yourself. Why do you want to be an early childhood educator? What are your strengths? What are your weaknesses? What are your interests? What are your values? What are your expectations of yourself and others? Are you willing to put forth effort to satisfy yourself and others? How much time and effort do you think is appropriate to put into caregiving? Consider the results of research by Izumi-Taylor, Lee, and Franceschini (2011) which found that early childhood teachers in the United States believed more strongly that infants should be cared for by a parent than did similar educators in Japan. How might those beliefs impact interactions with children and families?

Research has been conducted on the link between beliefs and classroom behaviors. Teachers who self-identified as "tone-deaf" were equally likely to engage in singing with young children in their classroom. However, they reported greater feelings of being self-conscious when singing and more often altered their singing behavior (Swain & Bodkin-Allen, 2014). Relatedly, when early childhood teachers were asked to rate their perceived competence in each of the content areas, they reported significantly less competence in various art strands (e.g., drama, dance; Garvis & Pendergast, 2011). These researchers then discovered that those who reported less competence were less likely to regularly engage with the various art strands in their classrooms.

What are your beliefs about these topics, and how do you think they impact your interactions with children and families?

5-2a Knowledge about Children and Families

Child development research continuously provides new information about children. The information helps identify each child's individual characteristics and levels of development. Your knowledge of physical, emotional, social, and cognitive development patterns influences how you plan for and interact with children. Yet, because children do not live in isolation, teachers must also learn about each individual family they're working with.

Each family situation is unique and affects your caregiving. As a caregiver, you can expect families to represent a great deal of diversity: single parent, grandparent as head of household, gay/lesbian parents, homeless families, and adoptive families with Caucasian parents and Asian children. Preservice teachers were found to hold deficit perspectives about homeless children and families (Kim, 2013). Fortunately, sustained interactions with children and families in homeless shelters caused the preservice teachers to reexamine their views about young homeless children and their families and positively develop their professional perspectives on the children.

You will work with families that reflect your own culture and those that are different from it. You should continually seek information from and maintain communication with family members. Families have special needs, desires, and expectations of themselves, their children, and you.

5-2b Knowledge about Early Child Care and Education

Developmentally appropriate practice (Copple & Bredekamp, 2009; Copple et al., 2013) encompasses emotional interaction, instructional planning, and

developmentally appropriate practice Process of making educational decisions about the well-being and education of young children based on information or knowledge about child development and learning; the needs, interests, and strengths of each individual child in the group; and the social and cultural contexts in which the individual children live.

licensing regulations Official rules on teacher-child ratios, safety, health, and zoning that an individual or organization must follow to be granted a license to provide care for children.

NAFCC An association offering professional recognition and distinction to family child care providers whose services represent high-quality child care.

NAEYC A professional organization that offers professional resources and development for early childhood educators, as well as recognition for programs that represent high-quality care.

accreditation Process of demonstrating and validating the presence of indicators of quality as set out by national standards.

various types of teaching and learning techniques involving children, families, colleagues, and the community. How do we create experiences that are responsive to the needs of toddlers? How do we identify which materials are appropriate for the various development levels of infants? Answers to these questions, while not always straightforward, can be found in a number of sources, including licensing laws and accreditation standards. State or county agencies design **licensing regulations** to standardize the care and education of young children in group settings in both home- and center-based programs. These regulations govern such things as teacher-child ratios, space, safety and health requirements, fire codes, and zoning ordinances. Licensing identifies a set of minimum standards that the program meets; it does not guarantee quality of care. However, many states, such as Indiana, are working to include important characteristics of quality programming in their licensing regulations. In addition, many states have created early learning standards as a way to help teachers appropriately focus their attention on development and learning.

The **National Association for Family Child Care** (**NAFCC**) and the **National Association for the Education of Young Children** (**NAEYC**), respectively, have well-established accreditation programs for family child care programs and center-based care. **Accreditation** standards are significantly more stringent than licensing regulations and serve to recognize high-quality programs that meet the physical, social, emotional, and cognitive development of children as well as the needs of the families being served.

Becoming familiar with licensing regulations, early learning guidelines, and accreditation standards is a necessary but insufficient condition for being a professional early childhood educator. Teachers should have time set aside each day to reflect on and analyze the events of the day. This slow, contemplative time away from children and other responsibilities can significantly increase knowledge of the profession. This time can be used individually, in small groups of teaching teams, in small groups by teaching levels (e.g., all infant teachers), and in a large group of all teachers in the program. According to Whitington, Thompson, and Shore (2014), this time should be:

> ... regarded as a way of further engaging with the challenges they face on a daily basis, rather than another work requirement. Teachers need to accept the uncertainty that professional learning brings, and allow themselves slow time to think and learn about professional practice. (p. 71)

Time should be devoted to clarifying the various roles that teachers of infants and toddlers play on a daily basis. You will need to balance these many roles to provide high-quality care and education. Understanding the responsibilities of the various hats you wear will help determine your strengths and how to increase knowledge and personal growth. Learn more about the various responsibilities by reading and discussing NAEYC's Code of Ethical Conduct (NAEYC, 2011b) with colleagues. This document, created with significant input from teachers working directly with young children, provides guidance on balancing and resolving any conflicts among your professional responsibilities.

5-2c Knowledge about Partnerships

Early childhood educators cannot work in isolation and provide high-quality care (Bove, 2001; Colombo, 2006; Copple & Bredekamp, 2009). **Partnerships** with families, colleagues, and community agencies are a must. Family members possess knowledge about the child that you often do not have access to, unless you ask. Do not expect the process of building relationships to be smooth and unidirectional—it is more often bumpy and met with frequent starts and stops (Hadley, 2014). However, everyone benefits when teachers consistently pursue reciprocal or bidirectional relationships with families because information flows freely, and better decisions can be made (Sewell, 2012). Colleagues are also invaluable resources whether you have worked in the early childhood profession five minutes, five months, or five years. Chapter 7 devotes significant space to building professional relationships with family members and colleagues.

PHOTO 5–2 Seek partnerships with other agencies when a child is suspected of needing specialized educational services.

partnerships Alliances with family and community members to support and enhance the well-being and learning of young children.

Partnerships with community agencies and organizations will add value and resources to your program (see, e.g., Friedman, 2007) (Photo 5–2). The number and type of agencies you form partnerships with will be determined by the characteristics of your families and community. When children or families have specific needs, such as speech, mental health, or nutritional, help them locate services in the community. Another great community resource is your local public library. Introduce yourself to both the children's librarian and the adults' librarians. They can offer assistance with books, websites, magazines, and journals to help you stay on top of the dynamic field of early childhood education. Some librarians will bring their resources directly to you and the children, providing story hour in the classroom. They can also apprise you of state and federal funding sources. Many communities have city- or county-wide consortiums that can offer educators services such as mentoring or educational opportunities. Moreover, do not forget to participate in your local and state Association for the Education of Young Children. Networking through those organizations can provide additional avenues for partnerships.

5-2d Knowledge about Advocacy

Professionals employ informal advocacy strategies in their daily work with children and families. As mentioned previously, every time you interact with family members, colleagues, and community members, you are a

TABLE 5–1 ▶ Brief List of Organizations That Provide Advocacy Resources and Support

National Association for the Education of Young Children	The National Children's Advocacy Center
First Candle	Child Welfare League of America
The Child Advocate	Children's Defense Fund
National Association of Child Care Resource and Referral Agencies	The Immigrant Child Advocacy Center

© Cengage Learning

teacher-leader. Careful consideration must be given to your practices, as others look to you for examples of how to treat infants and toddlers. Engaging in developmentally appropriate practice, for example, demonstrates your beliefs about the capabilities of children and your positive influence on their development and learning. Your dedication to engaging in and sharing professional knowledge and practices makes you an advocate for young children, families, and the early childhood profession as a whole.

Formal advocacy involves working with parents, community members, other professional organizations, and even policy makers to improve the lives of children and families and the early childhood profession. Learning to be an effective advocate takes time, dedication, and the acquisition of skills (NAEYC, 2005; Robinson & Stark, 2005). But don't worry because many organizations provide resources to assist you in acquiring or honing advocacy skills. Table 5–1 provides a sample of such resources. Children continue to benefit when teachers help parents learn to be advocates, especially for children identified with special rights (Wright & Taylor, 2014).

5-2e Professional Skills

Early childhood educators must possess a variety of skills related to caring and educating infants and toddlers. Teachers should employ proper strategies for routine activities such as diapering and feeding. They need to learn and implement each child's preferred strategies for being soothed and put to sleep. Regarding instructional strategies, infant-toddler teachers should possess the skills to gather data, analyze it, and plan responsive curriculum. In addition, they should be able to facilitate development in all domains and learning in each content area. Information on these skills will be discussed in Chapters 8, 9, 11, 12, 13, and 14.

5-2f Professional Dispositions

disposition Frequent and voluntary habits of thinking and doing that represent a particular orientation to the work and responsibilities of teaching.

Dispositions are not merely positive beliefs and actions (such as curiosity or generosity) or negative beliefs and actions (such as arguing or devaluing children). Rather, they are frequent and voluntary habits of thinking and doing. Murrell, Diez, Feiman-Nemser, and Schussler (2010) expand this definition by adding that dispositions represent a particular orientation to the work and responsibilities of teaching. In other words, dispositions result in the motivation to put beliefs into action so that commitments and habits of thought are visible in decisions, practices, leadership, and advocacy (Swim & Isik-Ercan, 2013).

Positive professional dispositions develop over time as teachers analyze their knowledge and experiences and intentionally bump into an event or belief that provokes a need to resolve one's own disequilibrium about a learning event (Swim & Merz, in press). For example, Terrance (continuity of care teacher) was attending to DeVonta's (21 months) desire to paint by refilling the green paint container when Sarina (13 months) started to cry. He immediately began to talk to Sarina from across the room in a soothing voice, could see that she was upset (not hurt), and invited her to join him. She moved by his side, and he continued to sooth her verbally. Terrance thought his response to both children was effective. Later, his co-teacher questioned why he didn't stop filling the paint container when Sarina "demonstrated a clear communication." This caused Terrance to question his decision, which made him feel uncomfortable. After reflecting and analyzing the situation from a number of different perspectives, Terrance decided his course of action was acceptable and met both children's needs. He decided to have additional conversations with his co-teacher to better understand her analysis of the situation. Engaging in this reflective process over time leads to the development of professional dispositions in which the educator is responsive and intentional, as well as an advocate for each and every child (Swim & Merz, in press). Using a critical lens during this reflective process can transform not only dispositions but also understanding of young children, theories, and practices in early childhood education (Anderson, 2014).

Before moving on with your reading, make sure that you can answer the following questions about the material discussed so far.

1. What important knowledge bases, skills, and dispositions should professional educators have? Why?
2. How do partnerships with families and community agencies help to promote the development and well-being of very young children?
3. Discuss with someone your understanding of the concept "developmentally appropriate practice." How can you learn more about this construct?

READING CHECKPOINT

5-3 Professional Preparation of the Early Childhood Educator

Both informal and formal educational opportunities are available to teachers of infants and toddlers. Informal experiences may be spontaneous or planned. A magazine article may stimulate your thinking by providing new information and raising questions. You may take time to do further thinking and discuss your ideas with colleagues, or you may think of the ideas periodically and begin changing your caregiving practices to incorporate what you have learned.

Formal educational opportunities are those that are planned to meet specific goals. You choose experiences to gain important knowledge and

Spotlight on Organization

WORLD ASSOCIATION FOR INFANT MENTAL HEALTH

The World Association for Infant Mental Health (WAIMH) is a professional organization whose mission is to promote education, research, and study of the effects of mental, emotional, and social development during infancy and on later development.

They support their mission through international and interdisciplinary cooperation, professional publications, and professional meetings (which they call congresses). They also have affiliates throughout the world and within several states in the United States. For a listing of affiliates and to learn more about this organization, visit its website.

skills. The following learning opportunities can contribute to your professional preparation:

- Work with a mentor or more-experienced caregiver. This person assists you with observing, reflecting on, and discussing effective techniques.
- Attend workshops, seminars, speakers, or continuing education courses. These may be sponsored by many different agencies, but they usually focus on a single topic or skill.
- Complete vocational school courses and programs in child care.
- Finish community college and university courses in early childhood education and/or child development.

Child Development Associate (CDA) A credential provided by the Council for Early Childhood Professional Recognition when a person has provided evidence of meeting the national standards for caregiver performance.

- Acquire a Child Development Associate Certificate. The **Child Development Associate (CDA)** is an entry-level certification which communicates that the person holding it meets the specific needs of children and works with parents and other adults to nurture children's physical, social, emotional, and intellectual growth in a child development framework. "Becoming a CDA is a process that you work at, learn, and nurture until it grows from within. It is a process by which you grow as an individual and as a professional" (Council for Professional Recognition, 2010).
- Complete early childhood education degrees. Associate, bachelor's, master's, and doctorate degrees can be completed at colleges or universities. NAEYC (2011a) created guidelines for the educational preparation of teachers based on seven core standards and a common set of professional knowledge, skills, and dispositions. Table 5–2 demonstrates the overlap of the CDA and NAEYC core standards. While the table signifies a great deal of shared vision for professional preparation, the expectations of teachers increase with each level of education attained (NAEYC, 2009).

5-3a Impact of Teacher Education on Quality of Care and Education

Does teacher preparation make a difference in the quality of care and education provided and child outcomes? Evidence is mounting that it does; after conducting a review of the literature, Hall-Kenyon, Bullough, MacKay, and Marshall (2014) concluded that "… higher levels of education

TABLE 5-2 ▶ Overlap of the CDA and NAEYC Standards

CDA COMPETENCY AREAS	NAEYC TEACHER PREPARATION STANDARDS					
	1. PROMOTING CHILD DEVELOPMENT AND LEARNING	2. BUILDING FAMILY AND COMMUNITY RELATIONSHIPS	3. OBSERVING, DOCUMENTING, AND ASSESSING	4. USING DEVELOPMENTALLY EFFECTIVE APPROACHES	5. USING CONTENT KNOWLEDGE	6. BECOMING A PROFESSIONAL
I. Safe, healthy learning environment	X			X		
II. Advance physical and intellectual competence	X			X	X	
III. Support social and emotional development; positive guidance	X			X		
IV. Positive and productive relationships with families		X				
V. Well-run, purposeful program			X			X
VI. Commitment to professionalism						X

© Cengage Learning

lead to higher quality classrooms" (p. 156). However, differences in variables studied and research methodologies make the answer to this question far from definitive (Hyson, Horm, & Winton, 2012; Washington, 2008). Head Start Teachers with higher educational levels were found to significantly impact the development of early math skills for immigrant preschool children (Kim, Chang, & Kim, 2011). Teachers who participate in learning experiences that reflect developmentally appropriate practices during their teacher-preparation program expressed more confidence in transforming curriculum from inappropriate to appropriate (Cunningham, 2014). Research on elementary teacher-preparation programs have found that those with a stronger practice focus (e.g., stronger supervision of student teaching and a practice-focused capstone project) had better outcomes, at least during their first year of teaching (Boyd, Grossman, Lankford, Loeb, & Wyckoff, 2009). In other samples, teachers with the greatest knowledge of developmentally appropriate practice had academic training in early childhood education and/or child development as well as supervised practical experience with young children (Buchanan, Burts, Bidner, White, & Charlesworth, 1998; McMullen, 1999; Snider & Fu, 1990). Taken together, these results suggest that higher levels of specialized (i.e., early childhood) education and specifically designed learning experiences during teacher-preparation programs influence practices employed with young children.

Do particular practices have a positive effect on child outcomes? Again, investigations have shown the positive impact of teachers' engaging in developmentally appropriate practices. For example, cross-cultural comparisons found that children in classrooms with more child-initiated activities and small group activities (e.g., two important components of developmentally appropriate practices) had improved language and cognitive performance (Montie, Xiang, & Schweinhart, 2006). Similarly, low-income children in classrooms that balanced both child-initiated activities and small group activities engaged in more language, literacy, and math activities and had higher language scores (Fuligni, Howes, Huang, Hong, & Lara-Cinisomo, 2012). Children whose teachers used approaches that fit their level of development had significantly higher letter-word identification and applied problem solving (Huffman & Speer, 2000) than those children whose teachers used developmentally inappropriate practices. Moreover, children who experienced preschool programs that were characterized by more active, child-initiated learning experiences (i.e., developmentally appropriate) had more success in their sixth year of school (Marcon, 2002). While the research reviewed in this section shows positive effects on child development when teachers engage in child-centered practices, these findings are not without controversy (see, e.g., Van Horn, Karlin, & Ramey, 2012; Van Horn, Karlin, Ramey, Aldridge, & Snyder, 2005).

The results discussed were for older children; how does research on Early Head Start help inform teachers' practices? Early Head Start programs have great variability in program quality (Love, Raikes, Paulsell, & Kisker, 2004) and child outcomes (Cline & Edwards, 2013; Raikes, Love, Kisker, Chazan-Cohen, & Brooks-Gunn, 2004; Raikes et al., 2014). This

Family and Community Connection

As a family child care provider, you value growing as a professional. You recently graduated with an associate of science degree in Early Childhood Education from a local community college. You plan to take a year off before pursuing a bachelor's degree in the same field. Your accreditation mentor mentions that the local Association for the Education of Young Children's conference is coming up soon. Specifically, they need providers to present on issues related to family child care. You are interested but apprehensive—"What could I talk about?" you wonder. What can you do to learn more about what is expected of presenters? How could you involve other family child care providers you know in delivering sessions at the conference?

variation could be due to the complex influence of teacher characteristics, participant characteristics (e.g., race, mental health), and program characteristics (e.g., home- or center-based) (see, e.g., Elicker, Wen, Kwon, & Sprague, 2013; Harden, Sandstrom, & Chazan-Cohen, 2012; Jung & Stone, 2008). All in all, this research indicates that higher levels of education and experience for the caregiver are associated with more appropriate practices with young children, and those are related to better child outcomes.

Because teachers of infants and toddlers are more likely to have lower levels of education than teachers of older children (Berthelsen, Brownlee, & Boulton-Lewis, 2002), and the early years are critical to brain development (see Chapters 1 and 2), we can no longer ignore the links among education, developmentally appropriate practice, and child outcomes. While this may seem obvious, learning to be a teacher of infants and toddlers poses particular challenges not found with teaching other ages. Infants and toddlers have special developmental needs. Here are four reasons to support that claim.

1. As discussed in Chapters 2 and 3, this period of growth and development is rapid—noticeable changes occur monthly, weekly, and, in some cases, daily.

2. Physical, social, emotional, and cognitive developments are more interrelated for infants than for older children.

3. Infants are more dependent upon a consistent relationship with a caregiver to meet all of their needs.

4. Infants have no effective skills for coping with discomfort and stress, so they are more open to harm (Gunnar, 2006; Shonkoff & Phillips, 2000) or abuse (Casanueva et al., 2014; Simonnet et al., 2014).

Many of these issues were highlighted by beginning teachers as challenges. Recchia and Loizou (2002) found that for teachers in their sample, adjusting to the physical and emotional intensity of nurturing very young children, setting limits and guiding the behavior of toddlers, and collaborating with others to ensure continuity of care were particular issues. This line of research, then, highlights the need for infant and toddler caregivers to receive specialized education, mentoring, and ongoing support during the early years of teaching.

READING CHECKPOINT

Before moving on with your reading, make sure that you can answer the following questions about the material discussed so far.

1. Name at least five different experiences that early childhood professionals can have that result in the growth of their professional knowledge and skills.
2. How does formal and informal education help early childhood teachers to be more effective in their various roles?

5-4 Observing Young Children to Make Educational Decisions

The previous chapters have laid the groundwork for taking a scholarly approach to your work with infants and toddlers. You cannot, for example, plan appropriate curriculum or be attuned to a toddler if you have not observed what the child is trying to accomplish. Yet, early childhood educators are not in the business of testing children (NAEYC, 2003). Care should be taken to act prudently in this age of testing and judging children. You should pay close attention to why you are gathering the data, how you gathered it, and how to analyze it. Then, careful attention must be placed on how you use the data. This approach can be referred to as scholarly.

Scholars or researchers—like young children—are curious and inquisitive; they think, wonder, and ask lots of questions. They also gather data to answer their questions. What do you wonder about infants and toddlers? Use your curiosity to drive, inspire, and sustain your work because, according to Maguire-Fong (2006), "Curious infants do best when matched with curious adults who are just as intent in their desire to learn about the infants in their care as the infants are to learn about the world before them" (p. 118). This section will provide you with knowledge, skills, and tools for gathering data about infants and toddlers.

5-4a Observe and Record

Why Observe?

Observations provide important information needed for decision-making and communicating with others. Planning a responsive, developmentally appropriate curriculum requires specific, detailed knowledge about each child in your care. Observation occurs before, during, and after your experiences with young children. This creates a continuous loop of observing, planning, implementing, observing, and so on (see Chapter 9 for more details).

Observations that include details of your own behavior, the curriculum, the materials, and the physical environment can provide particularly important information that is often overlooked. You may have observed that on Tuesday Jessica cried for ten minutes after being separated from her father. Including the fact that her father and primary caregiver were unable to locate her transitional object (a stuffed elephant) that day would help to explain her sudden, intense reaction to being separated.

In addition, effective communication with families, colleagues, and other professionals requires that you provide thorough reports (written and verbal) of what you observed. Making global or general statements without specific examples can break down communication rather than support it.

Who to Observe?

Each child in your care needs to be observed. All program plans and implementations start with what the teacher knows about each child and family. Setting aside time each day to observe each child provides you with a wealth of information. Observing how families interact with children and adults helps teachers plan responsive curriculum. However, because family members participate to varying degrees in a child care program, you might have more information on one or two members rather than all who have a significant impact on the child.

What to Observe?

Children's behavior helps us learn about them. Infants and toddlers often cannot use words to tell about themselves. Each child is unique. Early childhood educators must identify the characteristics and needs of each child because the child is the focal point of decisions and plans regarding time, space, and curriculum. Each child is continuously changing. This growth and development produces expected and sometimes unexpected changes. Living with someone every day, you may not notice some important, emerging developments. Therefore, it is important to make periodic informal and formal observations and to record them so that the changes in the child can be noted and shared. This information will affect your plans for, and interactions with, the child.

A caregiver's behavior provides needed information to analyze the child's behavior as well as her own behavior. You should record how you assisted the children with accomplishing a new skill or task. Vygotsky's theory (discussed in Chapter 1) necessitates that data be gathered on both the independent level of performance and the assisted level of performance. Teachers also need to gather data to improve their own practices and effectiveness as caregivers. For example, Ms. Josephine wanted to involve Monroe more when she shared a book with him. She selected a book she thought he would like and wrote down three questions to ask Monroe that would focus his thinking and questioning on objects from the book. She set up a digital audio recorder where she and Monroe would be sitting and invited Monroe over to share the book. Later, when Ms. Josephine listened to the audio, she discovered that she had talked all the time and told everything to Monroe rather than allowing him to talk, share, and question. Observations like these provide information about the kind of responses one person has to another person, showing if the desired interaction was stimulated or inhibited.

The entire child care setting, including equipment, materials, and arrangement of space, should be examined to determine their impact on children. Look at who is using what space and how it is being used to determine whether the space is being used effectively. Ask yourself questions such as, is the addition of musical instruments near the art area having a positive influence on the work being accomplished by the older infants? Additionally, children can impact their own outcomes or the outcomes of other children. Do toddlers, for example, cause disruptions to others who are reading because they have to walk through the area to get to the bathroom? After you gather data to answer your question, respond to what you find by making necessary adjustments.

Every early childhood professional is learning and continually developing skills. One caregiver may observe another one to learn new strategies or to reinforce those she already uses. Other people's observations can let caregivers know whether their actual practice matches the behavior intended. Ongoing evaluation and reflection, along with feedback, can help caregivers increase their effectiveness.

Why Record?

Making observations without having a method for recording your data is inviting trouble. You may work with between 6 and 12 different children throughout the course of a day and make hundreds of observations. If you don't write down the important ones, you run the risk of incorrectly remembering what you saw or attributing skills or development to the wrong child. In addition, infants and toddlers change quickly. They add skills on a daily basis, so failing to record them might mean missing this accomplishment altogether. Moreover, teachers, like young children, elaborate—add additional information based on previous knowledge and assumptions—to fill in any gaps (McDevitt & Ormrod, 2013). Thus, you may "see" something that really didn't happen but fits with what you already know about the child. These examples should help you understand the importance of recording what you observed as quickly as you can. The following section provides guidance on methods of observing and recording.

5-4b Tools for Observing and Recording

Observations may be spontaneous or planned, but they must be ongoing and regular. You may glance across the room and see Sammy roll over. This the first time you have seen that happen. You record this example in his portfolio and/or home-school journal. Other times, a staff member will arrange to spend a few minutes specifically observing a child, materials, or space (Photo 5–3). These observations can provide valuable information. Because infants and many toddlers cannot tell us in words what they have learned, we must attend carefully to their behaviors for clues. Writing what you observe gives you and other people access to that information later on.

Descriptions may be brief or very detailed and extensive. In either case, the focus is on reporting the exact behavior or situation in narrative form. You must learn to distinguish descriptive and

© 2017 Cengage Learning

PHOTO 5–3 Recording your observations are important caregiver behaviors.

interpretative phrasing. **Descriptive phrasing**, the preferred type for reporting observations, involves using words or phrases to describe observable behaviors, that is, behaviors that another observer (or reader) could easily verify. On the other hand, **interpretative phrasing** makes a judgment or evaluation but gives little or no observable data to justify the conclusions (Marion, 2004). An example of interpretative phrasing is, "Eva refused to eat her cereal at breakfast." The reader has no way to verify the word *refused* in this description of this meal. Compare that to the following: "Eva sat in her chair with her eyes squinted, mouth pursed, and her arms crossed. She stated, 'No, oatmeal' and pushed her bowl away from her. I offered her a banana, and she smiled and nodded 'yes.' She ate the entire banana and drank her milk." The difference in language is important because evaluative or interpretative phrasing is "emotionally loaded" and often leads to misunderstandings, whereas factual, descriptive statements can rarely be disputed.

Early childhood teachers can use three main categories of tools to observe and record the behaviors of young children: narratives (i.e., running and anecdotal records), checklists and rating scales, and authentic documentation. The first two methods are narrative because you observe an interesting incident and record essential details to tell a story.

Narrative

Running records are long narratives. They tell a story as it unfolds over a significant period of time for a child, a group, or an activity (Marion, 2004). This tool is useful for learning about child development. When you focus your attention on a child for a specific time period, say an hour, you can gather valuable information that might otherwise go unnoticed. Due to time considerations, running records are rarely used spontaneously. Teachers create schedules to routinely observe the development and behavior of every infant and toddler. Running records are closely related to an ethnographic report because they describe a total situation. An *ethnographic report* describes a total situation: the time, place, people, and how the people behave. A description of the total situation lets the reader know about things that may not be evident in just one part of a specific incident.

Adults unfamiliar with infants and toddlers may think that a young child does not do anything. An early education student observed the behaviors described in Table 5–3 during outdoor play in a family child care home one summer afternoon. She was to focus on one child and write down everything she saw and heard that child do and say. The purpose of this assignment was to identify and categorize the various experiences initiated by a 13-month-old child. The observer was not to interject her own interpretations into the narrative.

An **anecdotal record** is a brief narrative of one event. As the definition implies, you look for or notice one event and then write a short story about it. Anecdotal records are great for understanding individual child characteristics and how contextual variables impact the learning, development, and behavior of a child. With spontaneous anecdotal records, something happens that you did not anticipate, but that you want to record for possible use later. For example, you have planned to watch Julio's interactions with peers today, but he is sick. You then notice how Thomas John and

descriptive phrasing A technique for reporting observations that involves using words or phrases to describe observable behaviors.

interpretative phrasing A form of reporting that makes judgments without providing observable data to justify the conclusions.

running record A long narrative account of a significant period of time for a child, a group, or an activity written using descriptive language.

anecdotal record A brief narrative account of one event written using descriptive language.

TABLE 5–3 ▶ Running Record with Observational Data

CONTEXT	OBSERVATIONS (BEHAVIORAL DESCRIPTIONS OF WHAT YOU SEE AND HEAR)	ANALYSIS/INTERPRETATIONS/ QUESTIONS
The play yard contained the caregiver Lynn, the observer, and six children ranging from 7 months to 6 years of age.	**2:20** • Lynn puts mat out and stands Leslie up in yard. • Leslie looks around (slowly rocking to keep balance). • Reaches hand to Lynn and baby talks. • Looks at me and reaches for me. • Takes two steps, trips, and falls on mat, remains sitting on it. • Turns around to face me. • Cries a little. • Reaches for Lynn, then to me. • Looks around and watches Jason (4-year-old who is riding trike). • Reaches hand toward Lynn. • Watches Jason and sucks middle two fingers on right hand. • Looks around. • Swings right arm. **2:45** • Takes Lynn's fingers and stands. • Walks two steps onto grass. • Swings right arm and brushes lips with hand to make sound—baby talk. • Turns toward Lynn and babbles. • Lane arrives. Leslie watches and rubs left eye with left hand. • "Do you remember Leslie?" Lynn asks Lane. • Leslie reaches out arms to Lynn and walks to her. Hugs her. • Listens and watches Lynn. Holds onto her for support. • Turns around and steps on mulch and lifts foot to see what it is. • Watches Lynn tie Jason's shoe. • Lynn lifts her in air, and then sets her on her knee. • She lies back in Lynn's lap and laughs.	Leslie initiates a variety of interactions with people and materials. She is physically, emotionally, socially, and cognitively involving herself in her world. Teacher planning and facilitating can stimulate and build on Leslie's self-initiated behaviors. Wants to be picked up?

© Cengage Learning

Erika were sharing the space and materials while in the block area. You record the anecdotal record shown in Table 5–4.

Checklists and Rating Scales

Checklists and rating scales are quick, efficient tools for gathering data. They bypass details and merely check or rate development and progress (Marion, 2004). They can be used to gather data on specific behaviors that

TABLE 5–4 ▸ Anecdotal Record

Child's Name: Thomas John	Age: 22 months
Observer's Name: Rachel	Date: October 1
Setting: Block area	

What actually happened/What I saw: Thomas John is building a block tower using the square blocks. Erika toddled into the area and picked up a rectangle block. She held it out to Thomas John. He took it from her hand and placed it on top of the tower. They both smiled as if to say, "It didn't fall." Thomas John then picked up another rectangle block and placed it on top. The structure wobbled but did not fall. He looked at Erika, smiled, and knocked over the structure. They each began to build their own tower. They worked in the same area for 12 more minutes. Occasionally, they would hand blocks to one another and, like before, they did not verbalize.

Reflection/Interpretation/Questions: Thomas John is new to the class, and he has not yet spoken. His parents have reported that he tells them all about his day on the ride home. Erika tends to verbalize frequently. She seemed to respect the fact that he was working in silence. I wonder if they will continue to work together and form a friendship.

© Cengage Learning

you value (e.g., self-help skills) or might be concerned about (e.g., aggressive behaviors). In addition, many commercially designed tools for analyzing a child's progress on developmental milestones are checklists or rating scales. In fact, the Developmental Milestones tool in Appendix A was designed to help you gather data in all developmental domains for children 36 months old and younger. This is a combination of a checklist and a rating scale, so learning more about each will help you understand how to use this important tool.

A **checklist** is a record of behaviors that a child can perform at a given point in time. When you observe a child or group of children, you note whether each child does or does not show that characteristic or behavior. Placing a checkmark beside an item indicates that you observed the child perform that behavior during the observation. Leaving the item blank tells others either that the child cannot execute the behavior or that you did not observe the execution of it at that particular time. Suppose you are particularly interested in the children acquiring self-help skills. Thus, you create a checklist to monitor progress in this area. Table 5–5 shows just part of your checklist for infants.

Rating scales share many characteristics with checklists, but they are a listing of qualities of characteristics or activities (Marion, 2004). For example, instead of just knowing that Raji can lift the spoon to his mouth, you can rate the frequency (i.e., never, seldom, sometimes, often, always) of

checklist A method for recording observational data that notes the presence of specific predetermined skills or behaviors.

rating scale Method of recording observational data similar to checklists, but that lists frequencies (e.g., never, seldom, always) or qualities of characteristics or activities (e.g., eats using fingers, eats using spoon, eats using fork).

TABLE 5–5 ▸ Sample Checklist with Data

	DAKOTA	TRAVIS	COLBY	RAJI	SARAH	LAKINTA	JOSE
Holds bottle	X		X			X	X
Holds spoon		X	X			X	
Lifts bottle to mouth				X	X		
Lifts spoon to mouth				X	X		

© Cengage Learning

TABLE 5–6 ▶ Example of a Rating Scale for Brushing Teeth

Name of Child: _____			Age: _____
Date of Observation: _____			
	NEVER	SOMETIMES	FREQUENTLY	ALWAYS
Squeezes toothpaste on brush				
Brushes teeth independently				
Rinses mouth after brushing				
Rinses toothbrush				
Returns toothbrush to proper location				

© Cengage Learning

this behavior or its quality (i.e., all food on spoon placed in mouth, some of food on spoon placed in mouth, none of food on spoon placed in mouth). Table 5–6 is an example of a rating scale.

Returning to the Developmental Milestones in Appendix A, you should now recognize which part of the tool is a checklist and which part is a rating scale. When you note the date of the first observation, the tool serves as a checklist. When you evaluate the performance level at a later time (i.e., practicing or proficient), you are using the tool as a rating scale.

Authentic Documentation

"Documentation refers to any activity that renders a performance record with sufficient detail to help others understand the behavior recorded.... The intent of documentation is to explain, not merely display" (Forman & Fife, 2012, pp. 247–271). Documentation is a research story, built upon questions about the development and learning of children (Wien, Guyevskey, & Berdoussis, 2011). As such, it reflects a professional disposition of not presuming to know, of asking how the learning occurs, and of wondering. This form of assessment involves gathering work samples, taking photographs or video recordings of the children, and organizing the data to ask and answer using methods such as documentation panels. Educational portfolios will also be discussed in this section because of their clear connection to using authentic documentation.

documentation panel A visual and written explanation of children's learning displayed to others (family members, children, colleagues, and/or community members).

A **documentation panel** includes visual images and, whenever possible, narratives of dialogue that occurred during the experiences that were documented. The goal of creating documentation panels is to make visible to you, the children, and family members the development and learning that has been occurring in the classroom. As such, documentation panels include not only the objective record of your observations but also your reflections and interpretations of those events (Rinaldi, 2001b). As you make visible your reflections and interpretations through the panels, they, too, become part of the data that can be read, reread, and analyzed (Rinaldi, 2001b). The sharing of documentation panels with children, families, colleagues, and community members "moves learning from the private to the public realm" (Turner & Krechevsky, 2003, p. 42), which is something that traditional forms of observing and recording did not accomplish.

Documentation has been shown to increase memories regarding learning and on-topic speech for preschool and kindergarten children—demonstrating potential benefits to learning for young children (Fleck, Leichtman, Pillemer, & Shanteler, 2013). Furthermore, documentation advocates seeing children as rich, capable learners who actively participate in their own development and learning (Swim, 2012; Swim & Merz, 2011). Documentation, like portfolios, can be used for children of all ages and ability levels (Cooney & Buchanan, 2001; Stockall, Dennis, & Rueter, 2014).

A **portfolio** is a tool for collecting, storing, and documenting what you know about a child and her development and learning (Marion, 2004). All of the information gathered using the methods described previously can be added to the photographs and work samples to create a more complete picture of the child's capabilities (Photo 5–4). However, not all portfolios need be in paper form; arranging photos and videos on DVDs for families can provide a more complete picture of the child's development in the context of everyday interactions (Appl, Leavitt, & Ryan, 2014). Storing all of the data in one location allows for easy access and reflection. While originally designed for use with older children, portfolios can and should be used with very young children because they serve a number of purposes, including but not limited to the following:

© 2017 Cengage Learning

PHOTO 5–4 Labeling this artwork provides evidence of the child's language and representation skills. This artifact can be used as an entry in the child's portfolio.

portfolio Tool for collecting, storing, and documenting what you know about a child and her development and learning.

- Show the quality of the children's thinking and work.
- Document children's development over time (one year or more).
- Assist when communicating with families and other professionals (Appl et al., 2014).
- Support developmentally appropriate practice by giving teachers "a strong child development foundation on which to build age- and individually appropriate programs" (Marion, 2004, p. 112).
- Provide a tool for teacher reflection (e.g., expectations, quality of planned experiences).
- Make available information for evaluating program quality and effectiveness (Helm, Beneke, & Steinheimer, 2007; Marion, 2004).

Other Observation Tools

Time and event sampling techniques can be used to record events or behaviors quickly that you are interested in tracking. Use time sampling, for example, if you want to know what a group of toddlers does after waking from their naps. Create a chart of the areas of your classroom, and, then, for two weeks, record the first area selected by each child after waking. Doing this over a number of days would provide insight into the children's interests. Event sampling is very similar to time sampling in that you are recording specific behaviors that occur. With event sampling, however, you typically watch one child and record every time a particular behavior occurs. To illustrate, Lela is interested in understanding how Savannah responds when angry. Lela made a chart of the behaviors that Savannah typically engages in when angry. Then, whenever Lela sees that she is getting angry, she charts the behaviors she observes. To better understand the possible causes of

time and event sampling techniques Strategies for quickly recording events or behaviors that you are interested in tracking.

home-school journal A notebook or journal in which teachers and family members write notes about key happenings and which they send back and forth on a daily or weekly basis.

Savannah's anger, Lela also notes what she sees as triggers to Savannah's anger (Marion, 2004). Together, this information can provide Lela with insights into how to assist Savannah with gaining anger-management skills.

Home-school journals can also be used to record useful information for both families and teachers. The journals are used to record daily or weekly information about key happenings, such as developmental milestones, that might be of interest to family members and teachers. Teachers write in the journal, and then the family members take the journal home to read it. They are strongly encouraged to write back responses or questions, or to explain behaviors or events happening at home. These journals can be a fabulous tool for creating partnerships between teachers and families. Of course, teachers must pay close attention to how they describe events and behaviors; descriptive language is a must.

daily communication log A log for communicating with family members that covers routine care events such as eating, sleeping, toileting, and other.

Other records kept on a daily basis serve particular purposes, such as communication with families, but they often yield little data for use in evaluating development or learning. The daily message center of your classroom, for example, contains a clipboard for each child. The clipboard contains a daily communication log that covers routine care events such as eating, sleeping, toileting, and other. For consistency of care between family life and school, families and teachers have designated locations for recording information (see Table 5–7). Use the chart by writing down each

TABLE 5–7 ▶ Sample Daily Communication Log

Routine Care for _____ on _____.		
	HOME EVENTS	**SCHOOL EVENTS**
Eating		
Sleeping		
Toileting		
Other routine care		
Important information to know		

© Cengage Learning

time you perform a routine care event (e.g., change a diaper) and details about that event (e.g., record whether the diaper was wet or soiled). This can often be a useful place for noting supplies that are needed at school (e.g., diapers, dry formula).

5-4c Analysis

After you gather your data, the next component of a scholarly approach is reviewing, reflecting on, and analyzing the data. Set aside time on a regular basis, preferably each day, to analyze and evaluate the data (Photo 5–5). When analyzing, in general, your attention should be placed on coming to understand what the child can currently do. You can approach this aspect of your work by asking, "What is she capable of doing alone and with assistance?"

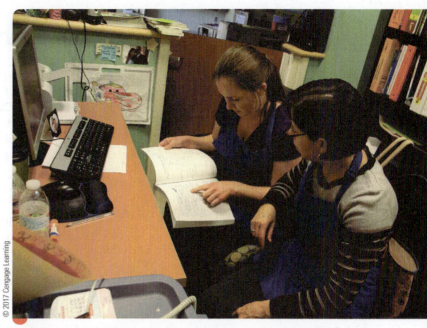

© 2017 Cengage Learning

PHOTO 5–5 Set aside time on a regular basis to share information with colleagues who work with the same children.

Analysis also means comparing the data gathered with what we know about child development and learning, as well as what you currently know about the child's context, especially family characteristics and circumstances. You may focus your analysis on one area of development, such as cognition and language, or the whole child, for example, physical, emotional, social, and cognitive/language. Although you can compare the child's level of development and behaviors to developmental milestones or expected patterns of development based on chronological age, be cautious with this approach. The age when children accomplish developmental norms varies greatly due to the influence of variables ranging from genetic predispositions to access to resources to family beliefs and practices. Nevertheless, knowing the expected age range for a milestone will help you determine how to use the data gathered. For example, infants typically produce their first word at 12 months of age; however, this can occur as early as 9 months or as late as 16 months and still be considered normal development. Typically, there is a three- to six-month range on either side of the developmental milestone, but this will vary depending on the particular behavior. Knowing this information is vital because it provides you with a context for distinguishing warning signs from red flags. *Warning signs* are those behaviors that, although you and family members should monitor, are not of great concern yet. *Red flags* are those behaviors that deviate from both the developmental milestone and the expected range. When a number of behaviors within a particular area of development are found to be red flags, it is time to invite other professionals with specialized knowledge in observation, assessment, and early intervention, to join the conversations.

Few caregivers have received the specialized training required to use standardized assessment techniques. If your program wants to carry out specialized assessment, obtain the necessary training first. However, remember

Spotlight on Research

CULTURALLY APPROPRIATE ASSESSMENT

As a teacher, you are not trained to screen and diagnose developmental delays or other special needs. You will need to understand, however, the ethical use of observational and screening tools. The NAEYC's position statement on ethical conduct (2011b) includes the use of assessment data to make decisions regarding the care and education of young children. This statement included the following ideals regarding the assessment of children:

I-1.6—To use assessment instruments and strategies that are appropriate for the children to be assessed, that are used only for the purposes for which they were designed, and that have the potential to benefit children.

I-1.7—To use assessment information to understand and support children's development and learning, to support instruction, and to identify children who may need additional services.

The statement also sets out the ideal that each child's culture, language, ethnicity, and family structure are recognized and valued in the program (I-1.10). Taking these three ideals together suggests that teachers should intentionally advocate for culturally appropriate screening of infants and toddlers. Unfortunately, this is easier said than done.

Most screening tools have been validated with White, middle-class populations with little investigation of the cultural aspects of screening (Lyman, Njoroge, & Willis, 2007). For example, Sturner, Albus, Thomas, and Howard (2007) argue for the revision of the *Diagnostic Classification of Mental Health and Developmental Disorders of Infancy and Early Childhood* (which is currently under way with the new edition expected in 2016; see the Zero to Three website for more information). They want the assessment to be graduated more finely to classify a range of symptomatology. In addition, they would like the tool refined to assess the families' strengths more accurately, not just their weaknesses. Although these are excellent modifications for this assessment instrument, none of the changes addresses the cultural bias that it most certainly contains.

Autism is a rising concern for early intervention specialists, teachers, and families in the United States. Much research has been conducted to create reliable and valid assessment tools that accurately diagnose autism during infancy and toddlerhood. For example, the Quantitative Checklist for Autism in Toddlers (Q-CHAT) was validated on a large sample of toddlers with and without a history of autism (Allison et al., 2008). The Modified Checklist for Autism in Toddlers (M-CHAT) compared older and younger toddlers of low- and high-risk for autism (Pandey et al., 2008).

Kara and colleagues (2014) understood the challenges of using a tool that was not culturally appropriate and adapted the M-CHAT to Turkish culture. They tested the adapted tool by having parents provide answers in two ways. First, parents were asked to complete it while waiting at a clinic for their child to have a well-child examination. The second parents in the second group were interviewed by health-care personnel who recorded the answers. Given the rates of false-positives of both methods of administrating the tool, the authors concluded that the tool was useful in Turkey for screening of pervasive developmental disorders in primary care, but that it was completed more accurately when health-care personnel ask the parents the questions (Kara et al., 2014). This study shows that screening tools can and should be adapted based on specific cultures and settings.

While researchers warn that "it is difficult to maintain an efficient level of sensitivity and specificity based on observational data from a single screening" (Honda et al., 2009, p. 980), as a member of the interdisciplinary assessment team, teachers must share their understanding of the profession's ethics for assessing children. Specifically, Ideals **1.6**, **1.7**, and **1.10** (described previously) would lead a teacher to advocate for additional observations of a child when a screening tool indicates areas of concern as well as work to ensure the assessment data accurately reflect what is known about the families' cultural background and practices. Other team members may be unaware of potential stereotyping that may come as a result of their using assessments designed for a particular population with culturally diverse individuals/families (Lyman et al., 2007). These authors go on to say that "screening for risks to development involves a complex interaction of the dynamics of the parent-child relationship, the effects of culture on those dynamics and growth, and cultural definitions of normalcy and risk" (p. 48). Each individual culture may have different expectations and definitions of what is considered developmentally on target. Cross-culture research must be done carefully to avoid a multitude of potential biases and to maximize the ecocultural context (Matafwali & Serpell, 2014). Researchers who design assessment tools must work with community members to identify

(continued)

shared concerns, understand how they view particular behaviors, and modify assessments accordingly
(Haack & Gerdes, 2011). When a tool is used in a classroom setting, teachers can help others to remember that
the results of each assessment are interpreted through
a particular cultural lens. By openly acknowledging
the ethnocentricity of our assessment tools and taking
steps to be more culturally competent in our screening,
we can better help children from all ethnic groups to
have a chance to grow up healthy.

that these tools are often not as valuable as your careful, ongoing observations,
records, and analysis of observational data from your specific classroom.

5-4d Using the Data

As mentioned previously, the data gathered on very young children should
be used to benefit them (NAEYC, 2011b). Teachers use this information to
organize care and educational plans on a daily and weekly basis, develop an
individual (and flexible) schedule that meets each child's needs, and create
responsive learning environments—indoors and outdoors—to support and
challenge the growth and development of each child. Each use of data just
mentioned will be addressed more completely in future chapters of this book.

Before moving on with your reading, make sure that you can answer the following
questions about the material discussed so far.

1. Why must teachers observe and record the behavior of infants and toddlers?
   What observation tools will (or do) you use most often? Why? What are the
   benefits to you, the children, and families when using these tools?
2. How will you ensure that all assessment tools you use in your work as an
   early childhood educator are culturally appropriate?

READING
CHECKPOINT

Summary

5-1 Describe the characteristics necessary to become a competent caregiver.

Competent caregivers take care of themselves
as much as they do others (e.g., young children,
family members) and strive to develop a positive
self-image regarding the work they do.

5-2 Specify the various types of knowledge, skills, and dispositions professional educators should possess.

Being an early childhood educator requires a
strong grounding in professional knowledge, skills,
and dispositions. Not only should you know what

to do in a given situation and have the skills to act
in a particular way, but you should value acting in
that manner.

5-3 Defend the importance of formal educational experiences for teachers on child outcomes.

Working independently and effectively with
young children comes after receiving extensive
instruction, investigating theories, writing papers,
and getting mentoring. It comes after your positive
intentions and caring have been transformed into
a firm educational base of understanding. Learning should be ongoing as you seek the answers to

more questions, and you see the impact of your behavior, curriculum, and relationships on the children's development and learning.

5-4 Justify how to match observational tools with your data needs.

Teachers gather data to make educational decisions that benefit each and every child. Many tools exist for gathering data about very young children. Each tool should be evaluated to ensure that it is appropriate for the child being observed; if it is not, modify the tool or select another one.

CASE STUDY   Eric

Eric, 4-and-a-half months old, is lying on the floor when he starts to cry. His teacher, Audrey, looks at the clock and picks him up. She "eats" his tummy, and he laughs. She holds him up in the air, and he smiles. She says, "Are you getting hungry?" Eric swings his arms as if to say, "Not right now, I want to play." Audrey "eats" his tummy again. Ria toddles over and looks at Eric. Audrey tells Eric what Ria is doing to provide a language-rich environment. Ria toddles away, and Eric begins to fuss. Audrey asks again if he is hungry. This time he continues to fuss, so she gets his bottle, sits in a chair, and feeds him. Eric gazes at Audrey and smiles between sips.

Grasping her finger, Eric looks around the room. Audrey notices he is looking toward Ria. She comments,

"Ria is painting. She is making large circles." Audrey stands him in her lap facing Ria. "Can you see better now?" He laughs. She holds him while he dances and laughs. Audrey turns him around so that he is facing her. She holds his hands to pull him to and fro, and kisses him. He watches Audrey's mouth and responds as she talks to him. He leans on her shoulder and burps as he fingers the afghan on the back of the chair.

1. What observation tool(s) would you use to gather information on Eric's interest in Ria? Why?
2. What suggestions would you give to Audrey for organizing the environment to support Eric's social and emotional development? Why?

Lesson Plan

Title: *Reading with My Friend*

Child Observation:

Leslie is outside with her caregiver Lynn. She "watches Jason (4 years old) and sucks middle two fingers on right hand." Then, Leslie "walks two steps onto the grass." See Table 5–3 for more details.

Child's Developmental Goal:

To develop (and practice) walking skills

To interact with another child

Materials: Blanket, basket of books

Preparation: Place blanket in grassy area with the basket where it cannot be reached while sitting on it.

Learning Environment:

1. When you take the children outside, sit Leslie on the blanket.
2. Draw her attention to the basket of books by using descriptive language. To illustrate, you could say:
   "Your favorite book is in the basket. I brought it out just for you."

3. Invite the child to get the book, if she hasn't already moved toward the basket, by asking prompts or open-ended questions such as these:
   a. I wonder where the book is.
   b. Why don't you walk over to the basket and look for it?
4. When she returns to the blanket, comment on her walking abilities and begin to read the book.
5. When Jason comes near the area, invite him to join Leslie. Engage them in looking at the same book. Invite conversation by asking questions of both of them. You might say, for example:
   a. Do you both have a dog at home?
   b. The girl in the story likes to be outside like us. What is your favorite thing to do outside?

Guidance Consideration:

If Leslie loses interest in Jason's story, build Jason's understanding by explaining that she cannot (yet) listen to a story as long as he can. If Leslie becomes excited and tears a page in the book, remind her to be gentle. If Jason is interested, enlist his assistance with repairing the book.

Variations:

Take pictures of Leslie and Jason interacting throughout the day/week. Make a book of their friendship.

Additional Resources

Benner, S., & Grim, J. C. (2013). *Assessment of young children with special needs: A context-based approach* (2nd ed.). New York: Routledge.

Boylan, J., & Dalrymple, J. (2009). *Advocacy for children and young adults.* Philadelphia, PA: Open University Press.

Isham, S. R. (2014). *Child and family advocacy: The complete guide to child advocacy and education for parents, teachers, advocates, and social workers* [electronic book]. Retrieved from amazon.com.

Nilsen, B. A. (2014). *Week by week: Plans for documenting children's development* (6th ed.). Belmont, CA: Cengage.

Voress, J. K., & Maddox, T. (2013). *Dayc-2: Developmental Assessment of Young Children* (2nd ed.). Austin, TX: Pro-Ed.

Zaslow, M., Martinez-Beck, I., Tout, K., & Halle, T. (2011). (Eds.). *Quality measurement in early childhood settings.* Baltimore, MD: Paul H. Brooks Publishing Company, Inc.

6
CHAPTER

Building Relationships and Guiding Behaviors

Learning Objectives

After reading this chapter, you should be able to:

6-1 Explain the philosophy and principles of the Reggio Emilia approach.

6-2 Summarize a developmental perspective on child guidance.

6-3 Apply strategies for communicating with very young children about emotions.

6-4 Match methods for helping children gain self-regulation skills to a situation.

Standards Addressed in This Chapter

naeyc **NAEYC Standards for Early Childhood Professional Preparation**

1 Promoting Child Development and Learning
4 Using Developmentally Effective Approaches

DAP **Developmentally Appropriate Practice Guidelines**

1 Creating a Caring Community of Learners

In addition, the NAEYC standards for developmentally appropriate practice are divided into six areas particularly important to infant/toddler care. The following area is addressed in this chapter: *relationship between caregiver and child.*

© 2017 Cengage Learning

As this book emphasizes, children need strong, positive relationships with adults in order to thrive in all areas of development. Although these relationships are supported through family grouping, continuity of care, and primary caregiving, those are not enough. The ways in which you interact with very young children need to become a focus of your attention. The first guideline for developmentally appropriate practice, creating a **caring community of learners**, speaks directly to the type of relationships adults need to establish with and among children (Copple & Bredekamp, 2009). In a caring community, each learner is valued, and teachers help children learn to respect and acknowledge differences in abilities and to value each other as individuals (Copple & Bredekamp, 2009). Teachers need to select a variety of strategies for helping children acquire the skills for interacting with others, such as emotional management and perspective-taking. How a teacher guides the behavior of the children sends a clear message about what actions are socially acceptable; we demonstrate through our interactions how to treat one another.

Another aspect of creating a positive environment involves what psychologists have labeled **mastery climate**. This term is used to describe how adults create a context that focuses on self-improvement, effort, persistence, and task mastery by providing challenging tasks (see, e.g., Smith, Smoll, & Cumming, 2007). In this context, mistakes are seen as opportunities for learning because of the valuable feedback they provide to the learner. In other words, an intentional emphasis is placed on internal motivation rather than external motivation. When investigating the impact of coaching behaviors within a mastery climate, Smith et al. (2007) found that athletes in such an atmosphere reported lower levels of anxiety. Applying the mastery climate concept to an educational setting should result in teachers focusing more on performance and movement toward achieving goals (rather than just the product or end point reached). Another logical assumption is that reduced levels of anxiety might result in more focused, risk-taking behaviors and thus greater levels of learning. Research, in fact, confirms that a mastery climate is an effective instructional approach that fosters a child-centered achievement environment, provides freedom of choice, and supports positive attitudes and self-perception toward movement, social interaction, and problem-solving skills (Robinson, Webster, Logan, Lucas, & Barber, 2012).

Creating positive learning environments and providing conscious, purposeful caregiving to individual children has been a leading premise of this book since its inception. One of the finest child care programs in the world operates in Reggio Emilia, Italy. That program and this text clearly share a common focus on promoting the highest-quality care for our youngest citizens.

6-1 Reggio Emilia Approach to Infant-Toddler Education

After World War II, the women of a village in Europe decided to build and run a school for young children. They funded the project with salvaged, washed bricks from destroyed buildings and money from the sale of a tank,

caring community of learners One of the five guidelines for developmentally appropriate practice which focuses on creating a classroom context that supports the development of caring, inclusive relationships for everyone involved.

mastery climate Adults create a context that focuses on self-improvement, effort, persistence, and task mastery by providing challenging tasks.

trucks, and horses left behind by the retreating Germans (Gandini, 2012b). They desired "to bring change and create a new, more just world, free from oppression..." (Gandini, 2004). This school formed the foundation for the later development of the municipal infant/toddler and preschool programs in Reggio Emilia, Italy. A series of national laws related to women's rights, workers' rights, and children's rights created a context that supported the establishment of nationally funded infant-toddler and preschool programs (see, e.g., Gandini, 2004; Ghedini, 2001). While creating nationally funded programs for preschoolers was a challenge, it was less of a battle than they faced with infant-toddler care. The Italian public feared potential damage to children or to the mother-child relationship (Mantovani, 2001). However, these attitudes changed with time, and now infant-toddler centers are viewed as "daily-life contexts with the potential to facilitate the growth and development of all children" (Mantovani, 2001, p. 25). As recently as 1997, laws were passed to establish local projects and services that address the needs of all children and youth (0–18 years old; Ghedini, 2001). These advancements continued the view that care and education of very young children is the responsibility of the broader community (New, 1998).

6-1a Philosophy

The programs of Reggio Emilia are built on educational experiences consisting of reflection, practice, and further careful reflection leading to continual renewal and readjustments (Gandini, 2004). Similar to the theoretical grounding of this book, several theorists influenced their philosophy, including but not limited to Dewey, Ferriere, Vygotsky, Erikson, Bronfenbrenner, Brunner, Piaget, Hawkins, and more contemporary people such as Shaffer, Kagan, Morris, Gardner, and Heinz (Gandini, 2012b). Reading and discussing the writings of these educational leaders assisted them in forming their views about the route they wanted to take when working with young children.

The educators in Reggio Emilia strive to reflect on and recognize in their practices the 14 principles shown in Table 6–1. Some of these principles have been discussed in previous chapters (e.g., Chapter 5), some will be addressed later (e.g., Chapters 8 and 9), and some are covered in this chapter because they relate to how we build relationships with very young children.

6-1b Image of the Child

The educators in Reggio Emilia first and foremost speak about the image they hold of the child and how this affects their interactions, management of the environment, and selection of teaching strategies (Edwards, Gandini, & Forman, 2012; Gandini, 2004; Wien, 2008; Wurm, 2005). Take a moment and think about three words or phrases that you would use to describe the characteristics, abilities, or expectations you hold of infants and toddlers. While looking over the list, ask yourself, "What do these words say regarding my beliefs about young children?" Does your list include words such as *active, possessing potential, independent, curious, competent, capable,* or *problem solvers*? The teachers in Reggio believe that all children are unique in their own ways, and their job as teachers is

TABLE 6–1 ▶ Fourteen Principles for Educators in Reggio Emilia, Italy

1. The image of the child
2. Children's relationships and interactions within a system
3. The three subjects of education: children, parents, and teachers
4. The role of parents
5. The role of space: an amiable school
6. The value of relationships and interaction of children in small groups
7. The role of time and the importance of continuity
8. Cooperation and collaboration as the backbone of the system
9. The interdependence of cooperation and organization
10. Teachers and children as partners in learning
11. Flexible planning vs. curriculum (*progettazione*)
12. The power of documentation
13. The many languages of children
14. Projects

Source: Adapted from Gandini, 2004.

to recognize and support these differences (Photo 6–1). More specifically, according to Rinaldi (2001c), their image is of "a child who is competent, active, and critical; therefore, a child who may be seen as a challenge and, sometimes, as troublesome" (p. 51). Children need adults who assist

© 2017 Cengage Learning

PHOTO 6–1 How do you respect and support the developing capabilities of very young children?

image of the child Beliefs about children that teachers hold; these beliefs are examined for how they impact teacher-child interactions, management of the environment, and selection of teaching strategies.

in the acquisition of skills that support an active construction of their own worlds (White, Swim, Freeman, & Norton-Smith, 2007). Young children must come to understand how they receive as well as produce change in all systems with which they interact (Rinaldi, 2001c). This **image of the child**, then, is a social, ethical, and political statement about active participation in a democratic society, not just an educational one (Gandini, 2012b; Swim & Merz, 2011).

According to Rinaldi (2001c), their creation of the image of the child "...was developed by the pedagogy that inspires the infant-toddler centers..." (p. 50). For educators in Reggio Emilia, there is a constant back and forth between theory (i.e., the image) and practice. Knowledge and meaning are never static but rather generate other meanings (Gandini, 2012b). Hence, you should not despair if your image of the child is not quite fully developed. By reading, reflecting, reading some more, interacting with children, analyzing interactions, and so on, you will facilitate this development.

6-1c *Inserimento*

inserimento A period of gradual "settling in" or "transition and adjustment" that includes strategies for building relationships and community among adults and children when the child is first entering a Reggio Emilia–inspired child care program.

Educators in these programs have deeply respectful ways in which they relate to children and parents. **Inserimento**, which can be roughly translated as "settling in" or "period of transition and adjustment," is used to describe the strategy for building relationships and community among adults and children when the child is first entering an infant-toddler center (Bove, 2001). While this period is individualized for each family, a general model is available to support educators' decision-making: parent interviews and home visits before the child starts at the center; parent-teacher meetings before, during, and after the initial transition process; documentation; large or small group discussions with families; and daily communication between families and teachers (Bove, 2001). The model is an attempt "to meet each family's needs, to sustain parental involvement, and to respond to the parents' requests for emotional support in caring for their young children" (Bove, 2001, p. 112). This process is flexible in order to respond to individual family needs as well as cultural variations found in families (Goldsmith & Theilheimer, 2015). Some families transition to school quickly as the need to return to work becomes pressing, while other families may make several visits to the school over a number of weeks before actually leaving the child with the teachers. In any case, teachers need to engage in open communication to encourage the family members to share their hopes and concerns about their child and group care (Goldsmith & Theilheimer, 2015). When communication is paired with careful observation of family members and the child, the adults can collaborate to determine the best way to proceed with each family (Bove, 2001; Kaminsky, 2005).

As the *inserimento* model demonstrates, parents are viewed as integral partners in caring for and educating the youngest citizens. It is part of our responsibility as professional educators to devise routines that help infants and toddlers simultaneously separate from and form strong bonds with family members; understanding that each goodbye will be followed with a hello (Balaban, 2006; Duffy, 2004). In other words, we must do all we can to assist in building and maintaining strong, healthy attachments at home and school. Helping parents, other relatives, siblings, and children become full participants of the program community is viewed as vital because this supports the well-being and development of not just the infant or toddler but the entire family.

Research on toddlers' transition to child care in Korea suggests that teachers and family members play an important role in helping the child adapt to the new environment. Teacher beliefs about the process and their perceptions of the toddler's adaptation strongly influenced their practices during the adaptation process (Bang, 2014). Specifically, when teachers believed that the adaptation program itself was enough for toddlers to adjust to the new environment, they focused only on providing the program. On the other hand, teachers who perceived soothing crying toddlers as a main concern and a significant part of their role used several strategies to stop the crying (Bang, 2014). As with the inserimento process described earlier, toddlers' successful adaptations to the new setting were supported by strong teacher-parent collaborations. Without such relationships, caregivers could not respond sensitively to toddlers' needs during this critical transition period (Bang, 2014).

Before moving on with your reading, make sure that you can answer the following questions about the material discussed so far.

1. Why should infant-toddler teachers focus their attention on creating a caring community of learners?

2. Review the principles of the Reggio Emilia approach to early education in Table 6–1. Which of the principles support the practices of inserimento?

READING CHECKPOINT

6-2 A Developmental View of Discipline

Newborns do not arrive in this world knowing how to behave. Yet, they immediately begin to investigate the world around them and their role in it. Infants and toddlers work minute by minute to construct their understanding of socially acceptable behaviors. The development of behavior from birth to 2 years old is characterized by stops-and-starts and periods of increased aggression, yet there are within-child and between-child variations that are influenced by family characteristics (e.g., sibling within 5 years of age of toddler, mental distress of parents) (Nærde, Ogden, Janson, & Zachrisson, 2014). While aggression is normative to some extent, it is your responsibility to help each child learn to be socially competent with peers and other adults. You may recall from Chapter 3 that toddlers who demonstrated high levels of effortful control were lower in externalizing behaviors and higher in social competence (Spinrad et al., 2007). Thus, the skills underlying effortful control such as response inhibition and delay of gratification are important for teachers to support. The primary avenue adults have to assist very young children with gaining effortful control and, in turn, social competence is to carefully plan their indoor and outdoor learning environments (see Chapter 8) and use positive strategies for guiding their behavior.

discipline (1) Approach to teaching appropriate behavior and setting limits on inappropriate behavior; (2) the ability to focus on an activity in the face of obstacles to reach a desired outcome.

Many experts in infant and toddler development avoid discussing discipline out of fear that their comments will be used inappropriately with children. Although a valid reasoning, it is essential that teachers use developmentally appropriate guidance strategies to help children learn to follow rules that keep themselves, other people, and property secure and safe (Marion, 2014). Therefore, discipline is an indispensable aspect of helping children develop. The term **discipline** is used here to mean teaching appropriate behavior and setting limits on inappropriate behavior. It *does not* mean punishing children or controlling their behavior. The purpose of guidance or discipline is to help young children learn about themselves (e.g., emotions, feelings) and to teach them ways to interact successfully with others (Keyser, 2006).

Everyone holds implicit, unexamined theories and beliefs regarding discipline (Marion & Swim, 2007). These have developed over time as the result of how we were treated as members of our own families and how we have treated others in our care. Some teachers were punished harshly as a child and remember the negative emotions that accompanied such treatment. As a result, they do not treat children in the same manner. However, some teachers have not acknowledged their emotional response to inappropriate care and continue to use those strategies (or aspects of them, such as sarcastic remarks) in their interactions with children. As a professional, it is time to take stock of your personal experiences and how they have shaped your beliefs.

Do so by remembering a time when you were "in trouble" as a child. Write down all that you can remember about this event: the setting, who was involved, how people acted and reacted, what the outcomes were for you and others. Then, answer the following questions as a strategy for reflecting on and evaluating the impact of the experience. What discipline or punishment strategies did the adults use? Did you think the outcome was fair or appropriate? Why or why not? How do you think that event impacted you as a child? As an adult? What did you learn from this event? How does that learning impact your behaviors with children today? Provide at least one example.

Sometimes reflecting on past experiences can be painful. However, the exercise is intended to assist you in acknowledging and uncovering your hidden, implicit theories about how to guide the behavior of young children. Doing so should highlight aspects of your theories that are useful to you as a professional educator and aspects that you should consciously address to improve. In any case, without reflecting to bring hidden theories to light, new information is often openly discarded because it doesn't fit with an existing worldview (Pintrich, Marx, & Boyle, 1993). Instead, use the information in this chapter to help change your beliefs and practices as you strive to adopt a developmental perspective on child guidance.

6-2a Mental Models

Different mental models help teachers understand their role when guiding the behavior of young children. Resources and Instruction for Staff Excellence (RISE; 2000) created a videoconference series about guiding the behavior of young children. This series promoted the mental model of

Family and Community Connection

As an Early Head Start provider, you provide services to family members and very young children in their homes and at your center. You have worked with Xolo's family for 14 months now. On your most recent visit, his mother, Mia, mentioned that she is struggling with his behavior. She mentioned that he says "no" to everything and runs away when she wants him to do something. You empathize with her regarding how stressful it can be to have a toddler in the home! You invite her to stay in the classroom the next time Xolo comes to school to observe him and you. You promise to talk about her observations at the next home visit. What questions would you ask Mia to find out her observations? Then, what questions would guide the conversation to thinking about and discussing RISE's mental model (i.e., self, environment, and child)?

self, environment, and child. When a situation arises, a teacher must first evaluate her responses and determine who owns the problem. If the adult owns the problem, she must determine how to solve it by examining the situation more carefully. The adult can ask, for example, do I just want to control the child? It is essential to accept the fact that even young children largely control their own behavior. If control is an issue, then this is your problem, and you need to find other ways to view and respond to the way the child behaves. If you do not own the problem, then you should move to the next level of the mental model: an evaluation of the environment. Can the issue be resolved by changing an aspect of the environment? For example, is the block area too small for the number of children who want to use it at one time? If so, then alter the physical arrangement of the room to accommodate the children's interest in building. If you can't resolve the situation by changing your behavior or the environment, then it is time to consider specific strategies to assist the child in acquiring a missing skill. To illustrate, if an infant is biting others, then your intervention might be talking *for* the infant, describing her wants and needs to others. Doing so would provide a language-rich context and promote the acquisition of vocabulary and communication skills.

The second mental model is offered by Powell, Dunlap, and Fox (2006). The first level of this model (see Figure 6–1) focuses on building positive relationships among children, families, and caregivers. This builds on the importance of fostering relationships with young children discussed in previous chapters and forms the foundation for the prevention of challenging behaviors. Recall also how those chapters linked the building of quality, secure relationships with the acquisition of positive social skills. The second level of this mental model is the building of high-quality environments. "Classroom schedules, routines, and activities also provide valuable tools for preventing the development and occurrence of problem behaviors" (Powell et al., 2006, p. 29). Every day should be carefully planned to minimize transitions as "[c]hallenging behavior is more likely to occur when there are too many transitions, when all the children transition at the same time in the same way, when transitions are too long and children spend too much time waiting with nothing to do, and when there are not clear instructions" (Hemmeter, Ostrosky, Artman, & Kinder, 2008, p. 1). In other words, when teachers carefully plan transitions and the rest of their day, they decrease opportunities for disruptive behavior.

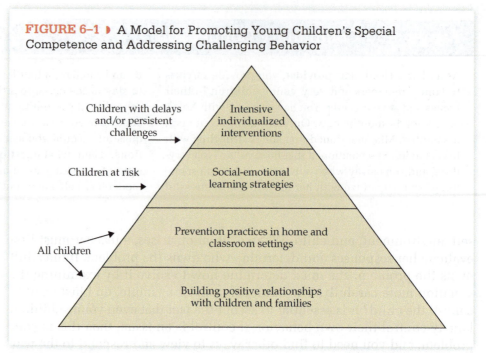

FIGURE 6–1 ▶ A Model for Promoting Young Children's Special Competence and Addressing Challenging Behavior

From: Diane Powell, Glen Dunlap, & Lisa Fox (2006). "Prevention and Intervention for the Challenging Behaviors of Toddlers and Preschoolers," *Infants and Young Children, 19*(1), 25–35 (page 27). Used with permission from Wolters Kluwer Health.

You may have noticed that levels one and two of this model are intended to address behaviors that may be considered challenging when displayed by any child. The next two levels address behaviors that are unresolved by positive, stable relationships and a carefully planned learning environment. These remaining behaviors need specific interventions to assist children in acquiring more positive social interaction or emotional regulation skills.

Teachers can learn to implement promotion, prevention, and intervention practices related to the pyramid model successfully and with positive impacts on children's behavior (Fox, Hemmeter, Snyder, Binder, & Clarke, 2011). The difficulty with this model was learning to implement it with fidelity. Reaching a level of consistency with the complex and comprehensive array of evidence-based practices required ongoing education and coaching (Fox et al., 2011). However, the importance of such levels of engagement should not lead to discouragement; rather, it should heighten your desire to support social, emotional, and behavioral development for young children who are learning to be members of a group. The next section describes some specific strategies teachers can use when faced with challenging behaviors.

READING CHECKPOINT

Before moving on with your reading, make sure that you can answer the following questions about the material discussed so far.

1. Why is taking a developmental approach to guidance beneficial for children and teachers?
2. Compare and contrast the two mental models for guiding children's behaviors.

6-3 Strategies for Communicating about Emotions

Creating a caring community involves attending to the social, emotional, and behavioral environments of a classroom or home setting. Infants and toddlers communicate their needs using a combination of verbal and non-verbal strategies. We do the same as we communicate with them. The strategies discussed in this section are an outgrowth of the theories presented earlier as well as the three *A*s. The purpose of your acquiring these strategies is to make strong relationships between you and the children possible and to promote optimal development and learning.

One important aspect of optional development and learning for infants and toddlers is coming to **self-regulate** their own behavior (Photo 6–2). Our culture expects individuals to behave in ways that are not harmful to themselves, other people, or the environment. These expectations are taught to infants and toddlers by their families, caregivers, and society. To live successfully with other people, children must learn to control their desires and impulses (self-control), and to take responsibility for themselves appropriately for their age and developmental abilities. The extent to which people perceive their lives as within their own control determines what is called **locus of control**. The word *locus* in this context means perceived location, so children who learn to take responsibility for themselves have an internal locus of control. Conversely, people who perceive their lives to be controlled by others have an external locus of control.

For infants and toddlers to internalize for themselves that certain behaviors are acceptable and others are not, they must feel that they have the power to choose their own actions. Unfortunately, many adults believe that they must control children's behavior to care for children and keep them safe. The consistent emotional message communicated to children by adults who feel responsible for the child's behavior is, "You have no choice but to do what I tell you." This belief is problematic for the development of self-regulation.

Child psychologists and counselors observe external locus of control in many children referred for behavior problems. In two studies conducted with older children, researchers found that the more parents espoused an external locus of control (i.e., attempted to control their children's behavior), the higher the likelihood their children had externalizing behavior problems (e.g., increased aggression with peers, lack of frustration tolerance) as they got older (McCabe, Goehring, Yeh, & Lau, 2008; McElroy & Rodriguez, 2008). Similarly, mothers who reported lower levels of efficacy when dealing with their child's aggressive behavior resorted to high-control techniques such as corporal punishment or punitive strategies such as removing privileges without explaining why (Evans, Nelson, Porter, Nelson, & Hart, 2012). Research on the effects of high-control techniques reveals that children of parents who use spanking and

self-regulate The skills necessary to direct and control one's own behavior in socially and culturally appropriate ways.

locus of control The extent to which a person perceives his or her life as within his or her own control.

© 2017 Cengage Learning

PHOTO 6–2 Infants and toddlers have to learn to self-regulate their own behavior.

other types of corporal punishment are especially likely to endorse aggressive problem-solving strategies with peers (Simons & Wurtele, 2010), engage in more aggression with peers, and engage in other deviant behaviors (Straus, 2001). Data from the Early Head Start Research and Evaluation Study revealed that aggressive behaviors were stable from infancy through toddlerhood, and that, for Caucasian families, maternal spanking was associated with parental reports of aggressive behaviors (Stacks, Oshio, Gerard, & Roe, 2009). In contrast, parents who actively supported their toddler's autonomy had children with greater executive functioning, including impulse control (Bernier, Carlson, & Whipple, 2010). What other parenting behaviors might help young children develop an internal locus of control? In a research study, mothers were asked to hold conversations with their preschool child about peer conflicts involving relational aggression. Those conversations were coded for coaching skills such as maternal elaboration, emotion references, and discussion of norm violations. They found that mothers with average to high levels of coaching skills about peer conflicts were associated with children's decreasing displays of relational aggression over a one-year period (Werner, Eaton, Lyle, Tseng, & Holst, 2014). What early childhood educators should take away from this research is that (1) all children, regardless of their ages, need to feel a sense of power over their lives; (2) the characteristics of the adult-child relationship relates to the child's self-regulation capabilities; and (3) building an internal locus of control during the infant-toddler period is easier than attempting to replace an external locus of control in the future.

Development of an internal locus of control requires that caregivers respect the right of young children to make many choices within their environment, including choosing their behavior. Many effective strategies are available for developing an internal locus of control. The next section provides an explanation of two guidance strategies that can be used to assist young children in communicating about their emotions—skills that will help build a strong foundation for more competent and self-regulated interactions with others.

6-3a Labeling Expressed Emotions

Caregivers should label feeling states from the time children are born. A good way to teach states is to verbalize your own feelings and your impressions of others' feelings. "I'm feeling rushed today," "Jaime seems sad," and "You really look excited!" are examples of labeling feeling states or **emotional talk** (Marion, 2014). Teachers should also model and mirror feeling states. Giving children feedback by repeating their words or mimicking their facial expressions helps to develop self-awareness and sensitivity to other people's feelings.

Feelings are inborn, but emotional reactions are learned. It is important to teach young children to identify their feeling states accurately and express those feelings in healthy ways. It is often easy to determine the emotions of even young infants. For example, young babies often "beam" when happy, have a "tantrum" when frustrated or angry, and "coo and

emotional talk Labeling feeling states to help young children understand their emotions and how they are expressing them.

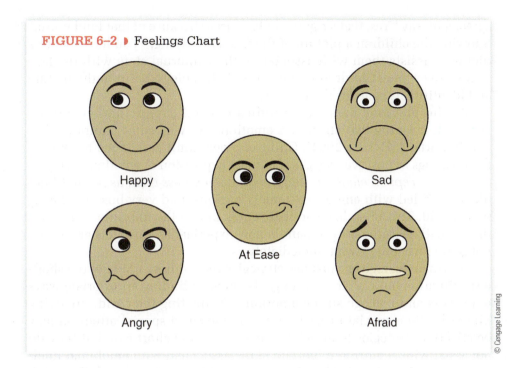

FIGURE 6–2 ▶ Feelings Chart

Happy

At Ease

Sad

Angry

Afraid

© Cengage Learning

smile" when happy and at ease. Caregivers should label feeling states for nonverbal infants, and as young children develop language, they should be taught to label and express their emotions accurately. One effective tool for helping young children pay attention to and identify feelings is to use a chart such as the one shown in Figure 6–2. This chart illustrates five primary emotions—Happy, At Ease, Sad, Angry, and Afraid—and can be used to help children accurately label their internal feelings. All human emotions are normal and are therefore healthy; a feeling state is neither bad nor good. The main goal is to help children be consciously aware of their feelings and to express them in ways that are helpful to them and not harmful to others.

The ultimate goal of affective education is for children to identify their own body responses and discuss when they started to experience a feeling. This gradual process starts with bringing attention to the child's internal state and labeling the child's feelings. Often the physical meter for children's feeling states are their whole bodies as they respond to different situations. A skilled observer can easily identify children who are experiencing different emotions by their body language. Share your observations with the children. Ask children how their bodies feel. State the feeling you sense with nonverbal children and infants and connect it to the nonverbal cues they are displaying. To illustrate, you can say, "I think you are at ease because you are concentrating hard on putting the puzzle together. Your body is relaxed."

At other times, you want them to learn to connect their feelings with symbols of those feelings. When you see a child expressing an emotion, show him or her the five faces (Happy, At Ease, Sad, Angry, and Afraid). Identify afraid, and point to it, saying, "You're afraid." If the child indicates agreement, say "Yes, that's right; you feel afraid because of that loud noise." Showing the children a picture of the face and saying, "You look like this picture," assists them with associating their internal state with the face symbol over time. Children will eventually be able to point to the picture and identify this state for themselves.

emotion-centered Children's emotions are viewed as natural, valid, and an important part of the curriculum.

As the previous paragraphs indicate, good caregiving is **emotion-centered**, meaning that children's emotions are viewed as natural, valid, and important (Hyson, 2004). Children need adult assistance to express their feelings in positive ways. To facilitate expression of emotions in a positive way, *accept all emotions and the need to express them as normal*. Toddlers are filled with energy, extremely curious, and very busy exploring their world. This often leads to frustration and all the unbridled emotions that go with learning how to handle new experiences. Conflicts arise from not getting what they want immediately.

A primary caregiver must use strategies that address not only the short-term situation but also long-term goals, such as finding appropriate ways to express and manage strong emotions. Distracting the child, involving him or her in a special project, or giving the child special attention may be effective strategies to alleviate emotions in the short run, but they do not assist with acquiring important skills associated with emotional intelligence (see Chapter 3). Therefore, you need to consider carefully which strategies to employ in a given situation to balance immediate needs with more long-term learning and development.

An excellent example of needing to be careful when selecting instructional strategies occurs when a toddler has a temper tantrum. Toddlers are known for expressing strong emotions such as frustration and anger through tantrums. These episodes are very scary for a young child. Using emotional talk at the first sign of the emotion can often alleviate the child's feeling of being emotionally overwhelmed and prevent a tantrum in the first place. However, when a child does have a temper tantrum, make sure all furniture and harmful objects are out of the way. Remove undue attention from her until she is through, ask her privately to tell you what she felt if she can verbalize, and then welcome her into the group again. Articulate your observations of the child's emotional state and how it changed over the episode. For example, you could say, "You were very angry with me. I wouldn't let you paint. You like to paint. It must've been frightening when you were so out of control. Now you are calm." This is the most appropriate way to deal with tantrum behavior after it has started because it doesn't cause further emotional harm to the child. This calm approach communicates that the child is still important to the teacher and the group. It is important that adults never hold a grudge against a child. This only demonstrates their lack of emotional skills. If they become overwhelmed by the intensity of the situation, then they should find a way to regain their emotional balance and return to a state of at ease.

emotional regulation Learning to control and manage strong emotions in a socially and culturally acceptable manner.

6-3b Teaching Emotional Regulation

Teaching infants and toddlers to soothe themselves and manage their emotions, known as **emotional regulation**, may be the single most challenging

Spotlight on Research

INFANTS AND DIVORCE

Divorce is difficult and can have long-term outcomes for a child of any age. However, given the importance of infants and caregivers establishing a healthy attachment, the impact of divorce on very young children should not be overlooked. This Spotlight on Research box will examine possible correlates of divorce as well as some consequences of divorce for infants.

As modern technologies assist with infertility issues and increase the survival rate of very low birth weight (VLBW) babies, families can experience increased financial and psychological stress. Of course, families respond differently when facing the birth of a VLBW child. For some, it brings the family members closer together. For others, it causes a change in the roles of the family members. Mothers, for example, may not continue or seek employment as they assume more responsibility for caring for the infant. Still, for other families, the stress becomes too great, and they seek a divorce. Swaminathan, Alexander, and Boulet (2006) found that the occurrence of divorce or separation following the birth of a VLBW infant was twofold greater compared to parents whose infants were born at greater than 1,500 grams. At "two years after the birth of a VLBW infant, approximately 90 percent of the marriages were still intact, while 95 percent of the marriages remained stable for families with a non-VLBW infant" (Swaminathan et al., 2006, p. 476). In addition, whether or not the pregnancy was wanted significantly impacted the occurrence of divorce. Specifically, those parents who reported that the pregnancy was unwanted had an 84 percent chance of their marriage being intact at two years postdelivery. Given the consequences of divorce for children and adults, "family-oriented policies and programs are [needed] to assure that families with VLBW infants have more reasonable prospects of staying intact and being self-sufficient" (Swaminathan et al., 2006, p. 478).

Family situations leading up to and following a divorce are complex. The difficulty of the situation is felt by everyone involved. Infants and toddlers clearly do not understand what is happening around them on a cognitive level, but they do experience it on an emotional level. Solchany (2007) used three case studies to discover that infants also experience divorce on a physical level. Growth, as measured by height, weight, and head circumference, was monitored at each well-baby checkup. Each of the three infants in the study experienced growth faltering or a failure to grow at the expected rate of development. Although each family had different custodial arrangements, all of them experienced high conflict and a deterioration of communication. At some point, each of the three babies refused to eat and experienced difficulties with breastfeeding as well as sleep disruptions (Solchany, 2007). When these families were referred to infant mental health services, and visitation schedules were altered to reflect the needs of the child more, two of the three infants showed some recovery growth. The author concluded that

> Divorce impacts all children, but infants are especially vulnerable to emotional and physical effects. Professionals—medical, mental health, and legal—as well as parents need to be aware of these possible effects and take proper steps to protect the well-being of infants in the midst of their parents' divorces. (p. 40)

Research has substantiated the positive impact of both mothers and fathers on developmental outcomes for infants and toddlers. When adults dissolve a marriage, it is necessary for them to devise ways for both parents to remain active in the child's life. Sano, Smith, and Lanigan (2011) found that the ability to maintain a positive adult-adult relationship in the midst of a divorce predicted greater father involvement in infants' lives. Unfortunately, even for adults who can maintain such positive relationships, the court system is the entity that more often than not determines how involved a parent can be in the postdivorce life of very young children. As the adults are the ones participating in the court proceedings, it is not inconceivable that rulings are made in their interests and not the child's. Lee, Kaufman, and George (2009) theorized that conflicted divorce might lead to more instances of disorganized attachment, especially if caregiving capabilities of parents aren't considered by the courts when making custody decisions. Investigating the situation of overnight visitation by nonresident parents, Strous (2011) concluded, from the perspective of attachment theory, that

> …the necessity for overnight contact may be more a case of parental or legal demands than in the best interests of the child. In instances where a very young child's relationship with a secondary attachment figure can be adequately safeguarded through regular, non-prolonged contact, insisting on overnight access that is more protracted than daytime contact may be a case of overkill. (p. 203)

(continued)

Spotlight on Research (*continued*)

This debate is far from over, as a recent research provided a mixed view of outcomes for infants. For example, McIntosh, Smyth, and Kelaher's (2013) finding supported an association between a greater number of shared overnight and lower levels of emotional regulation for children aged 0–1 and 2–3, when controlling for parenting style, parental conflict, and socioeconomic factors. In contrast, a meta-analysis of 11 research articles concluded that overnight stays with the father were not associated with negative outcomes for infants and toddlers and was actually associated with positive outcomes for preschoolers (Nielsen, 2014).

---

task a caregiver faces. Infants and toddlers, like all other humans, are unique in the ways in which they express their emotions. As discussed previously, this can be related to their temperament (see Chapter 3), family, community, and culture. Professional early childhood educators honor this individuality when they modify their curriculum to build on each child's preferences and strengths (Hyson, 2004).

Infants rely almost exclusively on other people for their need fulfillment, so they are not developmentally prepared at birth to soothe themselves. They must gradually learn that they can calm and soothe themselves through the feedback provided by their caregivers. Recall the three As from Chapter 4. Professional early childhood educators who sensitively administer the three As and systematically teach children to use the three As for themselves promote and develop **self-soothing**.

self-soothing Comforting and making oneself at ease.

You should encourage children's actions and help them manage emotions as they progress toward set goals. For example, when a child indicates the desire to hold an object and finally succeeds after trying several times with your help, the work is validated in a sense of achievement by your attention, approval, and attunement. This builds a feeling of confidence and a willingness to try the next time when the child reaches for the same object. The child may attempt the task on his own, or he may look for your encouragement or help, but eventually he will feel confident enough to succeed without your help.

Appropriate words of encouragement help children of all ages. Timing of when to give approval depends on the needs of the child. The child may start out wanting something but becomes too tired to finish. If the child is too tired, the primary need must be cared for first (holding the child until he or she goes to sleep). After the primary needs have been met, children will once again bring their attention to other activities.

Early childhood educators can help build strong self-images for the toddlers in their care. By being good role models and using reinforcing, positive self-talk, they can build language for the child to adopt. **Positive self-talk** is the internalization of messages we hear about ourselves from others. These messages represent how children feel about themselves and what they are capable of over time. If the messages are positive and encouraging, the child will become confident, but if they are negative, the child feels limited in the ability to succeed. These messages become the belief system of the child and the foundation for self-concept and future success or failure.

positive self-talk The internalization of positive messages we hear about ourselves from others.

TABLE 6–2 ▶ Approval Validates Mastery

CHILD BEHAVIOR	CAREGIVER RESPONSE	OUTCOME
1. eyes an object	observes child	caregiver attention
2. reaches for object	encourages with words such as "You can do it."	approval for mastery attempt; increased child motivation
3. looks at caregiver; tries to grasp objects again	continues to encourage, softly saying "Try again; you can do it!" models success	approval for mastery attempt; increased child motivation
4. successfully grasps object	compliments effort, makes eye contact, makes gentle hug	approval and affection for mastery of task
5. smiles and shows excitement—brings object to mouth	says "Nice job! I knew you could do it!" give three *A*s	validation of mastery; observable self-approval

© Cengage Learning

Scaffolding, or building sets of ideas and demonstrating how to use them, can be used to promote positive self-talk. Table 6–2 illustrates how scaffolding works when approval sustains the infant's attention. This approval validates children's mastery of their environment. Children internalize the validation they hear and make it their own as you reduce feedback.

Before moving on with your reading, make sure that you can answer the following question about the material discussed so far.

1. What strategies can be used to support communication about emotions?

READING CHECKPOINT

6-4 Self-Regulation as a Foundation for Perspective-Taking

Successful relationships and social acceptance depend on controlling impulses for actions and words that could harm another as well as developing an awareness of other people's perspectives. Children must learn to act without harming themselves, others, or the environment because internal controls are not innate. Children need to be taught the foundations of **perspective-taking** skills to have successful, positive relationships (Photo 6–3).

One way of helping children is to explain how their behavior may make others feel. By announcing out loud how others are reacting to a given behavior, you help all of the children involved begin to understand the others' perspectives. For instance, Ms. Barbara works in a licensed family child care center. She waits for 3-year-old Eroj to come home from the Head Start center at the bus stop with his 2-year-old sister Inara. She greets Eroj with a smile and hug. His sister is happy to see him too. He has his art projects in both hands, but drops them when he hugs Ms. Barbara. Inara grabs the papers and, in the excitement of the moment, she crumples one of them. Eroj becomes angry and yells at his sister, who starts to cry. As Ms. Barbara helps him gather up his work, she places Inara on her hip and places her hand firmly on Eroj's shoulder. She says to him, "I'm so sorry

perspective-taking Acquiring the skills for recognizing and responding to the perspectives of others; not a skill to be expected of infants and toddlers, but the foundations for skills should be set.

© 2012 Cengage Learning

PHOTO 6–3 Animals help toddlers learn perspective-taking skills and responsibility.

you dropped your papers. I can tell that you worked so hard on them (looking at papers he is showing her while walking). You should be proud of them. When we get back, you can show everyone your work and then put them on the wall if you like."

To show Inara's perspective, Ms. Barbara continues by saying, "You know, Eroj, Inara did not mean to crumple your papers. I know she misses you when you go to school because several times during the day she stands by the door and says your name. She loves you and wants to be with you. I don't think that she meant to crumple your paper. She just got so excited to see you."

This example has a very specific theme. The teacher provided Eroj and Inara information they would not have had and dealt with them in a very careful way. She greeted Eroj warmly, validated his feelings of anger and self-worth, soothed his sister by picking her up, and discussed the situation openly and honestly with both children. She expressed positive observations about their relationship. In addition, the teacher was acting as Inara's advocate.

Caregivers can offer similar comfort to very young children by using statements like, "Oh, I know Michael didn't mean to knock down your block pile, Dori; he just lost his balance." The key to successful use of this strategy is to know the child, know the facts of the situation, and communicate, as best as possible, the intentions and actions of the people involved.

While very young children may be able to consider another child's perspective with assistance, it is inappropriate to expect them to do so independently. The goal of your behaviors is not to teach them how to take someone's perspective but rather to lay a foundation for it because acquiring perspective-taking skills is a long, arduous task that lasts through adulthood.

6-4a Setting Limits

After children become mobile, they must learn to accept "no" about certain behaviors. Adults must help them learn that some behaviors are not acceptable, while recognizing ourselves that many of their behaviors are the result of acting on their natural instinct to explore their world (Walsh, 2007). For example, a mobile infant should be firmly—but kindly—told, "No. Leave the trash in the can," if she were reaching for an item that had been disposed of. *However, the number of behaviors they must accept "no" to is much smaller than many adults demand.* The main principle to use in selecting which behaviors children must accept "no" to is to start with only those behaviors that are directly harmful to themselves, other people, or property.

Limits and rules, while they help children to accept "no" about certain behaviors, are best followed if stated positively. Let the children know what to do in as specific language as possible (Marion, 2014). When you see an infant pulling on the lamp to stand, say, "Couches are for pulling up on" and move the child to the couch. Your behavior will help the child construct an understanding of safe furniture for pulling on. Limits, then, are for stopping inappropriate behaviors and replacing them with more appropriate ones.

Not enough can be said about the importance of stating limits positively. Many children spend time in classrooms where all limits start with the word no. This not only creates a negative environment (who wants to be told no all of the time?) but also does not teach the children the behaviors that will help them be successful. They are told not to run, so they hop. They are told not to hop, so they crawl. It seems as if they are playing a guessing game with the adult. When adults want children to do something, it is best to state, positively and directly, expectations for a desired behavior. For example, if you want toddlers to park their tricycles on the cement slab beside the toy shed, then tell them: "It is time to put the tricycles up. Park them at the sign beside the toy shed."

While each classroom and early childhood program needs rules or limits, these should be few in number (Photo 6–4). Infants and toddlers typically lack the cognitive skills to recall more than a few limits (Marion, 2014). Even with a few rules, however, teachers

> **limits** Positively worded statements about desired or acceptable behavior that help children acquire appropriate behaviors for a particular setting.

© 2017 Cengage Learning

PHOTO 6–4 There should be classroom rules and limits, but there shouldn't be too many. Teachers should remind children of the rules to support memory and understanding.

should not expect the toddlers to remember them. Pure recall is the most challenging type of memory skill to develop, taking several years. Therefore, educators should make the effort to remind the children of the rules gently as preventative measures. For example, if you notice that Kennedy is looking out the window and getting excited because she sees her grandmother coming to pick her up, you could say, "Let's walk to the door to greet her." This gentle reminder assists Kennedy both in walking and in expressing her love toward her grandmother.

6-4b Establishing Consequences

consequences The natural and/or logical outcomes of actions.

After limits have been defined, discussed, and modeled, **consequences** for each limit need to be established. The most effective consequences for learning appropriate behaviors are natural and logical (Marion, 2014). Natural consequences are those outcomes that occur without teacher intervention. Elisabetta runs through the block area of the classroom, trips over a wooden truck, and falls on the carpet. She is surprised but unhurt. Elisabetta has experienced a natural consequence of running in the classroom. Early childhood educators cannot allow all natural consequences to occur because they are too dangerous. Permitting a toddler to fall (i.e., experiencing a natural consequence) because he climbed over the top railing of the climbing structure is obviously not acceptable.

Logical consequences are outcomes that are related to the limit but would not occur on their own. For example, your rule is for the children to put their toys back on the shelf when they are done. If a child does not put her puzzle back on the shelf after being reminded, she will not be able to choose another activity until the first one is cleaned up.

Establishing consequences helps young children become autonomous, self-regulated individuals. Toddlers should be allowed and even encouraged to voice their own opinions and have a say in what happens to them. Unfortunately, this developmental phase is often referred to as the "terrible twos." This important period of personality and self-development is mislabeled as "terrible" by controlling adults who have difficulty accepting children saying "no" to them. It is vital that children be allowed to say "no" to teachers and other adults to develop a healthy sense of self. Caregivers who do not accept "no" from a child when he is not harming himself, others, or property do great harm to the child's sense of self-responsibility. Young children must learn to make decisions and establish boundaries with other people. Two additional guidance strategies to use with children who say "no" to practically everything are giving choices and redirection.

6-4c Providing Choices

People learn to make wise choices by being able to choose. Caregivers who give children choices that they can handle for their age avoid many confrontations and teach children to choose wisely (Marion, 2014). Yes/no questions are often problematic, as is a statement that commands the child. For example, "Do you want lunch?" is likely to result in "no," as is the statement "You're going to eat your lunch now." A much more effective approach is to give a choice, such as "Do you want a banana or apple slices with your grilled cheese sandwich? You choose." Much research has been conducted investigating the impact of choice on internal control and motivation.

In a meta-analysis of 41 research studies, Patall, Cooper, and Robinson (2008) found that choice does have a positive impact on internal motivation as well as effort, performance, and perceived competence. In addition, choices that allowed for the expression of individuality (e.g., what color of paper or pens to use) were particularly powerful motivators. Moreover, "the largest positive effect of choice on intrinsic motivation was found when participants made two to four choices in a single experimental manipulation" (Patall et al., 2008, p. 295). Thus, it seems that having too few choices does not allow children to feel a sense of control over their environment, while having too many may result in cognitive overload. Although none of the research studies included in the meta-analyses specifically studied infants and toddlers, the results are nonetheless instructional for teachers of very young children. Early childhood educators need to consider when they are providing choices throughout their day and how many choices are being provided at any one given time. In addition, the choices need to teach the children a sense of self-control and self-responsibility while encouraging self-expression. In general, providing choices increases people's internal motivation to complete a task because they feel they are more in control of their destiny (Patall et al., 2008). This is the exact outcome we seek for young children: they will learn that they are powerful people with opinions to share. In other words, providing choices fosters the development of young children's self-efficacy.

6-4d Redirecting Actions

There are two different types of redirection strategies (Marion, 2014). First, you can divert and distract a young child's attention to safe and acceptable activities to prevent confrontations. This strategy is useful for very young children with underdeveloped object permanence because for them out-of-sight is equivalent to out-of-mind. Older toddlers are not always so easy to distract because they can continue to think about the desired object even if they cannot see it. For example, if you take a young child into a setting with many breakable objects, diverting the child's attention to objects and activities in the setting that are not breakable can avoid problems. Your attention and interest most often evokes interest on the child's part, so rather than attending to all the breakable things, pay attention and draw the child into activities that are safe and appropriate.

The second type of redirection involves finding a substitute activity based on the child's underlying desire. If a toddler is chewing on a wooden block, find her a teething ring to chew on. If a child wants to climb and jump from the shelf, take him outside to jump. Redirecting attention to the appropriate location recognizes children's underlying needs and can help them learn to monitor and regulate their expression of emotions (Hyson, 2004).

6-4e Solving Problems

Infants and toddlers encounter problems frequently throughout their day. These can originate from physical objects, their abilities or lack thereof, and interactions with others. Although some adults may not recognize all of these situations as problems to be solved, it can be helpful to reframe their issues in this way. Doing so often makes adults and young children feel more powerful and directly in control of outcomes.

Consider this example. Susanna, 7 months old, awakes from her morning nap. Her teacher, Yu-Wen, picks her up while saying soothing words. Susanna begins to cry in earnest. Yu-Wen shifts positions and decides to check her diaper even though it was a short nap, but she is dry. Yu-Wen offers Susanna a bottle, but she refuses it. Then she holds her while gently swaying back and forth, a motion that Susanna typically likes, but not right now. Her crying intensifies. After 20 minutes of trying to solve the problem and strained emotions, Yu-Wen asks her co-teacher if she will take Susanna for a few minutes while she goes to get a drink of cold water. Yu-Wen uses that time to regain her composure and decides to try a strategy that she recently read about in a teacher journal. She prepares a soft blanket on the floor with two soft toys on it. She takes Susanna from her co-teacher and places her tummy up on the blanket. Susanna continues to cry, but the intensity lessens. Within a few moments she is staring at her feet; a small smile plays on the corner of her lips. Yu-Wen is pleased that the strategy of giving children the freedom to move to solve their own problem worked (Gonzalez-Mena, 2007).

Toddlers are moving from being dependent to being independent; from wanting to play alone to playing parallel or even cooperatively with others; and from thinking simplistically to thinking in more complex ways. All of these developmental advances provide them many opportunities to problem solve. Because toddlers are more skilled than infants, they should be more involved in the problem-solving process. The following are guidelines for how to solve a problem (Epstein, 2007; Marion, 2014; Swim & Marion, 2006):

1. Describe what you saw; have children verify if you are accurate.
2. Ask yes/no questions to engage children in the process of identifying and labeling the problem to be solved.
3. Volunteer an idea, choice, or solution to the problem.
4. Help the children select one solution.
5. Help the children implement the solution.
6. Ask yes/no questions to reflect on whether or not the solution worked for everyone.

As with the other guidance strategies described in this chapter, teachers are always the "more knowledgeable others," to use Vygotsky's term, and thus must assume the responsibility for providing children with necessary language and processes for solving problems.

Not all problems can be solved quickly. Change takes time for everyone. You should not try to solve all problems independently; seek guidance from colleagues or your director. As part of creating positive, reciprocal relationships with families, you should also seek their input and guidance. For example, if an infant or toddler shows signs of discomfort for more than two hours, family members should be consulted. The goal of this conversation is to obtain more information and to seek advice on additional strategies that work for them. As demonstrated earlier, professional teacher journals are another source of information on ways to solve problems.

As you are guiding the behavior of young children, remember that achieving social and emotional competence is a long journey. Do not expect perfection from yourself, the families, or the children. Observe what the children can do on their own and what they can do with assistance (i.e., identify their zones of proximal development). Then, use teaching strategies to scaffold them to the next level of development. Persistent, small gains add up to big changes over time.

Before moving on with your reading, make sure that you can answer the following question about the material discussed so far.

1. List and explain three strategies for positively guiding and supporting the development of very young children's self-regulation skills.

READING CHECKPOINT

Summary

Creating a caring community of learners is an important aspect of the work that teachers of infants and toddlers do. This involves building positive relationships with each child and using positive guidance strategies to facilitate the development of self-regulation and socially acceptable behaviors.

6-1 Explain the philosophy and principles of the Reggio Emilia approach.

The philosophy of the schools in Reggio Emilia, Italy, challenges teachers to reflect on and recognize in their practice concepts such as the image of the child. *Inserimento* is a collaborative process used in Italy for transitioning infants and toddlers to an educational program.

6-2 Summarize a developmental perspective on child guidance.

Two mental models were presented as ways to take a developmental view of discipline.

6-3 Apply strategies for communicating with very young children about emotions.

Teachers should help each and every child come to understand their emotions and the emotions of others. Infant and toddler teachers help to set a strong foundation for self-regulation by labeling emotions and teaching emotional regulation skills.

6-4 Match methods for helping children gain self-regulation skills to a situation.

Self-regulation skills serve as a foundation for perspective-taking skills. While infants and toddlers can demonstrate perspective-taking skills with assistance, they should not be expected to do so independently. Strategies such as setting limits, providing choices, and redirecting inappropriate behaviors help children learn to regulate their own behavior.

CASE STUDY   Regina's Biting Behaviors

"Should I call her mother again?" Enrique, a toddler teacher, asks his co-teacher as Regina struggles to free herself from his gentle hold. Regina has just bit the same peer for the second time today.

"Yes, I think you should. We could use some information." Although Regina is 27 months old, this is her first time attending child care.

Enrique calls to share how happy he is to have Regina in his classroom. He asks Ms. Gonzalez what strategies they use when she is upset. She provides him several things to try.

Ms. Gonzalez arrives about 30 minutes earlier than normal for pickup looking frazzled and upset. Enrique greets her and tells her that her suggestion to sing quietly worked wonders. He also asks if she came early because of the phone call. They discuss how the call was not intended to upset her but rather was to gather more information to help Regina.

They move closer to Regina who is working by herself at a table lining up clowns. Enrique and Ms. Gonzalez take a few moments to watch her work. Regina methodically lines the clowns around the perimeter of a piece of construction paper. She seems not to notice the other activities around her. The other children have divided themselves into two groups, working with blocks and pouring water through waterwheels.

Enrique asks Ms. Gonzalez what she is noticing. She replies by asking, "Does she usually play alone?"

"No. She typically works in the same area as other children. This is expected because as children get older,

they usually begin to play in small groups. Regina's interactions with the other children sometimes result in her biting them, like today. I am wondering if you can tell me how she interacts with you and your husband at home."

"We usually interact with her. If we ask her a question, she will nod yes or no. She is very quiet and does not seem to have many wants. But, if she does want something, she will point at the object."

"I'm wondering if she is biting because she does not have the language to tell her classmates what she wants. I'm also wondering what I can do to best help her. Can we both take some time to think about Regina and meet early next week to talk further?"

"That would be nice. Is it okay if my husband comes also?" inquires Ms. Gonzalez.

"Of course. Let me know what times work best for your schedules. And, thank you so much for making the extra time in your schedule to speak with me today. The more we work together, the better we can support Regina's needs."

1. How did Enrique's approach serve to value the relationships among Mr. and Ms. Gonzalez, Regina, and himself?
2. Describe what you believe is Enrique's image of the child. What information from the case did you use when drawing this conclusion?
3. What strategies would you suggest Enrique use to support Regina's acquisition of socially accepted behaviors? Why?

Lesson Plan

Title: *Where can I ride my trike?*

Child Observation:

Forrest (32 months old) is outside riding a tricycle on the cement path. He veers off the path and rides the trike through the sand area. When asked to get back on the cement path, Forrest screams "no" and tightly grabs the handlebar.

Child's Developmental Goal:

To develop an internal locus of control

To follow a limit

Materials: Tricycle, "Tricycles Stay on the Path" sign on a stand or otherwise able to be displayed in sand area.

Preparation: Place "Tricycles Stay on the Path" sign on the edge of the sand area.

Learning Environment:

1. When you take the children outside, invite Forrest to look at the sign by saying, for example:
   a. I put this sign out just for you. It says "Tricycles Stay on the Path." That means the tricycle should stay on the cement path (point to path). The sand is for walking and playing.
2. If Forrest wants to ride the tricycle, assist him with putting on his helmet, if necessary.
3. Stand near the sign so that you can talk with Forrest when he drives by the area. To illustrate, you could say:
   a. You are riding fast on the trike path.
   b. The trike rides better on the concrete, doesn't it?
4. If Forrest begins to ride in the sand, remind him of the limit, by saying, for example:
   a. Ride the tricycle on the cement path.

❯❯ **Professional Resource Download**

5. When first possible, talk with Forrest about how he followed the limit. Engage him to think about when he stayed on the path and when he wanted to ride in the sand. Discuss how he showed impulse control—define that in a simple way such as, "You wanted to ride in the sand but stopped because it was not the right thing to do at the time."

Guidance Consideration:

If Forrest begins to violate the rule and tries to drive the tricycle in the sand, get on his level and stop the trike. Start the problem-solving process by saying, "We have a problem that we need to solve. I want the tricycle ridden on the cement path, and you want to ride in the sand. What can we do to solve this?" Engage in the next steps of the problem solving process with Forrest.

Variations:

Introduce a new area for riding the tricycle and state the rules for that location.

Additional Resources

Brodey, D. (2007). *The elephant in the playroom: Ordinary parents write intimately and honestly about the extraordinary highs and heartbreaking lows of raising kids with special needs*. New York: Hudson Street Press.

Feeney, S. (2012). *Professionalism in early childhood education: Doing our best for young children*. Boston: Pearson Education.

Medina, J. (2014). *Brain rules for baby: How to raise a smart and happy child from zero to five* (updated and expanded). Seattle, WA: Pear Press.

Pfieffer, J. (2013). Dude, you're a dad!: How to get (all of you) through your baby's first year. Fort Collins, CO: Adams Media.

Weissbourd, R. (2009). *The parents we mean to be: How well-intentioned adults undermine children's moral and emotional development*. Boston: Houghton Mifflin Harcourt.

7

CHAPTER

Supportive Communication with Families and Colleagues

Learning Objectives

After reading this chapter, you should be able to:

7-1 Understand the active listening process and other skills for effective communication.

7-2 Develop procedures for informal and formal communication with families.

7-3 Describe specific family situations that might require additional support.

7-4 Analyze your own skills when communicating with colleagues.

Standards Addressed in This Chapter

naeyc **NAEYC Standards for Early Childhood Professional Preparation**

2 Building Family and Community Relationships

6 Becoming a Professional

DAP **Developmentally Appropriate Practice Guidelines**

5 Establishing reciprocal relationships with families

In addition, the NAEYC standards for developmentally appropriate practice are divided into six areas particularly important to infant/toddler care. The following area is addressed in this chapter: *reciprocal relationship with families*.

© 2017 Cengage Learning

Caregivers and family members* have a common goal: to provide high-quality experiences for children. When children are being cared for by someone other than an immediate family member, all persons involved must join in partnership to achieve this goal. The fifth guideline for developmentally appropriate practice as outlined by NAEYC is "establishing reciprocal relationships with families" (Copple & Bredekamp, 2009). Recognizing the complexity of this guideline is necessary for beginning teachers. Oversimplifying and regarding the objective as just parent education on the one hand, or total parent control on the other, minimizes the role of the teacher in joining with parents to provide the best care and education for their very young children. The primary components of this guideline are highlighted here.

- Reciprocal relationships require mutual respect, cooperation, shared responsibility, and negotiation of conflicts to achieve shared goals.
- Frequent two-way communication must be established and maintained between early childhood teachers and families.
- Families are welcomed into the program and invited to participate in decisions about their children's care and education as well as program decisions.
- Family members' choices and goals are responded to with sensitivity and respect, without abdicating professional responsibility.
- Teachers and families share their knowledge of the child, including assessment information, to maximize everyone's decision-making abilities.
- Professionals having educational responsibility for a child should, with family participation, share information (Copple & Bredekamp, 2009).

My experiences with preservice teachers and beginning educators demonstrate that building relationships with families can provoke fear. "I'm comfortable with children, not adults" is a common statement. Thus, this chapter is devoted to assisting you in considering this topic more in depth and developing the skills to be successful.

Effective communication between caregivers and families and among the early childhood program staff is a must. Communication is a two-way process. It requires listening, empathy, and effective expression of thoughts and feelings. The nonverbal, emotional messages that are sent in the questions asked and the statements made will either help or hinder successful communication. We must listen to uncover cultural diversity because families differ in how they communicate (Christian, 2006). The attitudes, beliefs, and biases caregivers and families have toward each other are reflected through the communication process. The goal of coming to understand our own and the families' cultures is to communicate effectively about children's strengths and needs, not to change the children or the families (Im, Parlakian, & Sánchez, 2007).

To be an effective caregiver, it is necessary to communicate well with children, families, colleagues, professionals, and other adults. "Communication

---

*In this chapter, the terms *family, families, family member,* and *family members* will be used interchangeably to refer to people who interact with and impact the learning and development of infants and toddlers in their home settings. These terms should be understood to include mother(s), father(s), legal guardian(s), grandparent(s), sibling(s), aunt(s), uncle(s), and so on. The term *parent* or *parents* is used to refer specifically to a mother and/or a father.

between parents and child care center staff is clearly integral to trust, yet it is complicated by differing communication styles and expectations, as well as by emotions" (Reedy & McGrath, 2010, p. 353). This chapter teaches you important communication skills such as rapport building, "I statements," and active listening. These skills will assist you in communicating successfully with other people in a sensitive and accepting style. Practicing these skills will help you listen to and understand others and be able to express yourself so that other people will understand and accept what you say.

7-1 Skills for Effective Communication

Figure 7–1 shows the general communication process. A *sender* (A) sends a message verbally and nonverbally to a *receiver* (B), who interprets the message and gives the sender feedback as to what the message means to the receiver.

7-1a Rapport Building

rapport An agreement between two people that establishes a sense of harmony.

calibrating Carefully observing the specific behaviors demonstrated by another during an interaction to build rapport.

pacing Matching complementary behavior to that of another person to build rapport.

Rapport is an agreement between two people that establishes a sense of harmony. This harmonious agreement with infants and toddlers has been discussed in previous chapters as interactional synchrony. When you learn to build rapport with an adult, just as you've done with an infant or toddler, you must follow the person's lead while you carefully observe his or her movements. Think of this as learning to dance well with another person. Rapport building involves two components: calibrating and pacing. **Calibrating** means carefully observing the specific steps, and **pacing** means carefully moving in harmonious synchrony. Three specific sets of behaviors must be calibrated and paced for you to build rapport and dance well with another person.

1. Posture. Align yourself in a complementary physical posture with the adult. If he is sitting, sit also. Change your posture to "dance" with the person face to face.

2. Nonverbal communication. Listen carefully to the tone of voice, tempo of speech, and intensity of the physical and emotional undertones of the gestures. What is the adult trying to tell you? Do the nonverbal communication strategies match the verbal ones?

3. Representational systems. This set of behaviors is hardest to learn to calibrate and pace because it includes all ways that the adult represents his or her beliefs, perceptions, and understanding of the world. These systems are culturally based, so it is imperative that you spend considerable time learning how culture influences communication for the families with whom you are working.

FIGURE 7–1 ▶ The Communication Process

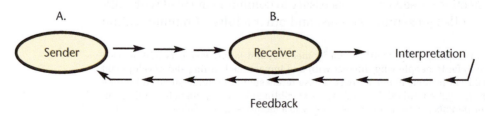

© Cengage Learning

7-1b I Statements versus You Statements

We also communicate to other people from the perspective of expressing our own thoughts and feelings through **I statements**, or giving advice or judgments about the other person by making **you statements**.

I statements usually start with the word *I* and express responsibility for our own perceptions without judging the other person. For example, "I am angry" is an I statement because it expresses a feeling without blaming another person. You statements are often disrespectful and tell the other person how he or she is thinking, feeling, or behaving. You statements often start with the word *You* and offer advice or an opinion about the other person. For example, "You make me angry" is a you statement because it offers an opinion about the other person (he or she is doing or saying something wrong), and it makes the other person responsible for the speaker's feeling (anger).

When you want the other person to feel accepted and understood, make I statements. I statements are respectful and take responsibility for the speaker's thoughts, feelings, and behaviors. You statements, on the other hand, offer opinions, advice, and judgments about the other person and often close off further communication.

We can also make disguised I and you statements. *Disguised you* statements sometimes sound like I statements and may even start with the word *I*, but they always end up judging or giving advice to the sender. For example, "I'm angry because you did that" is a disguised you statement because it blames and judges the other person.

Listen carefully so that you can provide feedback in response to the other sender's words. These responses can be *disguised I* statements when our feedback clearly takes responsibility for our own perceptions and map of the world. For example, if a person sends the message, "I can't stand Mary, she is always complaining," a good active listening response might be, "It sounds like Mary's complaining is making you feel angry." Notice that, although neither *I* nor *you* were used, the feedback takes responsibility for the receiver's perception by using the words "It sounds (to me) like…" without blaming or criticizing the sender. I statements keep communication open by giving nonjudgmental feedback, which allows the sender to confirm that the message was understood ("That's right, I really get angry with her") or correct the message ("Well, I don't really get angry, just a little annoyed"). While this form of communication might seem easy to use, it is not often a component of college students' active speech competence (Borodachyova, 2011). Therefore, you will need to practice this skill so that it becomes a natural component in your communication patterns.

7-1c Active Listening: The "How" in Communication

Most common communication errors can be avoided by applying a technique called **active listening**, which is "feeding back" the deeper feeling message (not the words) of the sender in the words of the receiver. This simple definition of active listening requires further explanation because, although it may sound simple, it takes practice to learn to give deeper feedback effectively.

I statements Expressions about one's own thoughts and feelings without judging the other person.

you statements Sentences that give advice to or judgment about another person, often closing off further communication.

active listening The skill required to simply "feed back" the deeper felt message (not words) of the sender in the words of the receiver.

Active listening differs from most common types of communication in the kind of feedback given to the sender. The two most common types of feedback are a *reaction* to the words in the message or a *defense* of your position. With either of these types of feedback, the communication process is closed off because we become emotionally involved in the words of the message. Common reactionary feedback messages include "How can you say that?" "You're wrong!" and "I don't think you meant what I heard." Defensive feedback might sounds like, "In my classroom, we all nap at the same time" or "Children should not need a pacifier when they are 3."

Active listening, on the other hand, involves objectively listening, in a nondefensive way, for the deeper message of the sender and then giving *reiterating* feedback. Rather than reacting to the words of the sender, the active listener interprets the entire message of the sender and gives it back to the sender. Because the active listener looks for the deeper message, most feedback starts with words such as "It sounds like...," "You seem to feel...," "I hear you saying...," and other phrases that reflect the sender's feelings. Beginning feedback in this manner allows the sender to affirm, reject, or clarify his message. By continuing to feed back the total message of the sender, the receiver can help the sender clarify the problem and, in most cases, arrive at his or her own solution.

An active listener also looks at body language. The look on a person's face, the position of the body, and what the person does with his or her hands and arms can help you understand the full message on the deepest level. Nonverbal behavior, as well as words, feelings, and attitudes, combine to transmit the complete, deep message.

Although active listening may sound simple enough to learn, it requires practice because most of us have learned to respond with reactionary and defensive feedback. Whiteman (2013) suggests that using positive communication strategies such as active listening, being empathetic, and choosing nonconfrontational language is especially important when discussing difficult topics with family members. These communication strategies can be learned well by teachers if practiced in classroom settings with family members and if given the opportunity to reflect on their effectiveness (Symeou, Roussounidou, & Michaelides, 2012). Therefore, with continued practice and analysis, you will find the rewards of active listening worth the effort it takes to master the technique. The following are some ways to analyze your communication with others:

1. Listen to the way you now respond to people. Did you react to the words of messages, or did you listen for the deeper meaning? Did you listen for the whole, deep message, including the words, feelings, attitudes, and behaviors?

2. Listen to the words you used in your response. Did you judge, criticize, or blame another?

3. Listen to the message you sent. Did you respond to the message with advice or personal feelings, or did you seek to understand completely what the other person thinks and feels?

4. Listen for when you have received the entire message. Did you add information to a message when you were ready, when the other person directly asked for it, or after that person had completely expressed

the entire message? You will know you have received the entire message when you hear real feelings and concern about what to do. At this point, questions such as "Have you thought about what you can do?" or "How would you solve this?" will give the person a chance to ask for advice or begin problem solving on his or her own.

Before moving on with your reading, make sure that you can answer the following questions about the material discussed so far.

1. What are the benefits of using effective communication skills and why?
2. Compare and contrast two of the communication skills discussed.

READING CHECKPOINT

7-2 Communications with Families

Teachers hold different beliefs about the responsibilities of those involved in the educational process. Korkmaz (2007) surveyed 148 teachers concerning their beliefs about the responsibilities teachers, parents, and schools have in facilitating learning. A theme running through the responses was the importance of communication for all involved parties. More specifically, she discovered that two-thirds of the teachers believed that parents should have good communication with teachers. They also thought that parents should be willing to participate in meetings held at school. When asked about the responsibilities of the school, 56 percent of the teachers expressed the importance of the school keeping parents informed about the progress of their child as well as the curriculum being implemented. Interestingly enough, only 44 percent of the teachers reported their responsibilities to "communicate clearly with students and have positive dialogue and interactions with them inside and outside the classroom... [listening] attentively to students' questions, comments, and views" (Korkmaz, 2007, p. 397). There were no examples provided of teachers saying that they held responsibility for communicating well with family members.

As you can see, this text deviates from those research results as it places particular emphasis on the decisive role teachers play in creating a positive context that supports open and ongoing communication with family members and children. Yet, our text does not differ from other research on "instructional communication competence" (Worley, Titsworth, Worley, & Cornett-DeVito, 2007) with award-winning teachers who explained and demonstrated that the use of active listening with students was extremely important to develop productive relationships. Our text also agrees with more recent research that found when parents and teachers shared positive perceptions of their relationship, parents participated in more communication with the school, and teachers held a more positive view of the child (Minke, Sheridan, Kim, Ryoo, & Koziol, 2014). Good teaching, at any level, relies on the skilled use of active listening to build positive relationships.

7-2a Using Active Listening with Families

Families tell you much information about their children and themselves when you have created a welcoming, supportive environment (Photo 7–1).

© 2017 Cengage Learning

PHOTO 7–1 Families will be more willing to share information about their children and themselves when caregivers create a welcoming environment.

Details about what the child does at home are needed by the caregiver each day. Ask open-ended questions, listen carefully to their responses, and record the information as soon as possible. In addition, using active listening helps caregivers understand families as they express their concerns and raise questions about parenting. Family members are often isolated from other support systems and need the caregiver to listen to them and help them come up with solutions. The next sections outline five situations in which active listening can be especially beneficial for families and caregivers.

Gathering Information

Families have a wealth of information about their children. For continuity between home and school, teachers need to know how the family typically responds to the child's needs. Many states require that licensed infant/toddler programs have families complete and regularly update questionnaires that ask about child characteristics, habits, and preferences, as well as family routines, goals, and expectations for the child. For example, knowing that Oliver has difficulty relaxing for a nap if he does not have his favorite blankie with him and his back patted will help the early childhood educator meet his body's needs for sleep.

While questionnaires are effective means for gathering information, going beyond the minimal requirements will help you form effective partnerships, meeting the guidelines for developmentally appropriate practice. Teachers should inquire regularly to gather observations of development that family members have noticed at home or other contexts. Use this information to provide a more complete picture of the child and her capabilities. Add those observations to yours, and then modify your understanding as necessary. Such conversations can occur informally during drop-off and pick-up and include other information about the child's experiences at home and school. This feedback helps caregivers maintain updated information that will shape their reactions to the child's behavior. When face-to-face interactions are not possible, home-school journals, mentioned in Chapter 5, are valuable tools for sharing and gathering information. This two-way communication strategy involves family members writing a few notes about the child's day(s) when at home, and then the caregiver responds with information about the child's experience while at the early childhood program. Of course, it is overly optimistic to think that caregivers and families will write in the journal every day. Yet those who do this on a regular basis develop a strong sense of partnership (Gandini, 2001).

Spotlight on Organization

CHILD CARE RESOURCE AND REFERRAL AGENCIES

The National Association of Child Care Resource and Referral Agencies (NACCRRA) is a professional organization that works with more than 700 state and local child care resource and referral agencies throughout the United States. These agencies help ensure that families have access to high-quality, affordable child care by providing information on what high-quality care looks like and how to locate such programs in their community, as well as by advocating for child care policies that positively impact the lives of children and families. The organization also supports professional educators by providing access to professional development opportunities to increase the quality of care.

A current focus for the organization is working with US military services to help personnel (e.g., service women and men) find high-quality, affordable child care that suits their unique needs.

For more information on this important organization, visit the NACCRRA website.

Sharing Information

Families need information about the daily experiences their child has in your care. Many tools are available (see Chapter 5) to help organize and record important things the child has done and share them with family members. Special experiences, such as the child's excitement about a visiting rabbit, may go into the written record, or the caregiver may tell a family member.

The child's rate and pattern of development should be shared with family members. Refer to the child's Developmental Milestones (see Appendix A) to focus on recent developments and identify developmental tasks the child may soon be mastering. When communicating effectively with family members, deliver this information without using professional jargon, slang, or fad expressions; any of these can lead to misunderstanding rather than a common understanding (Clements & Kuperberg, 2008). Moreover, learning key words in the family's native language can help reduce misunderstandings, build rapport, and minimize some barriers (Risko & Walker-Dalhouse, 2009). When we share common knowledge about the child and set goals together, then everyone can do things in her environment that support or enhance the child's development. However, when working with families, you should be clear in emphasizing the difference between facilitating and pushing the child. Families are often very interested in ideas for appropriate experiences and homemade toys (see Chapters 11–13; Herr & Swim, 2002).

When you communicate your observations with the family members, ask questions and use active listening when they share their observations as well. Mabel may have noticed that her 2-month-old child isn't distressed at all by being left at child care, and she wants more information relating to the effect of child care on young infants. Phyllis may be ready for information about separation anxiety because Branson is starting to show distress. Arlene may be interested in information to help her understand that Pearl's sharing Mommy with the new baby involves much more than practice in getting used to babies. Changing sleeping and eating patterns and toilet learning are other areas families frequently raise questions about. Of course, if your assessments reveal that a child is ahead of or behind age-expected levels, special emphasis should be placed on communicating with families. As discussed in previous chapters, deciding together when and how to proceed with involving other professionals is vital.

Families need information about the child care program. Before the child is admitted, the program director shares with families program goals, policies, descriptions of the daily program, and the practical use of Developmental Milestones. Many programs will include a developmental screening as part of the initial evaluation of the incoming child. This will help guide caregivers as they make their decisions about program implementation. Many situations occur that family members need to clarify and discuss with caregivers. For example, Sal wants his 23-month-old daughter Gabriele to stop using her fingers when she eats. The caregivers can help Sal by listening actively and, when it is appropriate, assuring him that eating with fingers is perfectly normal at this age but that you will continue to offer her utensils at every meal to support her development of fine motor control.

Expressing Feelings

Family members may want the caregiver to agree with them or reassure them, to confirm or reject ideas, and to respond to pressures from family and friends. For example, Lisha rushed in one morning with her son and said, "I called my mother last night and told her I went back to work this week. She had a fit. She said it was too soon and that right now my place was at home." Listen to Lisha's words and her tone of voice; read her nonverbal cues, her facial expressions, and degree of tenseness. She may be telling you that she is feeling frustrated and guilty, or she may be stating her mother's view while feeling fairly comfortable with her own choice of going back to work. You must listen to the whole message to interpret accurately what Lisha is telling you.

Caregiving undoubtedly involves feelings and emotions. Family members want to know that you are knowledgeable and concerned about their child and about them (Huber, 2003). In a variety of ways, let families know that you like and respect their child. Families look for caregivers who accept and like their child and who provide emotional security.

Determine how to share the child's new developments with family members. The first time you see children pulling themselves up on the table leg, teetering on two steps, holding utensils, riding a tricycle, turning book pages, hugging a friend, asking to go to the toilet, or catching a ball, you should be excited and pleased with their accomplishments. How might family members feel about missing the "big event"? Use your knowledge of each family to determine whether you report these experiences with elation or with caution. If the family wants to know all of the "firsts" exactly when they happen, then report your observations with enthusiasm. But, remember Lisha from earlier? Does she feel secure in returning to work, or does she feel uncomfortable? Many family members, especially mothers, feel guilty about needing or even wanting to return to work. They may feel that they are missing the most important moments of their children's lives. Sharing "firsts" with them would only serve to reinforce these feelings. When this situation arises, an alternative approach would be to alert families for behaviors to look for at home without explicitly stating that you saw the accomplishment first. Although some readers might interpret this as lying by omission, the news should be reframed so that you help family members see and share an important event for their child.

Uncovering Families' Expectations and Setting Goals

Actively listen to family members so that you will fully understand what care they expect you to provide. All families have expectations for their children; some will be explicitly stated, while others may not be fully articulated (Christian, 2006; Cheatham & Ostrosky, 2013).

Engage families in ongoing conversations to uncover these expectations and support them in achieving their goals. Listen to what a father is saying about the child and about his own needs. Some family members have very definite ideas and will tell you about them. One parent might say, "I want Velma to be happy. It bothers me to see her cry when I leave." Others do not say anything until they disagree with something, and then they may express frustration or be angry with you. Another mother may tell you, "I told you I want Pearl to get used to babies because my baby is due next month. Please do not start transitioning her to the preschool room yet." If this happens, use active listening to account for the family members' emotions as well as the words they say to you.

Not all families will have realistic or developmentally appropriate expectations for their child. Some families, especially first-time parents, set goals that are too high, while other families set their expectations too low. Either case can lead to poor child outcomes. It is your responsibility as a professional early childhood educator to work with them to realign their expectations. The communication skills discussed earlier are very important in these situations. You want to establish rapport as well as use active listening and I statements. When asked your opinion, you can be ready to guide them toward more developmentally appropriate expectations. This approach reflects the guidelines for establishing reciprocal relationships with families, especially that parents' choices and goals are responded to with sensitivity and respect without abdicating professional responsibility (Copple & Bredekamp, 2009).

Work together with family members to create goals that are acceptable to both of you. Sometimes that means taking baby steps toward meeting your personal goals for the child. In an educational context, that is far more acceptable than ignoring the family members' goals. Expect to devote considerable time in negotiating the goals that you will work toward together. Partnering means working until a common ground is found. This should be a win-win situation, not a hostile takeover of the families' goals in favor of your own or vice versa (see, e.g., Gonzalez-Mena, 2001).

Unfortunately, recent research found that for one sample of Head Start teachers' goal-setting practices during parent-teacher conferences did not reflect either a partnership or a negotiation. Rather, Cheatham and Ostrosky (2013) discovered that the teachers' practices tended to disallow parents' priorities and expertise regarding their children's educational planning. Native Spanish-speaking parents were particularly silenced. However, it is possible that cultural differences in understanding the role of teachers in setting educational goals or the lack of understanding of the need for educational goals might play a role for some families (Cheatham & Ostrosky, 2013). In any case, early childhood educators must adopt strategies that accommodate for parent-educator cultural and linguistic differences and result in each family member being involved in goal setting. This is particularly important during the infant-toddler period given that children grow and change rapidly; caregivers should expect to engage in goal setting and other such negotiations two to three times a year.

Sharing Expectations

After working to uncover the families' expectations and create goals together, explain what those goals might look like in practice. Your casual statements may take on more meaning than formal, written goal statements. When explaining how to encourage a toddler's independence, you might say: "We want to help children become as independent as they can, so when Louella resists my helping her take off her bib, I will let her try to take it off by herself. If she gets stuck, I will help her lift one arm out, and then encourage her to do the rest by herself."

Families are interested in what you expect of yourself as a caregiver. What kinds of things do you do? How committed are you? How friendly are you? Do you think you are more important than they are? Do you extend and supplement the roles of families, or do you expect to supplant them? You communicate these expectations through your words, attitudes, mannerisms, and interactions with children and family members.

What do you expect of the children in your care? A child care program using a developmental perspective emphasizes the development of the whole child and of individuality among children. Assure families that development does not follow a rigid schedule and is not identical among children. Adults often compare their child's development with another child's and gloat or fret at what they see. Caregivers who show that they believe children behave differently within a broad range of normal activity communicate to families that adults can challenge children without putting harmful pressure on them.

Caregivers expect many things of family members. Some expectations you may express; others you should keep to yourself. You might expect them to do the following:

- Love and like their child
- Want to hear about special occurrences in their child's day
- Want to learn more about their developing child
- Be observant of the child's health or illness
- Be willing to share information about the child with you
- Use respect as a basis for forming relationships

Some families will not meet your expectations. Because caregiving occurs in the family as well as in the child care program, you will need to resolve your differences with important people in the child's life. In some cases, you may need to change your expectations of family members. We speak of accepting children as they are, so we need to take the same attitude toward family members. They come to the child care program because they need love and care for their child outside the home. While they often need and want additional information about parenting and a sense of community, they usually are not looking for situations that place additional demands and expectations on them as parents (Mantovani, 2001). Creating systems to serve families and build a stronger community is an important advocacy function that early childhood programs can easily provide (Galardini & Giovannini, 2001). Information to help family members grow can be given when requested but not offered indiscriminately or forced upon them. You may increase your awareness of the unique situation each family faces simply by actively listening to them without making judgments.

7-2b Partnering with Families

Teachers should be intentionally inviting so that strong, positive relationships are created with and among families. These partnerships exist to facilitate the well-being of children and families.

In Decision-Making

Some programs involve family members in decision-making. Many not-for-profit child care centers have policy boards that include family representatives. These boards may make recommendations and decisions about center policy. Sometimes family members even serve on boards that make administrative decisions about hiring and firing staff and selecting curricula. However, few family child care homes and for-profit child care centers involve families in decision-making about policy, staff, or curricula.

Families of infants and toddlers must be involved in some decisions relating to their child's care. The family or pediatrician selects the infant's milk or formula; the caregiver does not make that decision. Families and caregivers must share information about the child's eating and sleeping schedules. The length of time from afternoon pick-up to mealtime and to bedtime varies among families. Because late afternoon naps or snacks may improve or disrupt evening family time, early childhood educators should set aside time to discuss what schedule is best for the child and family. Toilet learning must be coordinated between families and caregivers. Both parties share information about the appropriateness of timing, the failures and successes of the child, and the decision to discontinue or continue toilet learning.

About Children

Most adult family members of infants and toddlers in child care are employed. Therefore, family involvement during the child care day is often limited to arrival and pick-up time. They can help the child take off a coat or unpack supplies when leaving the child in the morning, and they can share with the caregiver information about the child's night, health, or special experiences. At pick-up time, the caregiver initiates conversations about the child's experiences and projects during the day, while the family member helps the infant or toddler make the transition back to home life by hugging the child or helping to put on outdoor clothes. Sharing written notes and photographs taken of work that occurred during the day is always a good way to start conversations.

7-2c Family Education

Some programs intentionally have a parent education component as part of their mission. Including parent education often reflects the goal of building strong partnerships between families and caregivers so that optimal child growth and learning results. These programs set aside time on a regular basis to provide information directly to groups of families. The focus of such meetings should be based on parental recommendations so that it is personalized. To ascertain that information, programs can conduct a survey that asks parents about parenting topics they would like more information on. The survey can also ask them how they might like that content delivered (e.g., guest speakers, videos, facilitated discussions). You may discover, for example, that half of the families in the infant and toddler rooms want more information on choosing and creating safe, developmentally appropriate, and growth-producing environments for their children, while the preschool families want to learn more about appropriately supporting emergent literacy skills. The director, advisory board, or teams of teachers should decide how to disseminate the information to the families, given stated preferences. Keep in mind that information should be delivered by someone the families trust and whose competence and experience will meaningfully affect the decisions they make. The decision about how to communicate this information should also reflect how adults learn. Making resources available that they can read, listen to, view, and/or discuss will help them further construct their ideas about the care and education of very young children. As part of this education, they may also want a designated time and place to discuss ongoing concerns, such as balancing work and family commitments, with other families with similarly aged children. Having a monthly coffee klatch might be just the thing for the parents in your program.

It is not unreasonable to expect that such parental educational efforts might raise the family members' awareness of related state and national concerns. How might their problem solving on the local level help others solve the related larger-scale problem? Informing families of whom to communicate with at local, regional, and national levels to share their solutions or lobby for other solutions will empower them and can benefit everyone involved in early childhood education.

If the program does not have parent education as part of the stated mission, then it should be offered individually to parents who express interest in wanting specific information. Avoid providing parenting advice if not asked. That can be seen as intrusive and disrespectful. However, including brief articles on child development in your newsletter is a nonintrusive way to inform parents about issues that might relate to their child's care and education.

7-2d Supporting Relationships between Families

As will be discussed later in this chapter, many families face stressful situations. One way to help alleviate stress is to create ways for families to get to know one another and build relationships among themselves. For example, you can plan events for families at the end of the day or on the weekends. These events need not be elaborate; in fact, meeting at a nearby park for a play date and picnic can be enjoyable for children and families. Similar to building relationships between teachers and families, families should be encouraged to engage with each other in formal and informal situations.

Programs can also help families provide support for each other by redefining individual "problems" as opportunities for community problem solving. For example, when a family has unreliable transportation, how can other families help them get to a well-baby doctor appointment? Or, how can families share babysitting assistance so that each family gets a mental and physical break from the stresses of caring for very young children?

7-2e Family-Caregiver Conferences

When a primary caregiving system is used in conjunction with regular conferences, the teacher is able to be a well-informed advocate for each child in her care. Having specific knowledge about a child that can be shared with family members strengthens relationships between teachers and families (Huber, 2003).

It is important that **family-caregiver conferences** have structure and occur at least twice per year. Preparing and sharing in advance an agenda and checklist, being a good listener, and keeping confidences are some of the important factors to consider when planning a conference. As you would treat children differently based on their individual characteristics, the same approach is vital when conducting a family-caregiver conference. Varying communication strategies for your audience, assisting intercultural communication by having translators available, avoiding specialized terminology, and following agendas in a flexible manner can prevent miscommunications and build rapport with families (Garcia-Sanchez, Orellana, & Hopkins, 2011; Howard & Lipinoga, 2010).

Busy families often have difficulty scheduling formal conferences. To make the most efficient use of time, plan what will be discussed. Identify the major purpose of the conference. Gather background information to discuss the topic. Caregiver records of observations, both formal and informal, should be consulted. Outside sources such as articles, books, pamphlets, tapes, and videos may provide information for the caregiver and can be shared with the family members. You may also need information on community agencies or organizations in your region.

Providing an agenda, checklist, and feedback sheet at least three days in advance helps to prepare everyone involved in the meeting. This will give them time to look over what you want to accomplish and to understand their active role in the conference. A sample agenda for a teacher-initiated conference might resemble the following:

1. Welcome

2. How do you see _____ (Rodney) _____ developing at home?

3. Do you have any questions or concerns about his development?

4. Review checklist sent home to discuss what behaviors and skills have been noticed at school.

family-caregiver conferences Periodic meetings between family members and caregiver to review documentation and interpretation of each child's developmental progress as well as to create plans for supporting development in the future.

5. What developmental and learning goals should we set for _____ (Rodney) _____?

   a. Discuss: family's goals.

   b. Discuss: teachers' goals.

   c. Create list of our goals together.

6. Brainstorm: How can we work on these goals together?

7. Do you have any feedback to share about the program or our (family-teacher and teacher-child) relationships?

The format of this agenda highlights many important aspects of good conferences. First, a conference starts with engaging the family members in reporting their observations and evaluations of the child. Then, the teacher shares some of her observations. In this way, two-way communication is used as an essential tool for developing a positive family-caregiver relationship as everyone should feel free to bring up concerns, problems, or issues, as well as joys, accomplishments, and strengths of the child (Markström, 2011). Step 4 serves the purpose of interpreting with family members each child's progress from a developmental approach to help them understand and appreciate developmentally appropriate early childhood programs (Markström, 2011; NAEYC, 2011a). The most important part of the conference is the negotiation of developmental and learning goals. Allow plenty of time to engage in this aspect of the conference because it typically has a large influence on whether or not the family members feel that the teacher has listened to them.

Sometimes situations warrant a conference outside of the "normal, twice-a-year" conferences. If the teacher requests the conference, tell the family members why and provide some observations to give them time to think about the concern beforehand. If a family member requests a meeting, ask what concerns need to be discussed so you can prepare ahead of time. Provide them with a sample agenda and ask them to modify it for their needs. In any case, the goal is the same as a regularly scheduled conference: to support listening of family members and work together to find solutions to the issues being raised. A sample agenda might include the following:

1. Welcome and thank you for calling this meeting.

2. What are your concerns? (*Then, be sure to listen actively.*)

3. Respond with information or observations if it is appropriate and helpful to the discussion.

4. How can we deal with these concerns?

5. Create a plan of action together.

6. Set up a follow-up meeting to monitor progress.

While conducting any conference, it is vital that you minimize power differences between you and family members. One way to do so is to arrange the physical environment so that all adults are sitting next to one another with no barriers. Placing chairs in a circle with no desk or table between you accomplishes this. Physical comfort should also be considered. Early childhood educators are accustomed to sitting in child-size chairs on a regular basis. However, family members rarely are. Providing adult-size chairs can help everyone feel more at ease and be physically comfortable. Having water, coffee, or juice, and a box of tissues nearby may also add to everyone's comfort.

7-2f Home Visits

Home visits are a regular part of Early Head Start and Head Start programs as well as many different early intervention programs, but other child care programs seldom make them. Home visits can be valuable opportunities for the family and the caregiver to learn more about each other; family members have reported that home visits are valuable because they afford personal time for asking questions and sharing concerns (Quintanar & Warren, 2008). Research on a Head Start program found that collaborative goal setting was associated with greater participation in the home visiting portion of the program (Manz, Lehtinen, & Bracaliello, 2013). This means that well-planned family-caregiver conferences impact the family members' engagement with other program aspects. Teachers also use home visits to learn more about how the family members and child relate to each other in their own home. To maximize the benefits of each home visit, teachers must plan them carefully to respect the family's time and space.

> **home visits** A meeting in the child's home providing an opportunity for the caregiver to see how the family members and child relate to each other in the home setting.

1. Identify and discuss with the family members the purpose for the visit: To get acquainted? To gather information? To work with the parents, child, or both?

2. Negotiate a time that is convenient for all family members and yourself. It can often be helpful to have a couple of dates in mind when you call to schedule the home visit.

3. Gather background information the visit requires. Do you need to take along any forms to be filled out? Will you be sharing your program goals? If so, do you have a flyer or pamphlet, or will you just tell them? Are there specific problems or concerns you want to discuss? Do you have written documentation of the child's behavior to share, such as daily reports or notes, or resource and referral information?

4. Conduct the home visit as you would a family-teacher conference. For example, ask questions to elicit information from family members, work together to create solutions for any issues of concern, and ask for feedback.

When you make a home visit, you are a guest in the family's home. You are there to listen and learn. While you want to be friendly, this is not a social call; families have busy lives, and you do too. Therefore, when you have finished talking about the issues, thank them for their interest, time, and hospitality, and then leave.

Before moving on with your reading, make sure that you can answer the following questions about the material discussed so far.

1. Why is effective communication with families important?
2. Write an agenda for a family-teacher conference initiated by you to discuss a child's toilet learning.

READING CHECKPOINT

7-3 Family Situations Requiring Additional Support

This section discusses four types of families that may need additional support from early childhood educators: grandparents as parents, families who have children who are at risk for later difficulties, families where abuse or neglect is present, and teenage parents. For all of these families, it is imperative that you use the positive communication skills discussed earlier.

7-3a Grandparents as Parents

Statistics indicate that grandparents are taking care of children more than ever before. According to the Children's Defense Fund, more than 2.9 million grandparents are responsible for raising their own grandchildren; almost 1 million of those grandparents do it without the child's parent present in the home (Children's Defense Fund, 2014). Of these grandparent-headed homes, 67 percent of the head-of-households were under the age of 60, and one in five of the families (20 percent) live in poverty (AARP, 2015).

You should extend a special invitation to grandparents who are now facing the challenge of raising grandchildren as primary caregivers because outcomes associated with this family situation are not always obvious. According to a study by Harnett, Dawe, and Russell (2014), grandparents reported higher levels of personal distress in the caring role and significantly less emotional and practical support than they would like. They are often balancing the demands of working full time and the pressures of being impoverished with being in the role of primary caregiver. All of these factors increase the grandparents' stress. They need encouragement, support, and someone to confide in. AARP has created fact sheets that provide important data regarding the prevalence of grandparent-headed households in each state as well as lists of useful resources. These fact sheets are free and easy to download, print, and share with families as they might need them.

7-3b At-Risk Families and Children

Children can be *at risk* for a number of reasons, including genetic or chromosomal disorders and environmentally produced problems (see Chapter 10 for more information). Significant contributors to being at risk are living in poverty, having one or more caregivers who have low levels of education, having parents with mental health issues (Beeber, Schwartz, Martinez, Holditch-Davis, Bledsoe, Canuso, et al., 2014; Simeonova, Attalla, Nguyen, Stagnaro, Knight, Craighead, et al., 2014), experiencing malnutrition or being undernourished, and lacking positive environmental stimulation (for reviews, see Duncan & Brooks-Gunn, 1997; Shonkoff & Phillips, 2000). Many families, especially single-parent households, struggle financially to meet the basic needs of their infants and toddlers, so they, rightfully, focus their attention on survival rather than on strategies for promoting optimal development and learning. Families who are poverty-stricken care deeply for their children. They may work two or

Family and Community Connections

When conducting a home visit with Valerie's family, you learned that she lives in a home with her mother, father, sister, paternal grandmother, and maternal aunt. You learned that Valerie's grandmother will be dropping her off and picking her up two days a week. Other days will be shared between her mother, father, and aunt, depending on work schedules. How would you help Valerie's family members create a consistent routine for pick-up and drop-off to minimize stress for Valerie?

three jobs to provide shelter, food, and clothing, and, even then, those may not be completely adequate.

Supporting families in these situations involve not only listening actively but also having contact information for community resources readily available (Photo 7–2). Including these resources regularly as part of your communication with families (e.g., in a section of your newsletter) is relatively simple for you but can have a significant impact on them. Knowing when and where to receive free immunizations, for example, can be key to promoting the physical well-being of infants and toddlers. In addition, providing strategies for interacting with the child during the car or bus ride home can facilitate the development of language and cognition skills and has the advantage of being free (Herr & Swim, 2002).

Families Experiencing Child Abuse or Neglect

Child abuse and neglect, while often closely linked in discussions, are two distinct constructs. Abuse is an action that causes harm to another and comes in three forms: physical, sexual, and emotional/psychological.

© 2017 Cengage Learning

PHOTO 7–2 Early childhood educators can provide support and information to families in at-risk situations.

Spotlight on Research

PROLONGED SEPARATIONS FOR YOUNG CHILDREN: PARENTAL INCARCERATION AND MILITARY DEPLOYMENT

In 2009, the Bureau of Justice Statistics reported that more than 800,000 prisoners or 53 percent of those being held in US prisons were parents of children under the age of 18, a rate which represents a 113 percent increase for mothers since 1991 (Glaze & Maruschak, 2009). Mothers in state prisons reported that 18 percent of the children were 4 years old or younger, while that percentage was 14 percent for those in federal prisons (Glaze & Maruschak, 2009).

Hundreds of thousands of US troops and reservists have been deployed around the world in the "Global War on Terrorism." Approximately 1.2 million children live in US military families (Kelly, 2003), and at least 700,000 of them have had at least one parent deployed (Johnson et al., 2007, both cited in Lincoln, Swift, & Shorteno-Fraser, 2008). In addition, approximately 6 percent of active duty and 8 percent of Reserve and National Guard military personnel are single parents (Yeary, 2007). Thus, young children whose parents are incarcerated or in the military often experience serious, prolonged separations and disruptions in their lives.

Recent research reveals that increased rates of mental health, behavioral, and stress problems were found in children during parental deployment (Gorman, Eide, & Hisle-Gorman, 2010). The most frequently reported manifestation of distress among young children is night waking (Lieberman & Van Horn, 2013). In addition, separation anxiety is heightened for some children by the fear of losing their other parent (Lieberman & Van Horn, 2013). In general, however, the literature reveals mediated results when measuring the impact of having a prolonged separation due to incarceration or military deployment on child outcomes such as social, emotional, and intellectual development. For example, children who already had a secure attachment to their incarcerated mother and received more stable continuous care in her absence were able to create secure emotional attachments with another adult (Poehlmann, 2005a). This strong, new relationship seemed to provide a protective factor against negative developmental outcomes.

Similarly, infants and toddlers who experienced separation due to military deployment tended to respond to the remaining parent's or caregiver's reaction (Lincoln et al., 2008). In other words, when the caregiver expressed high levels of sadness or anxiety,

infants were more likely to be irritable or unresponsive, and toddlers were more likely to experience sleep disruption or increased periods of crying. In contrast, when the child had a positive relationship with the parent at home, higher levels of psychological well-being were noted (Lincoln et al., 2008). When military families with children younger than 6 years of age created a plan for maintaining the father–child relationship during the deployment, they experienced less parenting stress after the deployment than did those families who did not create a plan (Louie & Cromer, 2014).

Another study also underscored the impact of the current family environment on mediating intellectual outcomes for children of incarcerated mothers. Poehlmann (2005b) discovered that the children's intellectual outcomes were compromised by their high-risk status at multiple contextual levels and that their intellectual outcomes were also mediated by the quality of their current family environment. In other words, even if a child experienced several risk factors, if she was being currently cared for in a positive, supportive environment, she was more likely to have better intellectual outcomes.

Some children appear to be more vulnerable before the separation and demonstrate this continued vulnerability during it. For example, children with disorganized attachments (see Chapter 3) were more likely to continue the pattern of disorganization during their mothers' incarceration, which placed them at further risk for social and emotional difficulties (Dallaire, 2007). Likewise, children who had a history of needing psychological counseling were more likely to need it again during the deployment of a parent (Lincoln et al., 2008).

As just discussed, separation from family members can be very stressful because the loss is felt deeply. However, research found that reuniting with family members after a deployment can be equally stressful as new roles and responsibilities have been negotiated and assumed in the parent's absence (Faber, Willerton, Clymer, MacDermid, & Weiss, 2008; Willerton, Schwarz, MacDermid, Wadsworth, & Oglesby, 2011; Williams & Rose, 2007). Similarly, parents who were once incarcerated have to rebuild a relationship with their child and assume their parental responsibilities. As this can be an overwhelming task, researchers have become interested in determining whether programs can be developed to assist incarcerated mothers with

(continued)

Spotlight on Research (*continued*)

being better parents after they are released. According to the Bureau of Justice Statistics, "Mothers (27 percent) were about two and a half times more likely than fathers (11 percent) to attend parenting or childrearing classes" (Glaze & Maruschak, 2009, p. 9). Participation in postsecondary education programs while in prison was correlated with participation in parenting classes and child visits (Rose & Rose, 2014). A recent review of literature on parent education and child-visitation programs for incarcerated parents demonstrated positive changes for mothers who participated (Bruns, 2006). It appears that family bonds may be particularly important for mothers as they work to better themselves as parents and employees.

As educators, we must assume a supportive role for family members and children when they experience a prolonged separation. In this situation, using the positive communication techniques described previously is vital to determining how to talk with young children. The children will experience a period of sadness (Poehlmann, 2005a) that should be discussed openly, honestly, and sensitively. Yet, you must collaborate with the family members to know what words to use during the conversations. Specific activities can be planned at school and home to encourage open communication such as drawing or reading picture books on the topic. Activities that engage children and family members together can help ease the burden for everyone (Guzman, 2014). Moreover, technology can greatly improve parent-child relationships during this time by having parents record their reading of children's books for the child to enjoy later, or the use of various social platforms can help maintain the parent-child connection (Yeary, Zoll, & Reschke, 2012).

Neglect is failing to provide for the basic needs or affection of a child or not adequately supervising children's activities (McDevitt & Ormrod, 2013). According to the Children's Defense Fund (2014), 1,825 children are confirmed abused or neglected each day. Abuse and neglect can and do occur in families of any racial and ethnic background, socioeconomic status, and community. Several factors are significantly associated with increased risk of child abuse for children under 5: race (White), inadequate housing, receiving public assistance (Palusci, 2011), maternal depression and substance abuse, as well as domestic violence (Azzi-Lessing, 2013). As mentioned in Chapter 2, infants under the age of 1 are at greatest risk of injury from shaking, a severe type of abuse. Early childhood educators are often the child's first line of defense for preventing and identifying abuse and neglect (Photo 7–3).

Continually communicating about and modeling strategies for implementing the three *As* can foster family members' thinking about capabilities and appropriate expectations for children from birth to age 3. Oftentimes, children are abused because family members do not know what is reasonable to expect of children at a certain age (McElroy & Rodriguez, 2008). For example, not knowing that it is unreasonable to expect a toddler to sit quietly in a restaurant and not interrupt the after-dinner conversation can result in stress and anger for the adult and abuse for the child. In addition, understanding that infants cry to communicate needs and that crying can oftentimes be frequent or of long duration can help parents to cope in those situations. Participation in Early Head Start has been found to be effective in reducing incidents of physical and sexual abuse when the

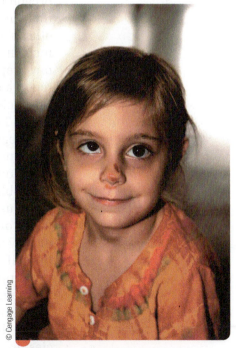

PHOTO 7–3 Early childhood educators are often the first line of defense for preventing and identifying abuse and neglect.

© Cengage Learning

children were 5–9 years of age (Green, Ayoub, Bartlett, Von Ende, Furrer, Chazan-Cohen, et al., 2014). It is possible that Early Head Start provides such powerful protections for young children because of the strong parent education component; parents are provided information to help them understand patterns of typical development.

Identifying children who are being abused or neglected is part of your professional and ethical responsibilities. Use your observation skills to inspect the child's body during routine care times to notice physical or sexual abuse. For example, while diapering, look at the child's arms, body, and legs. Any suspicious marking should cause you to inquire politely and discreetly of family members as to how the marks occurred. Immediately after your conversation, write down in the child's file exactly what you asked and what you were told. The use of descriptive language (see Chapter 5) cannot be overemphasized in this situation. Interpretative language will make the record of little use to other professionals who may need to investigate the case. Reread your entry and reflect on the conversation. Ask yourself: Does this seem like a reasonable event to have happened to a child of this age and mobility? If your answer is yes, then do nothing. However, if your answer is no, you need to involve the appropriate authorities.

Each early childhood program should have a written policy on how to handle suspected cases of child abuse that follows all state laws. In some states, it is proper procedure for a teacher to inform the program director or staff social worker of the situation and then that person is the one to report the incident to the appropriate community agency. This policy is often set in place to protect the teacher-family relationship. However, it is not the program director's or staff social worker's job to decide whether or not the incident needs reporting. If it is reported to them, they must report it. In other states, the person suspecting the abuse must be the one to report the incident. Thus, if you believe that an incident should be reported, then you must report it to protect you from being accused of neglect (i.e., failure to report a crime).

Deciding whether or not to report an incident can be emotionally difficult. The ethical dilemma stems from the fact that you are responsible for safeguarding the health and well-being of the children *and* maintaining relationships with families (NAEYC, 2011b). To ease your mind, the determination of whether intentional abuse has occurred has nothing to do with your obligation under the law to report it. Your responsibility is to report your suspicions. Therefore, you are not to launch a full investigation to verify or disprove your suspicions; this is the responsibility of the community agency. If you report an incident in good faith, you are not legally liable if it is not substantiated by other professionals.

Supporting families who are experiencing abuse or neglect is essential for them to acquire more positive ways of interacting and meeting each other's needs. Reporting child abuse to the appropriate community agency can be the first step in intervention. Contrary to popular belief, these agencies do all they can to assist parents in making good parenting choices. Linking families to other community resources, such as support groups or agencies that can provide education, is a way to facilitate the acquisition of positive parenting strategies.

7-3c Teenage Parents

According to the Annie E. Casey Foundation (2014), the teenage birth rate in 2012 was 29 births per 1,000 women aged 15–19. This figure represents a 40 percent decrease from the 2005 rate. While the occurrence of US teenage pregnancy is still the highest among economically advantaged nations, this figure continues to represent a record low birth rate for US teens (Annie E. Casey Foundation, 2014). See Table 7–1 for information on the states with the highest and lowest rates of teenage pregnancies.

The consequences of teenage pregnancy can be severe for both the teens and the infants. Teenage mothers are more likely to drop out of school and live in poverty, as evidenced by the fact that nearly 80 percent of teen mothers receive public assistance, while teen fathers are more likely to engage in delinquent behaviors such as alcohol abuse or drug dealing (Planned Parenthood Federation of America, 2014). Both teen mothers and teen fathers complete fewer years of schooling than their childless peers (Planned Parenthood Federation of America, 2014). Thus, the results of teenage pregnancy should be seen for what they are: a consequence for society through the perpetuation of the increasing inequalities in health and social opportunities (Paranjothy, 2009).

Researchers have long been interested in public norms about nonmarital pregnancy. When surveyed, teenagers reported levels of embarrassment that were stronger than those of adults (Mollborn, 2009). In addition, for teens, perceived levels of embarrassment predicted their reports of possible sanctions in their family through the withholding of needed material resources (Mollborn, 2009). Although this research study used hypothetical situations to assess embarrassment and sanctions, it is reasonable to assume that such outcomes are realistic for many teens.

The stress of limited financial resources coupled with a lack of life experiences can impact a teen parent's ability to interact with his or her

TABLE 7–1 ▶ Teen Pregnancy Rates (Number) in 2012*

HIGHEST NUMBER OF TEENAGE PREGNANCIES			
NUMBER			**NUMBER**
15–17 year olds		18–19 year olds	
Texas	12,938	Texas	27,513
California	10,345	California	24,545
Florida	4,221	Florida	11,731
Illinois	3,562	New York	9,081
Ohio	3,006	Ohio	8,431
LOWEST NUMBER OF TEENAGE PREGNANCIES			
Vermont	85	Vermont	276
Wyoming	141	North Dakota	454
North Dakota	149	New Hampshire	469
Maine	172	Wyoming	481
Alaska	182	District of Columbia	552

*Most recent year available.
Source: The Annie E. Casey Foundation, KIDS COUNT Data Center, http://datacenter.kidscount.org. Reprinted with permission.

infant or toddler. As any family member knows, raising children can be trying and very difficult even under the best of circumstances. Possessing sound coping mechanisms and the ability to make informed decisions is vital. These skills develop over time with life experiences and emotional maturity. Thus, parenting can be very challenging for teen parents, especially those who do not have family support. Add to this the necessity to set aside dreams and aspirations and place a baby's needs before their own, and it is no wonder that a large majority of teenage parents have emotional conflicts that decrease their ability to provide good parenting.

The role of the early childhood educator cannot be underestimated in these situations. Teenage parents (both mothers and fathers) need you to encourage their positive parenting abilities and acknowledge their efforts, successes, and challenges. This requires you to set aside additional time to empathize with and actively listen to the teen parent. In addition, providing contact information for community services (e.g., parenting courses, financial management, and social service agencies) as part of your regular communication with families can be invaluable for both the teen parents and their offspring.

Teenage parents need vital information, support, and role models that teach, through example, the daily competent care of infants and toddlers. This modeling should include the conscious application of attention, approval, and attunement in addition to the mechanics of care. A competent child care professional will help the teenage parents develop by appropriately extending positive attention, approval, and attunement to them. Teenage parents are not yet adults and need to be accepted, not judged or labeled, for who they are as individuals.

READING CHECKPOINT

Before moving on with your reading, make sure that you can answer the following questions about the material discussed so far.

1. List two family situations that would require extra support from you. What can you do to minimize stress for a family in those situations?
2. Regarding your answer to question 1, explain why many of these situations raise ethical dilemmas for educators.

7-4 Communicating with Colleagues

When a child care program has more than one staff member, effective communication among staff is essential. Arranging to meet with staff members regularly enhances communication. Although family child care providers often work alone in their own homes, they can contact licensing staff and other family child care providers for support. Group family child care arrangements employ at least two people who work with a larger group of children in the home. Child care centers usually have a staff that includes a director and one or more caregivers. The size of enrollment determines the number and kind of additional staff; these may be caregivers, cooks, custodians, bus drivers, early childhood educators, social workers, and health personnel. No matter if the staff is 2 or 22, regular, uninterrupted time to communicate, solve problems, and make decisions is necessary.

Similar to your relationship with children and family members, each caregiver needs to be a listener to fellow staff members. Staff can exchange information and discuss program issues in a reasonable way only if all are active listeners. How you listen to one another reflects how you respect one another.

7-4a Collaborating with Colleagues

Share Information and Areas of Expertise

Your educational and professional experiences give you information, insights, and perspectives that will help others understand issues and deal with problems. Each person has special talents and unique insights to share with colleagues, children, and families. Nobody appreciates know-it-alls, but we all benefit from people who are willing to share ideas that can be discussed, accepted, modified, or rejected.

Share Feelings and Solve Problems

As a part of a team, everyone benefits from sharing pleasurable experiences and tactfully expressing frustrations, disappointments, and anger (Photo 7–4). Keeping negative feelings bottled up can harm the entire program because it impacts the ability to meet program goals. Determine what is distressing you and discuss the issue. Using I statements and active listening strategies can help you focus on how to solve the problem at hand. You will be more likely to clear up misunderstandings and misperceptions if you focus your discussion on issues rather than on personalities.

Share Feedback

Both informal and formal observations provide you with feedback to share with your colleagues. Noting how other caregivers behave with people and materials in various settings, schedules, and routines can help the entire staff evaluate the current program and make necessary adjustments. Feedback can highlight caregiver actions that are helpful and effective, but you should use tact when commenting on a situation in which you believe your colleagues might act differently. Focus on what is best for the children and what changes can improve the situation, not on what a caregiver did wrong. Actions are more often *inappropriate* than wrong. Because all caregivers are developing their skills, comments that make colleagues feel incompetent are not helpful; however, focusing on appropriate alternative actions is productive.

PHOTO 7–4 Early childhood educators benefit from sharing both pleasant and challenging experiences with each other.

Share Responsibilities

Your colleagues will notice whether you are willing to carry your load. Not all of your responsibilities are explicit in your job description. Martha is responsible for getting snacks ready, but today she is rocking Natalie, who after crying and fussing has finally settled down but does not seem quite ready to be put

© 2017 Cengage Learning

PHOTO 7–5 Sharing ideas and assisting a colleague when help is needed helps to reduce stress.

down to play. If another caregiver volunteers to set up snacks, Natalie will not become distressed again and so will not disturb the other children.

7-4b Supporting Colleagues

Caregiving is physically and emotionally draining. Remember to put into practice the three *A*s of caregiving presented in Chapter 4 to help yourself and your colleagues cope with stress. For example, assisting a colleague when extra help is needed reduces stress. You can provide positive emotional support by listening, using honest compliments, giving credit, and reassuring colleagues about ideas or actions of theirs that you think are appropriate. Knowing that you are working together rather than against each other is in itself powerful emotional support (Photo 7–5).

7-4c Making Decisions

Early childhood educators need information to make intelligent program and curriculum decisions. Meet with other staff members regularly. Study issues and learn to identify relevant factors so that you will be able to discuss subjects intelligently and make wise decisions. Raise questions with colleagues; listen, think, and take an active part in making decisions related to delivering professional care and education for very young children.

READING CHECKPOINT

Before moving on with your reading, make sure that you can answer the following questions about the material discussed so far.

1. Why is effective communication with colleagues important?
2. How can you contribute to effective, positive staff relationships?

Summary

7-1 Understand the active listening process and other skills for effective communication.

Early childhood educators are responsible for interacting positively with family members and colleagues. I statements and active listening are just two strategies to master to help maximize understanding and build strong relationships.

7-2 Develop procedures for informal and formal communication with families.

Developing reciprocal relationships with families is one of the five aspects of developmentally appropriate practices. Teachers build such relationships by actively engaging family members in sharing information, setting goals, and involving them in decisions that impact their child. Communication should occur during informal meetings (e.g., drop-off time) and formal meetings (e.g., family-caregiver conferences or home visits).

7-3 Describe specific family situations that might require additional support.

Many factors such as grandparents raising grandchildren, prolonged separations, child abuse, and teenage pregnancy provide challenges to families. Learn how each family is responding to the situation and, if invited, provide information on community resources.

7-4 Analyze your own skills when communicating with colleagues.

Learning to work with colleagues as a member of a team can alleviate some negative outcomes and stress for teachers, families, and, most importantly, the children.

CASE STUDY   Angelica's Medical Needs

Angelica, just over 2 years of age, is relatively new to Sasha's class of mixed-age infants and toddlers. She joined the class for part-time care (three days a week) about three months ago after she was formally adopted by her aunt (her biological mother's sister) and uncle. Angelica is now the youngest of three children. She is obviously adored by her parents and siblings. Sasha is concerned because she is having difficulty forming a close attachment with Angelica in the child care setting.

Angelica has missed more than two-thirds of the days that she was scheduled to be at child care due to her illness, sickle cell anemia (SCA). This is an inherited disorder that profoundly affects the structure and functioning of red blood cells for African Americans (Hardman, Drew, & Egan, 2006). Angelica's disorder was identified at birth, yet is progressing at a rapid rate; she seems to be experiencing frequent and serious complications. Angelica misses school when she has to get partial-exchange blood transfusions. These treatments tend to cause her to throw up. In the past three months, she has needed eight such transfusions. After the last treatment, she had to be admitted to the hospital overnight because of dehydration. Angelica had experienced only three partial-exchange transfusions before being adopted.

When Angelica enrolled in her class, Sasha began to find out more about SCA and how she could best meet the toddler's needs. Her first source of information was Angelica's parents, of course, but they are just learning about this disorder as well. Next, she searched the web, but found conflicting information and not much about partial-exchange blood transfusions and their side effects. She did discover that minimizing stress, fatigue, and exposure to cold temperatures can assist those with a history of SCA crises. So, while she has gained some information, Sasha is still nervous about working with Angelica.

1. Given Angelica's family history, should Sasha be concerned about forming a close attachment with her? Why or why not?
2. Plan a family-caregiver conference to set plans for Angelica's care as well as shared goals for her development when she returns.
3. What strategies would you suggest Sasha use to help develop a strong relationship with Angelica's parents?

Lesson Plan

Title: *Waiting Patiently*

Child Observation:

Miles toddled over to his cubbie, took out his coat, and toddled to the classroom door. He stood by the door with his coat in hand for two full minutes. He then began to cry.

Child's Developmental Goal:

To develop a coping strategy for missing a loved one

To demonstrate attachment to another person

Materials: Pictures of granddad alone or with Miles, construction or typing paper, tape, clear plastic sleeves (like for a three-ring binder).

Preparation: Invite Miles's grandfather to provide pictures of himself along and/or with Miles. If that is not available, obtain permission to take a few photos during drop-off or pick-up. Tape the photos to the paper. Then, place the photos in the plastic sleeve to protect them. Tape the photos to the back of the classroom door at Miles's eye level.

Learning Environment:

1. When you notice Miles missing his granddad, invite him to look at the pictures you posted on the door.
2. Draw his attention to pictures by using descriptive language. To illustrate, you could say:

   "This is a picture of your granddad and you reading a book."

⌄ **Professional Resource Download**

3. Invite the child to look at and gently touch the pictures by asking prompts or open-ended questions such as the following:
   a. I wonder what you are doing in this photograph.
   b. You are eating a snack in this picture. What is your favorite thing to do with your granddad?
4. Talk about how important his grandfather is to him. Discuss why missing him is hard. Remind him that granddad misses him too and will come to get him right after work.
5. Describe how Miles can use the pictures when he misses his granddad. You might say, for example:
   a. Looking at these pictures help you when you are sad. You can visit them whenever you want.
   b. When I get sad, I like to look at pictures of my family. You can too. These will be here on the door. You can look at them whenever you want.

Guidance Consideration:

If Miles becomes distressed and hits a person or the property, calmly yet firmly tell him it is okay to be upset, but it is not okay to hit. Then, redirect him to the window to watch for his granddad.

Variations:

Make a book of favorite things Miles and his granddad like to do together or of their daily routines. Read the book when Miles misses his granddad.

Additional Resources

Birney, J. M. (2011). *Parenting from prison: A hands-on guide for incarcerated parents.* Charleston: CreateSpace Independent Publishing Platform.

Dunlap, G., Wilson, K., Strain, P. S., & Lee, J. (2013). *Prevent-Teach-Reinforce for young children: The early childhood model of individualized positive behavior support.* Baltimore, MD: Paul H. Brookes Publishing Co.

Lindsay, J. W. (2008). *Teen dads: Rights, responsibilities, and joys* (3rd ed.). Buena Park, CA: Morning Glory Press.

McCoy, M. L., & Keen, S. M. (2013). *Child abuse and neglect* (2nd ed.). New York: Psychology Press.

Newton, S., & Gerrits, J. (2011). *Straight talk about… child abuse.* St. Catharines, Ont.: Crabtree Publishing Company.

Zehr, H., & Amstutz, L. S. (2011). *What will happen to me?: Every night, approximately three million children go to bed with a parent in jail or prison: Here are their thoughts and stories.* Intercourse, PA: Good Books.

8 CHAPTER

The Indoor and Outdoor Learning Environments

Learning Objectives

After reading this chapter, you should be able to:

8-1 Create high-quality and developmentally appropriate indoor and outdoor learning environments from the teacher's perspective.

8-2 Improve a learning environment based on the child's perspective.

8-3 Describe why teachers should consider society's perspective when creating high-quality indoor and outdoor learning environments.

8-4 Select materials for use in a classroom based upon criteria.

8-5 Evaluate policies and procedures for protecting the health and safety of very young children.

Standards Addressed in This Chapter

naeyc **NAEYC Standards for Early Childhood Professional Preparation**

1 Promoting Child Development and Learning
4 Using Developmentally Effective Approaches

DAP **Developmentally Appropriate Practice Guidelines**

1 Creating a Caring Community of Learners
2 Teaching to Enhance Development and Learning

© 2017 Cengage Learning

In addition, the NAEYC standards for developmentally appropriate practice are divided into six areas particularly important to infant/toddler care. The following areas are addressed in this chapter: *exploration and play,* and *environment.*

". . . the issue is not simply having space but how it is used."
V. Vecchi, quoted in Gandini, 2012a, p. 320

Reflecting on the role of space is imperative, as has been demonstrated as a principle of the schools in Reggio Emilia, Italy (see Chapter 6). The classroom environment is considered the "third teacher" (e.g., Gandini, 2012a), a concept that acknowledges the role of adults in carefully preparing and selecting materials for indoor and outdoor learning environments. Teachers should consider three aspects—physical, social, and intellectual—of learning environments when making decisions. All three must be considered in unison because together they provide guidance to the children and adults about appropriate behavior.

Consider for a moment how your actions are influenced differently by being in a place of worship, a library, a shopping mall, or a family restaurant. All of these environments reflect messages of appropriate behavior. For example, a library may have special sections designated for individual quiet reading, small group gatherings for enjoying stories, and larger group gatherings for acting out stories with puppets. The way space and materials are arranged provides clues for appropriate behavior regarding physical movement, social interactions, and experiences with materials (Photo 8–1). The adults responsible for managing the space seldom have to remind others of their expectations; the environment does it for them. Similar to the designer of the library, a teacher's careful classroom environment planning will help children meet expectations for the use of the space and promote optimal development and learning.

We must design learning environments so that they facilitate the best care and education of young children. As discussed in previous chapters, the importance of environmental factors on brain development cannot be underestimated. In fact, Marshall (2011) argues that permanent deficits in the developing neurosensory systems can result from disruption, damage, or deprivation in the infant's social and physical environment. It is imperative that early childhood educators create spaces that support the development of social relationships and cognitive development, while resisting

"the drive to protect our children [that] is profound and easily can lead to cleansing their lives of challenge and depth. Early childhood is a time when children begin to live in the world and hopefully learn to love the world. They can't do this when fenced off from the messy richness of life to live in a world of fluorescent lights and plastic toys, two-dimensional glowing screens, and narrow teaching instruction." (Greenman, 2005, p. 7)

© 2014 Cengage Learning

PHOTO 8–1 Having a book basket with developmentally appropriate materials available continuously can foster a love of reading.

Think about what the classroom environment you created says about your educational values, your beliefs about the capabilities of young children, and the role of families. The focus of this chapter is on answering the following question: *How do teachers create meaningful learning environments that facilitate optimal development for very young children?*

8-1 The Teacher's Perspective

Many teachers prepare their indoor and outdoor areas for learning, but do they prepare these areas to promote optimal learning? Teachers create environments to promote all areas of development as well as learning in particular content areas, such as mathematics or social studies. Therefore, a thorough understanding of child development and learning theories will guide you in planning how to use your classroom space. When making educational decisions such as the arrangement and selection of materials, you should begin by reflecting on the age of children in your classroom; their needs, interests, and abilities; your program's philosophy; licensing and accreditation standards; and guidelines for developmentally appropriate practice. Each of these factors helps you shape the various areas in which the children will grow and learn.

An important question to begin your work is "How do I want the children to use this space?"

8-1a Learning Centers

Learning centers organize the space and materials and encourage specific types of behaviors in one location. For infants and toddlers, you can organize centers in several ways. A popular approach for toddlers involves dividing the indoor and outdoor space into use areas. A quiet zone or private space, a construction center, a wet center, a project area, a reading and listening center, or a dramatic play center can be created by using tables, short shelves, transparent dividers, and flooring to indicate an area inside. For infants, these areas may be less well defined. For example, a manipulation area will allow for exploring toys with the hands, while a more open space becomes a gross motor area. The room might be further subdivided into areas for specific types of routine care times such as diapering or napping. The outdoor space should also be divided into learning centers. Any experience done inside can be done outside; teachers should not overlook the importance of the outdoor learning environment (Nelson, 2012; Rivkin with Schein, 2014). Painting, riding trikes, climbing and jumping, playing in sand and water, growing vegetables or flowers in a garden, dramatic play, and storytelling are all centers that should be outside (Nelson, 2012). More importantly, outdoor learning environments should instill a passion in each child to explore, ask questions, and care for the environment (Honig, 2015). Given the importance of learning centers for promoting development, it is assumed that your child care setting will be flexibly organized into them.

When planning your learning environment, base the number and type of learning centers on the size of the space and the age of the children. In general, to maximize choice and minimize conflict over possessions,

learning centers A particular part of the environment where materials and equipment are organized to promote and encourage a specific type of learning, for example, music or science.

a rule of thumb to follow for toddlers is to provide one-third more work spaces than the number of children in your classroom. To illustrate, if you have 10 toddlers in your group, you will need at least (10 × 1/3) + 10 or 13 spaces for working. This might mean including two spaces at the sensory table, two at the easel, two or three at the art center, three or four in blocks/construction, three or four in dramatic play, two in the music/movement area, and one in the library/private spot. You can set up learning centers outside but will not need as many because you will want to maximize the amount of time children are moving and exercising; you can intentionally plan games and movement activities outdoors or indoors (Dow, 2010).

8-1b Real Objects versus Open-Ended Materials

Children need a balance of novel and familiar materials to attract and maintain their attention (see the next section for a more in-depth discussion). When children are engaged with materials and ideas, they have less opportunity to create mischief or misbehave, thus enabling teachers to change their supervision from guidance of behavior to guidance of learning. Developmentally, throughout the early childhood period, young children are learning to use objects as tools for representing their thoughts and theories about how the world works. Therefore, providing a balance of real and open-ended materials promotes cognitive development. Making available real objects such as child-size shovels for digging in the garden, Navajo pottery for storing paintbrushes, or child-size glass tumblers for drinks during meals (for older toddlers) serves two further purposes: (1) it demonstrates trust in the children's ability to care for objects, and (2) it connects home and school environments. Real objects, when provided in response to the children's expressed interests, can also facilitate thinking about a particular topic or concept.

Open-ended materials, on the other hand, can be used by the children to expand their understanding of concepts and demonstrate creative uses of materials (Photo 8–2); these materials cause children to problem solve and be inventive as they answer the question of "what if" (Daly & Beloglovsky, 2015). Open-ended materials include collected items such as fabric, cardboard, plastics, pebbles, shells, pinecones, or egg cartons, as well as commercially produced objects such as wooden blocks, animal and people figurines, or connecting manipulatives. Open-ended materials can spark, support, and enhance learning and development in any learning environment. Neatly arranging them in baskets or clear containers and displaying them on a shelf at the children's height will make them easily accessible to the children whether they are working indoors or outdoors. Of course, some open-ended materials might pose a choking hazard for infants and toddlers, so never leave the child unattended during the experience.

Independence versus Dependence

A primary goal for adults is that children become independent, self-regulated learners. For this to occur, teachers must carefully plan the physical environment with this in mind. As mentioned

© 2012 Cengage Learning

PHOTO 8–2 Open-ended materials can provide extensive opportunity for play and representation of ideas.

earlier, providing easily accessible open-ended materials promotes cognitive development. This practice also promotes social and emotional development because the children can independently select the materials they need for their work and can more easily help with cleanup before they leave the learning area. Moreover, modifying the bathroom so that all necessary hand-washing supplies can be reached fosters the children's independence. Outside faucets that have an attachment allowing children to serve themselves encourage the toddlers to get water whenever they need it for their work.

© 2012 Cengage Learning

PHOTO 8–3 Messy experiences for young children build cognitive structures through sensorimotor and hands-on, minds-on experiences.

Messy versus Dry

Designing space for daily opportunities to explore messy materials is a must. In fact, Bredekamp and Copple (1997) suggest that toddlers should have daily experiences with sand and water because of their educational value. Messy experiences are particularly significant for young children because they build cognitive structures or schemas (i.e., tightly organized sets of ideas about specific objects or situations) through sensorimotor and hands-on, minds-on experiences (Photo 8–3). Some typical messy centers include water and/or sensory tables, painting easels, and art. Water play, for example, provides opportunities for learning about quantity, building vocabulary, and negotiating the sharing of materials.

What does a teacher need to consider when managing messy experiences in a classroom setting? First, setting up messy experiences in an area with vinyl or linoleum flooring allows for ease of cleanup when spills occur. Second, placing these experiences near a water source can aid in cleaning up and refilling containers or even adding a new element to an experience. For example, if a sensory table is filled with dry sand, children can transfer water from the source using pitchers, thus transforming the properties of the sand. Third, placing a hand broom and dustpan nearby prompts children to keep the area clean.

If you do not have an area with flooring that allows for easy cleanup, you will need to be creative to provide such valuable learning experiences. Placing newspaper, towels, or a shower curtain under a sensory table or easel can resolve this issue. Another way to address this challenge is to plan daily experiences with messy materials outside.

Noisy versus Quiet

Some classroom experiences are noisier than others. Cooperating and negotiating requires children to interact with one another. Although sometimes interactions can become heated, a caregiver's goal should be to enable such interactions so that the children gain necessary perspective-taking and problem-solving skills, not to stop the interactions or prevent them in the first place. To manage the environment and facilitate learning, teachers can place noisy areas close together. Noisy centers include blocks and construction, dramatic play, music and movement, and project work space. Placing these centers adjacent to one another serves two purposes. First, the higher noise levels will be located in a particular section of the room. This allows children to concentrate better in the quiet areas, with fewer distractions close by. Second, placing areas that require more supervision and support together permits the teacher to engage in these interactions (e.g., assisting children with problem solving) without having to travel between different parts of the room.

Quiet centers consist of the library, listening centers, and private spaces. For your mental health and that of the children, you must provide both indoor and outdoor areas for children to be alone. These private spaces allow the children to regroup and gather their thoughts before rejoining others. A note of caution is needed here. You should never send a child to the quiet or private areas as a consequence for misbehavior. Children should freely choose these areas to help them relax. If you use the areas for punishment, or the children perceive them as such, they will not serve their purpose of helping them to relax and regroup.

Play in some other centers, such as with manipulatives or science/discovery, fluctuates between quiet and noisy, depending on the type of materials provided and the children's levels of engagement. These areas can be used to transition between the noisy and quiet centers.

When deciding where to place learning centers, teachers also need to consider the needs of the different types of centers. To illustrate, the music and movement center needs an electrical outlet for a CD player, shelves for musical instruments, baskets for scarves or strips of fabric, mirrors for observing motions, and space for creative movement and dance. Teachers often have limited resources and need to maximize the use of equipment and materials they do have. Locating the music and movement center near the dramatic play area is one way to do this: these two centers can share materials such as a mirror or basket of fabric.

8-1c Calm, Safe Learning Environment

Another question that you will encounter is "How can I create a calm, safe environment that provides stimulating learning experiences for the children?" In this section, we will focus attention on the last part of this question: "stimulating learning experiences."

Novel versus Familiar

Teachers and children deserve to be surrounded by beautiful objects and materials that are displayed in an aesthetically pleasing fashion. A well-planned environment should offer a mix of novel and familiar experiences and objects that each infant can explore at her own pace (Copple & Bredekamp, 2009). In other words, some of these objects should be part of the environment on a regular basis, while others can be included occasionally to spark interest. For example, hanging a framed print of Monet's sunflowers on the wall near the easel will create a beautiful environment for toddler children. Surprising the children with a display of Pueblo Indian pottery one day will create a different motivation to use the easel.

Learning spaces should be varied so that children have the opportunity to explore different perspectives. To illustrate, having the ability to change one's physical location by climbing up the stairs to a loft or playscape and looking down on a teacher provides a child with a new view of the world. Another way that teachers can vary the space and provoke thinking is by providing a new display or object to explore and discuss. A ground covering with two or more variations can naturally demonstrate hard versus soft and warm versus cold. Sitting on soft, lush grass on a hot summer day will feel cool to an infant's touch, thus providing him an opportunity to experience his environment in a different way.

Another way to conceptualize the familiar is to create spaces that parallel those found in home environments. For example, placing a couch, rocking chair, and end table with a lamp in the entryway mimics a living room in a home. A cozy nook like this not only adds warmth and comfort to the learning environment but also helps to create a sense of security at school: a home away from home. Having a hanging swing, the kind families might have on their front porch, gives the adults and children a place to snuggle and relax on a warm springtime afternoon.

Pathways versus Boundaries

As you are planning your layout, you need to consider how you will define your learning centers. Having visible boundaries for centers provides children with a clear message about the use of materials in a particular area. Use a variety of dividers, such as short shelving units, bookcases, transparent fabrics, and sheets of decorated acrylic. Flower beds, raised gardens, or cobbled pathways make great dividers for outdoor learning centers. Transparency, or the ability to see between centers, both allows teachers to supervise and facilitates children's play because they can make connections between materials in different centers in each environment. Even though materials are organized into learning centers, caregivers should be flexible in allowing the children to move materials that they need from one center to another. When planning the boundaries for a learning center, you must carefully consider how much space to devote to that area. As described earlier, the noisier areas often require more space than quieter areas because these areas tend to elicit more parallel and associative play, requiring two or more children at a time.

A teacher also needs to consider how to use open space. Because we need gathering spaces for toddlers that can easily accommodate most of the children and caregivers in the room at one time, we often set aside this space for that one purpose. However, it is more logical, when not being used for a gathering, to convert that space to a place for "rough and tumble" play (see the Spotlight on Research box).

Pathways into and out of the room as well as between centers need to be carefully considered. When children arrive for the day, they should be able to complete a gradual transition from home to school. Having to walk to the opposite side of the classroom to store their belongings in their cubbies can

Spotlight on Research

ROUGH AND TUMBLE PLAY

From birth, children learn by using their bodies. They kick their feet and move a blanket; they roll over and get to a toy that was originally out of reach; they learn how to balance their body when standing for the first time. They also learn a great deal by wrestling with each other, jumping on a mattress, and playing chase. Rough and tumble play supports the development of the whole child: physical, cognitive, social, and emotional. Carlson (2011) considers boisterous, physical play a "developmental necessity" (p. 11). Teachers are often suspicious of having children engage in rough and tumble play for fear that it will lead to real fights, aggressive acts, or injury. Carlson's (2011) extensive review of research suggests that these are not typical outcomes and that there are many more benefits to engaging in such behaviors than limitations, especially for children who are experiencing social difficulties.

Flanders and his colleagues have investigated the impact of rough and tumble play on children's level of aggression and emotional regulation. Their research found that the amount of time fathers spent with their child was negatively associated with the child's level of reported aggression. In other words, the more time fathers spent with their children, the lower they rated their child on frequency of aggressive acts (Flanders, Leo, Paquette, Pihl, & Séguin, 2009). More importantly, "when fathers asserted a minimum amount of dominance, rough and tumble play is not associated with adverse consequences [aggression or lack of emotional regulation] concurrently and overtime" (Flanders, Simard, Paquette, Parent, Vitaro, Pihl, et al., 2010, p. 365). Paquette (2013) investigated this relationship based on activation relationship theory. This theory focuses on parents balance the stimulation of risk-taking behaviors with parental control during exploration or interactions. When fathers more optimally activated their sons during interactions in toddlerhood, the more the father-child dyad engaged in rough and tumble play at the age of 3 (Paquette, 2013). This body of research suggests that rough and tumble play is very exciting and engaging for young children, but that they need assistance in learning to regulate those strong emotions. When fathers do not contain these

play interactions, the children can become excited to the point of being out of control or physically aggressive and, therefore, do not develop the skills required to regulate these states (Flanders et al., 2010).

Rough and tumble play should occur not only in homes. Early childhood educators should intentionally set up space and plan ways to encourage such interactions (Carlson, 2011; Swim, 2014). In interviews with teachers, Tannock (2008) found that they could articulate the benefits of rough and tumble play, allowed children to engage in it, but they did not actively plan for it. The author concluded that these teachers needed more guidance to increase their comfort level with this type of play. Carlson's and Flanders's research provides some guidelines. A few important ones are the following: (1) set up the environment to support rough and tumble play, (2) provide constant supervision for infants and toddlers, (3) coach them at reading each other's nonverbal cues (especially faces), (4) create limits for this type of play and help children follow them, and (5) engage yourself in this type of play with individual children, especially those at risk for social difficulties.

When studying rough and tumble play in a university-sponsored child care center, Lindsey (2014) discovered that peer acceptance depended not only on the type of play but whether the play was with same- or opposite-gender peers. In general, for this group of preschoolers, boys' rough and tumble chasing was associated with peer acceptance. When analyzed more deeply, he found that boys who engaged in rough and tumble fighting with same-gender peers were better liked by peers, whereas boys who engaged in rough and tumble chasing with other-gender peers were less liked by peers. Thus, teachers much consider multiple variables when planning rough and tumble play experiences to maximize the positive benefits for young children.

In addition, all teachers should be familiar with state regulations related to rough and tumble play. Although these regulations must be followed to remain in compliance, if they are too limiting, work with colleagues and family members toward amending those laws/guidelines so that each child can experience this invaluable play (Carlson, 2011).

be stressful, especially if they must pass by noisy centers. When considering movement between centers, remember that walking through one center to get to another can cause children to become distracted. Do you want the children to walk through a center such as the block/construction area to get to the music center? It would quickly become evident from the children's behavior that such an arrangement does not work well.

8-1d Basic Needs

As you are considering the educational needs of the children, you must also dedicate space for meeting the children's basic needs for eating, toileting, resting, and playing. The question here is "How do I plan the environment to meet these basic requirements?"

Eating versus Toileting

Some infant and toddler classrooms separate the changing table and food preparation counter with a small sink. This practice may seem to be an efficient use of counter space, but it could jeopardize both the early childhood educators' and the children's health. For hygienic purposes, it is imperative that the eating and toileting areas are separated (Photo 8–4). Although this is relatively simple in a preschool classroom, it may be more difficult in an infant and toddler classroom because the typical restroom just does not have enough space for toilets, sinks, and a changing table. Because infant and toddler teachers must both continually supervise the children and also spend a significant amount of time diapering, changing tables are often placed in the classroom. Where should a changing table be located? Placing it next to a water source assists with good hand-washing practices. You should also position it away from a wall, so that your back is not to the rest of the children when you are changing a diaper.

PHOTO 8–4 Teachers must plan the environment and adopt practices to protect their own health and the health of the children.

The food area can require a number of small appliances such as a mini-refrigerator or microwave (per licensing regulations); therefore, cabinet space near electrical outlets is very important. For toddlers and older children, space for eating can be shared with other areas of the classroom. For example, the tables that are used for art can be cleaned and sanitized when it is snack time or mealtime. Infant teachers must address other issues when planning the environment. Depending on your state regulations, you may or may not need a separate high chair for each infant. Finding storage space for mealtime equipment must be given careful consideration.

Sleep and Comfort versus Play

Children and adults need locations to store special items and belongings from home. This not only reaffirms the importance of both environments but also teaches respect for one's own and others' belongings. Switching between environments can be stressful for people of all ages, so plan for comfortable places for children to make the transition from home to school, snuggle, relax, and enjoy reunions with family members. Couches and rocking chairs located in a variety of classroom areas provide an excellent avenue for this.

All children need time throughout the day to rest and rejuvenate. Teachers should create a calm relaxing environment during nap or rest time. Closing blinds on the windows, plugging in a night light, playing soft instrumental music, and providing comfort items for each child (e.g., blankets, favorite stuffed animals) might assist with shifting from play to sleep. You should also organize the environment to address the needs of children who require less sleep during the day, by creating baskets with books, paper and pencils, and other quiet toys that can be used by a child lying on a cot or sitting at a table.

At times, children may prefer to nap outdoors after exerting themselves during activities and play. A shady and easily supervised space made soft with quilts or blankets should be readily available for resting.

We have now considered the learning environment from the teacher's perspective, but it is time to consider the child's perspective. Although presenting the material in this manner may create paradoxes (seemingly contradictory messages), keep in mind that these are different sides of the same coin. In other words, consider and prepare to articulate the common focus of each perspective.

READING CHECKPOINT

Before moving on with your reading, make sure that you can answer the following question about the material discussed so far.
1. When planning classroom environments, why do we need to balance opposites such as real objects versus open-ended materials, noisy versus quiet, and novel versus familiar?

8-2 The Child's Perspective

First and foremost, the educational space has to guarantee the well-being of each child and of the group of children. Children have the right to educational environments that facilitate their social, emotional, moral, physical, linguistic, and cognitive development; they also have the right to environments that are free of excessive stress, noise, and physical and psychological harm (Gandini, 2012b). At the same time, according to Loris Malguzzi, the space should reflect how the school is a "dynamic organism: it has difficulties, controversies, joys, and the capacity to handle external disturbances" (Gandini, 2012b, p. 41). The following section explains 10 principles that are important to consider when creating your educational environment from the child's perspective. You may notice that these principles are not restricted to a particular learning center but rather apply across educational spaces.

Consider each of the general principles in relationship to the specific children in your care. The environment must reflect and be responsive to the unique developmental characteristics of children of specific ages as well as the individual children within that age group (Copple & Bredekamp, 2009). Although the general principles are relevant to all environments for young children, they may manifest themselves differently for the various age groups. One or two principles may be more relevant for a particular age group or setting. To briefly illustrate, continuity of care between home and school environments is vital for the appropriate care of infants (see, e.g., Bergen, Reid, & Torelli, 2001; Bove, 2001; Essa, Favre, Thweatt, & Waugh, 1999). Thus, plenty of space needs to be devoted to areas where family members and teachers can comfortably communicate and ease each infant's transition. Less space may be required for this purpose with preschoolers.

Before providing detailed explanations of each principle, a general overview of each will be provided, highlighting questions that a child might ask:

- **Transparency**—Can I see my friends, teachers, and family members from almost any place in the room? Is there a place I can have some time alone? Can I quickly find the materials I want to use?
- **Flexibility**—Can I find areas that support my interests in the classroom?
- **Relationships**—Can I build relationships with other people in my classroom?
- **Identity**—Am I an important person in this environment?
- **Movement**—Can I move my body freely?
- **Documentation**—Do the important adults in my life communicate about me frequently?
- **Senses**—Is the environment warm and welcoming and a place that I want to spend 4 to 10 hours of my day?
- **Representation**—Can I tell you in multiple ways about my understanding of and theories about the world?
- **Independence**—Can I do things myself?
- **Discovery**—Can I find interesting things to examine closely and learn about?

8-2a Transparency

Can I see my friends, teachers, and family members from almost any place in the room? To support connections and relationships, children need to be able to see materials and one another. From the adult's viewpoint, transparency adds to the ease of supervision. You should be able to see from one side of the room to the other. This should not remove all privacy, however. Children and adults need secluded spaces to be alone and gather their thoughts (Marion, 2014). To achieve this principle, you can use translucent fabrics, shelves with the backing removed, or sheets of decorated acrylic to divide areas (Photo 8–5) (Curtis & Carter, 2015).

A second concern a child might have is, "Can I quickly find the materials I want to use?" This aspect of transparency considers the amount and the presentation of materials in the environment. In general, you want the room to be as uncluttered as possible. You should regularly analyze your environment to identify unused toys or materials and then locate places to store those items to minimize clutter (Cutler, 2000).

For those items that are being used regularly, carefully observe the quantity of material being used by the children; have you provided too many objects or not enough? You should strive to provide a sufficient amount of material. The definition of *sufficient* is guided by your professional interpretation; realize that it differs for each group of children. The aim is to provide materials to spark older toddlers' interests, yet not totally satisfy them, thus provoking them to use their emerging skills of imagining,

© 2012 Cengage Learning

PHOTO 8–5 "Hiding" behind the transparent barrier.

pretending, and transforming objects for use. The phrase "less is more" is key to this principle. Try to display the materials and supplies in baskets or clear containers on shelves that are low and open so that children can see what is available and can select and clean up materials independently (Isbell & Exelby, 2001; Marion, 2014; Topal & Gandini, 1999).

8-2b Flexibility

Can I find areas that support my interests in the classroom? The environment should change in response to individual children and each group of children living in it (Copple & Bredekamp, 2009). To illustrate, an infant-toddler teacher modified her classroom as the children got older and she noticed particular interests. For example, to support and further enhance the children's interests in building, she designed her room with two separate construction areas. This seemed to work well for this group because they could spread out to work in the distinct spaces. As one of the children's projects grew, she altered another area of the classroom to support their representation of a city surrounded by train tracks. For a short period of time, this teacher had three classroom areas devoted to construction! She flexed her environment to best meet the needs of the children.

To many teachers' dismay, child care programs often lack adequate space for all that the children and teachers want to do. Combining or rotating learning centers is one way to maximize learning opportunities without overloading the setting (Isbell & Exelby, 2001). For example, a toddler teacher in a church-based program had to combine the writing and art center, while her colleague decided to carefully select materials to merge science exploration and reading/library into one center. In contrast, another of their colleagues provided space in the outdoor environment for daily experiences at the sensory table and easel to better use classroom space.

Related to that idea of combining centers is the notion of providing open-ended materials that can be used in many areas of the classroom (Curtis & Carter, 2015). Encouraging the children to borrow or move material among the learning centers is another way to demonstrate the flexibility of the environment. Hence, another question a child might wonder is, "Can I move the materials and supplies around the room to do my work?"

A final aspect of flexibility highlights the teacher's role in building engaging learning environments. DeViney, Duncan, Harris, Rody, and Rosenberry (2010) suggest that teachers should create displays in the learning environment to spark engagement and creativity. These displays should be changed frequently so that they relate to current topics of study. In addition, each display should be aesthetically pleasing and use real items and/or natural materials. For example, Lois teaches a group of toddlers. They are very interested in cars. She decided to go to a local auto salvage yard and gather some items. She found a rear view mirror, fuzzy dice, and a stick-shift knob. She then went to a local fabric store and found cloth similar to what is on her car seats. The next week, she created a beautiful display of these items in the dramatic play area. The children spotted the display immediately upon arrival and began to talk about the materials.

8-2c Relationships

Can I build relationships with other people in my classroom? The environment needs to support and facilitate the development of strong, enduring relationships among children, families, and staff members (Honig, 2002; Galardini & Giovannini, 2001; Gandini, 2012a). As discussed in previous chapters, continuity of care should be a priority to support optimal social and emotional development. Space needs to be allocated and arranged so that adults and children have soft, warm areas for gathering, snuggling, communicating, or just being together (Photo 8–6). This space also serves to create an "at home" feeling, which is important because it helps high-quality child care programs avoid an institutional feel.

To illustrate this principle, consider the infant teacher who reorganized the entry to his classroom to include two rocking chairs and a small table. This provided space for him to speak with families at the beginning of the day, gathering information about family events and sharing anecdotes from the previous day. He also noticed that some families would linger in this area to say their goodbyes. Moreover, he used the same chairs to read to and snuggle with individual children before naptime.

© 2017 Cengage Learning

PHOTO 8–6 Space needs to be allocated so that adults and children have soft, warm areas for gathering, snuggling, or just being together.

8-2d Identity

Am I an important person in this environment? Learning space should provide traces of those who live in it. Providing special spots for belongings is also a must, because it tells children that items of value from home are welcomed and respected in the classroom. Photographs of children working and playing, as well as family members and staff members both at work and at home, should be displayed in prominent locations around the classroom. Pedagogical panel documentation makes visible the work of the children and teachers; provides explanation and evidence of the persons living and learning in the space; and provokes dialogue and interpretation about the work and the participants (Dahlberg, 2012; Forman & Fyfe, 2012; Turner & Krechevsky, 2003). Such documentation also communicates that it is important to understand the children and their work and adds to their sense of self (Project Zero & Reggio Children, 2001).

Do not restrict yourself to displaying traces of the children, families, and staff on classroom walls. No space should be considered marginal (Gandini, 2012a). Using the door of the playground shed, a shelf in the entryway, bathroom walls or stall doors to display photographs or works of art, for example, demonstrates to children the importance of that space and can provide additional information to help them build their identities (see Wien, Coates, Keating, & Bigelow, 2005). For example, a toddler teacher created a hand-washing chart using photographs of the children engaged in the various steps of the process. This chart not only provided the necessary information required to be posted by the state regulatory agency but also assisted the children with independently completing this self-help task.

An additional idea is to place mirrors around the classroom in strategic places, so that children notice their work or actions from another perspective (Photo 8–7).

Another way to conceptualize identity is to consider the ways in which individual children think about and engage with the world. Some children are persistent when faced with a challenging task, while other children are incredibly inventive and use materials in ways others would never consider. Children, like teachers, must develop a variety of important **dispositions**; good environments assist young children with this ongoing task. Teachers must plan environments to support social dispositions such as being cooperative, empathetic, and accepting, as well as intellectual dispositions such as being creative and curious, asking questions, solving problems, investigating, and communicating (Da Ros-Voseles & Fowler-Haughey, 2007).

dispositions Frequent and voluntary habits of thinking and doing that represent a particular orientation to the work and responsibilities of teaching.

© 2012 Cengage Learning

PHOTO 8–7 Mirrors also provide valuable information that contributes to the development of children's identity.

8-2e Movement

Can I move my body freely? The environment needs to reflect the National Association for Sport and Physical Education's (NASPE) guidelines by providing plenty of structured and unstructured opportunities for physical activity and movement experiences (see Table 8–1). High-quality environments provide space for large-muscle movements such as climbing, dancing, and acting out stories. Such environments also minimize, or

TABLE 8–1 ▸ NASPE Guidelines for Physical Activity

GUIDELINES FOR INFANTS

a. Infants should interact with caregivers in daily physical activities that are dedicated to exploring movement and the environment.

b. Caregivers should place infants in settings that encourage and stimulate movement experiences and active play for short periods of time several times a day.

c. Infants' physical activity should promote skill development in movement.

d. Infants should be placed in an environment that meets or exceeds recommended safety standards for performing large-muscle activities.

e. Those in charge of infants' well-being are responsible for understanding the importance of physical activity and should promote movement skills by providing opportunities for structured and unstructured physical activity.

GUIDELINES FOR TODDLERS

a. Toddlers should engage in a total of at least 30 minutes of *structured* physical activity each day.

b. Toddlers should engage in at least 60 minutes—and up to several hours—per day of *unstructured* physical activity and should not be sedentary for more than 60 minutes at a time, unless sleeping.

c. Toddlers should be given ample opportunity to develop movement skills that will serve as the building blocks for future motor skillfulness and physical activity.

d. Toddlers should have access to indoor and outdoor areas that meet or exceed recommended safety standards for performing large-muscle activities.

e. Those in charge of toddlers' well-being are responsible for understanding the importance of physical activity and promoting movement skills by providing opportunities for structured and unstructured physical activity and movement experiences.

Source: Reprinted from *Active Start: A Statement of Physical Activity Guidelines for Children from Birth to Age 5*, 2nd edition (retrieved September 16, 2011 from http://www.aahperd.org/naspe/standards/nationalGuidelines/ActiveStart.cfm), with permission from the National Association for Sport and Physical Education (NASPE), 1900 Association Drive, Reston, VA 20191, www.NASPEinfo.org.

eliminate entirely, equipment that confines children. A playpen, for example, not only physically limits a child but creates a barrier that socially and emotionally isolates the child from others. Holding a child offers more safety and security than the most expensive playpen. In addition, wheeled walkers do not enhance upright mobility development of infants; they can actually promote bad habits such as walking on tiptoes. Before using equipment that confines children (indoors or out), check with your state and local licensing regulations.

Creating multilevel spaces inside and outside provides additional ways for the children to explore their bodies in space. Adults should be mindful of how the architecture of the room intersects with their educational goals (Zane, 2015). Playscapes, platforms, and lofts, for example, not only provide a quiet space for reading or writing but also offer a different viewpoint of the room and the objects within it (Curtis & Carter, 2015). When standing in a loft, many toddlers are larger than their caregivers for the first time, thus filling them with a new sensation: power!

8-2f Documentation

Do the important adults in my life communicate about me frequently? Some classroom space should be dedicated to communicating and record keeping because reciprocal relationships are built on open, ongoing communication among the adults in the children's lives (Copple & Bredekamp, 2009). Adults require comfortable places to read and send messages, record observations, and store or display documentation about each child, such as portfolios and pedagogical panels. Returning to the example provided in the "Relationship" section earlier, the teacher also used his entryway as a place for providing written communication with families. Beside one chair, he placed a basket that held the home-school journals (see Chapter 5). In addition, he had a bookshelf where all of the children's portfolios were stored. The table provided space for him to spread out artifacts collected over the week and make decisions about what to add to the portfolio or use in this pedagogical panel documentation.

8-2g Senses

Is the environment warm and welcoming—a place that I want to spend 4 to 10 hours of my day? The environment should be pleasing to the senses. There needs to be a balance of hard and soft, rough and smooth, novel and familiar, simple and complex, quiet and noisy (Bergen et al., 2001). Neutral or natural tones are preferable for both furniture and walls. Young children bring plenty of colors to the environment; their natural beauty should be a focal point rather than having it compete with "loud background noise."

The principle of the senses also includes the use of natural light. As often as possible, rely on natural sunlight to supply lighting for the classroom because it is less harsh on the senses for you and the children. However, when this is not possible, you can provide additional lighting in the form of lamps. Place them on shelves, end tables, or on the floor to create smaller areas for work and gatherings. Avoid relying on overhead, fluorescent lighting, which tends to be less warm and welcoming.

To provide complexity and aesthetic pleasure, you can include paintings, sculptures, or photographs in the environment (Curtis & Carter, 2015). Pillows, nontoxic potted plants, and fabrics can also be used to soften the environment and lower the height of the ceiling. Moreover, scented potpourri, oils, or plug-ins (kept out of the reach of the children, of course) can be used to provide a pleasant aroma.

You also need to provide opportunities for infants and toddlers to explore and learn using their senses (Photo 8–8). You can't be afraid to get dirty or to let the children get dirty. For example, imagine that an

© 2012 Cengage Learning

PHOTO 8–8 A developmentally appropriate environment supports young children in making decisions and in doing things alone.

older infant is crawling outside on a small mound of dirt. She repeatedly pats the dry dirt flat. If you pour a bit of water in one area to see how she responds, she is likely to squish the mud between her fingers and giggle in delight. Adding water may make the child dirtier, but it enhances the experience for her.

8-2h Representation

Can I tell you in multiple ways about my understanding of and theories about the world? Children need multiple opportunities to express their current understanding of the world. Representation of ideas can occur through painting, drawing, dramatic play, music, writing, sculpting, or any of the other "hundred languages" (New, 2003; Edwards et al., 2012). The environment, then, needs to provide space and open-ended materials for these purposes.

8-2i Independence

Can I do things myself? Children desire independence (Photo 8–9). This is a natural and healthy aspect of socioemotional development. A developmentally appropriate environment supports young children in making decisions, doing things alone, solving problems, and regulating their own behavior (Copple & Bredekamp, 2009; Marion & Swim, 2007). Use care in selecting where to place materials, supplies, and learning areas because this is one way to foster independence. As mentioned previously, displaying materials and supplies in baskets or clear containers on low shelves allows children to select and clean up materials with assistance from others (Isbell & Exelby, 2001; Marion, 2014).

Careful placement of learning centers adds to this sense of independence. One toddler teacher placed her easel on the tile floor closest to the sink. Not only was this more convenient for her, but it also encouraged the children to take responsibility for cleaning up spills or splatters. In the beginning of the year, she discussed with children where paper towels and sponges were kept, while assisting them in cleaning up the paint. In no time at all, many of the children were cleaning up after themselves, often without even notifying her.

8-2j Discovery

Can I find interesting things to examine closely and learn about? As mentioned in the "Senses" section, the environment needs to provide a balance of novel and familiar materials, permitting new discoveries that keep the learners engaged.

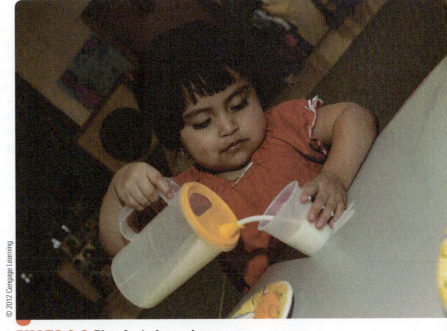

© 2012 Cengage Learning

PHOTO 8–9 Plan for independence.

Providing unique things to explore, examine, and learn about does not have to be expensive. Arranging familiar materials in a new location or display is one technique for renewing interest. Another method to cultivate interest in infants and toddlers is to offer treasures or items from nature that they can explore and investigate (McHenry & Buerk, 2008). Rocks, feathers, flowers, tree branches, and things that sparkle or shine are all worthy of investigation (Curtis & Carter, 2015). In addition, providing recycled or found materials in aesthetically pleasing arrangements or containers provokes children to think about them in new ways (Topal & Gandini, 1999). The intention is to help the children with "finding the extraordinary in the ordinary" (L. Gandini, personal communication, January 26, 2001). Of course, remember to examine each item or material carefully for sharp edges and the like to ensure that it is safe for the infants and toddlers. If an item is a choke hazard, never leave a toddler unsupervised while handling it (see the "Selecting Equipment and Materials" section later in this chapter).

Before moving on to the last perspective on environmental design, Table 8–2 recaps the major components from the first two perspectives: teacher and child.

READING CHECKPOINT

Before moving on with your reading, make sure that you can answer the following questions about the material discussed so far.

1. Why is it important to consider the child's perspective when designing a learning environment?
2. What can teachers do to make sure that their environment addresses each child's development and learning?

TABLE 8–2 ▶ Key Aspects of Environmental Design by Perspective

Teacher's Perspective	Learning Centers
	Real Objects vs. Open-ended materials
	Independence vs. Dependence
	Use of Space
	Messy vs. Dry
	Noisy vs. Quiet
	Calm, Safe Learning Environment
	Novel vs. Familiar
	Pathways vs. Boundaries
	Basic Needs
	Eating vs. Toileting
	Sleep and Comfort vs. Play
Child's Perspective	Transparency
	Flexibility
	Relationships
	Identity
	Movement
	Documentation
	Senses
	Representation
	Independence
	Discovery

8-3 Society's Perspective

This section focuses on making decisions about the environment that are good for the greater society. In other words, I am asking you to consider ways in which you can "go green" or "reduce your carbon footprint" when working with infants and toddlers in educational settings. Some changes to consider might seem very small, and others might seem more than a teacher can do alone. That is okay. Each teacher has to make changes at her own pace. However, each of us should consider what we can do to make long-term differences in the future world of the infants and toddlers that we work with today. If we don't think big and do our part, we run the risk of permanently changing the earth's climate in negative directions (Sivertsen & Sivertsen, 2008).

8-3a Environmental Changes for the Classroom

Teachers can take many steps to build an earth-friendly environment in their learning environments (i.e., indoors and outdoors). One suggestion for reducing energy use in a classroom is to plug appliances such as a CD player, microwave, and computers into one or two plug strips. Turn the strips off at the end of the day. Another idea is to use natural sunlight to light the classroom during the day. This was mentioned earlier as being good for the children, not just the environment. Taylor (2008) provided evidence that older children are able to concentrate better when they are in a green school that uses natural light. A logical extension of this finding would be that the infants and toddlers also learn and grow better in natural light. When additional light sources are needed, use lamps with compact fluorescent lightbulbs (CFLs). As CFLs now come in a variety of color spectra, try out a few different types until you find one that you prefer. Some CFLs give off a warm light similar to the old incandescent lightbulbs, so they are more pleasing in the environment. In addition, you can consider using light-emitting diodes (LEDs) such as rope lights to provide a small amount of light in specific areas of the classroom. Stringing rope lights around the book corner provides additional light on overcast days and makes the area feel warm and cozy.

Plants were discussed earlier as a way to soften the environment. They should also be included in the environment as a way to improve air quality. Plants naturally clean the air that we breathe. In addition, if you select flowering plants or herbs, they can emit pleasant aromas.

Teachers can also make decisions about how to create recycling areas in their learning environments. In an infant classroom, create the space based on how you use items. For example, it might be most convenient for you to have three containers side by side: one for trash, one for plastic (e.g., baby wipes or baby food containers), and one for glass (e.g., baby food jars). Have small containers near the phone and documentation area to hold recycled paper for writing notes. In a toddler classroom, make an area for recycling containers that the toddlers can access independently or with supervision. For example, you could put a box in the art center to collect paper that can be reused. Help the toddlers to learn to distinguish paper that is reusable from that which should be recycled in another area. At other times, guide the toddlers to place items to be recycled in the proper areas.

Family and Community Connections

A small group of families in your toddler class are interested in being more "green." They would like to start a community garden on the land to the south of the building. This land is owned by the center but not currently used in any meaningful way. How would you support these families in advocating for using the land in this way? What information would you share with them about the importance of outdoor experiences for young children? Who else in your community could you obtain information from? What might be benefits of this project for families, the center, and the greater community?

8-3b Curricular Changes

Many young children grow up in homes where food is purchased entirely from grocery stores and where the outdoors is viewed as a dangerous place. It is our responsibility as educators to help them feel safe and to connect appropriately with nature. Yet, there is so much more to be learned by engaging with nature (see, e.g., Honig, 2015; Nelson, 2012; Rivkin with Schein, 2014). Nimmo and Hallet (2008) argue that planting and tending to a garden teach young children about "play and inquiry, safe risk taking, the building of relationships, and deeper understandings of diversity" in nature and society (p. 1). Relatedly, other authors suggest that a lifetime of healthy eating habits can sprout from teaching young children how to garden (Kalich, Bauer, & McPartlin, 2009). Thus, teachers must intentionally incorporate this into their curriculum (to be discussed in Chapter 9) opportunities for engaging with nature.

Infants and toddlers explore their world and work hard to understand it and their role within it. As discussed previously, one way to address their interest in the natural world is to create spaces both inside and outside for exploring nature. However, teaching about the environment goes beyond providing selected items from nature; young children need ongoing, meaningful experiences. To illustrate, you could plant a garden to attract butterflies in your outdoor learning space. You could place magnifying glasses outside for the children to use along with paper and pencils for recording their observations. These experiences over time would afford the children the opportunity to talk about what they see, create hypotheses, and search for answers. For example, if the toddlers notice that the butterflies fly back to the garden each morning, you could ask, "Where do the butterflies go at night?" Together, you could search for answers through observations or in books.

Toddlers are also very interested in how things grow. They cognitively link their own personal experiences to explain their observations of changes in other living things. Growing a vegetable garden is a particularly engaging experience for toddlers because of this interest. You could enlist the assistance of the toddlers to plant fruits and vegetables that the children are familiar with as well as novel ones. Encourage them to assist in tending to the crops, harvesting them, preparing and cooking them, and, of course, eating them. Toddlers understand, albeit in a primitive way, that they eat food to grow. You can assist them in discovering that plants need food also. To extend this thinking and further help the environment, you can compost their uneaten food from snack and lunch to enrich the soil. Thus, the toddlers will come to see that they can play an active role in helping to sustain their environment (Honig, 2015). More importantly, however, learning to care for plants and the environment is part of developing a disposition to care (Noddings, 2005), and, as the following quote reminds us:

> The human heart and the environment are inseparably linked together. If you think only of yourself, ultimately you will lose. (Dalai Lama XIV, 2002)

8-3c Partnerships and Advocacy

Teachers cannot tackle some of the bigger environmental issues without creating partnerships with family members, colleagues, directors, and/or licensing agents. For example, instead of needing to recycle individual baby food jars, it may be possible to make the baby food in the kitchen at the center or family child care home. Whenever possible, you should shop locally at farmers' markets or directly from farmers to obtain fresh fruits and vegetables in addition to those available at your local supermarket (Marriott, 2008; Taylor, 2008). Clean, cook, and mash the food as necessary before serving it to the children. Involving children in the process also tends to increase their desire to eat the "fruits of their labor," which can be a real benefit if you are introducing new vegetables to a group of toddlers. When you need to begin with frozen vegetables, you can quickly thaw a serving of peas, for example, from the larger package, cook, and then mash them for an infant. Not only would this practice be better nutritionally for the infant, but it would also eliminate the need to recycle jars.

Another option is for child care centers to reduce their reliance on disposable napkins, paper towels, and baby wipes. Much waste is created each day in an infant/toddler classroom. Teachers can rethink their practices to eliminate some of the waste. To illustrate, just imagine how much paper would be saved if you switched to cloth napkins at lunchtime. In addition, instead of cleaning up children with paper products, consider the warmth and softness of a warm, wet washcloth on the skin after snack or lunch. This may also start the soothing, calming process before naptime. When paper products cannot be eliminated entirely, purchase those manufactured with recycled materials, such as office paper products, toilet paper, and paper towels.

Consider all of the waste with each diaper change. Given the yet-unresolved-controversies regarding cloth versus disposable diapers, if a family wants to use cloth diapers, you should make every attempt to support this decision. Consult your local licensing representative for specific procedures that should be followed. Beyond that issue, there are other ways to reduce the use of diaper wipes. When an infant is just wet, it is better for the child's skin to be cleaned with a washcloth that has been dampened with warm water. You could place a lidded clothes basket next to the diaper pail and dispose of the cloth much as you would the soiled diaper. Then, the clothes are washed at the end of each day so that they can be reused.

Child care centers and family child care homes should consider speaking with their licensing representatives to find ways to reduce the use of harsh chemicals. According to Taylor (2008), research shows that when hospitals use green cleaning products, patients recover faster and spend less time in the hospital. It would seem logical that subjecting infants and toddlers to harsh cleaning products to disinfect surfaces may not be the best option. (Taylor [2008] also provides a list of cleaning products that are considered environmentally friendly.) In addition, it is important to remember that washing children's hands with soap and warm water is the best defense against spreading germs. Programs should avoid using antibacterial soap with very young children as recent animal research suggests that it alters hormone regulation. While the effects on humans are being investigated, the FDA is not suggesting that the product be pulled from the market, yet the agency clearly states that they have limited evidence that antibacterial soaps provide benefit over washing with regular soap and water (US Food and Drug Administration, 2010).

This section has provided just a few ways to start thinking about how teachers and programs can "go green" to build a more sustainable society for the next generations. Table 8–3 provides a list of suggestions that have the potential to have a greater positive impact on the environment.

An environment should never be considered "finished" or "complete." You should frequently (i.e., at least once a month) consider the primary question of this chapter, "How do teachers create meaningful learning environments that facilitate optimal development for the children?" Regularly review all the ways that the physical environment impacts the children's development and learning and vice versa because the answer is constantly evolving. Teachers must continually assess and respond to the changing developmental needs and interests of young children.

READING CHECKPOINT

Before moving on with your reading, make sure that you can answer the following questions about the material discussed so far.

1. What are three things that teachers could do to "go green" in their classrooms?
2. Compare the teacher's perspective, the child's perspective, and society's perspective on environmental design. How are they alike and different?

TABLE 8–3 ▸ Changes for "Going Green" Making a Positive Environmental Impact

Utilize solar or wind power to provide part of your electricity needs. Research available rebates and incentives at the state and federal levels.
Order an energy audit from your local utility company. Follow as many of the suggestions as you can. For example, install a programmable thermostat to minimize heating/cooling the building at night.
Join a purchasing group with other child care centers/family providers to purchase paper and food items as well as bulk equipment.
Create partnerships with families and local businesses to recycle nonhazardous "beautiful stuff" that can be used in unique ways by the children.

© Cengage Learning

8-4 Selecting Equipment and Materials

Early childhood educators must carefully select the equipment and materials they make available to the children, based on the children's needs and abilities (Table 8–4). For example, with young infants, you should have a high chair available for feeding; infants who can sit unassisted skillfully can sit on a low chair at a table. Select materials to use based on your

TABLE 8–4 ▸ Basic Equipment for Infants and Toddlers

CHILD CARE CENTER CLASSROOM	CHILD CARE HOME
	Indoor
EATING	
high chairs	low chairs and tables
	booster seats for kitchen and dining room chairs
low chairs and tables	kitchen and dining room table
SLEEPING	
rocking chair	rocking chair
cribs	cribs
cots	family beds and sofa covered with the child's sheet and blanket for naps
TOILETING	
changing table sink and hand-washing supplies	changing table or counter space in the bathroom for changing
free-standing potties	diapers, hand-washing and storing supplies
supply storage	
toilet seat adapter	toilet seat adapter
steps (if needed at sink)	steps (if needed at sink)
STORAGE	
coat rack	coat rack near door
cubbies shelves: toys, books	especially designated shelves in the family room, living room, and/or bedroom where books and toys are kept for the child care children
RECORD KEEPING	
bulletin boards	corked wall and refrigerator door space to exhibit art treasures
record-keeping table, counter	table, counter, drawer
	Outdoor
CLIMBING STRUCTURES	
wood, tile, rubber tires, steps, tied ropes	rubber tires, steps, tied ropes
CONTAINERS	
sand table or box water table	large plastic trays or tubs for sand and water

© Cengage Learning

TABLE 8–5 ▸ Types of Equipment and Materials

SOFT	HARD
puppets	blocks
cloth and soft plastic dolls	hard plastic dolls
dress-up clothes	cars, trucks
mats and rugs	cardboard books
cloth or foam scraps	wood
ribbon or yarn	plastic bottles
stuffed animals	sandpaper
rubber or sponge balls	metal cans
OPEN-ENDED	**CLOSED/REAL OBJECTS**
clay	stacking rings
blocks	zipper
water	button/buttonhole
sand	lidded containers
SIMPLE	**COMPLEX**
one-piece puzzle	wooden blocks
doll	doll clothes
HIGH MOBILITY	**LOW MOBILITY**
bike	water
toy cars, trucks	slide
stroller, buggy	books

© Cengage Learning

choke tube Plastic tube used to determine safe sizes of objects for child play.

© 2012 Cengage Learning

PHOTO 8–10 Many states require a choke tube in all child care settings.

observations of the children to support their individual needs and interests (Table 8–5). Kate, for example, is exploring peer relationships and would benefit from a toy that puts her into contact with others, such as a rubber ball. When Adrianna is upset, she may need a soft, cuddly toy that encourages seclusion, such as a teddy bear. Manendra is working on representing complex ideas, so clay would be a good open-ended material to offer him.

Materials and equipment must be selected with special care because very young children put everything they touch to a hard test: they bite, pinch, hit, fling, bang, pound, and tear at whatever they can. In their exploration, they focus on actions and do not think initially in terms of consequences. Therefore, caregivers must take care to provide only materials and equipment that can safely withstand intense use by children.

When purchasing equipment for any child care setting, consider buying a **choke tube**; many states require its use (Photo 8–10). Loose toy pieces are dropped through an opening in the device; if the pieces go through the tube, they are considered a swallowable hazard and are discarded or used only when toddlers are under constant supervision. Toys with pieces larger than the opening are presented to the child as part of the regular learning environment.

In other words, items that are not a choking hazard can be put on a shelf for a child to select independently.

8-4a Age-Appropriate Materials

When purchasing materials, be aware that the age classifications provided will not accurately fit each child. This brings up the crucial distinction between age and individual appropriateness. An item that is right for many other infants may not be appropriate for a specific infant in your care because of the developmental skills she possesses. Caregivers must determine when an item is appropriate for a particular child.

Selection of appropriate equipment and materials involves a cost-benefit analysis. To determine whether an item is cost-effective, analyze the following factors for each item:

- The areas of development facilitated
- The ages of children who can use it
- The number of senses it engages
- The number of ways it can be used
- Safety factors
- The type, quality, and durability of construction

Table 8–6 provides an example of deciding whether to purchase a wooden telephone. The telephone was evaluated as supporting two areas of development: social and cognitive. When program goals emphasize the development of the whole child, a variety of items facilitating physical, emotional, social, and cognitive development are needed. Some materials attract interest at particular ages. The telephone can be used with a wide range of ages, thus is a better buy than materials with a limited age range.

Because infants and toddlers interact with their environment through their senses, they need items that stimulate the senses. Children of different ages make use of their senses in different ways. In the first few months of life, infants see many things and need items that stimulate their interest in seeing. They do not have much control of their hands and fingers, so touching is limited to bumping, banging, and eventually grasping. A limited number and kind of items are needed to stimulate touching. However, 18-month-olds actively use all their senses, so they need a wider range of items to stimulate each of their senses. How many senses does the telephone stimulate?

Some equipment and materials can be used in only one way; others have flexible uses (refer to the discussion of open-ended materials versus real objects in previous sections). Children and caregivers can adjust and adapt open-ended materials in a variety of ways to facilitate development. Single-use materials, like the telephone in the example, are in themselves neither good nor bad, but they may be costly.

It is important to analyze how materials and equipment are constructed. What they are made of and how they are put together will determine their durability when used by the children. This in turn will determine whether the item can serve the purposes for which it is intended in the program. Poorly constructed items that fall apart are frustrating, often unsafe for

TABLE 8–6 ▶ Guide for Analyzing Equipment or Materials

ANALYSIS	
FACILITATED DEVELOPMENT	**TELEPHONE (EXAMPLE)**
physical	
emotional	
social	X
cognitive	X
AGE GROUP	
0–6 months	
6–12 months	
12–18 months	X
18–24 months	X
24–30 months	X
30–36 months	X
SENSES APPEALED TO	
seeing	
hearing	X
touching	X
tasting	
smelling	
NUMBER OF USES	
single	X
flexible	
SAFETY FACTORS	
nontoxic	X
sturdy	X
no sharp edges	X
CONSTRUCTION	
MATERIAL	
fabric	
paper	
cardboard	
rubber	
plastic	
wood	X
metal	
QUALITY	
fair	
good	
excellent	X
DURABILITY	
fair	
good	
excellent	X
COST—$	
commercial	$15.00
homemade	
COMMENTS:	

children, and costly. The telephone is of high quality, wood construction that should be durable for many years.

The cost of equipment and materials has become astronomical. Therefore, most programs must decide which commercially made items they can purchase and which items they can make themselves.

8-4b Homemade Materials

Homemade items should meet high standards for construction, durability, and safety. The items we make can be more individualized than commercially prepared items, stimulating the interest and development of children in the program. For example, using cardboard-mounted color photographs of each child to identify space for storing belongings will appeal to the children more than a commercially produced label. Resources such as Herr and Swim (2002) and Miller and Gibbs (2002) are available that explain how to make homemade materials. In addition, Part 3 of this text includes ideas for homemade materials.

Diligent scrounging of free and inexpensive materials from parents, friends, and community businesses and industries can greatly reduce the cost of homemade items. One group that has developed a very creative and beneficial support system to help child care programs locate and use scrounged materials is the St. Louis Teachers' Recycle Center. The organization operates a recycling center for discarded or excess industrial materials that can be used by teachers, parents, and youth groups to provide learning activities for children for free or at a fraction of the usual cost. Because of the demand, they have a traveling recycle center for delivering materials or displaying them at educational events.

Before moving on with your reading, make sure that you can answer the following questions about the material discussed so far.

1. How can caregivers determine whether a piece of equipment or material is useful in the program?
2. List safety factors caregivers must consider in selecting toys and equipment for infants and toddlers.
3. Describe how a toy or piece of equipment may be safe for one child and unsafe for another.

READING CHECKPOINT

8-5 Protecting Children's Health and Safety

All early childhood education programs must have clearly defined policies and procedures for protecting children's health and safety. The child care program should be a model for families to duplicate. These policies should be well thought out and designed from the viewpoint of the child and with prevention as the underlying tenet for health and safety.

Policies will need to be determined on such issues as these:

- Respectful care and treatment of children, families, and staff
- Confidentiality of children's records

- Detection and prevention of child abuse
- Emergency care and training for staff
- Communicable diseases
- Keeping medical records and files for children and staff up to date

8-5a Emergency Procedures

Each program should have policies and procedures in place and practice them regularly to ensure that the needs of the children can be immediately and effectively met in the event of natural disasters that are common to the area (e.g., hurricane, tornado) as well as fire. Emergency numbers, evacuation routes, and established meeting places should be up to date and posted in a convenient place for staff to see.

Materials or supplies needed during an emergency, such as fire extinguishers, need to be organized in an accessible location and tested periodically to ensure they are in proper working condition. In addition, you should practice evacuating the building safely with the children. Many state licensing regulations require fire drills to be performed, timed, and recorded on a monthly basis. Talk with the children about times when all of you might need to get out of the building quickly; be careful, however, not to scare them. Discuss how the sirens or signals might be loud and hurt their ears. When practicing a fire drill, warn the children in advance to minimize feelings of fright. If you have nonwalkers, select one crib that can fit through doorways, put heavy-duty wheels on it, and put a special symbol on it. When you need to evacuate, put the nonwalking children in this special crib and wheel it outside. If you have toddlers, hold hands, talk calmly, and walk the toddlers as quickly as possible out of the building to the designated spot.

8-5b Immunization Schedule

Program policies for immunization should reflect the requirements set forth by the appropriate state licensing agency. The immunization schedule in Figure 8–1, from the American Academy of Pediatrics, provides a general guide of immunizations for very young children.

8-5c Signs and Symptoms of Possible Severe Illness

Each center or family home program that provides care to young children must have policies and procedures in place to recognize and respond to illnesses and communicable diseases. Teachers should watch carefully for the signs of severe illness such as having a temperature; coughing, wheezing or breathing difficulties; vomiting or diarrhea; or a rash.

Children who exhibit any of these symptoms or who demonstrate unusual behavior in relation to any of these symptoms should be removed to a predetermined place of isolation, where they should be cared for until a family member takes them home. Given the contagious nature of some illnesses, programs must report to other families as well as the local health department that children have been exposed.

FIGURE 8–1 ▸ Recommended Immunization Schedule

Recommended Immunization Schedule for Persons Aged 0 Through 6 Years—United States • 2009
For those who fall behind or start late, see the catch-up schedule

Vaccine ▼ Age ▶	Birth	1 month	2 months	4 months	6 months	12 months	15 months	18 months	19–23 months	2–3 years	4–6 years
Hepatitis B[1]	HepB	HepB		see footnote 1		HepB					
Rotavirus[2]			RV	RV	RV[2]						
Diphtheria, Tetanus, Pertussis[3]			DTaP	DTaP	DTaP	see footnote 3	DTaP				DTaP
Haemophilus influenzae type b[4]			Hib	Hib	Hib[4]	Hib					
Pneumococcal[5]			PCV	PCV	PCV	PCV				PPSV	
Inactivated Poliovirus			IPV	IPV		IPV					IPV
Influenza[6]						Influenza (Yearly)					
Measles, Mumps, Rubella[7]						MMR		see footnote 7			MMR
Varicella[8]						Varicella		see footnote 8			Varicella
Hepatitis A[9]						HepA (2 doses)				HepA Series	
Meningococcal[10]										MCV	

Range of recommended ages

Certain high-risk groups

This schedule indicates the recommended ages for routine administration of currently licensed vaccines, as of December 1, 2008, for children aged 0 through 6 years. Any dose not administered at the recommended age should be administered at a subsequent visit, when indicated and feasible. Licensed combination vaccines may be used whenever any component of the combination is indicated and other components are not contraindicated and if approved by the Food and Drug Administration for that dose of the series. Providers should consult the relevant Advisory Committee on Immunization Practices statement for detailed recommendations, including high-risk conditions: http://www.cdc.gov/vaccines/pubs/acip-list.htm. Clinically significant adverse events that follow immunization should be reported to the Vaccine Adverse Event Reporting System (VAERS). Guidance about how to obtain and complete a VAERS form is available at http://www.vaers.hhs.gov or by telephone, 800-822-7967.

1. Hepatitis B vaccine (HepB). *(Minimum age: birth)*
At birth:
• Administer monovalent HepB to all newborns before hospital discharge.
• If mother is hepatitis B surface antigen (HBsAg)-positive, administer HepB and 0.5 mL of hepatitis B immune globulin (HBIG) within 12 hours of birth.
• If mother's HBsAg status is unknown, administer HepB within 12 hours of birth. Determine mother's HBsAg status as soon as possible and, if HBsAg-positive, administer HBIG (no later than age 1 week).
After the birth dose:
• The HepB series should be completed with either monovalent HepB or a combination vaccine containing HepB. The second dose should be administered at age 1 or 2 months. The final dose should be administered no earlier than age 24 weeks.
• Infants born to HBsAg-positive mothers should be tested for HBsAg and antibody to HBsAg (anti-HBs) after completion of at least 3 doses of the HepB series, at age 9 through 18 months (generally at the next well-child visit).
4-month dose:
• Administration of 4 doses of HepB to infants is permissible when combination vaccines containing HepB are administered after the birth dose.

2. Rotavirus vaccine (RV). *(Minimum age: 6 weeks)*
• Administer the first dose at age 6 through 14 weeks (maximum age: 14 weeks 6 days). Vaccination should not be initiated for infants aged 15 weeks or older (i.e., 15 weeks 0 days or older).
• Administer the final dose in the series by age 8 months 0 days.
• If Rotarix® is administered at ages 2 and 4 months, a dose at 6 months is not indicated.

3. Diphtheria and tetanus toxoids and acellular pertussis vaccine (DTaP). *(Minimum age: 6 weeks)*
• The fourth dose may be administered as early as age 12 months, provided at least 6 months have elapsed since the third dose.
• Administer the final dose in the series at age 4 through 6 years.

4. Haemophilus influenzae type b conjugate vaccine (Hib). *(Minimum age: 6 weeks)*
• If PRP-OMP (PedvaxHIB® or Comvax® [HepB-Hib]) is administered at ages 2 and 4 months, a dose at age 6 months is not indicated.
• TriHiBit® (DTaP/Hib) should not be used for doses at ages 2, 4, or 6 months but can be used as the final dose in children aged 12 months or older.

5. Pneumococcal vaccine. *(Minimum age: 6 weeks for pneumococcal conjugate vaccine [PCV]; 2 years for pneumococcal polysaccharide vaccine [PPSV])*
• PCV is recommended for all children aged younger than 5 years. Administer 1 dose of PCV to all healthy children aged 24 through 59 months who are not completely vaccinated for their age.

• Administer PPSV to children aged 2 years or older with certain underlying medical conditions (see MMWR 2000;49[No. RR-9]), including a cochlear implant.

6. Influenza vaccine. *(Minimum age: 6 months for trivalent inactivated influenza vaccine [TIV]; 2 years for live, attenuated influenza vaccine [LAIV])*
Administer annually to children aged 6 months through 18 years.
• For healthy nonpregnant persons (i.e., those who do not have underlying medical conditions that predispose them to influenza complications) aged 2 through 49 years, either LAIV or TIV may be used.
• Children receiving TIV should receive 0.25 mL if aged 6 through 35 months or 0.5 mL if aged 3 years or older.
• Administer 2 doses (separated by at least 4 weeks) to children aged younger than 9 years who are receiving influenza vaccine for the first time or who were vaccinated for the first time during the previous influenza season but only received 1 dose.

7. Measles, mumps, and rubella vaccine (MMR). *(Minimum age: 12 months)*
• Administer the second dose at age 4 through 6 years. However, the second dose may be administered before age 4, provided at least 28 days have elapsed since the first dose.

8. Varicella vaccine. *(Minimum age: 12 months)*
• Administer the second dose at age 4 through 6 years. However, the second dose may be administered before age 4, provided at least 3 months have elapsed since the first dose.
• For children aged 12 months through 12 years the minimum interval between doses is 3 months. However, if the second dose was administered at least 28 days after the first dose, it can be accepted as valid.

9. Hepatitis A vaccine (HepA). *(Minimum age: 12 months)*
• Administer to all children aged 1 year (i.e., aged 12 through 23 months). Administer 2 doses at least 6 months apart.
• Children not fully vaccinated by age 2 years can be vaccinated at subsequent visits.
• HepA also is recommended for children older than 1 year who live in areas where vaccination programs target older children or who are at increased risk of infection. See MMWR 2006;55(No. RR-7).

10. Meningococcal vaccine. *(Minimum age: 2 years for meningococcal conjugate vaccine [MCV] and for meningococcal polysaccharide vaccine [MPSV])*
• Administer MCV to children aged 2 through 10 years with terminal complement component deficiency, anatomic or functional asplenia, and certain other high-risk groups. See MMWR 2005;54(No. RR-7).
• Persons who received MPSV 3 or more years previously and who remain at increased risk for meningococcal disease should be revaccinated with MCV.

The Recommended Immunization Schedules for Persons Aged 8 Through 18 Years are approved by the Advisory Committee on Immunization Practices (www.cdc.gov/vaccines/recs/acip), the American Academy of Pediatrics (http://www.aap.org), and the American Academy of Family Physicians (http://www.aafp.org).
DEPARTMENT OF HEALTH AND HUMAN SERVICES • CENTERS FOR DISEASE CONTROL AND PREVENTION

Department of Health and Human Services - Centers for Disease Control and Prevention

8-5d First Aid

First aid refers to treatment administered for injuries and illnesses that are not considered life threatening. Before an event occurs, programs must have in place policies and procedures to prepare the adults to act. For example, programs need to keep a completed Emergency Care Permission form on file for all children. This allows emergency medical personnel to administer life-saving care if the situation calls for it. In addition, all teachers and program staff (e.g., administrators, cleaning staff, and cooks) should be educated in first aid, universal precautions, and cardiopulmonary resuscitation (CPR) and keep their certification up to date. Thus, first-aid procedures should be based on principles that are familiar to everyone involved in the care setting. Take the following steps in the event of an emergency:

1. Summon emergency medical assistance (call 911 in most areas) for any injury or illness that requires more than simple first aid.
2. Stay calm and in control of the situation.
3. Always remain with the child. If necessary, send another adult for help.
4. Keep the child still until the extent of injuries or illness can be determined. If in doubt, have the child stay in the same position and await emergency medical help.
5. Quickly evaluate the child's condition, paying special attention to an open airway, breathing, and circulation.
6. Carefully plan and administer appropriate emergency care.
7. Do not give any medications unless they are prescribed to save a life in certain life-threatening conditions.
8. Record all the facts concerning the accident and treatment administered on the appropriate form; provide one copy to the child's family member(s) and one in the child's file.

First-aid kits should be visible and easily accessible to teachers but out of the reach of children. Kits should be available in all indoor and outdoor environments. If the playground is large, you should consider having two kits so they are more easily reached. The contents of first-aid kits should reflect your particular state's licensing regulations, but they might include the following:

adhesive tape	bandages of assorted sizes
cotton balls	roller gauze, 1″ and 2″ widths
flashlight	gauze pads, sterile, 2″ × 2″, 4″ × 4″
latex gloves	instant ice pack or plastic bags
blunt-tipped scissors	tweezers
spirits of ammonia	splints
tongue blades	first-aid book

8-5e Universal Precautions

universal precautions Medical term for a series of standard procedures used to keep the patient and staff as healthy and safe as possible during physical care.

Universal precautions must be understood and used by every person in the care setting who is around body fluids. Each caregiver is responsible for receiving the training and updates necessary to be aware of current policies. Universal precautions are a set of procedures to prevent coming into contact with bodily fluids. Infectious germs may be contained in human waste (urine, feces and body fluids, saliva, nasal discharge, tissue and injury discharges, eye discharges, and blood). Because many infected people carry communicable diseases without symptoms, and many are contagious before they experience symptoms, everyone must protect himself or herself and the children he or she serves by routinely carrying out sanitation and disinfection procedures that prevent potential illness-spreading conditions.

Medical gloves must be worn every time bodily fluids are present, such as when changing diapers or controlling a bloody nose (Photo 8–11).

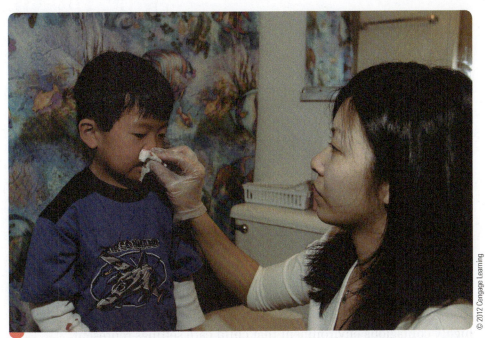

PHOTO 8–11 Medical gloves must be worn every time bodily fluids are present.

Blood contaminants such as hepatitis B are found in blood and blood fluid (watery discharge from lacerations and cuts) and pose a real health threat. Other fluids, such as saliva, may present health dangers as well. Procedures for handling spills of bodily fluids—urine, feces, blood, saliva, nasal discharge, eye discharge, and tissue discharges—*after putting on the medical gloves*, are as follows:

1. For spills of vomit, urine, feces, blood, and/or blood-containing bodily fluids: Anything that had the potential to come in contact with the substance (e.g., the floor, tabletop, toys, diaper-changing table) should be thoroughly cleaned and disinfected, even if contaminants are not visible to your naked eye. Use a solution of 1/4 cup liquid chlorine bleach to 1 gallon tap water when cleaning contaminated surfaces. Even if the area looks clean, anyone involved in cleaning contaminated surfaces must wear gloves to protect herself from exposure to disease.

2. Blood-contaminated material and diapers should be disposed of in a plastic bag with a secure tie, and labeled with a tag.

3. Mops should be cleaned, rinsed in sanitizing solution, wrung as dry as possible, and hung to dry.

4. After you have removed your gloves, engage in established hand-washing procedures (see Chapter 9) for yourself and with the children.

5. Because of the frequency of children touching objects to their mouths, toys and all equipment should be sanitized and disinfected on a regular basis. Rooms with nondiapered children should be cleaned weekly. For example, individual children's items for personal care and hygiene should be sent home with parents to be cleaned weekly. Crib mattresses should be cleaned at least weekly. Thermometers, pacifiers, and the like should be disinfected between uses.

It is important to realize that having policies and procedures for universal precautions may not be sufficient for guaranteeing compliance if everyone is not held accountable for following them. Alkon and Cole (2012) discovered that child care providers in their sample demonstrated the lowest level of compliance with national health and safety standards for washing children's hands and cleaning and sanitizing counters. Everyone working in a child care program must come to value these policies and procedures for what they really are: personal protection. As will be discussed in the next section, adults can be at higher risks for contracting contagious diseases than children are at getting them from us.

Human Immunodeficiency Virus (HIV) Infection

HIV infection Immune disease that attacks white blood cells and is transmitted through open sores or other bodily fluid sources.

This infection attacks and destroys white blood cells, making the person more susceptible to illnesses. Acquired Immune Deficiency Syndrome (AIDS) is the final stage of the **HIV infection**. No cases of transmission through casual contact have been reported in child care anywhere in the world (National Network for Child Care, 2014). HIV-positive adults may care for children. However, the HIV caregiver is at great risk due to the highly contagious environment that child care settings represent.

Parents of HIV-infected children should be alerted to any exposure to communicable diseases such as measles and chicken pox. Their pediatrician will probably want to take special precautions to protect them. As with any other child, universal precautions are used in every incident of spilled blood or possible blood exposure.

8-5f Playground Safety

The National Program for Playground Safety (NPPS) provides resources to child care teachers as they work to keep playgrounds safe for children. This organization suggests that when teachers use S.A.F.E., they uphold their responsibility for keeping children safe (NPPS, 2015). S.A.F.E. stands for:

1. **Supervision.** Does not mean standing back and watching. Actively engage in learning experiences with the infants and toddlers to support their play and provide necessary redirection to prevent injuries.

2. **Age-Appropriate.** All equipment should be designed for the age of children who are using it. The steps on a slide or a climber, for example, should be spaced at the appropriate distance depending on how long the children's legs are. Of course, just because it is age-appropriate does not always ensure that it is individually appropriate. Provide extra supervision as necessary.

3. **Fall Surface.** The American Academy of Pediatrics, American Public Health Association, and the National Resource Center for Health and Safety in Child Care (2011) suggest these modifications to make safer playgrounds: place climbing structures closer to the ground (i.e., 1 foot per year of age for intended users); mount them over 9–12 inches of uncompressed, shock-absorbing material such as pea gravel, or tree bark; have enough space for each child using the playground at any one time (amount varies depending on the child's age) to place all equipment far enough away from other structures and child traffic patterns to prevent collisions; cover sharp

edges and exposed bolts; and teach children to play safely. Mack, Sacks, Hudson, and Thompson (2001) found that child care centers with indoor equipment were using mats designed for exercising or tumbling as fall surfaces. When tested, those mats were found to be insufficient for preventing injuries. Thus, attention to selecting the correct type of fall surface is just as important indoors as out.

4. Equipment Maintenance. All pieces of equipment, indoors and outdoors, should be examined daily to ensure that they are functioning properly and pose no hazards to the children. Unsafe climbers, slides, and other equipment should be removed until repaired. The Massachusetts Department of Public Health has developed a Site Safety Checklist and a Playground Safety Checklist that can be used or adapted for assessing and providing safe and healthy indoor and outdoor environments for infants and toddlers (see Appendix A).

As discussed earlier, everyone should also know how to complete an injury report properly. Completed reports should be routinely examined by all providers to identify and correct trouble spots. More importantly, this regular, systematic study of injury in child care centers and in home child care is needed to enhance prevention efforts because very young children do not understand how to be safe (Waibel & Misra, 2003) and because children 2–5 years of age cared for in child care centers experience more injuries than children that age cared for by parents in their own home (Davis, Godfrey, & Rankin, 2013).

Before moving on with your reading, make sure that you can answer the following question about the material discussed so far.

1. Explain how universal precautions serve to protect everyone's safety, but especially the safety of the caregivers.

READING CHECKPOINT

Summary

8-1 Create high-quality and developmentally appropriate indoor and outdoor learning environments from the teacher's perspective.

Teachers must consciously plan indoor and outdoor learning environments to support the physical, social, emotional, and intellectual needs of children. To do that, they must consider many different aspects.

8-2 Improve a learning environment based on the child's perspective.

Preparing high-quality indoor and outdoor learning environments should also consider the child's perspective. How is the environment experienced by the children? Many questions from the child's perspective were provided to help spark thinking and analysis about learning environments.

8-3 Describe why teachers should consider society's perspective when creating high-quality indoor and outdoor learning environments.

Learning environments need to reflect our society's need for sustainability. Strategies for "going green" were provided.

8-4 Select materials for use in a classroom based upon criteria.

Selecting appropriate equipment and materials requires planning and reflecting. Items should be appropriate for the age of the children as well as reflect the needs, abilities, and culture of individual children.

8-5 Evaluate policies and procedures for protecting the health and safety of very young children.

Teachers have to collaborate with colleagues to implement policies and procedures to protect the health and safety of themselves and very young children. Sometimes teachers also have to create or modify such policies and procedures for their specific classroom, group of children, and/or individual children.

CASE STUDY Ena's Medical Challenges

Ena Robson, who was 7 1/2 months old, had an unusual first day in the group family child care center. One of the helpers got sick in the middle of the day, and another provider was called on to take her place. The first provider had been ready to begin an assessment of Ena, but her replacement was not told of this, so she did not conduct one.

Ena was small, frail, and odd-looking. Her skull was box-shaped, her eyes were set far apart, and her mouth seemed to be in an unusual position when you looked straight at her. She had only a wisp of hair, she was mostly inactive, and her eyes appeared to be slow in reacting to visual changes. On her first day, Ena was dressed in a tattered but clean outfit with strawberry patches and a hat.

Because the regular provider was sick again the next day, the director took care of Ena and noted her appearance after checking her medical records. She performed a developmental assessment with the following results.

Physical, cognitive, and language skills were at the four-month level. Her social and emotional skills were at the six-month level.

Because there was a significant delay in three areas (two months with a 7 1/2-month-old), the director decided that a conference was needed soon so that appropriate referrals for further evaluation could be made.

A conference was arranged with Ena's mother to obtain permission in writing for the referrals. Mrs. Robson arrived with Ena's grandmother, who was a trained nurse's aide, early in the morning for the conference. The director had reviewed the medical and family records in advance and found no unusual medical or family history. Della, Ena's mother, was tall but appeared to have been sick because she needed help walking, had deep circles under her eyes, and had a rather gray color to her skin. Della explained that Ena had experienced many fevers off and on but that she was well at present. The director began asking questions from an interview form, and after a short time, Della became visibly stressed. Her voice changed, her arms and hands waved when she spoke, and she refused to answer questions about the pregnancy and Ena's birth. When the director rephrased the question to ask if Ena was a full-term baby, Mrs. Robson became agitated, and Ena's grandmother answered in a calm voice that it would probably be best if they stopped the conference but that she would like to set up an evening appointment. A home visit was scheduled for that evening in Ena's home, and her grandmother said she would speak to Della in the meantime.

The apartment where Della and Ena lived was small and sparsely furnished. The grandmother and a registered nurse were administering an intravenous injection to Mrs. Robson when the director arrived. When Mrs. Robson saw the director, she began to cry, and Ena's grandmother sadly explained that both Della and Ena had AIDS. The director maintained a professional demeanor and actively listened to the grandmother as she discussed her sadness, anger, and disappointment. It was obvious that both Della and her mother were very fearful that the director would not allow Ena to stay in the child care setting. The director learned that Della's disease was progressing rapidly in spite of medications, and that Ena would start on medication the next day. Both Della and her mother asked the director to please keep Ena.

The director assured them that they would keep Ena in the child care center as long as she was not running a fever or showing other disease complications. She assured the family that all of her staff used universal precaution techniques, and they were all aware that blood was the only transmitter of the disease. She reassured the family that her staff would hold, feed, and play with Ena in both the indoor and outdoor environments. They discussed the importance of having Ena take her medication as prescribed by her doctor, on a regular basis, and at the same time of day. As long as Ena was without disease symptoms, the director assured them that Ena was welcome to attend the center. Both Della and her mother were relieved to hear that the staff would keep the illness confidential because that was permitted by law.

The result of the home visit was that no further referrals were made at that time. The director and teacher decided that Ena might need more time to adjust to her new routine before another assessment could be made. In the meantime, Ena was cared for in both indoor and outdoor environments at the child care center, just like the other children. The staff provided her with more rest and activities to enhance her physical, cognitive, and language skill areas, and Ena showed improvement in her growth and development.

1. Discuss your feelings about working with a child like Ena, who has AIDS. How do you feel you would handle such a responsibility?
2. What should the teacher consider changing in her environment to make it more individually appropriate for Ena?
3. What information should the caregivers use when selecting equipment or materials for Ena?
4. What other steps or help might the director have provided to this family?

Lesson Plan

Title: *A Sculpting We Will Go!*

Child Observation:

Charlie was at the outdoor table making a pile of dough into a tall tower. The dough was soft from the heat of his hands and from the warm fall day. The dough kept squishing down on the table, getting flatter rather than taller. Charlie showed he was frustrated by saying "No" and "Don't," but he continued to work for another six minutes.

Child's Developmental Goal:

To develop fine motor skills

To demonstrate creative use of materials

Materials: Clay for sculpting, wire with handles for cutting clay, placemat for each area at the table or a cloth to cover the entire table, smock or shirt to cover child's clothing, wet sponge

Preparation: Put placemats or cloth on the table. Place clay and wire near the end of the table so that adult and child can cut off pieces together. Hang a smock or shirt over the back of each chair to signal that it is needed for this experience. Use the wet sponge to clean up the area as needed.

Learning Environment:

1. When you notice a child at the table, join the child. If necessary, assist with the smock.
2. Draw the child's attention to the clay by using descriptive language. To illustrate, you could say:
   "This is clay. We can cut off a piece for you to use. Can you help me cut it?"
3. Invite Charlie to use the clay with the child at the table, if he hasn't already.
4. By using prompts or asking open-ended questions, encourage the child to touch and manipulate the clay. Say something such as:
   a. I wonder how the clay feels on your fingers.
   b. How can you use your fingers to pinch or shape the clay?

5. Talk about how the clay compares to other dough they've used.
6. If a toddler tries to eat the clay, redirect the child's attention to manipulating the clay. You might say, for example:
   a. The clay is for using with our fingers.
   b. Please keep the clay on the table.
7. When the child is done with the experience, invite her or him to clean up the area for the next child. Be specific about how that should be done. For example, say:
   a. "Please put your clay beside the block of clay" (while pointing).
   b. "Use this sponge to wipe the table beside your placemat" (while pointing).

Professional Resource Download

Guidance Consideration:

If a toddler attempts to take the clay to another area, explain why it needs to stay at the table (e.g., it is messy).

Variations:

When the child is ready, introduce other tools for working with or carving the clay. Talk about how the tools work, and demonstrate how to use them, if necessary.

Important Note:

The focus of the toddlers' work with clay should be on the sensory experience. Toddlers typically do not focus on representing a particular object or idea before they start working or even after they complete their work. This will come later.

Additional Resources

Bergen, S., & Robertson, R. (2013). *Healthy children, healthy lives: The wellness guide for early childhood programs.* St. Paul, MN: Redleaf Press.

Broadhead, P., & Burt, A. (2012). *Understanding young children's learning through play: Building playful pedagogies.* New York: Routledge.

Bullard, J. (2014). *Creating environments for learning: Birth to age eight* (2nd ed.). Upper Saddle River, NJ: Merrill.

Kuh, L. P. (Ed.) (2014). *Thinking critically about environments for young children: Bridging theory and practice.* New York: Teachers College Press.

Quon, E., & Quon, T. (2013). *Little cooks: Fun and easy recipes to make with your kids.* San Francisco, CA: Weldonowen.

Williams, D., & Brown, J. (2012). *Learning gardens and sustainability education: Bringing life to schools and schools to life.* New York: Routledge.

Young, S. T., & Dhanda, K. (2013). *Sustainability: Essentials for business.* Thousand Oaks, CA: Sage Publications, Inc.

9 — Designing the Curriculum

CHAPTER

Learning Objectives

After reading this chapter, you should be able to:

9-1 Identify major influences on the curriculum.

9-2 Defend why routine care times are important for facilitating development and learning.

9-3 Plan daily or weekly, integrated lesson plans that are individualized for each child.

Standards Addressed in This Chapter

naeyc NAEYC Standards for Early Childhood Professional Preparation

1 Promoting Child Development and Learning

4 Using Developmentally Effective Approaches

DAP Developmentally Appropriate Practice Guidelines

2 Teaching to Enhance Development and Learning

3 Planning Curriculum to Achieve Important Goals

In addition, the NAEYC standards for developmentally appropriate practice are divided into six areas particularly important to infant/toddler care. The following areas are addressed in this chapter: *play routines,* and *exploration.*

© 2017 Cengage Learning

curriculum Everything that occurs during the course of the day with infants and toddlers; planned learning experiences and routine care.

Having already discussed how teachers actively construct the physical and social environments for infants and toddlers (Chapters 8 and 6, respectively), let's turn our attention to the intentional design of the intellectual environment. **Curriculum** is everything that you do with a child or that a child experiences through her interactions with the environment from the time she enters the classroom until the time she leaves it (Greenman, Stonehouse, & Schweikert, 2008). While this definition may seem simplistic, it is actually complicated because it requires teachers to consider all of their actions and reactions throughout the day.

You should plan curriculum based on what you know about each child's development, that is, what the child can do now independently and what he can do with assistance. Your teaching or caregiving strategies should scaffold or challenge the child to move toward the next level. In this way, it may be helpful for you to think about how the "curriculum is the child."

Infants and toddlers participate actively in selecting their curriculum and initiating their activities. When Jessie babbles sentence-like sounds and then pauses, Ms. Howard looks over at her, smiles, and answers, "Jessie, you are excited about finding the red ring." Jessie is playing with a large, colored plastic ring that Ms. Howard has set near her. Jessie determines what she will do with the ring and what she will say. Her sounds attract Ms. Howard's attention. Ms. Howard then makes a conscious choice to attend and become attuned to her, engaging her as a competent communicator. Daily experiences provide an integrated curriculum for children to be actively involved with learning about the world around them.

Because the infant and toddler curriculum involves the whole child, the child should have experiences that enhance his or her physical, emotional, social, and cognitive/language development. In addition, infants and toddlers are working on understanding important concepts such as gravity, cause and effect, and directionality. The caregiver is responsible for planning and facilitating this holistic curriculum.

Each child is a distinct being, differing from others in some ways, yet sharing many of the same basic needs. *There is no single curriculum for all infants.* Caregivers have a special responsibility to design each child's curriculum by observing, analyzing, and planning. They can meet these individual needs best when they adopt a developmental perspective. This entails gathering observational data continually, analyzing the data, and then using that data as the justification when selecting materials and planning curricular experiences. Thus, careful, ongoing observation on the part of the adults (e.g., caregivers and family members) facilitates child contributions to the curriculum; it is responsive to the needs, abilities, and interests of each child. Curriculum should also be designed with a purpose in mind. In other words, you should balance meeting areas of development and areas of learning so that the development of the whole child is addressed.

9-1 Influences on the Curriculum

Cultural expectations, the setting, the child, and the caregiver all influence the infant and toddler curriculum. Each of these influences on the child is discussed in detail in the following sections.

9-1a Influences from Cultural Expectations

Families feel pressure from their friends, relatives, strangers (i.e., looks in a restaurant), and the media about their child-rearing activities. They receive comments, praise, suggestions, scolding, and ridicule on a variety of topics. Sometimes they hear conflicting comments on the same topic, such as the following:

- The parent should stay home with the newborn and very young infant *versus* it is acceptable for the parent of a child of any age to work outside the home.

- The parents are wasting their time when talking to and playing with a young baby *versus* the parents should talk to and play with the infant.

- The infant should start solid foods at 4 months of age *versus* the infant should start solid food after 9 months of age.

Parents must reconcile their attitudes and expectations with those of people around them, including their child's teacher. This is a long and laborious task that often results in inconsistent beliefs and practices. It may seem that parents are wishy-washy or flip-flop about what they do versus what they want you to do. When you understand the various pressures on families and use active listening, you can help them resolve these parenting conflicts. Using the other positive communication skills discussed earlier (Chapter 7) will help family members share their expectations with you.

Cultural variations will be evident during your conversations with family members. Family members, even within the same family, hold various ideas about child-rearing and parenting techniques. Some family members, for example, expect to be perfect parents. The realities of parenting often cause them to feel guilty when they fall short of perfection or when they leave their child with another caregiver. Their frustrations may affect their attitudes about themselves and their interactions with their children and teachers. Sometimes jealousies develop. Early childhood educators can discuss more realistic expectations when a family member raises an issue. On the other hand, some family members seem very casual about their responsibilities. They move from one parenting task to the next with seemingly little thought of goals or consequences. Some of these family members seem to place their children into child care with the attitude, "Do what you want to with them; just keep them safe." The caregiver may need to emphasize the worth of the child in his daily conversations and encourage the family to consider how important it is for them to demonstrate in multiple ways how they value the child. Between these two extremes are family members who want to engage in positive parenting behaviors and who actively invite caregivers to assist them and their children.

Family members look to teachers to reinforce and extend their own child-rearing practices, which is a realistic expectation, within certain boundaries, given the guidelines for developmentally appropriate practice (Copple & Bredekamp, 2009) as well as standards for teacher preparation (NAEYC, 2011a). Our goal is to create partnerships with families, and supporting child-rearing practices, whenever possible, is part of the process. Another aspect of partnering with families involves using what family members believe to inform your interactions with and curriculum

PHOTO 9–1 Each child is a unique being who deserves positive support to reach his or her full potential.

culture Values and beliefs held in common by a group of people.

bias A prejudgment concerning the style and forms of a specific culture.

planning for the child. For example, if a family feeds their toddler from their laps, then it is an acceptable practice for you to hold the child during meals and snacks.

Like families, each caregiver brings unique cultural experiences and expectations to the caregiving role (Photo 9–1). Be aware of how these are similar to or different from those of the families and other staff to plan and provide meaningful curriculum.

Cultural Diversity

Culture can be described as the shared, learned, symbolic system of values, attitudes, and beliefs that shape and influence a person's perceptions and behaviors shared by groups of people (Espinosa, 2010). The group of people referenced in the definition can be large, such as African Americans or Blacks, or it can be small, such as an individual family. Child care settings offer many opportunities to experience cultural diversity because of how this setting raises important issues for discussion around the care and education of very young children. Every culture has somewhat different customs, mores, beliefs, and attitudes toward child care. Although the style and form may vary from one culture to the next, all cultures have healthy child care practices.

Some cultures do not talk to young children as much as other cultures. Some do not smile at them or expect a response. Some carry their babies on their backs; other cultures carry them over their hearts. Father involvement is different from one culture to another, as is the way family members interact with each other. Families also differ on how they define independence for their child. Brainstorming and other problem-solving techniques, along with active listening, will help to address any misunderstandings that may occur. Moreover, valuing and supporting these differences, as well as working to understand child-rearing practices within every culture, are important for being a competent early childhood educator.

Your job is to be sensitive to cultural diversity, seek additional information when values or beliefs clash, and facilitate open conversations between and among family members. This will not be easy because strongly held beliefs are often hidden, even from ourselves, and, therefore, seldom examined. Through shared experiences, readings, and conversations with others, the adults can examine carefully their beliefs and then decide what changes to embark on. In contrast, if you are embarrassed about discussing differences or prejudices, you will continue to (unknowingly) act on your **biases**—negative judgments about the style, form, and content of another person's culture that are made without a thorough investigation. More importantly, however, is that not discussing these issues can actually result in children forming biases. You could, through omission, perpetuate oppressive beliefs and behavior (Derman-Sparks & Edwards, 2010).

To prevent the development of biases, teachers need to take an active role in helping very young children develop to their fullest potential. Optimal development will not happen by chance or naturally as the result of getting older. Human differences can impede children receiving all of the rights they deserve (see Chapter 6) from teachers, other adults, and other children due to inequity of resources and the invisibility of certain kinds of people and cultures within educational systems (Derman-Sparks & Edwards, 2010). Thus, teachers should implement an **anti-biased curriculum** to challenge children's current understanding about identity, fairness, diversity, prejudice, and discrimination. Children should learn how to think critically about unfairness and how to take action to remedy unfair situations. Derman-Sparks and Edwards (2010) and Derman-Sparks, LeeKeenan, and Nimmo (2015) outlined four goals of an anti-biased curriculum for children:

1. Each child will demonstrate self-awareness, confidence, family pride, and positive social identities.

2. Each child will express comfort and joy with human diversity; accurate language for human differences; and deep, caring human connections.

3. Each child will increasingly recognize unfairness, have language to describe unfairness, and understand that unfairness hurts.

4. Each child will demonstrate empowerment and the skills to act, with others or alone, against prejudice and/or discriminatory actions.

An anti-biased approach understands that teachers, both alone and together, can make a huge impact on child outcomes. However, the process is not simplistic; the society beyond their classrooms challenges change because it "has built advantages and disadvantages into its institutions and systems" (Derman-Sparks & Edwards, 2010, p. 3). Child care programs are no exception. Early childhood programs must reconstruct their culture to move away from a dominant-culture-centered program that pushes other viewpoints to the margin to one that intentionally pulls many cultures into the center of all that happens (Derman-Sparks et al., 2015). To accomplish a many-cultures, anti-biased approach, teachers have to acknowledge that each of us is biased toward what we have always known or our own experiences. We must find ways to be open to looking at other ways of doing things that might be equally valid. Many researchers and teachers refer to the idea of tolerating different cultures as considering people and ideas that are different from our own and finding ways of living together. However, King (2001) asks that we transcend toleration and move to being empowered by understanding the following:

1. Culture is learned. Children learn rules both directly by being taught (e.g., "Hold your fork in your left hand and your knife in your right") and through observation. It can be a mistake to assume a person's culture from his or her appearance.

2. Culture is characteristic of groups. Cultural rules come from the group and are passed from generation to generation. Do not mistake individual differences for cultural differences. We share some characteristics

anti-biased curriculum An approach to curriculum development that involves directly addressing issues of identity, fairness, diversity, prejudice, and discrimination through critical thinking and taking action.

with our cultural group, but we are also defined by our individual identities.

3. Culture is a set of rules for behavior. Cultural rules influence people to act similarly, in ways that help them understand each other. Culture is not the behavior, but the rules that shape the behavior.

4. Individual members of a culture are embedded to different degrees in that culture. Because culture is learned, people learn it to different degrees. Family emphasis, individual preferences, and other factors influence how deeply embedded one is in one's culture.

5. Cultures borrow and share rules. Every culture has a consistent core set of rules, but they are not necessarily unique. Two cultures may share rules about some things but have very different rules about other things.

6. Members of culture groups may be proficient at cultural behavior but are unable to describe the rules. People who are culturally competent may not know that they are behaving according to a set of cultural rules; they have absorbed the rules by living them. However, teachers must do the extra work to reflect on and identify the cultural rules, beliefs, and practices that they bring to their work (Im, Parlakian, & Sànchez, 2007).

9-1b Influences from the Care Setting

Family Child Care Home

The setting has a variety of influences on your curriculum. Physical location, financial limitations, family work schedules, and other factors influence the schedule, environment, and curriculum in family child care homes. Establishing a positive learning environment is essential to quality care no matter which resources and limitations you find in your particular setting. Establishing a consistent, warm, friendly environment where large doses of the three *As* (Attention, Approval, and Attunement) are administered is the way to create the most powerful positive influence in any physical setting.

Family child care homes provide a homelike situation for the infant or toddler. During the transition for a child to a new caregiver and a new situation, the caregiver should quickly establish a setting that is familiar to the child: crib, rooms, and routines of playing, eating, and sleeping. A warm, one-on-one relationship between the teacher and the child provides security in this new setting.

Child Care Center

Child care centers care for multiple infants and toddlers in a group setting. Some centers care for infants 6 weeks of age and older, and a few centers are even equipped to care for newborns. The very young infant must receive special care. One caregiver in each shift needs to be responsible for the same infant each day. The caregiver should adjust routines to the infant's body rhythm rather than try to make the infant eat and sleep according to the center's schedule. The early childhood educator will need to work closely with family members to understand the infant's behavior and changing schedule of eating and sleeping. Consistently recording and sharing information with the family is necessary to meet infant needs and involve the family in their child's daily experiences.

Time

The number and age of children in a group will affect the amount of time the caregiver has to give each child. The needs of the other children also affect how the time is allocated. Schedules in the child care home or center should be adjusted to meet the children's needs and the family members' employment schedules. For instance, if the father works the 7:00 a.m. to 3:00 p.m. shift, special planning may be required for the infant who awakens from a nap at 2:45 p.m. to be ready when he arrives. Through the use of attunement, the quality of interaction can remain high, even when time for interaction is limited.

Educational Philosophy of Program and Teachers

The **philosophy** of the program needs to be clearly articulated to teachers and families. Educational decisions should be evaluated in light of the program's philosophy. However, philosophy statements are often broad, leaving much room for interpretation. This is where your personal educational philosophy, including your *image of the child*, comes into play. You must consider your beliefs and how they apply to daily interactions with children, family members, and colleagues.

philosophy Set of educational beliefs that guide behaviors and decision-making for individual teachers and groups of teachers (e.g., programs).

Programs vary in how the teachers approach curriculum (Photo 9–2). Recent research on family child care providers will be used to help us understand the variations. Some family providers approach curriculum as a parent might. They don't plan extra learning activities but focus on what happens in the normal course of the day (e.g., free play, then work together to prepare

© 2017 Cengage Learning

PHOTO 9–2 The caregiver facilitates each child's development by planning experiences that match his interests and skill level.

lunch). In contrast, other family child care providers intentionally create more of a "preschool" atmosphere with multiple planned learning activities that follow a set time schedule. As Freeman (2011) discovered, when she inquired into the daily life of four family child care providers, many providers adopt aspects of both extremes. She found that their curriculum was characterized by responsiveness, play, reflection, and didactic teaching. When considering the first three aspects of the curriculum, the providers regularly made decisions based on what attracted children rather than preparing teaching objectives in advance and holding children to them (Freeman, 2011). These aspects were in contrast to their use of didactic teaching when asked about teaching as an intentional act (Freeman, 2011). Thus, the providers fluctuated between being responsive to the children's needs and interests by using strategies such as listening, negotiation, and encouragement to using direct instruction, cued recall (e.g., verbal questions on first letter of a word), and sequenced craft activities. Adopting an educational philosophy that makes young children's learning a stronger and more natural, integrated dimension of the program would help teacher support optimal learning. Freeman and Karlsson (2012) suggest that family child care providers should adopt four recommendations, grounded in the Reggio Emilia approach to early education, to improve the quality of their program:

1. Provide active, hands-on learning experiences.
2. Support play that promotes strong development and learning.
3. Offer opportunities for challenge within children's potential.
4. Capitalize on the benefits of the home's natural environments.

Those recommendations serve to further support the educational philosophies that serve as the basis for this book. Important aspects of this book include the following:

1. All people are viewed developmentally. From the moment of birth to the time of death, every person is constantly growing in many ways. Focusing on the positive changes resulting from growth helps maintain a positive learning environment.

   a. Each infant and toddler progresses through development at his or her own rate.

   b. Each family member and caregiver adds to his or her knowledge and skills. Caregivers have knowledge obtained from talking, reading, and studying, as well as individual experiences with children and families.

2. Development and growth occur through active interaction with one's environment and can be observed through the four major areas of development (see Table 1–1, page 4).

   a. Each person is an active learner with rights and responsibilities.

   b. Each person constructs knowledge through active interactions with people and materials.

   c. Each person adapts previous experiences to current situations.

   d. Each person builds on the knowledge and skills learned from previous experiences.

e. Each person initiates interactions with other people and materials in the environment.

f. Each person uses multiple modes of representation to express understanding about the world.

9-1c Influences from the Child

Every child has an internal need to grow, develop, and learn. During the first years of life, children's energies are directed toward those purposes consciously and unconsciously. Although children cannot tell you this, observers can see that both random and purposeful behaviors help them.

The children look, touch, taste, listen, smell, reach, bite, push, kick, smile, and take any other action they can to involve themselves actively with the world. The fact that children are sometimes unsuccessful in what they try to do does not stop them from attempting new tasks. Sometimes they may turn away and begin a different task, but they will keep seeking something to do.

Infants learn from the responses they get to their actions. When the caregiver consistently answers cries of distress immediately, infants begin to build up feelings of security. Gradually these responses will help infants learn to exert control over their world. If caregivers let infants cry for long periods before going to them, the infants remain distressed longer, possibly causing them to have difficulty developing a sense of security and trust. Remember from Chapter 3 that research demonstrates unresponsive, harmful, stressful, or neglectful caregiving behaviors affect the development of the brain negatively. Children who experience unresponsive and stressful conditions, either in a home or in a child care setting, were found to have elevated cortisol levels. You can't love a child too much or address their cries of distress too quickly.

Joey, age 7 months, is crying hard. Paulette is speaking softly to him as she checks to see if he is wet, tired, hungry, too hot, or too cold. None of these are the source of his discomfort, so she picks him up and holds him close. She walks with him slowly around the room, rocking him gently in her arms. Joey soon calms down. We can see how Paulette's actions influenced Joey. A child can influence her caregiver in many ways as well. Eden, 30 months, has started to hide and make faces during her bowel movements. Mrs. Frank has noticed and recorded it in Eden's daily log. Mrs. Frank soon begins to introduce Eden to toilet learning as a result of the child's own influence.

As you will learn in your day-to-day work with children, influence runs in many directions. The family can influence your behavior just as society can, and all come into play within the four walls of your classroom.

Before moving on with your reading, make sure that you can answer the following questions about the material discussed so far.

1. List and explain three influences on the curriculum. Make sure that your answer provides examples from three different types of influences.
2. Write a brief newsletter article for a child care center explaining its approach to cultural diversity.

READING CHECKPOINT

9-2 Routine Care Times

Infants and toddlers have needs that must be met on a regular basis. Some needs, such as eating and eliminating, occur frequently throughout the day. Infant and toddler teachers often think that all they do is feed, rock, and diaper children. Our traditional notion of teaching seems—and is—inappropriate for very young children (Swim & Muza, 1999). That is why our definition of curriculum presented earlier is so important. You must come to understand that everything you do facilitates development and learning. As discussed in previous chapters, using the three As—Attention, Approval, and Attunement—while meeting the basic needs of infants and toddlers promotes optimal development and learning. This section provides examples of ways to organize and plan the **routine care times** of the curriculum. First, however, we will discuss aspects of the daily schedules.

routine care times Devoting attention to the developmental needs of children while attending to their biological needs. For example, using diapering times as opportunities for building relationships with a child and not just meeting her need to be clean.

9-2a Flexible Schedule

The schedule you create for the day should reflect each individual child's physical rhythms. Thus, your schedule depends on the infant or toddler you are caring for (Photo 9–3). The goal is not to coordinate the children's physical schedules but rather to have a flexible plan for meeting the needs of each child. During the first months, the infant is in the process of setting a personal, internal schedule. Some infants do this easily; others seem to have more difficulty. So when a child is first entering your care, ask family members what the infant or toddler does at home. Write this down to serve as a guideline. Next, observe the child to see whether he or she follows the home schedule or develops a different one.

The daily schedule must be individualized in infant and toddler care. It focuses on the basic activities: sleeping, feeding, and playing. Andrea arrives at 7:45 a.m.; Novak is ready for a bottle and nap at 8:00 a.m.; Myron is alert and will play until about 9:00 a.m., when he takes a bottle and a nap; and Savannah is alert and will play all morning but is ready for a nap immediately after lunch. As their caregiver, noting these preferences will provide you with guidelines for your time.

Children's schedules and preferences for routines change over time. Each month infants sleep less. This affects when they eat and when they are alert. As infants change their sleeping schedules, they will adjust to allow more time for exploration and engagement with materials.

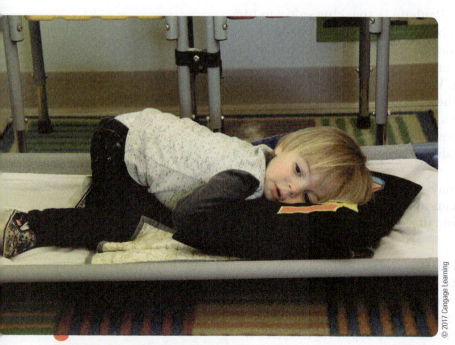

© 2017 Cengage Learning

PHOTO 9–3 The schedule teachers create each day should be flexible to meet the needs of each child.

Spotlight on SIDS

SUDDEN INFANT DEATH SYNDROME (SIDS)

SIDS is a tragic event in which a very young child dies after going to sleep for a nap or at bedtime with no indication of having discomfort. The peak *age* for SIDS is 2–4 months; however, SIDS can occur as late as 12 months. The peak *time* of occurrence is in the early morning (Cornwell & Feigenbaum, 2006). Research suggests that SIDS may be related to sleep apnea, a condition in which breathing momentarily stops (Sawaguchi, Franco, Kadhim, Groswasser, Sottiaux, Nishida, et al., 2004) or hippocampal asymmetry (Rodriguez, McMillan, Crandall, Minter, Grafe, Poduri, et al., 2012). Research on apnea in infants indicates that the baby's brain is not mature and therefore periods of instability occur. Young children spend a great deal of the day sleeping, yet REM cycles do not stabilize into a regular pattern until 3 months of age. The development of the central nervous system facilitates the synchronization of sleeping patterns (Cornwell & Feigenbaum, 2006). Regarding hippocampal asymmetry, Rodriguez and colleagues (2012) believe that some cases of SIDS might be analogous to sudden unexpected death in epilepsy due to a possible link with temporal lobe pathology; this suggests a possible role for seizures in the events leading to sudden death for some very young children.

Fortunately, the incidence of SIDS is very low (2 infants per 1,000 births between 1 week and 1 year of age), but the American Academy of Pediatrics has found that infants who are placed on their backs on a firm mattress to sleep have a lower incidence of SIDS. Recently, the American Academy of Pediatrics expanded its recommendations from being only SIDS-focused to addressing safe sleep environments in the hope of reducing the risk of all sleep-related infant deaths. The recommendations continue to include infants sleeping on their backs on a firm sleep surface, but they also endorse breastfeeding, room-sharing without bed-sharing, staying up to date on routine immunizations, using a pacifier, and avoiding soft bedding, overheating, and exposure to tobacco smoke, alcohol, and illicit drugs (American Academy of Pediatrics Task Force on Sudden Infant Death Syndrome, 2011). In addition, this organization continues to promote "tummy time" at home and at child care as long as the child is awake and closely supervised, as this supports the development of chest and neck muscles.

All early childhood educators are expected to follow the recommendations of the American Academy of Pediatrics when it comes to safe sleep environments for infants. Barriers to following those recommendations include perceived parental objections, provider skepticism about the benefits of infants sleeping on their backs, and lack of program policies and training opportunities (Moon, Calabrese, & Aird, 2008). Educators, directors, family members, and licensing agencies can join together to overcome those barriers, such as revising statewide regulations and monitoring and creating systematic advocacy campaigns.

© Cengage Learning

Toddlers will also differ in how much time they spend asleep and awake. Morning and afternoon naps do not fit into a rigid schedule from 8:30 to 9:45 a.m. or from 12:00 to 2:00 p.m. You can identify blocks of time for specific types of activities but should keep in mind that no schedule can fit each child's needs.

Arrival Time

During this special time, the primary caregiver greets the parent and child and receives the infant or toddler. This is the time for the caregiver to listen to the family member who tells about the child's night and about any joys, problems, or concerns. They should write down important details, for example, "celebrated birthday last night."

Arrival time is also a time to help the infant or toddler make the transition from home to school. The caregiver's relationships with the child should provide a calming, comfortable, accepting situation so that the child will feel secure. Touching, holding, and talking with the child for a few minutes helps the child reestablish relations with the caregiver. When the child is settled, the caregiver can help the child move on to whatever activity she is ready to do. If the child is upset during the transition, use emotional talk (Chapter 6) to address emotional needs and the desire to maintain a strong connection with family members. Do not rush to distract the child with other activities.

Sleeping

Newborns sleep an average of 16 to 17 hours per day. Sleep periods range from 2 to 10 hours. By 3 to 4 months of age, infants regularly sleep more at night than during the day. As children become more mobile and begin to crawl and walk, their sleep patterns change, and they require less sleep. Children should still be encouraged to rest every day, and a well-planned child care program provides nap times that meet the individual needs for children who are under 3 years of age.

If you are responsible for several infants or toddlers, plan your time carefully so you are available to help each child fall asleep by providing what they desire (Photo 9–4). Each child has preferences that you must learn to build your curriculum. Ask family members how they put their child to sleep at home so that you can coordinate your routines at school. Some children like quiet time with a favorite stuffed animal or blanket; others want to be held, sung to, and rocked; still others like their backs rubbed. Because of the risk of SIDS, place the baby on her back on a firm mattress.

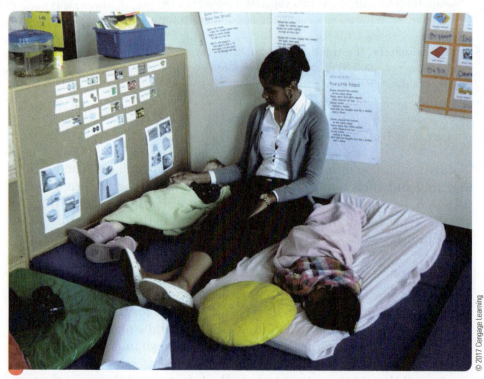

PHOTO 9–4 Caregivers should plan their time so they are available to help each child fall asleep.

© 2017 Cengage Learning

Record when each child went to sleep and when she or he woke. Family members need to know how long and at what time their child slept, and the caregiver needs to know when each infant or toddler can be expected to sleep.

Some infants and toddlers have difficulty relaxing and falling asleep. You will need to work with the family to create strategies that work in those situations. Some teachers have found that various relaxation techniques such as visualization, progressive muscle relaxation, and massage (Berggren, 2004; Mayo Clinic Staff, 2011) work with young children. Of course, making sure that infants and toddlers have sufficient opportunity for exercise and full-body play can positively impact sleep patterns as well (see Chapter 8).

Eating

The very young infant may eat every two to four hours. They should eat when they are hungry, which is called **demand feeding**. Demand feeding involves more flexibility for the caregiver and is one of the first steps to building a bond between that person and the children in his or her care. It is also the first step toward the child internalizing a sense of trust and security. Ask family members how often the baby eats at home. Infants will tell you when they are hungry by fussing and crying. Learn their individual schedules and their physical and oral signals, so you can feed them when they cry but before they become too distressed. Record the time of feedings and the amount of milk, formula, or food the baby consumed.

demand feeding Providing solid or liquid foods when an infant or toddler is hungry.

This curricular time is to meet the nutritional needs of the child. All food offered to the children should be nutritious. State licensing regulations often provide plenty of information on how to address the children's nutritional needs. But eating is also a curricular time for nurturing physical, emotional, social, cognitive, and language development. Always hold the infant when you are giving a bottle. Maintaining eye contact, talking to, and building a relationship with the child creates a secure foundation for the child.

Infants are born with their primary teeth. The first primary tooth usually erupts between 4 and 8 months of age, but individuals vary widely in teething. New teeth erupt every month or so after the first one. The average age for having all 20 baby teeth is around 33 months. Figure 9–1 shows the order and age at which teeth typically erupt. As children get older, they begin to exert independence while eating. They no longer want you to hold the bottle for them or feed them with a spoon. This is normal behavior and should be supported as much as possible. During this time, however, parents and caregivers often worry that the child is not getting enough to eat. You may find that a child in this situation wants to eat more often; providing additional opportunities to eat can ensure that the child's need for food is being met. Children may also want to exert their independence by skipping a meal or snack occasionally. Encourage community involvement by having the child stay in the area where the other children are eating, or allowing the child to sit on your lap.

All eating must be supervised, as the chance of choking is high for very young children who are learning to eat solid foods. Food for older infants should be cut into pieces no larger than a quarter of an inch. Older toddlers can have half-inch pieces. But the best way to supervise is to eat with the older infants and toddlers. Sit at the table and engage them in conversation.

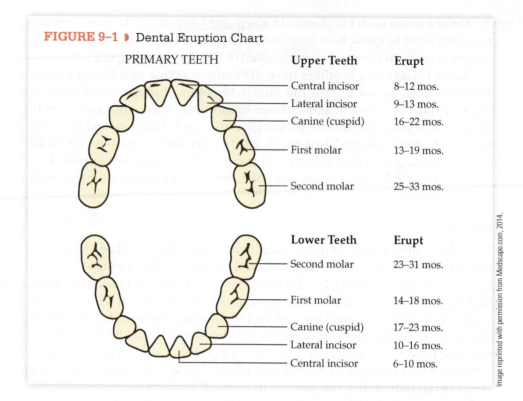

FIGURE 9–1 ▶ Dental Eruption Chart

PRIMARY TEETH

Upper Teeth	Erupt
Central incisor	8–12 mos.
Lateral incisor	9–13 mos.
Canine (cuspid)	16–22 mos.
First molar	13–19 mos.
Second molar	25–33 mos.

Lower Teeth	Erupt
Second molar	23–31 mos.
First molar	14–18 mos.
Canine (cuspid)	17–23 mos.
Lateral incisor	10–16 mos.
Central incisor	6–10 mos.

Image reprinted with permission from Medscape.com, 2014.

Toothbrushing

Helping infants' and toddlers' brush their teeth after each meal and providing information to family members about the importance of oral hygiene will support the development of lifelong, healthy dental habits. Encourage each family to have their child's first dental checkup at least 6 months after the first tooth erupts or at 12 months.

There are multiple steps for helping a toddler brush her teeth. First, prepare the environment by putting a small swipe of toothpaste on the toothbrush. Put a stepstool in front of the sink, if not already available. Wet a washcloth with warm water for cleaning up afterwards. Then, encourage the toddler climb up on a stepstool at the sink so she can reach everything needed. Turn on the faucet and have the toddler wash her hands; you wash your hands also. Next, remind the toddler that first she brushes and then you get to brush her teeth. Encourage the toddler to wet her own toothbrush and brush all of her teeth (not just the front ones). Singing a song or speaking a chant you created about how to brush your teeth can promote longer brushing. Then, it is your turn to brush the child's teeth. Encourage the toddler to spit out the extra toothpaste, but this is not a necessity. Turn on the faucet and allow the toddler to rinse her own toothbrush. Have the child wipe off her face and mouth with the warm washcloth. Return the toothbrush to its proper place for use later.

Diapering and Toileting

Most infants and toddlers cannot communicate that they need a curricular experience involving a diaper change. You must be vigilant about checking.

Spotlight on Dental Health

ACCESS TO DENTAL CARE

The American Dental Association (ADA) recommends that a dentist examine a child within six months of the eruption of the first tooth or no later than the first birthday (ADA, 2014). This first dental visit is a "well-baby checkup." Besides checking for tooth decay and other problems, the dentist can demonstrate how to clean the child's teeth properly and how to evaluate any adverse habits, such as putting a child to sleep with a bottle or consuming too many sugary drinks (including fruit juice), which are significant factors in dental caries. Protecting the primary teeth is important because they create a foundation for the health of the permanent teeth.

Access to dental care, while improving, is not uniform within our society. Children who are Black or multiracial, lower income, and lack a personal dentist were significantly less likely to have a preventive dental visit within the previous year (Lewis, Johnston, Linsenmeyar, Williams, & Mouradian, 2007). Access to appropriate dental care, however, might not just be based on family or child characteristics. Two other factors to be considered are availability and attitudes of oral health providers.

Not all children live in close proximity to an oral health provider, even if their services are covered by Medicaid. Most US states have expanded oral health services to include physician-based preventive oral health services for infants and toddlers to fight inequalities in oral health and access to care. But has this increased rates of utilization of these services? Among North Carolina's 100 counties, 4 counties had no physician-based oral health services and 9 counties had no dental practice (Kranz, Lee, Divaris, Baker, & Vann, 2014). These researchers learned that children who lived farther from the nearest dental practice were less likely to make dental visits, yet distance from physician-based oral health services did not predict utilization (Kranz et al., 2014). They concluded that, for very young children, oral health services provided in medical offices can improve access and increase utilization. But what happens when a child who needs more than preventive care goes to a pediatrician?

Long, Quinonez, Rozier, Kranz, and Lee (2014) discovered that pediatricians in North Carolina were challenged to refer 1-year-old children to a general dentist if the child already had dental caries. The general dentists were more willing to accept referrals when they could focus on providing preventive care and when the parents saw the importance of dental referrals. Thus, finding a dental home after the child has caries might be a great challenge for families.

This research demonstrates that a complex interaction of variables is at play when discussing access to oral health care for infants and toddlers. Helping families gain access so that the primary teeth are well cared for is important both now and for later oral health.

© Cengage Learning

Diapers should always be changed when wet or soiled. With young children, it is common to have seven or eight changes within a 12-hour period. Some children may have several bowel movements per day, while others may have only one. If a child does not have a bowel movement each day, the family should be notified because constipation can be a problem in some cases. Diarrhea can also be a problem because of the possibility of rapid dehydration. As with other areas of physical development, accurate daily records should be kept on elimination and shared with family members.

Attending to this routine care time requires planning. Doing so will allow you to talk and sing and engage in positive experiences while you are providing for this basic need (see, e.g., Herr & Swim, 2002). Make this a pleasant time for both of you (Photo 9–5). The steps in the diapering process (Aronson, 2012; Swim, 1998) are as follows:

1. Gather all of the supplies (e.g., latex gloves, diaper wipes, clean diaper, and change of clothes) you will need, and place them in the changing area within reach.

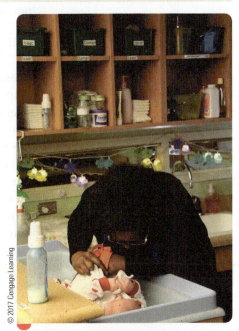

PHOTO 9–5 Make diapering a pleasant time for both of you.

2. Put on latex gloves. Remove the infant's clothes or pull them up to the chest level. Remove the soiled diaper and place it on the edge of the area out of the infant's reach.

3. *Keep one hand on the infant at all times.*

4. Wipe off the bowel movement with a diaper wipe or toilet tissue, going from front to back. Put this wipe on the soiled diaper. Continue until the child's bottom is clean.

5. Take off your gloves and wrap the soiled disposable diaper and wipes inside of them. Do this, for example, by holding the diaper in your right hand and using your left hand to pull the glove over and around the diaper. Then, put the diaper into your left hand and pull the glove over them again.

6. Throw away a soiled disposable diaper immediately in a foot-activated, covered, plastic-bag-lined container. Put a soiled cloth diaper in a plastic bag, which will be closed with a twist tie when you are finished. When using cloth diapers, throw away the soiled wipes separately in the trash container.

7. Wash your hands with a diaper wipe. If at any time from this point forward you notice bodily fluid, *put gloves on*.

8. Put a clean diaper on the child, fitting it snugly around the child's legs and waist. Dress the infant again or put on new clothes, as necessary.

9. Wash the child's hands in running water and carry the child to the next activity.

10. Return to the changing area to clean it. Spray the changing area with disinfectant. Wash your hands thoroughly with soap and running water before you do anything else.

11. Record the time and consistency of bowel movements. You and the child's family members need this information to determine patterns of normalcy and to look for causes of irregularities.

toilet learning The developmental process for gaining control of bladder and bowels; complex process involving physical, cognitive, social, emotional, and language skills.

Toilet learning should begin when the toddler is developmentally ready. The muscles that control bowel and bladder, called sphincter muscles, are usually not mature until after 18 months of age. Toilet learning requires two major functions—biofeedback and muscular control. Toddlers learn to recognize the feelings their bodies have before they urinate or have a bowel movement. They can use this biofeedback to decide what to do. At first, they seem to just observe the feelings and afterward label what has happened. When the child is aware of the sensations of the sphincter muscles and can control them until the appropriate time, he or she is ready for toilet learning. Timing and control must be coordinated. Toddlers may have some control at first but not enough to last as long as it takes to get into the bathroom, get clothes out of the way, and get seated or standing. Through feedback and adjustments, toddlers learn what their bodies are doing and what they can control and plan.

Toddlers tell you through their behavior and words that they are ready for toilet learning. Behaviors include staying dry for a few hours;

demonstrating awareness that they are going to the bathroom (e.g., squatting); telling you that they have urinated or had a bowel movement after they have; and showing a desire to be dry and wear underpants. Research by Barone, Jasutkar, and Schneider (2009) suggested that toilet learning should be initiated prior to the age of 32 months for children who display these signs of toilet learning because starting after that time was associated with increased rates of urge incontinence for children in their sample. However, there is no right age by which all children should be using the toilet independently. Schum, Kolb, McAuliffe, Simms, Underhill, and Lewis (2002) found that the median age when girls could independently enter the bathroom and urinate by themselves was 33.0 months, whereas the same skill for boys was achieved at 37.1 months.

When the child starts toilet learning, use training pants at home and at the child care program. Do *not* put diapers on the toddler during nap time. Outer clothes must be loose or easily removed to facilitate independence. Help the toddler acquire self-help skills by instructing her how to pull down necessary clothes and how to get seated on the adapter seat or potty chair. For the boy who can reach while standing, determine where he should stand and direct his penis. If the child needs to have a bowel movement, use your knowledge gained from family members to decide whether to give the child a sense of privacy or whether you should stay near. If he wants you to be nearby, read a book to support literacy development (being sure to clean the books on a regular basis), or engage the child in a conversation about his work so far or what he is planning to do next to support reflection and planning. To support understanding of diversity, you could also engage in a conversation about how the child is similar to and different from you (Aldridge, 2010). For example, you could discuss hair color versus hair texture. When the child is done, put on your gloves before proceeding. Teach how to get toilet paper and how to wipe from front to back. Then let the child try to do it alone. Check to see if assistance is needed in cleaning the child's bottom. Support independence in getting clothes back up. Remove gloves. Both you and the child should wash your hands thoroughly.

Throughout the toilet learning process, toddlers will need special reminders, especially during play, regarding when they typically need to go to the bathroom. A good approach to toilet learning is to provide specific feedback on success and avoid punishing or shaming for mistakes. The child should participate as much as possible for his or her age in cleaning up when accidents happen.

Of course, toilet learning is not a skill that can be learned only while in your care; it takes a concerted effort by everyone to achieve independence. Both the home and the child care program need to begin at the same time and use the same procedures. Let the toddler's family direct the timing. All human relationships are bound to involve conflicts and disagreements. Toilet learning is an area ripe for such conflicts because it is accompanied by such a great deal of variability in cultural beliefs (Gonzalez-Mena, 2001; Gonzalez-Mena & Eyer, 2007). Cultural groups and individual families within those groups often have strong beliefs

© 2017 Cengage Learning

PHOTO 9–6 Caregivers should make hand washing a routine for themselves and the children.

about when and how to assist with toilet learning. One family will start toilet learning at 1 year of age and another will wait until the child is "ready," while still another may not provide any formal assistance until the child is 4 years of age. None of these perspectives on timing is definitively correct or incorrect; they reflect different belief systems. As a parent, member of a cultural group, and/or a teacher, you have beliefs about toileting also. Open communication and respectful listening are the beginning steps in addressing cultural conflicts, but they are not enough. You must be clear about your own views and the philosophy of the program so that you can truly listen and work toward solutions with the families. Issues such as toilet learning will not be resolved in one conversation. Sustained dialogue is necessary for resolving the conflict (Gonzalez-Mena, 2001).

Hand Washing

Frequent hand washing is a vital routine for caregivers and children to establish because failure to do it is directly related to the occurrence of illness (Photo 9–6). Hand-washing procedures should be thorough: a quick rinse with clear water does not remove microorganisms.

The caregiver must wash hands before	The child must wash hands before
• working with children at the beginning of the day. • handling bottles, food, or feeding utensils. • assisting child with face and hand washing. • assisting child with brushing teeth.	• handling food and food utensils. • brushing teeth.
The caregiver must wash hands after	The child must wash hands after
• feeding. • cleaning up. • diapering (remove gloves first). • assisting with toileting (remove gloves first). • wiping or assisting with a runny nose (remove gloves first). • working with wet, sticky, dirty items (remove gloves first).	• eating. • diapering or toileting. • playing with wet, sticky, and/or dirty items (e.g., sand, mud).

Proper procedures for hand washing include wetting the whole hand with warm water, applying soap, and rubbing the whole hand—palm, back, between fingers, and around fingernails. Rinse with clean water, rubbing the skin to help remove the microorganisms and soap. Dry hands on a disposable paper towel that has no colored dyes in it. Throw away the towel so others do not have to handle it. You can also use small washcloths as towels, with each child using his own once and then putting it in the laundry basket.

Toddlers who can stand on a stepstool at the sink can be somewhat independent in washing their own hands. Stay nearby so you can verbally remind them of the steps and provide physical assistance when needed. Singing a favorite song or reciting a nursery rhyme can help make this time enjoyable. In addition, to support scientific understanding, allow time for the toddlers to explore the water; how it feels on their arms versus their hands, how it splashes, and what it takes to clean up spills.

End of the Day

At the end of each child's day, collect your thoughts and decide what to share with family members. To help you remember, or to gather information for other caregivers who work with the child, review the notes in the child's portfolio or on the report sheet. This sharing time includes the family members in the child's day and provides a transition for the child from school to home.

As mentioned several times throughout this section, routine care times can be designed to support and enhance both development and learning. Singing songs, reciting nursery rhymes and fingerplays, and exploring the properties of water can support various aspects of learning. We will turn our attention to planning learning experiences in the next section.

READING CHECKPOINT

Before moving on with your reading, make sure that you can answer the following questions about the material discussed so far.

1. Why is flexibility in schedules important in an infant and toddler program? How would you explain this need for flexibility to a child's family member?
2. List three routine care times. Explain how each event can be used to promote the development of the child.
3. How is toilet learning a complex developmental accomplishment?

9-3 Planned Learning Experiences

In between sleeping and eating, infants and toddlers have **alert times** when they are very aware and attracted to the world around them. This is the time when the caregiver does special activities with them (see Part 3). The infant or toddler discovers himself or herself, plays, and talks and interacts with you and others. Children have fun when in an alert state, as they actively involve themselves in the world.

Determine the times when the infants and toddlers in your care are alert. Decide which times each individual child will spend alone with appropriate materials you have selected and which times you will spend together one-on-one or in a small group. Each infant or toddler needs some time during each day to play with his or her primary caregiver. This

alert times Times during the day when a child is attending and attracted to the world around him or her.

playtime is in addition to the time you spend changing diapers, feeding the child, and helping the child get to sleep.

As you play with the infant or toddler, you will discover how long that child remains interested. Stop before the child gets tired. The child is just learning how to interact with others and needs rest times and unpressured times in between highly attentive times. With an infant, you might play a reaching-grasping game for a couple of minutes, a visual focusing activity for about a minute, and a standing-bouncing-singing game for a minute. Watch the infant's reactions to determine when to extend the activity to two minutes, five minutes, and so on. Alternate interactive times with time spent playing alone. Infants will stay awake and alert longer if they have some times of stimulation and interaction.

Toddlers spend increasing amounts of time in play. There should be opportunities for self-directed play as well as challenge and interaction with the caregiver. Toddlers also need quiet, uninterrupted time during their day. Constant activity, especially in a group setting, is emotionally and physically wearing on them.

NAEYC's guidelines for developmentally appropriate practices support our understanding of how to create learning experiences:

1. Providing experiences for all areas of development: physical, cognitive, language, social, and emotional

2. Building on what the children already know and are able to do

3. Promoting the development of knowledge and understanding, processes and skills, as well as dispositions toward learning

4. Supporting home cultures and languages while developing a shared culture of the learning community

5. Setting goals that are realistic and attainable for each child (Copple & Bredekamp, 2009).

In addition, Freeman and Swim (2009) challenge teachers to evaluate the intellectual integrity of their work. Examining educational rituals and classroom practices often uncovers instructional strategies that are more about the teacher than for an individual or a group of children. Giving infants copies or pages from a coloring book, for example, focuses on the perceptions of the teachers and other adults (e.g., family members) rather than the learning needs of infants. When infants are able to hold a spoon, they are able to hold a chunky crayon. Yet, they should be encouraged to make their own marks on blank paper.

The following sections discuss the specifics of how to create curriculum for infants and toddlers.

daily plans An approach to curriculum in which planned learning experiences are designed daily based on specific observations of the children.

planned experiences Curricular experiences designed to enhance and support the individual learning needs, interests, and abilities of the children in an early childhood program.

9-3a Daily Plans

For infants and young toddlers, you should plan experiences daily for each child (Photo 9–7). Assess the four areas of development for children by gathering observational data using the Developmental Milestones (Appendix A). Analyze your data and determine the skills that the child can do independently and with assistance. Translate these skills into **daily plans**.

After implementing some **planned experiences**, you can use the data gathered and recorded to plan new experiences for the next day. This is called the assessment-planning-teaching loop. As a loop, caregivers can begin anywhere in the process. However, infant and toddler teachers are becoming more and more accountable for using evidence-based practices. If you start with observational data, you can more easily explain to your director, co-teacher, or family members the rationale or justification for your planning. Imagine that you implemented one or both experiences outlined on Table 9–1. What data did you collect and record after the experience, and how would you use that information to plan the next learning experience?

When planning experiences, you should not only consider the children's developmental needs and abilities but also their interests and culture. If you want an infant to practice finding hidden objects, for example, hide a rattle that the child likes. Curricular experiences should balance practicing or reinforcing skills with introducing new ones. Introducing too many new experiences can overstimulate the infant or make him overtired. Carefully read the child's nonverbal communication to know when to stop the experience. Regarding cultural appropriateness, you should select materials for learning experiences that reflect the cultures and backgrounds of the children in the classroom. For example, when working with dough, select various shades of brown and pink/peach, or use chopsticks or Splayds (Australian name-brand sporf—a spork with a knife edge) instead of forks and knives.

In addition, with each planned experience, consider extensions or adaptations so that you can be flexible in addressing the children's

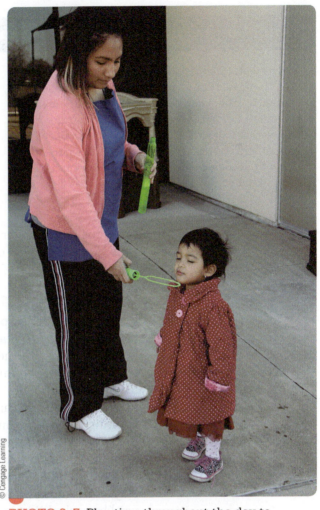

PHOTO 9–7 Plan time throughout the day to interact one on one with each infant or toddler.

TABLE 9–1 ▶ Sample Section of a Weekly Plan for Two Individual Children

EXAMPLE:

CHILD'S NAME:		WEEK:
AREA OF DEVELOPMENT	**MATERIALS**	**CAREGIVER STRATEGIES AND COMMENTS**
Physical: (Seeing) Roberto: Visual tracking	Red ribbon bow	Hold bow where infant can focus. Slowly move bow to side, to front, to other side. Observe eyes holding focus. Stop. Talk to infant, and repeat moving bow.
Naomi: Changing focus	Red and blue ribbon bows	Hold red bow where infant can focus. Lift up blue bow and hold a few inches to side of red bow. Observe eyes changing focus. Continue changing positions with both bows.

Family and Community Connections

You have decided to follow Schwarz and Luckenbill's (2012) suggestion to help your materials be more authentic and accurate by inviting family members to donate items that reflect their background. You decide that you would like to have materials for your dramatic play area. You invite them to share "extra" items from their homes that would work in the children's kitchen. You suggest that they could consider "extra" eating utensils, pans for cooking, and materials for reading/writing (e.g., cook books, menus for favorite restaurants). The response is overwhelming! How will you decide which materials to put out first, knowing that your choice will communicate your values regarding identity and dominant culture? How might you involve the families in making this decision?

reactions to the materials. How, for example, could you make the experience less challenging or more challenging?

9-3b Weekly Plans

weekly plans Approach to curriculum where experiences are planned on a weekly basis based on specific observations of the children.

For older toddlers, you can plan experiences by the week, but you must modify the weekly plans throughout the week to respond to the children's needs. Planning for the entire week affords you the ability to carefully plan the learning environment (see Chapter 8) and make available appropriate materials, equipment, and supplies. Materials are a vital part of the curriculum; they should be carefully selected to provoke the children's thinking and learning (White, Swim, Freeman, & Norton-Smith, 2007). The infants and toddlers learn by interacting with materials; the construction of knowledge comes from holding, tasting, shaking, hitting, throwing, taking apart, and listening to objects. Select open-ended materials, such as wooden unit blocks, clay, and sand, because they provide a variety of experiences and can be used by each child to meet his or her needs and ideas (Curtis & Carter, 2015).

Learning Centers

As discussed in Chapter 8, learning centers organize the room and materials and encourage specific use of a particular space. Select materials for each learning center by matching them with the needs, interests, and abilities of the children. Do so carefully because a poor selection of materials can actually impede the children's development. Materials that are too easy can be boring, while those that are too difficult can be frustrating. Using currently popular materials or those labeled "educational" may or may not be appropriate or effective for promoting development for your group of toddlers or a particular toddler. On the other hand, selecting developmentally appropriate materials for each child can facilitate growth and skill advancement (see Part 3).

For example, you notice that José seems to attend carefully to the wind chime outdoors. You want to promote his reaching and grabbing of objects, so you secure a wind chime in the manipulative area just within his reach. In Elizabeth's case, however, you want her to practice transferring objects from hand to hand, so you put out attractive clear blocks with interesting materials inside. You anticipate that when she picks one up to examine it, the material inside will shift locations, encouraging her to switch hands for a better view.

Spotlight on Research

INFANT BRAIN DEVELOPMENT

As mentioned several times throughout this book, infants and toddlers use everything within their realm—people, materials, equipment—to develop their brain. When we view very young children as competent, constructors of their own development, it emphasizes the role of adults in opening "a world of possibilities that lay the groundwork for their development" (Lewin-Benham, 2010, p. 1). In her book, *Infants and Toddlers at Work: Using Reggio-Inspired Materials to Support Brain Development*, Lewin-Benham demonstrates how certain materials are essential resources for infants and toddlers to build neural networks that, in time, enable them to use higher-order thinking skills and build complex relationships between and among concepts. She especially advocates for the use of open-ended materials "because they allow many approaches; therefore, they reach children with diverse interests" (p. 11). These materials also stimulate long engagement, which provides evidence of prolonged attention, and any experience that facilitates attention also builds the brain's capacity to learn.

Lewin-Benham advocates for using more natural materials, such as fabric, wood scraps, leaves, and clay, as well as man-made materials such as foil, paper, cardboard tubes, netting, and paint, as tools for engaging the senses and building the brain. Short- and long-term memory is constructed, in part, through the adult's intentional use of language to mediate meaning-making during experiences. Infants and toddlers need words to provide content "because to think, you have to think about something" (p. 31). As the teacher expounds on what is happening, asks questions, waits for answers,

and provides powerful descriptive language, she entices the infant/toddler brain to create pathways for remembering the experience and ideas associated with it. For example, an infant is manipulating clay with her hands. The teacher says, "You nipped off a small piece this time using just your thumb and pointer finger. You are rolling the clay into a ball using your hand and the table. How will you get it to stick to the large flat piece? (pause) Oh, you just pushed down hard on it. Will it work?"

Teachers also promote brain development through their intentional planning of curricular experiences. Teachers must carefully observe the children to learn what they are interested in, what they can do independently and with assistance, and what confuses them. Because feeling disoriented is an essential prerequisite for learning, teachers should create experiences that produce results that are counter to what the child might expect, given their current level of understanding. "The teacher, like an administrative assistance to children's brains, reminds, refocuses, and provokes them to remember" (p. 148). On the other hand, teachers must balance provocations with repetition. Adults often have difficulty deferring their work so toddlers can engage in theirs—namely, repeating an activity. Teachers need to be intentional about following the pace set by the children and not just impose their own.

Lewin-Benham concluded her book by stating children's extensive experiences with materials "trigger the brain functions that from 0 to 3 lay the groundwork for increasingly complex learning" (p. 158), and a large vocabulary of materials helps children to "imagine, build relationships, realize ideas for projects, make constructions and contraptions, and in a word *think*" (p. 159).

© Cengage Learning

Projects

After you know the children's interests and abilities, you can plan a week's worth of engaging curriculum. Instead of selecting themes, you should identify *moments* that can be developed into an ongoing project. Many projects have no clear beginning; they emerge (with much teacher observation and reflection) slowly over time from the documentation (see Chapter 5) that the teacher has collected or from her experiences interacting with the children (Photo 9–8). Small moments encountered by one or two children can become projects in their own ways (May, Kantor, & Sanderson, 2004). Following our approach about the daily plans, projects should be individualized for each child or a small group of children.

project An ongoing investigation that provokes infants, toddlers, and teachers to construct knowledge.

You can outline experiences and questions to support the project or line of thinking and integrate the areas of development. In the infant-toddler

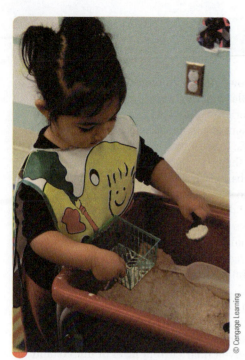

© Cengage Learning

PHOTO 9–8 To plan engaging and challenging experiences, create curriculum based on your prior observations of each individual child.

progettazione Italian term that is loosely translated as "flexible planning."

centers of Reggio Emilia, teachers have constructed a particular approach to curricular planning referred to as **progettazione**, or flexible planning (Rinaldi, 1998). This curriculum is characterized by uncertainty, no predetermined outcome, and multiple directions for the work. Teachers there plan open-ended experiences to facilitate the co-construction of knowledge for children and themselves. They view the teacher's role as that of a resource who does not simply satisfy needs or answer questions but instead helps children discover their own answers and, more importantly, helps them learn to ask good questions (Rinaldi, 1998). Therefore, this "is a dynamic process based on communication that generates documentation and is regenerated by documentation" (Gandini & Goldhaber, 2001, p. 128).

As discussed earlier, a key principle of the educational approach used in Reggio Emilia, Italy, involves the many languages of children. Children are provided with multiple opportunities and avenues for expressing their understanding of the world. Thus, children use their "one hundred languages" to tell adults and peers what they know. Some avenues for expression include, but are not limited to, sculpting with clay or wire, painting, building with found materials, sketching, acting out stories, and dancing with scarves. These types of curricular experiences serve to cultivate and elaborate on the image of the child as a competent, capable, active learner who is constantly creating and re-creating theories about the world.

Sample Project

This section provides two examples of projects that can be done with a group of children. The number and types of projects appropriate for children this age are only limited by teachers' thinking. The first example extends from the butterfly garden discussed in Chapter 8. The toddlers were curious about the butterflies that come and go in their garden, asking many questions about how they fly. You notice that the children have discovered that they can see the butterfly garden from a window in the classroom. You decide to extend their interest by placing a small table near the window. On this table, you place a book about butterflies, two pairs of binoculars, and two clipboards with blank paper/pencils for drawing and writing. This proves to be a popular area, with many children visiting it for 10–15 minutes at a time. You decide to post a large piece of easel paper on the wall and record all of the questions you hear being asked. After reviewing the list, you decide to provide a new provocation and add a bird feeder to the garden. The children immediately notice it and wonder who else might visit the garden. When the yellow finches come to feed, the opportunity to discuss and compare how the butterflies and birds fly arises.

The other example is a project about wheeled vehicles that was created for a group of older toddlers. Joan and Derek displayed interest when the wheels fell off a vehicle in the block area. They immediately noticed that the car didn't move as easily without the wheels, and after about five minutes of "hard" pushing, left it lying on the edge of the carpet.

Picking up on the children's frustration about the car, Sue decided to provoke the children's thinking about wheels further. She placed a full-size car tire (that had been cleaned) in the center of the room and waited to see what the children would do. Derek ran right to it and began to climb on it. Sue stood back and watched as other children began to join in the excitement. After about seven minutes, she sat on the floor near the children and asked questions such as "What is this?" "What is this for?" "How does it help a car move?" "Can a wheel help you move?" "What helps you move?" and recorded their answers. Later that day when the children were napping, she took a few moments to review her notes. She began to *web* what the children knew about the movement of wheels and people (Figure 9–2).

Sue decided to build on the children's interest in the wheels and planned the curricular experiences for the following week. To "kick off" the project, she planned to take the children on a walking field trip in their neighborhood to look for wheels. She mapped out the route to take so they would pass by the used car dealership and the playground with the tire swings. She prepared a clipboard (e.g., a piece of cardboard cut to 9″ × 12″ with unlined paper held on by a binder clip) with a pencil for each child to sketch what he or she saw. Later in the week, they were going to work with clay to represent wheels and possibly cars. She would put books about transportation in the reading/listening center and in the art center for when they worked with paint or clay. She planned to add wheels to the construction area that fit on the unit blocks so children could build their own cars.

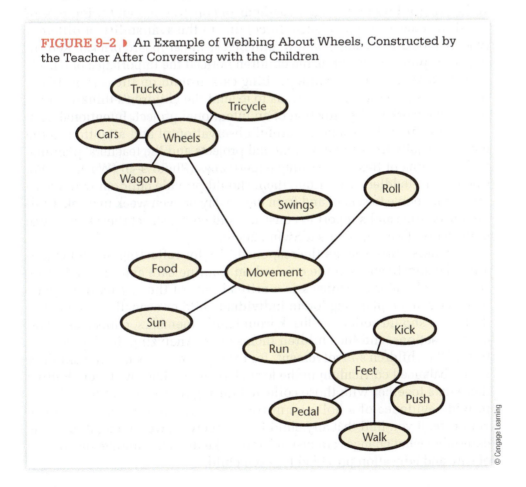

FIGURE 9–2 ▸ An Example of Webbing About Wheels, Constructed by the Teacher After Conversing with the Children

© Cengage Learning

Of course, Sue and her co-teacher, Joni, will document these classroom events using their digital video camera (which takes still photographs as well), running records of conversations, and work samples. These data will be reviewed daily during nap time and on Friday before planning experiences for the next week.

As mentioned in Chapter 8, the educators in Reggio Emilia speak of the importance of finding the "extraordinary in the ordinary" (L. Gandini, personal communication, January 26, 2001). In other words, early childhood educators should balance novel and familiar objects in the environment. Exploring flashlights on a dreary, rainy day meaningfully engages the children in investigating light, dark, and shadows. Wurm (2005) explains that teachers and children in Reggio engage in four types of overlapping projects on a regular basis: intentional, daily life, self-managed, and environmental projects. The ones most important to infants and toddlers are daily life and environmental, which can both lead into intentional projects. Daily life projects are those events that occur repeatedly or on an ongoing basis for very young children. Learning to eat and dress independently and to separate from and rejoin family members, for example, are daily life projects. May et al. (2004) provide additional examples of daily life projects about object permanence and identity development.

Environmental projects are inherently built into the classroom as part of the learning environment (Wurm, 2005). In other words, these projects emerge directly from the space and materials in which the children live and work. Children investigate methods of construction and principles of physical sciences (e.g., balance, force) due to the availability of different types of blocks (e.g., large, hollow, unit blocks or cardboard bricks). Returning to our previous example, the children noticed the importance of wheels to make a vehicle move while pushing cars around on the carpet. When the teachers provided provocations to extend the children's thinking, they moved the work in the direction of an intentional project. Intentional projects result from the teachers' careful observation of and attention to the children's daily life and environmental projects and the teachers' planning and designing of flexible learning experiences (Photo 9–9) (Wurm, 2005). Good infant-toddler curriculum, then, should provide children with continuity from home to school and from day to day or even week to week. Children need time and support to construct and co-construct their knowledge of the world (see, e.g., Cross & Swim, 2006).

Teachers must assume the responsibility for reflecting on and evaluating the effectiveness of the curriculum (routine care and planned experiences). Therefore, feedback is a critical part of the curriculum cycle, whether you are planning for an individual child or a small group of children. You should solicit feedback from family members, colleagues, your own reflections, and the children themselves. Analyzing the documentation of the children's involvement, for example, ensures that the children have a balanced curriculum in the formal, planned times with you. Putting these data together with those collected during routine care times should provide evidence of a holistic, nurturing curriculum for each child in your care. If you find that any child is not receiving well-thought-out care, determine what changes are needed and make them to improve the quality of care and education provided for each child.

© Cengage Learning

PHOTO 9–9 Intentional projects arise from a teacher's observation and attention to each child's daily life and environment.

Before moving on with your reading, make sure that you can answer the following questions about the material discussed so far.

1. List three reasons for creating daily plans for infants and young toddlers.
2. How can a project be used to involve a child physically? Emotionally? Socially? Cognitively?

READING CHECKPOINT

Summary

9-1 Identify major influences on the curriculum.

Infant-toddler curriculum, or everything that happens with a child during the time in an early childhood program, covers routine care times (e.g., eating and diapering) and planned learning experiences (e.g., daily plans or projects). Multiple forces, such as family culture, program philosophy, and child characteristics, influence how the curriculum is developed.

9-2 Defend why routine care times are important for facilitating development and learning.

Routine care times (e.g., diapering, feeding, sleeping) should be designed to facilitate development

and learning of each individual child. Specific guidelines for select routines were provided.

9-3 Plan daily or weekly, integrated lesson plans that are individualized for each child.

Caregivers also plan daily or weekly, integrated lesson plans. Like routine care times, daily or weekly plans should be individualized for each child.

CASE STUDY   Challenging Lukaz and Tyler

April is a teacher in a birth to 2-year-old, mixed-age classroom at a local university. Lukaz has been in her class since he was 6 weeks old, so she is very familiar with him and his family. He is a healthy 21-month-old child who has outstanding verbal skills. He speaks in full sentences and possesses an extensive vocabulary. He has a close friend in Tyler who is almost 2. The two boys are almost inseparable: they both love to read books, build ramps, and play chase games. She has noticed lately that these two children seem bored in the classroom and have disrupted others who were working on two different occasions. For example, on Monday, Mackenzie was painting at the easel, and Lukaz pushed her arm as he walked by. Tyler laughed when Mackenzie started to cry. As these behaviors are not typical for either boy, April decided to spend the next two days watching them closely and gathering some additional data.

Here are some data April gathered along with her wonderings.

1. Lukaz is in the book area. He picked up a board book, opened one page, and tossed it back toward the basket. He said "These are for babies." Tyler responded with, "Yeah, babies. Let's go." They left the area. [April's wonderings: When did I last add new books? Are they ready for stories with more words or more complex artwork?]
2. In the block area, Tyler has built a simple ramp using unit blocks. Lukaz helped him line up the plastic people at the end of the ramp. They have one car and are taking turns pushing it down the ramp to knock over the people. [April's wonderings: What else could challenge them with ramps? What questions should I ask? Should I be concerned about running over people—doesn't seem very caring?]
3. Mackenzie, Lukaz, and Tyler are sitting at the art table working with clay. Lukaz is making a car. He is challenged by the wheels not rolling. His voice is getting louder as he rolls a wheel between his palms. Mackenzie tells him to "Stop." He reaches over and pounds on her creation. She begins to cry.

   a. Before addressing the specifics of the case, think about planning curriculum in general. What must be accomplished before an individualized curriculum can be developed for any child? Why?

   b. Do you think that April's initial conclusion that Lukaz and Tyler are bored is accurate? Why or why not? Use the data she gathered to help provide evidence for your conclusion.

   c. What curricular experiences would you plan to challenge Lukaz and Tyler? How would these experiences build on the boys' strengths? Provide examples of daily plans as well as plans for an ongoing project.

Lesson Plan

Title: *Comforting Jack*

Child Observation:

Jack, 17 months, started in the program two weeks ago; he attends four full days a week. He fell asleep in his primary caregiver's arms but startled awake when she put him in his crib. He cried hard for the next 18 minutes.

Teacher Interpretation:

This fits the patterns of other days; Jack has never slept more than 30 minutes at a time. He doesn't seem to have a favorite item to use at nap time; a new blanket is brought to the program each day. I have been in constant communication with his grandmother since he joined our program. She told me that Jack moved in with her and her husband when her son, Jack's father, was deployed as part of the National Guard. Her son is expected to be away for 12 months.

Child's Developmental Goal:

To facilitate the development of trust

To find comfort in a new situation

Materials: Item that Jack finds comforting at home; Dad's favorite scent (e.g., cologne or body spray)

Preparation: Invite Jack's grandparents to determine an item that he finds comfort in, such as a blanket or stuffed animal. Have them spray a bit of his Dad's cologne or body spray on the item before bringing it to the program.

Learning Environment:

1. When Jack is ready for his nap, prepare his bottle and retrieve the item (i.e., blanket) provided by his grandparents.
2. Draw his attention to the blanket by using descriptive language. To illustrate, you could say:

   "Your grandmother thought you would like this special blanket. It smells good, like your Daddy. Would you like to smell it?
3. Invite Jack to touch and cuddle with the blanket, if he hasn't already.

▼ **Professional Resource Download**

4. While feeding Jack his bottle, talk with him about how scary it is to be in a new program but how you want to help him. Say something such as:
   a. It is scary to be here. You miss your dad, grandmother, and grandfather. Your grandmother will be back to pick you up later. I'll stay with you until she comes for you.
   b. New faces are scary. You don't know me well yet. I am here to help you. I feed you, keep you clean, and help you find toys to play with.
5. Explain that you will rock and hold him until his bottle is finished. Then, tell him that you will put him in his crib with his special blanket.
6. When you put him in the crib, make sure that his blanket is close by. Place him on his back and stay nearby to continue comforting him. Pat his belly or gently rub his arm if that seems to help him.

Guidance Consideration:

If Jack becomes overly upset when placed in his crib, pick him up and comfort him. As soon as possible, return him to his crib.

Variations:

Use the scented blanket throughout the day to provide comfort when Jack becomes upset.

Additional Resources

Derman-Sparks, L., & Ramsey, P. G., with Edwards, J. O. (2011). *What if all the kids are white: Anti-bias multicultural education with young children and families* (2nd ed.). New York: Teachers College Press.

Helm, J. H. (2014). *Becoming young thinkers: Deep project work in the classroom.* New York: Teachers College Press.

Lickey, D. C., & Powers, D. J. (2011). *Starting with their strengths: Using the project approach in early childhood special education.* New York: Teachers College Press.

Marotz, L. R. (2015). *Health, safety and nutrition for the young child* (9th ed.). Stamford, CT: Cengage Learning.

de Melendez, W. R., & Beck, V. O. (2013). *Teaching young children in multicultural classrooms: Issues, concepts, and strategies* (4th ed.). Belmont, CA: Wadsworth Cengage Learning.

Topal, C. W., & Gandini, L. (1999). *Beautiful stuff! Learning with found materials.* Worcester, MA: Davis Publications.

10

CHAPTER

Early Intervention

*Co-written with
Heloise Maconochie*

Learning Objectives

After reading this chapter, you should be able to:

10-1 Describe early intervention.

10-2 Discriminate between different types of intervention.

10-3 Summarize the notion of special needs and special rights.

10-4 Explain why family capacity-building is a vital component of early intervention.

10-5 Identify the steps involved in the evaluation and assessment process, and apply this to your own practice.

10-6 Describe the characteristics and care of children with special rights related to physical, cognitive, emotional, and social development.

Standards Addressed in This Chapter

naeyc **NAEYC Standards for Early Childhood Professional Preparation**

1 Promoting Child Development and Learning

DAP **Developmentally Appropriate Practice Guidelines**

2 Teaching to Enhance Development and Learning

In addition, the NAEYC standards for developmentally appropriate practice are divided into six areas particularly important to infant/toddler care. The following areas are addressed in this

© 2017 Cengage Learning

chapter: *relationship between caregiver and child;* and *exploration and play.*

CASE STUDY	Kierston's Mother Is Depressed

Kierston, 2 1/2-months-old, has just arrived at the child care home. She sits in her infant seat, which is on the floor by the sofa. Kierston's fists are closed, and her arms and legs make jerky movements. As each of the other children arrives, they smile and "talk" to her, with the caregiver watching close by. Kierston does not make eye contact with any child, and after a few minutes, she starts to whimper, then cry. Bill, the caregiver, picks her up and says, "Are you getting sleepy? Do you want a nap?" Bill takes Kierston into the bedroom and puts her in her crib, where she promptly falls asleep.

Continue to think about Kierston as you read this chapter; we will return to her situation at the end.

10-1 What Is Early Intervention?

Early intervention (EI) can occur at any time in a child's life. For example, health-care professionals may seek to intervene early in the lives of adolescents at risk of developing Type 2 diabetes. However, as it pertains to early childhood, EI means to intervene early, and as soon as possible, in the lives of young children and their families who are experiencing difficulties or who may be "at risk" for poor developmental outcomes. In its broadest sense, EI refers to policies, services, and programs applied to vulnerable children and their families to promote a child's healthy development and to reduce or prevent specific problems before they become intractable (Smith & Guralnick, 2007).

In the United States, under the provisions of *Part C of the Individuals with Disabilities Education Act* (**IDEA**), the notion of EI is associated with a system of services to help **disabled children** (in our case, infants and toddlers) and those at risk of **developmental delay**. This includes children from birth until their third birthday who are experiencing developmental delays in one or more domain—cognitive, physical, communicative, social, emotional, or adaptive—or who have a physical or mental impairment that has a high probability of resulting in delay, such as Down syndrome or cerebral palsy. As discussed in previous chapters, all young children learn through social interaction with their primary caregivers and others, as well as through exploration of their environment. However, for disabled children, their learning experiences are likely to be more restricted than their nondisabled peers due to the interaction between features of their **impairment** and the disabling features of the society in which they live. In other words, a **disability** is evident when an individual with an impairment is prevented from maximum participation in society by environmental, social, and attitudinal barriers. Specific intervention is therefore required to remove the environmental and social barriers disabled children face and to support them in achieving their optimal development. IDEA, therefore, provides for **special education** or specifically designed instruction for children over the age of 3 with an impairment, disability, or developmental delay.

At state discretion, *Part C* of IDEA can also apply to infants and toddlers who are at risk of poor health and/or social-emotional difficulties

early intervention
Comprehensive services for infants and toddlers who have special rights or are at risk of acquiring a disability. Services may include education, health care, and/or social and psychological assistance.

IDEA Federal law in the United States that provides rights and protections for a free and appropriate public education to all children, ages 3–21. *Part C* outlines provisions for infants, toddlers, and their families.

Spotlight on Terminology

TALKING ABOUT EARLY INTERVENTION

impairment A medical condition, diagnosis, or description of functioning that could be related to a difficulty with physical, sensory, cognitive/communicative, adaptive, or social-emotional functioning. Examples of impairment include cerebral palsy, deafness, learning difficulties, speech and language difficulties, and depression.

disability A dynamic interaction between individual impairment and the social effects of impairment as a consequence of environmental, social, and attitudinal barriers that prevent people with impairments from maximum participation in society. Examples of disabling barriers include buildings without ramps or lifts, discriminatory attitudes, segregated education, and inadequate health care.

disabled children Children who are treated differently because of an individual impairment. See disability definition above.

developmental delay A child who is experiencing a delay as defined by the state in which he or she resides and as measured by appropriate diagnostic instruments in one or more of the following areas: physical development, cognitive development, communication development, social or emotional development, or adaptive development (IDEA, 2004).

early intervention Comprehensive services for disabled infants and toddlers and those at risk of developmental delay. Services may include education, health-care, and/or social and psychological assistance (Hardman, Drew, & Egan, 2014).

infant mental health The capacity to regulate and express emotions, form secure attachments, and explore the environment and learn. These skills develop in the context of family and community. Infant mental health is synonymous with healthy social and emotional development from birth to age 3.

special education Specifically designed instruction provided to children over the age of 3 with an impairment, disability, or developmental delay at no cost to the parents and in all settings (e.g., the classroom, physical education facilities, the home, and hospitals or institutions).

---

due to environmental factors such as poverty, homelessness, substantiated child abuse, poor attachment to caregivers, and parental mental illness and substance abuse. Indeed, research evidence suggests that infants and toddlers who experience adverse circumstances and maltreatment are six times more likely to have a developmental delay than the general population (Hebbeler, Spiker, Bailey, Scarborough, Mallik, Simeonsson, et al., 2007). The Adverse Childhood Experiences (ACE) Study shows that young children having a difficult start to their lives can experience lifelong personal and social problems leading to high economic costs for society (Centers for Disease Control and Prevention, 2014). Therefore, there is strong justification for intervening early to promote infant mental health and to reduce the risk of children's development being hampered by poverty, abuse, neglect, or other early parent-child relationship difficulties.

The rationale for investing in EI is based on the premise that acting early on in a child's life results in important effects not gained if action is delayed (Smith & Guralnick, 2007). Thus, intervention can pay dividends in the long term by improving a child's overall development, including their social and emotional well-being and educational attainment, as well as helping to prevent problems in later life. Indeed, in recent years, there has been recognition by policy makers internationally that investing in early years' prevention and intervention makes sense economically, as

Spotlight on Research

INFANT MENTAL HEALTH

As defined previously, infant mental health focuses on promoting optimal social and emotional development of infants and toddlers. Chapter 3 outlined numerous social and emotional skills that need to be acquired for health development as well as how family and community factors influence that development. This Spotlight on Research box will investigate when development goes off the expected trajectory and intervention strategies to address areas for growth.

The mental health of infants and toddlers are impacted by the context in which they are being raised. Family crises, such as divorce (see Spotlight on Research box in Chapter 6), abuse or neglect (Osofsky & Lieberman, 2011), domestic violence (Brinaman, Taranta, & Johnston, 2012; Ellison, 2014), or homelessness (Brinaman et al., 2012) can disrupt the parent-child relationship and/or obscure the infant's needs. Similarly, issues on either side of the relationship can be disruptive: maternal depression (Bydlowski, Lalanne, Golse, & Vaivre-Douret, 2013), maternal substance abuse (Flykt, Punamäki, Belt, Biringen, Salo, Posa, et al., 2012; Siqveland, Haabrekke, Wentzel-Larsen, & Moe, 2014), infant sleep and eating disorders (Christl, Reilly, Smith, Sims, Chavasse, & Austin, 2013) as well as aggression in very young children (see Bolten, 2013, for a review). Even though the vast majority of this research focused on the mother-child relationship, Fitzgerald, Bocknek, Hossain, and Roggman (2015) remind us of the important role fathers play in development, from pregnancy on, both directly and indirectly through their marital relationship.

As you will read later in this chapter, infant mental health is most often a problem of the relationship between adults and children. As such, interventions must be through bi-generational services (e.g., services that simultaneously address the needs of adults and children). The Parenting Interactions with Children: Checklist of Observations Linked to Outcomes (PICCOLO) measures parenting strengths that have been shown to improve outcomes for children, such as increased language and attention to emotions. When used with a protocol of therapeutic interactions and observations and analysis of parent-child interactions (mostly through videotaped interactions), parents gained a deeper understand of their strengths and received guidance on areas for improvement (Wheeler, Ludtke, Helmer, Barna, Wilson, & Oleksiak, 2013). Although working with the video recordings can be challenging at first, the therapists and parents realized the benefits of immediately reviewing concrete behaviors of the parents and their child and saw measurable gains in parent-child interactions (Wheeler et al., 2013).

Another intervention strategy, kangaroo mother care, is used to address infant mental health issues. This strategy focuses specifically on attachment and depression issues that often accompany a premature birth. Kangaroo mother care involves prolonged and ongoing skin-to-skin contact between the mother and infant. Botero and Sanders (2014) believe that this type of care promotes a healthy mother-child relationship because it is an external extension of life in the womb. Bera and colleagues (2014) found that premature infants with the lowest birth weights responded best to 40 weeks of kangaroo mother care in terms of weight gain and cognitive development. More specifically, the lowest weight children met the control infants in terms of growth at their corrected birth age and then continued to surpass the control infants throughout the next 12 months (Bera, Ghosh, Singh, Hazra, Mukherjee, & Mukherjee, 2014). In addition, at 1 year, the infants who received kangaroo mother care also exceeded the control group in terms of cognitive development. While those results are important to the infants' development, how did the intervention impact the mothers? In a meta-analysis of research, Athanasopoulou and Fox (2014) concluded that kangaroo mother care was beneficial to mothers due to its positive reduction of maternal stress and depression as well as the promotion of more positive interactions with their preterm infants. Thus, the intervention of kangaroo mother care has resulted in positive benefits to both the infant and mother within the first year of life. Given the importance of attachment history in the first year of life, it would seem that such positive outcomes would set a foundation for future social and emotional development.

well as ethically, because it can reduce later public spending on expensive specialist services in health, social care, education, and the criminal justice system (Cunha & Heckman, 2010; Heckman, 2004; Schweinhart, 2004; Shonkoff & Phillips, 2000; Uren, 2014).

10-2 Types and Tiers of Early Intervention

Multiple forms of EI exist depending on the nature of the difficulty experienced by the child and the level of severity (Gore, Hastings, & Brady, 2014; Baker & Feinfield, 2003). Part C of IDEA, Section 303.13, lists a range of different types of intervention available, including audiology and vision services; assistive technologies; family training, counseling, and home visits; health, medical, nursing, nutrition, and psychological services; occupational, physical, and speech therapies; social work services; and special instruction, such as the design of learning environments and curriculum activities. As you might imagine, different types of personnel with specialized knowledge are needed to deliver each type of interventions. This could include the following:

- Qualified audiologists
- Vision specialists
- Family therapists
- Nurses
- Occupational therapists
- Physical therapists
- Speech and language pathologists
- Orientation and mobility specialists
- Pediatricians and other physicians for diagnostic and evaluation purposes
- Psychologists
- Registered dieticians
- Social workers
- Special educators and other suitably qualified professionals, such as autism specialty providers and developmental specialists

multidisciplinary Intervention teams that are comprised of professionals from two or more separate disciplines or professions working in partnership with the child and his or her family.

universal services Programs that are routinely available to all children and their families to promote children's healthy development.

targeted interventions Programs that target specific families or communities who are experiencing greater levels of difficulty or stress and need additional support.

In many cases, intervention teams are **multidisciplinary**, inasmuch as they involve two or more separate disciplines or professions working in partnership with the child and his or her family.

Levels of EI are often grouped into three tiers: universal, targeted, and specialist (see Figure 10–1). **Universal services** are provided to, or are routinely available to, all children and their families to promote children's healthy development. Universal services are generally expected to make reasonable adjustments to include disabled children and those with additional needs. Countries and states (within the United States) differ as to the extent of universal early interventions available to young children and their families, but, in general, the United States lags behind other nations by providing few universal services. Examples provided in other countries include free or heavily subsidized early childhood care and education programs; national/regional health promotions and immunization programs; and mainstream schools.

On the other hand, **targeted interventions** are not universal, rather, they are targeted at specific families or communities who are experiencing greater levels of difficulty or stress and need additional support. Targeted interventions apply to disabled children and those at risk of developmental

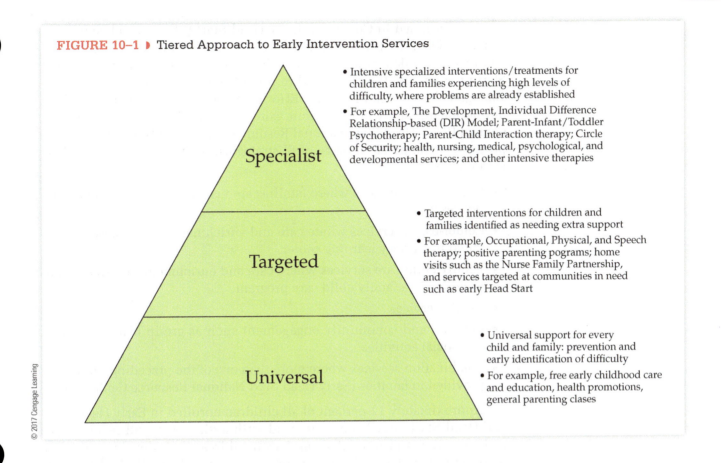

FIGURE 10–1 ▶ Tiered Approach to Early Intervention Services

Specialist

- Intensive specialized interventions/treatments for children and families experiencing high levels of difficulty, where problems are already established
- For example, The Development, Individual Difference Relationship-based (DIR) Model; Parent-Infant/Toddler Psychotherapy; Parent-Child Interaction therapy; Circle of Security; health, nursing, medical, psychological, and developmental services; and other intensive therapies

Targeted

- Targeted interventions for children and families identified as needing extra support
- For example, Occupational, Physical, and Speech therapy; positive parenting pograms; home visits such as the Nurse Family Partnership, and services targeted at communities in need such as early Head Start

Universal

- Universal support for every child and family: prevention and early identification of difficulty
- For example, free early childhood care and education, health promotions, general parenting clases

© 2017 Cengage Learning

delay or of developing social and emotional difficulties, such as attachment disorders and challenging behavior. Examples of targeted interventions in the United States include First Steps and Early Head Start. The aim of these often short-term interventions is to provide specific support and guidance to maximize a child's cognitive, physical, communicative, social, emotional, or adaptive functioning, and to prevent or minimize the risk of negative outcomes.

Finally, **specialist or specialized interventions** tend to be more long term and are provided to families with children who experience persistent challenges or to families in crisis. Specialist interventions offer systematic and sometimes intensive therapeutic treatment and other services to children and families with acute, complex, or very high-level needs who would otherwise be at great risk of poor outcomes.

For many children, a portfolio of interventions across the tiers is likely to be most effective because these interventions can address multiple risk factors by acting at the individual, family, school, and community levels. This is consistent with the ecological systems perspective advocated by Bronfenbrenner (2001) (see Chapter 1), which is integral to the multidisciplinary approach of EI programs such as Early Head Start (EHS) and other integrated early education, health, and social care programs such as the Chicago Child-Parent Centers. However, whether children and families participate in **mixed early child development interventions** like these, or in other EI programs, it is vital that the range of early interventions they do receive are coordinated and flexible (Chen, 2014).

specialist or specialized interventions Long-term, systematic services that are provided to children or families with acute, complex, or very high-level needs who would otherwise be at great risk.

mixed early child development intervention Intervention which includes a mix of approaches that can be center-based and home-based and/or directed at both children and parents.

As mentioned in Chapter 1, Early Head Start (EHS), which started in 1994, is a federally funded program for low-income pregnant women and families with infants and toddlers. This program evolved from the Head Start program and the clear need to provide early intervention for disadvantaged children and families. EHS is built on four cornerstones: child development, family development, community building, and staff development (Early Head Start National Resource Center, 2014). In addition, the program encompasses a range of EI strategies, including services such as the following:

- Home-based services where families are visited weekly by a home visitor provider
- Center-based services where care and enrichment experiences are provided in an early learning center
- Family child care services where care and enrichment experiences are provided in a family child care program
- Health services
- Parental and community engagement such as group learning events and social activities
- Combination services where more than one of the preceding services is provided to families (Early Head Start National Resource Center, 2014)

Approximately 12 percent of all children enrolled in Early Head Start and Head Start have been diagnosed with a disability and receive special education and/or related services to address their developmental or learning issues (Early Head Start Program Facts Sheet, 2011). However, this figure does not include the number of children who are at risk for developmental or learning issues due to being victims of child abuse or neglect.

Even though far too few children are served by this important program, the children who are enrolled have documented positive outcomes in all areas of development. For example, they have higher immunization rates, larger vocabularies, and better social-emotional development as indicated by lower rates of aggression with peers and increased attunement with objects when playing (National Head Start Association [NHSA], 2014). They had higher early reading and math scores than peers who were not enrolled in EHS (Lee, Zhai, Brooks-Gunn, Han, & Waldfogel, 2014). African American children who were in EHS programs had better cognitive outcomes (e.g., increased receptive vocabulary and sustained attention) and social outcomes (e.g., increased engagement with parents during play; reduction in aggressive behaviors; Harden, Sandstrom, & Chazan-Cohen, 2012).

In addition, EHS has been found to have positive effects on parents, including decreased rates of depression, increased participation in educational or job training, and higher rates of employment (NHSA, 2014). They have been found to score higher on measures of parenting supportiveness (Harden et al., 2012), especially for mothers with less initial attachment avoidance or attachment anxiety (Berlin, Whiteside-Mansell, Roggman, Green, Robinson, & Spieker, 2011). NHSA (2014) research found that EHS parents were more likely to read to their child on a daily basis and provided a more stimulating home-learning environment. Indeed, research from evaluations of EHS and other EI programs in the United States indicates that programs which combine center-based intervention with home visiting have greater benefits for families than those that rely on home-visiting alone (Love, Kisker, Ross, Raikes, Constantine, Boller, et al., 2005).

10-3 From Special Needs to Special Rights

Taking a developmental perspective in our work with young children means valuing all of the individual characteristics for each infant and toddler in our care. In addition, it means being able to identify strengths and areas of growth for each child to support optimal growth, development, and learning. In the current context within the United States, educators tend to think about providing services to meet a child's identified special needs. This perspective has its origins in federal law, specifically IDEA, in which the discourse of early intervention is associated with making provision for "children with disabilities" and "special needs." However, professionals inspired by educators in Reggio Emilia, Italy, prefer to use the term "children with special rights," as this further supports a strong, positive image of the child (see Chapter 6). Using this phrase shifts the emphasis away from a deficit model of childhood (i.e., that disabled children are "needy") and toward a credit model in which all children have rights, including disabled children who have special rights. We would like you to reframe the issue of EI from a deficit approach (i.e., focusing on what disabled children lack and their educational needs) to a special rights approach (i.e., focusing on disabled children's strengths and their educational rights).

The special rights approach of Reggio Emilia also draws on the concepts of children's rights as articulated within the United Nations Convention on the Rights of the Child, 1989. The UN Convention guarantees three types of rights for children: provision, protection, and participation (Lansdown, 1994). For example, each child has the right to be provided with an education, to be protected from harm, and to participate in decisions that affect his or her life. Thus, educators in Reggio Emilia expand on our basic value of individual rights to include the concept of special rights (Vakil, Freeman, & Swim, 2003). In that educational context, children with special rights have "immediate precedence" for admission into programs (Gandini, 2001, p. 55) and are included in classrooms alongside their nondisabled peers. This practice reflects how teachers in Reggio Emilia wanted to "embrace, not ignore, the concept of differences among children" (Soncini, 2012, p. 189). Soncini (2012) continues that while an impairment brings with it a difference, this is just one of many differences that every child, disabled and nondisabled, exhibits: "We want to have an encounter with these and all exceptions. Each child has his or her own exceptionality" (p. 190). We add to this understanding of special rights the idea that teachers must start their work focusing on what each child can do independently and adding on what she is entitled to learn with assistance (refer to the Vygotsky discussion in Chapter 2). When teachers, children, and family members discuss differences and come to terms with

special needs A deficit model that focuses on what children are not able to do, their limitations, or what they need, oftentimes to the exclusion of their strengths or abilities.

special rights A credit or strength-based model in which all children have rights, including disabled children who have special educational rights.

conflicting ideas, then everyone can see the child's possibilities and limits realistically (Soncini, 2012). Thus, giving some children the status of special rights is seen as a way to improve everyone's participation and inclusion within the community.

10-4 The Need for Family Capacity-Building

Traditionally, EI programs have been concerned with targeting individual children who have been deemed eligible for services under the criteria defined by the nation/state/region in which they reside. Interventions may include the provision of educational and/or therapeutic services, healthcare, and/or social and psychological assistance (Hardman et al., 2014). However, in more recent years, awareness of the vital role that parents play in fostering children's well-being, learning, and development has increased and subsequently broadened the term to include interventions targeted at both children and their parents (Photo 10–1). Indeed, there is a growing recognition among early childhood and EI programs that "in order to truly address the best interests of the children, they must also serve the best interests of their parents" (Summers and Chazan-Cowen, 2012, p. 52). This realization has led to the provision of high-quality family support and other **bi-generational services** and therapeutic programs that focus on parenting practices as well as children's well-being, education, and development. Consequently, effective EI programs have a twofold focus: (1) to promote the best possible outcomes for the child, and (2) to enhance the capacity of families (and communities) to meet their child's needs. Early Head Start and the Nurse-Family Partnership in the United States and Sure Start Children's Centres in England are good examples of **family capacity-building** programs that seek to intervene early in the lives of families with infants and toddlers.

Building the capacity of families to support their child's development is important not only in mixed intervention programs such as EHS but also in therapeutic interventions with disabled children and programs targeted at children with emotional difficulties. Rather than leaving "intervention" to the specialists/clinicians (e.g., through the child participating in a one-hour clinical session once a week with a therapist), professionals should work in close collaboration with families so that parents are able to incorporate specialists' strategies into their child's everyday routines and activities. For example, a physical therapist could introduce and illustrate to the parent of a child with mobility difficulties how to use a four-point kneeling exercise and then have the parent use this practice with his or her child and evaluate the experience. Alternatively, for a pre-verbal toddler with behavioral difficulties, a specialist could model and explain how to attune and respond to a child's communicative cues, and then film the parent attempting this with his or her toddler. The parent and specialist could then watch the film together to evaluate how the interaction went. These intervention strategies can then be implemented by parents (and teachers) on an ongoing basis rather than being conducted solely by a specialist on an

bi-generational services When services are provided to adults and children through the same program, often at the same time.

family capacity-building When professionals work in close collaboration with families to uncover each family members' goals and wishes for the child. Then, strategies are designed for the everyday routine and activities so that parents are able to improve their lives and the daily lives of their child.

PHOTO 10–1 Parents play a vital role in fostering children's well-being.

Spotlight on Research

EARLY INTERVENTION AND BUILDING COLLABORATIVE PARTNERSHIPS

After a child has been evaluated and deemed to benefit from early intervention, family members, clinicians, and teachers must find ways to build working partnerships. A literature review revealed three aspects of building partnerships: (1) starting from a strength-based perspective, (2) sharing expectations, and (3) meeting emotional needs.

Working from a strength-based perspective means that professionals use language and communications to demonstrate what a child can do or is working on. For example, instead of saying that the child cannot sit unassisted, you could reframe the situation to say that the child is rolling over independently. Both observations might be true, but the latter one highlights what the child can do. In this way, reframing provides a way for teachers to build a new perspective around the child and family (Weishaar, 2010).

The second aspect of building this partnership is for teachers and clinicians to shed their expert roles and co-construct with families a shared frame of reference (Lyons, O'Malley, O'Connor, & Monaghan, 2010; McWilliam, 2015). In other words, all parties must share their goals, fears, concerns, and so on, as a starting point for the work. Parents are often uncertain about their roles, especially how to participate in therapy sessions and how they are expected to carry over strategies (Lyons et al., 2010). Being clear about what you expect from them and what they expect from you can create a stronger foundation from which to work.

Creating a partnership also involves finding ways to address and fulfill the emotional needs of the participants. Brotherson et al. (2010) found that families and professionals had four types of emotional needs:

(a) a need for a sense of hope in the child's progress, (b) a sense of urgency to provide timely early

intervention and prevent or ameliorate the child's disabilities, (c) a feeling of stress arising from multiple or complex challenges experienced by families, and (d) a sense of overload on the part of professionals based on feeling inadequate to deal with complex needs or demands of the job. (p. 38)

Unfortunately, not all emotional needs are addressed equally in all partnerships. Sometimes the professionals' needs were met, sometimes the families' needs were met, sometimes both the professionals' and families' needs were met, and sometimes neither had their needs met (Brotherson et al., 2010). Systems of practice must be put in place better to ensure that everyone's needs are appropriately addressed in the partnership. Epley et al. (2010) discovered in their research that administrative practices and procedures had a significant impact on providers' ability to serve families of young children with disabilities. If the goal of the early intervention is to promote optional development in children, then professionals at all levels must create working partnerships that help everyone engage fully in the therapy process.

The collaborative relationship is not just between families and intervention professionals. Early childhood teachers are a vital part of the process, often providing intervention strategies on a regular basis in their program or classroom. In a recent inquiry, Mattern (2015) discovered that early childhood educators were knowledgeable about evidence-based practices in early intervention. Unfortunately, they did not feel that such practices were being implemented in their programs/classrooms. Mattern concluded that early childhood educators need additional education and guided practice to increase their ability to deliver high-quality early intervention strategies. This study demonstrates the importance of each member of the intervention team receiving support so that her or his needs are met.

occasional basis. When intervention strategies are built into the fabric of the families' daily life and respond to family members' reported goals and challenges with daily routines, parents are more apt to implement them on a regular basis (Siller, Morgan, Turner-Brown, Baggett, Baranek, Brian, et al., 2013). The researchers also found that building on the families' daily life "fostered the density of treatment hours, facilitated generalization across activities, and expanded opportunities for families and children to participate together in meaningful everyday activities" (Siller et al., 2013, p. 373).

Family and Community Connections

In your center-based classroom, you serve two children with special rights. Both children are sociable and show good emotional regulation. They are each challenged by physical movement, but for different reasons and to different degrees. A physical therapist and an occupational therapist provide intervention services each week. You try to implement the strategies shown but they do not always work smoothly in your classroom routine. How can you communicate your issues to the therapists without appearing unsupportive of their work or unwilling to implement the strategies? What will you specifically do and say during a conversation?

READING CHECKPOINT

Before moving on with your reading, make sure that you can answer the following questions about the material discussed so far.

1. What are the benefits of intervening early (1) for the child, (2) for the family, and (3) for society?
2. How does the family capacity-building approach described here compare to the EI practice you have observed or been involved with?

10-5 The Evaluation and Assessment Process

Children diagnosed with a specific condition, or who experience significant prematurity, low birth weight, illness, or surgery, are eligible for EI services from birth. In other cases, if an infant or toddler acquires an impairment later, or if a parent, caregiver, or other professional suspects a child is entitled to additional support, the family may be referred for assessment. Eligibility is ascertained by evaluating the child to see if she does, in fact, have a delay in development or a disability. Part C eligibility is determined by each state's definition of "developmental delay" and whether it includes children "at risk" in the eligibility formula.

10-5a The Role of Teachers

Teachers have particular responsibilities regarding the identification of special rights, especially for children who experience poverty because they have been found to be at higher risk of disability, behavioral and emotional difficulties, and ill health (Spencer, 2008; Shahtahmasebi, Emerson, Berridge, & Lancaster, 2011; World Health Organization, 2011). Peterson, Mayer, Summers, and Luze (2010) identify six recommendations for teachers:

1. Monitor children closely, especially when their families face multiple risks.
2. Develop clear procedures to determine when and how to refer families to disability-related services.
3. Collaborate closely with community partners.
4. Collaborate with the health-care community to address health issues and identify potential disabilities.

PHOTO 10–2 Teachers should report observations to family members, rather than try to diagnose a particular disorder or delay.

5. Focus on early intervention strategies to prevent problems from becoming delays.

6. Provide services and support to families of children with disabilities.

After carefully observing, teachers should report their observations to family members and, in partnership with the family members, enlist the assistance of experts trained in clinical diagnoses (Photo 10–2). First Steps (a federally funded intervention program), Early Head Start, private agencies, and public schools should all have qualified personnel on staff to assess, evaluate, and provide diagnoses as appropriate. Only such experts can diagnose a child. As a teacher, you should never tell a family member that you think her child has a particular disorder or delay. In fact, doing so oversteps your areas of expertise and exposes you to specific legal liabilities. Your job is to explain what you have observed and allow the family member to draw her own conclusions. You can note, however, if any of the behaviors "raise a red flag" (i.e., item of concern) or "raise a yellow flag" (i.e., item to be watched further) for you and why. You should also note the child's unique strengths and interests, celebrating and building on these with the child, family members, and any other professionals involved.

10-5b The Individualized Family Service Plan (IFSP)

After the qualified person has completed an assessment, the need for a specific educational plan will be determined. If such a plan is warranted, a conference of all necessary professionals and family members will be convened. The goal of this meeting is to create an Individualized Family Service Plan (IFSP) that outlines how professionals will provide services and assist the family in supporting the child's growth, development, and learning.

Depending on the nature of the difficulty, these assessments may involve professionals from a variety of different disciplines. Under IDEA, evaluations and assessments are to be provided at no cost to the parent. At each stage of the process, professionals need to collaborate with parents/caregivers (Gore et al., 2014) and to be culturally responsive to children and families in all screening, assessment, and intervention practices (Lynch and Hanson, 2011).

After the IFSP has been constructed, it is your responsibility as an educator to carry out the aspects of the early intervention plan that are assigned or designated to you. According to the Center for Parent Information and Resources (2014), the IFSP should contain the following elements:

- The child's present physical, cognitive, communication, social/emotional, and adaptive development levels and needs
- Family information (with consent from parents), including the resources, priorities, and concerns of the child's parents and other family members closely involved with the child
- The major results or outcomes expected to be achieved for the child and family
- The specific services the child will be receiving
- Where in the natural environment (e.g., home, community) the services will be provided (if the services will not be provided in the natural environment, the IFSP must include a statement justifying why not)
- When and where the child will receive services
- The number of days or sessions he or she will receive each service and how long each session will last
- Who will pay for the services
- The name of the service coordinator overseeing the implementation of the IFSP
- The steps to be taken to support the child's transition out of EI and into another program when the time comes (e.g., how the child will transition from EI to preschool special education after his third birthday)

10-5c Natural Environments

Early intervention programs and services may be delivered in a variety of settings. Part C of IDEA requires that "to the maximum extent appropriate to the needs of the child, EI must be provided in natural environments, including the home and community settings in which children without disabilities participate" (34 CFR Para 303.12(b)). It is therefore a legal requirement that EI must be provided in settings that are natural or typical for a nondisabled infant or toddler to the maximum extent appropriate (Photo 10–3). Only when this cannot be achieved satisfactorily in a natural environment may services be provided in other settings.

There are a number of benefits to this approach. As sociocultural psychologists suggest, the social and temporal context of everyday environments, such as home or child care center, are vital for child development (Donaldson, 1978; Bronfenbrenner, 1979; Hogan, 2005). These scholars assert that when children are placed in experimental or clinical settings, they often appear less competent compared to when they are in their real-world contexts. Familiar surroundings help children feel more comfortable and thus exhibit their competences more readily. Furthermore, **natural environments** promote family-centered practices because the focus is on helping families learn how to foster their child's learning and development as part of the child's daily routines and activities in their everyday settings. Finally, natural environments promote **inclusive practices** because children are not excluded from their non-disabled peers.

10-6 Characteristics and Care of Children with Special Rights

In virtually every community in the United States, early interventions for disabled and at-risk infants and toddlers are currently available (Odom, Teferra, & Kaul, 2004). These children sometimes require specialized equipment, care, and curricula, and the child care specialist must learn how to care for children with specific special rights. Because it is impossible to cover all the special conditions and procedures necessary to care for children with special rights in one text, an overview of categories and characteristics is provided here as related to: (1) physical and cognitive/language development, and (2) social and emotional development. However, the first source of information should be the child and family. Observe carefully and closely to understand the child. The partnerships you create should encourage the family members to freely exchange information with you. When you know the child well and need additional information about the disability in general, contact the appropriate local and national associations and organizations for information on how to care for an individual child with that specific special right. In other words, you should become an expert on each individual child first and then familiarize yourself with the effects of the impairment or difficulty (Brekken, 2004).

PHOTO 10–3 As much as possible, EI services must be provided in natural, typical settings.

natural environments Legal requirement that EI must be provided in settings that are natural or typical for a nondisabled infant or toddler to the maximum extent appropriate.

inclusive practices The act of educating and providing supports and services to disabled children in settings with their nondisabled peers.

10-6a Physical and Cognitive Development

The following categories help to explain several of the common special rights infants and toddlers may have regarding physical and cognitive/language development. However, note that every child with one or more of the impairments discussed next is unique in terms of the characteristics she possesses and the care she is entitled to.

1. **Children with Motor Difficulties.** Infants and toddlers with motor difficulties exhibit delayed motor development, retention of primitive reflexes, and abnormal muscle tone as the result of central nervous system (CNS) damage or malformation. The three major conditions that are

accompanied by motor difficulties are cerebral palsy, myelomeningo-cele, and Down syndrome. Infants and toddlers with motor difficulties usually exhibit delays in other developmental areas as well because learning occurs through active exploration of the world. Research on interventions involving systematic exercise and sensory stimulation and integration indicates that early intervention can improve motor and sensory development and encourage parent support and acceptance. For more information, contact the American Medical Association, American Academy of Pediatrics, and local chapters of specific organizations such as the United Cerebral Palsy Foundation.

2. **Biologically At-Risk Infants and Toddlers.** Some children experience central nervous system (CNS) damage, for example, from CNS infections, trauma, ingestion of toxins, and sustained hypoxia (lack of oxygen). Research results on interventions ranging from special nursery settings and free nursing and medical care to infant stimulation by parents yield mixed results, with very short-term, positive effects. Interventions for this population appear to be more effective with parents than with children. For more information, contact the American Medical Association, the county health department, the American Academy of Pediatrics, or local pediatricians.

3. **Children with Visual Impairments.** Infants and toddlers who are blind or have low vision are found in approximately 1 out of 3,000 births, with a wide range of severity and etiology. The most important consideration is visual efficiency, which includes acuity, visual fields, ocular motility, binocular vision, adaptations to light and dark, color vision, and accommodation. Research findings indicate that early intervention helps visually impaired infants and toddlers perform closer to typical developmental expectations. Interventions using a team approach, including parents, child care specialists, and other professionals, are more effective than individual treatment approaches. For more information, contact the National Society for the Prevention of Blindness, the National Council for Exceptional Children, the local health department, and agencies for the blind or those with low vision.

4. **Children with Hearing Impairments.** Hearing impairments are classified by type (sensorineural, conductive, or mixed), time of onset (at birth or after), severity (mild to profound), and etiology. Research indicates that early intervention programs should include parent counseling, staff with training in audiology, speech and language training, sign language as a normal program component, the flexibility to help each family, and the involvement of deaf adults as resources for children. For more information, contact the Council for Exceptional Children, the local health department, and the National Association of the Deaf.

5. **Children Who Are Medically Fragile.** A new subgroup of health disorders, referred to as medically fragile, has emerged in recent years (Hardman et al., 2014). These individuals are at risk for medical emergencies and often require specialized support. For example, children with feeding tubes need highly trained individuals to provide necessary nutritional supplements. Other times, medically fragile children have progressive diseases (e.g., AIDS or cancer) or episodic conditions (e.g., severe asthma or sickle cell disease; Hardman et al., 2014). Such disorders have an impact

not only on the way the infant or toddler forms his or her own identity but also on how others see and treat him or her. Seeking information from families or community agencies/organizations can help to alleviate your concerns and educate the child's peers about the specific disorder, improving peer relationships (McDevitt & Ormrod, 2013).

6. **Children with Cognitive and General Developmental Disorders.** Some infants and toddlers exhibit delays in several facets of cognition, such as information processing, problem solving, and the ability to apply information to new situations. These issues may have environmental or genetic sources such as Down syndrome or teratogenic damage. Global delays in motor, cognitive, language, and socioemotional areas are common. Children with cognitive and general developmental disorders tend to reach milestones but at a much slower rate, with lower final levels of development. Research strongly indicates that EI programs prevent the decline in intellectual functioning found in children with mild learning difficulties who do not receive intervention. Programs for children with moderate and profound learning difficulties are more effective with active parental participation and training, but overall they appear to be less effective with infants and toddlers with mild learning difficulties. For more information, contact the American Association on Intellectual and Developmental Disabilities, the local special education administration, or local chapters of specific associations such as the Down Syndrome Association.

7. **Children with Language and Communication Disorders.** Infants and toddlers who exhibit problems with the mechanics of speech (phonation, moving air from the lungs through the mouth, and articulation) have speech disorders, and children with problems using the rules of language (labeling or forming sentences) have language disorders. Results of studies on various kinds of interventions suggest that the course of communication disorders can be modified through early intervention. For more information, contact the American Association for Speech and Language, the American Speech-Language-Hearing Association, the Association for Speech and Hearing, and local chapters of associations for speech and language disorders.

10-6b Social and Emotional Development

This section outlines just a few of the ways in which infants and toddlers might exhibit special rights with regard to emotional and social development. However, the categories here are not exclusive to social and emotional development because the domains of development interact differently for each individual (Photo 10–4).

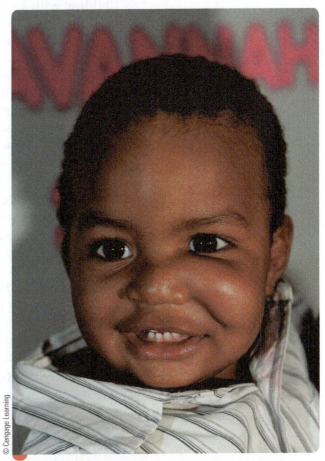

© Cengage Learning

PHOTO 10–4 Children have different social and emotional abilities and needs.

1. **Children with Autistic Spectrum Disorders (ASD).** Infants and toddlers with ASD exhibit disturbances in developmental rates and sequences, social interactions (i.e., extremely withdrawn), responses to sensory stimuli, communication, and the capacity to relate appropriately to people, events, and objects. The incidence of ASD in the general population is rising, yet estimates of prevalence rates vary widely: from 1 child out of 68 (Centers for Disease Control and Prevention, 2014a) to 1 in 143 (Hardman et al., 2014). Overall, however, males outnumber females three to four (American Psychiatric Association, 2014). Data on early assessment suggest that children as young as 18 months can be reliably diagnosed with ASD, but that the tools fail to recognize the disorder in many toddlers who will later show clear symptoms (Watson, Baranek, & DiLavore, 2003). Much research has continued to create tools and increase the reliability of diagnosing ASD for infants and toddlers (see, e.g., Brian, Bryson, Garon, Roberts, Smith, Szatmari, et al., 2008; Honda, Shimizu, Nitto, Imai, Ozawa, Iwasa, et al., 2009; Wetherby, Brosnan-Maddox, Peace, & Newton, 2008). Research on structured EI programs, which include parents, has yielded highly encouraging results. For more information, contact the Autism Society of America, Autism Speaks, or your local psychological association.

2. **Reactive Attachment Disorder.** This term describes children who have experienced severe problems or disruptions in their early relationships. Children with an attachment disorder fail to form normal attachments to primary caregivers. Attachment disorders appear to be the result of "grossly inadequate care" during infancy and toddlerhood (Hardman et al., 2014, p. 190). This disorder results in serious problems in emotional attachments and developmentally incompetent social relationships (Cain, 2006). For more information, contact your state Infant Mental Health Organization, local mental health providers, and community-specific organizations, such as an EHS program. In addition, the American Academy of Child and Adolescent Psychiatry (AACAP) website provides useful information as well as resources for families and teachers.

3. **Mental Health Disorder.** This describes a wide range of unique child characteristics that can begin during the infant-toddler developmental period, such as Reactive Attachment Disorder that was just described. Although the prevalence of such disorders is very, very low for this age group, serious disorders such as depression, childhood schizophrenia, and anxiety disorders have been known to occur. However, some research suggests that the interaction of particular parent characteristics (e.g., depression symptoms) and infant traits (e.g., components of temperament) predict higher levels of depression-like symptoms in toddlers (Gartstein & Bateman, 2008).

4. **Children with Multiple Disabilities.** As defined by IDEA federal regulations, many children experience multiple disabilities or concomitant impairments, meaning that they have more than one identified exceptionality. The particular combination causes such severe educational issues that the individual cannot be accommodated in special education programs designed solely for one of the special

needs (34 Code of Federal Regulations 300.8(c)(7) [2006], as cited in Hardman et al., 2014).

5. **Children with Fetal Alcohol Spectrum Disorders (FASD).** Children with FASD were exposed to an adverse environmental agent—alcohol—during the periods of prenatal development. Children with more severe cases typically have growth delays, facial abnormalities, mental retardation, impulsivity, and behavioral problems (McDevitt & Ormrod, 2013). Other children, while exposed to alcohol prenatally, do not demonstrate the same severity of outcomes. The difference seems to be the amount, frequency, and duration of alcohol consumption by the mother as well as other maternal and child characteristics (e.g., nutrition). Researchers and medical professionals do not know how much alcohol needs to be ingested to produce a small effect versus a large effect. Because of the diversity of characteristics for these children, a number of different intervention programs have been created (see Chandrasena, Mukherjee, Raja, & Turk, 2009; Davis, Desrocher, & Moore, 2011, for reviews).

Before moving on with your reading, make sure that you can answer the following questions about the material discussed so far.

1. Explain three special rights infants and toddlers might have in relationship to physical development, cognitive/language development, and social-emotional well-being. What would you do if you suspected a child had one of these special rights?

2. What is your role as a professional educator in supporting children with special rights and their families?

READING CHECKPOINT

Summary

10-1 Describe early intervention.

EI programs are based on the premises that intervention is likely to be more effective and less costly when provided earlier in life rather than later. High-quality EI can minimize potential delay by promoting children's development in key domains (physical, cognitive, communicative, adaptive, social, emotional).

10-2 Discriminate between different types of intervention.

This chapter discussed universal, targeted, and specialist types of intervention for disabled children and those experiencing adverse circumstances. Mixed, bi-generational approaches that focus on children and parents appear to be the most effective

in enhancing child outcomes (Geddes, Haw, & Frank, 2010).

10-3 Summarize the notion of special needs and special rights.

We have reframed EI from a deficit approach (focusing on children with special needs) to a credit or strength-based model (focusing on children's special rights). This has important implications for practice. In our efforts to support children and their families, we should avoid pathologizing "at risk" and "poor" families, and/or children with "disabilities," "developmental disorders," "behavioral problems," and "special needs." Rather we should acknowledge each child's unique strengths, rights, and interests.

10-4 Explain why family capacity-building is a vital component of early intervention.

High-quality EI enhances the capacity of families to support their children's development. Appropriate bi-generational intervention, applied early, can change a child's developmental trajectory, leading to higher achievement and greater independence, as well as promoting family competence and well-being. Working as partners with families in EI means listening actively to uncover each family member's goals and wishes for the child. It also requires that families and other professionals collaborate to address the many structural and environmental factors that place children "at risk" of poor developmental outcomes.

10-5 Identify the steps involved in the evaluation and assessment process, and apply this to your own practice.

Teachers have particular responsibilities regarding the identification of special rights, yet they are not the ones to make a specific diagnosis.

Teachers often start the process by explaining to family members what they have observed and allowing family members to draw their own conclusions. You should always note the child's unique strengths and interests, celebrating and building on these with the child, family members, and any other professionals involved. When families pursue a diagnosis, teachers participate on teams with other professionals who have diagnostic responsibilities. The process for evaluation, assessment, and treatment was explained in detail.

10-6 Describe the characteristics and care of children with special rights related to physical, cognitive, emotional, and social development.

The chapter ended by summarizing aspects or characteristics of common impairments, disorders, or disabilities. It is vital that you understand that every child with one or more of the items discussed is unique in terms of the characteristics she possesses and the care she is entitled to.

CASE STUDY	Kierston's Mother Is Depressed

You were introduced to Kierston in the beginning of this chapter, but this section provides additional information to assist with understanding her behavior. She is the youngest of eight children, and the sibling she is closest to is 17 years her senior. Both of her parents are first-generation immigrants. Her mother is over 45, and during the pregnancy, her husband, who was 57, suddenly died of a heart attack. Kierston was delivered by cesarean. Since her birth, her mother has provided minimal care for the newborn due to deepening depression. The majority of the care she receives is from siblings, cousins, and other extended family members. The grief of the family is obvious to anyone observing them. The well-meaning but numerous caregivers provide very inconsistent care for Kierston. The variety of different faces and personalities who

care for her may help explain her lack of desire to interact with others.

The child care home she attends is owned and operated by a married couple, Hurika and Bill. They have compensated for the lack of consistency in Kierston's home environment by assigning a primary caregiver to her. Bill will establish a consistent daily routine around her needs; he plans to handle and speak to her gently to enhance her sense of trust and security.

Kierston's mother is clearly concerned that her daughter is not developing like her other children but seems unable to act because of her depression. Luckily, Hurika and Bill participate in an Early Head Start partnership and were able to encourage Kierston's mother to request an evaluation of

Kierston. The developmental specialist assigned to the family meets with the mother and older siblings next week.

1. What effect do you think a depressed family member has on the social and emotional development of a 2-month-old? Support your thoughts with evidence.

2. Referring to the list of recommended elements for an IFSP, what would you expect the family plan to cover in terms of services, location, and strategies? Why?

3. How should Bill continue to develop a relationship with Kierston's mother? What is the benefit for Kierston of them having a strong partnership?

Lesson Plan

Title: *Sorting Socks*

Child Observation:

Imani, 22 months, works with a speech and language pathologist each week. She is growing in her ability to pair sounds and gestures to communicate her needs and wants. For example, today at snack she said "ape" while pointing to the grapes in the center of the table.

Child's Developmental Goal:

To facilitate the development of spoken language

To use gestures to communicate desires

Materials: 10–11 pairs of children's socks, basket for holding socks

Preparation: Separate 5–6 pairs and mix in basket; place basket on floor; if necessary, clear space around the basket to work; reserve other pairs of socks to use if child(ren) need an additional challenge.

Learning Environment:

1. When Imani is looking for an experience, draw her attention to the socks by using descriptive language. To illustrate, you could say:

   "I brought these socks for you. What can you do with them?"

2. Invite Imani to touch the socks, if she hasn't already. Describe what she touches. Say something such as:
   a. Oh, you touched the red sock with the white polka dots.
   b. Is the striped sock soft?

3. Encourage Imani to match the socks. Explain what is a match by telling her to find the two socks that are alike.

4. When she makes a match, describe the socks.

5. To encourage her to speak, ask her about the sock she is touching.

6. If she is holding a sock but hasn't matched it yet, ask her where the match is. Encourage her to point to the sock she needs.

7. Describe her matching successes by saying something such as:
   a. You worked hard and matched all five pairs of socks.
   b. You matched both pairs of polka dot socks.

8. Invite other children to match the socks with Imani. When possible, encourage the children to describe their socks or ask each other for assistance finding a particular sock.

Guidance Consideration:

If Imani becomes upset, use emotional talk to describe her feelings. For example, if she is frustrated, you can say, *"It is frustrating when I can't understand your communications. Tell me again, I really want to know."*

Variations:

Roll the socks into balls and toss them into the basket. Count the number of socks or describe the socks that make it in the basket.

Additional Resources

Dunst, C. J., Bruder, M. B., & Espe-Sherwindt, M. (2014). Family capacity-building in early childhood: Do context and setting matter? *School Community Journal, 24*(1), 37–48.

Early Childhood Technical Assistance Center (ECTA). (2015). *The effectiveness of early intervention.* Retrieved February 9, 2015, http://ectacenter.org /topics/effective/effective.asp

Helms, C. (2011). *The effectiveness of early intervention programs' poverty capstone.* Retrieved February 9, 2015, http://www2.wlu.edu/ documents/shepherd/academics/cap_11 _Helms.pdf

Keilty, B. (2010). *The early intervention guidebook for families and professionals: Partnering for success.* New York: Teachers College Press.

11

CHAPTER

Teaching Children Birth to Twelve Months

Learning Objectives

After reading this chapter, you should be able to:

11-1 Select materials appropriate to the development of infants at that age level.

11-2 Devise strategies appropriate to infants (birth to 12 months of age) that are responsive to individual developmental levels.

Standards Addressed in This Chapter

naeyc **NAEYC Standards for Early Childhood Professional Preparation**

1 Promoting Child Development and Learning

4 Using Developmentally Effective Approaches to Connect with Children and Families

DAP **Developmentally Appropriate Practice Guidelines**

2 Teaching to Enhance Development and Learning

3 Planning Curriculum to Achieve Important Goals

In addition, the NAEYC standards for developmentally appropriate practice are divided into six areas particularly important to infant/toddler care. The following area is addressed in this chapter: *exploration and play*.

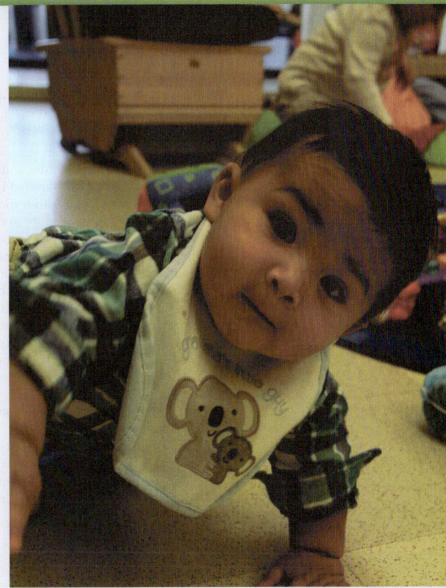

© 2017 Cengage Learning

CASE STUDY   Theresa

Theresa, 6 months old, is lying on her stomach on the floor, kicking her legs and waving her arms. She looks at a toy radio and drools. She fingers the toy radio, chews, and drools some more. She "sings" with the music. Ellie, the caregiver, winds up the toy radio. Theresa kicks her feet and smiles. She watches the radio and kicks her feet. Ellie smiles at Theresa, and Theresa smiles back. She kicks her feet rapidly. While Theresa looks at Wayne, another infant, Ellie speaks to her. Theresa tries to lift herself by pushing on the floor with her arms. She turns herself around, still on her tummy. She kicks her feet and keeps trying to lift herself up onto her knees to a crawling position. She presses her feet against furniture. During this time, she has turned about 180 degrees.

11-1 Materials

Infants under the age of 2 to 3 months of age tend to not require a great number of toys to remain happy. What they need are sensitive, responsive interactions with others. It has been said that the most important toy for a newborn is the human face. They can stare at it, it expresses emotions, and they can react in kind. As they get older and have longer periods of being awake and alert, they become more interested in exploring the world around them.

Children older than 4 to 8 months of age must be provided materials that are safe for the infants to mouth and hit and bang on themselves. These infants have developed some manual skills, but their limited control of their arm and hand muscles causes them to be rather rough on their toys and themselves. Attention-catching toys stimulate the interest of these infants and lengthen their playtime.

As infants grow and gain mobility, they will encounter an expanded world. All objects within reach must be safe to taste, touch, and move. Older infants need space as they continue to develop control of gross motor movements, such as crawling, standing, pulling, and throwing objects. Attention-catching materials stimulate infants to select and use those materials. Materials to manipulate must be small enough to grasp with the palm and fingers or with thumbs and forefingers, but not small enough for them to swallow.

Thus, materials given to infants younger than 1 year must be both challenging and safe. Every object infants can grasp and lift will go into their mouths. *Before* you allow an infant to touch a toy, determine whether it is safe. Each toy should meet *all* of the following criteria:

1. Too big to swallow (use a choke tube to measure objects; see Chapter 8)
2. No sharp points or edges to cut the skin or eyes
3. Can be cleaned
4. No movable parts that can pinch
5. Nontoxic paint on painted surfaces
6. Sturdy enough to withstand biting, banging, and throwing

After you have established that a material is safe, you must next evaluate its level of challenge. Look for toys and materials that the infant can use in several different ways. These provide greater opportunities for the infant to practice and develop new skills. Change the toys often so they seem new and interesting. To be challenging for the young infant, each material should do the following:

1. Catch the infant's attention so that she will want to interact with it in some way, such as reaching, pushing, grasping, tasting, or turning, and being able to practice these movements over and over again.

2. Be movable enough to allow the infant to successfully manipulate the object and respond to it with arms, legs, hands, eyes, ears, or mouth.

3. Be usable at several levels of complexity, so that the infant can use it with progressively more skill.

11-1a Types of Materials

Small toys and objects to grasp	Mirrors, unbreakable
Foam blocks	Sound toys
Rattles	Pictures, designs
Yarn or texture balls	Crib gym
Soft balls that are safe to throw	Teething toys
Furniture to climb on, over, pull self up on, or walk around	Toys that make sounds
	Materials to crawl over
Toys for banging and hitting	Textured objects
Stacking or nesting objects	Crayons
Puppets	Pictures to talk about
Pail and objects for filling and spilling	One- to four-piece puzzles

Materials may be homemade or commercially made. Figure 11–1 provides suggestions for making some of your own materials.

11-2 Caregiver Strategies to Enhance Development

Observations provide important information needed for decision-making, especially when planning a responsive, developmentally appropriate curriculum (see Chapters 5 and 9). This ongoing process or continuous loop of observing, planning, implementing, observing, and so on is vital to being a professional educator. Yet, assessing young children can be challenging. Because of the difficulties inherent in assessing what is expected of young children, some authorities advise caregivers not to assess children at all! Avoiding assessment is not only impossible but also results in care and education without any clear goals. The best approach, then, is to observe children formally and informally on a daily basis and make frequent adjustments in curriculum according to their progress in development, while honoring the uniqueness of each child. When teachers plan curricula that balance experiences for supporting and challenging skills in all developmental areas, then they are meeting the core concept of "teaching

FIGURE 11–1 ▶ Examples of Homemade Materials

RATTLES

Film canister (plastic or metal): Put in one teaspoon uncooked cereal. Replace the cap and tape it on with colored tape.

FABRIC TWIRLS

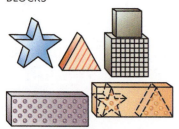

Cut out the center of a lid from a margarine tub. Cut carefully, leaving a clean, smooth edge. Use the remaining rim ring. Sew on three strips of printed washable fabric 3 inches long by 2 inches wide. Hang from the crib gym or put on the infant's wrist.

BLOCKS

Cut foam rubber into squares, circles, rectangles, triangles, and other shapes. Cover the foam with printed fabric sewn to fit the shapes. Large shapes can be stacked as blocks.

Cut 1-inch-thick sponges into shapes. Make sure the finished pieces are a good size to handle but too big to swallow.

CLUTCH BALL

Cut a circle of colorful, washable fabric. Put polyester filling on one part of the fabric and sew around it, creating a lump. Repeat, making a second lump. Baste around the edge of the circle and pull the circle almost closed. Stuff in polyester filling to pad the ball. Sew through the fabric and wind thread around the gathered end, creating a tuft of fabric.

PUZZLE

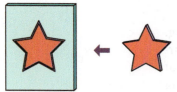

Glue a picture of one simple object on a piece of thick cardboard (use white glue and water mixture to cover the whole picture and cardboard). Cut out the object, making a simple shape. Place the object into the frame.

PUPPET

On a child-sized white sock, use a nontoxic waterproof marker to draw a face on one side, hair on the other side.

Spotlight on Organizations

ZERO TO THREE

This professional organization is dedicated to helping professionals and parents learn more about (1) the development of infants and toddlers, (2) methods for providing appropriate care for infants and toddlers, and (3) current topics in public policy. In addition, this organization has many resources for individuals who want to advocate for infants, toddlers, and their families.

Zero to Three produces many high-quality resources for teachers, families, intervention specialists, and other professionals who might work with infants and

toddlers, including books, videos, and the journal, *Zero to Three*. Moreover, this organization provides many professional training opportunities. It has a train-the-trainer format for some of its programs such as *Cradling literacy: Building teachers' skills to nurture early language and literacy birth to five* and *Preventing child abuse and neglect: Parent/Provider partnerships in child care* (PCAN). In addition, you can schedule an on-site trainer at your center for topics such as reflective supervision or identifying developmental difficulties of infancy and toddlerhood.

to enhance development and learning" as outlined in the guidelines for developmentally appropriate practices (Copple & Bredekamp, 2009).

Remember, however, that developmentally appropriate practice also involves building relationships with family members. As such, you will often need more than just observations to be a responsive educator. You will need to listen to family members and gain a deeper understanding of the contextual issues (e.g., family or community characteristics) that impact the child's development and learning. As you gain more information about a child's context or a particular developmental issue or challenge, you may have to engage in Internet searches or read scholarly resources to learn more. Many resources are available at local universities, public libraries, or through professional organizations. The Spotlight on Organizations box provides information on one organization that can greatly assist teachers in building their professional knowledge.

11-2a Physical Development

Infants from birth to 4 months of age show a very rapid rate of physical development that varies widely from infant to infant. One baby may turn from stomach to back early while another may reach for objects early and turn over later. Starting at birth with reflexive movements, infants rapidly gain an increasing level of **muscular control** over much of their bodies. In general, development moves from the simple to the more complex movements.

The control begins with the infant's head and neck and continues to his shoulders, back, waist, and legs. For example, infants first lift their heads up before they have the muscular control to sit, and they sit before they can use their legs for standing (Photo 11–1). Muscular control also develops from mid-body out to the hands and feet. Gradually infants are able to control their arm and leg movements to some degree, before they develop control of their hands, and to control their hands before they can grasp or pick up things with their fingers. Infants use these developing motor skills along

muscular control Gaining conscious control over muscles so that behaviors such as reaching, grabbing, and releasing can occur when the infant or toddler wants them to.

© 2017 Cengage Learning

PHOTO 11–1 Infants rapidly gain an increasing level of muscular control.

with their other senses (e.g., seeing, hearing, touching, smelling, and tasting) to notice differences and experience their world.

As infants get older, they become more motivated to master physical skills and explore their environments (McDevitt & Ormrod, 2013). This development is fostered by being awake and alert for longer periods and for a greater portion of the day. By 6 months, for example, infants can sit in a high chair, grasp an object intentionally, and bang it purposefully. During the last half of the first year of life, their muscles become more coordinated as the head, neck, arm, chest, and back muscles are used simultaneously to maintain an independently sitting position. They begin to move their bodies through space using all of their muscles, until eventually they can take their first unassisted step.

From Reflexes to Voluntary Control

Newborns' movements are reflexive; they occur without the infants' control or direction. These reflexive movements are necessary for the survival of the human species. For example, if infants had to be taught to suck and swallow, they would more than likely starve to death before they had gained the necessary muscular control to perform the skill. In a less dire example, reflexive hand and arm movements develop into a grasping-groping action, which can be independent of vision. Yet, over the next several months, hand and arm movements will become directed, voluntary activities that are visually controlled. Figure 11–2 provides information on when reflexes typically appear and disappear. If an infant is not gaining voluntary control of his or her reflexes as expected, it can be a sign of neurological problems (Ohgi, Arisawa, Takahashi, Kusumoto, Goto, Akiyama, et al., 2003).

FIGURE 11–2 ▶ Summary of Reflexes for Infants and Toddlers

Appears	swallow,* gag,* cough,* yawn,* blink suck rooting Moro (startle) grasp stepping plantar elimination tonic neck reflex (TNR)	Landau tear* (cries with tears)	parachute palmar grasp pincer grasp				
(Age)	(birth)	(1–4 mos)	(4–8 mos)	(8–12 mos)	(12–18 mos)	(18–24 mos)	(3–4 years)
Disappears		grasp suck (becomes voluntary) step root tonic neck reflex (TNR)	Moro (startle)	palmar grasp plantar reflex	Landau	parachute	elimination (becomes voluntary)

* Permanent; present throughout person's lifetime.

Source: Marotz & Allen, *Development Profiles: Pre-Birth through Adolescence*, 8th Edition, Fig. 4–3, p. 72, © 2016, Cengage Learning

Newborns are unable to control or independently support their head—it is just too large and heavy in comparison to the rest of their body. Yet, within the first month, infants gain enough strength and control to lift their heads when lying on their stomachs. Soon after, they are using their arms to push against the floor or bed to raise their heads and chests.

During these first three months, infants are also busy coordinating their legs. The legs have been kicking and pushing in the air and against anything within range. Infants roll and kick their legs from side to side. Their upper and lower back muscles are developing so that one day when they kick and roll to one side, they keep going right onto their backs or their stomachs. The baby has rolled over!

With continued practice, the infant can intentionally roll from stomach to back, and by the sixth month, most infants can roll from back to stomach. As mentioned previously, they are also working on developing stability in relation to the force of gravity (sitting assisted and independently); simultaneously, they are attempting to move their bodies forward through space (**locomotion**). **Creeping**, which is considered the first locomotor movement (see Appendix A), involves moving the body through space by pulling the body with the arms or sometimes pushing with the legs to help move. Regan is lying on her stomach, reaching for a toy. She twists her body, pulls with her arms, and pushes with her legs. Slowly she moves forward to the toy. To accomplish this major task, Regan used her head, neck, back, arm, and leg muscles to move and lift the top part of her body up and down without tipping over. She may even get up on her hands and knees and rock. Infants can be encouraged to move at this stage by placing toys just out of reach.

During the last five months of the first year, infants are rapidly developing muscular control. A formerly low-activity baby may show a sudden spurt of activity during this time as she learns to sit alone or as creeping evolves into **crawling**, where the arms and legs are used in opposition. On hands and knees, the infant first slowly moves one limb and then another. With increased control, crawling can become a very fast and efficient means of locomotion, providing the infant with a new world of possible experiences. Quickly after learning to crawl, infants begin to pull themselves up and stand with the assistance of objects and people. When infants have gained stability in standing upright, they can turn their efforts toward moving forward (walking). Many months of movement precede the actual accomplishment of walking.

DeQuavon is standing next to a chair watching a bright toy on the floor sparkle in the sunshine. He leans toward it and reaches for it, but he cannot reach it. He takes one step away from the chair while still holding on to it. He still cannot reach the toy. He takes another step, and his hand slips off the chair. He is now on his own. He takes another step, stops, weaves, takes another step, and then falls down. DeQuavon is beginning to walk. His first attempts at locomotion are filled with standing, stepping, weaving, sitting or falling down, pushing himself back up to standing, and trying again.

A dynamic systems framework helps us understand that multiple layers of child-environment interaction influence both the long-term and short-term changes that infants experience in their movements and actions

locomotion The attempt to gain stability when moving forward or upward (e.g., crawling and walking) against the force of gravity.

creeping Strategy for moving the body through space that involves infants pulling their body with their arms or sometimes pushing with the legs to help move.

crawling Strategy for mobility where the infant or toddler moves on hands and knees while using arms and legs in opposition.

(Newell, Liu, & Mayer-Kress, 2001). DeQuavon will repeat this cycle thousands of times, a process that strengthens his muscles and develops his coordination. Infants quickly, within the first month of walking, move from making short steps from a wide-base stance with feet pointed outward to longer steps made from a smaller base with feet pointed forward (Adolph, Vereijken, & Shrout, 2003). These authors believe that the experience of walking over and over again is what assists infants with developing the more adult-like walk. To accomplish this developmental task, DeQuavon needs open floor space, where he can walk without bumping into furniture or having to step around toys on the floor.

To promote optimal physical development, infants' basic needs for proper nutrition and sleep should be met. Adults should provide adequate floor space where they can roll, crawl, climb, reach, stand, and walk as they want. Of course, the caregiver does not need to tell the infants to arch their backs, to creep toward a toy, or pull themselves up on the sturdy furniture. Infants do this naturally. The caregiver facilitates infant movement by making sure their clothes do not limit movement, by providing a circle of safety, and by offering the infant materials and toys that are safe and appropriate. Conscientious caregivers are also cautious about the equipment they provide. Playpens can very easily become prisons that restrict movement. Wheeled walkers or stationary jumpers can put undue strain on the infant's back, restricting the development and coordination of head, neck, arm, chest, back, leg, and foot muscles, while putting too much emphasis on leg movement. Safe floor place for engaging in physical development is what is needed most.

Fine Motor Manipulation

As stated previously, the best toy for a newborn is the human face. They are fascinated by looking at it. They will often attempt to touch it. Because newborns grasp reflexively, their hands will close on anything that touches them. They will grasp objects with either hand. Gradually infants begin to open their hands and use the whole hand to "palm" a toy. During the first six months, arm movement develops from erratic waving to carefully controlled reaching. Infants use shoulder, elbow, wrist, and hand movements to coordinate with what they see to reach purposefully and successfully grasp an object. Control of reaching must accompany the task of grasping. Therefore, as they become more skilled at reaching and voluntarily grasping objects, their attention often turns to **manipulation**, or touching, moving, banging, and otherwise using an object. This is no simple task to accomplish. As Healy (2004) states:

manipulation Includes reaching, grasping, and releasing objects; in the first year of development, the control of objects moves from reflexive to voluntary.

> Although the baby starts practicing muscle control almost immediately, integrating reflex motor movements into controlled patterns takes a long time. The baby needs many things to see and to touch with body, mouth and hands. At first the infant's movements seem random, but as he gets the feel of his own body in space, connections build...to help the child organize his muscles around independent plans of action. (p. 43)

As the child develops, the manipulation process becomes more complex. For example, the child learns how to move toys from one hand to the other. They often hold a finger straight and poke at themselves and objects around them. They push and pull and may keep repeating their actions. In addition, they use their thumb and fingers to grasp objects, perfecting the **pincer grasp**. Using this skill often, they continue to develop their finger muscles and eye-hand coordination. Because they do not have good control of the strength of the pinch, they may sometimes pinch another child hard enough to hurt.

pincer grasp The physical skill of using the thumb and pointer finger to grasp objects.

These infants are also developing control of their arms; now they can clap and bring both hands to mid-body repeatedly. Their hands can grasp some objects, so they may bang objects together. They can hold crayons and make marks with them (refer to Appendix A). By about 8 months of age, infants have gained enough control of their arm and hand movements to be able to touch lightly or stroke objects.

Infants 8 months to 1 year old are also beginning to use each hand for different tasks. They may pick up a toy with one hand, transfer it to the other hand to hold, and then pick up another toy. By the end of the first year, an infant will be able to use thumb and forefinger to assist in grasping objects (see Appendix A). For example, Stanley is holding a car in his right hand. He reaches out with this left hand, picks up a block using a pincer grasp, and stacks it on top of another block. Then he transfers the car to his left hand, picks up a block with his right, and places the second block on the tower.

Caregivers must provide materials that support the development of fine motor skills, such as a variety of rattles, soft and foam blocks, balls of different sizes and textures, clean stuffed animals, and open-ended items to engage their interest. See Table 11–1 Suggestions for Implementing Curriculum—Physical Development for additional ideas. In any case, the items provided must be safe, free of hazards, and not small enough to be swallowed.

Sleep

Most newborns sleep between 14 and 17 hours a day (Photo 11–2). They get those hours from sleeping anywhere from 2 to 10 hours at a time. Like adults, infants experience different states in the sleep-wake cycle. Table 11–2 outlines six states in the sleep-wake cycle. Infants' living patterns usually take on regularity in the first months of life. The infant who establishes a regular, though slowly changing, schedule for eating and sleeping creates a predictable world into which the caregiver can easily fit. Infants whose feeding and sleeping times remain erratic create stress for themselves and their caregivers.

Newborns are relatively light sleepers, and deep sleep periods are only about 20 minutes long. By 3 to 4 months old, infants regularly sleep more at night than during the day, but night awakenings are common throughout infancy and early childhood (Goodlin-Jones, Burnham, Gaylor, & Anders, 2001). As children become more mobile and begin to crawl and walk, their sleep patterns change and they require less sleep. Children should still be encouraged to rest every day, and a well-planned early

© 2017 Cengage Learning

PHOTO 11–2 Most newborns sleep up to 17 hours per day.

TABLE 11–1 ▶ Suggestions for Implementing Curriculum—Physical Development

CHILD BEHAVIOR	MATERIALS	EXAMPLES OF CAREGIVER STRATEGIES
Reflex		
Grasp reflex (hand closes)	finger, rattle	Lift infant's body slightly. Place object in palm of infant's hand.
Startle reflex	mirror, mobile	Touch and hold infant to calm him.
Muscular Control		
(develops from head to feet)		
Head and Neck		
Turns head	stuffed toy	Place infant on back or stomach. Place toy to one side.
Holds head upright with support		Support infant's head when holding infant upright.
Lifts head slightly when on stomach		Place infant on stomach.
Holds head without support		Set and hold infant upright.
Holds head in midline position	mobiles, crib gyms	Put some objects above center of crib.
Trunk		
Holds up chest		Place infant on stomach.
Sits with support; may attempt to raise self; may fuss if left lying down with little chance to sit up		Place infant in sitting position. Support head and back with arm or pillow. Lengthen sitting time as infant is able.
Leans back and forth	toys within reach	Keep area around infant free of sharp objects. Infant topples over easily.
Sits in a chair	chair with back	Use chair strap for safety. Let infant sit in chair, but for a short time because the infant's muscles tire quickly.
Sits unsupported for short time	safe, flat sitting space	Place in safe area where infant can sit and play or watch. Infant will tire soon and lie down.
Raises self to sitting position	flat surface	Keep area clear of objects that would hurt the infant if child falls on them.
Sits alone		Provide a short time to sit. Infant may tire soon.
Leg		
Lifts legs when on back and stomach		Provide clothes that allow free kicking.
Rolls from stomach to back		Place where infant can move freely and safely. Keep crib sides up. Keep hand on infant while changing diapers.
Straightens legs when standing		Hold infant in standing position for short periods. Hold infant's sides firmly when child bounces.
Stamps feet when standing		Firmly hold infant upright and provide flat surface for infant to push and move feet against.
Rolls from back to stomach		Place where infant can move freely and safely. Keep crib sides up. Keep hand on infant while changing diapers.
Raises to hands and knees		Place on flat, firm surface.
Stands with support		Hold infant's sides or hands while infant is standing on flat surface.
Pulls self to standing position		Hold infant's hands and allow infant to use his or her own muscles to pull self up. Check furniture and shelving to make sure neither will tip over when infant pulls on them to stand up.
Stands holding on to furniture or hand	sturdy chair, bench, table	Remove furniture that could tip over on infant.
Stands without assistance	flat surface	Allow infant to stand alone.
Squats and stands		Watch sharp-cornered furniture. Pad corners as needed. Infant often stands up underneath furniture (tables) and bumps head.

(continued)

CHILD BEHAVIOR	MATERIALS	EXAMPLES OF CAREGIVER STRATEGIES
Muscular Control		
(develops from mid-body to limbs)		
Arm		
Moves randomly	toys	Place objects within reach of infant.
Reaches	bright toys that make noise	Place objects slightly beyond reach of infant; give to infant when child reaches for it.
Visually directs reaching, hitting	crib toys, movable toys	Provide toys that infant can reach and hit. Provide large toys infant can accurately hit against.
Throws objects	soft, light toys and objects	Select toys that are light and will not go far and hit other children. Place infant in an area where child can safely throw objects.
Hand		
Opens and closes	toys with handles that fit in fist	Place handle in fist; help infant close fist around object.
Plays with hands	colorful plastic bracelet	Place on infant's hands and fingers colorful, safe objects that attract infant's attention.
Uses hand to grasp object, whole hand, and fingers against thumb	toys with bumps to hold on to	Place object within reach of infant.
Uses thumb and forefinger	toys that can be grasped with one hand	Place object within reach of infant.
Uses thumb and two fingers	toys, dolls	Provide objects small enough to pinch and lift.
Uses finger to poke	pillow, ball, small box	Provide soft objects to poke into. Watch carefully because infant may poke other children's faces, eyes, and so on.
Holds and uses pen, crayon	flat surface, fat felt marker, fat crayon, paper	Provide materials and space. Demonstrate where marks go (on paper, not floor or table). Remain with infant when child is using marker or crayon. Allow child to make the kind and number of marks he or she wants to. Praise child for the interest and effort. Put materials away when child decides he or she is finished.
Reaches, touches, strokes object	textured objects	Provide objects of different textures. Infants can stroke, not just grasp and pinch. Demonstrate gentle stroking. Describe the texture, for example, "the feather is soft." Allow infant to gently stroke many objects.
Stacks blocks with dominant hand	blocks, small objects	Allow infant to choose which hand to use in stacking objects.
Takes off clothes	own clothes with big buttonholes, zippers	Infant's fingers are beginning to handle buttons, zippers. Allow infant to play with these. Infant does not understand when to undress and when to keep clothes on. Discourage undressing when you want infant to stay clothed.
Eye-Hand Coordination		
Moves arm toward object; may miss it	toy, bottle	Place within reach of infant.
Reaches hand to object; may grab or miss it	toy, bottle	Place within reach of infant.
Picks up object with one hand; passes it to the other hand	small toys of any shape	Place toys around infant so child will use both hands. Ask for toy from one hand. Give toy to each hand.
Uses objects in both hands	banging toys	Play banging game with blocks, bells, balls.
Uses one hand to hold object, one hand to reach and explore	objects small enough to grasp	Provide several objects at once that stimulate infant's interest.

© Cengage Learning

TABLE 11–2 ▶ Sleep-Wake Cycle

Quiet sleep. Respirations are regular, eyes are closed and not moving, and the child is relatively motionless.

Active sleep. Muscles are more tense than in quiet sleep, the eyes may be still or display rapid eye movements (REM), breathing is irregular, and there are spontaneous startles, sucks, and rhythmic bursts of movement.

Drowsiness. Eyes open and close, and there is increased activity, more rapid and regular breathing, and occasional smiling.

Quiet alert. Eyes are open, scanning the environment; the body is still, and respiration is more rapid than in sleep. During this state, infants are most attentive to the environment, focusing attention on people or objects present. As infants get older, they spend more and more time in this state.

Active alert. The child is awake and has body and limb movements, although the child is less likely to attend to external stimulation and focuses eyes less often than in the quiet alert state.

Crying. Activity and respiration rate are elevated, and the child exhibits cry vocalization and a facial expression of distress.

© 2014 Cengage Learning

childhood program provides nap times that meet the individual needs for children who are under 3 years of age. Around 1 year of age, infants typically take more defined morning and afternoon naps that allow for more time awake in which to be alert and play. Each infant has a personal sleep schedule that is affected by the child's own body needs for sleep, as well as by the sleep routines at home. If the infant is awakened at 5:00 a.m. to get ready to come to child care, that child may need a morning nap earlier than an infant who is able to sleep at home until 7:00 a.m.

Gradually gaining stability in the sleep-wake cycle is not only important for growth and physical development but also for social development (Feldman, 2006). Infants who are more consistent in their sleep-wake cycles were associated with greater mother-infant synchrony at 3 months of age. When analyzed separately, high-risk premature infants displayed disorganized biological rhythms, lower thresholds for demonstrating negative emotions, and lower levels of mother-infant synchrony (Feldman, 2006). With increases in infants born prematurely, teachers and parents must find ways to assist these infants with organizing their sleep-wake patterns.

Eating and Teething

From birth to around 6 months of age, infants should be fed breastmilk or formula exclusively. Plan carefully with family members to have enough breastmilk/formula available every day and properly store it. You can also encourage mothers who are breast-feeding to feed their infant at the program. Do this by providing a comfortable, private (if desired) space. A screen can be used, for example, to temporarily separate the couch from the rest of the room. After the baby is fed, return the screen to where it is normally used or stored. Please see the Spotlight on Research Box: Breast-feeding and Later Development for more information.

Many pediatricians recommend that infants begin solid foods at about 6 months of age, which can be around the time of the first tooth eruption. Mouthing and swallowing solid foods involves a coordination of muscles different from those used for sucking. Begin solid foods when family members request it. Use the same kind of spoon they use at home so the infants do

Spotlight on Research

BREAST-FEEDING AND LATER DEVELOPMENT

"You are what you eat" is a slogan many of us have heard quite frequently throughout our lives. This saying is the basis for the long-standing belief that, to be healthy, you have to eat well. Breast-feeding—a natural resource for mothers—is considered by many to be the best for meeting infants' nutritional needs. Recent research suggests that it also has long-term health benefits. For example, Jing, Lin, Yun, Guowei, and Wang (2014) conducted a meta-analysis of the relationship between breast-feeding and obesity using research studies from 12 different countries. They discovered that breast-feeding was a significant factor associated with lower incidents of obesity in children.

Research has examined also whether or not this practice has benefits beyond physical development to other areas, such as cognitive, social, or emotional development. Extending the focus from nutrition to other areas of development highlights the feeding relationship (i.e., the dynamic interactions that parents and children establish around food), which influences lifelong habits (Parlakian & Lerner, 2007). This extended focus is also important because it helps parents understand their influential role (Passehl, McCarroll, Buechner, Gearring, Smith, & Trowbridge, 2004).

Much research has supported the link between breast-feeding and later cognitive development (see Benton, 2008, for a review). The mechanisms for this link are not yet understood. Some researchers hypothesize that the high levels of fatty acids in breastmilk impact later cognitive development because the fatty acids are incorporated into the brain during growth spurts, and those fatty acids play an important structural role in cell membranes, helping cells communicate more easily with each other (Benton, 2008). Tanaka, Kon, Ohkawa, Yoshikawa, and Shimizu (2009) investigated the relationship between levels of DHA (a type of fatty acid) in red blood cell membranes and the cognitive functioning of very low birth weight infants at 5 years of age. The results showed that the levels of DHA at four weeks were significantly lower from formula-fed infants than breast-fed infants. At 5 years of age, breast-fed infants scored significantly higher on three different measures of cognitive functioning. In his review of research, Benton (2008) concluded that "in preterm babies the diet of the neonate can have lasting implications for brain development…and hence cognitive functioning" (p. 35).

The impact of breast-feeding on social and emotional development is also of interest to many researchers. In 2008, research was conducted on early determinants of mental health issues for young children (Robinson, Oddy, Jianghong, Kendall, de Klerk, Silburn, et al., 2008). Of interest to this discussion is the result that shorter durations of breast-feeding were associated with greater mental health issues, specifically internalizing (withdrawn/depressed) and externalizing (aggressive/destructive) behavior problems. A more recent study of children age 8–11 found that breast-feeding was a protective factor in terms of externalizing behaviors and being diagnosed with attention-deficit hyperactivity disorder. Specifically, breast-feeding, after controlling for child and maternal IQ, was associated with decreased internalizing, externalizing, and overall behavioral problems as well as the diagnosis of ADHD (Park, Kim, Kim, Shin, Yoo, & Cho, 2014). These studies suggest that early childhood and middle childhood mental health is affected by a variety of prenatal, perinatal, and postnatal variables within a child's environment, including breast-feeding. Do maternal beliefs about breast-feeding matter?

Bai, Middlestadt, Joanne Peng, and Fly (2009) examined mothers' beliefs about exclusive breast-feeding for at least six months. They found that mothers in the study reported valuing the emotional benefits of breast-feeding for themselves and their infants. Thus, it may be that mothers who breast-feed are more attuned to their infants' emotional needs. It may also be that these beliefs are held very strongly within their social contexts because these mothers also reported receiving approval from family members to continue this practice, even though they felt disapproval from others within their community. Thus, this strong emphasis on caring for the nutritional and emotional needs of their infants overrode the negativity they perceived from others outside their family.

The difficulty in drawing conclusions from this line of research is that many women who breast-feed, especially in the United States, tend to be more economically well-off, tend to have higher levels of education, and tend to be of higher intelligence, making it "difficult to distinguish the provision of mother's milk from a range of environmental benefits" (Benton, 2008, p. 28). However, there is a push in the United States and around the world to encourage breast-feeding for lower-income families as a way to reduce economic costs of babies (see, e.g., Fornasaro-Donahue, Tovar,

(continued)

Spotlight on Research *(continued)*

Sebelia, & Greene, 2014, and Bbaale, 2014). Mortensen's (2007) commentary regarding recent articles on the impact of breast-feeding on social competency suggested that there are effects of breast-feeding on mental health that are independent of global measures of cognitive abilities and maternal intelligence. More research needs to be conducted to understand this complex relationship more clearly.

Nonetheless, practitioners need to evaluate their practices and policies so that they provide another source of support for families who want to breast-feed.

Having quiet spaces where mothers can visit and breast-feed during the day would be one important type of support. In addition, following all guidelines for storing and preparing breastmilk for feedings while the infant is at child care would be beneficial. Another example of support could be holding ongoing discussions with families about the benefits and challenges of breast-feeding. While this is the most "natural" way to feed an infant, it is by no means an easy process to start and maintain for today's busy families because a majority of mothers return to work within the first year.

not have to adjust to different sizes and shapes of spoons while they learn to retrieve food from a spoon and swallow it without spitting it out or choking.

Eating patterns may or may not be disrupted by teething because infants react differently to it. Sometimes an emerging tooth causes an infant to be very fussy and irritable, while other times a new tooth just seems to appear with no change in the infant's behavior. Teething infants often like to bite on something—even the spoon as you are feeding them. If an infant seems to be hurting, a cold teething ring or crushed ice in a clean cloth provides coldness as well as hardness for the child's gums. Because teething infants may drool profusely, they may need to wear a bib at nonmeal times; changing it frequently will keep their clothes dry.

Feeding time presents an opportunity to socialize; the infant may be distracted from eating to coo and gurgle with his caregiver between eating spurts. This social exchange is very important to concurrent and subsequent social development. Encourage interactions by describing what they are doing or how they are helping with eating. For example, an early childhood educator could say, "Robin, you are holding the bottle all by yourself today," or "James, you are working hard to drink from a cup. Tip it slowly. That's it. What a new challenge!" Even when an infant attempts something new (e.g., cup), he may not be ready to give up the old (e.g., bottle).

Advances in motor control, both fine and gross, assist infants with eating over the next few months. Most infants express an interest in wanting to feed herself or himself and will show resistance to being fed, even though it is too early for them to use a spoon with accuracy. Follow the child's cues and let her hold and use the spoon! Also offer **finger foods** so that some food has a chance of being consumed, if that is culturally appropriate for the family and child. In fact, even when some skill is gained in using a spoon, infants often use fingers and a spoon at the same time. Infants want to get the food into their mouths, and they use every way they can to accomplish this task. So be prepared for spills, dropped food, and other messes by carefully planning the eating environment. Most importantly, because so little food is actually making it to their stomachs, recognize that the infants might be hungry sooner than expected.

Caution should be used when selecting eating utensils. Infants typically have four to eight teeth by the end of the first year and they tend to

finger foods Foods that older infants and toddlers can easily feed to themselves such as crackers or dry cereal.

use their new teeth to bite anything put into their mouths (see Figure 9–1, Dental Eruption Chart, in Chapter 9). Plastic or disposable utensils often cannot withstand the infants' biting. Infants should be skilled at holding their own bottles and, around their first birthday, may be beginning to use a cup without a lid. Provide child-size cups so they can complete these skills independently or with minimal assistance.

READING CHECKPOINT

Before moving on with your reading, make sure that you can answer the following questions about the material discussed so far.

1. Deborah, a 5-month-old, is sitting up against a pillow on the floor. She is looking at the toy she has just thrown out of her reach. She leans forward, tips over, and cries. Describe what you would do next. Explain why you would do it.
2. List three caregiver strategies that facilitate fine motor manipulation of the infant between 7 and 11 months old.

11-2b Cognitive Development

Early childhood educators provide for the care and education of very young children. What we do matters immensely to the developing child, especially when considering brain development. Neuropsychologist Jane Healy discusses brain development of an infant in her book *Your Child's Growing Mind* (2004).

> Amazingly, although the number of cells actually decreases, brain weight can double during the first year of life. As neurons respond to stimuli seen, heard, felt, or tasted, they fire off messages that build new physical connections to neighboring cells, linking them into efficient relay systems....During the first six months after birth, they become extremely active as sensory messages bombard the infant brain, which must learn to receive them and then pass them from one area to another....Synaptic connections are strengthened by repeated use; if they fail to connect, they die off....Every response to sights, sounds, feelings, smells, and tastes make more connections. (pp. 17–20)

This means that caregivers take every opportunity to teach, knowing that to increase an infant's experiences with the living and nonliving world is to increase ultimate human intelligence.

Piaget's theory of cognitive development categorizes the first two years of life as a part of the sensorimotor stage. Infants get information in this stage through their senses and motor activity. "At this stage, thought and action are indistinguishable. The infant's first cognitions are sensory and motor oriented" (Bergin & Bergin, 2012, p. 98). Infants use and refine all their senses—seeing, hearing, smelling, tasting, and touching—to build physical knowledge about objects, the world, and their place in it. Moving themselves, moving others, and handling objects become coordinated with their senses (Photo 11–3). For example, when hearing a sound, infants turn their heads in the direction it comes from.

As discussed in Chapter 2, the sensorimotor stage has been divided into six substages; the first four are evident in the first year of life. In each stage, the infant develops new behaviors. In Substage 1, the newborn's behavior is reflexive. Infants quickly start to change their behavior from passive reactions to active searching. Each of the senses operates independently. During

© 2017 Cengage Learning

PHOTO 11–3 A ball poses particular challenges, cognitive as well as physical, for a newly mobile child.

Substage 2, infants begin to coordinate their senses. They begin to develop hand-mouth coordination, eye coordination, and eye-ear coordination. One behavior can stimulate another; for example, a reflexively waving arm may attract the infant's attention so that he visually focuses on his own hand.

During the next two substages, infants continue to use information gained from sensory and motor actions to develop their ideas about the world. However, they now act to repeat an interesting reaction or to sustain interesting sights (Substage 3, reproduction). This begins as empty repetition and develops into organized, goal-directed behavior during Substage 4 (coordination). Piaget hypothesized that the concept of object permanence develops toward the end of the coordination substage as infants purposefully search, either visually or manually, for interesting items. When the object an infant is watching disappears, she will typically search for it visually, but not manually. When the object she is holding disappears, she will search for it manually.

Piaget's theory has generated a great deal of research on children's cognitive development. With advancements in technology, recent research on object permanence has caused a revision in how we look at the capabilities of infants. Baillargeon (2004) and Charles and Rivera (2009) found that 2- to 6-month-old infants demonstrated signs of object permanence and gradually solidified this knowledge and linked it to their reaching behaviors. Johnson and Munakata (2005) suggest that infants develop cognitively due to error-driven and self-organizing learning mechanisms, or as Healy (2004) states, babies are born "with the 'need to know'" (p. 50). In other words, infants learn from mistakes and repeatedly try to obtain a desired reaction. This active construction of knowledge is "heavily constrained by...interactions with the physical (e.g., objects, space) and social ('pedagogy') environment" (p. 156). More recent research using an

Family and Community Connection

You and your co-owner care for six children, including two infants. The infants are approaching 7 months of age, and you want to prepare their parents for upcoming cognitive, social, and emotional changes, especially separation anxiety. How will you start the conversation with the families? What do you want them to understand at the end of the conversations? Why is it important to start the conversation now, before stranger anxiety is evident in either of the infants?

object discrimination task suggests that infants of clinically depressed mothers were less skilled at discriminating between novel and familiar views of the object (Bornstein, Mash, Arterberry, & Manian, 2012). Infants of nondepressed mothers successfully discriminated, raising questions about how the social environment impacts cognitive development, especially the understanding of objects. The importance of creating optimal environments for facilitating cognitive development should not be underestimated. In addition, the research reviewed here suggests that Piaget underestimated the capabilities of young children, even though the construction of knowledge and the expected sequence of behaviors develop as he theorized (see, e.g., Xu, 2013). These results demonstrate the importance of early childhood educators continuously engaging in research-based professional development so that they value and support the capabilities of young children.

Infants take in and process a great deal of information on a daily basis. The processes of assimilation and accommodation help them to make sense of new information and store it for future reference. Information that is stored can be about the property of objects and people (e.g., how they act or behave, how they move, how they feel), as well as the results of their observations or interactions with objects and people (e.g., how causing certain actions leads to somewhat predictable consequences; McDevitt & Ormrod, 2013). Infants combine different aspects of their stored knowledge to develop theories about cause-and-effect relationships.

The establishment of **object permanence** is a major development during Substage 4, even though, according to Piaget, the process will not be complete until later. People and toys are perceived, more and more, as real entities that continue to exist even when the infants cannot see them. With this concept, infants now actively search visually and manually for people or objects that are no longer visible. Infants mentally construct a representation of the person or object. This mental representation of the real entity forms the foundation for increasingly complex forms of representation.

object permanence The understanding that people and objects exist even if they are currently out of sight.

Because of these budding representation skills, infants imitate people and things that are not present. They have established **deferred imitation**, which requires sufficient cognitive skills to remember and reproduce things they have seen and heard in the past that interest them. Many researchers, parents, and teachers believe that infants have poor or ill-defined memory skills. However, research on deferred imitation reveals that infants attend to the actions of the model (rather than the model's face; Kolling, Óturai, & Knopf, 2014) and produce highly detailed memory

deferred imitation Imitation of another person's behavior even when that person is no longer present.

representations (Jones & Herbert, 2006) that are functional in nature, rather than arbitrary (Kolling et al., 2014). Thus, infants are able to attend to the "right" information to imitate it at a later time. In addition, when infants observe a complicated behavior but are not able to immediately imitate it, they can reproduce the observed actions in similar situations when encountered at a later time. The accuracy of and details featured in the behaviors demonstrate that their memory must be of equally high quality (Jones & Herbert, 2006).

Researchers have been interested in strategies for challenging and improving the deferred imitation of infants. Patel, Gaylord, and Fagen (2013) investigated whether changing the auditory and visual context impacted infants' ability to imitate. They discovered that 6-month-old infants generalized imitation with the puppet only when the music and room on the test day were identical to the earlier learning environment; 9-month-olds could generalize deferred imitation across a change in music but not a change in room; whereas the 12-month-olds were able to defer imitation across a change in both the room and music. Thus, they showed that infants are less dependent on contextual cues to engage in deferred imitation across the last half of the first year of life.

Herbert (2011) investigated whether pairing language with modeled behaviors on the imitation behaviors of 12- and 15-month-old children would improve imitative behaviors. She found that the young children who received the verbal cues demonstrated better representational flexibility than those who did not receive the verbal assistance. The results suggest that infants may be able to express their knowledge better in novel situations when language cues are paired with behavioral modeling (Herbert, 2011). Barr, Rovee-Collier, and Campanella (2005) investigated the impact of active retrieval (i.e., physically imitating demonstrated behavior) or passive retrieval (i.e., observing the same behavior again) one day after observing the modeled behavior on longer-term imitation of the behavior. More specifically, 6-month-old infants were shown a three-sequence behavior using a puppet while sitting on their caregiver's knee. The next day, the researchers returned to their home and allowed one group to observe the same sequence of behaviors again (i.e., passive retrieval) and one group to interact with the puppet and imitate the behavior (i.e., active retrieval). Infants in both groups "reproduced the target actions 2 to 2.5 months later" (Barr et al., 2005, p. 273). In this experiment, repeated exposure to the modeled behavior—active and passive—resulted in greater ability to imitate the behavior even months later. Taken together, these research projects demonstrate that infants in the first year of life may possess deferred imitation skills to a greater degree than previously thought, suggesting that teachers may need to rethink how they describe and support the capabilities of young children.

The sensitive educator uses several strategies to enhance cognitive development. Selecting items for and arranging an attention-catching environment stimulates the infant to respond in any way possible at his or her particular stage. Repeating and discussing the infant's behaviors provides them with a responsive and language-rich environment. Please see Table 11–3 Suggestions for Implementing Curriculum—Cognitive Development for additional ideas.

Spotlight on Practice

VOICES FROM THE FIELD

I work in a mixed-age classroom with children age 6 weeks to 18 months. Paul and Abraham are both 8 months of age. They were sitting on a mat playing with toys from a nearby shelf. I took a small receiving blanket and joined them on the mat. As Paul sat down, I covered up the small stuffed dog he was playing with, using the blanket, and said, "Where did the dog go?" Paul looked at me with a nervous look on his face. I then replied, "Let's find the dog," as I slowly pulled the blanket off the stuffed animal. During this time, Abraham was sitting beside Paul, watching the dog being covered and uncovered by the blanket. When I covered up the dog again, Paul reached over and grabbed a different toy.

I then turned to Abraham and placed the blanket over his toy. Abraham immediately grabbed the blanket and pulled it off the toy. He began smiling and clapping his hands. We repeated this game several times. I then added a variation by placing the blanket over Abraham's face. He responded in a similar manner by pulling it off, smiling, laughing, and clapping his hands.

This experience was important for me because prior to this, I had been treating Paul and Abraham in very similar ways. If I planned an activity for one, I immediately invited the other to join. I learned that not all 8-month-olds are at the same developmental level for all skills. While I should've known this, I think I am more aware of this now.

TABLE 11–3 ▶ Suggestions for Implementing Curriculum—Cognitive Development

CHILD BEHAVIOR	MATERIALS	EXAMPLES OF CAREGIVER STRATEGIES
Piaget's Stages of Sensorimotor Development		
SUBSTAGE 1 (Reflex)		
Carries out reflexive actions—sucking, eye movements, hand and body movements		Provide nonrestricting clothes, uncluttered crib to allow freedom of movement.
Moves from passive to active search	visually attractive crib, walls next to crib, objects; occasional music, singing, talking, chimes	Provide environment that commands attention during infant's periods of alertness.
SUBSTAGE 2 (Differentiation)		
Makes small, gradual changes that come from repetition		Provide change for infant; carry infant around, hold infant, place infant in crib. Observe, discuss, record changes.
Coordinates behaviors, for example, a sound stimulates looking	face and voice, musical toy, musical mobile, rattle	Turn on musical toy; place where infant can see it.
Puts hand, object in mouth and sucks on it	objects infant can grasp and are safe to go in mouth	Place objects in hand or within reach. Infants attempt to put everything in their mouths. Make sure they get only safe objects.
Moves hand, object to where it is visible	objects which infant can grasp and lift	Provide clothes that allow freedom of movement. Place objects in hand or within reach.
Produces a pleasurable motor activity and repeats activity		Provide time, space for repetition.
SUBSTAGE 3 (Reproduction)		
Produces a motor activity, catches interest, and intentionally repeats the activity over and over	objects that attract attention: contrasting colors, changes in sounds, variety of textures, designs	Watch movements the infant repeats. Waving arm may hit the crib gym; the infant may wave arm more to hit the crib gym again. Watch which movements the infant repeats. Provide materials that facilitate it, for example, new items on the crib gym.

(continued)

TABLE 11–3 ▶ Suggestions for Implementing Curriculum—Cognitive Development (*continued*)

CHILD BEHAVIOR	MATERIALS	EXAMPLES OF CAREGIVER STRATEGIES
Repeats interesting action		The infant may pound fists on legs. Watch to see that child's actions are safe.
Develops hand-eye coordination further; looks for object, reaches for it, and accurately touches it	toys	Place blocks, dolls, balls, other toys near the infant where child can reach them.
Imitates behavior that is seen or heard	toy, food, body	Initiate action; wait for infant to imitate it; repeat action, for example, smile, open mouth.
Piaget's Concept of Object Permanence		
SUBSTAGE 4 (Coordination)		
Visually follows object. Searches visually for short time when object disappears	toys, bottle, or objects that attract visual attention	Show infant a toy. Play with it a minute and then hide the toy. Bring it out and play with it again. (You will not *teach* the infant to look for the toy. Enjoy playing with the infant and toy.)
Does not search manually		
Sees part of object; looks for whole object when object disappears	familiar toy, bottle, rattle, teething ring, ball, doll	Cover up part of object with a blanket or paper. Infant will pull object out or push off blanket, that is, play peekaboo.
Follows moving objects with eyes until object disappears; looks where object has disappeared; loses interest and turns away; does not search for it	toys and objects that attract visual attention	Place object in range of infant's vision. Allow time for infant to focus on object. Move object slowly back and forth within child's field of vision. Move object where infant cannot see it, for example, roll ball behind infant.
Establishes object permanence, that object exists when it is no longer visible, for example, child seeks toy that rolls behind box		Play hiding games, for example, hide the doll under the blanket; place the block behind you.
Causality		
Learns that others cause actions		Verbalize caregiver's own actions, for example, "I put the ball behind me."
Imitation and Play		
Imitates other's actions; uses actions as play		Introduce new copying games. Allow time and space for infant to play.

© Cengage Learning

11-2c Language Development

productive communication
Using actions to express messages to others. Infants progress from using noises, cries, and gestures to using babbling and words.

Productive communication involves actions to express messages to others. Infants use noises, cries, and gestures as their earliest forms of productive communication (e.g., Southgate, van Maanen, & Csibra, 2007). Research suggests that infants vary the pitch and duration of their cries as well as the number of pauses between bursts of crying to communicate the depth and intensity of the emotions they are experiencing (Cecchini, Lai, & Langher, 2007). Even newborns cry in different ways, depending on whether they are startled or uncomfortable. Empirical research supports that adults are able to read the cries of infants to determine whether it is a communication of anguish, anger, annoyance, or care-seeking (Cecchini, Lai, & Langher, 2010). Although this line of research is not definitive, holding the belief that one is skilled in reading cues may assist caregivers in providing responsive care.

Infants use several kinds of sounds as part of their language. They produce sounds as they eat and as they play with their tongues and mouths.

They use their throats, saliva, tongues, mouths, and lips to produce gurgling, squealing, smacking, and spitting noises. Within the first two months of life, they begin to produce repetitive, vowel-like sounds that can be classified as cooing. While spontaneous smiles occur within days of birth, even for preterm infants (Kawakami, Takai-Kawakami, Kawakami, Tomonaga, Suzuki, & Shimizu, 2008), laughter (smile plus vocalization) tends to occur later. It was once believed that spontaneous smiles and laughter were precursors to more intentionally social behaviors and were replaced in early infancy. However, recent research found spontaneous smiles being produced by 15-month-old children (Kawakami, Kawakami, Tomonaga, & Takai-Kawakami, 2009), calling into question that conclusion.

When infants hear someone talk to them, it stimulates them to make sounds (see the parental selection hypothesis in Locke, 2006). This dialogue is very important. Effective dialogue can occur when the caregiver looks at the infant while alternately listening to and answering the child's talk. The one-to-one dialogue is what stimulates the infant to engage in more positive vocalizing at later ages (Henning, Striano, & Lieven, 2005). Talking that is not directed to the infant personally is not as effective as a stimulator. Adults conversing with each other in the presence of the child, or turning on a radio or television show, do not involve the child in language dialogue.

Over time, the crying, cooing, and babbling of the infant help develop the physical mechanisms that produce speech. Developmentally, the cooing period is followed by an extended period of babbling. Babbling continues the diversification of sounds begun in cooing yet with the addition of consonants (e.g., *g, t, k, b, r*). For the uninformed, infant babbling might seem meaningless. However, according to Whalley (2008), babbling is an important step in the acquisition of language because these motor behavior explorations help infants learn to control the muscles that are required to produce speech.

Infants seem to produce sounds first and then discover them to reproduce over and over again. They experiment with these sounds and begin to make changes in them. The difference may consist of the same sound made from a different part of the mouth. Babbling is playing with speech sounds. It is spontaneously produced rather than planned. While babbling, infants use and learn to control their physical speech mechanisms. They babble different speech sounds and combine them into two- and three-syllable sounds. They control air flow to produce word-like sounds and change the intensity, volume, pitch, and rhythm of their babbling sound play.

Babbling does not occur in social isolation. Infants listen to the sounds around them. When you repeat the sounds infants have just made, they may imitate your sound. Contingent (i.e., attuned) maternal behavior was found to facilitate more frequent, complex, and phonologically advanced vocal behavior by infants 6 to 10 months in age (Goldstein, King, & West, 2003). Vocal stimulation that is relevant to the infant's behaviors and vocalizations seems to increase their babbling and, therefore, their control over their language. This stimulation also helps infants begin the two-way communication process of talking-listening-talking. They are finding that when they talk, you will listen; infants make you talk to them (Photo 11–4). Cooing and babbling sounds are used to provide pleasure as well as to convey feelings. Conversations include pitch and volume added to strings of sounds that seem like syllables or words. Infants imitate and initiate private and social talking.

© Cengage Learning

PHOTO 11–4 The caregiver listens to and records the infant's new sounds.

lexical words Words that have a concrete or abstract connection to objects or events (e.g., nouns, verbs, and adverbs).

grammatical words Function words that have little meaning on their own yet affect the meaning of other words (e.g., articles, prepositions, or conjunctions).

Researchers have discovered that by 6 months of age, infants can distinguish **lexical words**, which are words that have a concrete or abstract connection to objects or events (e.g., nouns, verbs, and adverbs), from **grammatical words**, which are function words that have little meaning on their own yet affect the meaning of other words (e.g., articles, prepositions, or conjunctions; Shi & Werker, 2001). Moreover, infants demonstrate a distinct preference for lexical words (Shi & Werker, 2001, 2003), which may be related to the acoustic and phonological salience of these words. In response to this developmental preference, teachers should label and describe objects and events in the environment using rich language. For example, when an infant is lying on her back looking at a sun catcher, you could say, "You are looking at the shimmering sun catcher. It sparkles in the sunlight." More importantly, this is a primary reason to read to infants daily; many board books pair one or two words with a large picture of the object, reinforcing lexical words. Every child should have a one-on-one book experience each day (Vukelich, Christie, & Enz, 2012).

Around 1 year of age, infants typically speak their first recognizable words and use a combination of sounds, babbling, and single words to communicate with themselves and others (McDevitt & Ormrod, 2013). The impact of early oral communication (e.g., babbling, first word) on later language development has been studied extensively. For example, in a study of 12 late talkers (LT; i.e., children who failed to produce at least 50 words or any two-word combinations) and 12 typically developing talkers (TDT), LT and TDT were found to produce equivalent amounts of spontaneous vocal productions (Fasolo, Majorano, & D'Odorico, 2008). What was important in distinguishing capabilities was the phonetic complexity of the speech produced (higher rates of complexity by TDT); more specifically, the LT had a significantly higher proportion of the simplest syllable structure (i.e., consonant-vowel) and a lower proportion of syllables containing two different consonants compared to TDT (Fasolo et al., 2008). What other variables have been found to relate to language development?

A newly studied type of babbling focuses on what researchers are calling object-directed vocalizations (ODVs). When babies utter a noncry, prelinguistic vocalization when looking at an object that is within reach or is being held, it is defined as an ODV. Recent work has shown that contingent social responses to infants' ODVs have different relations to vocabulary size at 15 months, depending on the match between caregiver labeling and the object at which the infant is babbling (Goldstein & Schwade, 2010). More specifically, mothers who provided object labels that matched what the child was looking at had children with a greater vocabulary at 15 months when compared to mothers who reacted to ODV with words that were similar to the sound produced but unrelated to the object being vocalized (Goldstein & Schwade, 2010). This study, along with countless others, supports the idea that responsiveness to babbling and attentional focus by caregivers during the first year of life predicts language development.

Professional caregivers use several strategies to enhance the infant's language development.

1. Talk: Say words, sentences, and repetitive chants; read stories aloud, and show the baby pictures of different faces and designs.

2. Sing: Hum; sing words set to your own music, favorite tunes, lullabies, and songs; play African drums or recorded bagpipe music.

3. Recite: The rhythms of nursery rhymes can be used to respond to the infant's behavior. If he is soothing himself by rubbing his hands together, select a nursery rhyme with a slow rhythm. If she is vigorously bouncing her legs, select one with a fast, steady beat.

4. Read: Books should be every child's favorite tool. Support a love of reading by reading often to the children in your care. See Appendix D for a list of board books for very young children.

5. Listen and respond: Infants will produce sounds; this talk will decrease if they do not have someone to listen to them and to "answer" them.

6. Initiate conversation: Almost every encounter with an infant is an opportunity for conversation. Routine physical care, such as feeding, changing diapers, and rocking, all present the necessary one-on-one situations where you and the infant are interacting. It is not necessary or helpful to talk all the time or to be quiet all the time. The infant needs balance between times for language and conversation and times to be quiet.

See Table 11–4, Suggestions for Implementing Curriculum—Language Development, for additional strategies for supporting language skills.

11-2d Emotional Development

Positive interactions with caregivers help infants develop good feelings about themselves. During the first months of life, infants develop their basic feelings of security as they attend to many different events and draw a general conclusion about their ability to trust another. While this process takes several months, it is important to develop these feelings of security right from birth. Feelings of security and trust develop out of relations with others, not by infants on their own. Infants develop these feelings from the way other people treat them. Two caregiver behaviors of special importance are responding immediately to the infant's distress signals and responding unfailingly to the infant's signals of stress, need, or pleasure. Family members and early childhood educators should coordinate in providing the kinds of relationships and experiences that enable the infant to develop this basic security.

Beginning around 4 months of age, infants express a wider and wider range of emotions. Pleasure, happiness, fear, and frustration are displayed in a variety of sounds, such as gurgles, coos, wails, and cries, along with

TABLE 11–4 ▶ Suggestions for Implementing Curriculum—Language Development

Initiating-Responding	
Initiates making sounds	"Answer" infant with sounds or words.
Responds vocally to another person	Hold infant: look at infant eye to eye; make sounds, talk, sing to infant; listen to infant's response; talk, sing again; listen, and so on.
Makes sound, repeats sound, practices the sound for a few minutes, and then lengthens the practice to longer blocks of time	Talk with infant, show interest, look at infant.
Responds to talking by cooing, babbling, and smiling	Talk directly to infant.
Imitates sounds	Make sounds, talk, sing to infant.
Looks for person speaking	Place yourself so that the infant can see you when you converse together.
Looks when name is called	Call the infant by name and talk with child.
Makes consonant sounds	
Responds to own name	Use infant's name when you start talking with that child.
Repeats syllables, words, for example, *bye-bye*	Label frequent behaviors and respond to infant's use, for example, say "bye-bye" and wave; repeat occasionally.
Makes sounds like conversation	Respond verbally to infant's "conversation," for example, "Holly is talking to her truck."
Connects words with objects, for example, says "kitty"—points to kitty familiar toys, objects	Point or touch objects you verbally label.
Crying	
Cries automatically when distressed or frustrated	Empathize with the infant. Respond to infant's crying immediately and consistently.
Cries differently to express hunger, discomfort, anger	Attend to the need infant expressed by crying.
Cries to gain attention	Find out what infant wants.
Productive Language	
Coos using repetitive vowel-like sounds	Imitate, respond, and talk with infant
Babbles syllable-like sounds	Respond with talk.
Babbles conversation with others	Respond with talking.
Babbles two- and three-syllable sounds	Respond with talking.
Uses intensity, volume, pitch, and rhythm	Use normal speaking patterns and tones when talking to the infant.
Shouts	Respond to infant's feelings.
Uses names: Mama, Dada	Reinforce by talking about Mama and Dada.
Makes sounds like conversation	Respond verbally to infant's "conversation," for example, "Holly is talking to her truck."
Repeats, practices word over and over	Allow infant to play with words.
	Respond and encourage.

© Cengage Learning

stranger anxiety Fear exhibited by older toddlers around 9 months of age toward people who are different or unknown; demonstrates their growing cognitive abilities.

physical movements such as kicking rapidly, waving arms, bouncing, rocking oneself, and smiling.

Many infants experience what is called **stranger anxiety** in the latter half of the first year and well into the second year of life (McDevitt & Ormrod, 2013). People the infant doesn't know or does know but doesn't often see may find that the infant fears them. The infant may cry, cringe, hide, or move away. This very normal infant behavior occurs at a time when the infant is beginning to construct the idea of self as separate from others. It is important that "strangers" not feel something is wrong with them. A substitute teacher may experience this infant withdrawal because the infant has established familiarity and attachment to the primary caregiver, whereas he is different and unknown.

It is also during this period that the infant may demonstrate **separation anxiety** at being left by his mother or other primary caregiver. The infant may become nervous or distraught if the caregiver is too far away or out of sight. Take every opportunity to tell the child that you will leave and will return. Introduce the other early childhood educator and explain that this person will take good care of him until you return. It is important to tell the infant when you have returned.

Anger is also experienced more because of cognitive advancements. Infants can now conceive of goals or desires and actively pursue them; when these goals are blocked, anger and frustration result. For example, when Tomas does not want his father to leave at drop-off time, he might crawl over and cling to his father's leg. Or he might crawl to the door and bang on it after his father has left. Tomas is clearly communicating his desire to keep his dad near and sadness (most often expressed through anger) at not being able to do so. Teachers must help infants and family members create rituals for coping with the emotions that stem from being separated on a daily basis (Balaban, 2006). Infants will express their anger, anxiety, and fear in a multitude of ways; teachers must learn to crack the message encoded in their behaviors (Marion, 2014).

At the end of the first year, infants are better at communicating their preferences and are showing signs of budding independence. Providing toys they like not only adds to their pleasure in playing with the toys but also enhances their feelings of asserting some control over their world. As discussed previously, developing physical skills also make infants more independent in feeding and dressing themselves. Allowing them to accomplish as many tasks as possible on their own helps them strengthen their identity or who they are as an individual.

Temperament

Temperament, or the infant's basic style of behavior, gradually emerges in the first four months. As discussed previously, infants have different temperaments or characteristic ways of approaching their surroundings. You will need to know where a child falls in each of the nine behavioral categories (activity level, regularity, response to new situations, adaptability, sensory threshold, positive or negative mood, response intensity, distractibility, and persistence; for descriptions, see Chapter 3) so that you can adjust to the child's approach to the world and help him or her cope with daily situations. As discussed previously, the important issue surrounding temperament is the teacher's ability to create a *goodness of fit* between the child and her environment (Marion, 2014). When family members provided responsive care despite infants' negative reactions, children were more eager and less angry in interactions as they became toddlers (Kochanska, Aksan, & Carlson, 2005). It is logical to deduce that similar outcomes would result when early childhood educators provide responsive care (Photo 11–5).

separation anxiety Fear exhibited at the loss of physical or emotional connection with the primary caregiver.

© 2017 Cengage Learning

PHOTO 11–5 Family members and caregivers can accept and return an infant's affection with a smile, hug, or cuddle.

Determining where a child falls on each category requires focused observations. Some styles are easily recognized, whereas others may be more difficult to observe. The activity level of infants is obvious. They may kick, wriggle, and squirm a great deal, or they may lie quietly while either asleep or awake. Highly active infants may kick their covers off consistently and get tangled in their clothes. Their bodies get plenty of activity. They may need to be checked frequently to be sure they can move freely and aren't tangled in a blanket or article of clothing. A blanket may be more of a bother than it is worth because it seldom covers the infant. Infant suits or long smocks and socks may keep the active infant just as warm. Very quiet infants may seem easy to care for. They seldom kick off their covers or need their clothes adjusted. They may, however, need to be picked up and moved around to stimulate their physical movement.

Infants characteristically use differing levels of energy when responding to stimuli. One infant will cry loudly every time. Another infant will whimper and fuss and occasionally cry more loudly when very distressed. The caregiver, when responding to the infant's cries, will need to learn cues other than loudness to determine the type and severity of stress. The caregiver may need to check infants who fuss and cry quietly to make sure their needs are being met. The teacher must attend and be attuned as well as use her understanding of each child's temperament to create appropriate learning experiences.

Persistence can be a challenging aspect to observe as it is often tied to other behaviors. Take trying to stand upright and stepping forward, for example. Very persistent infants will try again and again to stand or step. Falling down becomes a deterrent only after many tries. Other infants persist only a few times, then stop their efforts and change to some new task or interest. So, their lack of persistence could look like more like lack of attention. Early childhood educators must use the three *A*s to help infants with low persistent levels keep trying so that necessary skills can be mastered (see Chapter 4).

Behavior Regulation

Around the first birthday, external influences such as a verbal "no" or a firm look may sometimes cause infants to change their behavior. Follow up your restrictive words or looks with an explanation. For example, when an infant throws food on the floor, the caregiver can say, "No. You need the carrots in your dish to eat. Please put a carrot in your mouth." Sometimes infants will stop their own negative action. You may see them pick up food or a toy, start to throw, and then stop their arm movement and put the object down carefully. This early self-restriction may be caused by distraction rather than self-control. Nevertheless, acknowledge such actions to help the child better understand the acceptable behavior.

As soon as the child has a modicum of verbal skills, promote perspective-taking skills and apply the three *A*s to elicit positive emotions. Remember that the most powerful way to promote behavioral self-regulation is to *provide attention for appropriate behavior*. Redirecting negative behaviors to positive or desired behaviors works better than drawing attention to negative ones (see Chapter 6). Be sure to trust the child's motives. Children are doing the best they can at all times.

The caregiver can use several strategies to enhance the infant's emotional development. Whereas physical development can be enhanced by moving the infant, toys, and oneself around, emotional development demands more than manipulation; it requires consistent interactions. When relating to the infant, the three *As*—Attention, Approval, and Attunement—play a most crucial part in the daily emotional development of the child. The following strategies will help the caregiver to be conscious of the three *As* while engaged in routine care, planned learning experiences, and general interactions:

- Focus your attention on the child's needs and interests.
- Engage the child—make eye-to-eye contact.
- Move slowly and with intention.
- Make meaningful physical contact.
- Reflect vocal expressions, sounds, and words back to him or her.
- Try to sense how the child is feeling—is the child excited, happy, frustrated?
- Get attuned with the child. Let him or her lead you vocally.
- Involve the child directly in the experience/interaction.
- When leaving the infant, indicate where you'll be in the room or when you will be back.

See Table 11–5 Suggestions for Implementing Curriculum—Emotional Development for additional ways to support emotional development.

11-2e Social Development

The caregiver must become emotionally involved with infants to provide for their social needs. In fact, during the first few months of life, the most important plaything for infants is a responsive caregiver (Herr & Swim, 2002). The caregiver can use several strategies to enhance the social development of infants of this age. The caregiver can respond quickly to the infant's needs and can initiate interactions by looking, holding, stroking, talking, playing, carrying, and rocking the infant. While interacting, teachers should remember to use positive communication skills such as active listening and mirroring. In fact, the positive outcomes for mirroring have been established through research. High-affect-mirroring mothers were associated with infants (2- to 3-month-olds) who ranked high on prosocial behavior and social expectancy—responded more frequently with smiles, vocalizations, and gazes (Legerstee & Varghese, 2001).

According to attachment theory, just as infants develop a unique attachment to their mothers and fathers, they can develop an additional attachment to their primary caregivers in child care settings. Thus, many of the caregiver strategies previously discussed for building emotional relationships between infants and teachers involve frequent use of looking and touching, which serve a dual function of supporting attachment.

TABLE 11–5 ▶ Suggestions for Implementing Curriculum—Emotional Development

Types of Emotions–Feelings		
Shows stress	calming touch, talk, music, singing	Determine cause. Change situation to reduce stress, for example, change diaper, change position, talk to infant (child may be bored).
Shows enjoyment	interesting, challenging toys, objects	Provide pleasant experiences, for example, give infant a bath, snuggle, converse, smile.
Shows anger or frustration		Determine cause. Remove or reduce cause. Divert infant's attention; for example, turn infant around to look at something else.
Shows fear		Hold, comfort infant. Remove fear-producing object or change situation, for example, hold infant startled by sudden loud noise.
Shows pleasure in repetitive play	favorite toys	Provide favorite toys. Share pleasure in repetitive actions, for example, clapping hands.
Shows fear of strangers		Introduce new people carefully. Do not let strangers hover closely. Give the infant time to become accustomed to the stranger at a distance.
Shows happiness, delight, joy; humor expressed with laughs, giggles and grins		Share laughing, giggling. Play funny games, for example, "Touch your nose"; hold your finger by your head and slowly move it to touch the infant's nose while you say excitedly, "I'm going to touch your nose."
Shows rage		Allow infant to kick legs, flail arms, scream, and cry for a short time. Determine the cause of the rage. Reduce or eliminate the cause if possible. Use touching, rocking, soothing talk to help the infant calm down. Verbally affirm and acknowledge the infant's anger and distress. Remain calm and present soothing support.
Shows anxiety		Use calm, quiet talking, singing. Cuddle and stroke the child. Remove the child from situation if necessary.
Shows anger or frustration through tantrums		Determine and remove cause if possible. Use calm talking about child's goal and other ways to pursue it. May sometimes hold and soothe infant. Help infant start a new activity. Keep child safe, but ignore a tantrum.
Shows independence—helps with feeding and dressing self	cup, spoon, clothes that child can manipulate	Allow infant to help feed and dress self. This takes much time and patience. Lengthen eating time to adjust to self-feeding skills.
Shows affection		Accept and return affection with smile, hug, cuddle.
Control of Emotions–Feelings		
Decreases crying	activities, toys that catch infant's attention and that infant likes	Involve infant in an activity.
Reflects feelings in sounds		Respond to the feelings expressed, for example, comfort (by talking) a whining child, change situation.
Feels comforted when held		Consistently hold, caress, cuddle, and comfort when infant needs it.
Sometimes stops crying when talked to, sung to		Talk calmly, soothingly to crying infant.
Control of Behaviors		
Begins to learn to obey "No"		Use "no" sparingly so infants can determine important situations when they must control their behavior. Use firm, not angry, voice and matching nonverbals so message is clear.
Sometimes inhibits own behavior		Provide detailed feedback to infant about self-control; for example, infant raises arm to throw something, but puts it down on table so say, "You thought about throwing the crayon but did not. Now, Zachary can use the crayon."

Spotlight on Research

ATTACHMENT TO OBJECTS

"Do security blankets belong in child care programs?" is a question frequently posed by teachers and directors/owners. The issue of children being attached to objects has been hotly debated by researchers, teachers, and families for more than the past four decades. Given the complexity of the matter, it does not appear that it will be resolved soon.

Children might come to use an attachment object for a wide variety of reasons. College students who had a strong attachment to an object during their childhood reported greater smell sensitivity, higher tactile thresholds, and higher levels of seeking tactile stimulation than participants without a comfort object (Kalpidou, 2012). Thus, for some children, sensory stimulation through touch might be soothing. Other children may turn to an attachment object to relieve stress. Young children who attended all-day child care were more likely to have an attachment object than children who attended only half-day (Fortuna, Baor, Israel, Abadi, Knafo, Gagne, et al., 2014). When faced with moderately upsetting medical procedures, children with attachment to an object mitigated distress by having the object or their mother present compared to having no supportive assistance available (Ybarra, Passman, & Eisenberg, 2000). Yet, having both present at the same time did not provide additional levels of soothing. On the other hand, nonobject-attached children demonstrated no benefit to having a blanket nearby; they were just as distressed as children with no supportive assistance available (Ybarra et al., 2000).

Parenting attitudes and behaviors have been studied extensively as potential reasons for differences in the use of transitional objects. Early research found that most parents studied held positive views regarding the significance of transitional objects in the life of their child, especially when it was time to go to sleep (Triebenbacher, 1997). There were differences between mothers and fathers regarding other times that having/ using a transitional object would be acceptable and in when young children should be expected to give up their transitional object, with mothers supporting greater and longer access to transitional objects (Triebenbacher, 1997). There were also group differences for mothers; White mothers reported a wider variety of situations in which their children want/need transitional objects than did either Black or Hispanic mothers. More current research suggests that Caucasian mothers living in New York were significantly more likely to have a child who was attached to a transitional object than children of Japanese mothers living in Tokyo (62 percent and 38 percent, respectively; Hobara, 2003).

In a study of parenting behaviors, mothers who used four high-contact parenting behaviors (breastfeeding, feeding on child's cues, sleeping with infant, and holding/nursing during transitions to sleep) were found to have children with significantly lower rates of attachment to objects compared to mothers who used three or fewer of the high contact behaviors (Green, Groves, & Tegano, 2004). Sleeping arrangements were an important variable in Hobara's (2003) cross-cultural study. The Japanese mothers in her study slept in the same room (60 percent) or shared a bed (38 percent) with their babies significantly more than the American mothers (4 percent and 2 percent, respectively). If mothers are available throughout the night for physical comfort, infants would not need to seek it from another source. Additionally, because of the co-sleeping arrangements, "bedtime is not likely a time of stress or fear for Japanese children...," further diminishing the need for a security item (Hobara, 2003, p. 186).

Other researchers have investigated whether the infant's attachment history with a primary caregiver is related to the need for an attachment object. No significant relationship was found between blanket attachment and attachment to mother (Donate-Bartfield & Passman, 2004). What was interesting in this research study is that blanket-attached children used their attachment object differently depending on their attachment with their primary caregiver. Avoidant, blanket-attached children, while initially appearing to be adjusting better than other children in the upsetting situation (e.g., during separation from mother during the Strange Situation), demonstrated being conflicted. When given the chance to reunite with their parent, they remained separate from their mother and in contact with their special, inanimate object. The results demonstrated that, although being conflicted, avoidant, blanket-attached children appear better able than secure, blanket-attached children to use inanimate objects to remedy their discomfort (Donate-Bartfield & Passman, 2004).

When should children give up objects they are attached to? The study by Triebenbacher (1997) found that both mothers and fathers reported that their children should give up transitional objects two to three years younger (e.g., prior to formal school) than the age they gave up their own attachment object. Qualitative

(continued)

Spotlight on Research (*continued*)

responses indicated that the parents want their children to be more self-confident, mature, and independent as they approach school age. This seems to contradict other research that attachment objects are common throughout adolescence. In the sample, 37 percent of adolescent girls had transitional objects, and those girls reported greater levels of sadness than girls who did not have a transitional object (Erkolahti & Nyström, 2009). The underlying nature of that relationship needs additional research to better understand what it could mean for adolescent development.

If transitional objects are used by children to cope with stressful situations, why would we deny the use of them in a home child care or center-based child care center? As research reviewed in Chapter 3 suggests, many children experience high levels of stress throughout the day in child care settings. Making attachment objects accessible continuously during the day may serve to alleviate some of the stress and assist young children with healthy emotional and social development.

Attachment theory and research have identified phases in the development of attachment. Ainsworth (1982) identified infants' social behaviors during the first few months of life that relate to developing attachment.

Phase 1: Undiscriminating Social Responsiveness (2 to 3 months of age)

- Orienting behaviors: visual fixation, visual tracking, listening, rooting, postural adjustment when held
- Sucking and grasping to gain or maintain contact
- Signaling behaviors: smiling, crying, and other vocalizations to bring caregiver into proximity or contact

Phase 2: Discriminating Social Responsiveness (at 6 months or older)

- Discriminates between familiar and unfamiliar persons
- Responds differently to them
- Exhibits differential smiling, vocalizing, crying

Phase 3: Actively Seeking Proximity and Contact (around 7 months)

- Signals intended to evoke response from mother or attachment figure
- Locomotion that facilitates proximity seeking
- Voluntary movements of hands and arms
- Following, approaching, clinging—active contact behaviors

Social Interactions

Because infants are social at birth, their interactions with others increase over the first year of life. Budding skills allow them to be engaged in several new social experiences. Their developing physical skills of manipulating objects contribute to the cognitive development of constructing a concept of self and not-self. As they gain mobility, infants encounter different people or move away from these people. They can now initiate interactions with other children and adults as well as respond to others' interactions with them.

Infants are challenged to clearly separate others' desires and needs from their own. Therefore, they are often fearful, uncertain, and occasionally clingy. They can be very possessive of materials and people. Such materials

TABLE 11–6 ▶ Suggestions for Implementing Curriculum—Social Development

CHILD BEHAVIOR	MATERIALS	EXAMPLES OF CAREGIVER STRATEGIES
Attachment		
Shows special closeness to parent; differentiates response to parent—voice, touch, presence, absence		Accept that the infant will respond differently to you than to parent. Closely observe the parent-infant interaction, and then model some of the caregiving behaviors, sounds, and other characteristics of the parent.
Develops familiarity with one primary (significant other)		Same caregiver provides most of infant's care, although other caregivers may share responsibility occasionally.
Shows strong attachment to family members Differentiates response to family members		Reinforce attachment to family members.
Shows familiarity with one specific caregiver		Assign a specific, primary caregiver to a specific infant. One caregiver can be a primary person (significant other) to four or fewer infants. Primary caregiver assumes responsibility for emotional involvement with the infant while providing care for the whole child.
Shows intense pleasure and frustration with person to whom attached		Accept and share pleasure; calm, soothe, stroke, and sing during infant's frustrated periods.
Others		
Recognizes voice of parent		Hold infant. Smile, talk with infant.
Watches people		Place infant where you can be seen moving about. Carry infant around to see others.
Shows longer attentiveness when involved with people		Spend time during infant's alert times interacting with infant.
Behaves differently with parent than with others		Accept different responses.
Interacts with people		Initiate interactions, respond; place or carry infant where infant can meet people.
Laughs		Play with infant, laugh with infant, respond to infant's laugh.
Seeks family's and caregiver's attention by movement, sounds, smiles, and cries		Respond immediately and consistently to happy, sad, or angry pleas for attention.
Resists pressures from others regarding feeding and eating		Encourage but do not force the infant to eat. Adjust the time to stop and start according to the infant's rhythm.
Acts shy with some strangers		Hold and provide security to the infant when meeting a stranger. Allow the infant time to hear and see the stranger before the stranger touches the infant or even gets too close.
May fear strangers		Keep strangers from forcing themselves on infant, who may not want to be held by stranger.
Keeps parent or caregiver in sight		Allow infant to follow you around. Arrange room so infant can see you from different areas of the room.
Becomes assertive; initiates action to fill needs		Encourage infant's assertiveness. Observe to determine whether infant is getting aggressive and will need cautions.
Is possessive of people		Verbally assure infant you will be here and will come back to talk and play with infant again.
Is possessive of materials	many toys	Provide enough toys and materials so infant does not need to share.
May demand attention		Provide positive verbal attention even though you may be busy with another child.

PHOTO 11–6 Caregivers help children who can sit upright to explore materials and interact with others.

and people still seem part of the infant, not completely separate, and thus they seem to belong to the infant.

Low teacher-child ratios and a primary caregiving system help meet the social needs of infants (Gallagher & Mayer, 2008). When these characteristics are in place, teachers are more familiar to the infant and thus can better meet each infant's need for security and social interaction (Photo 11–6). You will see hints of the quality of the teacher-child relationship by watching the infants' behaviors. Securely attached mobile infants, for example, will stay "with a trusted caregiver, watching newcomers with a healthy suspicion" (Gallagher & Mayer, 2008, p. 82).

See Table 11–6 Suggestions for Implementing Curriculum—Social Development for additional strategies for supporting the social development of children up to one year of age.

READING CHECKPOINT

Before moving on with your reading, make sure that you can answer the following questions about the material discussed so far.

1. When an infant engages in productive language such as cooing or babbling, what additional caregiver strategies are needed? Explain your rationale for at least three strategies.
2. Describe cognitive development for infants between 3 and 10 months old. Match two developmental changes with caregiver strategies.
3. When an infant begins to show strong emotions such as anger at blocked goals, what additional caregiver strategies are needed? Explain your rationale for at least three strategies.
4. Describe social development for infants between 8 and 12 months old. Match two developmental changes with caregiver strategies.

Summary

11-1 Select materials appropriate to the development of infants at that age level.

Early childhood educators must select materials that support development, challenge development, and are safe. In addition, the materials should be open-ended so that they can be used in multiple ways.

11-2 Devise strategies appropriate to infants (birth to 12 months of age) that are responsive to individual developmental levels.

Teachers make educational decisions based on specific observations of an infant's development.

This not a simple task because multiple milestones are reached in each area of development for infants between birth and 12 months. Early childhood educators must observe frequently, formally and informally, to note changes or modifications in desires, needs, skills, interests, and so on. For example, as the infants become mobile, begin to babble, develop stranger anxiety, and express strong emotions, teachers must plan a responsive curriculum that reflects the capabilities of the ever-changing infant.

CASE STUDY   Theresa's Attachment to a Blanket

Theresa's parents both work at home. Her mother works late evenings and her father works early mornings. Theresa's mother is breast-feeding her on demand except for one day a week, when both parents are out of the house. During that day, she gets thawed, previously frozen breastmilk from a bottle.

Both parents care for Theresa. They both manage to take breaks at the same time to give quality time to "Terry Bear," as she is affectionately called. Sometimes they all take walks together, taking turns carrying the baby. She enjoys the movement and facing her parents in her infant front carrier, but she is also curious about the sights and sounds around her. She has really begun to wiggle on these walks, so her parents are considering a new backpack where she can ride on their back and look around better.

While her parents really liked this schedule, work changes now require that Theresa attend child care two mornings a week. She has recently started going to a family child care and is learning to adjust and make the transition. She seems to be building a strong bond with Ellie, her caregiver. Ellie quickly discovered that Theresa is easily calmed by being given her satin blanket and talking in a soothing voice. Theresa really chews on her blanket when upset or trying to go to sleep.

1. Should Theresa be allowed to keep her blanket and chew on it?
2. What would happen to Theresa if you took away her blanket? Why do you think that would happen?
3. How old should a child be before she or he no longer needs "attachments" to favorite things? Why?

Lesson Plan

Title: *Pull Up and See*

Child Observation:

Marcel is a fast crawler, using his skills to move around the room to engage with people and objects. For example, he crawled to the block area, stacked five blocks, and put a person figurine on top. He then crawled to the block shelf and sat on the floor, whimpering and pointing to the book sitting open out of reach on the top shelf.

Child's Developmental Goal:

To develop the skills to pull self to a standing position

To demonstrate problem-solving strategies

Materials: Favorite book and a sturdy piece of furniture.

Preparation: Place the piece of furniture in a convenient location in the room. Set the book open in the middle of the furniture.

Learning Environment:

1. When Marcel crawls to the new furniture, point out his favorite book on top. Invite him to look at the book. To illustrate, you could say:

   "That is your favorite book about cats. Do you want to look at it?"

2. Encourage Marcel to consider how he can reach the book. Use open-ended prompts to promote problem solving such as:
   a. *I wonder how you can reach the book.*
   b. *How can you move your body to reach the book?*

3. Scaffold his attempts to move his body. You can scaffold by
   a. Verbally describing what he is attempting (e.g., "You are pulling on the furniture with your arms. That's it. Keep going.")
   b. Providing suggestions to help him (e.g., "You are on your knees. Push up and put your foot flat on the floor.")

    c. Offering physical guidance (e.g., place hand behind child's back, touching his body only when support is needed)

    d. Encouraging persistence (e.g., "You are trying hard to reach the book. One more time and I think you can reach it.)

4. Pay close attention to Marcel's emotional reactions to the challenge. If he seems to be going beyond a "helpful frustration level," then give him a choice of how to solve the problem. You can say, for example, "You worked really hard to get that book. It was too hard to reach. Do you want me to stand you up, or do you want me to hand you the book?"

❯❯ Professional Resource Download

Guidance Consideration:

Watch closely for signs of physical or emotional overload or exhaustion. If either occurs, redirect Marcel to another favorite book that is easily within reach. Enjoy one-on-one time by reading that book with him.

Variations:

Place a favorite toy or musical instrument on top of a sturdy shelf or piece of furniture for him to obtain.

Additional Resources

Banning, W., & Sullivan, G. (2011). *Lens on outdoor learning*. St. Paul, MN: Redleaf Press.

Epstein, A. S. (2014). *The intentional teacher: Choosing the best strategies for young children's learning* (rev. ed.). Washington, DC: National Association for the Education of Young Children.

Essa, E. L., & Burnham, M. M. (Eds.) (2009). *Informing our practice: Useful research on young children's development*. Washington, DC: National Association for the Education of Young Children.

Ochshorn, S. (2015). *Squandering America's future: Why ECE policy matters for equality, our economy, and our children*. New York: Teachers College Press.

Roffman, L., & Wanerman, T., with Britton, C. (2011). *Including one, including all. A guide to relationship-based early childhood education*. St. Paul, MN: Redleaf Press.

12
CHAPTER

Teaching Children Twelve to Twenty-Four Months

Learning Objectives

After reading this chapter, you should be able to:

12-1 Select materials appropriate to the development of young toddlers.

12-2 Identify strategies appropriate to young toddlers (12 to 24 months of age) that are responsive to individual developmental levels.

Standards Addressed in This Chapter

naeyc **NAEYC Standards for Early Childhood Professional Preparation**

1 Promoting Child Development and Learning

4 Using Developmentally Effective Approaches to Connect with Children and Families

DAP **Developmentally Appropriate Practice Guidelines**

2 Teaching to Enhance Development and Learning

3 Planning Curriculum to Achieve Important Goals

In addition, the NAEYC standards for developmentally appropriate practice are divided into six areas particularly important to infant/toddler care. The following area is addressed in this chapter: *exploration and play*.

© 2017 Cengage Learning

CASE STUDY | Lennie Bites

Lennie, 23 months old, walks to a child-sized rocking chair, backs up to it, and sits down. He rocks and watches the other children. He gets off the chair and sits on his legs while picking up blocks. He picks up a block wagon, stands up, and walks around. He holds the block wagon in his left hand, tries to put in another block with his right hand, and succeeds. He puts the wagon on the floor and pushes it. He takes off one block and then takes off five blocks; he puts them back on. Jasper walks past, and Lennie says, "Noooo." While distracted, Tracey takes the block wagon. Lennie reaches for it but does not get it. He bites Tracey on the arm; when she lets go of the wagon, he picks it up and begins putting blocks in it. He picks up the block wagon and a block bag, gets up, and walks around, talking to himself.

Toddlers learn with their whole bodies—not just their heads. They learn more through their hands than they do through their ears. They learn by touching, mouthing, and trying out, not by being told. They learn by doing because it leads to thinking. As such, they can become absorbed in discovering the world around them. If you are convinced that toddlers have short attention spans, just watch them with running water and a piece of soap. Hand washing can become the main activity of the morning! Early educators, then, need to value and respect the unique time period of toddlerhood. They can demonstrate their value and respect by intentionally doing the following:

- Practicing the three *As* of child care—Attention, Approval, and Attunement
- Being skillful, patient observers who help with problem solving and promote a positive perspective
- Increasing their knowledge of toddler development so that they may understand toddlers' daily struggles and challenges
- Sharing in the toddler's delights and discoveries
- Demonstrating their genuine fondness of toddlers

12-1 Materials

Toddlers solve problems on a physical level. Watch toddlers at play for just five minutes, and you will see them walk (which looks like wandering), climb, carry things around, drop things, and continually dump whatever they can find.

Walking is a major development for toddlers who have just turned 1. They are fascinated with toys to pull or push as they toddle around. They climb over objects. They may ride wheeled toys. They grasp and throw and drop objects again and again. These large-muscle activities are not done to irritate adults—they are the legitimate "big body" activities of toddlers (Carlson, 2011). Over the next twelve months, they will develop increased competence as they practice moving their bodies in new and varied ways.

FIGURE 12–1 ▶ Examples of Homemade Materials

PULL TOY

Use plain or painted empty spools. Thread and knot spools on a length of clothesline rope.

TOSS BOX

Collect several small, soft toys and place in a cardboard box. Show child how to take out objects, stand away from the box, and throw the objects into the box. Paint the inside of the box as a target to attract the child's attention.

EXPLORING TUBS

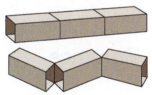

Place one solid object in a margarine tub. Put lid on. When children shake it, they hear a noise. Encourage the children to take off the lid to discover what is inside. Put lid back on. Have several tubs available with different objects inside, e.g., plastic clothespins, large wooden spools.

TUNNELS

Use a sturdy, long cardboard box large enough for child to crawl through. Cut out ends and tape edges to prevent scraping the child and tearing the box. Place several boxes end to end or in a square or zigzag pattern.

PUPPET

Use a paper plate. Tear colored paper, cut pieces of yarn, and paste the pieces on the paper plate making a silly face. These puppets are safer without a wooden stick handle.

Their imaginations are expanding as they construct internal representations of their world. Their play will change over the next few months as they begin to use toys for imaginative play. Teachers will need to provide materials that can facilitate this type of play. Figure 12–1 provides examples of homemade materials that support young toddlers' development.

VOICES FROM THE FIELD

I am a teacher in a Continuity of Care classroom (birth–age 22) at a university-affiliated center. The children and I have been working on a paper project for the past few weeks. We've explored paper of different weights (e.g., stock, tissue, typing, newspaper) by touching, tearing, marking on, painting, and so on. Today, I wanted them to paint a paper bag. Because I thought it would be easier for them, I taped the flat bags to a larger sheet of paper. Two children, ages 13 and 15 months, immediately began to pick at the tape. I read this communication as they didn't want the bag taped. I helped them undo the tape and opened up the bag. Shasta, 15 months old, proceeded to apply paint to four sides of the bag (not the bottom). After the bags dried, I invited the children to find items in the classroom to put in their bags. We have had many conversations about the items they are collecting.

12-1a Types of Materials

pull toys, push toys	low, wide balance beam
trucks, cars	toy people or figurines
low, riding wheel toys	tools: hammer, broom, shovel
low, three-step stairs to climb	pail with objects to put in and take out
blocks	snap toys
area with water and sand toys	sand and water play equipment
soft objects to throw	balls
mirrors	telephones (if real, cut off cords)
dolls and puppets	stuffed animals
puzzles	containers with caps or lids to twist off
picture books and cards	CDs, digital audio devices
paper, nontoxic markers, crayons	tempera paint

12-2 Caregiver Strategies to Enhance Development

12-2a Physical Development

An expanding world opens up to toddlers as they become mobile. They walk, lurch, run, fall, bump into things, and persist in moving around in their world. They are unstable when they walk. They may topple over from stepping on an object, by leaning too far, or walking too fast. They are learning to make adjustments so that they can remain upright. They toddle about for the pure pleasure of practicing their new skills as much as to get from one place to another. The experience gained from walking results in their walking becoming more stable and adult-like (Adolph, Vereijken, & Shrout, 2003). Falling is a valuable learning experience as well (Joh & Adolph, 2006), so avoid rescuing the child too quickly; let her get back up and try again.

Toddlers practice walking by pushing and pulling objects in their environment. Child-size grocery carts, wagons, and even chairs become objects of their efforts. Avoid making rules such as "The chairs stay at the table" because this will frustrate the child who is trying out his new skills; it will also frustrate you when the behavior isn't easily redirected. To illustrate, Roberto, a 14-month-old in a family child care program, likes to combine emptying with transporting things. He finds favorite spots or hiding places: under the bed, in the wastebasket, or even in the sink and toilet bowl. His teacher provides him with equipment and materials for filling and spilling, rather than trying to stop the behavior. Specifically, she gave Roberto a basket of items to hide and then challenged him to collect all of the items back in the basket before the end of the day.

During the last half of this year, toddlers gain much more stability and coordination. They can stand up, squat, reach over, and stand upright again without toppling. They climb on just about everything and even try to climb out of areas where adults put them, such as their cribs. They will soon succeed. They climb up and down stairs by holding onto a rail or hand to maintain balance, but they still do not alternate their feet. These children can now move rapidly, both walking and running, and jump with both feet. They become increasingly more adept at kicking balls. By around 22 months, they can pedal cycles such as Big Wheels, and they love to push and pull toys and objects. They can throw objects at targets rather than randomly throwing and tossing, although they seldom hit the intended target.

Toddlers are also developing their fine motor skills, so they have increased control of their fingers and wrists. They probe, twist, and turn objects (Photo 12–1). They can consciously tell their muscles to relax, so they can more easily release the objects they have grasped, allowing them to drop or throw objects when they choose to. They also are more accurate in directing the objects dropped or thrown. These increased fine motor skills allow toddlers, around 18 months of age, to turn several pages of a book at a time; by 24 months, most will be able to turn pages one at a time.

PHOTO 12–1 Physical development promotes cognitive development.

Some children may favor using one hand over the other. If a child shows such preferences, allow her to use the dominant hand. The child may occasionally use the other hand when using a spoon, for example; if the child occasionally chooses to do so, this will not be harmful. The caregiver should allow the child to develop and maintain the handedness that is comfortable. Do not attempt to make a left-handed child use utensils and toys with the right hand. That child's neurological patterns have developed with his or her left-handedness. Attempting to change a child's handedness may cause both neurological and muscular stress.

Please see Table 12–1 Suggestions for Implementing Curriculum—Physical Development for additional ways to support physical development.

Before moving on with your reading, make sure that you can answer the following question about the material discussed so far.

1. Describe a gross motor and a fine motor skill a 16-month-old would do that shows she is gaining additional muscular control.

READING CHECKPOINT

12-2b Cognitive Development

According to Piaget's theory, cognitive and physical development are linked. Substages 5 and 6 mark the onset of experimentation and mental trial and error, respectfully. Toward the end of this year, some toddlers begin

TABLE 12–1 Suggestions for Implementing Curriculum—Physical Development

CHILD BEHAVIOR	MATERIALS	EXAMPLES OF CAREGIVER STRATEGIES
Locomotion		
May prefer crawling to walking		Allow toddler to crawl when desired. It is faster than walking when the child is just beginning to walk.
Walks alone		Allow toddler to walk alone when desired. Provide a hand to hold onto when child seeks help.
Climbs up stairs with help	stairs	Provide handrail or your hand to assist child with balance.
Climbs down stairs with help	stairs	Provide handrail *and* your hand. Balance is still poor when walking down stairs.
Climbs over objects	low, sturdy furniture, equipment, boxes	Provide low climbing equipment, furniture, for example, ottoman, sturdy cardboard boxes, covered foam incline.
Walks backward	flat floor, ground; clear of toys	Encourage child to walk backward; caution child about obstacles.
Runs with stops and starts	clear area	Provide *flat* running space. On incline. child may run down too fast and fall on face.
Jumps with both feet	low steps, box, block, plastic crate	Keep other children away from jumping spot when one child is jumping to the floor. Sometimes catch child as he or she jumps. Release and steady child so he or she can climb and jump again.
Kicks object	large ball: beach ball, Nerf ball, soccer ball, volleyball, rubber ball	Provide space where child can kick the ball and it will not go too far, for example, into a big cardboard box or into a corner.
Walks up stairs holding railing; walks down stairs holding railing	steps and rail	Provide equipment and time for child to safely walk up and down.
Throws object at target	bean bag; ball, box, cardboard or wood shape with large holes cut in it	Place target at edge of play area so object is thrown away from children.
Pedals cycle	low riding cycle; not high tricycle	Provide space for fast and slow riding, for turning curves and in circles. Keep children on foot away from the area.
Fine Motor Manipulation		
Shows hand preference		Allow toddler to use whichever hand he or she chooses.
Points with finger	pictures, books, objects	Play pointing game, for example, open picture book, "Point to the tree."
Throws objects	soft, small objects	Provide a place and target where toddler can throw objects.
Rolls and catches objects	large, small balls	Sit on floor with legs open and outstretched and roll ball back and forth with toddler.
Helps more in dressing and undressing	buttons, snaps, zipper, cards, books, clothing frame board, large dolls with clothes	Allow toddler to do as much as possible. Assist when toddler needs help.
Pulls zippers	zipper board, book, clothes with large zipper with tab	Provide large zipper with tab large enough for small fingers to pinch and pull. Demonstrate where to hold fabric in other hand.
Increases wrist flexibility; turns wrist to turn object	small objects to twist and turn; jars and screw-on lids	Provide toys that stimulate manipulating, for example, attractive, textured on several sides. Demonstrate twisting jar lid on and off.

(continued)

CHILD BEHAVIOR	MATERIALS	EXAMPLES OF CAREGIVER STRATEGIES
Establishes right- or left-handedness		Allow child to pick up objects and use them with hand child chooses. Do not change object into other hand.
Turns book pages	sturdy pages in books	Read to child, carefully turning each page by grasping the upper right-hand corner and moving hand down to middle of page to gently turn the page.
Digs with tool	shovel, scoop, spoon; sand, dirt	Provide tools that are not sharp and will not bend. Provide space designated for digging. Demonstrate where sand or dirt may and may not go.

the transition to preoperational thinking. The child deliberately begins to invent new actions she has never tried before and to explore the novel and unique features of objects. In other words, she constructs new uses based on past knowledge of outcomes with objects. She tries to find out what will happen if she uses objects in new ways. She combines objects with other objects to create new ways of doing things and uses mental trial-and-error approaches to discover new solutions to problems. Mental trial and error is much faster than the sensorimotor trial and error, in which children had to manipulate objects. A toddler can now make decisions mentally about how something might work or how he or she might affect an object. Clearly, newly acquired physical and mental skills combine to allow the toddler to explore objects in new ways and therefore construct new understandings of the world.

As you can see, this is a time for learning, so opportunities to learn should be provided, including learning how to learn. Too often, adults give children answers to remember rather than problems to solve. This is a grave mistake. "Unless children develop the art of problem solving...their brains will remain underdeveloped" (Healy, 2004). Children construct their knowledge and understanding of the world through their experiences with the environment (Elkind, 2003). According to Piaget, however, people engage in **individual constructivism**, in which a single person individually creates new understandings, interpretations, and realities through interactions with materials, equipment, and people in their environment (McDevitt & Ormrod, 2013). Adults must provide developmentally appropriate learning experiences that challenge toddlers' current level of development but are achievable (Copple & Bredekamp, 2009), causing disequilibrium and influencing their development now and in the future. For example, as object permanence becomes more firmly established, toddlers may search for an object they have seen moved and hidden. So playing hiding games such as "Doggie, doggie, where's your bone?" engages and challenges the children. They will also explore the hiding locations of objects both on their own or when an adult prompts them. May, Kantor, and Sanderson (2004) described a curriculum project that grew from two children's ritualistic investigation of object permanence. In this project, teachers supported the children's interest by planning activities that provided new or novel opportunities for hiding and promoted development by scaffolding the toddler's learning.

Young toddlers are interested in observing the effects of their own and others' actions, learning about **cause and effect**. These little explorers try, probe, and practice activities and observe the results of their actions.

individual constructivism Piaget's belief that each person individually creates new understandings, interpretations, and realities through interactions with materials, equipment, and people in their environment. This is also referred to as cognitive constructivism.

cause and effect In sensorimotor development, observation allows a child to identify the relationship between an action and its effect.

Spotlight on Organizations

NATIONAL ASSOCIATION FOR THE EDUCATION OF YOUNG CHILDREN

This national organization began in the 1920s and was originally called the National Association for Nursery Education (NANE). This group of dedicated volunteers organized conferences, bulletins, and publications. In addition, they developed and implemented nursery school and child care programs through the Works Progress Administration (WPA) during World War II. In 1964, NANE was reorganized and renamed the National Association for the Education of Young Children (NAEYC). That year, a great deal of attention was focused on early childhood education as the federal Head Start program was launched as part of the war on poverty. This organization currently has expanded to include a wide number of services for its 100,000

plus members. For example, this organization supports two annual conferences and four publications, *Young Children, Early Childhood Research Quarterly, Beyond the Journal,* and *Teaching Young Children.* The organization also supports the development of teachers by producing books, videos, and pamphlets that can be shared with families and community members. High-quality early childhood programs can be accredited through this organization (see Chapter 5). Another way that NAEYC impacts the field of early childhood education is through its national standards for teacher preparation. In other words, NAEYC works closely with faculty in universities and colleges to identify the knowledge, skills, and dispositions that all early childhood educators, whether in an initial or advanced program, should possess.

A trial-and-error approach to the world can result in guidance encounters with adults as they experiment with new ways to do things. For example, what happens when sand is thrown? Can I go down the slide head first?

Researchers have found that stimulating playthings are more important for cognitive development after age 1 than in earlier months. According to Healy (2004), availability of interesting and challenging play materials in the child's environment after the first year "predict[s] later IQ and school achievement in reading and math" (p. 53). Toddlers are now able to follow one- and sometimes two-step *oral* directions (recall that 6-month-old infants could imitate three sequenced behaviors after observing a model; see Chapter 11). Pairing toys with their increasing ability to store and recall mental representations results in mastering deferred imitation. Imitative behaviors often show up in the children's play. For example, the caregiver washing the child's face is imitated later by the child as the child washes a doll's face. However, it is important to recognize that children intersperse novel ideas (or ones they have individually constructed) with imitative behaviors. Early childhood educators should watch children's play carefully for themes and insights into their inner world without overreacting to one child's display of negative or troubling behavior. While observing, teachers may also notice that toddlers use some play behaviors repeatedly in the same pattern and develop their own ritual play.

Play begins to move from imitative to symbolic during this time period. **Symbolic play** is children's representation of objects or feelings or ideas. They begin to connect past experiences into their current world as they take on simple roles. Infants and toddlers begin symbolic play by imitating actions associated with particular props, learning to substitute one thing for another, and acting as if they are someone else who is familiar to them (Isenberg & Jalongo, 2001; Van Hoorn, Nourot, Scales, & Alward, 2003).

symbolic play Children's symbolic representations of objects, feelings, or ideas.

Simone might pretend to be a cook and make soup by stirring a spoon in a pot. You might hear Simone say, "More salt" just as a cook might say after taste-testing. Symbolic play serves several functions: Children can express conflicts and work them out in the pretend world. They can pretend to be other people or objects, thereby reflecting their understanding of other people or objects as separate from themselves and trying behaviors similar to or different from their own (See Table 12–2). For those reasons, play is a window for adults to observe and tune into the children's emotional lives (i.e., their worries, fears, and joys; see Honig, 2005). Yet, caution must be exhibited when teachers observe a child's play. While toddlers often imitate a person's behavior, they also put their own spin on the situation by joining together reality and fantasy. For example, a toddler who has never been spanked or hit by a family member might hit a doll. So, for accuracy purposes, teachers should watch play behaviors over a period of time before making interpretations (Marion, 2004). If troubling behaviors are frequently noted, then it should serve as a warning sign, and assistance from a professional specializing in play therapy should be sought, as children with preverbal trauma may retain those memories and reenact events even when they cannot verbally describe the experience (Green, Crenshaw, & Kolos, 2010).

At around 22 to 24 months, a caregiver can determine what is going on with a child cognitively by **role playing** with puppets or dolls. Often the troubled child explains (verbally or nonverbally) very clearly to the caregiver a situation that might have been disturbing or upsetting. Role playing is also a good way for the child to get feedback in a positive way, a good place to use the three *A*s, and a good way to help them solve problems and continue to develop good self-esteem.

role playing When children represent their ideas by acting them out using props such as puppets, dolls, or other dramatic play materials.

12-2c Language Development

Language in toddlers expands from less reliance on sounds and babbling to more use of recognizable words. Children learn language through positive relationships with others. Cuddling, unconditional love, and attuned interactions all serve to create a strong need to communicate with others. When children have positive relationships, they want to interact more with others and therefore gain greater knowledge of spoken language and of the topics being spoken about (McGee & Richgels, 2012). Children learn the rules of spoken language when adults speak distinctly, convey meaning clearly, and use appropriately challenging words. A toddler uses many word approximations, which, when acknowledged and expanded upon, become a usable part of his or her expressive vocabulary. In addition, caregivers must be careful not to criticize children's speech patterns. Forcing a child to repeat a sentence or word "correctly" often serves to shut down her desire to communicate. Recent research suggests using sign language and picture symbols with a late-talking child resulted in more verbal outputs without any direct prompts to speak (Leech & Cress, 2011). Thus, the child spontaneously produced expressive language even when other forms of communication were available. Persisting in the use of signs or picture symbols even after a child is producing expressive language can continue to support language development.

TABLE 12–2 Suggestions for Implementing Curriculum—Cognitive Development

CHILD BEHAVIOR	MATERIALS	EXAMPLES OF CAREGIVER STRATEGIES
Piaget's Substages 5 and 6 of Sensorimotor Development		
Object Permanence		
Watches toy being hid and moved. Looks for it where it was moved.		Play game with child. Hide the object while child watches. Let the child watch you move the object to a different place under the blanket. Ask questions such as, "Where is it? Can you find it?" Observe and allow child to find the object. Describe their behaviors of watching and thinking.
Sees object disappear, mentally remembers object, and figures out where it went		Allow the child to think and search for object. Give clues, ask questions only after the child has acted and still needs assistance. Play hiding games with child.
Causality		
Investigates cause and effect		Allow and encourage child to search to identify the relationship between an action and the effect of it, for example, "What made the ball go under the table?"
Sees self as causal agent		Verbally identify the child as cause of the action, for example, "Laquata kicked the ball."
Explores various ways things happen	water toys, water basin	Allow the child time to play with the water and toys to discover different actions of water and of objects in the water.
Employs active trial-and-error approach to solve problems	narrow-neck milk carton, different sizes and shapes of objects	Provide time and materials that stimulate child to think and try out ideas. Ask questions but do not tell answers or show child.
Experiments with objects		Provide open-ended toys and materials that encourage several uses. Encourage child to see how many ways he or she can use them. Ask questions and allow time for the child to experiment; ask "What happens?"
Mental trial and error		
Tries out ideas mentally, based on past concrete experiences		Allow child time to figure out solutions. If child seeks assistance, help child think about the problem, for example, "What can you use to reach that block?"
Imitation and Symbolic Play		
Copies behaviors of others		Encourage child to pretend: to drink from a pretend bottle like baby Gwen, to march like Pearl, to pick up toys. Think about your own behaviors; child will copy what you do. Be sure your actions are the kind of actions you feel comfortable seeing the child copy.
Turns play with imitation into rituals		Allow child to repeat own play and develop own preferences. For example, a child may see you hug a child who comes in the morning and imitate your hugging. The child may repeat this imitation and develop the ritual of hugging the child who has just arrived.
Plays roles		Encourage children to act out or talk about problems through dramatic play props or materials (e.g., puppets).
Tries on new roles		Provide clothes and materials that help child pretend to be someone else.

© Cengage Learning

overgeneralize The use of one word to mean many different things.

Toddlers may **overgeneralize** or use one word for many different things. *Wawa* may mean anything to drink. *Mama* may mean any woman. Word meaning is usually flexible. The toddler may call anything that is round a *ball*. This is the time the vocabulary of the toddler can be expanded by

© 2017 Cengage Learning

PHOTO 12–2 Make available various types of materials for children to read and talk about.

your use of words to label actions and objects. It is also a time to make them more aware of the world around them by pointing out sounds to listen to and naming what these sounds are. By 18 months, toddlers will be asking what things and sounds are as they categorize their world.

The young toddler's vocabulary is expanding rapidly: at 18 months, typically developing children usually have 5–20 words in their vocabulary, whereas by 24 months, that has expanded to 150–300 words (Vukelich, Christie, & Enz, 2012). Thus, this rapid growth is often referred to as a language explosion. Toddlers direct their own language growth through constantly asking, "What's this?" While this may exhaust the adults in their lives, toddlers should be supported in learning labels for objects and people in their environment as well as those they read about in books.

Young children use their oral language in functional ways, like adults. They use it to express needs, direct others, seek information, and interact with others (see Table 12–3). Toddlers now use nouns, verbs, and pronouns (e.g., me, mine, you) as they combine words into two- and three-word sentences. These children produce telegraphic speech, that is, a sequence of several words that conveys a thought or action but has omitted words. In general, telegraphic speech is almost exclusively made up of lexical words, rather than grammatical words (McDevitt & Ormrod, 2013; see Chapter 11 for the difference between lexical and grammatical words). For example, Cameron says, "Key go car" when he sees his mother take the key ring out of her purse. She responds, "Yes, I have my keys. We're going in the car." It is important to attend to the entire context when a toddler uses telegraphic speech because the same phrase can be used to communicate two different ideas. For example, "my ball" might mean "Where is my ball?" "Give back my ball," or even "My ball is rolling down the ramp."

language explosion The time during which toddlers experience a rapid growth in the size of their vocabulary and can use those words to converse.

telegraphic speech When infants and toddlers combine two or three words into a sentence including only key words (e.g., "go daddy").

TABLE 12–3 Examples of Functional Use of Oral Language and Caregiver Responses

CATEGORY	EXAMPLE	MEANING	EXAMPLE CAREGIVER ELABORATION
Express needs	More.	I'd like more juice.	More juice, please.
Direct others	Go Di (abbreviated caregiver's name).	Please leave me along right now.	You want to play alone with the doll.
Seek information	Where go?	Where did grandpa go?	Grandpa had to go to work. He'll be back after nap.
Interact with others	Peek boo.	Let's play my favorite game, Peekaboo.	Peekaboo is a fun game. Let's play.

© Cengage Learning

See Table 12–4 Suggestions for Implementing Curriculum—Language Development for additional ways to support language development.

READING CHECKPOINT

Before moving on with your reading, make sure that you can answer the following questions about the material discussed so far.

1. List three ways symbolic play helps a child develop cognitively.
2. Identify two possible developments in the child's language and state two strategies for each that a caregiver can use to facilitate that development.

12-2d Emotional Development

Toddlers seek both dependence and independence. Erikson (1963) called this developmental crisis the need to resolve Autonomy versus Shame and Doubt, his second stage of development. For many tasks, toddlers need help. The caregiver can provide toddlers with emotional strength and security, accepting their very real dependence while helping them to become independent. For example, most toddlers do not possess the fine motor skills to zip their coat. However, we can engage them in helping to put it on, bringing the sides together, and then zipping after we've threaded the zipper and closed it about half way. Emotionally they need support that affirms their importance as individuals who can make some choices and accomplish certain tasks all by themselves. As they approach their second birthdays, toddlers are able to care for themselves more (e.g., dressing and undressing, feeding self) leading to further separation from their caregivers. Their growing sense of achievement enhances their developing positive feelings of self-worth and demonstrates an understanding of cause and effect.

Emotions are felt and expressed intensely. Toddlers can swing between extremes, such as smiling or laughing, followed by screaming or crying, as they gain skills related to the five domains of emotional intelligence (see Chapter 3). They also can experience more than one emotion at a time, which is confusing for them. When introduced to a new material, they might be simultaneously excited and fearful. Many fears at this age are learned from adults because our reactions influence the toddler's response. Toward the end of the second year, children's fantasies increase. They are very real and may sometimes be frightening, resulting in increased levels of stress. Toddlers may feel fearful of being separated

TABLE 12–4 Suggestions for Implementing Curriculum—Language Development

CHILD BEHAVIOR	MATERIALS	EXAMPLES OF CAREGIVER STRATEGIES
Babbles sentences		Respond to toddler's babbling.
Repeats, practices words		Repeat toddler's word. Occasionally expand it to a sentence, for example, "gone-gone," "The milk is all gone."
Imitates sounds of other people, objects		Enjoy toddler's sounds. Play sounds game: point to objects and make sound of object, for example, dog barking.
Uses word and gestures in conversation, expects others to understand meaning		Become very familiar with toddler's words and gestures. You often have to guess what the toddler is saying. Make a statement or ask a question to determine if you are interpreting correctly, for example, "Taylor, do you want to go outside?"
Responds to many questions and commands even if he or she cannot say them		Choose a few questions and commands you can use often and consistently. The toddler will learn what they mean through many experiences, for example, "Go get your coat."
Uses word approximations for some words		Watch the toddler's behavior to help you experience what the child is experiencing. What do you see at the point where the child is looking, pointing, reaching? Say a word or sentence to test whether you are interpreting the word correctly.
Uses words in immediate context		Notice what the toddler is doing, saying, or needing right now. Toddler's talk is about immediate needs and desires, not past or future situations.
Identifies familiar pictures	pictures, picture book	Orally label objects. Ask toddler to point to or name familiar pictures.
Expands vocabulary rapidly, labeling objects		Verbally label objects and actions in child's world. Point to and touch the objects. Also expand the label into a sentence, for example, "Ball. Michael has a ball."
Learns social words such as *hello, please, thank you*		Consistently use social words in their correct context. Say "please" and "thank you" to the child.
Uses language to express needs, desires, or direct others		Listen to child's expression of needs and her commands. Verbally respond so child knows that his or her words get your attention and you understand them. Use words and actions to meet child's needs or explain why you cannot meet them, for example, "The milk is all gone." Or "We can't go outside now. It is raining."
Questions; asks "What's that?"		Answer child's frequent and persistent questions. This is how the child learns labels and other information about the world. Provide answers that reflect the child's language abilities, for example, "That is a flower" might be great for one child while another might benefit more from, "That is a daisy. Look at the delicate petals."
Uses nouns, verbs, pronouns		Speak normally with the child so child can hear complete sentence patterns.
Learns prepositions		Use in natural contexts, for example, "The ball rolled under the table," "Put the book on the shelf."
Makes two- and three-word sentences		Use both short and long sentences with the child. Encourage the child and respond to child's sentences with elaboration, for example: Child: "Coat on?" Caregiver: "Yes, you need your coat on."

© Cengage Learning

or abandoned by family members, monsters, loud noises, being sucked down the toilet, or of losing control. They may act out these feelings during play. Additionally, research with older children suggests that having anxious feelings may negatively impact the quality of play exhibited

Family and Community Connections

You work in a ministry that serves children from birth to age 12. You specifically work in one of the classrooms with infants from birth to 18 months. The young toddlers are so much fun but also a challenge for you—they are extremely joyful and loving as well as angry and fearful. The extremes are evident each day for almost each child. You have noticed in conversations with family members that they share some of your struggles with how to respond to these emotional displays. You decide to invite all of the parents for a meal at the end of the day (others will be available to help care for the children). You want to hold informal conversations at the tables, so you decide to write questions on cards to help guide the conversations. What questions would you ask and why? How does helping the family members speak with each other help them deal with their child's emotions and their own strong emotions?

(Christian, Russ, & Short, 2011). More specifically, higher levels of anxious feelings were significantly associated with lower levels of organization and affective processes during play. Teachers of toddlers should observe play carefully to determine if the child's emotional state is negatively impacting a play episode. If that is the case, emotional talk (see Chapter 6) may alleviate some of the negative emotional state and help the child engage in higher quality play.

Adults play a significant role in helping young toddlers deal with strong emotions (See Table 12–5). They interpret responses from caregivers and other children as reflecting their self-worth. Children's feelings can be easily hurt by criticism, and they are afraid of disapproval or rejection. Even though they become easily frustrated, they are learning to communicate some feelings and desires. As always, early childhood educators should accept and acknowledge their emotions. If you want to help them find alternative ways to express their emotions, focus on teaching the behaviors you would rather them display, being respectful of cultural differences in such expressions.

Research showed that higher levels of compliance to cleanup tasks by toddlers were related to both child characteristics (lower levels of anger proneness and social fearfulness) and maternal characteristics (sensitivity and structuring of the task; Lehman, Steier, Guidash, & Wanna, 2002). Hence, adults help children learn to control strong emotions and comply to requests when they use the three *A*s of caregiving—Attention, Approval, and Attunement. Caregivers must take an inventory of themselves and recognize what emotional messages they are conveying to an impressionable toddler. It is the continued responsibility of the caregiver to promote a positive learning environment.

Teachers can also respond to signs of emotional distress by creating new routines or maintaining existing routines (Simpson & McGuire, 2004). For example, Ms. Linda helps each family create their own good-bye routines that include hugs, kisses, and waving good-bye from the good-bye window (Balaban, 2006; Herr & Swim, 2002). Because shared reading provides security and calms children's emotional agitation (Rosenkoetter & Barton, 2002), Ms. Linda uses books to calm children after they are separated

© Cengage Learning

PHOTO 12–3 What part of tying his shoe can he do so that he feels independent?

TABLE 12–5 Suggestions for Implementing Curriculum—Emotional Development

CHILD BEHAVIOR	MATERIALS	EXAMPLES OF CAREGIVER STRATEGIES
Types of Emotions-Feelings		
Recognizes emotions in others		Be consistent in showing emotions, for example, happiness—smile and laugh; anger—firm voice, no smile.
May fear newness or strangeness		Introduce new people, new experiences to toddler. Caution others not to rush the child. Allow child to approach or withdraw at his or her own rate.
Shows excitement, delight		Respond with similar excitement, for example, touching a pretty flower, an animal.
Expresses sense of humor		Giggle and laugh with toddler.
Shows affection		Accept and return physical and verbal shows of affection.
Has tantrums		Determine and remove cause if possible. Proceed calmly with involvement with other children, activities.
Uses play to express emotions, resolve conflicts	blocks, dolls, home objects, clothes, toy animals	Provide props for acting out fear, frustration, insecurity, joy.
Seeks dependency, security with adults		Provide touching, holding, stroking interactions; respond quickly and consistently to toddler's needs.
Seeks to expand independence		Allow toddler to attempt activities by himself or herself, providing only necessary scaffolding.
		Do not assist if toddler can be successful without you.
Shows one or more emotions at the same time		Identify the child's emotions. Respond to the child's needs.
Seeks approval		Provide verbal and nonverbal approval of child as a person and of child's behavior when it is positive.
May develop new fears		Listen to child's fears. Accept them as real. Comfort child. Reassure child of your concern and of your presence.
Increases fantasy		Listen to child's fantasies. Accept them as real to the child. Enjoy funny, happy fantasies. Comfort and reassure child of his or her safety when child has scary fantasies, for example, "There's a monster in the kitchen."
May increase aggressiveness		Remain nearby to caution, remind, and sometimes remove object or child from situation.
Seeks security in routines		Provide consistent routines that involve child completing tasks that she has mastered to increase competence and promote independence.
Sometimes rejects family members or caregiver		Allow child to express rejection in words and behaviors. Continue to express your affection for the child.
Control of Emotions-Feelings		
Begins to learn right and wrong		Verbalize which behavior is right and which behavior is wrong. Give reasons. Because toddlers are only just beginning to conceptualize right vs. wrong, only occasionally can they apply the concept to control their own behavior.
Reinforces desired behavior		Provide positive feedback when a toddler controls his own behavior.
Uses reactions of others as a controller of own behavior		Use words, facial expressions, gestures to indicate approval and disapproval of child's behavior.
May resist change		Explain change *before* it happens. Provide reason for the change and whenever possible, provide choices.
Moves to extremes, from lovable to demanding		Allow child to express swings in mood and behavior. Show acceptance of child as a person. Help child positively communicate her demands by suggesting alternative behaviors.

from their family. She keeps in reach a few favorite books about emotions and being separated from favorite objects or possessions (for book suggestions, see Zeece & Churchill, 2001) that she reads individually to children after they have been dropped off at her family child care center. Ms. Linda also helps families provide security objects (e.g., blankets, stuffed animals) when a child responds positively to their presence (see Chapter 11).

Because toddlers are still gaining the skills to regulate their strong emotions, their anger and frustration may overwhelm them at times and be displayed through temper tantrums. Adults should prevent temper tantrums whenever possible by attending to and changing the conditions that caused the child's frustrations, providing choices, and using emotional talk (see Chapter 6). Of course, not all sources of emotional upheaval can be modified or removed. In those cases, tantrums often occur. It was once believed that children had tantrums because they were angry and then, when it was over, expressed sadness. New research suggests that anger and sadness occur simultaneously in rhythm to one another—sad sounds tended to happen throughout a tantrum with expressions of anger overlaid in sharp peaks (Green, Whitney, & Potegal, 2011). Understanding the rhythm can help adults know when to intercede. In general, it is best to let the child experience the tantrum after it starts. Remove any items that might cause a safety issue and then refrain from interacting with her until the tantrum is winding down. Trying to interact while the toddler is still angry tends to increase the anger and adds further confusion to an already overloaded cognitive system (Green et al., 2011). When the tantrum is over, she will probably seek comfort. Provide it and quietly talk about the emotions being experienced, the cause of the tantrum, and how scary it feels to be out of control of one's emotions and body.

As stated many times before, children learn concepts of right and wrong through their interactions with adults; they use that information to guide their peer interactions (see Chapter 3). Toddlers are just beginning to use words, and they respond to some labels and commands. But words alone will not control their behavior until they internalize the language and construct concepts of right and wrong. These concepts are constantly being revised and expanded as the toddlers try to understand adults' reaction to that behavior. At this age, toddlers are still learning to separate themselves from their actions enough to understand the idea, "I like you, but I do not like what you are doing." Therefore, caregivers need to find ways to help toddlers discriminate between right and wrong while still accepting each child as a worthy person no matter how he or she behaves.

Use Positive Guidance Strategies

Toddlers may also express negativism by saying "No!" Their pursuit of independence may result in doing the opposite of what was requested or carrying out their own ideas (not the adult's). Rephrase command statements by providing choices or by refocusing attention to something of interest to the toddler. For example, you might rephrase "Put the doll away" to "Mary Jane, do you want to put the doll in the bed or on the blanket?" Allowing the child to choose between two positive and equally desirable outcomes helps the child learn to make decisions as well as to have more control over his or her environment (Swim & Marion, 2006).

Yet, don't depend on words alone; use physical touch or intervention when necessary. For example, prevent a harmful behavior before it occurs by holding back a child's threatening arm before he has a chance to hit. Lead a child by the hand back to the table to clean up after a snack. In general, providing adequate supervision should allow you to prevent many situations that might have resulted in a child being "in trouble." In addition, consistently using the three *As* of caregiving—Attention, Approval, and Attunement—when the child has behaved correctly will help the child know what is right. If you find yourself saying "I knew that was going to happen,"…next time, don't predict it, *prevent* it (Marion, 2014).

READING CHECKPOINT

Before moving on with your reading, make sure that you can answer the following question about the material discussed so far.

1. List four fears a toddler who is between 12 and 24 months of age might have. Explain how you would respond to these fears.

12-2e Social Development

Toddlers see the world from their own point of view or perspective. As they develop the concept of object permanence, they begin to differentiate *self* from other objects and people. They start to use words that identify them as individual people, such as *I, mine,* and *me*. This major development provides the basis for lifelong expansion of their concept of self and their interactions with others and provides the child with one of his or her earliest experiences with self-image. Caregiver acceptance is extremely important at any stage of development. This acceptance is internalized and becomes part of the child's self.

Yet, at the same time they are struggling with a sense of self, they have to negotiate living and learning as part of a group—me to we. In other words, young toddlers are expanding their relationships with others. This requires a beginning recognition of other people's feelings, and they are working slowly at understanding another person's intentions. Some have argued that infants and toddlers cannot engage in prosocial behaviors because they do not have the capacity to intentionally decide to positively impact others. McMullen, Addleman, Fulford, Moore, Mooney, Sisk et al.'s (2009) research provides clear evidence that infants and toddlers engage in positive social interactions with one another—sharing, caring, rule following, and cooperation. Thus, they challenge us to redefine **prosocial behaviors** as communications and behaviors on the part of a baby that help create a positive emotional climate in the group and that involve reaching out—positive, discernable, outward social expression on the part of one baby toward one or more other individuals, whether infant or adult (p. 21).

prosocial behavior
Spontaneous communications and behaviors on the part of an infant or toddler that benefit others.

This definition clearly supports viewing infants and toddlers as socially capable of building strong bonds with each other (see Photo 12–4). Infants and toddlers demonstrate distinct preferences for friends (Riley, San Juan, Klinkner, & Ramminger, 2008) and exhibit this by greeting each other in special ways (e.g., hugs) and by being sad or asking for the friend who isn't present. Thus, they behave differently with friends than with peers or classmates.

Another group of researchers (Kärtner, Keller, & Chaudhary, 2010) wanted to know if prosocial behaviors could be predicted best by

Spotlight on Research

PEER INTERACTIONS OF YOUNG TODDLERS

Many researchers are interested in how young children acquire complex social skills over the course of their first few years of life, examining this development from a wide variety of perspectives. For example, Deynoot-Schaub and Riksen-Walraven conducted a research study where 70 toddlers were observed with their peers during 90-minute free play situations at their child care center. They found that the 15- and 23-month-old children were significantly more likely to have contact with a child care provider than with their peers (Deynoot-Schaub & Riksen-Walraven, 2006a) and that the rate of negative interactions with their caregivers, but not positive, decreased from 15 to 23 months of age (Deynoot-Schaub & Riksen-Walraven, 2006b). In addition, those interactions with caregivers were predominantly positive, whereas interactions with peers were balanced across positive and negative interactions (Deynoot-Schaub & Riksen-Walraven, 2006a, 2006b).

When examining the factors that might relate to peer-initiated peer contacts, these researchers discovered that more peer-initiated peer contacts occurred in classrooms with higher child-caregiver ratios (Deynoot-Schaub & Riksen-Walraven, 2006a). According to Wittmer (2012), when toddlers have warm, caring relationships with their teachers, they show higher levels of social competence. In addition, children directed more negative initiative toward peers in environments that were rated lower on the learning activities and social interactions subscales of the Infant Toddler Environmental Rating Scale (Deynoot-Schaub & Riksen-Walraven, 2006a). When examining the longitudinal data, the researchers also found that ratings of aggressive/disruptive behaviors at 23 months were predicted by higher rates of negative initiative toward peers at 15 months (Deynoot-Schaub & Riksen-Walraven, 2006b). In other words, when more children are present in a lower-quality classroom environment, children initiate negative interactions with peers more often, and the earlier negative behaviors are predictive of later aggressive behavior with peers. These authors concluded that "the quality of childcare appears to affect children's contact with peers during childcare at a very early age. Early peer contacts can thus contribute to children's well-being

and socio-emotional adjustment or maladjustment" (Deynoot-Schaub & Riksen-Walraven, 2006a, p. 725).

The research examined earlier evaluated children's interactions from a dyadic perspective. In other words, they carefully examined the interactions between two people: toddler and teacher or toddler and peer. Can toddlers successfully interact within a small group of three people? Ishikawa and Hay (2006) examined social behaviors when three toddlers, unknown to each other, interacted in a laboratory observation room. Of the 715 episodes identified, 193 (27 percent) were found to be triadic. This research demonstrated that toddlers can actively and successfully engage in triadic interactions of two- and three-move sequences (Ishikawa & Hay, 2006). Contrary to research with adults, toddlers were more likely to engage in triadic interactions when there was no conflict present. This research demonstrates that toddlers are able to engage in complex social interactions with peers. Further research which uncovers factors that explain changes in triadic interactions could be helpful in understanding the importance of early peer relations for children's later social development (Ishikawa & Hay, 2006).

This text has clearly argued for children to be cared for in family groupings (see Chapter 1) as it most closely mimics how relationships naturally form in many families. But, what does the research say about such arrangements on peer relationships? McGaha, Cummings, Lippard, and Dallas (2011) discovered that toddlers demonstrated a strong sense of empathy and caring for infants (helping to soothe a crying infant or bringing a toy to an infant). Pairs of toddlers and infants seemed to create mutually desirable relationships as particular children would seek each other out for play or assistance. However, the most important aspect in this research was that the caring behaviors that were started in toddler-infant dyads were extended to age-mates. After interacting with infants, the toddlers were more caring and gentle in their interactions with each other (McGaha et al., 2011). Other research has found that toddlers are more likely to respond to the cries of another toddler if the peer was familiar (i.e., the toddlers know each other) and if the peer tended to not cry frequently (Mayuko, Kenji, Tadahiro, Toshihiko, & Tetsuhiro, 2012).

(1) measures of self-concept and self-other differentiation, or (2) measures of mothers' relational socialization goals (SGs) concerning interpersonal responsiveness (obedience, learning to help others). For children growing up in Berlin, early self-concept was correlated with toddlers' engaging in prosocial behaviors. In contrast, children with mothers who placed emphasis on obedience had children who were more prosocial (regardless of where they lived, Berlin or Delhi). The way toddlers are socialized to think about others impacts how they interact with another during a time of emotional distress.

Not all interactions with peers are positive, though. Hay, Castle, and Davies (2000) discovered that when toddlers (age 18 to 30 months) attributed a hostile intent to familiar peers during interactions, they were more likely to use personal force. In other words, if a peer pointed toward or reached for an object that the toddler was using, she was likely to protest, withdraw the object, or physically harm the peer. This pattern of outcomes is particularly noteworthy because it suggests that some toddlers may be prone to attributing hostile intent, which may interfere with their ability to form positive relationships with new acquaintances, and that "social misunderstandings and processes of peer rejection might begin even before a child enters formal group care" (p. 465).

Caregivers should help the toddlers interpret the emotions and behaviors of their peers by providing descriptive language. To illustrate, if a toddler reaches for the toy of another, the teacher should describe what he sees and provide an alternative perspective and possible strategies. "Burke, you are watching Libby smash the play dough with the rolling pin. Do you want to roll? Here is another rolling pin for you." You should then involve Libby in the conversation to facilitate her interpretation of Burke's reaching behaviors by saying, "Burke likes the way you are flattening the dough. He was watching you work. He wants to use the rolling pin also. I found one for him." Chapter 6 discussed the importance of communicating the intentions and actions of the people involved to assist very young children with beginning to learn perspective taking.

Young toddlers play with toys and materials and sing and talk during play. Toddlers engage in **solitary play** (playing alone), engage in **parallel play** (playing near but not with other children), and enjoy social interactions with friends as described previously. Toddlers should be the ones to decide what kind of interaction they want with others. However, research suggests that teachers can create a positive verbal environment that supports social development by using a variety of instructional strategies such as showing interest in a child's activity and asking open-ended questions (Meece & Soderman, 2010).

© Cengage Learning

PHOTO 12–4 Toddlers use familiar games such as peekaboo to initiate interactions with peers and teachers.

solitary play Playing alone; a child may periodically look at other children, but they do not yet interact.

parallel play Type of play in which older infants and toddlers engage with similar materials and share physical space but do not interact with one another.

Those strategies are key because they provide entry points into the child's thinking and play themes—allowing an opportunity for you or another child to join the ongoing play in a way that is welcoming to the child and not disruptive to the flow of the play. It is important to remember, however, that toddlers are still working on showing ownership and are not yet ready to share. Provide multiple supplies and equipment so that, if desired, they can engage alongside each other in parallel play.

See Table 12–6 Suggestions for Implementing Curriculum—Social Development for additional ideas to support social development.

TABLE 12–6 Suggestions for Implementing Curriculum—Social Development

CHILD BEHAVIOR	EXAMPLES OF CAREGIVER STRATEGIES
Self	
Is egocentric: understands only his or her own viewpoint	Help toddler to feel sorry for hurting someone else by using emotional talk.
Working on perspective taking, sees things from own point of view	Recognize that child thinks others think and feel the same way he or she does. Help child identify own ideas and feelings. Explain how another child might see the same situation.
Identifies materials as belonging to self	Recognize and allow ownership of toys.
Uses *I*, mine, *me*, *you*	Verbally respond to child's use of pronouns, reinforcing distinction child makes between self and others.
Relations with Others	
Seeks presence of family members or caregiver	Allow toddler to follow you around. Tell child when you are going out of sight.
Initiates and plays games	Play games with toddler. Respond and play child's games.
Occasionally shares	Provide enough materials and equipment so sharing can be encouraged but not required.
May be shy with some people	Do not force toddler to interact with all people. Allow child to keep his or her distance and watch.
Engages in parallel play	Provide materials and space so toddlers can play with own materials but near each other.
Begins to be aware of others' feelings	Help child identify and verbalize the feelings he has that appear in his behavior, for example, "Allen is crying; he is sad."
Expands social relationships	Encourage child to interact with others. Be present and provide your support when child encounters a new child or adult.
Looks to others for help	Consistently provide assistance when needed. Praise child for seeking help with something child would not be able to do for self, for example, putting on shoe and then seeking help for tying laces instead of fussing and crying.
Wants to help, assist with tasks, clean up	Encourage the child to help put toys away, clean up, and so on. Work along with child. Child can be a very good helper if he or she sees how you do it.
May do opposite of what is requested	Carefully word your requests, providing choices whenever possible. Negativism often comes out in a frequent "no" when given commands ("Do this now.")
Has difficulty sharing	Provide enough toys and materials so child does not have to share. Suggest allowing another child to play with toy when child finishes. Provide alternative toys to the child who must wait for a desired toy.
Engages in parallel play	Provide toys, materials, and space for children to play near each other. Talk to each of them. Allow them to choose if they want to trade toys or do something else.

© Cengage Learning

Before moving on with your reading, make sure that you can answer the following question about the material discussed so far.

1. Describe two situations in which a toddler interacts with others. Describe two situations in which a toddler plays alone. What is the adult role in each situation and why?

READING CHECKPOINT

Summary

12-1 Select materials appropriate to the development of young toddlers.

Early childhood educators must select materials that support development, challenge development, and are safe. In addition, the materials should be open-ended so that they can be used in multiple ways during parallel play. As young toddlers become more interested in playing beside each other, insure that you have multiple, identical materials to minimize the need for sharing.

12-2 Identify strategies appropriate to young toddlers (12 to 24 months of age) that are responsive to individual developmental levels.

Between the age of 12 and 24 months, toddlers spend most of their waking moments exploring their environment. They investigate objects with their hands, mouth, eyes, and ears. They are eager to discover how many objects fit into a given space as they constantly fill and spill containers. Responsive caregivers plan the learning environment carefully to encourage such repetitive, explorative practices. In addition, toddlers are becoming more interested in interacting with adults and peers. They seek out people to "talk" with, show objects, and demonstrate affection. Adults play an important role in helping toddlers gain control of their emotions and interact positively with peers.

CASE STUDY   ## Lennie Bites

Lennie, whom you met earlier in the chapter, continues to struggle with expressing his desires appropriately. He has learned that biting can be very effective for getting what he wants. Louise and her colleagues are very frustrated with Lennie's biting behavior as well as his frequent tantrums. Louise has recorded every biting and tantrum event over the past two weeks. During that time period, Lennie bit four times; once hard enough to break the skin on one child's body. He had five tantrums the first week under observation and four

the second. Louise is concerned that some children are beginning to avoid him, some have verbally refused to play with him, and one child who has been bitten more than once becomes visibly upset when Lennie is near him. As Lennie's primary caregiver, Louise decided to invite Lennie's parents and the center's director to a conference to discuss her observation, to find out how he behaves at home, and to discuss possible ways to address these behaviors.

On the day of the meeting, Lennie's father was unable to attend the meeting due to a medical emergency with his own father. Louise opened the conversation by expressing her concern for Lennie's grandfather and then by sharing some positive anecdotes about Lennie and his development. She then asked Lennie's mother about the types of behaviors they were seeing at home. Lennie's mother was very defensive and provided few details. When asked directly about biting behaviors, she spoke loudly saying, "No matter how many times we spank him, we can't get him to stop biting his older sister. It worked with his hitting." When probed, she stated, "We solved his hitting by spanking him each time. He doesn't hit us anymore."

Louise asked Lennie's mother about other strategies they use at home that she might be able to use at school, explaining that ethically and legally she would not hit a child because it might cause harm. Lennie's mother was unable to come up with any other strategies. Louise changed the subject slightly to ask about potential causes of his biting and tantrums. His mother was unclear what the potential causes of his biting and angry outbursts might be. At home, Lennie bites only his older sister but it seems to happen in a wide variety of situations.

Louise and Lennie's mother agreed they needed more data on the potential triggers or causes of his biting and tantrums. They agreed to carefully observe him and then set a follow-up meeting for the next week.

They collected the following data:

- Bit two children at school who took his toys
- Three tantrums at school when told it was time to stop playing and clean up
- Two tantrums at school when stopped from riding trike in the grass
- Two tantrums at home when sister wouldn't let him play with her toys

- Three tantrums at home when he didn't want to go to bed
- Bit sister two times when she took a toy of hers away from him

The data showed some clear patterns of behaviors for Lennie. It appeared to Louise and his mother that he doesn't deal well with frustration or not being able to carry out his personal goals or ideas. They created a plan that involved using the following tools: labeling and expressing feelings, providing a toy for self-soothing, giving warnings before a change in behavior was expected, and setting clear, positive limits. The plan also involved talking weekly about how the strategies were working at home and at school.

After a month of implementing the plan, Lennie's behavior had improved significantly at school but not at home. Louise began to model, whenever she could, some of these techniques for his parents. She also invited them to spend more time in the classroom. They slowly improved in their use of the strategies and reported that the biting and tantrums had decreased at home.

1. How did you react emotionally to Lennie's behaviors at the start of the case (beginning of this chapter)? How would you deal with and express these feelings?
2. How did Louise's behavior during the first conference impact the outcomes of that meeting? What do you think made a positive difference?
3. Do you think it was a good idea for Louise to suggest using four new strategies at one time? Why or why not?
4. Neither Louise nor the parents described Lennie's language skills. What might be the relationship between language development and acts of frustration/anger that Lennie displayed?

Lesson Plan

Title: *Playing Side-by-Side*

Child Observation:

Asmara and Gesang are best friends. They have been coming to your program since they were infants. Now, at 20 months, they express strong emotions for each other. For example, yesterday, Gesang was later than normal to arrive. Asmara asked two times, "Where Gesang?" You reassured her that he should be on his way. When he arrived, she broke into a smile and ran to greet him with a hug. Gesang's dad apologized to her for being late. "We overslept because Gesang had a bad dream last night. He missed you also," he said.

Child's Developmental Goal:

To continue developing prosocial skills

To engage in parallel play

Materials: Wooden unit blocks and people figurines

Preparation: Place figurines in the basket and put it on the block shelf. Before the children arrive, set out a few blocks and stand a few figurines around the blocks. This should draw their attention to the new materials and spark their interest in exploring them.

Learning Environment:

1. When one or both children notice the new materials, encourage them to look more closely. To illustrate, you could say:

   "What are those people for? How could you use them? Go on over and touch them."

2. Watch as the children explore the materials. Take pictures and record in your notes how each child explores and begins to use the figurines.

3. Support parallel play by letting them use the materials individually.

⌄ **Professional Resource Download**

4. Encourage them to talk to you while working with the materials. Use open-ended prompts to promote conversations such as:

   a. I wonder what Gesang's person is doing on top of that tower.

   b. Asmara, you set the persons down on the block. Are you pretending the block is a car? (listen to answer) Oh, where are they going in the car?

5. Acknowledge prosocial behavior, if it occurs. You can do that by verbally describing what you observed (e.g., "Asmara, you put that figurine beside Gesang's block. He is using it now. You shared the figurine with him.")

Guidance Consideration:

Because Asmara and Gesang are close friends, their emotions can be strong both positively and negatively. Watch closely for signs of irritation or annoyance when using the new figurines. If negative emotions arise, be prepared to engage in emotional talk, give choices, or redirect them to other figurines.

Variations:

Add cars or animals to the area to support role playing.

Additional Resources

Armstrong, L. J. (2011). *Family child care homes: Creative spaces for children to learn.* St. Paul, MN: Redleaf Press.

Honig, A. S. (2009). *Little kids, big worries: Stress-busting tips for early childhood classrooms.* Baltimore, MD: Brookes.

Kersey, K. C., & Masterson, M. L. (2013). *101 Principles for positive guidance with young children: Creating responsive teachers.* Washington, DC: National Association for the Education of Young Children.

Meier, D. (2009). *Here's the story: Using narrative to promote young children's language and literacy learning.* New York: Teachers College Press.

Wein, C. A. (2014). *The power of emergent curriculum: Stories from early childhood settings.* Washington, DC: National Association for the Education of Young Children.

Vecchi, V. (2010). *Art and creativity in Reggio Emilia: Exploring the role and potential of ateliers in early childhood education.* Contesting Early Childhood series. New York: Routledge.

13

CHAPTER

Teaching Children Twenty-Four to Thirty-Six Months

Learning Objectives

After reading this chapter, you should be able to:

13-1 Select materials appropriate to the development of older toddlers.

13-2 Devise strategies appropriate to older toddlers (24 to 36 months of age) that are responsive to individual developmental levels.

Standards Addressed in This Chapter

naeyc **NAEYC Standards for Early Childhood Professional Preparation**

1 Promoting Child Development and Learning

4 Using Developmentally Effective Approaches to Connect with Children and Families

DAP **Developmentally Appropriate Practice Guidelines**

2 Teaching to Enhance Development and Learning

3 Planning Curriculum to Achieve Important Goals

In addition, the NAEYC standards for developmentally appropriate practice are divided into six areas particularly important to infant/toddler care. The following area is addressed in this chapter: *exploration and play.*

© 2017 Cengage Learning

318

CASE STUDY   Ming Learns English

Twenty-six-month-old Ming picks up a fire truck and walks up on the porch with it. She pushes it around on the floor, and then picks it up and takes it out into the yard. Ms. Tao asks her what she has. Ming responds, "A truck," and smiles. Ms. Tao asks what kind of truck. Ming says, "Red," and smiles. Ming picks up a ball and says, "Watch me throw it." She moves the fire truck and tells Ms. Tao, "Can't find ladder." Ms. Tao finds the ladder and starts to put it on the fire truck. Ming requests, "Me do it." Ming puts a toy firefighter in the truck and plays with it. She says to Ms. Tao, "See the truck," and then, "See if it goes?" As Ming plays with the fire truck, the ladder falls off again, and she says, "Oh, no," and looks at Ms. Tao. She takes the truck to Ms. Tao to fix the ladder, saying "It fall off" and pointing to the ladder. She watches Ms. Tao fix the ladder and plays with it again. Another child gets the fire truck and begins to play with it. Ming tells the child, "I want the truck." Bill gives the fire truck back to Ming, who says, "Thank you, Bill."

13-1 Materials

Children this age are active, eager learners. They practice newly acquired skills and develop new ones. They like large muscle activities (e.g., riding toys and playing chase) and are developing their fine muscles for more controlled manipulation of objects such as stringing beads or marking with crayons. They focus on the process rather than the producing of a product. They enjoy playing imaginatively and exploring their world. Their play incorporates their imagination, language, new ideas, behaviors they have observed, and understanding of themselves and others. They construct sentences to share their ideas. They listen to stories and enjoy participating in rhymes, fingerplays, music, and singing. Thus, adults must carefully select materials and equipment to further their development and learning.

13-1a Types of Materials

balance beam	puzzles
riding toys or cycles	climbing equipment
wagon	rocking boat
different types of blocks (wooden, foam, cardboard)	barrel to climb through
large trucks for hauling items	trucks, cars
jars with twist lids	dolls, people, animals
knobs	items to put together or pull apart
large beads and string	large pegs and boards
clay and utensils	markers, crayons, pens, chalk
construction material: wood, Styrofoam, glue	paint and variety of utensils
rhythm instruments	pictures to look at and talk about
puppets	music sources (iPod, CDs, etc.)
	dress-up clothes
	matching games

FIGURE 13–1 ▶ Examples of Homemade Materials

BALANCE BEAM

Put masking tape on the floor to indicate a line on which the child can walk. In the yard, partially bury a tree trunk so that several inches remain above ground. Place so that no branch stubs are on the top walking surface.

PEG BOARD

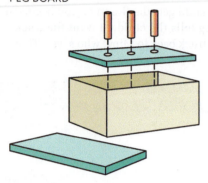

Cut a piece of heavy cardboard to fit in the bottom of a box (such as for shoes or gifts). Cut holes in the cardboard. Cut a ½-inch dowel rod into roughly 2-inch lengths. Paint if desired. Store cardboard and pegs in the box and use the lid.

MARACAS

Collect gourds in the fall. Allow to dry. The seeds will rattle when the gourd is shaken.

SOAP PAINT

Use one part soap flakes, one part water, and food coloring. Beat the mixture with a hand eggbeater. Skim off soap suds to paint on tabletop, shelf paper, or freezer paper.

PUZZLE

Cut out one uncluttered colored picture from a magazine. Gather two pieces of cardboard that are slightly larger than the picture.

a. Glue the picture to the center of one piece of cardboard.
b. Cover the picture and cardboard with clear adhesive. Outline three to five sections that are visually recognizable (head, legs, tail) with a pencil. Cut around the picture, being careful to cut cleanly through the cardboard.
c. Cut the remaining hole in the cardboard slightly larger.
d. Glue a backing onto the cardboard with a second piece of cardboard the same size. Fit the puzzle pieces into place. If necessary, trim so the pieces come out easily.

MATCHING GAME

Cut two 2-inch squares from each page of a wallpaper sample book. Make about six pairs, using different pages. Store the pieces in an envelope. To play, mix up the pieces and then select squares that match.

FIGURE 13–1 ▶ *(continued)*

DRAMATIC PLAY BOX

Gather props for a specific story or role. For example, put a stethoscope, white shirt, and small pad of paper in a shoebox for doctor props. In a larger box, put a child-size firefighter's hat, boots, and poncho. Gather the materials based on your observations of the children's play. Select items that will enhance and promote development.

BOOK: JOURNAL

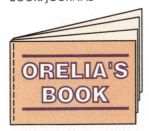

Sew or staple sheets of unlined paper together. Each morning, ask a child to identify one toy he or she wants to play with or an activity to do. Write a sentence identifying what the child chose. Allow the child to scribble and draw on the page. Read the sentence to the child. Label the journal with the child's name. To promote partnerships with families, send the journal home each Friday. Encourage the family members to add sentences and illustrations for the days the child is not at school.

WOODEN PEOPLE OR ANIMALS

Draw or cut out of a magazine pictures of people (infants, children, adults; firefighter, police officer, doctor) or animals or other objects (e.g., cars or houses).

Glue pictures on a piece of 1-inch-thick white pine board. With a jigsaw, cut around the outside of the picture on three sides, cutting the bottom straight across. Sand the edges smooth. Apply two coats of nontoxic sealer. The object will stand up by itself.

13-1b Activity Ideas

The following are examples of activities that help children construct knowledge, along with some of the items, concepts, and actions involved.

Exploration

Cooking

recipe chart	stir	see
oral language	beat	hear
measure	smell	taste
sift	feel	

Growing Plants

carrots	bean sprouts	observations
sweet potatoes	food	comparisons
beans	care	charting
lettuce	rate of growth	

Representations

Oral Language

conversation	poetry	singing and rhythms
information gathering	nursery rhymes	dramatic play
storytelling	fingerplays	

Objects

painting rocks, seeds, pine cones
creating prints with found objects or body parts such as feet, hands,
fingers

Pictures

magazines, photographs
art media: crayons, painting, tear and paste

Books

wordless picture books
naming books
books with a story line to read or tell in your own words

13-2 Caregiver Strategies to Enhance Development

Early childhood educators recognize the importance of ongoing curriculum planning. They plan for the next day or the next few days, rather than developing curricular experiences weeks or even months in advance. This approach is valued because curricular experiences must be based on current knowledge of what the child can do, what the child is interested in, and what challenges the child is ready for in each area of development.

13-2a Physical Development

Children of this age are increasing their stability in both fast and slow movements, running, and walking. They can walk backward. They run quickly and usually maintain their balance (Photo 13–1). Thus, older toddlers are more flexible and stable in their movements than before (Adolph, Vereijken, & Shrout, 2003). They can alternate feet going upstairs. While riding toys still poses developmental challenges at the beginning of the year, by the end, they most likely have mastered a tricycle. They jump up and down, they jump off objects, and they jump forward. They spend hours using climbing and jumping equipment. Kicking and throwing are increasingly accurate and enjoyable for the children. It is important to remember that there may be cultural differences in the acquisition of motor skills. African and African American children have been observed to be advanced in motor competence, and children from some Asian cultures are slower to acquire some motor skills; these variations are probably the result of the complex

© Cengage Learning

PHOTO 13–1 The young child is becoming more coordinated and can balance on smaller surfaces.

interplay between "parenting values and practices, family life, and genetic contributions from ancestors" (Trawick-Smith, 2010, p. 108).

Older toddlers continue to develop their fine motor skills as well. Their eye-hand coordination is more accurate, so they can reach, grasp, and throw objects with accuracy, but they still have difficulty using each finger independently. They can twist and turn to dress and undress, and they can use their small muscles to hold clothes and begin buttoning, snapping, and zippering. They are able to fit objects together and like to put them together and pull them apart. Toddlers may use either their right or left hand, but most do not firmly establish handedness until between 3 and 4 years of age (Marotz & Allen, 2013).

Toddlers use these newly acquired motor skills to demonstrate their independence and engage in daily routines (see Table 13–1). They use a spoon when eating and are learning to use a fork. Some children this age have all 20 baby teeth and should be taught how to brush their own teeth. At this age, children can establish sleep routines that they can do themselves in the child care setting. Before their nap, they can go to the bathroom and wash their hands. They can sit on their cots, take their own shoes off, and put their shoes under the cot. They can lie down with their heads near the top of the cot. When they awaken, they can go to the bathroom and return to put on their shoes (needing assistance with tying, of course). If others are still sleeping, they can choose a quiet activity, such as looking at books or listening to a story or music with earphones.

Many children this age also exhibit signs of being interested in toilet learning, and most children are fully engaged in the process by 36 months of age. When you see such behaviors, share your observations with family

TABLE 13–1 ▶ Suggestions for Implementing Curriculum—Physical Development

CHILD BEHAVIOR	MATERIALS	EXAMPLES OF CAREGIVER STRATEGIES
Locomotion		
Bends at waist	objects to drop and pick up: pail and plastic rings	Encourage child's interest in the materials. Play game with child and then have child play independently or with another child.
Climbs	low objects: steps up to slide, tires	Select safe materials and safe height.
Jumps	two- to three-step equipment	Keep floor or ground space clear where children jump. Block off higher levels so jump is safe distance for muscles and balance.
Stands on one foot	song for lifting one foot	Make up rhyme or song about standing on one foot. Child will stand on one foot for only a few seconds. Provide feedback and encourage child to repeat or try again.
Dances to music	music, scarves or fabric	Play favorite music and provide scarves or fabric for moving rhythmically.
Throws	target: large paper sack or plastic basin; objects: Nerf ball, yarn ball	Provide space for child to throw objects at target. Decorate target so child is aiming at hoop or door.
Fine Motor Manipulation		
Turns pages	books	Encourage child to turn pages of book when you are reading together.
Dresses and undresses self with assistance		Allow time for child to manipulate clothes. Demonstrate how to hold button and buttonholes, zipper and cloth, and so on.
Twists	jars and cans with lids; large plastic or metal nuts and bolts	Provide objects that twist on and off easily.

members to determine how to approach this developmental skill. As discussed in Chapter 9, families vary greatly in their beliefs regarding when and how to support children's toilet learning, so be prepared to have ongoing conversations throughout this process. When the decision has been made to support toilet learning, encourage family members to dress the toddler in clothes she can remove quickly and easily. She will need easy access to the bathroom as well as occasional questions and reminders to go to the bathroom.

13-2b Cognitive Development

Many children between 24 and 30 months are entering Piaget's **preoperational stage** of cognitive development. The first substage of the preoperational stage is **preconceptual**, which occurs from about 2 to 4 years of age. These children can mentally sort some objects and actions. The mental symbols are partly detached from experience. Early nonverbal classifications are called *graphic collections*, in which children can focus on figurative properties. These children form some verbal preconcepts, but the meaning of words may fluctuate from one time to another. Verbal reasoning is from the particular to the particular.

Preconceptual children are constructing and organizing knowledge about a wide range of areas in their world. They are beginning to classify objects and to develop very limited ideas of quantity, number, space, and time. Due to their preference for routines and sameness, their sense of time is based more on what happens after an event rather than on an understanding of *later* or minutes of time passage.

The development of the symbolic function occurs in the preconceptual stage. It involves the following mental representations, presented here in increasing order of complexity, and some that were evident during the sensorimotor period. In the child's search for hidden objects, the object remains permanent (does not cease to exist) in the child's thinking even when the child cannot see it. These experiences form the basis for more specific representational thinking. In deferred imitation, the child imitates another person's behavior even when that person is no longer present. A child engaged in symbolic play may give the caregiver a stone and tell the caregiver to "eat this apple"; the stone represents the real object. The child's *drawings* may be scribbles, experiments with the media, or begin to be graphic representations; a child may point to a mark he or she has made on a piece of paper and say his or her own name. **Mental images** are pictures in the mind with which children can carry out action sequences internally. Language is used easily to represent objects or behaviors. As children develop language, they internalize words, meanings, mental images, and thoughts; from a Vygotskian perspective, language plays a critical role in cognitive development. This internalization of thoughts permits toddlers to use private speech to guide and regulate their behaviors (see Chapter 2).

Children at this age are active explorers, seeking information through manipulating and observing their world. As problem solvers, they now move beyond trial and error to mental manipulation of ideas and physical manipulation of objects to construct their reasoning. They are seeking to discover what makes things

preoperational stage Piaget's second stage of cognitive development, during which toddlers and preschoolers reason based on perception.

preconceptual The first substage of Piaget's preoperational stage of cognitive development, in which children can mentally sort some objects and actions.

mental images Pictures in the mind with which children can carry out action sequences internally.

© Cengage Learning

PHOTO 13–2 Blocks, beads, and other manipulatives support the development of mathematical concepts such as one-to-one correspondence and sorting.

Spotlight on Practice

VOICES FROM THE FIELD

I am a preservice teacher at a local university as well as an assistant teacher in a toddler room. I have been learning about language and cognitive development of toddlers and decided to try out a learning experience with the children. I planned a game with two parts. First, I would name a body part and have the children point to that part of their body. If they were successful, I would then point to a body part and see if they could name it. The second part of the game should be more challenging, but it would help me authentically assess their language and concept development.

When invited to play a game with me, three different children told me "no" and went to play elsewhere. Finally, Armani came over to me and sat on my lap. I began the game. She easily pointed to all of the body parts that I named. She was able to label her belly and head when I pointed, but not her nose, before getting bored and moving on to another area. I then noticed Sam playing with Mr. Potato Head. I went over and picked up different body parts, asked "What is this?" while holding up the arm. Sam said "Hand." Then, I asked, "Do you have one of these too?" He said "No." Then, I said "Well, why not?" Sam said, "Because it does not match." I said, "Do you have fingers?" He said "Yes" and showed me where they were. Then I said, "Does the Potato Head arm have fingers?" Sam said "Yes." I looked at him and said, "Well what is this?" and pointed at the hand. Sam replied, "A hand." I asked, "Do you have a hand?" He smiled and said "Yes." He looked at me and said, "They are the same."

Although my plan did not go exactly as planned, I was able to have positive interactions with two different children. I learned that teachers should find ways to deliver their plans in ways that match what the toddlers want to accomplish. I also learned that Armani knew the labels of belly and head while Sam knew the label of hand. Sam independently compared his body parts to those on a toy.

---

tick, what objects are made of, and how actions happen. As discussed previously, they observe, question, manipulate, classify, and measure to learn about their world (Photo 13–2). According to Piaget, children construct or learn three different types of knowledge.

Children construct physical knowledge by moving objects and observing changes in objects. They observe the effects of their pulling, pushing, rolling, kicking, jumping, blowing, sucking, throwing, swinging, twirling, balancing, and dropping objects. Knowledge about physical events requires inferences drawn from observations. The source of physical knowledge is partly in the object, and the reaction depends on its properties (DeVries, 2000). Offer materials and activities that help children discover the physical characteristics of objects.

In the preconceptual stage, children may attempt to put objects in an order, such as placing a group of three buttons from biggest to smallest, but when more objects are provided, the children may not be able to determine the logic of ordering. Arranging objects in a series, or **seriation**, is guesswork for young children because they do not understand the relationships in a series of objects: an object that is simultaneously smaller than and larger than other objects is placed in the middle of the series. However, physical knowledge about the properties of objects develops through their continued interactions with materials.

seriation Ordering items in sequence based on criteria such as color, length, or size (e.g., small, medium, large).

The second type of knowledge children construct, logico-mathematical knowledge, is gained by discovering relationships among objects. Comparisons of quantity, number, space, and time are explorations in relating two or more objects or events in a new and abstract way. Children can seek relationships among any kinds of materials. Games and activities that use invented relationships help stimulate and reinforce their constructions.

For example, providing a group of objects to sort and classify might lead a child to notice color relationships.

Children learn the third type of knowledge, social-arbitrary knowledge, from other people through various forms of communication (DeVries, 2000). They learn the names of objects, meanings of words, and days of the week, for example, from others. They learn the classroom rules from their caregivers, who bear the major responsibility in the child care program for providing this type of information and helping the child construct social-arbitrary knowledge.

Because toddlers still reason prelogically, adults and children construct experiences differently. Even if both a child and an adult were present during the same experience, each would learn and experience something different. Jane Healy, in her book *Your Child's Growing Mind* (2004), gives several ways to help "bridge the schema" gaps (p. 57), or fill in missing information.

1. As you solve problems together, talk through your own questions. "I wonder how I should start?" "Could I put them together?" "Is it working?" "What's going to happen?" "How did I do this?"

2. Ask the child similar questions. Phrase them simply, and give the child plenty of time to think and answer.

3. Let the child repeat each solution several times to understand it.

4. Encourage understanding. Ask "Why do you think that happened?" "Why did (or didn't) that work?"

Interacting in this manner not only bridges informational gaps but also, by its very nature, engages toddlers emotionally and intellectually. Older toddlers need curriculum, environments, and interactions that engage them emotionally and intellectually because successfully completing a challenge provides valuable information about their capabilities. Carefully planning learning experiences that give value to the tools of the learning disciplines (e.g., mathematics, social studies) gives curriculum intellectual integrity (Freeman & Swim, 2009). Toddlers should be given opportunities to investigate scientific topics they have questions about (e.g., living creatures, microorganisms, gravity; see, e.g., Youngquist, 2004) and use scientific tools/ processes such as observing, recording, and testing hypotheses. They should have daily experiences with mathematical concepts such as problem solving, measurement, and geometry. These experiences can be completed separately or integrated into learning experiences and projects (see Chapters 9 and 14).

A note of caution should be introduced here. In no case should toddlers be forced or required to engage in these activities. These learning experiences should be among the many choices in the environment. Moreover, designing curriculum in this manner ensures that the content is contextualized at all times.

See Table 13–2 Suggestions for Implementing Curriculum—Cognitive Development for additional ways to support cognitive development.

13-2c Language Development

Children of this age are rapidly increasing their vocabulary. Their vocabulary may include as many as 200 to 300 words. Their daily experiences provide opportunities for them to construct meanings of new objects and to extend previously learned concepts. The labeling process is now part of

TABLE 13–2 ▶ Suggestions for Implementing Curriculum—Cognitive Development

CHILD BEHAVIOR	EXAMPLES OF CAREGIVER STRATEGIES
Piaget's Preoperational Stage, Preconceptual Substage	
NONVERBAL CLASSIFICATION	
Makes graphic collections	Allow child to create own classifications. Encourage child to use art media to represent objects, ideas, and so on. Listen to child's explanation of his or her own classification system.
VERBAL PRECONCEPTS	
Uses words differently at different times	Listen and ask for clarification of words used differently. Ask for clarification of meaning if necessary.
Uses words with private meanings	Listen to child's words in context; reword or question to find meaning.
Begins to label classes of objects	Repeat and identify class of object. Extend child's label to include other objects. Remember that child's meaning may not be as inclusive as yours, so interact to determine exactly what child meant.
Focuses on one attribute	Reinforce classifications. Child has not yet formed stable classes of objects.
VERBAL REASONING	
Reasons from particular to particular	Understand and accept child's classification of behaviors that seem alike. Ask for clarification if needed.
Reasons from effect to cause	Think backward from action to previous action to understand child's reasoning.
QUANTITY	
Understands *some, more, gone, big*	Use quantity words in context with objects, as part of daily experiences. Respond and expand on child's use.
NUMBER	
Understands *more*	Use objects and words to identify *more* in a comparison. Use daily situations, for example, "There are more rocks in this pail than in that pail."
SPACE	
Understands *up, down, behind, under, over*	Use spatial-position words with actions, for example, "I will lift you up," and to describe actions, for example, "Merrilee is behind the box."
TIME	
Understands *now, soon*	Label actions in terms of time, for example, "Let's wash your hands now."
Understands *before, after*	Use time words in daily experiences, for example, "We wash our hands before we eat," and "We go to the bathroom after naptime."

© Cengage Learning

children's construction of the identity of objects. During this time, older toddlers typically begin to include grammatical (e.g., functional or space) words when speaking (refer to Chapter 11 for a definition of "grammatical words"). As toddlers move from telegraphic speech to communicating complete ideas through sentences, sentence length increases as they begin to use subject-verb-object sentences and include grammatical or function words, such as *on, in, a,* and *the.* As such, they speak more complete sentences and are able to express several ideas in a sequence of sentences.

Toddlers do not merely reproduce sentences from memory; they *construct* them given their understanding of **syntax** or the underlying rules for how to produce and comprehend sentences in their language (McGee & Richgels, 2012). Thus, the child has to think and select words that express his or her ideas in ways others can understand. This may not be smooth, as the toddler has to plan and coordinate all the parts (words) of the sentences.

syntax How words combine into understandable phrases and sentences.

Spotlight on Research

ADULT DEPRESSION AND INFANT COGNITIVE DEVELOPMENT

This text has discussed in previous chapters the importance of quality infant-parent interactions. When adults are attuned to infants, the infants have better social-emotional developmental outcomes. Mothers who are depressed tend to have more difficulty in creating and maintaining positive, synchronous interactions (see Wanless, Rosenkoetter, & McClelland, 2008, for a review). However, do such interactions impact other areas of development?

Koutra, Chatzi, Bagkeris, Vassilaki, Bitsios, and Kogevinas (2013) found that maternal postpartum depressive symptoms were associated with a decrease in cognitive development at 18 months of age; this result was independent of reports of depression during the pregnancy. In contrast, Kaplan, Danko, Everhart, Diaz, Asherin, Vogeli, et al. (2014) discovered that mothers who scored higher on maternal depression were more likely to have a toddler with lower levels of expressive communication skills. Depression was not associated with measures of cognitive skills. The authors concluded that their results suggest that problems with expressive communication precede, and may partially account for, apparent deficits in general cognitive development (Kaplan et al., 2014). In a longitudinal study, Feldman and Eidelman (2009) studied 126 infant-mother pairs from birth through age 5. All of these infants had a healthy low-risk, yet premature birth. Mothers were asked to report their depressive symptoms prior to being discharged from the hospital. Mother-infant interactions were captured on videotape at 6, 12, and 24 months of age. Those tapes were analyzed for maternal sensitivity (e.g., positive affect, acknowledgment of child communication) and child social engagement (e.g., social initiation, gaze, alertness). Cognitive development was measured by the Bayley Scales of Infant Development at 6, 12, and 24 months of age and the Wechsler Preschool and Primary Scale of Intelligence at 5 years of age. The results of the analyses showed that maternal depression impacted the children's cognitive development. More specifically, those mothers reporting more symptoms of depression had children who showed slower rates of cognitive growth from infancy through 5 years of age. In contrast, another longitudinal study examining the relationship between maternal depression and cognitive outcomes found a weak relationship, even though maternal depression was negatively related to parenting behaviors (Kiernan & Huerta, 2008).

Wanless et al. (2008), in their review of literature, examined current studies on *paternal* depression and discovered that the research results are somewhat mixed. For example, some studies demonstrated that fathers who were depressed spent less time in parenting, including playful and cognitively stimulating activities, while others found no difference in parental behaviors. Research by Roggman, Boyce, Cook, and Jones(2004; see Spotlight on Research box in Chapter 3) uncovered the importance of participating in Early Head Start programs on fathers' ability to create complex play situations with their toddlers. Thus, it appears that paternal interaction is important to the cognitive outcomes of infants and toddlers, and adults who are depressed have more difficulty in being engaged with their young child.

Teachers should be supportive of all families and children in their care. Making available information on mental health resources to everyone on a regular basis reduces the need for families to seek assistance in finding the help they may need. In the United States, seeking mental health support is still viewed as a sign of weakness. Infant and toddler professionals should advocate for such behavior as a sign of strength and should create policies and practices for their own school/classroom from a strength-based perspective that emphasizes resilience and protective factors over symptomatic behaviors (Lamb-Parker, LeBuffe, Powell, & Halpern, 2008).

The more words used, the more difficult it is for the toddler to construct a sentence. While toddlers learn to use word order patterns common to their language during interactions with others who are more skilled, toddlers cannot tell you the basic rule or principle of word order they are using. These are abstract principles that will be uncovered during the school-age years.

Children also extend their construction of language to include two ways of forming new words. They begin to use the plural and the past tense forms of words (see Table 13–3). By now, children understand that there is more than one hand, eye, or foot. They listen to others talking and learn that the word changes when referring to more than one hand. They then construct their words to include plurals, for example, *hands*, *eyes*, and so forth. However, at this age, they apply the same plural rule to all words, making words such as *foots*. Obviously, they have never heard an adult use the word *foots*, so this highlights how children are using their understanding of language to actively constructing meaning. Applying the same rule to all words is called **overregularization**. Older toddlers are very gradually constructing concepts of time, and most of their new time words come during this period. The past is still an abstraction they are attempting to understand grammatically. Therefore, toddlers frequently overregularize past tense forms, constructing words like *goed* and *seed or* saying things like, "Jim bited me" and "I bringed these out." Some adults may be concerned when a child creates a word that violated the established pattern and will want to correct her. As discussed before, it is more effective for language development to repeat the child's statement substituting the correct form of the word. Early childhood educators should

overregularization Strategy of applying one standard grammatical rule to an irregular word, for example, "goed" for the past tense of "go."

TABLE 13–3 ▶ Suggestions for Implementing Curriculum—Language Development

CHILD BEHAVIOR	EXAMPLES OF CAREGIVER STRATEGIES
Increases Vocabulary	
Points to and labels objects, for example, "a foot," "my nose"	Be attuned to their intentions and elaborate: "Mary has a foot. This is a foot." Introduce new toys or objects for exploration and labeling. Describe objects using a single word, and then use in a sentence.
Combine labels, for example, "red car," "big book"	Extend to sentences how they are interacting with toys or objects: "Ray has the red car; Twila has the green car."
Uses action words	Identify and label a child's or another child's actions with a toy or object: "Urvi rolled the ball to Cassandra" (adult). "Stewart is eating."
Says "more" or "a lot"	Use word patterns that indicate repeating or additional, for example, at snack ask each child if he or she wants *more* apple.
Uses proper word order	Elaborate on child's phrase "Move truck" to "Yes, the truck moves."
Learns prosodic patterning	Use expression when talking. Accent the proper syllables. The child will imitate you.
Improves Syntax	
Uses subject-verb-object pattern	Engage in conversation with the child. Help the child expand his or her ideas.
May omit grammatical words	Repeat the child's words in a complete sentence.
Experiments with word order	Repeat the child's sentence, using proper word order.
Uses longer sentences, including grammatical words	Respond to the child's meaning. Comment on his or her ideas, or ask question to continue conversation.
Improves word forms	
Uses plurals	Use correct plural form. When the child says "foots," restate the word, for example, "See your feet."
Uses past tense	Use correct past tense. When the child says "He bited me," restate: "He bit you? Show me where he bit you."

© Cengage Learning

Family and Community Connections

You work in a child care program that is associated with the local elementary school. You are the lead teacher in one of the classrooms with toddlers from 18 to 36 months of age. The older toddlers are so much fun, but you are finding collaborating with families a challenge—they seem to be very focused on school readiness. In your past conversations, you have been left unsatisfied with how school readiness is being defined almost exclusively in terms of identifying colors, writing their name, and learning the ABCs. You decide to focus your documentation panels exclusively on school readiness for toddlers. The panels include

current research and classroom examples of how skills such as problem solving, vocabulary development, phonological awareness, self-control, and the development of friendships relate to current and later success. The families who have read the documentation panels have really opened up in conversations and seem to relish this more open definition of school readiness. In fact, they seem more relaxed about how the program is benefitting their child. Unfortunately, not all families have read the documentation panels. How can you engage them with the panels? Or, how can you devise alternative methods for providing this information to them?

advocate for children in this situation and explain that these "mistakes" demonstrate the child's growing capacity to apply challenging language rules as they distinguish between quantities, and present and past tense.

prosodic patterning
Communication strategy in which toddlers learn how to use the appropriate stress and intonation to express their specific ideas.

Children also have to learn **prosodic patterning** or how to use the appropriate stress and intonation to express their specific ideas. They learn emphasis and rhythm of word parts, words, and sentences along with the words themselves and syntax. For example, "*my* ball" means something different from "my *ball*."

The ability to produce or express language during the toddler years has been associated with larger vocabularies and better reading outcomes during the early elementary years (Rescorla, 2002; see also Pullen & Justice, 2003). Although the pathways are not completely understood, adult styles of interactions and literacy behaviors at home and at school are believed to play significant roles in literacy outcomes (Britto & Brooks-Gunn, 2001; Dodici, Draper, & Peterson, 2003; Murray & Yingling, 2000; Williams & Rask, 2003). Teachers must develop partnerships with families to support and enhance the language and literacy development of children. Although many strategies exist for helping parents read to children at home (Darling & Westberg, 2004), creating literacy bags that contain high-quality children's literature and a guidebook for parents with questions for discussion has been shown to increase both the quality and frequency of reading books at home for older children (Dever & Burts, 2002). Logically, if parents are helped early on to carve out time daily to read to their infants and toddlers, greater literacy outcomes might be gained (see, e.g., Raikes, Pan, Luze, Tamis-LeMonda, Brooks-Gunn, Constantine, et al., 2006).

phonological awareness The conscious attention to the sounds of spoken language.

To promote **phonological awareness** or the conscious attention to the sounds of spoken language (McGee & Richgels, 2012), early childhood educators should play language games with the children. Songs, chants, and nursery rhymes, which have been discussed many times throughout this book, assist with this awareness because their natural rhythms highlight and segment speech sounds. Help toddlers think about the words that make up songs, fingerplays, or nursery rhymes by clapping for each word when you say it; the next step is to segment syllables in individual words by clapping them (Vukelich, Christie, & Enz, 2012). When the toddlers are familiar with a song, chant, or nursery rhyme, repeat a verse, leave out the rhyming word, and ask the children to fill it in (Pinnell & Fountas, 2011). Phonological awareness is tied to literacy development, so that connection will be discussed more in Chapter 14.

READING CHECKPOINT

Before moving on with your reading, make sure that you can answer the following questions about the material discussed so far.

1. Explain why an early childhood educator should be concerned if a parent of a toddler in his or her care appears to be depressed. How might that impact the development of the whole child?
2. Imagine that a colleague questions why you read to the toddlers in your family child care every day. What would you say and why?
3. Compare how children learn physical knowledge, logico-mathematical knowledge, and social-arbitrary knowledge.

13-2d Emotional Development

Older toddlers continue to develop their feelings about self. Emotional development includes positive and negative self-image, competence, and acceptance. Children this age are becoming more independent while simultaneously recognizing their need for help. They attempt to please and show affection (Photo 13–3). At 24 months, they make fewer demands and are better able to express themselves. They can attend for longer and longer periods of time as they fully engage their minds and bodies in learning. However, by 30 months, these easier-going children can seem to suddenly become more demanding and more possessive about their things. They may become frustrated, say "no" to almost everything, and have temper tantrums. They may suddenly want help with things they previously could do and want to do things they are not yet able to do successfully. In quick succession, they may be aggressive, then shy, and then act younger than they actually are; they may be affectionate at one moment and want no affection the next. They sometimes struggle when provided too many choices at once and many demand sameness and consistency. In fact, meeting their need for sameness may well be the best way to handle 30-month-old children. *Routines* provide children this age with consistency and security. Here, the caregiver's skills of being well organized, consistent, and flexible may be challenged. Be sure to use plenty of the three *A*s for your own benefit, as well as that of the children. Furthermore, remind yourself and family members that toddlers do not

© Cengage Learning

PHOTO 13–3 Friends show affection for each other.

use their emotional expressions or reactions to manipulate others (see, e.g., Brophy-Herb, Horodynski, Dupuis, Bocknek, Schiffman, Onaga, et al., 2009); they are trying to find ways for coping with their ever-changing feelings.

Most adults who work with older toddlers wonder when and how children begin to be able to look at situations from another person's viewpoint. Some toddlers may seem to behave in an empathetic fashion occasionally or briefly. Such behavior is probably indicative of the sociocultural context they are being raised in (Kärtner, Keller, & Chaudhary, 2010) and reflects an emergent understanding of what someone else is feeling. An older toddler may, for example, look concerned if another child cries, may rush over to pat the unhappy one, may offer a cracker or toy, or may even burst into tears. Spinrad and Stifter (2006) found that when mothers were more responsive in their interactions with very young children, the toddlers displayed more concerned attention to a crying doll baby and to maternal distress. Logically, teachers who are responsive to the toddlers' emotional needs will assist them in learning to be empathetic and to display empathy with peers.

As they get closer to their third birthday, children let you know how they feel and then may move beyond their anger or happiness to express a wide variety of different feelings. They express their emotions and feelings strongly, but they are becoming more skilled at expressing their emotions in a socially acceptable manner. And, depending on their temperament, some children's emotional responses become calmer. They become less resistant and use words such as *yes* and *will* to replace the earlier *no* and *won't*. However, significant differences exist in how different cultures socialize children to express emotions. According to Day and Parlakian (2004), the following attributes of emotional expression tend to vary across cultures:

- Intensity of emotional expression
- Loudness or volume of speech
- Directness of questions
- Directness of eye contact
- Degree to which touching is involved
- Use of gestures
- Amount of personal space desired

Thus, teachers should be aware of and respect the differences that children bring with them to school. The goal is not to establish consistency among the children in the room but rather to provide cultural continuity from home to school (Day & Parlakian, 2004).

Within this context of cultural differences, toddlers, like older children, express negativism in several ways. Sometimes negative behavior is a way of asserting themselves and their independence. They may begin or continue to display physical aggression (Baillargeon, Zoccolillo, Keenan, Cote, Perusse, Wu, et al., 2007; Tremblay, Nagin, Seguin, Zoccolillo, Zelazo, Boivin, et al., 2004). Their widening world presents many new experiences. Older toddlers may use aggression in their attempts to assert some control over their world.

Because of the link between aggression and concurrent and future mental health issues, child development and early childhood experts are particularly concerned about aggression in toddlers (see, e.g., Collins,

Mascia, Kendall, Golden, Schock, & Parlakian, 2003). Differential patterns of stability and predictability have been found for boys and girls (see Baillargeon et al., 2007; Gill & Calkins, 2003; Hay, Castle, & Davies, 2000). Much research has been conducted to understand the causes of aggression and patterns of trajectories. Tremblay et al. (2004) found that the best predictors of high, stable physical aggression were maternal variables (e.g., history of antisocial behavior during mother's school years, early child-bearing, and coercive parenting behavior) and family variables (e.g., low income and family dysfunction). In contrast, Van Aken, Junger, Verhoeven, Van Aken, Deković, and Denissen (2007) found that self-reports of parenting behaviors were associated with boys' externalizing behaviors. Specifically, the more both parents used verbal punishments (i.e., negative comments and threats) and the less they created structure, the more toddlers displayed externalizing behaviors. In a cross-cultural study, parental problem-solving and parenting behaviors were studied for their impact on the display of aggressive behaviors by their firstborn toddlers (Feldman, Masalha, & Derdikman-Eiron, 2010). These researchers found, similar to Van Aken et al. (2007), that the use of ineffective parenting behaviors was related to child aggression in both Israeli and Palestinian families. In addition, for both groups, higher marital hostility and more co-parental undermining behaviors were associated with increased levels of child aggression. Cultural differences were found in what predicted lower levels of aggression in the toddlers; for Israelis, for example, family compromise and marital empathy predicted less aggressiveness, whereas for Palestinians, engaging in more resolution by consent predicted lower aggression. The authors concluded that understanding the cultural basis of conflict resolution within close relationships may expand understanding of the roots of aggression for young children (Van Aken et al., 2007).

This text has described some of the behavioral components of healthy emotional development in toddlerhood, a stage during which a child works on becoming an autonomous individual, capable of competently functioning in an environment appropriately geared to his or her needs and abilities. It should be clear that children who are given sufficient opportunities to explore, use their senses, be physically active, use expressive materials, and develop language skills may often—through the very nature of these activities—be destructive, messy, noisy, impudent, and defiant. These behaviors reflect directly the crisis they are experiencing in regard to their identity development: autonomy versus shame and doubt. During these times, early childhood educators must demonstrate respect for the toddler while providing extra helpings of the three *As* to meet the toddlers' developmental needs. Even when frustrated by the toddlers' inconsistent behaviors, teachers should continue to use positive guidance strategies (see Chapter 6) because successfully resolving this emotional crisis is vital for healthy emotional intelligence.

As toddlers develop cognitive skills that allow for symbolic play and mental images, they can more easily recall and imagine fearful events or situations. They express concerns with darkness, monsters, and specific animals or other things they might have read about in a book or watched on TV. Unfortunately, some children have experienced frightening behaviors firsthand. Some events such as being in a car accident where they or a family member was hurt are isolated experiences. On the other hand, some frightening events occur frequently. War; physical, emotional, or sexual abuse; and observing parental violence are examples of events that can have long-term negative impacts on children's development due to heightened fear and chronic anxiety. According to the National Scientific Council on the Developing Child (2010), "Science shows that exposure to circumstances that produce persistent fear and chronic anxiety can have lifelong consequences by disrupting the developing architecture of the brain" (p. 1). Children in those circumstances experience greater levels of stress, and increased stress has been shown to affect the amygdala, hippocampus, and prefrontal cortex. These brain structures are intimately involved in emotional expression, emotional regulation, executive functions, and decision-making (see Chapter 3). Early childhood educators, family members, and community members can positively impact developmental outcomes for highly stressed children by learning effective strategies from early intervention programs. Early intervention programs that focus on parenting skills, parent-child interactions/attachment behaviors, and preventing abuse have been shown to improve cognitive and socioemotional outcomes for children (Goldsmith, 2010; Mercy & Saul, 2009).

Another strategy for helping stressed children is to have a class pet. Toddlers can be encouraged to display caring behaviors (i.e., their own use of the three *A*s) and responsibility through them (Photo 13–4). Teachers should select a pet only after she is certain no children have allergies. Sometimes teachers select pets that tend to be allergy free, such as fish. Toddlers should be closely supervised in the beginning and until they demonstrate the ability to care for the pet appropriately. Set specific, positively worded limits so that expected behaviors are clear. Telling a child to "Be nice" is not specific enough. It is better to say, "Pet the bunny on her

© 2017 Cengage Learning

PHOTO 13–4 Toddlers can learn to show caring behaviors to class pets.

TABLE 13–4 ▸ Suggestions for Implementing Curriculum—Emotional Development

CHILD BEHAVIOR	EXAMPLES OF CAREGIVER STRATEGIES
Types of Emotions and Feelings	
Feels positive self-worth	Provide experiences that appropriately challenge children; when they succeed, they often feel pleased with themselves. Give the child positive feedback concerning performance and worth as a person.
Feels negative self-worth	Be sensitive to the child's frustrations with tasks and with social encounters. Provide reassurance of the child's worth.
Feels fear	Accept emotion as real and provide comfort as well as strategies for coping with emotion (e.g., talking, reading a story, or snuggling with an attachment object).
Reacts strongly	Accept the child's initial response. Help the child keep within bounds of appropriate behavior; for example, let the child express anger by vigorously riding a Big Wheel for a while or drawing an angry picture.
Acts negatively	Rephrase suggestions to the child. Stimulate interest in a different activity. Describe emotions the child is feeling.
Learns enthusiastically	Reinforce the child's excitement for learning. Provide (repeated) opportunities for challenging, developmental, and content-rich experiences that help the child master skills and develop understanding.
Control of Emotions and Feelings	
Expresses emotions	Accept the child's feelings as honest rather than manipulative.
Is physically aggressive	Provide activities for the child to work out feelings and the need to control, such as using a puppet for imaginary play or letting the child be a leader in a structured activity. Have the child paint, draw, use clay, dance, or go outdoors to run, jump, and yell.

© Cengage Learning

back. She likes to be petted from her head to her tail." If a class pet is not possible, consider inviting the children to share their pets from home.

See Table 13–4 Suggestions for Implementing Curriculum—Emotional Development for additional ways to support emotional development.

13-2e Social Development

Twenty-four-month-olds enjoy the company of other children; they are beginning to interact while playing but also continue to engage primarily in parallel play (see Table 13–5). It is possible to involve children this age in group activities, such as painting individual pictures while sitting at the same table. Because toddlers still have some difficulty sharing, they need support during their interactions with others. Facilitating interactions between the toddlers will contribute to the toddlers initiating and engaging in cooperative interactions. By 30 months of age, these children interact with each other but may spend more time quarrelling over possessions rather than participating in a cooperative effort.

Play, according to child development experts, offers children a way to discover who they are and who they can be (Elkind, 2007; Honig, 2005). Toddlers become graceful and coordinated as they dance with scarves, explore gender roles as they play superheroes, and learn to control

Spotlight on Research

CONFLICTS WITH PEERS

Infants and toddlers have strong desires and they work to fulfill them. In group settings such as child care centers, these desires can often be in conflict with what others want or need them to do. Responding with strong emotions or harmful behaviors when a desire cannot be fulfilled does not necessarily mean that children are aggressive or antisocial. When fighting over objects, the intention is rarely to harm another; the children act to protect their own desires. Although it may seem counterintuitive, this can be a positive learning situation because the children begin to consider why others may be resisting them. In other words, "as their everyday social interactions increase in frequency and complexity, young children must learn how to engage in a process of responsible decision-making as they negotiate their relationships with others" (Warren, Denham, & Bassett, 2008, p. 34).

While we know that infants and toddlers experience conflicts with their peers, minimal empirical data exist on the content of these conflicts. Licht, Simoni, and Perrig-Chiello (2008) conducted a longitudinal investigation with 28 infants. These infants were observed and videotaped during free play situations in their child care center at 8, 14, and 22 months of age. Then, the videotapes were coded for instances of conflict. These researchers defined conflict as needing at least three actions: (1) Child A does something that influences Child B, (2) Child B resists, and (3) Child A persists. Ninety-eight incidents of conflict were found (14 at Time 1; 26 at Time 2; and 58 at Time 3). Then, the behaviors of the target child and peer were analyzed for each conflict.

At Time 1, the 8 month olds' motivations for conflict were characterized by "interruption of activity" and "exploration." In both cases, infants sought to continue their interactions with a given toy and either resisted their activity being interrupted by a peer or persisted with wanting to explore the toy that a peer possessed. At Time 1, the researchers concluded that infants at this age were too young to understand possessions or jealousy. Therefore, the infants focused on their desired interactions with a toy.

At Times 2 and 3, the most frequent displays of motivations for conflict continued to be those identified with the infants: interruption of activity and exploration. The toddlers also exhibited other motivations (e.g., Time 2: "awoken needs" and the "will to effect," and Time 3: "contact and sensation seeking" and "dominance") but at less than a 6 percent frequency each. At Time 3, however, another motivation was identified as occurring at 24 percent possession. This motivation was described as the display of the desire to control the object along with intense emotions. When experiencing these types of conflicts, the older toddlers' verbal and nonverbal expressions referred to the child's own self (e.g., "mine"; pointing to object and to herself).

Licht et al. (2008) conclude from this research that "the role that the urge to explore plays in conflicts between peers in the first two years of life has been underestimated" (p. 245). Furthermore, "ascribing conflicts among children in this age group solely to a motive such as possession is a reductive and misleading interpretation of children's capacities and their social life" (p. 245). Toddlers are working on being able to infer another's emotion, use emotional language, and solve social problems, all of which are crucial to positive peer relationships (Warren et al., 2008). To attribute all of their conflicts to possession minimizes their efforts.

impulses and persist at difficult tasks through play (Honig, 2005). Children who are given the chance to enjoy a variety of experiences of play—role playing, make-believe play, social play with peers, individual creative and artistic play, dyadic play with an adult—develop emotionally, physically, cognitively, and socially. In fact, one study found that symbolic play of preschool children is related to their executive functioning (Kelly & Hammond, 2011). More specifically, the production of symbolic play was positively associated with the ability to inhibit an initial response to a situation or object in order to engage in pretend play.

The ability to interact with and respond to emotional communication from peers during play has been hypothesized to vary depending upon a number of different variables. Levine and Conway (2010) measured a group of toddlers' (22–26 month olds) self-other awareness through mirror self-recognition, perceptual role taking, pronoun recognition, and pronoun use. They found that girls who were higher on self-other awareness engaged in more duplicate toy play with a peer (i.e., parallel play with identical objects) than did girls who were lower on self-other awareness. Boys' level of self-other awareness was not related to the nature of their peer interactions as measured in the study (Levine & Conway, 2010). In addition, no significant correlations between self-other awareness and toy claiming (e.g., demonstrating possession of an object) were found for either boys or girls. In other words, measures of self-recognition were not consistently associated with declaring objects as "mine" or protecting them from another child.

Another study examined how toddlers use social referencing from a peer to guide their interactions with a toy (Nichols, Svetlova, & Brownell, 2010). In this study, 12-, 18-, and 24-month-old children were shown videos of a child expressing a positive, negative, and/or neutral reaction to a specific toy. The children were then presented two toys (one of which was in the video), and their interactions with the toys were recorded. The results showed that 12-month-olds decreased their play with toys toward which a peer had expressed either positive or negative emotion, whereas 24-month-old children increased their toy play after watching a peer display negative affect toward the toy (Nichols et al., 2010). The authors concluded that children of this age are not as skilled in using social referencing from peers as compared to adults. In comparison, however, when very young children were shown a video of a peer expressing fear about a toy, children with siblings decreased their play with the toy, regardless of their age, demonstrating the typical social-referencing response. Thus, children with siblings may be more skilled at reading and responding to the emotion of fear.

When toddlers are helped with tasks, they learn to help others. In previous chapters (see, e.g., Chapters 3 and 12), prosocial behaviors were discussed from the perspective of engaging in spontaneous helpful or caring behaviors. Svetlova, Nichols, and Brownell (2010) classified prosocial behavior into three categories: instrumental (action-based), empathic (emotion-based), and altruistic (giving up an object on their own). While 18- and 30-month-old toddlers more readily engaged in instrumental prosocial behaviors, they both needed more adult assistance with empathetic and altruistic types of prosocial behavior (Svetlova et al., 2010). It is not a surprise, then, that toddlers tend to want to help with frequently repeated tasks such as cleaning up toys. Because of being able to predict what will happen, toddlers may be more cooperative if the early childhood educator establishes routines and rituals for certain repetitive experiences such as cleaning up. Signaling that it is almost clean up time via a warning, singing a short song two or three times in a row, and providing choices of how to help may result in more cooperative behaviors. Additionally, many toddlers desire to be helpful outside of routines. They want to help you sweep the floor, clean up spilled paint, or water the classroom plants. Accepting their offers to volunteer promotes their social as well as emotional development—they learn to see themselves as capable, helpful persons. It is understood that cleaning up the mess or completing the chore on your own would take less time. However, the benefits of patiently teaching such skills will last a lifetime.

TABLE 13–5 ▶ Suggestions for Implementing Curriculum—Social Development

CHILD BEHAVIOR	EXAMPLES OF CAREGIVER STRATEGIES
Self	
Realizes own skills	Provide materials and equipment that the child can use to own satisfaction. Provide challenging materials that the child can use.
Possessive of materials or people	Provide enough toys and materials so the child can control use of some of them for a time. Continue one-on-one time with each child.
Others	
Shows independence	Allow the child to accomplish as many tasks as possible by self. Assist when asked or when you anticipate you are needed.
Acts to please adult	Provide verbal and nonverbal descriptive feedback to the child. Recognize the child's need for your attention and attunement. Plan activities the child can help you with (e.g., clean up).
Shows feelings to others	Show feelings to the child. Show appropriate actions with feelings, for example, *happy*: laugh, physical excitement; *sad*: hug, pat, listen. Provide feedback when he or she uses those behaviors.
Recognizes emotions in others	Label children's behaviors. Verbalize about feelings of others. Provide appropriate responses to behaviors. Provide feedback when the child identifies or responds to others' emotions.
Understands *mine* and *yours*	Reinforce possession by the child and others. It is *mine* while the speaker is using it.
Directs others	Provide opportunities for the child to display leadership skills with peers.
Helps others	Praise the child's spontaneous helping. Ask for assistance so the child can help with routines and so forth.
Control of Self	
Starts to share	Provide materials and equipment so some sharing is necessary. Provide feedback when the child shares. Verbalize reasons for sharing. Recognize, however, that not all children can share yet.
Helps others	Provide opportunities for purposeful helping: cleaning up, passing out items, assisting with clothing. Thank the child for helping behaviors. Accept toddlers' offers to assist when they volunteer.
Engages in parallel play	Plan space and materials so children can play close to others without having to interact in play.
Engages in cooperative interactions	Provide toys, materials, and time for interacting. Engage the toddlers in conversations as they play. Describe, for example, what each child is doing with the materials (how alike and how different).
Shares	Encourage by providing opportunities to share, for example, when eating orange wedges or apple slices.
Takes turns	Use daily routines to help skill development, for example, taking turns to wash hands.

© Cengage Learning

Table 13–5 Suggestions for Implementing Curriculum—Social Development provides additional strategies for supporting helpful behaviors and other aspects of social development.

Does responding to communication from peers or engaging in prosocial behaviors mean that toddlers possess perspective-taking skills? Not completely, but they continue to gain skills in this area. Most toddlers (like other preoperational children) continue to believe that everyone sees the world in the same way they do. Even though young children can distinguish themselves from others, they are only slowly developing the ideas that follow from this. For example, they are just beginning to understand that others have feelings and thoughts different from their own (i.e., intentional states, see Chapter 2). They assume that when they speak, everyone understands the exact meaning of their words; they do not realize that others may give different meanings to the same words or experiences.

However, developing perspective-taking skills assists in peer interactions and the development of friendships. As children spend greater amounts of time in group care, they have the opportunity to develop friendships. McGaha, Cummings, Lippard, & Dallas (2011) demonstrated that infants and toddlers are quite capable of building enduring relationships with one another through both planned and spontaneous interactions. Although this article did not explicitly discuss characteristics of children within those friendships, research with preschool children suggests that friendships are developed based along race and gender lines (e.g., Barron, 2011). Data provided evidence that children's friendships were shaped by their interactions and conversations during classroom activities because during those interactions they internalized ways in which some children were familiar (e.g., like us) or unfamiliar (e.g., not like us). Thus, if toddler teachers want children to play with others of different races, ethnicities, and gender, then they have to create situations where children can play in pairs or triads and learn about one another.

Children continue to identify their "selfness" within their world. Their toys are a part of themselves, and they remain very possessive of the toys and materials they are using. However, their strengthening sense of self from 24 to 36 months of age also provides a foundation for expanding interactions with others. Children of this age are increasingly aware of others as individuals. They use adults as resources, seeking assistance from them when they decide they need help. They become directive with others, exerting control over people, animals, and toys as they learn ways to control their world. As discussed in the earlier emotional development section, toddlers can engage in instrumental, empathetic, and altruistic prosocial behaviors. This facilitates their social relationships as they become better at recognizing others' emotional needs and responding with assistance or even giving up a toy because another child desires it.

The children's self-control is increasing. Their desire for instant gratification is being restricted, so they sometimes accept delayed gratification. Toddlers' ability to exert greater effortful control was found to be related to higher levels of maternal effortful control and greater maternal time in caregiving in infancy (Bridgett, Gartstein, Putnam, Lance, Iddins, Waits, et al., 2011). The authors concluded that when caregivers capitalize more frequently on opportunities to interact with very young children, they promote the emergence of effortful control during toddlerhood. Likewise, early childhood educators should spend time each day with children in their care to be able to provide necessary emotional and social support during peer interactions. Having effortful control means that toddlers are capable of taking turns occasionally. At times they may decide to share, and they may play cooperatively for short periods of time (Photo 13–5). The research strongly suggests that what begins to ingrain the deepest sense of these prosocial qualities in that child is the felt experience, over and over and over again, of cooperation; the experience of having an important adult put aside his or

© 2017 Cengage Learning

PHOTO 13–5 Sometimes toddlers share and play cooperatively.

her own needs to meet the child's very real needs; and the experience of that important adult showing empathy, concern, respect, and nurturance toward the child. In other words, adults who consistently use the three *A*s help children learn how to positively interact in social situations.

READING CHECKPOINT

Before moving on with your reading, make sure that you can answer the following questions about the material discussed so far.

1. Provide two examples of cultural differences in expressing emotions. Describe which aspects of emotional expression those differences reflect.
2. Describe how you would assist a child in demonstrating ownership of toys or security items.
3. Describe a situation in which an older toddler is asserting independence. How should the teacher respond to the child's actions? Why?

Summary

13-1 Select materials appropriate to the development of older toddlers.

Early childhood educators must select materials that support development, challenge development, and are safe. In addition, the materials should be open-ended so that they can be used in multiple ways during parallel play or in the beginning of cooperative play.

13-2 Devise strategies appropriate to older toddlers (24 to 36 months of age) that are responsive to individual developmental levels.

Between the age of 24 and 36 months, toddlers are especially energetic in their learning. They ask questions (often through their behaviors, not their language) and inquire into possible answers as a way to learn more and be a "big kid." Responsive caregivers plan the learning environment carefully to encourage explorations. In addition, older toddlers are becoming more interested in interacting with peers. They seek out others to "talk" with, show objects, and demonstrate affection. As a part of learning to interact, they experience conflict and can be aggressive. Emotionally, they are up and down during this year. During the first half of the year, toddlers frequently demonstrate dependent behaviors, make more frequent demands, and challenge your requests; these are all typical behaviors as they resolve the identity crisis of autonomy versus shame and doubt. By the end of the year, they may be more emotionally calm. Adults play an important role in helping toddlers gain social skills and emotional control.

CASE STUDY Ming Learns English

You met Ming at the beginning of the chapter and might remember her strong verbal skills. She comes from a low-income family. The Department of Social Services provides her child care free of charge because of the severe poverty of her family. She often comes to the program without having eaten and insufficiently dressed for the weather. Her 24-year-old mother is a day laborer who has three other children under the age of 7.

Ming's teacher, Ms. Tao, has known from daily interactions that her mother has limited English proficiency. When the first parent conference was held, she called on the services of another parent who is bilingual in her specific dialect. While explaining her observations of Ming's development in all areas, she learned that Ming's mother was overwhelmed with all of the information. She slowed down and focused on what she believed were the most important pieces of information about Ming. For example, she shared that Ming was on target with her language and cognitive development but is often hungry and tired. Working through the interpreter, they created a plan to redesign the evening routine to help Ming get more sleep. The teacher also provided information on community resources such as a local food bank in case the family didn't have access to enough food resources.

1. What impact do poverty and/or a lack of food have on a child's development?
2. Which factors do you think have helped Ming to be on target with her cognitive and language skills? What strategies used by Ms. Tao may have helped at school?
3. What supports at both school and in the home could be provided to help Ming get and then stay on track with the other areas of development? What other supports could be offered to help Ming's family?

Lesson Plan

Title: *Me do it!*

Child Observation:

Logan wanted to go outside as indicated by his standing at the door and crying. He needed his raincoat and boots because of the large puddles in the yard (the water and air temperatures were too cold to go out without proper clothing). He resisted putting on the required clothing by holding his arms around his stomach and leaning against the door.

Teacher note: Logan loves to go outside. Our Seattle weather does not always support his desire, but I provide the necessary clothing so we can go out as often as possible. I believe he gets so emotionally upset that he cannot "see" a way to meet his goal. I am going to attempt to prevent the strong emotions by giving him choices and helping him plan for playing outside.

Child's Developmental Goal:

To align desires with emotional responses

To participate in actions that support obtaining the goal set

Materials: Raincoat, boots

Preparation: Place raincoat and boots beside the door.

Learning Environment:

1. When Logan arrives, discuss the rain with him. Describe how the rain is coming down and how we need to prepare to go outside. To illustrate, you could say:

   "It is raining gently outside. The weatherperson said it might rain all morning. I put the raincoat and boots that you like by the door. I'll let you know when we will be going outside so that you can get ready."

2. Watch Logan throughout the morning. If he goes near the coat and boots, join him. Remind him that we need the raincoat and boots to keep us dry from the rain. Ask him what he would like to do outside today. Elaborate on his answer, if necessary. For example, if he says "trike," reply with, "You want to ride the trike."

3. When it is five minutes until cleanup and time to go outside, give everyone a warning. Specifically, remind Logan that he wants to ride the trike and that everyone will go outside when properly dressed.

4. Encourage Logan to decide if he wants to put the raincoat or boots on first. Provide scaffolding, if necessary, for him to complete the task. Begin with verbal scaffolding by providing a suggestion (e.g., "I find it easier to put on my coat when it is all unbuttoned") or asking a question (e.g., "Do you want to put the boots on over your shoes, or do you want to take off your shoes first?"). If necessary, provide physical assistance to complete the task.

5. If Logan experiences frustration or anger during the process, use emotional talk to help him remain in control of his emotions. For example, you can say, "It is frustrating when the boots don't go on easily. Take a slow breath. You can get the boot on."

6. Provide acknowledgement for completing the task, and encourage Logan to enjoy "riding the trike" outside.

Guidance Consideration:

If Logan becomes aggressive with the materials or the adult because of his frustration, acknowledge his emotions but make it clear that aggressive behavior is not acceptable. Do so by saying, "It is okay to be upset. It is not okay to hit me. That hurts. What can I do to help you with the boots?"

Variations:

Help him plan another goal and carry it out.

∨ Professional Resource Download

Additional Resources

Dombrink-Green, M., & Bohart, H. (Eds.). (2015). *Spotlight on young children: Supporting dual language learners.* Washington, DC: National Association for the Education of Young Children.

Kagan, S. L., & Tarrant, K. (Eds.) (2010). *Transitions for young children: Creating connections across early childhood systems.* Baltimore, MD: Brookes.

MacDermid Wadsworth, S., & Riggs, D. S. (Eds.). (2014). *Military deployment and its consequences for families.* New York: Springer.

Ochshorn, S. (2015). *Squandering America's future: Why ECE policy matters for equity, our economy, and our children.* New York: Teachers College Press.

Ramsey, P. G. (2015). *Teaching and learning in a diverse world: Multicultural education for young children* (4th ed.). New York: Teachers College Press.

Developmentally Appropriate Content

Learning Objectives

After reading this chapter, you should be able to:

14-1 Articulate "big ideas" for infants and toddlers that are associated with each content area.

14-2 Differentiate central concepts of each content area.

14-3 Devise a broad range of strategies for children to acquire developmentally appropriate content knowledge through integrated projects.

Standards Addressed in This Chapter

naeyc NAEYC Standards for Early Childhood Professional Preparation

4 Using Developmentally Effective Approaches
5 Using Content Knowledge to Build Meaningful Curriculum

DAP Developmentally Appropriate Practice Guidelines

2 Teaching to Enhance Development and Learning
3 Planning Curriculum to Achieve Important Goals

In addition, the NAEYC standards for developmentally appropriate practice are divided into six areas particularly important to infant/toddler care. The following area is addressed in this chapter: *exploration* and *play*.

© 2017 Cengage Learning

| CASE STUDY | Andrea's Explorations |

Andrea, 22 months old, stands looking around. She walks over to Jenny, a fellow toddler, who is sitting on the sofa. She stands between Jenny's legs and bounces up and down to Hokey Pokey music from the CD player. Andrea and Jenny dance around. Jenny lies down on the floor and Andrea crawls on top of her. Jenny moves and Andrea follows. They both lie quietly for a minute. Andrea walks to a dramatic play shelf with toys. She picks up a toy plastic milk bottle and lifts it to her mouth to drink. She sits down and puts three lock blocks in the bottle. Allen, the caregiver, says, "What do you have?" Andrea shakes the bottle, and it makes a noise. She shakes it again. She stands up and begins to dance to her "shaker." She toddles over to the child's rocking chair beside Allen, climbs up, turns around to sit down, and starts rocking. She leans over, picks up a book from the basket, and turns the first page. Allen leaves to attend to another child who just woke from a nap. Andrea "reads" (looks at the pages of the book while talking) while rocking, then looks over to where Allen was sitting. She looks around the room, spots him, and returns to reading the book.

Infants and toddlers continue to be active, eager learners as they use repetition to master old skills and acquire new ones. The areas of development impact each other. For example, their developing fine muscles allow for more controlled manipulation of objects such as blocks, tweezers, and pencils, furthering their understanding of communication, scientific, and mathematical concepts. When play is the basis for the curriculum, they learn foundational concepts in all of the content areas while engaged in imaginative, explorative interactions. Well-designed early education curriculum encourages toddlers to represent their ideas through play, language, drawing, structures, and various art mediums.

14-1 Big Ideas That Guide Work

Teachers of infants and toddlers must be well versed in the essential content knowledge and resources in many academic disciplines. Caregivers must understand how very young children will investigate and express understanding within each content area, how each content area is organized, and how the content areas connect to one another. Because children are encountering those content areas for the first time, early childhood professionals set the foundations for later understanding and success.

Whereas literacy and mathematics have a central place in later academic competence, the arts, social studies, health and physical movement, and science are nonetheless important to introduce during the infant and toddler years. How concepts within these content areas are explored is vital to effective teaching and learning. "Big ideas" such as problem solving, writing for a purpose, expressing ideas through paint and movement, changing over time, exercising, and balancing objects should be the focus of open-ended learning experiences. Because toddlers are striving to understand how the world works, focusing on isolated facts within any of the content areas is not a useful strategy. Toddlers need to have

Family and Community Connections

You are working in a program that serves families from an affluent community. Some family members place significant emphasis on school readiness skills. You recently learned from your director that some families have complained that you "have refused" to teach their toddlers how to write their names and count. They are worried that their children will not get into the local preparatory school when they are 5. How will you share information on the "big ideas" that guide your work? Specifically consider what format you will choose to deliver the information and what information you will communicate. Explain why you made those decisions.

meaningful experiences to connect concepts between past and present interactions (recall information on project work from Chapter 9). Highly effective early childhood educators, therefore, understand that they must intentionally create learning experiences to facilitate the development of such connections.

As discussed in Chapter 9, early childhood educators plan effective curriculum to support optimal learning and meet educational goals. To do so, they need a broad repertoire of effective strategies and tools to help young children learn. Engaging conversations, thought-provoking questions, providing ordinary materials for novel uses, and capitalizing on both routine and spontaneous experiences are all strategies that help facilitate optimal learning. According to NAEYC (2011a), teachers should possess the following repertoire of teaching/learning approaches:

- Drawing from a continuum of teaching strategies
- Making the most of the environment, schedule, and routines
- Setting up all aspects of the indoor and outdoor environment
- Focusing on children's individual characteristics, needs, and interests
- Linking children's language and culture to the early childhood program
- Teaching through social interactions
- Creating support for play
- Using integrative approaches to curriculum

For infants and toddlers, embedding content area knowledge in these strategies makes it an implicit delivery method. In other words, you do not explicitly teach math or science through a direct-instruction model; rather, it is more naturally entwined as a part of everyday living and learning and the intentional learning experiences just described. Your questions help children to think deeply about the content area and to develop theories.

14-2 Central Concepts of the Content Areas

The following sections investigate central concepts for the content areas of literacy, mathematics, fine arts, social studies, and science. In addition, strategies are discussed for embedding these concepts in the curriculum.

14-2a Emergent Literacy

Without doubt, success in our society demands fluency in reading and writing. To reach that end, very young children need to have quality experiences in listening, speaking, reading, writing, and playing. Taken together, these five skills make up emergent literacy, which is the knowledge of reading and writing before the possession of skills to engage in conventional reading and writing. Telling a story, reciting a memorized book, and scribbling are examples of emergent literacy. Focusing on emergent literacy supports an image of the child as capable because it demonstrates a belief that even the youngest children are on a path to becoming literate.

Listening

Immediately upon birth (if a parent has not already begun), infants should be spoken to during routine care and alert times. As discussed in earlier chapters (e.g., Chapters 3, 11, 12, and 13), hearing spoken language develops the understanding of the sounds, forms, and patterns of their native language while also supporting listening skills. During the first three years of life, young children learn to attend to a speaker for longer and longer periods of time. Infants should also listen to things other than language. Listening to instrumental music, a wind chime tinkle in the breeze, chants or nursery rhymes, for example, provide infants with different discrimination tasks. Be prepared to chant beloved nursery rhymes over and over again.

Speaking

Efforts at producing sounds should not only be supported but also encouraged. As shown on the Developmental Milestones tool (see Appendix A), there are typical patterns in how infants begin to speak. They move from cooing to babbling to using jargon to speaking telegraphically. Adults can enhance the children's speaking skills through teaching sign language, engaging in conversations, and elaborating on their utterances. (See Chapters 11, 12, and 13 for more strategies.)

Reading

Infants should be read to from the day they are born, if it is not already an established practice within the family. It can be challenging to hold a newborn and a book simultaneously, but it is worth the effort. Reading aloud to infants not only facilitates the listening and speaking skills just described but also results in joint attention, reinforces basic concepts, and stimulates imagination (Zeece & Churchill, 2001). It is also an ". . . opportunity for adults and children to connect, for children to experience 'tranquility,' and a way to encourage continuity between the home and school environment" (Edwards, Cline, Gandini, Giacomelli, Giovannini, & Galardini, 2014, p. 35). Vukelich, Christie, and Enz (2012) elaborate on the importance of human interactions during story reading by saying, "Getting children to talk about the text or think about what is going on in the story is central to children's literacy growth" (p. 125). Book reading guides young children in the turn-taking patterns inherent in all conversations. Therefore, adults should actively engage with infants when reading. The Allen County

Public Library in Fort Wayne, Indiana, suggests that adults should follow the children's lead by following the "CAR" method:

Comment and wait.*
Ask questions and wait.*
Respond by adding a little more.

*Waiting gives the child time to respond (Allen County Public Library, 2009).

Many parents and teachers understand that they have to do the majority of the work while reading to infants. Pointing to things in pictures and labeling them orally is especially important because infants are acquiring so much receptive language and are beginning to produce expressive language as well. As mentioned earlier, you can add more to the story or book as you read. For example, relate what is in the book to the infant's experience. "You love your stuffed elephant. You sleep with her every day at nap time." [infant looks toward cubbie] "Yes, she is in your cubbie right now. Should we get her so she can hear the story also?" [take infant to cubbie to get elephant, based on response] If parents or other family members are not reading to their infant or toddler daily, early childhood educators should encourage it. Such book interactions are important for all children but especially for children with visual impairments (Murphy, Hatton, & Erickson, 2008).

For many decades, researchers have been interested in how parents (primarily mothers) engage in shared book readings with their infants and toddlers. Results have consistently shown that book behaviors vary with socioeconomic status. For example, mothers who lack financial resources tend to engage in less reading overall, and when they do read, they use a more limited range of vocabulary (e.g., talk less about the story or relate it less to other experiences the child might have had). However, more recent research suggests that there is a great deal of variability in reading patterns within a sample of low-income mothers. Specifically, mothers differed in their use of language strategies and language production while reading to their 6-month-old infant (Abraham, Crais, & Vernon-Feagans, 2013). The analyses also indicated stability within mothers, as maternal language use at the 6-month-old time point significantly predicted later maternal language when reading a book at the 15-month-old stage (Abraham et al., 2013). In a sample of Early Head Start families in the Midwest, parents' reading habits were evaluated based on two dimensions: instructional and emotional. The results suggest that there is a complex interaction between the two dimensions of parenting behavior, home language (i.e., English, Spanish) and child outcomes in terms of both cognitive and language skills (Cline & Edwards, 2013). When considering parental reading behaviors for middle- to upper-income families, Edwards (2014) found that mothers engaged in several emergent literacy behaviors (e.g., phonological awareness and written language awareness) while engaged in shared reading experiences in their home. Toddlers (18–36-month-olds) were also found to engage in these behaviors. These variations in parenting behaviors when reading highlight how children acquire different types of knowledge in their homes. Some family cultures are more expressive, while others are more reserved in how they interact around books. Neither approach is inherently right or wrong. Teachers should not judge, but rather come to understand these differences so that bridges between home and school can be built.

Choose reading materials for young children that cover a variety of topics, match the children's interests, and introduce new concepts (Photo 14–1). Straub and Dell'Antonia (2006) suggest that you pay close attention to what aspects of a book engage a child (e.g., colors, busy or simple pictures, animal or human characters, labels or story line, books by same author) and then look for those characteristics in another book. They advise not to overlook the obvious such as a favorite animal (refer to the Spotlight on Practice box). Recent research suggests that teachers tend to select a limited variety of books for reading with children. According to Pentimonti, Zucker, and Justice (2011), out of 426 titles read by preschool teachers, narrative texts were the dominate genre used during read-aloud time. In addition, there was low exposure to alphabet books, nursery rhymes, books featuring math concepts, and multicultural content (Pentimonti et al., 2011). In addition, adults should select e-books as a way to provide a different, yet still interactive, reading experience for toddlers (Hoffman & Paciga, 2014). These authors warn that adults should select "true e-books (those that actually function as books and include print) [because they] better promote language and literacy development" rather than entertainment applications where the literacy experience becomes superficial (p. 382). To reflect an anti-biased approach, books should represent different genders, races, ethnicities, and lifestyles in accurate, nonbiased manners (Derman-Sparks & Edwards, 2010; Pelo, 2008). According to Derman-Sparks, LeeKeenan, and Nimmo (2015), directors should assist teachers in reflecting on the books they select for the classroom and the messages conveyed through those choices as well as on building relationships with families to best select culturally relevant reading materials. Local librarians can also provide invaluable assistance when selecting books for young children. Intentionality when selecting reading materials assists children with acquiring knowledge, forming a strong personal identity, and developing a love of reading.

After carefully selecting a book, be prepared to read it multiple times. Repetition when reading books is essential. As infants experience multiple readings of the same book, they begin to join in the reading, identifying objects in illustrations by either pointing to or verbally acknowledging an object (Zeece & Churchill, 2001). Such behaviors provide clues to the infants' cognitive skills, especially their memory of prior events. As infants gain mobility skills, they will bring you books to read, indicating their preferences for specific books or stories.

© 2017 Cengage Learning

PHOTO 14–1 Teachers should make available books that reflect students' interests, cover a variety of topics, and represent different genders, races, ethnicities, and lifestyles.

VOICES FROM THE FIELD

I am a toddler teacher in a church ministry. I have the same five children each morning and a different group of five children each afternoon. The children in both of my groups love to look at books. I get new books every two weeks from the public library. I invite a librarian to read stories once a month. I've learned several skills from her such as how to ask open-ended questions throughout the book. It is amazing to me how the children's interests impact their reactions to the stories. For example, Selene is interested in books with a story line. She does not attend long to books with only one word on a page. Fiorenzo loves dinosaurs. I selected a book with different animals in it thinking that would attract his attention. He didn't show much interest until we got to the page with his favorite animal on it. When I pointed to the dinosaur and said its name, Fiorenzo smiled and began talking quickly using a combination of telegraphic speech and jargon.

To support language and literacy development, infant and toddler teachers must carefully plan their schedule to allow for daily, one-on-one reading. Although it can be a challenge to accomplish each day, the importance of such book interactions should not be underestimated (Vukelich et al., 2012). A list of board books (categorized by content) has been provided in Appendix C to assist you in planning for the daily, curricular event of reading.

As children get older, some will remain interested in board books as their desire to label objects and people in their environment (i.e., lexical words) is supported. However, others will expand their interests to include picture books because of a budding desire to hear stories. It is essential to select high-quality literature that appeals to the children's interests, evokes humor, and stretches their imagination (Vukelick et al., 2012; Appendix D contains a list of picture books that might be of interest to toddlers.). Because toddlers will be selecting books independently from the library shelf, teachers must have a wide variety of high-quality books available. Shelves should be stocked with different types of reading materials, such as magazines, board books and picture books, small books and big books, nonfiction, and storybooks. Although new research suggests that some parents are equating DVDs and books as equal tools for print exposure during the early years (Mol, Neuman, & Strouse, 2014), teachers should not include passive delivery of literacy (i.e., DVDs) in program experiences or routines.

Each toddler in your care needs time to snuggle up with a primary caregiver and a good book throughout the day (Photo 14–2). Because reading a book might be of short duration, plan to read several different times throughout the day. Books contain language patterns that serve as examples to children who are busily constructing language. While one-on-one reading is obviously still important, you may find that two or more toddlers are interested in hearing a book at the same time. Snuggle on the couch or in an oversize chair to read together.

© 2017 Cengage Learning

PHOTO 14–2 It's important for caregivers to take the time to read with just one or two toddlers at a time.

Gathering time (or circle time) may not be the best time for reading stories with children of this age due to differing attention spans and interests. Instead, gathering time for toddlers should be about coming together as a group to positively interact, not about reading a story from beginning to end.

Before reading a picture book, show the toddler the cover and read the title and objects or events in the child's environment to help them understand the meaning behind the words. You should expect the toddlers (beginning around 15 months of age) to be more involved while reading books (Vukelich et al., 2012). When you ask a question and the child answers, expand on the answer or ask another question related to the first one.

As you may have experienced, toddlers are excited to associate what they already know with the pictures and words in a book. For example, if you read books of nursery rhymes that you have previously recited to them as infants, they will remember the rhymes and, more than likely, join in the reading. If they are not spontaneously reciting words, pause at the end of the line to see if they fill in the rhyming word (Pinnell & Fountas, 2011).

Notice, however, that toddlers differ in how they attend to the books. Some children are very engaged, pointing and vocalizing, while others are more passive. How toddlers demonstrated joint attention during book reading was associated with later language development (Fletcher, Perez, Hooper, & Claussen, 2005). Although more research needs to be conducted, it would be logical to hypothesize that these and other child characteristics influence the quality of the adult-child reading interactions. Thus, teachers may need to demonstrate extra patience when interacting with children who are more passive.

Early educators should provide reading experiences that transcend the book as a way to engage more passive participants. Making a flannel board or puppets with characters from familiar stories encourages toddlers to actively engage with the story (McGee & Richgels, 2012). Another strategy is to invite the children to tell the story using just the pictures. These experiences provide practice in putting thoughts into oral language.

bibliotherapy Reading books to toddlers with the goal of assisting them in solving life problems, gaining important socioemotional skills, and knowing how to behave with peers.

Books that are selected to help a child solve a problem can be particularly engaging. The term for using books in this manner is **bibliotherapy**. In bibliotherapy, books are read to toddlers with the goal of assisting them in solving life problems (e.g., death, birth of sibling), gaining important socioemotional skills (e.g., anger management, perspective taking), and knowing how to behave with peers (e.g., group entry, helping others). Research suggests that bibliotherapy can be effective for helping children with emotional growth (Heath, Sheen, Leavy, Young, & Money, 2005), incarcerated parents (Hames & Pedreira, 2003), abuse and neglect (Kanewischer, 2013), self-concept (Sridhar & Vaughn, 2000), racism (Mankiw & Strasser, 2013), anxiety (Rapee, Abbott, & Lyneham, 2006), and death of a loved one (Mankiw & Strasser, 2013; Martell, Witt, & Witt, 2013).

Books, therefore, play an increasingly important role in the lives of toddlers (Photo 14–3). Reading aloud provides examples of language patterns; reading the pictures encourages self-expression; and talking about the story or the pictures facilitates comprehension of the language. Having these experiences fosters larger vocabularies and better storytelling abilities in the children.

The ability to produce or express language during the toddler years has been associated with larger vocabularies and better reading outcomes during the early elementary years (Rescorla, 2002; see also Pullen & Justice, 2003) and up through age 13 (Bartl-Pokorny, Marschik, Sachse, Green, Zhang, Van der Meer, et al., 2013). As mentioned previously, adult styles of interactions and literacy behaviors at home are associated with literacy outcomes. As mentioned in Chapter 13, partnerships between families and teachers support and enhance the language and literacy development of children. One successful strategy to support a partnership is to send home literacy bags that contain high-quality children's literature and a guidebook for parents with questions for discussion. Such practices have been shown to increase engagement with home literacy activities (Brand, Marchand, Lilly, & Child, 2014).

© 2017 Cengage Learning

PHOTO 14–3 Books play an increasingly important role in the lives of toddlers.

Boyce (2014) took a different approach and engaged family members in bookmaking following a shared experience. For example, the toddlers showed their family members around the outdoor learning environment collecting items such as leaves and talking about nature. A staff member captured their experience in four or five photographs. Then, each family was invited to make a book using their home language that recorded what the child had to say about the photos (for more details on the other directions provided, see Boyce, 2014). When parents agreed, the books were copied so that the book could be used in the classroom. Family feedback showed the power of the bookmaking experience in three ways: (1) the families felt that their home language was valued, (2) the books could be used by the family to elicit new conversations with their toddlers, and (3) the books could be used to revisit memories of the classroom experiences at home (Boyce, 2014). Creating books in this manner might also spark early childhood educators and family members to make other books about the child's experiences, further supporting literacy development.

As a result of the push to help children learn to read sooner and sooner, early childhood educators need to assist family members in understanding the difference between emergent literacy skills and reading. New programs to teach infants how to read abound on the market. Current evidence suggests that babies cannot be taught to read, even when using programs such as Your Baby Can Read (Neuman, Kaefer, Pinkham, & Strouse, 2014). In fact, the children in the intervention group (those who participated in the Your Baby Can Read program over seven months) were no more skilled at receptive language knowledge or able to complete important skills such as letter-name knowledge, print awareness, and sight word reading than children in the control group. In contrast, if parents are helped early on to carve out time daily to read to their infants and toddlers, important emergent literacy skills, such as phonological awareness, might be gained.

phonological awareness The conscious attention to the sounds of spoken language.

As discussed in Chapter 13, to promote knowledge of **phonological awareness**, which refers to the conscious attention to the sounds of spoken language (McGee & Richgels, 2012), early childhood educators and family members should play language games with the children. You may recall that clapping for each word or to segment syllables in a word and pausing before saying the rhyming word helps toddlers think about the words that make up songs, fingerplays, or nursery rhymes (Vukelich et al., 2012; Pinnell & Fountas, 2011). Reading picture books with rhyming words also supports children's development of phonological awareness. As with spoken language strategies, you can point to words with your finger while reading to highlight individual words, or you can pause before reading the rhyming word at the end of a sentence to encourage the toddler to fill in the word. Appendix D provides you with a list of picture books that have rhyming patterns. Don't forget your childhood favorites, though, such as *Hop on Pop* or *Green Eggs and Ham* by Dr. Seuss. With extended practice, some toddlers might create their own rhyming words or songs. However, this is a skill most children acquire during the preschool years (McGee & Richgels, 2012; Pinnell & Fountas, 2011).

Writing

Literacy also involves learning to communicate ideas in writing. Teachers should plan daily opportunities for very young children to express their ideas using writing tools such as pencils/pens, crayons, markers, and paint/paintbrushes. Infants can be held on an adult lap at a table and given a pencil/pen and paper to mark on. Or, if they are able to pull up to stand, a coffee table can be covered with paper and writing tools can be placed in a basket on the table for easy access. **Scribbling**, which is often undervalued

scribbling Nonsense writing marks that are a precursor to writing.

by adults, involves nonsense writing marks that are a precursor to writing. Thus, scribbling is an important aspect of the language/reading/writing processes the infant is developing. Earliest marks on paper are not just random; they are early attempts at written communication. Like babbling, these written marks will eventually develop into a more conventional form of communication.

Encourage the infants' and toddlers' scribbling by providing time and attention to their use and enjoyment of writing. Avoid asking the child what her scribbles are. The scribbles at this stage may not represent anything. Rather, comment on what you see—lines from top to bottom or across the page, dots, and colors. You might make descriptive comments such as, "I like your orange and brown picture" or "What bold blue lines!" While the focus should be on the process of scribbling rather than the end product, do not forget to display some of the children's work in prominent locations in the environment to support the children's developing identities and respect their methods for representing ideas (see Chapter 8). This type of documentation assists the toddlers in valuing their own work and models the need to value such developmental milestones to other adults (e.g., family members and colleagues).

The interrelationships among language, reading, and writing are evident at an early age. Toddlers need open access to paper and writing utensils for drawing and writing as well as paint for expressing ideas. Toddlers use lines, circles, and other marks to represent objects in their world. This is a beginning stage of writing. When you support them as they talk about what they have drawn or written, they connect symbols (mental representations) with language. Furthermore, involving children via language as you write names, labels, and notes serves to model how cultures use written texts to communicate. Do this by saying, for example, "You want to paint after nap. Let's write a note and put it on your cubbie so we won't forget." Then, say each word as your write it on the paper. Joint interactions such as this assist toddlers in coming to understand the multifaceted dimensions of roles in literacy events: who does what, with whom, and for what purposes (Rowe, 2008). In fact, toddlers and preschoolers come to understand the purposes of written communication (e.g., tell another facts, ask for something, remember an idea or item) before they can produce conventional forms of writing (Vukelich et al., 2012).

As they grow, written language is becoming more and more a part of their world. They see print at home, at the grocery store, out the bus window, and at the child care home or center. They read cereal boxes and snack containers, look at the print in a book as the caregiver reads the story or tells the story line, and see their name on artwork, cubbies, and other prized possessions. They are eager to make their own marks.

Research over several decades suggests that infants' and toddlers' writing progresses in a predictable sequence. Figure 14–1 depicts the sequence and provides examples of young children's mark making. A synthesis of research concluded that, while each child develops scribbling at his or her own rate, there were statistically significant increases in the level and complexity of drawing between 1 and 3 years of age (Dunst & Gorman, 2009). There is a progression to their scribbles, which moves from random marks to controlled

FIGURE 14–1 ▶ Sequence and Examples of Mark Making, Scribbling, and Drawing Identified by Research

1. Marking
2. Dots
3. Random Marks
4. Random Circles
5. Controlled Marks
6. Controlled Strokes
7. Geometric Shapes
8. Simple Figures

Source: Reprinted with permission from Dunst, C. J., & Gorman, E. (2009). Development of infant and toddler mark making and scribbling. *CELL Reviews*, 2(2), 1–16. Retrieved February 8, 2012, from http://earlyliteracylearning.org/cellreviews/cellreviews_v2_n2.ppdf

© 2017 Cengage Learning

PHOTO 14–4 Provide students with a variety of opportunities to write.

marks and strokes, to geometric shapes and simple figures, and, eventually during the preschool and early primary years, to writing mock letters and words and writing conventionally (Dunst & Gorman, 2009; McGee & Richgels, 2012; Sturm, Cali, Nelson, & Staskowski, 2012). It is important not to underestimate the value of scribbling as a foundation for writing because young children demonstrate through their marks their understanding of the functions of written language even if they cannot produce conventional forms of it yet (Vukelich et al., 2012). However, by 3 years of age, young children are capable of rudimentary graphic representations of people, objects, and events that reflect personal meaning (Lancaster, 2007).

Children's drawing abilities were found to relate to the types of opportunities provided by adults. The more drawing opportunities children were afforded, the more they marked and scribbled, and the faster they made a transition to higher level prerepresentational and representational drawing (Dunst & Gorman, 2009). Thus, with repeated practice, many toddlers may begin to do controlled marks or geometric shapes, and some will draw simple figures.

Writing opportunities can be provided to children in several ways (Photo 14–4). Create a writing center and have recycled paper, printer paper, pencils, pens, crayons, and markers readily available. Provide a variety of choices in terms of those materials. For example, some toddlers push hard so they prefer chunky crayons that do not break easily while other toddlers grip and push more gently so they prefer a thin marker. Toddlers should be able to self-select and self-regulate the use of these materials with minimal guidance from you. Toddlers also enjoy opportunities to mark on an easel or chalkboard. As with the writing center, rotate the types of materials available (e.g., paint, oil pastels, markers). If you do not have a chalkboard available, make your own by painting a section of a low wall with chalkboard paint. Select the location carefully so that it will get a lot of use and is easily cleaned. Be sure to add a border so that children understand the boundaries of that space and that not any wall can be written on. Thick, soft chalk, while it is messier, makes dark marks more easily. Thin, regular-size chalk can break more easily and can cause frustration.

As stated previously, adults play an important role in children's development of writing. They model many uses of writing for children: writing names on artwork papers, recording dictated sentences on the pages of a classroom story, writing notes to remember things, charting the growth of beans that the children planted, and documenting daily experiences in the block area. In this way, the children experience multiple, meaningful uses of writing. As with reading, early childhood educators should partner with family members to support emergent writing skills.

Playing

While reading and writing centers are a necessary component of an infant and toddler classroom, teachers should go beyond those centers to incorporate emergent literacy experiences. Intentionally connecting shared storybook reading experiences with props in the other classroom areas supports emergent literacy skills. Older toddlers have been found to engage in, for example, more sociodramatic play with the blocks when there are props connected to stories that have been read recently (Heisner, 2005). Teachers should allow props to migrate from one area to another so that the toddlers can build elaborate structures using unanticipated supplies (Luckenbill & Schallock, 2015). Wellhousen and Giles (2005/2006) also suggest that teachers can provide reading and writing materials as part of the block center. Children can use the materials to record their ideas and draw the structures they have created, and then use books to support their construction (e.g., look at a picture of a city as they build one), thus expanding their play. Research by Hanline, Milton, and Phelps (2010) found that preschool children with and without disabilities who had greater representation skills in block constructions had higher reading abilities and a faster rate of growth in reading abilities during the early elementary years. These authors concluded the following:

> . . . representational construction, socio-dramatic play and literacy materials within block play provide experiences for young children that may help them build the cognitive structures that support later literacy learning. (p. 1014)

Emergent literacy skills can easily be incorporated into the dramatic play area as well. For example, if the area is designed as a home, you could include a bookshelf or magazine rack with books, magazines, and newspapers. If you were to create a communication center for the home, you could place a phone on a table with a phone book and notepad for recording messages. If the area was designed like a restaurant, you could include menus, cookbooks and recipe cards, paper for making grocery lists, and a pad for taking orders. The idea is for educators to meaningfully and naturally integrate reading and writing into the play topic for the area.

Teachers can also integrate literacy into a science area or outdoor learning environment (McLennan, 2012). When studying birds that visit the class bird feeder, toddlers can be encouraged to record their observations via drawings and their words can be dictated. In addition, the teacher can take pictures of the birds and record what the children say about them. Picture books also can be specifically selected for the library area, while informational books (with lots of pictures) can be placed near the bird feeder so that birds can be matched on characteristics such as color or size.

In general, early childhood educators should provide ample opportunities for toddlers to have experiences with reading and writing materials to support the development of emergent literacy skills. In addition, those experiences should reflect how adults engage with reading and writing on a regular basis.

Before moving on with your reading, make sure that you can answer the following questions about the material discussed so far.

1. Why should teachers focus on "big ideas" when developing and implementing curriculum instead of isolated facts?
2. Explain the role adults play in toddlers' acquisition of emergent literacy skills.

READING
CHECKPOINT

14-2b Mathematics

Teachers of very young children should focus their integrated curriculum around mathematical process and content standard areas. The National Council of Teachers of Mathematics (2000) identified process standards that support problem solving, representation, reasoning, connections, and communication across the number and operations core content standard and the geometry core content standard for preschool children. The discussion here will focus on how infants and toddlers do the following:

- Reason and build connections.
- Engage in mathematical problem solving.
- Communicate their thinking about mathematical concepts.

These process skills then will be used to understand how teachers can support the development of numeracy (e.g., quantity, counting, measuring) through strategies such as observing, questioning, and classifying.

Reasoning and Building Connections

Reasoning involves drawing conclusions or inferences based on the logical use of data or facts. Reasoning is often associated with problem solving because good problem solving uses logical reasoning to attempt to arrive at a solution (Butera, Friesen, Palmer, Lieber, Horn, Hanson, et al., 2014). It is long believed that adults and toddlers reason differently from each other, with toddlers demonstrating more immature reasoning. However, recent research calls at least one aspect of that conclusion into question. Casler, Hoffman, and Eshleman (2014) found that both toddlers and adults overattended to the role of function when selecting a tool for a task and ignored other properties, such as size, that would make the tool impractical. Thus both the toddlers and the adults made serious scale mistakes in selecting the tool. The authors argued the following:

> . . . it may be inaccurate to explain their scale errors in purely maturation-based or perceptual terms. Mounting research suggests that all humans are deeply biased toward categorizing and using objects according to functions . . ." (Casler et al., 2014, p. 1699).

For other types of reasoning, toddlers may need adult assistance to develop necessary skills and understanding.

Comparisons of quantity, number, space, and time are explorations in building connections between two or more objects or events in a new and abstract way. Children can seek relationships among any kinds of materials (Photo 14–5). Walker and Gopnik (2014) discovered that toddlers as young as 18 months can accurately infer a higher-order relational causal principle from just a few observations. This means that young toddlers not only attend to the features of the object but how the objects act in relationship to each other. These researchers also found that the toddlers would use this newly gained knowledge to guide their own subsequent actions with the objects (Walker & Gopnik, 2014). Games and learning experiences that use invented relationships help stimulate and reinforce their constructions. For example, providing a group of objects to sort and classify might lead a child to notice color relationships.

PHOTO 14–5 Provide children with a variety of opportunities to make comparisons and find relationships between objects.

Problem Solving

Toddlers should be given many opportunities to solve problems throughout the day. When these occur naturally because a material will not stick in the glue, a paintbrush breaks, a wheel falls off the trike, or a plant dies due to lack of water, they seamlessly fit into the flow of the day. However, early childhood educations should also intentionally plan for problem solving in the daily learning experiences. Butera et al. (2014) suggest that teachers should directly teach mathematical problem solving, which they say has five steps:

1. What is the problem?
2. Think of some solutions that might work.
3. Talk about each of the solutions and select the best one.
4. Try it!
5. Reflect by asking, "How did it work?"

Problem solving takes a great deal of mental concentration. Thus, teachers should find ways to minimize distractions when toddlers are problem solving. In a recent research study, Wyss, Kannass, and Haden (2013) tested how distracted toddlers would be when engaging in a variety of tasks. When toddlers were problem solving, they were more easily distracted. They also discovered that toddlers in the distraction situation were able to attend better during the second half of the testing period than the first. The authors concluded that the toddlers ". . . may have habituated to the distractor or were better able to resist distraction as the session progressed" (p. 423). With that in mind, early childhood educators should find ways to minimize distractions but should also realize that teaching a toddler how to re-attend to a problem is an important life skill, even for very young children.

You may recall that Chapter 6 discussed using problem solving for social issues. When you compare the steps in both approaches to problem solving, you should notice a great deal of similarities. Social problem solving is discussed here again because of its importance for toddlers. When we address problems encountered by toddlers (e.g., conflict, emotional dysregulation) as social problems rather than individual child problems, we work *with* toddlers to help them learn language, cooperation, perspective taking, and empathy (Gloeckler & Cassell, 2012). Most importantly, it fosters self-regulation skills that assist a child in persisting when faced with a problem be it social or cognitive. Furthermore, it supports mental problem solving as toddlers slowly gain foundational skills for mentally solving social problems.

Communicating about Thinking

Because toddlers can still reason prelogically at times, adults often misunderstand how they reached a conclusion or outcome. Adults and children construct understanding of experiences differently. If a child and an adult were present during the same experience, each would learn and experience something different. Toddlers attend to different aspects or salient features during an experience. Through various scaffolding techniques, adults can assist toddlers to attend to other aspects and to communicate about their thinking by doing the following:

1. As you interact with the materials, talk through your own questions. "I wonder how I should start." "Could I put them together?" "Is it working?" "What's going to happen?" "How did I do this?"

2. Ask the child similar questions. Phrase them simply, and give the child plenty of time to think and answer.

3. Encourage the child to repeat each solution several times to understand it. "Can you do it again?"

4. Foster understanding. Ask "Why do you think that happened?" "Why did (or didn't) that work?"

Toddlers can be asked to explain their reasoning for other conclusions they are drawing. When a toddler tells you at snack that you have more milk in your cup than she does, respond by using a prompt such as "How do you know?" or "Tell me more."

If a toddler says "Not fair" and points between two piles of sorting bears on the table, ask "How are the piles not fair?" The point is to be attuned to the toddlers' actions and words so that you can use a prompt to elicit an explanation of their thinking.

Numeracy

Toddlers need experiences to build mathematical understanding, not just talking about math (Franzén, 2014). When provided with open-ended materials, toddlers spend a great deal of time counting and sorting them.

They are just developing language to describe their actions, so they might not talk, they might use language in different ways than you, or they might reflect common usage. Recent research found that toddlers in Norway demonstrated fewer skills than expected in using number words and reciting number sequences; the authors wondered if this could be based on cultural differences (Reikerås, Løge, & Knivsberg, 2012). Toddlers, who are just learning that there are labels for grouping objects, may have repeatedly heard adults or older children say those labels. Yet, understanding that each label has a specific meaning and that it represents a particular group of items is still developing. For example, a toddler is working with blocks on the table. You overhear her say, "one, two, five, nine" while touching each of the four items. Some caregivers might want to correct the child's counting, but it is better to comment on what the child did accurately. You might say, for example, "You labeled each item as you counted it."

Toddlers often put objects in an order, such as placing a group of three buttons from biggest to smallest. They tend to be successful with three items, but when more objects are provided, the children may not be able to determine the logic of ordering. Arranging objects in a series, or **seriation**, is guesswork for young children because they do not understand the relationships in a series of objects: an object that is simultaneously smaller than and larger than other objects is placed in the middle of the series. However, physical knowledge about the properties of objects develops through their continued interactions with materials.

seriation Ordering items in sequence based on criteria such as color, length, or size (e.g., small, medium, large).

As discussed previously, comparisons of quantity, number, space, and time are explorations in relating two or more objects or events in a new and abstract way. When comparing two groups of sticks, toddlers will experience the concept of more and less. Sorting items can result in understanding the relationship of color to the items. Some mathematical knowledge, however, is not physical in nature. Some relationships are not easily touched or manipulated by toddler hands. Instead, toddlers must mentally construct logico-mathematical knowledge for the relationships among objects. Considering time, caregivers naturally talk about causal relationships when moving a child through the daily routine. This helps to develop an understanding of before and after. To illustrate, the caregiver says, "You are hungry after playing outside. Let's wash our hands before snack." Infants and toddlers do not seem to use time-related vocabulary until around the middle of the third year of life. Then, they begin to talk about "when I was a baby," or they may even pretend to be a baby again. They may also talk about events from their past by using terms in very general ways. Yesterday may by overgeneralized to mean any day in the past, rather than the previous 24 hours (as adults use the term). When the toddler uses the word in a general way, just reflect back the child's sentence using the proper time term (e.g., last week, last month, in January).

This growing ability to focus on the past allows the opportunity for early childhood educators to assist toddlers in reflecting on their recent behaviors. For children this age, reflection must be supported by concrete products (e.g., photographs) and artifacts (e.g., drawings or sculptures). Holsington (2002) discovered that taking photographs of block play assisted children with asking questions, thinking through problems, and making connections between building experiences.

Spotlight on Practice

VOICES FROM THE FIELD

I am the owner/teacher of my family child care center. I planned a musical experience for the two infants (9 and 11 months of age) and the toddler in my care. It was one of the first I've done with children this young. I just recently read an article about the importance of music for very young children, so I decided to try it out. In the middle of the kitchen floor, I put out several different types and sizes of bowls as well as plastic tubes of different lengths. I then placed wooden and metal spoons on the floor.

I didn't take the children to the materials but rather waited for them to discover them. Ethan found them first. He squealed with joy as he picked up two metal bowls and banged them together. He squinted his eyes and

dropped the pans. He had a scared look on his face as he gazed up at me. I said, "What a loud noise you made. Did that scare you? (pause) Maybe you should hit the bowl with your hand." He did just that and resumed smiling.

Kei crawled quickly into the room with a curious look on her face. She reached for a tube and a wooden spoon. She began banging the spoon on the tube.

Ethan and Kei passed materials back and forth between them on two separate occasions. I was impressed with their developing social skills and with how engaged they were with the materials. This was also an important cognitive experience for them as they produced music independently through their own actions. I will need to think about other ways to engage Maisy, as she never joined in the experience.

14-2c Fine Arts

Fine arts include visual art, dramatic play, music, and creative movement/dance experiences. Many states, such as Georgia and Indiana, have adopted guidelines for such experiences for very young children. Georgia's creative dance guidelines, for example, state that infants will respond to music, young toddlers (12–24 months) will move their body to music, and older toddlers (24–36 months) will dance to and become engaged in music and movement (Georgia Department of Early Care and Learning, 2015).

Unfortunately, we find ourselves in a climate where attention to fine arts continues to be questioned. Teaching and learning for young children has relied upon the creative subjects in making children aware of the world around them and of their own creative and artistic competences—even though emergent literacy and mathematics are viewed as more important (Samuelsson, Carlsson, Olsson, Pramling, & Wallerstedt, 2009). Early childhood educators need to advocate for focused attention, time, and space for experiences with the fine arts, starting in infancy. Samuelsson et al. (2009) argue that the fine arts should be domain-intrinsic knowing, or the use of arts to learn more about the arts. This is in contrast to domain-extrinsic knowing where the arts are a means for developing capabilities in domains outside of the arts. Many researchers have hypothesized that if the arts can be used to demonstrate more about literacy or mathematical understanding, then their value would increase. Phillips, Gorton, Pinciotti, and Sachdev (2010) investigated how a fine arts curriculum could be used to promote literacy and other school readiness skills. They found that their art curriculum in fact did provide small gains in literacy and school readiness for their sample of high-risk preschoolers. More recent research has found similar results in terms of school readiness skills (Nevanen, Juvonen, & Ruismäki, 2014). Whether you take a domain-intrinsic or domain-extrinsic knowing perspective, fine arts must be an integral component of your infant-toddler curriculum.

Visual Arts

As soon as infants can sit in your lap and use the pincer grasp, they are ready to explore art materials. They should be provided with a variety of materials, such as pencils, pens, paint, crayons, markers, clay, and dough so that they can experience drawing, painting, sculpting, and so on. Even though some might suggest that toddlers should be given fat or chunky versions of materials, it is better to encourage the young child to choose. Each toddler should determine what works best for her. Some toddlers are very aware of the type of pencil their siblings use at their schools, others want to "write like Dad," and still others prefer to use the chunky crayons because they break less often.

Infants should be encouraged to develop an understanding of the properties of the materials they are provided. Before they can use the materials to communicate an idea, they need to understand if it is sticky, cold, hard, malleable, and so on. In other words, gaining physical or functional knowledge about the materials precedes any creative processes. In addition, infants and toddlers do not need a full range of choices when initially experiencing art materials (Photo 14–6). For example, it is enough to provide one color of paint at a time at the easel so that the young toddlers' focus is on learning how the paint spreads and responds to a finger in comparison to a thick brush. When they have more experience, you can add in another color and begin to introduce additional tools (e.g., thin brush, Q-tip, feather).

By the end of the third year, many toddlers will begin to label aspects of their artwork, the entire product, or another person's artwork. For example, a toddler might say, "I made a whale" while showing you a drawing. This labeling represents a beginning understanding that she can communicate symbolic intentions and pictorial concepts as well as use materials expressively in art (Louis, 2013). Adults can also help the toddlers begin to appreciate another

© 2017 Cengage Learning

PHOTO 14–6 It is enough for young toddlers to use just one color of paint because they are just learning how paint spreads.

person's artwork by looking closely at it and describing what they see. The discussions might focus entirely on color, shape, and types of lines (straight, curvy), or they may expand beyond that to what the artist was representing ("It is a flower at night."). Discussions such as these may assist a toddler in valuing nature and specifically his own local environments (Ward, 2013).

Dramatic Play

dramatic play A form of play that provides opportunities to combine language with imagination.

This type of play provides opportunities to combine language with imagination. The positive impacts of **dramatic play** on problem solving, representational skills, divergent thinking, and mathematical readiness as well as language and literacy development have been well documented through decades of research. Children of this age use their language skills to describe their actions and take on new roles (e.g., say what they think others might say). They are simultaneously mastering their language and fitting it into a social context (Honig, 2005).

As such, the dramatic play area should not always reflect a "house" area; it should be expanded to include other play themes. This area can be used to support the inquiry focus for the curriculum. For example, a toddler teacher could change the house area into a child-generated art museum as a way to extend a recent field trip. This area could have children's artwork framed and hung on the walls, sculptures displayed on low counters, and pictorial maps of the "museum." Like many museums, the teacher could include space for observing and/or replicating the artwork.

Sociodramatic roles occur in many areas of the classroom. Block play has shown alternative avenues to positive developmental outcomes, possibly due to the ability of children to take on sociodramatic roles (e.g., construction worker, zookeeper, bird sitting on a nest) while building. When teachers intentionally connect storybook reading experiences with props found in the block area, children engage in more sociodramatic play with the blocks (Heisner, 2005).

Thus, teachers should provide materials that support dramatic play in areas of the classroom beyond the one area specifically designated for that purpose (Photo 14–7).

Music

Newborns are born with the capacity for distinguishing frequency and pitch (Healy, 2004), and they develop finer auditory discrimination during the first year. For example, Newman (2005) found that at 5 months of age, infants can separate speech produced by different talkers at the same time, although it is a capacity that develops greatly by 13 months of age. Additionally, mothers reported that

© 2017 Cengage Learning

PHOTO 14–7 Dramatic play can take place both inside and outside the dramatic play areas.

music was an important part of their interactions with their infants, especially in supporting learning, creating a positive atmosphere, and enhancing family traditions (Byrn & Hourigan, 2010). Music has also been found to be an important factor in developing a sense of self. Barrett (2011) discovered in her three-year longitudinal study that toddlers regularly invent songs and engage with music in their homes. The findings suggest that this musical storying and storytelling encourages young children to enact multiple ways of being. In fact, Morehouse (2013) suggests that young children should frequently engage in music-making behaviors. Teachers can support such behaviors by providing percussion instruments (e.g., drums, maracas) to reinforce the children's physical connection with music.

Just as we provide infants with a well-balanced diet, we should also provide a well-balanced auditory environment, as "soothing, pleasant and interesting sounds inspire curiosity and a receptive attitude" toward language (Healy, 2004, p. 46). Music is a great educational resource because you can select slow or fast music, depending on your needs (see Table 14–1). For toddlers, a great activity is to form a circle with classical music playing in the background and dance to the music. Adding scarves encourages full-body movements. For example, play "The Flight of the Bumblebee" (Rimsky-Korsakov), pretend everyone is a bumblebee, and buzz around the room. In contrast, playing this music right before nap time would not serve to assist children with relaxing and transitioning to sleep.

Additionally, too much noise, noises that are too loud, or nonstop noise can cause confusion and be detrimental to development. Thus, caregivers must carefully monitor background sounds (especially music) and discuss this issue with family members.

Creative Movement/Dance

Infants and toddlers should also be involved in creative movements and dance, which can be as easy as playing music and inviting the children to dance (if they had not already started). You can also make available scarves and ribbons for moving to the music. The National Coalition for Core Arts Standards (NCCAS, 2014) states that preschool children should respond to suggestions for changing movement through guided improvisational experiences. Thus, playing freeze or participating in guided movements such as hop like a bunny or crawl like a snake are reasonable expectations for toddlers. Toddlers can also be encouraged to act out a familiar nursery rhyme or story. Samuelsson et al. (2009) suggest that teachers should give children verbal feedback and challenge them to express their ideas in dance and aesthetic movements.

14-2d Social Studies

The National Council for the Social Studies (NCSS, 2010) has devised curriculum standards for preschool through grade 12. This organization has outlined 10 themes for those curriculum standards:

1. Culture
2. Time, continuity, and change
3. People, places, and environments

TABLE 14–1 ▶ Music Resources

The following is a list of music that can be used in a variety of ways with toddlers to support their development and learning.

Country/Folk Music

Arbo, Rani. (2010). [Recorded by Rani Arbo & Daisy Mayhem]. *Ranky tanky* [CD]. Middletown, CT: Mayhem Music.

Dobbins, J., & Huliska-Beith, L. (2013). *A farmer's life for me.* [Book with CD]. Cambridge, MA: Barefoot Books.

Dreyer Family Band. (2009). *Family photograph* [CD]. United States: Mighty Toad Music.

Fox and Branch. (2009). *Take time in life* [CD]. Milwaukee, WI: Fox and Branch.

Guthrie, Sarah Lee. (2009). *Go waggaloo* [CD]. Washington, DC: Smithsonian Folkways.

Mitchell, Elizabeth, vocalist. (2010). [Recorded by Elizabeth Mitchell; ft. Daniel Littleton, and Children of Agape Choir]. *Sunny day* [CD]. SI: Smithsonian Folkways.

Sleepytime Rangers. (2011). *Nashville for babies: Lullaby renditions of country music hits* [CD]. SI: Sleepytime Rangers Records.

Educational Music

Broza, J., Fink, C., & Marxer, M. (2012). *Someone else's shoes* [CD]. SI: Big Round Records.

Day, Roger. (2010). *Why does gray matter? And other brainy songs for kids!* [CD]. Franklin, TN: Roger Davis Productions.

Plume, J. (therapist). (2013). *Everybody has a story* [CD]. Nashville, TN: Monroe Carell Jr. Children's Hospital at Vanderbilt.

Harman, Mar. (2011). *Adding animals* [CD]. SI: Music with Mar.

Harman, Mar. (2011). *Subtracting animals* [CD]. SI: Music with Mar.

Hartmann, Jack. (2010). *Rockin' reading songs* [CD]. St. Petersburg, FL: Hop 2 It.

Feldman, Jean R. (2009). [Recorded by Children's choir]. *Going green* [CD]. Tampa, FL: Progressive Music.

Stephens, C. (2012). *Season sings!* [CD]. Portland, OR: CD Baby.

They Might Be Giants (2009). *Here comes science* [CD]. Burbank, CA: Walt Disney Records; Brooklyn, NY: Idlewild Recordings.

Exercise/Movement Music

Bari Koral Family Rock Band. (2014). *The apple tree & the honey bee* [CD]. Ann Arbor, MI: Loopylou Tunes by All Media Network.

Feldman, Jean R. (2010). *Better bodies and brains* [CD]. Tampa, FL: Manufactured by Progressive Media & Music.

Mr. Greg. (2010). *Lots of fun!* [CD]. United States: GregRoth/Greg BMI.

Pfeiffer, Tessa. (2009). *Dance it!* [CD]. SI: asseT Productions.

Smith, Aaron Nigel. (2010). *Everyone loves to dance!* [CD]. Redway, CA: Music for Little People.

Misc.—Children's Music

Bryce, D. (author). (2013). *Aheym: Kronos Quartet plays music by Bryce Dessner* [CD]. Los Angeles, CA: Wea Corp.

Father Goose. (2014). *Bashment time* [CD]. New York, NY: Goose Hut.

Hope, Charlie, musician. (2009). *I'm me!* [CD]. Ontario: Little Maple Leaf Productions.

Kidz Bop Kids. (2013). *Kidz Bop party hits* [CD]. New York: Razor & Tie.

Laurie Berkner Band. (2014). *The ultimate Laurie Berkner band collection* [CD]. New York: Two Tomatoes/Razor & Tie.

TABLE 14–1 ▸ Music Resources (*continued*)

Maggie G. (2010). *Around the house* [CD]. Burlington, Ontario: The Children's Group.

McCory, Peter. (2009). *Get all happy!* [CD]. Warrenton, VA: Peter McCory: Maranna Music.

Recess Monkey. (2009). *Field trip* [CD]. SI: Recess Monkey.

Roslonek, Steve. (2010). *Music time with Steve Songs. Vol. 2* [CD]. United States: PBS Kids.

Valeri, Michele. (2010). *Little ditties for itty bitties: Songs for infants and toddlers* [CD]. SI: Community Music.

Music for Little People (2010). [Recorded by Various performers]. *Giggling & laughing: Silly songs for kids.* [CD]. Redway, CA: Music for Little People.

Silverstein, Shel. (2010). *Twistable, turnable man: [A musical tribute to the songs of Shel Silverstein].* [CD]. Nashville, TN: Sugar Hill.

Yakobian, D. H., & Nelson, M. (2012). *Classical for today's kids* [CD]. Encino, CA: Worldwide Success Media.

Lullabies

Berkner, L. (2014). *Lullabies* [CD]. New York: Razor & Tie.

Hope, Charlie, musician. (2009). *World of dreams* [CD]. Ontario: Little Maple Leaf Productions.

Hot Peas 'n Butter, musical group. (2012). *Catchin' some peaz, the lullabies.* New York: Hot Peas 'n Butter.

Lite, Lori, & Jacopin, David. (2010). *Indigo dreams: Kid's relaxation music: Magical musical melodies relaxing children's bodies and minds* [CD]. SI: www.StressFreeKids.com.

Putumayo World Music. (2011). [Recorded by Putumayo Kids]. *Acoustic dreamland* [CD]. New York: Putumayo World Music.

Springfield, Rick. (2009). *My precious little one [sound recording]: Lullabies for a new generation* [CD]. New York: Gomer Records.

Various performers. (2011). *The rough guide to world lullabies* [CD]. London: World Music Network.

Rock Music

Billy, Mr. (2012). *A boy and his guitar* [CD]. SI: Flying Bounce House Records.

Billy, Mr. (2010). *H2O-go-go* [CD]. SI: GO Kids Music.

Billy, Mr. (2010). *Rock and roll railroad* [CD]. SI: GO Kids Records.

Milkshake. (2009). *Great day* [CD]. Baltimore, MD: Milkshake Music.

Not-Its! (2009). *We are the Not-Its!* [CD]. SI: Little Loopy Records.

Recess Monkey. (2011). *Flying!* [CD]. SI: Recess Monkey.

Sulinha. (2012). *Imagination* [CD]. SI: Sulinha Boucher.

Uncle Rock. (2010). *The big picture* [CD]. Chichester, NY: Jackpot Music.

World Music

Barbier, K., Debussy, C., Albéniz, I., & Schumann, R. (2014). *Evocation* [CD]. Germany: Oehms Classics.

Moona Luna. (2010). *Piñata party* [CD]. SI: Luchadora.

Putumayo World Music. (2009). *Picnic playground: Musical treats from around the world* [CD]. New York: Putumayo World Music.

Various singers and musicians. (2013). Based on Tchaikovsky, P. I. (composer), *Max & Ruby in The Nutcracker Suite* [CD]. United States: Koba Music, The Children's Group.

Various writers. (2010). [Recorded by Various performers]. *World music for children: Dance the world* [CD]. United States: World Music Network.

4. Individual development and identity

5. Individuals, groups, and institutions

6. Power, authority, and governance

7. Production, distribution, and consumption

8. Science, technology, and society

9. Global connections

10. Civic ideals and practices

It is the responsibility of an early childhood educator working with very young children to set a foundation for some of these concepts during the first three years of life. For example, a basic feature of understanding culture is observing similarities and differences among groups. Infant and toddler providers can foster such understanding through an anti-biased curriculum (see Chapter 9) that challenges children's current understanding of identity, fairness, diversity, prejudice, and discrimination that can result from actual or perceived differences in culture.

As discussed many times throughout this book, infants and toddlers are faced with the developmental task of identity formation. Thus, gaining important intellectual, physical, social, and emotional skills as well as dispositions such as perseverance or self-direction influences how a child perceives herself as well as how others perceive her. Thus, a curriculum that has a strong focus on supporting, guiding, and challenging children to develop social and emotional skills that support later abilities to successfully work in groups is also a curriculum that is strong in social studies.

The last theme to be discussed is civic ideals and practices. You may recall from Chapter 6 that the concept of the image of the child is a social, ethical, and political statement about active participation in a democratic society. It should be no surprise, then, that learning to participate in a democratic society is a focus in the infant-toddler curriculum. This participation looks different from how a preschool child would engage. The goal during the first three years of life is to assist very young children in understanding that they have a voice in decisions that impact them. For example, giving an infant a choice of blankets at nap time allows him to decide how to experience resting that day. Attending carefully to the child's desired behavior, acknowledging that desire, and redirecting her efforts to a more appropriate location helps her to understand that her desires are important to others (not just her!). Moreover, responsive caregivers engage infants and toddlers in the six steps of problem solving when necessary. This facilitates their understanding of the importance of listening, gathering data, and finding a common solution. No one would expect a toddler to fully participate in society, exercise democratic freedoms, or pursue the common good (NCSS, 2010). However, a strong curriculum supports skills that assist infants and toddlers to successfully participate in groups now, while setting a foundation for later learning.

inquiry Asking and answering questions as well as solving problems that arise as the result of investigations or unexpected outcomes.

14-2e Science

Science is **inquiry**—asking and answering questions as well as solving problems that arise as the result of investigations or unexpected outcomes. Very young children ask questions through their actions or behaviors,

Spotlight on Research

TODDLERS AND MEDIA

The American Academy of Pediatrics has suggested that the time infants and toddlers spend in front of televisions, computers, and educational games should be eliminated for children under 2 years of age (American Academy of Pediatrics, 2011) and limited to one hour a day for all other children (American Academy of Pediatrics, 2012). This policy statement cites three primary reasons for this recommendation; two of which will be examined further: (1) the lack of evidence supporting educational or developmental benefits for media use, and (2) the potential adverse health and developmental effects of media use. But first, the prevalent use of media by very young children will be investigated.

Toddlers are certainly consumers of media—television, videos, and computer games. A parent survey revealed that "By 23 months of age, 100 percent of the children in the sample watched television, and 90 percent watched videos. . . . children typically watched videos for 25 minutes per day, and those who watched television programs did so for more than one hour per day" (Weber & Singer, 2004, p. 32). In a recent survey of parents of infants and toddlers (birth to age 3), data suggests that this trend has not abated and that children are clearly growing up in media-rich homes (Vaala, Bleakley, & Jordan, 2013). Particularly high rates of media usage occurred for older toddlers (2–3 year olds), children with a bedroom television, and those whose parents believe in various benefits of viewing. When mothers were asked about their beliefs regarding television/video usage by infants and toddlers, they reported more positive than negative beliefs about the outcomes associated with these types of media usage (Vaala, 2014). These beliefs were predictive of the children's estimated viewing rates. In other words, mothers who held more positive beliefs had children who viewed television/videos more. While 47 percent of the parents in Weber and Singer's (2004) study noted that they watched every television program with their child, it remains unclear what developmental benefits there are for the toddlers' media usage.

The primary concern of media viewing for very young children is that it does not provide educational or developmental benefits, merely benefits for the companies producing the media (Cardany, 2010). Infants and toddlers have been found to gain little from watching television due to a phenomenon called video deficit, whereby they comprehend less than they would from equivalent real-life displays (see, e.g., Anderson & Hanson, 2010; Courage & Howe, 2010). Researchers have investigated strategies for helping very young children overcome video deficit and have discovered that when parents engaged in more shared focus and turn-taking, infants looked more at the program (Fidler, Zack, & Barr, 2010) and when parents who talked most about what was on screen (e.g., labeling or describing what was on screen), children's language learning was boosted (Fender, Richert, Robb, & Wartella, 2010; Linebarger & Vaala, 2010). In contrast, other research has found that mothers verbally interacted less when watching television with their child than when reading a book or playing (Nathanson & Rasmussen, 2011). Lavigne, Hanson, and Anderson (2015) found that co-viewing baby videos decreased the quantity of parent language to their infant but in some cases increased the quality of the language used. It is unclear how frequently family members use television intentionally as a medium for positive interactions instead of using it as a babysitter (e.g., child watches program while adult cooks dinner). Furthermore, in the lives of busy families, it is possible that television viewing takes the place of other activities that have been proven to promote development and learning: play and reading.

Children and adults have adverse health effects of spending too much time in sedentary activities, especially television viewing. Television viewing has been long associated with rates of obesity. To illustrate, in a meta-analysis of 21 studies focusing only on infants, toddlers, and preschoolers, more television viewing was associated with higher rates of obesity and decreased scores on measures of psychosocial health and cognitive development (LeBlanc, Spence, Carson, Connor Gorber, Dillman, Janssen, et al., 2012). Going beyond the obvious relationship to lack of exercise, researchers have been interested in the impact of television on eating habits. For example, in a sample of Early Head Start families, watching more TV during mealtime was predictive of adults and toddlers consuming more unhealthy foods (Horodynski, Stommel, Brophy-Herb, & Weatherspoon, 2010). Similarly, Arthur (2010) argued that watching television commercials influenced children's food preferences for sugary cereals and snack foods.

Television and videos have no place in educational settings for infants and toddlers. Unfortunately, a recent study found that children were, in fact, watching

(continued)

Spotlight on Research (continued)

television in center-based and home-based child care, not just at home. In center-based programs, infants did not watch TV while toddlers watched on average 6 minutes a day whereas TV viewing in home-based programs was 12 minutes for infants and 1.6 hours for toddlers (Christakis & Garrison, 2009). TV watching was found to be significantly lower when providers in home-based programs had a two- or four-year college degree (Christakis & Garrison, 2009). In their policy statement, the American Academy of Pediatrics concluded that "despite the explicit or implicit marketing claims of educational programs for infants, whether they are actually learning something from these programs is questionable" (pp. 1041–1042). Weber and Singer (2004) enhance this claim when they state there is no evidence that "media can be integrated into the lives of very young children in a developmentally appropriate way" (p. 36).

What about newer forms of technology? The technology world experienced by infants and toddlers today is much different from the world in which many of us grew up in and has been studied by scientists in the past (Robb & Lauricella, 2015). For example, when a baby or toddler becomes upset while in a restaurant, she is frequently handed a mobile device such as a smartphone or tablet. It seems as if she immediately knows what to do; she swipes or taps the screen and is no longer upset. While these devices require less manual dexterity or cognitive understanding to operate (e.g., cause an outcome to occur) than a computer or a television, how are they impacting brain development or self-regulation skills? The research reviewed previously involved primarily television viewing; we know little about how the use of mobile devices impacts development and learning for infants and toddlers. Err on the side of caution and advocate for no screen time for children under the age of 2 and no more than one hour of screen time (e.g., combined TV, video, mobile device, and/or computer)—total for home and school—a day for children older than 2. In addition, we must remind family members of the benefits of reading, playing, and otherwise interacting with young children. If half an hour or more is devoted to watching television or videos, this time might be more wisely spent on shared reading, for example, given the developmental and educational outcomes associated with that strategy (Dodici, Draper, & Peterson, 2003; Lawhon & Cobb, 2002; Rosenkoetter & Barton, 2002).

---

rather than merely verbally. Therefore, infant and toddler teachers must observe closely to plan responsive and engaging science experiences. As mentioned previously, children build physical knowledge through their interactions with objects. DeVries, Zan, Hildebrandt, Edmiaston, and Sales (2002) suggest that four criteria must be met to support physical knowledge, especially concepts related to physics:

1. Children must produce the movement through their own actions.
2. Children must be able to vary their actions.
3. Children must observe the reaction of the objects.
4. The reaction of the objects must be immediate.

Playing with sand, building with blocks, manipulating goop[1] with their hands, rolling a ball down a ramp, and filling/spilling water from different containers all provide children with physical knowledge. Thus, teachers must provide a variety of materials and experiences to both spark children's questions and to help them answer questions. According to Stoll,

---

[1]Goop can be made by mixing 1 cup of corn starch and 1/3 cup water. Double or triple the recipe depending on how many children will be playing with it.

Hamilton, Oxley, Eastman, and Brent (2012), teachers should also build on "children's natural inclination for problem solving" (p. 26). DeVries and Sales (2011) suggest that teachers should provide different lengths of plastic tubes, cove molding, and many different things that roll (cars, marbles, balls, pebbles, etc.) to challenge children's understanding of gravity. (NOTE: Monitor items for being a choke hazard if a child still places objects in her or his mouth.) As children get older, they will build more sophisticated mental relationships that consider the weight of the object, slope of the ramp, and how the pieces are connected to the outcome observed. While the toddlers may focus on those aspects in isolation, they will probably spend a great deal of time experimenting with the materials to understand their basic properties.

An inquiry-based science curriculum should expand beyond the physical sciences to include life sciences (e.g., animals and botany) and environmental sciences. In previous chapters (e.g., Chapter 8 and 13), the focus was on building aspects of life sciences into the learning environment. Doing so allows the teacher to intentionally focus the curriculum on these aspects. Having a class vegetable garden, for example, brings the interplay of plants and human nutrition into many different conversations: when tending to the garden, when harvesting the tomatoes, when cooking the green beans, and when eating a fresh salad. In other words, a carefully planned environment offers opportunities for asking and answering questions about healthy eating habits in a way that is natural and meaningful (Kalich, Bauer, & McPartlin, 2009). Yet, the curriculum does not have to be merely about nutrition. You can get into other important life science topics such as biodiversity, ecosystems (need for sunlight, earthworms to enrich and aerate the soil, or bees to pollinate the plants and flowers), and life cycles. Investigating these topics using inquiry helps to focus on scientific process skills such as observation and data collection (Hachey & Butler, 2012). Recall that our goal is not to fill toddlers' heads with random bits of knowledge (or "facts") but rather pose questions and problems and assist them in addressing them.

Similarly, environmental scientists use interdisciplinary tools and knowledge to solve problems of our environment. Chapter 8 covered ways to reduce, reuse, and recycle materials to address societal concerns in early childhood education programs. When a learning environment is planned with such concerns in mind, it becomes a natural part of adult-child conversations and can be used in forming engaging curriculum. For example, if a toddler begins to throw away a partially used piece of paper, an adult can engage them in a conversation about the need to recycle that paper. Environmental scientists focus on other issues as well that can naturally occur in early learning environments. If a child begins to drink dirty water from a sensory table, the caregiver can direct them to clean water from the drinking fountain. This could lead to conversation on water pollution. Moreover, when taking walks around the neighborhood, children often notice trash left behind by others. Bringing a bag to gather the trash (if appropriate) can demonstrate how we all need to work together to keep our community clean from another type of pollutant. As you can see, because many concepts studied by environmental scientists are abstract, we should help toddlers learn about and engage with them on a concrete, personal level. According to Pancheri-Ambrose and Tritchler-Scali (2013), the more personal their experiences with nature, the more children become innovative, responsible, and concerned about the environment.

READING CHECKPOINT

Before moving on with your reading, make sure that you can answer the following questions about the material discussed so far.

1. Explain two strategies for promoting mathematical knowledge.
2. Describe how you would assist a child in using fine arts to demonstrate their understanding in another content area or their understanding of that aspect of fine arts.

14-3 Teaching with Content Learning in Mind

Earlier in Chapter 2, you were asked to conceptualize and represent the relationship between development and learning (see Figure 2–1 on page 23). You may recall that learning was defined as the acquisition of knowledge and skills through systematic study, instruction, practice, and/ or experience. In this chapter, we have investigated learning in regard to the content areas such as literacy, mathematics, and fine arts. The conversation will be furthered by considering what instructional methods to use with infants and toddlers. Traditional methods of instruction for preschool or elementary-age children should *not* be used with toddlers. The principles discussed throughout this book—engaged, active exploration that is child-led—apply to learning content knowledge as well as our previous discussions of supporting development. Carefully planned learning experiences give value to the tools of the learning disciplines (e.g., mathematics, social studies) and give curriculum intellectual integrity (Bredekamp & Copple, 1997). Toddlers should be given opportunities to investigate scientific topics they have questions about (e.g., living creatures, microorganisms, gravity; see, e.g., Youngquist, 2004) and use processes such as observing, recording, and testing hypotheses. They should have daily experiences with mathematical concepts such as solving problems, measurement, and geometry. Integrated projects such as the ones described on the following pages are important to the learning of toddlers because the tools used allow children to do the following:

> . . . directly participate in study of the disciplines, for instance, by conducting scientific experiments, writing [observations], . . . collecting and analyzing data, . . . and performing other roles of experts in the disciplines. (Bredekamp & Copple, 1997, p. 20)

emergent curriculum Devising curricular experiences based on previous observations of the children's interests, needs, and questions.

To support learning, early childhood educations should build an **emergent curriculum** that is responsive to the ever-changing and evolving characteristics of children in the group (Wien, 2008). Emergent curriculum is created for a specific child within a group based on current knowledge of what the child can do, what the child is interested in, and what challenges the child is ready for. In other words, teachers create curriculum from their research on children (Wien, 2008). A holistic curriculum that addresses the development of the whole child (e.g., physical, cognitive/language, emotional, and social) as well as learning in each of the content areas is a must. Daily and weekly plans typically focus most on individual activities for toddlers, but some short small-group activities may be included, such as telling a story, reciting a nursery rhyme, or doing a fingerplay. Any small-group activity would be appropriate for use with individuals. In addition, short- and long-term **integrated projects**, which carry ideas from one day to another, provide a mechanism for toddlers to develop important dispositions and knowledge. Working on an ongoing project naturally results in challenges and problems to be solved. Therefore, projects assist toddlers in developing the disposition of **discipline** or the ability to maintain energy in and focus on an activity in the face of obstacles to reach a desired aim (Glassman & Whaley, 2000). An example of an integrated project is cooking. When caregivers provide opportunities for cooking, toddlers gain cognitive skills (e.g., transformations), mathematics skills (e.g., measuring), literacy skills (e.g., written communication for providing information), and life skills (e.g., making healthy food choices; Colker, 2005; Darbyshire, 2004; Houts, 2002). Brewer (2010) demonstrated how toddlers developed discipline as they investigated Canadian Geese over the course of several months. Building on the children's interests and working toward an aim are both necessary conditions for quality education. "Children who are not emotionally engaged with the material they are learning and by the teachers who instruct them, cannot grow intellectually" (Olfman, 2008, p. 62).

> **integrated project** Curriculum approach where ideas are carried from one day to another as a mechanism for developing important dispositions and knowledge.

> **discipline** the ability to focus on an activity in the face of obstacles to reach a desired outcome.

The rest of this section shares three projects designed specifically for toddlers to illustrate how scientific and mathematical knowledge can be explored with very young children. Examples of incorporating literacy and fine arts in the projects are included as well.

Shaffer, Hall, and Lynch (2009) investigated insects with a group of toddlers. The teachers intentionally decided to "value and foster the children's curiosity about insects," which was a challenge because the adults initially held negative views about bugs (p. 20). This project emerged because the toddlers spent a great deal of time searching their environments (indoors and outdoors; home and school) for insects. When an insect was found, it resulted in the opportunities to observe and record observations through drawings, create and revise hypotheses (e.g., where particular bugs like to live; what happens to insects in the wintertime), ask questions (e.g., "What happens if . . ."), and conduct experiments (e.g., try out an idea when safe for both child and insect). In addition, when a question arose that couldn't be answered via experimentation (e.g., is an orange bug with no spots really a ladybug?), they sought out an expert (e.g., parent who is an entomologist) or informational texts (i.e., nonfiction books). It is important to note that many informational texts exist about insects but are not written for toddlers; adult support and guidance to look at the pictures can make the books useful tools. The toddlers were then supported as they shared the information back with the whole group. Thus, the toddlers learned that finding scientific answers takes research of many different forms.

As mentioned previously, Brewer (2010) conducted a project on Canadian geese with a group of five children (one infant, three toddlers, and one preschooler) in her home-based child care center. On each visit to the dam/park she would take a "discovery bag" that typically contained card stock, pens/pencils, magnifying glasses, specimen containers (to bring back an item for future observation), and binoculars. Brewer (2010) describes how Alex (30 months) looked intentionally at the geese and then made marks on his paper. While the marks did not yet represent recognizable geese, he was engaging in important fieldwork—careful observation and records of them—just as a professional scientist does. Even the youngest child in the group engaged in scientific explorations as she noticed the animals' reactions to her honking like a goose and screaming like a gull. During a discussion with the oldest child in the group, the teacher suggested making a cast of footprints the geese leave in the mud. This provocation afforded not only a scientific exploration of the characteristics of the footprints but also provided opportunities for mathematical experiences (to be discussed shortly).

Grzegorzewska and Konieczna-Blicharz (2011) describe a light project they completed with 24 toddlers (18–36 months of age) and their parents. The children were initially provided with a question ("What shines in our classroom?") to provoke their thinking. They engaged with a variety of light sources (e.g., flashlight, candle, lamps) and made discoveries about how they work (e.g., turn switch, push button). Then, they tested and observed the results of their own actions (e.g., turning light switch on and off changed room from light to dark). Adults provided the children with a wide variety of lightbulbs and challenged them to guess if each would fit into a particular lamp. As another aspect of their fieldwork, they went on a field trip to a store with plenty of lights to observe, draw, and explore. In addition, they were able to ask questions of the experts who worked there.

Clearly, these projects abounded in scientific concepts and principles. For example, toddlers were given first-hand experiences to support their inquiry in all of these projects. They both asked questions and were asked questions to extend their thinking about how objects and living organisms work. They were provided experiences in how to gain information about a topic: observing, reading, and seeking out experts. In the insect and light project, the children were encouraged to compare fiction and nonfiction books. Toddlers in all of the projects drew to record observation and revisited them to consider changes in their thinking. All in all, the toddlers in these classrooms were provided rich experiences that afforded them the opportunity to act as scientists.

It is conceivable that these toddlers also had the chance to act as mathematicians during these projects. While not explicitly discussed in the articles, I will hypothesize how each of the science projects described here is connected with mathematical concepts (based on a review of literature). When examining and discussing the geese footprint casts or the various types of insects, the children might have compared and contrasted them by using descriptive language (e.g., tall, big, small, skinny) to tell how they were alike and different (Geist, 2009). In addition, the toddlers might have come to see that some footprints or insects could

Spotlight on Curriculum

HIGH-QUALITY PROGRAM MODELS

This textbook has provided you with guidance on how to create emergent, responsive curricula for infants and toddlers. The best way to create curricula for very young children is to develop it yourself based on careful observations of the children in your care. We also realize that there are some curriculum models that can provide you with additional structure and direction. If you were to select and implement a particular given model, it should be done only after careful consideration and investigation of the theories used to build the program. A program model should provide you with guidance (as this textbook has) without causing you to merely implement a series of predetermined curriculum activities.

There are a number of high-quality program models that might be useful to you as a classroom teacher or in a child care program; yet, this section will feature only a few for which information is readily available online. *High/Scope for Infants and Toddlers; Creative Curriculum for Infants, Toddlers, and Twos*; and the *Waldorf Curriculum* all build on the understanding that children are active meaning-makers who need open-ended materials to explore and develop their minds. Hence, play is a fundamental aspect of all of these models. In addition, planning for positive social interactions among adults and children is a significant component in each model.

Research is available for each program model. Of course, careful attention to who conducted the research and how outcomes were measured are important when evaluating the data and the conclusions drawn. Some research comparing program models, such as Edwards's (2002), is not affiliated with any particular program model and thus might be considered more objective.

In addition, the teachers in the infant-toddler and preschool centers of Reggio Emilia, Italy, have plenty to teach us about high-quality care and education. Although they are not a program model, they do offer, through a variety of publications, their experiences as a tool for analyzing and reflecting on your own practices.

be reclassified to fit into more than one category (e.g., small and then skinny) depending on what dimension was being attended to (Horst, Ellis, Samuelson, Trejo, Worzalla, Peltan, et al., 2009). Furthermore, the toddlers could have counted, with the assistance of a more knowledgeable other person, the number of different types of lightbulbs they examined or the number of different insects they collected. Such counting experiences are necessary for the development of number concepts such as number labels, counting, and one-to-one correspondence (Linder, Powers-Costello, & Stegelin, 2011). Howell and Kemp (2010) remind us that early number sense is an essential component of number sense prior to school entry. However, toddlers should not be expected to master any of those concepts. Instead, the goal is to create a rich, meaningful environment where mathematical concepts are discussed and explored. This stance emerges from research that found the more parents used "math talk" in their home, the more their toddlers understood cardinal number knowledge (i.e., understanding that the number 4 refers to a set of four items; Levine, Suriyakham, Rowe, Huttenlocher, & Gunderson, 2010). The authors concluded that the quality of the mathematical language environment can positively impact current understanding as well as future achievement. It is reasonable to expect that when early childhood educators create similarly high-quality mathematical environments, it will positively impact learning as well.

Thus, when planning an integrated project, teachers of very young children should consider how to support learning in each of the content areas. It is not enough to focus on one content area because such learning does not occur in isolation. Children's minds are working to connect new vocabulary, outcomes from measuring objects, and drawing of their theories to their understanding of a concept (e.g., how birds fly). However, Kogan and Pin (2009) remind us that project work for toddlers is different from that of preschoolers or older children. They theorized that teachers of very young children should focus on *project practice*, or experiences that introduced them to specific elements of project work. To illustrate, instead of engaging children in a discussion to find out what they already know about a given topic and what they want to know, toddler teachers used observations of the children to guide their brainstorming session of possible provocations. To account for the children's language skills, toddlers should be provided one provocation at a time and observed and listened to carefully as they engaged with the materials. Observation data were analyzed to determine the children's level of interest and implicit questions.

Opportunities for fieldwork should also reflect the budding capabilities of the children. As the three projects demonstrated, categories of fieldwork can include, but are not limited to, observational drawings and paintings, making clay or other models, building with blocks, and expressing ideas through dramatic play. Of course, expectations for performance during those experiences were based on what the teacher knows about the individual capabilities of the toddlers. One child might engage in an observational drawing by making random marks while another might use geometric shapes. Honoring and valuing both modes of expression supports these very young children in learning their personal power for creating written communication during project work. Because some toddlers are just beginning to play cooperatively, Kogan and Pin (2009) suggested that fieldwork experiences be primarily designed for solitary or parallel work with some opportunities for older toddlers to be more cooperative. Individual work can be combined and discussed in documentation and displays to represent the work of the entire group.

As you can see, project work provides an important avenue for toddlers to engage with content area knowledge and to support their developing capabilities as learners. In fact, they might come to understand that: "What I do, say, and think is important," or "My work is taken seriously," or "I can impact what happens in a group" (Grzegorzewska & Konieczna-Blicharz, 2011). Each child in our care has the right to such rich learning opportunities.

Closing Note

Even now in the twenty-first century, the huge gap between humankind's intellectual development and emotional development is obvious. Wars continue to rage, terrorists gain power from instilling fear, and people are killed because of the color of their skin. Educators who work with our youngest citizens are responsible for creating a strong foundation for development and learning, but especially for social and emotional skills.

Considering someone else's needs or perspective before taking action, for example, can serve not only that relationship but also the greater good. Thus, now that you possess the knowledge of the importance of teaching emotional intelligence, you must act to improve the humanity of the next generation. As a caregiver of infants and toddlers, you have an essential role in ensuring that our youngest citizens learn how to interact humanely and intimately with other people, develop sound mental health and healthy self-esteem, maintain a balance between thinking and feeling, and improve the quality of life.

You are in the unique position to assist the field of early childhood education and the greater society in changing from an exclusive emphasis on cognitive skills to a greater emphasis on being emotionally healthy and socially at ease when in the presence of others. By placing importance on the emotional and social development of children, as well as the other major areas of physical and cognitive development, you can significantly help create a social structure in which compassion, understanding, and ethical behavior are valued and practiced.

Caregivers of children from birth through age 3 are in an ideal position to lay the foundation for emotionally and socially intelligent individuals. Your abilities to practice the three *As* and care for young children sensitively will promote optimal development for individuals; in the process, society will truly be affected. Congratulations on your choice of the most important position in society!

Before moving on with your reading, make sure that you can answer the following questions about the material discussed so far.

1. What are the benefits to using integrated curriculum with toddlers?
2. Provide two examples of how you would integrate social studies into one of the projects described.

READING CHECKPOINT

Summary

14-1 Articulate "big ideas" for infants and toddlers that are associated with each content area.

"Big ideas" such as problem solving, writing for a purpose, expressing ideas through paint and movement, changing over time, exercising, and balancing objects should be the focus of open-ended learning experiences for very young children.

14-2 Differentiate central concepts of each content area.

In addition to development, teachers of infants and toddlers embed content area learning in the curriculum. The content should cover central concepts in emergent literacy, mathematics, fine arts, and social studies.

14-3 Devise a broad range of strategies for children to acquire developmentally appropriate content knowledge through integrated projects.

Toddlers should be provided challenging, ongoing learning experiences (i.e., integrated projects) that build on and stretch their capabilities in each content area.

CASE STUDY   Andrea's Explorations

Andrea, from earlier in this chapter, is a 27-month-old who comes from an upper-middle-class professional family. Both of her parents have successful professions and work full time, so Andrea is in child care full time. Observations by Allen, her primary caregiver, led him to conclude that Andrea is very interested in music and movement as well as reading. At the last conference with her parents, Allen learned that they also like music and often take her to free children's concerts held in local parks. Andrea participates less frequently in the science activities he provides. Allen hypothesizes that this may be because (1) he may be unconsciously supporting gender stereotypes, or (2) the science activities are often messy, and Andrea tends to not like to "get dirty."

Allen worked with Andrea's parents to establish a plan to help her engage in more scientific explorations. First, he created a beautiful display of two musical instruments. After she had time to explore, he added another instrument. He carefully chose the instruments so that there were different variations on themes (e.g., pitch or intensity of sound). Second, the strategy of integrating music and science was used to assist her with skills such as comparing and contrasting instruments and identifying different qualities of sounds. He created a list of questions to keep in his pocket as a reminder of potential links between the two content areas. Third, after much exploration of the "real" instruments, Allen put out a variety of materials that could be used for creating musical instruments. When Andrea worked in that space, he, again, asked questions to help her reason scientifically. For example, he asked, "What would happen if you used buttons instead of pebbles in your shaker?" Finally, he put books in the area with the musical instruments. The books were both fiction and nonfiction. He even selected some nonfiction books designed for adults but that had stunning photographs to look at.

Within a short time, Andrea made notable progress in her use of scientific thinking skills, and her interest in exploring other science materials expanded.

1. How important is it for girls, as well as boys, to learn to think like a scientist? Why?
2. Describe how and why each of these strategies helped to expand Andrea's interest in science.
3. What other strategies could be used to help Andrea think like a scientist?

Lesson Plan

Title: *Recordings of Stories*

Child Observation:

Nikolina is new to the classroom and to the community. Her family recently moved from Croatia. Although this has been a culture shock, Nikolina seems to be adjusting well to the classroom. Yesterday, her mother sent a book written in her native language to school; Nikolina looked at it nine times before lunch. She held it tightly when falling asleep for nap.

Child's Developmental Goal:

To promote emergent literacy skills

To engage with other members of the community

Materials: A picture book; device for recording family members reading the story and for playing the recordings.

Preparation: Send home with each family the book and recording device. Invite them to read the book in their native language, record it, and return the materials to school. After each family that wants to participate has recorded the book, select an area that can be easily supervised for displaying the book and the recording device.

Learning Environment:

1. When a child notices the book and recording device, join her or him in the area. Invite another child to listen to the story with you.

2. Explain how to play the recordings on the device. To illustrate, you could say:

    "Touch this symbol. When it opens, you can touch this arrow to hear the story."

3. Observe the children listening to the story. Talk about the story before inviting them to listen to other versions of the story.

4. Document using pictures, and record anecdotal records of how the children attend to the story.

5. As other children hear the recording and show interest, invite them to join in the experience.

6. After each reading, encourage them to talk about the book. The goal is to understand what they noticed about the different readings. Use open-ended prompts to promote conversations such as the following:

a. "I wonder who was reading the story. Do you recognize the person's voice? Does a friend here sound like the reader?"

b. "How did the story sound different with each reading?"

Guidance Consideration:

If the children argue over who will start the recording, use the social problem-solving protocol to determine a solution.

Variations:

Have family members select their child's favorite books to read and record. Make those books and recordings available to the children as they are preparing for nap or when they are missing their family members.

⌄ Professional Resource Download

Additional Resources

Ardizzone, L. (2014). *Science—not just for scientists!: Easy explorations for young children.* Lewisville, NC: Gryphon House.

Bentley, D. F. (2013). *Everyday artists: Inquiry and creativity in the early childhood classroom.* New York: Teachers College Press.

Gandini, L., Hill, L., Cadwell, L., & Schwall, C. (Eds.). (2014). *In the spirit of the studio: Learning from the atelier of Reggio Emilia* (2nd ed.). New York: Teachers College Press.

Lubawy, J. (2011). *Visions of creativity in early childhood: Connecting theory, practice and reflection.* St. Paul, MN: Redleaf.

Nemeth, K. (2012). *Many languages, building connections: Supporting infants and toddlers who are dual language learners.* Lewisville, NC: Gryphon House.

Neuman, S. B., & Dickinson, D. K. (Eds.) (2011). *Handbook of early literacy research* (Volume 3). New York: Guilford.

Shea, M. (2011). *Parallel learning of reading and writing in early childhood.* New York: Routledge.

A
APPENDIX

Tools for Observing and Recording

Appendix Outline

- Developmental Milestones (Combination of Checklist and Rating Scale)

  Approximately Birth to Four Months of Age

  Approximately Four to Eight Months of Age

  Approximately Eight to Twelve Months of Age

  Approximately Twelve to Eighteen Months of Age

  Approximately Eighteen to Twenty-Four Months of Age

  Approximately Twenty-Four to Thirty Months of Age

  Approximately Thirty to Thirty-Six Months of Age

- Running Record
- Anecdotal Record
- Indoor Safety Checklist
- Playground Safety Checklist

Developmental Milestones
(Combination of Checklist and Rating Scale)

Approximately Birth to Four Months of Age

CHILD BEHAVIOR	PRACTICING (RECORD DATE OBSERVED)	PROFICIENT (RECORD DATE OBSERVED)	OBSERVATION TO SUPPORT LEVEL
Physical Development			
MUSCULAR CONTROL			
Reflex			
Grasp reflex			
Startle reflex			
Tonic neck reflex			
Head and neck			
Turns head			
Holds head upright with support			
Lifts head slightly when on stomach			
Holds head to sides and middle			
Holds up head when on back and on stomach			
Holds head without support			
Trunk			
Holds up chest			
Sits with support			
May attempt to raise self			
May fuss if left lying down with little chance to sit up			
Holds up chest and shoulders			
Leg			
Rolls from stomach to back			
Arm			
Moves randomly			
Reaches			
Hand			
Opens and closes			
Keeps hands open			
Plays with hands			
Uses hands to grasp object			
Whole hand and fingers against thumb			
Thumb and forefinger			
Holds and moves object			
Eye-hand coordination			
Moves arm toward object; may miss it			
Reaches hand to object; may grab or miss it			

(continued)

Approximately Birth to Four Months of Age (*continued*)

CHILD BEHAVIOR	PRACTICING (RECORD DATE OBSERVED)	PROFICIENT (RECORD DATE OBSERVED)	OBSERVATION TO SUPPORT LEVEL
SEEING			
Focuses eight inches from eyes			
Follows with eyes			
Sees objects beyond eight inches			
Looks from object to object			
Looks around; focuses on object; then continues visual searching			
HEARING			
Responds to voice and range of sounds			
Reacts to hearing low- and high-pitched sounds			
Locates source of sound			
SLEEPING			
Sleeps much of the day and night			
Takes a long morning nap and a long afternoon nap			
May have irregular sleep habits			
EATING AND ELIMINATION			
Establishes regular time for eating and bowel movements			
Cognitive Development			
SENSORIMOTOR SUBSTAGE 1			
Reflexive actions			
Passive to active search			
SENSORIMOTOR SUBSTAGE 2			
Small, gradual changes come from repetition			
Coordination of behaviors, for example, looking toward sound			
Puts hand, object in mouth and sucks on it			
Moves hand, object to see it			
Produces a pleasurable motor activity and repeats activity			
OBJECT PERMANENCE			
Follows moving object with eyes until object disappears			
Looks where object disappeared			
Loses interest and turns away			
Language Development			
LANGUAGE INITIATION–RESPONSE			
Initiates making sounds			
Responds vocally to another person			
Makes sound, repeats sound, continues practicing sound and lengthening it			
Imitates a few sounds he or she already knows			
Experiments with sounds			
Coos in vowel-like sounds			
Adds pitch to cooing			

(*continued*)

CHILD BEHAVIOR	PRACTICING (RECORD DATE OBSERVED)	PROFICIENT (RECORD DATE OBSERVED)	OBSERVATION TO SUPPORT LEVEL
CRYING			
Cries apparently automatically in distress, frustration			
Cries differently to express hunger, discomfort, anger			
Cries less as vocalizing increases			
Emotional Development			
TYPES OF EMOTIONS AND FEELINGS			
Shows excitement			
Shows stress			
Shows enjoyment			
Shows anger			
Shows fear			
Protests			
CONTROL OF EMOTIONS AND FEELINGS			
Cries			
Increases sounds (talking)			
Reflects sounds (talking)			
Comforted by holding			
TEMPERAMENT (LIST BEHAVIORS TO INDICATE BASIC APPROACH)			
Activity level			
Regularity			
Response to new situations: Approach or withdrawal			
Adaptability to change in routine			
Sensory threshold			
Positive or negative mood			
Intensity of response			
Distractibility			
Persistence and attention span			
Social Development			
ATTACHMENT			
Shows special closeness to family members			
Develops familiarity with one primary caregiver			
SELF			
Becomes aware of hands and feet			
Smiles spontaneously			
Smiles at people (social smile)			
INTERACTIONS WITH OTHERS			
Interacts with people			
Laughs			
Initiates talking to others			

⌄ Professional Resource Download

Developmental Milestones
Approximately Four to Eight Months of Age

CHILD BEHAVIOR	PRACTICING (RECORD DATE OBSERVED)	PROFICIENT (RECORD DATE OBSERVED)	OBSERVATION TO SUPPORT LEVEL
Physical Development			
MUSCULAR CONTROL			
Head and neck			
Holds head up independently			
Holds head in midline position			
Holds head up when on back, stomach, and sitting			
Trunk			
Holds up chest, shoulders; arches back, hips			
Sits with support			
May attempt to raise self			
May fuss if left lying down with little chance to sit up			
Leans back and forth			
Sits in a chair			
Sits unsupported for short time			
Pushes self to sitting position			
Leg			
Straightens legs when standing			
Stamps feet when standing			
Rolls from back to stomach			
Raises self to hands and knees			
Stands with support			
Pulls self to standing			
Locomotion			
Kicks against surface to move			
Rocks on hands and knees			
Creeps on stomach			
Uses legs to pull, push self when sitting			
Arm			
Visually directs reaching, hitting			
Throws objects			
Hand			
Picks up object with one hand; passes it to the other hand			
Uses objects in both hands			
Grasps and releases objects			
Drops objects			
EATING			
Begins solid foods (new tongue and swallowing technique)			
Drinks from cup (new tongue and swallowing technique)			

(continued)

CHILD BEHAVIOR	PRACTICING (RECORD DATE OBSERVED)	PROFICIENT (RECORD DATE OBSERVED)	OBSERVATION TO SUPPORT LEVEL
Eats at "mealtimes"—solid foods, milk, juice			
Feeds self finger foods			
TEETH			
First teeth emerge: two middle lower, two middle upper			
Cognitive Development			
SENSORIMOTOR SUBSTAGE 3			
Repeats interesting action			
Refines hand-eye coordination			
Looks for object, reaches for it, and accurately touches it			
Imitates behavior he or she can see or hear			
OBJECT PERMANENCE			
Searches visually (not manually) for short time when object disappears			
Sees part of object; looks for whole object			
Language Development			
Babbles syllable-like sounds			
Responds to talking by cooing, babbling, smiling			
Imitates sounds			
Looks when name is called			
Babbles conversation with others			
Reflects happiness, unhappiness in sounds made			
Babbles two- and three-syllable sounds			
Varies intensity, volume, pitch, and rhythm			
Emotional Development			
TYPES OF EMOTIONS AND FEELINGS			
Shows pleasure in watching others			
Shows pleasure in repetitive play			
Shows depression			
Shows fear of strangers, of falling down			
Shows frustration with stimulation overload			
Shows happiness, delight, joy, humor			
Shows frustration, anger, and/or rage			
CONTROL OF EMOTIONS AND FEELINGS			
Sometimes stops crying when talked to, sung to			
TEMPERAMENT (LIST BEHAVIORS TO INDICATE BASIC APPROACH)			
Activity level			
Regularity			
Response to new situations: approach or withdrawal			
Adaptability to change in routine			
Sensory threshold			
Positive or negative mood			

(continued)

Approximately Four to Eight Months of Age (*continued*)

CHILD BEHAVIOR	PRACTICING (RECORD DATE OBSERVED)	PROFICIENT (RECORD DATE OBSERVED)	OBSERVATION TO SUPPORT LEVEL
Intensity of response			
Distractibility			
Persistence and attention span			
Social Development			
ATTACHMENT			
Shows strong attachment to family members			
Differentiates response to family members			
Shows intense pleasure and frustration to person with whom attached			
SELF			
Seeks independence in actions			
Plays self-designed games			
INTERACTIONS WITH OTHERS			
Imitates others			
Plays with people			
Seeks family's and/or caregiver's attention by movement, sounds, smiles, cries			
Follows family members and/or caregiver to be in same room			
Acts shy with some strangers			

⌄⌄ Professional Resource Download

Developmental Milestones

Approximately Eight to Twelve Months of Age

CHILD BEHAVIOR	PRACTICING (RECORD DATE OBSERVED)	PROFICIENT (RECORD DATE OBSERVED)	OBSERVATION TO SUPPORT LEVEL
Physical Development			
MUSCULAR CONTROL			
Trunk and leg			
Stands holding onto furniture or hand			
Stands without assistance			
Sits from standing			
Squats and stands			
Locomotion			
Crawls			
Steps forward			
Crawls up steps			
Steps sideways			
Walks with help			
Climbs on furniture			
Hand			
Brings both hands to middle of body			
Uses finger to poke			
Carries objects in hands			
Holds and uses pen and crayon			
Uses one hand to hold object, one hand to reach and explore			
Stacks blocks with dominant hand			
Takes off clothes			
EATING			
Holds bottle			
Holds cup			
Holds and uses spoon			
Uses fingers to eat most food			
Starts establishing food preferences			
Cognitive Development			
SENSORIMOTOR SUBSTAGE 4			
Differentiates goals			
Can focus on reaching and focus on toy			
Object permanence			
Child knows object exists when it is no longer visible; child seeks toy that rolls behind object			
Causality			
Understands that others cause actions			
Imitation and play			
Imitates others' actions in play			

(continued)

Approximately Eight to Twelve Months of Age (*continued*)

CHILD BEHAVIOR	PRACTICING (RECORD DATE OBSERVED)	PROFICIENT (RECORD DATE OBSERVED)	OBSERVATION TO SUPPORT LEVEL
Language Development			
Shouts			
Labels object sounds			
Uses names: *mama, dada*			
Responds to familiar sounds			
Responds to familiar words			
Repeats syllables, words, for example, *bye-bye*			
Engages in babble conversations			
Repeats, practices word over and over			
Says one or two words			
Emotional Development			
TYPES OF EMOTIONS AND FEELINGS			
May have tantrums			
Rejects items, situations			
Develops preferences for toys, people			
Shows independence—helps with feeding and dressing self			
Shows affection			
CONTROL OF EMOTIONS AND FEELINGS			
Obeys commands: *No-No, Stop*			
Sometimes inhibits own behavior			
TEMPERAMENT (LIST BEHAVIORS TO INDICATE BASIC APPROACH)			
Activity level			
Regularity			
Response to new situations: approach or withdrawal			
Adaptability to change in routine			
Sensory threshold			
Positive or negative mood			
Intensity of response			
Distractibility			
Persistence and attention span			
Social Development			
May fear strangers			
Keeps family members or caregiver in sight			
Focuses on own pleasure; may not consider others			
Imitates play			
Shows ownership of people			
Shows ownership of materials			
May become shy, clinging			
May demand attention			

⌄ Professional Resource Download

© Cengage Learning

Developmental Milestones

Approximately Twelve to Eighteen Months of Age

CHILD BEHAVIOR	PRACTICING (RECORD DATE OBSERVED)	PROFICIENT (RECORD DATE OBSERVED)	OBSERVATION TO SUPPORT LEVEL
Physical Development			
MUSCULAR CONTROL			
Locomotion			
May prefer crawling to walking			
Walks alone			
Climbs up stairs with help			
Climbs down stairs with help			
Climbs over objects			
Hand			
Shows hand preference			
Rolls and catches objects			
Eye-hand coordination			
Scribbles			
Helps in dressing, undressing			
Cognitive Development			
SENSORIMOTOR DEVELOPMENT: SUBSTAGE 5			
Object permanence			
Watches toy hidden and moved			
Looks for it where moved			
Causality			
Investigates cause and effect			
Sees self as causal agent			
Explores various ways things happen			
Employs active trial and error to solve problems			
Experiments			
Imitation and play			
Turns play with imitation into rituals			
Language Development			
Imitates sounds of other people, objects			
Responds to word and gesture conversation			
Responds to many questions and commands child cannot say			
Engages in jargon (babbling with a real word inserted)			
Uses word approximation for some words			
Uses words in immediate context			
Looks at board books independently			
Identifies family members in photographs			
Uses markers			

(continued)

Approximately Twelve to Eighteen Months of Age (*continued*)

CHILD BEHAVIOR	PRACTICING (RECORD DATE OBSERVED)	PROFICIENT (RECORD DATE OBSERVED)	OBSERVATION TO SUPPORT LEVEL
Emotional Development			
TYPES OF EMOTIONS AND FEELINGS			
Expresses emotions in behavior and language			
Recognizes emotions in others			
Expresses sense of humor			
Displays negativism			
May have tantrums			
Uses play to express emotions, resolve conflicts			
Seeks dependency, security with family and caregiver			
Seeks to expand independence			
CONTROL OF EMOTIONS AND FEELINGS			
Begins to understand right and wrong			
Reinforces desired behavior			
TEMPERAMENT (LIST BEHAVIORS TO INDICATE BASIC APPROACH)			
Activity level			
Regularity			
Response to new situations: approach or withdrawal			
Adaptability to change in routine			
Sensory threshold			
Positive or negative mood			
Intensity of response			
Distractibility			
Persistence and attention span			
Social Development			
SELF			
Has concept of self			
Is egocentric: understands only own viewpoint			
OTHERS			
Seeks presence of family or caregiver			
Plays games			
Acts differently toward different people			
Uses variety of behaviors to gain attention			
May be shy with some people			
Engages in parallel play			

❯❯ Professional Resource Download

Developmental Milestones

Approximately Eighteen to Twenty-Four Months of Age

CHILD BEHAVIOR	PRACTICING (RECORD DATE OBSERVED)	PROFICIENT (RECORD DATE OBSERVED)	OBSERVATION TO SUPPORT LEVEL
Physical Development			
MUSCULAR CONTROL			
Locomotion			
Walks backward			
Walks sideways			
Runs with stops and starts			
Jumps with both feet			
Kicks object			
Walks up and down stairs holding railing; both feet to one step			
Pushes and pulls objects while walking			
Climbs			
Pedals cycle			
Arm			
Throws object at target			
Hand			
Grasps and releases with developing finger muscles			
Pulls zippers			
Scribbles			
Increases wrist flexibility, turns wrist to turn object			
Turns book pages			
Digs with tool			
Makes individual marks with crayon or pen			
TEETH			
Uses toothbrush			
Cognitive Development			
SENSORIMOTOR DEVELOPMENT: SUBSTAGE 6			
Mental trial and error			
Tries out ideas mentally, based on past concrete experiences			
Object permanence			
Sees object disappear, remembers object, and figures out where it went			
Deferred imitation and symbolization			
Imitates past events			
Engages in symbolic play			
Uses symbolic play to resolve conflict			
Uses symbolic play to try on roles			

(continued)

Approximately Eighteen to Twenty-Four Months of Age (*continued*)

CHILD BEHAVIOR	PRACTICING (RECORD DATE OBSERVED)	PROFICIENT (RECORD DATE OBSERVED)	OBSERVATION TO SUPPORT LEVEL
Language Development			
Uses language to reflect own meaning; expects others to have same meaning			
Expands vocabulary rapidly, labeling objects			
Points to objects and pictures named by others			
Learns social words—*hello, please, thank you*			
Uses language to express needs, desires			
Uses language to direct others			
Asks questions			
Uses nouns, verbs, pronouns			
Is learning prepositions			
Calls self by name			
Follows directions of one step or two steps			
Uses telegraphic speech (two- to three-word sentences)			
"Reads" books			
Listens to stories and rhymes			
Scribbles			
Emotional Development			
TYPES OF EMOTIONS AND FEELINGS			
Views internal feelings and external behavior as same			
Shows one or more emotions at same time			
Seeks approval			
May develop new fears			
Increases fantasy			
May increase aggressiveness			
Seeks security in routines			
May become shy again			
Sometimes rejects family members or caregivers			
CONTROL OF EMOTIONS AND FEELINGS			
Uses reactions of others as a controller of own behavior			
May resist change			
Moves to extremes, from lovable to demanding and stubborn			
TEMPERAMENT (LIST BEHAVIORS TO INDICATE BASIC APPROACH)			
Activity level			
Regularity			
Response to new situations: approach or withdrawal			
Adaptability to change in routine			
Sensory threshold			

(continued)

CHILD BEHAVIOR	PRACTICING (RECORD DATE OBSERVED)	PROFICIENT (RECORD DATE OBSERVED)	OBSERVATION TO SUPPORT LEVEL
Positive or negative mood			
Intensity of response			
Distractibility			
Persistence and attention span			
Social Development			
SELF			
Shows strong ownership by identifying materials as belonging to self			
Uses *I, mine, me, you*			
OTHERS			
Begins to be aware of others' feelings			
Believes people have changes in identity			
Interacts with other children; expands social relationships			
Looks to others for help			
Imitates tasks of others			
Wants to help, assists with tasks			
May do opposite of what is requested			
Engages in parallel play			

⌄ Professional Resource Download

Developmental Milestones

Approximately Twenty-Four to Thirty Months of Age

CHILD BEHAVIOR	PRACTICING (RECORD DATE OBSERVED)	PROFICIENT (RECORD DATE OBSERVED)	OBSERVATION TO SUPPORT LEVEL
Physical Development			
MUSCULAR CONTROL			
Movement			
Bends at waist			
Climbs			
Jumps			
Stands on one foot			
Is learning to use fork			
ELIMINATION			
May show interest in learning to use toilet			
Cognitive Development			
PREOPERATIONAL STAGE: PRECONCEPTUAL			
Nonverbal classification			
Makes graphic collections			
Verbal preconcepts			
Uses words differently at different times			
Uses words with private meanings			
Labels objects in one class			
Focuses on one attribute			
Verbal reasoning			
Reasons from particular to particular			
Quantity			
Understands some, more, gone, big			
Number			
Understands more			
Space			
Understands up, down, behind, under, over			
Time			
Understands now, soon			
Language Development			
Uses demonstrative naming			
Uses attribution			
Uses possession			
Uses action			
Uses recurrence			
Uses negation			
Learns prosodic patterning			

(continued)

CHILD BEHAVIOR	PRACTICING (RECORD DATE OBSERVED)	PROFICIENT (RECORD DATE OBSERVED)	OBSERVATION TO SUPPORT LEVEL
Uses subject-verb combinations			
Uses verb-object			
May use subject-verb-object			
Selects and reads books			
Uses controlled scribbling			
Emotional Development			
TYPES OF EMOTIONS AND FEELINGS			
Self-esteem			
Feels comfortable with self			
Feels positive self-worth			
Feels negative self-worth			
CONTROL OF EMOTIONS AND FEELINGS			
Independently expresses many emotions in socially acceptable manner			
TEMPERAMENT (LIST BEHAVIORS TO INDICATE BASIC APPROACH)			
Activity level			
Regularity			
Response to new situations: approach or withdrawal			
Adaptability to change in routine			
Sensory threshold			
Positive or negative mood			
Intensity of response			
Distractibility			
Persistence and attention span			
Social Development			
SELF			
Realizes own skills			
Identifies self as boy or girl			
OTHERS			
Acts to please adult			
Recognizes the difference between *mine* and *yours*			
Shares, but not consistently			
Helps others			
Engages in parallel play			
May engage in brief episodes of cooperative play			

© Cengage Learning

⌄ Professional Resource Download

Developmental Milestones

Approximately Thirty to Thirty-Six Months of Age

CHILD BEHAVIOR	PRACTICING (RECORD DATE OBSERVED)	PROFICIENT (RECORD DATE OBSERVED)	OBSERVATION TO SUPPORT LEVEL
Physical Development			
MOVEMENT AND COORDINATION			
Runs smoothly			
Jumps in place and forward			
Has firmly established handedness			
ELIMINATION			
Is in process of or has completed toilet learning			
Cognitive Development			
PREOPERATIONAL STAGE: PRECONCEPTUAL			
Nonverbal classification			
Makes graphic collections			
Verbal reasoning			
Thinks one action is like another action			
Reasons from effect to cause			
Time			
Understands now, soon, before, after			
Language Development			
Has vocabulary of more than 200 words			
Creates longer sentences			
Includes functional words (e.g., *a, an, the*)			
Uses plurals with accuracy and overregularization			
Uses past tense with accuracy and overregularization			
Listens to stories, "reads" pictures, storybooks			
Emotional Development			
TYPES OF EMOTIONS AND FEELINGS			
Reacts strongly			
Acts negatively			
Learns enthusiastically			
CONTROL OF EMOTIONS AND FEELINGS			
Is physically aggressive			
TEMPERAMENT (LIST BEHAVIORS TO INDICATE BASIC APPROACH)			
Activity level			
Regularity			
Response to new situations: approach or withdrawal			
Adaptability to change in routine			
Sensory threshold			
Positive or negative mood			

(continued)

CHILD BEHAVIOR	PRACTICING (RECORD DATE OBSERVED)	PROFICIENT (RECORD DATE OBSERVED)	OBSERVATION TO SUPPORT LEVEL
Intensity of response			
Distractibility			
Persistence and attention span			
Social Development			
SELF			
Acts possessive			
OTHERS			
Seeks assistance			
Directs others			
Helps others			
CONTROL OF SELF			
Plays cooperatively			
Shares			
Takes turns			

⌄⌄ Professional Resource Download

© Cengage Learning

Running Record

CONTEXT	OBSERVATIONS (BEHAVIORAL DESCRIPTIONS OF WHAT YOU SEE AND HEAR)	ANALYSIS/INTERPRETATIONS/QUESTIONS

© Cengage Learning

Anecdotal Record

Child's name:	Age:
Observer's name:	Date:
Setting:	

What actually happened/What I saw:

Reflection/Interpretation/Questions:

Child's name:	Age:
Observer's name:	Date:
Setting:	

What actually happened/What I saw:

Reflection/Interpretation/Questions:

≫ Professional Resource Download

Indoor Safety Checklist

ITEM	YES/NO	CORRECTIONS/ COMMENTS	DATE CORRECTION MADE
General Environment			
Floors are smooth and have a nonskid surface.			
Pipes and radiators are inaccessible to children or are covered to prevent contact.			
Hot tap water temperature for hand washing is 110°F–115°F or less.			
Electrical cords are out of children's reach and are kept out of doorways and traffic paths.			
Unused electrical outlets are covered by furniture or shock stops.			
Medicines, cleansers, and aerosols are kept in a locked place, where children are unable to see and reach them.			
All windows have screens that stay in place when used; expandable screens are not used.			
Windows can be opened only six inches or less from the bottom.			
Drawers are kept closed to prevent tripping or bumps.			
Trash is covered at all times.			
Walls and ceilings are free of peeling paint and cracked or falling plaster; center has been inspected for lead paint.			
There are no disease-bearing animals, such as turtles, parrots, or cats.			
Children are always supervised.			
There is no friable (crumbly) asbestos releasing into the air.			
Equipment and Toys			
Toys and play equipment are checked often for sharp edges, small parts, and sharp points.			
All toys are painted with lead-free paint.			
Toys are put away when not in use.			
Toy chests have lightweight lids or no lids.			
Art materials are nontoxic and have either the AP or the CP label.			
Curtains, pillows, blankets, and soft toys are made of flame-resistant material.			
Hallways and Stairs			
Stairs and stairways are free of boxes, toys, and other clutter.			
Stairways are well lit.			
The right-hand railing on the stairs is at child height and does not wobble when held; there is a railing or wall on both sides of stairways.			
Stairway gates are in place when appropriate.			
Closed doorways to unsupervised or unsafe areas are always locked unless this prevents emergency evacuation.			
Staff are able to watch for strangers entering the building.			

(continued)

ITEM	YES/NO	CORRECTIONS/ COMMENTS	DATE CORRECTION MADE
Kitchen			
Trash is kept away from areas where food is prepared or stored.			
Trash is stored away from the furnace and water heater.			
Pest strips are *not* used; pesticides for crawling insects are applied by a certified pest control operator.			
Cleansers and other poisonous products are stored in their original containers, away from food and out of children's reach.			
Food-preparation surfaces are clean and free of cracks and chips.			
Electrical cords are placed where people will not trip over them or pull them.			
There are no sharp or hazardous cooking utensils (e.g., knives) within children's reach.			
Pot handles are always turned in toward the back of the stove during cooking.			
The fire extinguisher can be reached easily in an emergency.			
All staff know how to use the fire extinguisher correctly.			
Bathrooms			
Stable step stools are available when needed.			
Electrical outlets are covered with shock stops or outlet covers.			
Cleaning products, soap, and disinfectant are stored in a locked place, out of children's reach.			
Floors are smooth and have a nonskid surface.			
The trash container is emptied daily and kept clean.			
Hot water for hand washing is 110°F–115°F.			
Emergency Preparation			
All staff understand their roles and responsibilities in case of emergency.			
At least one staff person who is certified in first aid and CPR for infants and children is always present.			
The first aid kit is checked regularly for supplies and is kept where it can be reached easily by staff in an emergency.			
Smoke detectors and other alarms are checked regularly to make sure they are working.			
Each room and hallway has a fire escape route posted in clear view.			
Emergency procedures and telephone numbers are posted near each phone in clear view.			
Children's emergency phone numbers are kept near the phone, where they can be reached quickly.			
All exits are clearly marked and are free of clutter.			
Doors open in the direction of all exit travel.			
Cots are placed so that walkways are clear for evacuation in an emergency.			

Source: Statewide Comprehensive Injury Prevention Program (SCIPP), Massachusetts Department of Public Health.

⌄ Professional Resource Download

Playground Safety Checklist

ITEM	YES/NO	CORRECTIONS/ COMMENTS	DATE CORRECTION MADE
All Equipment			
Nuts, bolts, or screws that stick out are covered with masking tape or sanded down.			
Metal equipment is free from rust or chipping paint.			
Wood equipment is free from splinters or rough surfaces, sharp edges, and pinching/crushing parts.			
Nuts and bolts are tight.			
Anchors for equipment are stable and buried below ground level.			
Equipment is in its proper place and is not bent with use.			
Children who use equipment are of the age/developmental level for which the equipment was designed.			
Ground Surface			
All play equipment has 8–12 inches of shock-absorbing material underneath (e.g., pea gravel or wood chips).			
Surfaces are raked weekly to prevent them from becoming packed down and to find hidden hazards (e.g., litter, sharp objects, animal feces).			
Stagnant pools of water are not present on the surface.			
There is no exposed concrete where equipment is anchored.			
Spacing			
Swing sets are at least nine feet from other equipment.			
Swings are at least 1½ feet from each other.			
Slides have a 2½- to 3-yard run-off space.			
There is at least eight feet of space between equipment items.			
Boundaries between equipment items are visible to children (e.g., painted lines or low bushes).			
Play areas for bike riding, games, and boxes are separate from other equipment.			
Swing sets are at least six feet from walls and fences, walkways, and other play areas; there is a barrier to prevent children from getting into traffic (e.g., when chasing a ball).			
Slides			
Slides are six feet in height or less.			
Side rims are at least 2½ inches high.			
Slides have an enclosed platform at the top for children to rest and get into position for sliding.			
Slide ladders have handrails on both sides and flat steps.			
There is a flat surface at the bottom of the slide for slowing down.			

(continued)

ITEM	YES/NO	CORRECTIONS/ COMMENTS	DATE CORRECTION MADE
Metal slides are shaded to prevent burns.			
Wood slides are waxed, or oiled with linseed oil.			
The slide incline is equal to or less than 30 degrees.			
Steps and rungs are 7–11 inches apart to accommodate children's leg and arm reach.			
Climbing Equipment			
Ladders of different heights are available for children of different ages and sizes.			
Bars stay in place when grasped.			
The maximum height from which a child can fall is 7½ feet.			
Climbers have regularly spaced footholds from top to bottom.			
There is an easy, safe "way out" for children when they reach the top.			
Equipment is dry before children are allowed to use it.			
Rungs are painted in bright or contrasting colors so children will see them.			
Swings			
Chair swings are available for children under age 5.			
Canvas sling and saddle seats are available for older children.			
S-shaped or open-ended hooks have been removed.			
Hanging rings are less than five inches or more than ten inches in diameter (smaller or larger than child's head).			
The point at which seat and chain meet is exposed.			
Sandboxes			
Sandboxes are located in a shaded spot; only sterilized sand is used.			
Sandbox is securely covered, if accessible to pets or other animals.			
The frame is sanded and smooth, without splinters or rough surfaces.			
The sand is raked at least every two weeks to check for debris and to provide exposure to air and sun.			
The sandbox has proper drainage.			
Poisonous plants and berries are removed from play area.			
A source of clean drinking water is available in the play area.			
There is shade.			
The entire play area can be seen easily for good supervision.			

Source: Recommendations of Statewide Comprehensive Injury Prevention Program (SCIPP), Massachusetts Department of Public Health.

❯❯ **Professional Resource Download**

This section provides specific information about standards for practicing or preservice teachers. Covered in this appendix are the CDA Competency Goals and the NAEYC Standards for Early Childhood Professional Preparation: Initial Licensure Programs. Table B–1, which was provided initially in Chapter 5, is included to remind you of the relationships between these two sets of standards.

Appendix Overview

CDA Competency Standards for Infant/Toddler Caregivers in Center-Based Programs

NAEYC Standards for Early Childhood Professional Preparation: Initial Licensure Programs

NAEYC Initial Licensure Standards Summary

CDA Competency Standards for Infant/Toddler Caregivers in Center-Based Programs

The CDA Competency Standards are used to evaluate a caregiver's performance with children and families during the CDA assessment process (Council for Professional Recognition, 2010). The Competency Standards are divided into six **competency goals**, which are statements of a general purpose or goal for caregiver behavior. The competency goals are common to all child care settings. The six goals are defined in more detail in 13 **functional areas**, which describe the major tasks or functions that a caregiver must complete to carry out the competency goal (see Table B–2).

Each functional area is explained by a **developmental context**, which presents a brief overview of child development from birth to 3 years of age and provides a rationale for the functional area definition and examples of competent caregiver behavior that follow. Three different developmental levels are identified: young infants (birth–8 months), mobile infants (9–17 months), and toddlers (18–36 months). Children develop at different rates, and descriptions of these levels emphasize the unique characteristics and needs of children at each stage of development.

Each functional area is further explained by a list of sample caregiver behaviors (not included here). These examples describe behavior which demonstrates that a caregiver is acting in a competent way or exhibiting a skill in a particular functional area. During the assessment process, most candidates will exhibit other competent behavior, and a competent candidate might not demonstrate all the examples listed under a functional area. The

TABLE B–1 ▸ Alignment of the CDA and NAEYC Standards

CDA COMPETENCY AREAS	NAEYC TEACHER PREPARATION STANDARDS						FIELD EXPERIENCES*
	1. PROMOTING CHILD DEVELOPMENT AND LEARNING	2. BUILDING FAMILY AND COMMUNITY RELATIONSHIPS	3. OBSERVING, DOCUMENTING, AND ASSESSING	4. USING DEVELOPMENTALLY EFFECTIVE APPROACHES	5. USING CONTENT KNOWLEDGE	6. BECOMING A PROFESSIONAL	
I. Safe, healthy learning environment	X			X			X
II. Advance physical and intellectual competence	X			X	X		X
III. Support social and emotional development; positive guidance	X			X			X
IV. Positive and productive relationships with families		X	X	X			X
V. Well-run, purposeful program						X	X
VI. Commitment to professionalism						X	X

*NAEYC considers field experience an integral part of professional preparation.

© Cengage Learning

TABLE B–2 ▶ CDA Competency Goals and Functional Areas

I. To establish and maintain a safe, healthy learning environment.
1. Safe: Candidate provides a safe environment to prevent and reduce injuries.
2. Healthy: Candidate promotes good health and nutrition and provides an environment that contributes to the prevention of illness.
3. Learning Environment: Candidate uses space, relationships, materials, and routines as resources for constructing an interesting, secure, and enjoyable environment that encourages play, exploration, interaction, and learning.

II. To advance physical and intellectual competence.
4. Physical: Candidate uses a variety of developmentally appropriate equipment, learning experiences, and teaching strategies to promote the physical development (fine motor and gross motor) of children.
5. Cognitive: Candidate provides activities and opportunities that encourage curiosity, exploration, and problem solving appropriate to the developmental levels of each child.
6. Communication: Candidate actively communicates with children and provides opportunities and support for children to understand, acquire, and to use verbal and nonverbal means of communicating thoughts and feelings.
7. Creative: Candidate provides opportunities that encourage children to play with sound, rhythm, language, materials, space, and ideas in individual ways and to express their creative abilities.

III. To support social and emotional development and provide positive guidance.
8. Self: Candidate develops a warm, positive, supportive relationship with each child, and helps each child learn about and take pride in his or her individual and cultural identity.
9. Social: Candidate helps each child feel accepted in the group, helps children learn to communicate and get along with others, and encourages feelings of empathy and mutual respect among children and adults.
10. Guidance: Candidate provides a supportive environment and uses effective strategies to help all children learn and practice appropriate and acceptable behavior as individuals and as a group, and effectively provides support for children with persistent challenging behaviors.

IV. To establish positive and productive relationships with families.
11. Families: Candidate establishes a positive, cooperative relationship with each child's family, engages in two-way communication with families, encourages their involvement in the program, and supports the child's relationship with his or her family.

V. To ensure a well-run, purposeful program responsive to participant needs.
12. Program Management: Candidate is a manager who uses all available resources to ensure an effective operation. The candidate is a competent organizer, planner, record keeper, communicator, and a cooperative coworker.

VI. To maintain a commitment to professionalism.
13. Professionalism: Candidate makes decisions based on knowledge of research-based early childhood practices, promotes high-quality child care services, and takes advantage of opportunities to improve knowledge and competence, both for personal and professional growth and for the benefit of children and families.

Source: Statewide Comprehensive Injury Prevention Program (SCIPP), Massachusetts Department of Public Health.

examples are organized according to developmental stages of children from birth to 3 years to emphasize the importance of the special skills needed to work with young infants, mobile infants, and toddlers. Specific bilingual specialization examples are presented for several functional areas.

The samples of caregiver competency included in the standards should serve as a basis for recognizing other, more specific behaviors that are important to the individual candidate. CDA candidates and individuals conducting or participating in CDA training will be able to think of many different ways to demonstrate skill in the 6 competency goals and 13 functional areas.

Competent caregivers integrate their work and constantly adapt their skills—always thinking of the development of the whole child. In all functional areas, it is important for competent caregivers to individualize their work with each child while meeting the needs of the group. In every area, too, caregivers must promote multiculturalism, support families with different languages, and meet the needs of children with special needs. And, while demonstrating skills and knowledge, competent caregivers must also demonstrate personal qualities, such as flexibility and a positive style of communicating with young children and working with families.

The Council for Early Childhood Professional Recognition has designed both training and assessment systems for persons interested in the CDA credential. For more information, contact

Council for Professional Recognition
2460 16th St., NW
Washington, DC 20009-3547
Telephone: (202) 265-9090 or (800) 424-4310
Fax: (202) 265-9161
http://www.cdacouncil.org/

NAEYC Standards for Early Childhood Professional Preparation

The National Association for the Education of Young Children (NAEYC) has designed standards for teacher-preparation programs at the associate, initial, and advanced levels. The 2010 NAEYC Standards for Initial and Advanced Early Childhood Professional Preparation Programs are the national standards used to evaluate teacher-preparation programs. This process involves evaluating the preservice teacher's performance with children and families during annual program reviews. The expectations for knowledge, skills, and performance levels are divided into seven standards with supporting elements.

These standards were created to express a national vision of excellence for early childhood professionals who work with children and families birth through age 8. Teacher-preparation standards are just one avenue for tackling this monumental task of helping children learn and develop at optimal levels. Accreditation standards for early childhood programs, guidelines for developmentally appropriate practices, curriculum content and assessment, teacher-preparation standards, and a system for financing early childhood education all work together to create this context.

Because programs educate teachers to participate in a wide range of diverse settings and programs, for example, private nursery school programs, center- and family-based child care programs, kindergartens, public school programs, early intervention programs that include Early Head Start and Head Start, and so on, standards cannot be rigid or "one size fits all."

The following page outlines and summarizes the standards for early childhood professional preparation. Refer to the entire document for more specific guidelines and examples for each standard. More information about the standards can be downloaded from the NAEYC website.

NAEYC Standards for Early Childhood Professional Preparation Programs

Standard 1. Promoting Child Development and Learning

Candidates prepared in early childhood degree programs are grounded in a child development knowledge base. They use their understanding of young children's characteristics and needs, and of multiple interacting influences on children's development and learning, to create environments that are healthy, respectful, supportive, and challenging for each child.

Standard 2. Building Family and Community Relationships

Candidates prepared in early childhood degree programs understand that successful early childhood education depends upon partnerships with children's families and communities. They know about, understand, and value the importance and complex characteristics of children's families and communities. They use this understanding to create respectful, reciprocal relationships that support and empower families, and to involve all families in their children's development and learning.

Standard 3. Observing, Documenting, and Assessing to Support Young Children and Families

Candidates prepared in early childhood degree programs understand that child observation, documentation, and other forms of assessment are central to the practice of all early childhood professionals. They know about and understand the goals, benefits, and uses of assessment. They know about and use systematic observations, documentation, and other effective assessment strategies in a responsible way, in partnership with families and other professionals, to positively influence the development of every child.

Standard 4. Using Developmentally Effective Approaches

Candidates prepared in early childhood degree programs understand that teaching and learning with young children is a complex enterprise, and its details vary depending on children's ages, characteristics, and the settings within which teaching and learning occur. They understand and use positive relationships and supportive interactions as the foundation for their work with young children and families. Candidates know, understand, and use a wide array of developmentally appropriate approaches, instructional strategies, and tools to connect with children and families and positively influence each child's development and learning.

Standard 5. Using Content Knowledge to Build Meaningful Curriculum

Candidates prepared in early childhood degree programs use their knowledge of academic disciplines to design, implement, and evaluate experiences that promote positive development and learning for each and every young child. Candidates understand the importance of developmental domains and academic (or content) disciplines in early childhood curriculum. They know the essential concepts, inquiry tools, and structure of content areas, including academic subjects, and can identify resources to deepen their understanding. Candidates use their own knowledge and other resources to design, implement, and evaluate meaningful, challenging curriculum that promotes comprehensive developmental and learning outcomes for every young child.

Standard 6. Becoming a Professional

Candidates prepared in early childhood degree programs identify and conduct themselves as members of the early childhood profession. They know and use ethical guidelines and other professional standards related to early childhood practice. They are continuous, collaborative learners who demonstrate knowledgeable, reflective, and critical perspectives on their work, making informed decisions that integrate knowledge from a variety of sources. They are informed advocates for sound educational practices and policies.

Early Childhood Field Experiences

Programs seeking NAEYC Accreditation or Recognition must provide field experiences in at least two of these three early childhood age groups (0–3, 3–5, 5–8) and in at least two of these three early learning settings (P–12 schools, child care centers and homes, Head Start).

Source: Excerpted from NAEYC, "NAEYC Standards for Early Childhood Professional Preparation Programs," Position Statement (Washington, DC: NAEYC, 2009). Copyright © 2009 NAEYC. Reprinted with permission. Full text of this position statement is available on the NAEYC website.

The following is a list of board books that can be used with infants and toddlers. They are arranged by categories or topics. Those marked with "MC" also represent a variety of cultures or cultural experiences.

Alphabet

Bancroft, Bronwyn. (2010). *W is for wombat.* Little Hare Books, Surry Hills, N.S.W.
Davis, Sarah. (2015). *My first ABC.* DK Publishing, New York.
Hartman, Scott. (2010). *ABC dinosaurs.* Sterling Publishing, New York.
Heck, Edward. (2011). *A, B, C, D, eat!* Price Stern Sloan, New York.
Katz, Susan B. (2010). *ABC, baby me!* Robin Corey Books, New York.
Lewis, Jan. (2014). *My first ABC.* Armadillo Books, Wigston, Leicester.
Lluch, Alex. (2014). *Trace & learn the ABCs.* WS Publishing Group, San Diego, CA.
Mayer, Mercer. (2011). *Little critter ABCs.* Sterling, New York.
Powell, Sarah. (2013). *ABC: Alphaprints.* St. Martin's Press, New York.
Sirett, Dawn. (2015). *Sophie peekaboo! ABC.* DK Publishing, New York.
Thompson, Lauren. (2010). *Little Quack's ABC's.* Little Simon, New York.
Wynne Pechter, Lesley. (2011). *Alligator, bear, crab: A baby's ABC.* Orca Book Publishers, Victoria, BC.

Animals/Pets

Blair, Karen. (2014). *Baby animal farm.* Candlewick Press, Somerville, MA.
Boynton, Sandra. (2012). *Moo, baa, la la la!* Little Simon Books, New York.
Carle, Eric. (2009). *Have you seen my cat?* Little Simon, New York. MC
Davis, Sarah. (2015). *My first animals.* DK Publishing, New York.
Franceschelli, Christopher. (2010). *Oliver.* Lemniscaat USA, Brooklyn, NY.
Froeb, Lori. (2010). *Let's go to the farm.* Holiday House, New York.
Gillingham, Sara. (2010). *In my forest.* Chronicle Books, San Francisco.
Gillingham, Sara. (2009). *In my nest.* Chronicle Books, San Francisco.
Grogan, John. (2011). *Marley springs ahead!* Harper Festival, New York.
Husar, Lisa. (2011). *Zoo babies!* Farcountry Press, Helena, MT.
Katz, Karen. (2011). *Where is baby's puppy?* Little Simon, New York.
Kingfisher Publications. (2011). *In grasslands.* Kingfisher, New York.
Kingfisher Publications. (2011). *In the jungle.* Kingfisher, New York.
Mitter, Matt. (2014). *Who is on the farm?* Reader's Digest Children's Books, White Plains, NY.
Ohrt, Kate. (2011). *Hop, pop, and play.* Accord Publishing, Denver, CO.
Oxenbury, Helen. (2010). *It's my birthday.* Candlewick Press, Cambridge, MA.
Perrin, Martine. (2011). *Look who's there!* Albert Whitman, Chicago.
Root, Phyllis. (2010). *Hop!* Candlewick Press, Somerville, MA.
School Specialty Publishing. (2009). *Millie the millipede.* School Specialty Publishing, Columbus, OH.
Sirett, Dawn. (2009). *Baby: Woof! woof!* DK Publishing, New York.
Tafuri, Nancy. (2011). *Five little chicks.* Little Simon, New York.

Van Fleet, Matthew. (2010). *Heads*. Simon & Schuster Books for Young Readers, New York.

Weiss, Ellen. (2012). *Let's go to the zoo*. Reader's Digest Children's Book, White Plains, NY.

Bedtime

Asim, Jabari. (2010). *Boy of mine*. LB Kids, New York.

Asim, Jabari. (2010). *Girl of mine*. LB Kids, New York. MC

Benoît, Marchon. (2013). *Goodnight!* Houghton Mifflin Harcourt, Boston, MA.

Boynton, Sandra. (2012). *The going to bed book*. Little Simon Books, New York.

Clairmont, Patsy. (2014). *Sleep sweet my little one*. Thomas Nelson Publishers, Nashville, TN.

Dicmas, Courtney. (2014). *Wild bedtime!* Child's Play, Swindon, Australia.

Hill, Eric. (2011). *Spot says goodnight*. G.P. Putnam's Sons, New York.

Magsamen, Sandra. (2014). *I love you, snugglesaurus!* LB Kids, New York.

Quay, Emma. (2011). *Good night, sleep tight*. Dial Books for Young Readers, New York.

Shea, Bob. (2011). *Dinosaur vs. bedtime*. Hyperion, New York.

Shields, Gillian. (2010). *When the world is ready for bed*. Bloomsbury, New York.

Thompson, Carol. (2012). *Snug*. Child's Play, Swindon, Australia.

Thompson, Lauren. (2009). *Little Quack's bedtime*. Little Simon, New York.

Verdick, Elizabeth. (2010). *Bedtime*. Free Spirit Pub., Minneapolis, MN. MC

Verdick, Elizabeth. (2010). *Calm-down time*. Free Spirit Pub., Minneapolis, MN.

Colors and Shapes

Davis, Sarah. (2015). *My first colors*. DK Publishing, New York.

Ghigna, Charles. (2013). *The wonders of the color wheel*. Picture Window Books, North Mankato, MN.

Hawkins, Emily. (2008). *Rainbow fun!* Silver Dolphin Books, San Diego.

Heck, Edward. (2011). *Color-by-penguins*. Price Stern Sloan, New York.

Heck, Edward. (2011). *Shape up, pup!* Price Stern Sloan, New York.

Orla, Kiely. (2012). *Shapes*. Egmont, London.

Taback, Simms. (2009). *Colors*. Big Apple Books: Chronicle Books, Maplewood, NJ.

Family

Child's Play. (2009). *Look at me!* Child's Play, Swindon.

Child's Play. (2009). *Waiting for baby*. Child's Play, Swindon.

Gardner, Charlie. (2012). *My first busy home: Let's look and learn!* DK Publishing, New York.

Giles, Andreae. (2013). *I love my mommy*. Disney Hyperion Books, New York.

Hill, Eric. (2008). *Spot loves his grandma*. Putnam, New York.

Janovitz, Marilyn. (2010). *Baby baby baby*. Sourcebooks Jabberwocky, Naperville, IL.

Katz, Karen. (2010). *Baby's colors*. Little Simon, New York.

Katz, Karen. (2010). *Baby's shapes*. Little Simon, New York. MC

Lester, J. D. (2011). *Grandma calls me Gigglepie*. Robin Corey Books, New York.

Lester, J. D. (2010). *Daddy calls me Doodlebug*. Robin Corey Books, New York.

Lewis, Paeony. (2008). *I'll always love you*. Tiger Tales, Wilton, CT.

Mattingly, Wade A. (2013). *Sometimes, my dad and I*. Matting Leah Pub. Co., Warwick, NY.

Parry, Jo. (2015). *Mommy loves you so much!* Thomas Nelson Inc., Nashville, TN.
Price, Stern, Sloan. (2009). *Mommy loves me.* Price Stern Sloan, New York.
Rock, Lois. (2012). *We now have a baby.* Lion Hudson, Oxford.
School Specialty Publishing. (2009). *Sammy the snake.* School Specialty Publishing, Columbus, OH.
Steele, Michael Anthony. (2010). *Little dinosaur.* Barron's, Hauppauge, NY.
Steele, Michael Anthony. (2010). *Little penguin.* Barron's, Hauppauge, NY.
Thompson, Lauren. (2009). *Little Quack loves colors.* Little Simon, New York.
Wan, Joyce. (2013). *Hug you, kiss you, love you.* Cartwheel Books, New York.

Friendship/Teamwork

Bently, Peter. (2011). *Thank you for being my friend.* Parragon Inc, Bath, UK.
Bugbird, Tim. (2011). *Best friends.* Make Believe Ideas, Nashville, TN.
Dworkin, Brooke. (2011). *Furry friends.* Disney Press.
Liesbet, Slegers. (2012). *Friends.* Clavis Pub., New York.
Magsamen, Sandra. (2014). *Because I love you.* Little Brown and Company, New York.
Quay, Emma. (2011). *Yummy ice cream: A book about sharing.* Dial Books for Young Readers, New York.
Rohmann, Eric. (2011). *My friend Rabbit.* Roaring Brook Press, New York.
Slegers, Liesbet (2012). *Friends.* Clavis Publications, New York.
Verdick, Elizabeth. (2009). *Sharing time.* Free Spirit Pub., Minneapolis, MN. MC

Language/Vocabulary

Ackland, Nick. (2014). *First words.* Barron's Educational Series, Hauppauge, NY.
Brooks, Felicity. (2010). *Lift-the-flap word book.* EDC Publishing, Tusla, OK.
Gardner, Charlie. (2011). *Flaptastic first words.* DK Publishing, New York.
Heck, Edward. (2011). *Monster opposites.* Price Stern Sloan, New York.
Hudson, Wade. (2009). *Best friends.* Turnaround, New York; Marima, London. MC
Liesbet, Slegers. (2012). *Sounds.* Clavis Pub., New York.
Murphy, Mary. (2008). *I like it when/Me gusta cuando.* Harcourt, Orlando. MC
Oxenbury, Helen. (2010). *It's my birthday.* Candlewick Press, Cambridge, MA.
Roger, Priddy. (2012). *My big word book.* St. Martin's Press, New York.
Shaw, Pippa. (2010). *Weather.* Grosset & Dunlap, New York.
Snyder, Laurel. (2010). *Nosh, schlep, schluff: Babyiddish.* Random House Children's Books, New York.
Tankard, Jeremy. (2008). *Me hungry!* Candlewick Press, Somerville, MA.
Thompson, Lauren. (2010). *Little Quack's opposites.* Little Simon, New York.

Numbers/Counting

Blake, Quentin. (2009). *Quentin Blake's ten frogs.* Anova Children's, London.
Capote, Lori. (2013). *Monster knows numbers.* Picture Window Books, North Mankato, MN.
Davis, Sarah. (2015). *My first 123.* DK Publishing, New York.
Donaldson, Julia. (2012). *One ted falls out of bed.* Macmillan Children's, London.
Formento, Alison. (2011). *This tree, 1, 2, 3.* Albert Whitman, Chicago.
Giles, Andreae. (2013). *Giraffes can't dance: Number rumba counting book.* Cartwheel Books, New York.
Harris, Marian. (2010). *Ten little kittens.* Accord Publishing, Denver, CO.
Katz, Karen. (2011). *10 tiny babies.* Little Simon, New York. MC

Katz, Karen. (2010). *Baby's numbers.* Little Simon, New York.
Kingfisher Publications. (2010). *Animal 123: One to ten and back again.* Kingfisher, New York.
Lluch, Alex. (2014). *Trace & learn the 123s.* WS Publishing Group, San Diego, CA.
Mayer, Mercer. (2011). *Little critter numbers.* Sterling, New York.
Moerbeek, Kees. (2011). *Count 1 to 10.* Abrams Books for Young Readers, New York.
Petrlik, Andrea. (2009). *Animal airways.* School Specialty Publishing, Columbus, OH.
Stone, Kate. (2014). *Numbers.* Andrews McMeel Publishing, Kansas City, MO.
Thompson, Lauren. (2009). *Little Quack counts.* Little Simon, New York.
Tudor, Tasha. (2015). *1 is one.* Little Simon, New York.
Yoon, Salina. (2011). *One, two, buckle my shoe.* Robin Corey Books, New York.

Play/Adventure

Ackerman, Jill. (2010). *Welcome summer.* Scholastic, New York.
Allen, Constance. (2010). *Shake a leg.* Random House Children's Books, New York.
Broach, Elise. (2010). *Seashore baby.* LB Kids, New York.
Dicmas, Courtney. (2014). *Wild playtime!* Child's Play, Swindon, Australia.
Fujikawa, Gyo. (2010). *Let's play.* Sterling, New York.
O'Connell, Rebecca. (2010). *The baby goes beep.* Albert Whitman, Chicago.
Quay, Emma. (2009). *Puddle jumping.* Dial Books for Young Readers, New York.
Thompson, Lauren. (2010). *Mouse's first fall.* Little Simon, New York.
Yoon, Salina. (2011). *At the park.* Feiwel and Friends, New York.

Self-Awareness/-Emotions

Beauvisage, Alice. (2013). *My blankie.* Simply Read Books, Vancouver, British Columbia.
Boynton, Sandra. (2011). *Happy hippo, angry duck.* Little Simon, New York.
Cabrera, Jane. (2010). *If you're happy and you know it!* Holiday House, New York.
Church, Caroline. (2012). *Let's get dressed.* Scholastic, New York.
Crozier, Lorna. (2014). *Lots of kisses.* Orca Book Publishers, Victoria, British Columbia.
Dahl, Michael. (2013). *Little dinos don't bite.* Capstone Picture Window Books, Mankato, MN.
Dahl, Michael. (2013). *Little dinos don't hit.* Capstone Picture Window Books, Mankato, MN.
Dahl, Michael. (2010). *Duck goes potty.* Picture Window Books, Mankato, MN.
Dodd, Emma. (2010). *Dot and Dash eat their dinner.* Cartwheel Books, New York.
DwellStudio. (2011). *Good morning, toucan.* Blue Apple Books, Maplewood, NJ.
Ford, Bernette G. (2009). *No more blanket for Lambkin!* Sterling, New York.
Geis, Patricia. (2010). *Good-bye pacifier!* Windmill Books, LLC, New York.
Hächler, Bruno. (2010). *I am who I am.* NorthSouth Books, New York. MC
Juliet, David. (2013). *Sorry.* Candle Books, Oxford.
Juliet, David. (2013). *Thank you.* Candle Books, Oxford.
Magsamen, Sandra. (2010). *Twinkle, twinkle, you're my star.* Little Brown, New York.
Manushkin, Fran. (2011). *The tushy book.* Feiwel and Friends, New York.
McGee, Marni. (2011). *Messy me.* Good Books, Intercourse, PA.
Page, Claire. (2010). *Peek-a-boo! Happy baby.* Make Believe Ideas, Berkhamsted, Hertfordshire.

Patricelli, Leslie. (2011). *Higher! Higher!/¡Más alto! ¡Más alto!* Candlewick Press, Somerville, MA. MC

Patricelli, Leslie. (2011). *The birthday box/Mi caja de cumpleaños.* Candlewick Press, Cambridge, MA. MC

Perez, Monica. (2011). *Parade day.* Houghton Mifflin Harcourt, Boston.

Rippin, Sally. (2008). *Go baby go!* Allen & Unwin, Crows Nest N.S.W. MC

Schoenberg, Jane. (2010). *The baby hustle!* Little Simon, New York.

Spelman, Cornelia Maude. (2010). *When I feel scared.* Albert Whitman, Chicago.

Spelman, Cornelia Maude. (2010). *When I miss you.* Albert Whitman, Chicago.

Thompson, Lauren. (2010). *Mouse's first day of school.* Little Simon, New York.

Uzón, Jorge. (2010). *Not a baby anymore!* Groundwood Books, Toronto.

Verdick, Elizabeth. (2009). *Manners time.* Free Spirit Pub., Minneapolis, MN.

Verdick, Elizabeth. (2009). *Words are not for hurting/Las palabras no son lastimar.* Free Spirit Pub., Minneapolis, MN. MC

Wood, Hannah. (2010). *This little piggy.* Tiger Tales, Wilton, CT.

Sign Language

Anthony, Michelle. (2009). *My first signs.* Scholastic, New York. MC

Ault, Kelly. (2010). *Let's sign, baby! A fun and easy way to talk with baby.* Houghton Mifflin Harcourt, Boston. MC

Heller, Lora. (2012). *Sign language ABC.* Sterling Children's Books, New York.

Lewis, Anthony. (2013). *Jack and Jill.* Child's Play (International) Ltd, England.

Lewis, Anthony. (2013). *Old Macdonald.* Child's Play (International) Ltd, England.

Vance, Mimi Brian. (2010). *Baby and bunny: Sharing sign language with your child.* Bright Sky Press, Lancaster, Houston, TX. MC

Vance, Mimi Brian. (2010). *Boat and bath: Sharing sign language with your child.* Bright Sky Press, Lancaster, Houston, TX. MC

Vance, Mimi Brian. (2010). *Book and bed: Sharing sign language with your child.* Bright Sky Press, Lancaster, Houston, TX. MC

Vance, Mimi Brian. (2010). *Milk and more: Sharing sign language with your child.* Bright Sky Press, Lancaster, Houston, TX. MC

Miscellaneous

Alexander, Heather. (2010). *Allie Gator and the mixed-up scarecrow.* RP Kids, Philadelphia.

Allen, Constance. (2010). *Shake a leg.* Random House Children's Books, New York.

Bedford, David. (2012). *Opposites.* ChirpyBird, Richmond, Victoria.

Bondor, Rebecca. (2014). *It's time for….* Children's Press, New York.

Chandler, Shannon. (2011). *Dinosaurs.* Accord Publishing, Denver, CO.

Coble, Colleen. (2013). *The blessings jar: A story about being thankful.* Thomas Nelson Publishers, Nashville, TN.

Dismondy, Maria. (2014). *Spoonful of sweetness: And other delicious manners.* Making Sprits Bright: One Book at a Time, Dearborn, MI.

Jablow, Renée. (2011). *Hey, that's not trash! But which bin does it go in?* Little Simon, New York.

Lombardi, Kristine. (2010). *When I grow up: Mix and match.* Reader's Digest Children's Books, New York.

Underwood, Deborah. (2013). *The quiet book.* Houghton Mifflin Harcourt, Boston, MA.

The following is a list of picture books that can be used with infants and toddlers. They are arranged by categories or topics. Those marked with "MC" also represent a variety of cultures or cultural experiences.

Alphabet

American Museum of Natural History. (2014). *ABC insects.* Sterling Children's Books, New York.

Baker, Keith. (2010). *LMNO peas.* Beach Lane Books, New York.

Barbour, David Marchuck, & Bemisdarfer, Brian Lyle. (2014). *The gang of twenty and six: Alphabet adventures.* Millpond Ink, Highlands Ranch, CO.

Brown, Margaret Wise. (2010). *Goodnight moon ABC.* HarperCollins, New York.

Brown, Margaret Wise. (2010). *Sleepy ABC.* Harper, New York.

Carter, David A. (2014). *B is for box—The happy little yellow box: A pop-up book.* Little Simon, New York.

Concepcion, Patrick, Concepcion, Traci, & Ryski, Dawid. (2014). *Aesthetically awesome alliterated alphabet anthology.* Little Gestalten, Berlin.

Ghigna, Charles, & Jatkowska, Ag. (2014). *The alphabet parade.* Picture Window Books, North Mankato, MN.

Guéry, Anne. (2009). *Alphab'art.* Frances Lincoln Children's Books, New York.

Hatanaka, Kellen. (2014). *Work: An occupational ABC.* Groundwood Books, Toronto, ON.

Martin, Bill. (2009). *Chicka chicka boom boom.* Beach Lane Books, New York.

Seeger, Laura Vaccaro. (2010). *The hidden alphabet.* Roaring Brook Press, Brookfield, CT.

Sierra, Judy. (2009). *Sleepy little alphabet.* Alfred A. Knopf, New York.

White, Teagan. (2014). *Adventures with barefoot critters.* Tundra Books, Toronto, ON.

Animals/Pets

Bridwell, Norman. (2010). *Clifford the big red dog.* Scholastic, London.

Brown, Margaret Wise. (2009). *A child's good morning book.* HarperCollins, New York.

Capucilli, Alyssa Satin. (2009). *Katy Duck.* Little Simon, New York.

Carle, Eric. (2009). *The very hungry caterpillar pop-up book.* Philomel Books, New York.

Dodd, Emma. (2008). *I don't want a posh dog.* Little Brown, New York.

Domnauer, Teresa. (2013). *Wacky!: Pets.* Spectrum, Greensboro, NC.

Fox, Mem. (2010). *Where is the green sheep?* Sandpiper, Boston.

Fox, Mem. (2009). *Hello, baby!* Beach Lane Books, New York.

Gershator, Phillis. (2009). *When it starts to snow.* Henry Holt, New York.

Gillespie, Katie. (2014). *Pets.* AV2 by Weigl, New York.

Graire, Virginie. (2015). *Animals.* Simon & Schuster, New York.

Gravett, Emily. (2009). *The odd egg.* Simon & Schuster Books for Young Readers, New York.

Hayes, Susan, & Gordon-Harris, Tory. (2014). *Polar animals.* Scholastic, New York.

Jordan, Christopher. (2014). *Baseball animals.* Fenn/Tundra, Toronto, ON.

Lewin, Ted. (2014). *Animals work.* Holiday House, New York.

Minor, Wendell. (2009). *If you were a penguin.* Katherine Tegen Books, New York.

Nees, Susan. (2013). *Class pets.* Scholastic, New York.

Sheperd, Jodie, & Ovresat, Laura. (2011). *Playtime pets.* Readers Digest, White Plains, NY.

Storey, Rita. (2014). *Animals.* Smart Apple Media, North Mankato, MN.

Taback, Simms. (2009). *Simms Taback's city animals.* Blue Apple Books, Maplewood, NJ.

Van Fleet, Matthew. (2009). *Cat.* Simon & Schuster Books for Young Readers, New York.

Zenz, Aaron. (2011). *Chuckling ducklings and baby animal friends.* Walker & Co., New York.

Bedtime

Fox, Mem, & Quay, Emma. (2014). *Baby bedtime.* Beach Lane Books, New York.

Geringer, Laura. (2010). *Boom boom go away!* Atheneum Books for Young Readers, New York.

Gershator, Phillis. (2010). *Who's awake in springtime?* Henry Holt, New York.

Katz, Karen. (2009). *Princess baby, night-night.* Schwartz & Wade Books/Random House, New York.

McCue, Lisa. (2015). *Time for bed! A cozy counting bedtime book.* Simon & Schuster Merchandise, New York.

Radzinski, Kandy. (2009). *Where to sleep.* Sleeping Bear Press, Chelsea, MI.

Sanders, Rob, & Won, Brian. (2015). *Outer space bedtime race.* Random House, New York.

Sartell, Debra. (2010). *Time for bed, Baby Ted.* Holiday House, New York.

Scheffler, Axel. (2014). *The bedtime frog.* Nosy Crow, Somerville, MA.

Shea, Bob. (2010). *Race you to bed.* Dutton Children's Books, New York.

Sitomer, Alan Lawrence, & Carter, Abby. (2014). *Daddy's zigzagging bedtime story.* Disney/Hyperion Books, New York.

Viola, Karen. (2011). *Good night sun, hello moon.* Reader's Digest Children's Books, New York.

Behavior/Manners

Amant, Kathleen. (2010). *Anna brushes her teeth.* Clavis Books, New York. MC

Bridwell, Norman. (2010). *Clifford goes to dog school.* Scholastic, New York.

Buzzeo, Toni. (2010). *No T. Rex in the library.* Margaret K. McElderry Books, New York.

Chou, Yih-Fen. (2010). *Mimi loves to mimic.* Heryin Books, Alhambra, CA.

Chou, Yih-Fen. (2010). *Mimi says no.* Heryin Books, Alhambra, CA.

Clayton, Dallas. (2010). *An awesome book of thanks!* AmazonEncore, Las Vegas, NV.

Devlin, Jane. (2009). *Hattie the bad.* Dial Books for Young Readers, New York.

DiCicco, Sue. (2013). *Manners.* Silver Dolphin Books, San Diego, CA.

Elliott, David. (2009). *Finn throws a fit!* Candlewick Press, Somerville, MA.

Gassman, Julie. (2011). *Crabby pants.* Picture Window Books, North Mankato, MN.

Hargreaves, Roger. (2010). *Mr. Wrong.* Price Stern Sloan, New York.

Ingalls, Ann, & Rooney, Ronnie. (2013). *Basic manners.* The Child's World, North Mankato, MN.

Kaplan, Michael. (2011). *Betty Bunny loves chocolate cake.* Dial Books for Young Readers, New York.

Petersen, Christine, & Rooney, Ronnie. (2015). *The smart kid's guide to manners.* The Child's World, North Mankato, MN.

Raatma, Lucia. (2013). *Good manners.* Children's Press, New York.

Watson, Wendy. (2010). *Bedtime bunnies.* Clarion Books, New York.

Counting/Shapes

Boyd, Michelle, & Kenna, Kara. (2013). *Counting bunnies.* Silver Dolphin, San Diego, CA.

Cabrera, Jane. (2009). *One, two, buckle my shoe.* Holiday House, New York.

Capote, Lori, & Wass, Chip. (2013). *Monster knows shapes.* Picture Window Books, North Mankato, MN.

Donaldson, Julia. (2009). *One mole digging a hole.* Macmillan Children's, London.

Fleming, Candace. (2010). *Seven hungry babies.* Atheneum Books for Young Readers, New York.

MacDonald, Suse. (2009). *Shape by shape.* Little Simon, New York.

Pelham, Sophie. (2014). *Shapes.* Price Stern Sloan, New York.

Prochovnic, Dawn Babb, & Bauer, Stephanie. (2012). *Shape detective: Sign language for shapes.* Magic Wagon, Minneapolis, MN.

Schoenherr, Ian. (2009). *Read it, don't eat it!* Greenwillow Books, New York.

Urban, Linda. (2009). *Mouse was mad.* Harcourt, Orlando.

Weakland, Mark. (2014). *Hockey counting.* Capstone Press, North Mankato, MN.

Zubek, Adeline. (2012). *Counting lions.* Gareth Stevens Pub., New York.

Family

Appelt, Kathi. (2010). *Brand-new baby blues.* Harper, New York.

Bedford, David. (2010). *Mums.* Little Hare Books, Surry Hills, N.S.W.

Bennett, Kelly. (2010). *Your daddy was just like you.* Grosset & Dunlap, New York.

Brown, Margaret Wise. (2010). *The fathers are coming home.* Margaret K. McElderry Books, New York.

Cole, Joanna. (2010). *I'm a big sister.* Harper, New York.

Cole, Joanna. (2010). *Soy un hermano mayor.* Rayo, New York. MC

Cole, Joanna. (2010). *Soy una hermana mayor.* Rayo, New York. MC

Cora, Cat. (2011). *A suitcase surprise for Mommy.* Dial Books for Young Readers, New York.

Cordell, Matthew. (2012). *Hello! Hello!* Disney/Hyperion Books, New York.

Cusimano Love, Maryann. (2010). *You are my wish.* Philomel Books, New York.

Gore, Leonid. (2009). *Mommy, where are you?* Atheneum Books for Young Readers, New York.

Gore, Leonid. (2009). *When I grow up.* Scholastic Press, New York.

Havill, Juanita. (2009). *Just like a baby.* Chronicle Books, San Francisco, CA.

Hopkinson, Deborah. (2010). *First family.* Katherine Tegen Books, New York. MC

Konrad, Marla Stewart. (2010). *Grand.* Tundra Books, Toronto; Tundra Books of Northern New York, Plattsburg. MC

Konrad, Marla Stewart. (2009). *Mom and me.* Tundra Books, Toronto. MC

Modarressi, Mitra. (2010). *Taking care of Mama.* G.P. Putnam's Sons, New York.

Modesitt, Jeanne. (2009). *Oh, what a beautiful day!* Boyds Mills Press, Honesdale, PA.

Parr, Todd. (2010). *The family book*. Little Brown, London. MC
Peete, Holly Robinson. (2010). *My brother Charlie*. Scholastic Press, 2010, New York. MC
Rissman, Rebecca. (2013). *Family*. Capstone Raintree, Chicago.
Saltzberg, Barney. (2010). *Kisses*. Houghton Mifflin Harcourt, Boston.
Sayre, April Pulley. (2010). *One is a snail, ten is a crab: A counting by feet book*. Candlewick Press, Somerville, MA.
Unknown author. (2015). *Meet the hive*. Grosset & Dunlap, New York.

Friendship/Teamwork

Antle, Bhagavan. (2011). *Suryia & Roscoe: The true story of an unlikely friendship*. Henry Holt, New York.
Berenstain, Mike. (2015). *Hospital friends*. HarperCollins Children's Books, New York.
Bildner, Phil, & Watson, Jesse Joshua. (2014). *The soccer fence: A story of friendship, hope and apartheid in South Africa*. G. P. Putnam's Sons, New York. MC
Brown, Alan James. (2010). *Love-a-duck*. Holiday House, New York.
Carle, Eric. (2013). *Friends*. Philomel Books, New York.
Carlson, Nancy L. (2014). *Armond goes to a party: A book about Asperger's and friendship*. Free Spirit Publishing, Inc., Minneapolis, MN.
Carpenter, Tad. (2015). *Barnyard friends*. Sterling, New York.
DeSantis, Susan. (2014). *Little Too-Tall: A book about friendship*. The Child's World, North Mankato, MN.
Edwards, Amelia, & Conger, Holli. (2014). *Playground friends*. Teacher Created Materials, Huntington Beach, CA.
Engelbreit, Mary. (2014). *The blessings of friendship treasury*. Zondervan, Grand Rapids, MI.
Grossinger, Tania, & Esperanza, Charles George. (2013). *Jackie and me: A very special friendship*. Skyhorse, New York.
Kim, Cecil, & Jeong, Hajin. (2015). *Friendship quilt*. Norwood House Press, Chicago.
King, Stephen Michael. (2010). *You: A story of love and friendship*. Greenwillow Books, New York.
Kleven, Elisa. (2011). *The friendship wish*. Dutton Children's Books, New York.
Liu, Cynthea, & Peterson, Mary. (2013). *Wooby & Peep: A story of unlikely friendship*. Sterling Children's Books, New York.
Otoshi, Kathryn. (2014). *Two*. KO Kids Books. Navoto, CA.
Saltzberg, Barney. (2009). *Cornelius P. Mud, are you ready for baby?* Candlewick Press, Somerville, MA.
Sansone, Adele. (2010). *The little green goose*. NorthSouth, New York.
Shealy, Dennis. (2010). *I am a T. Rex!* Golden Book, New York.
Smith, Denny. (2010). *Dimitri's fleas: A story about friendship*. The author, Van Wert, OH.
van Hout, Mies. (2013). *Friends*. Lemniscaat USA, New York.
Zia, Farhana. (2011). *Hot, hot roti for Dada-ji*. Lee & Low Books, New York. MC

Language/Vocabulary/Poetry

Brown, Monica. (2011). *Pablo Neruda: Poet of the people*. Henry Holt, New York. MC
Canetti, Yanitzia, & Aggs, Patrice. (2012). *Uno dos tres: My first Spanish rhymes*. Frances Lincoln Children's, London, England. MC

Clay, Kathryn. (2014). *Signing around town: Sign language for kids*. Capstone Press, North Mankato, MN.

Lewis, Jan. (2015). *Action rhymes*. Armadillo, London, England.

Ohi, Ruth. (2010). *Chicken, pig, cow horse around*. Annick Press, Toronto, ON; Buffalo, NY.

Rampersad, Arnold, Blount, Marcellus, & Barbour, Karen. (2012). *African American poetry*. Sterling Children's Books, New York.

Ruddell, Deborah, & Rankin, Joan. (2015). *The popcorn astronauts: And other biteable rhymes*. Margaret K. McElderry Books, New York.

Scarry, Richard. (2014). *Lowly Worm word book*. Random House Books for Young Readers, New York.

Szekeres, Cyndy. (2010). *Melanie Mouse's moving day*. Sterling, New York.

Szekeres, Cyndy. (2010). *Nothing-to-do puppy*. Sterling, New York.

Wilson, Karma. (2009). *Bear snores on*. Spotlight, New York.

Wilson, Karma. (2009). *Bear's new friend*. Spotlight, New York.

Play/Adventure

Auerbach, Annie, Scotton, Rob, Farley, Rick, & Brantz, Loryn. (2013). *Splat the cat: On with the show*. HarperFestival, New York.

Carter, David A. (2010). *Opposites: A bugs pop-up concept book*. Little Simon, New York.

Coffelt, Nancy. (2009). *Big, bigger, biggest!* Henry Holt and Co., New York.

Cook, Gary, & Sward, Adam. (2013). *The best Saturday ever!* Scarletta Kids, Minneapolis, MN.

Davis, Nancy. (2009). *A garden of opposites*. Schwartz & Wade Books, New York.

Ditchfield, Christin. (2009). *"Shwatsit!": No one knows just what it means*. Golden Book, New York.

Frazier, Craig. (2011). *Bee & bird*. Roaring Brook Press, New York.

Gibbs, Edward. (2011). *I spy with my little eye*. Templar Books, Somerville, MA.

Gorbachev, Valeri. (2011). *Two little chicks*. NorthSouth Books, New York.

Guy, Ginger Foglesong. (2010). *Bravo!* Greenwillow Books, New York. MC

Hennessy, B. G. (2010). *Play ball, Corduroy*. Viking, New York.

Isadora, Rachel. (2010). *Say hello!* G.P. Putnam's Sons, New York. MC

Kawa, Katie. (2013). *My first trip to the beach = Mi primer viaje a la playa*. Gareth Stevens Pub., New York.

Konrad, Marla Stewart. (2010). *I like to play*. Tundra Books, Toronto; Tundra Books of Northern New York, Plattsburg. MC

Korda, Lerryn. (2010). *Into the wild*. Candlewick Press, Somerville, MA.

Lakin, Patricia, & Edmunds, Kirstie. (2014). *Bruno & Lulu's playground adventures*. Dial Books for Young Readers, New York.

LaRose, Melinda, & Batson, Alan. (2014). *Follow that sound!* Disney Press. Glendale, CA.

Mayer, Mercer. (2010). *Little Critter's Hansel and Gretel*. Sterling, New York.

Mayer, Mercer. (2010). *Little Critter's little red riding hood*. Sterling, New York.

Robertson, M. P. (2012). *Frank n Stan*. Frances Lincoln Children's, London, England.

Ross, Michael Elsohn. (2009). *Play with me*. Tricycle Press, Berkeley.

Rylant, Cynthia. (2010). *Brownie & Pearl get dolled up*. Beach Lane Books, New York.

Sakai, Komako, Hirano, Cathy, & Todd, Penelope. (2013). *Hannah's night*. Gecko Press, Wellington, New Zealand.

Self-Awareness/Emotions

Adler, Victoria. (2009). *All of baby nose to toes.* Dial Books for Young Readers, New York.

Bauer, Jutta. (2014). *Queen of colors.* NorthSouth Books, New York.

Bogart, Jo Ellen. (2009). *Big and small, room for all.* Tundra books, New York, London.

Burton, LeVar, Bernardo, Susan Schaefer, & Fletcher, Courtenay. (2014). *The rhino who swallowed a storm.* Reading Rainbow, Burbank, CA.

Conway, David. (2010). *Errol and his extraordinary nose.* Holiday House, New York.

Côté, Geneviève. (2014). *Starring me and you.* Kids Can Press, Toronto, ON.

Dahl, Michael. (2011). *Two heads are better than one.* Picture Window Books, North Mankato, MN.

Delacroix, Sibylle, & Li, Karen. (2015). *Prickly Jenny.* Owlkids Books, Toronto, ON.

Evans, Kristina. (2011). *What's special about me, Mama?* Disney/Jump at the Sun Books, New York. MC

Genechten, Guido van. (2014). *Odd one out: Happy angry sad.* Clavis Pub., New York.

Helakoski, Leslie. (2010). *Big chickens go to town.* Dutton Children's Books, New York.

Hodgkinson, Leigh. (2010). *Smile!* Balzer & Bray, New York.

Jones, Christianne C. (2011). *Maybe when I'm bigger.* Picture Window Books, North Mankato, MN.

Lester, Helen, & Munsinger, Lynn. (2014). *Hurty feelings.* Houghton Mifflin Harcourt, Boston.

Millar, Goldie, Berger, Lisa, & Mitchell, Hazel. (2014). *F is for feelings.* Free Spirit Publishing, Minneapolis, MN.

Moses, Brian, & Gordon, Mike. (2014). *Jayden jealousaurus.* Barron's, Hauppauge, NY.

Rubenstein, Lauren, & Hehenberger, Shelly. (2014). *Visiting feelings.* Magination Press, Washington, DC.

Rylant, Cynthia. (2010). *Brownie & Pearl see the sights.* Beach Lane Books, New York.

Savage, Stephen. (2011). *Where's Walrus?* Scholastic Press, New York.

Schubert, Ingrid, & Schubert, Dieter. (2010). *The umbrella.* Lemniscaat USA, Brooklyn, NY.

Stewart, Whitney, & Rippin, Sally. (2015). *Meditation is an open sky: Mindfulness for kids.* Albert Whitman & Company, Chicago.

Tafolla, Carmen. (2009). *What can you do with a paleta?* Tricycle Press, Berkeley, CA. MC

Teague, David. (2010). *Franklin's big dreams.* Disney/Hyperion Books, New York.

Thomas, Jan. (2009). *Can you make a scary face?* Beach Lane Books, New York.

Tompert, Ann. (2010). *Little Fox goes to the end of the world.* Marshall Cavendish Children's Books, New York.

References

AARP. (2015). GrandFacts: National. Retrieved January 25, 2015, from http://www.aarp.org/content/dam/aarp/relationships/friends-family/grandfacts/grandfacts-national.pdf

Abraham, L. M., Crais, E., & Vernon-Feagans, L. (2013). Early maternal language use during book sharing in families from low-income environments. *American Journal of Speech-Language Pathology, 22*(1), 71–83.

Abraham, M. M., & Kerns, K. A. (2013). Positive and negative emotions and coping as mediators of mother-child attachment and peer relationships. *Merrill-Palmer Quarterly, 59*(4), 399–425.

Acredolo, L. P., Goodwyn, S., & Abrams, D. (2009). *Baby signs: How to talk with your baby before your baby can talk* (3rd ed.). Chicago, IL: Contemporary Books.

Adolph, K. E., Vereijken, B., & Shrout, P. E. (2003). What changes in infant walking and why. *Child Development, 74*(2), 475–497.

Ainsworth, M. D. S. (1967). *Infancy in Uganda: Infant care and the growth of love.* Baltimore, MD: Johns Hopkins University Press.

Ainsworth, M. D. S. (1973). The development of infant-mother attachment. In B. M. Caldwell & H. N. Ricciuti (Eds.), *Review of child development research: Vol. 3. Child development and social policy.* Chicago, IL: University of Chicago Press. (pp. 1–94).

Ainsworth, M. D. S. (1982). The development of infant-mother attachment. In J. Belsky (Ed.), *In the beginning: Readings on infancy.* New York: Columbia University Press.

Ainsworth, M. D. S., Blehar, M., Waters, E., & Wall, S. (1978). *Patterns of attachment.* Hillsdale, NJ: Lawrence Erlbaum Associates.

Aldridge, B. (2010). Culture of the program and culture of the home: Infants and toddlers. In D. Derman-Sparks & J. O. Edwards, *Anti-biased education for young children and ourselves* (pp. 151–152). Washington, DC: National Association for the Education of Young Children.

Alkon, A., & Cole, P. (2012). Assessing Indiana's health and safety in early care and education programs: Identifying areas for improvement. *Maternal & Child Health Journal, 16*(3), 555–563.

Allen County Public Library. (2009). *Talking and reading to infants and toddlers: Follow the CAR* [Brochure]. Fort Wayne, IN: Author.

Allison, C., Baron-Cohen, S., Wheelwright, S., Charman, T., Richler, J., Pasco, G., et al. (2008). The Q-CHAT (Quantitative Checklist for Autism in Toddlers): A normally distributed quantitative measure of autistic traits at 18–24 months of age: Preliminary report. *Journal of Autism & Developmental Disorders, 38*(8), 1414–1425.

Alzahrani, M., Ratelle, J., Cavel, O., Laberge-Malo, M., & Saliba, I. (2014). Hearing loss in the shaken baby syndrome. *International Journal of Pediatric Otorhinolaryngology, 78*(5), 804–806.

American Academy of Pediatrics. (2011). Policy statement: Media use by children younger than 2 years. *Pediatrics, 128*(5), 1040–1045.

American Academy of Pediatrics. (2012). *Family life: The benefits of limiting TV.* Retrieved February 13, 2012, from http://www.healthychildren.org/English/family-life/Media/pages/The-Benefits-of-Limiting-TV.aspx?nfstatus=401&nftoken=00000000-0000-0000-0000-000000000000&nfstatusdescription=ERROR%3a+No+local+token

American Academy of Pediatrics, American Public Health Association, and National Resource Center for Health and Safety in Child Care. (2011). *Caring for our children: National health and safety performance standards: Guidelines for early care and early education programs* (3rd ed.). Elk Grove Village/Washington, IL/DC: American Academy of Pediatrics/American Public Health Association. Retrieved from http://cfoc.nrckids.org/StandardView.cfm

American Academy of Pediatrics Task Force on Sudden Infant Death Syndrome. (2011). Technical report: SIDS and other sleep-related infant deaths: Expansion of recommendations for a safe infant sleeping environment. *Pediatrics, 128*(5), e1341–e1367.

American Dental Association (ADA). (2014). *Oral health topics A-Z: Teething.* Retrieved July 2, 2015, from http://www.mouthhealthy.org/en/az-topics/t/teething

American Psychiatric Association. (2014). Autism spectrum disorders. Retrieved February 11, 2015, from http://www.psychiatry.org/mental-health/autism-spectrum-disorders

Anderson, D. R., & Hanson, K. G. (2010). From blooming, buzzing confusion to media literacy: The early development of television viewing. *Developmental Review, 30*(2), 239–255.

Anderson, E. M. (2014). Transforming early childhood education through critical reflection. *Contemporary Issues in Early Childhood, 15*(1), 81–82.

Annie E. Casey Foundation. (2014). *2014 Kids count data book.* Baltimore, MD: Author. Retrieved December 19, 2014, from http://www.aecf.org/resources/the-2014-kids-count-data-book/

Appl, D. J., Leavitt, J. E., & Ryan, M. A. (2014). Parent–child portfolios: "Look—This book is all about us!" *Early Childhood Education Journal, 42*(3), 191–202.

Aronson, S. S. (Ed.). (2012). *Healthy young children: A manual for programs* (5th ed.). Washington, DC: National Association for the Education of Young Children.

Arthur, N. (2010). Technology and television for babies and toddlers. *Children & Libraries: The Journal of the Association for Library Service to Children, 8*(2), 58–59.

Athanasopoulou, E., & Fox, J. R. E. (2014). Effects of kangaroo mother care on maternal mood and interaction patterns between parents and their preterm, low birth weight infants: A systematic review. *Infant Mental Health Journal, 35*(3), 245–262.

Azzi-Lessing, L. (2013). Serving highly vulnerable families in home-visitation programs. *Infant Mental Health Journal, 34*(5), 376–390.

Badanes, L. S., Dmitrieva, J., & Watamura, S. E. (2012). Understanding cortisol reactivity across the day at child care: The potential buffering role of secure attachments to caregivers. *Early Childhood Research Quarterly, 27*(1), 156–165.

Bai, Y. K., Middlestadt, S. E., Joanne Peng, C.-Y., & Fly, A. D. (2009). Psychosocial factors underlying the mother's decision to continue exclusive breastfeeding for 6 months: An elicitation study. *Journal of Human Nutrition and Dietetics, 22*(2), 134–140.

Baillargeon, R. (2004). Infants' physical worlds. *Current Directions in Psychological Science, 13*(3), 89–94.

Baillargeon, R. H., Zoccolillo, M., Keenan, K., Cote, S., Perusse, D., Wu, H., et al. (2007). Gender differences in physical aggression: A prospective population-based survey of children before and after 2 years of age. *Developmental Psychology, 43*(1), 13–26.

Baker, C. E. (2013). Fathers' and mothers' home literacy involvement and children's cognitive and social emotional development: Implications for family literacy programs. *Applied Developmental Science, 17*(4), 184–197.

Baker, B. L., & Feinfield, K. A. (2003). Early intervention. *Current Opinion in Psychiatry, 16*(5), 503–509.

Balaban, N. (2006). Easing the separation process for infants, toddlers, and families. *Beyond the Journal: Young Children on the Web.* Retrieved March 12, 2009, from http://journal.naeyc.org/btj/200611/pdf/BTJBalaban.pdf

Banerjee, P. N., & Tamis-LeMonda, C. S. (2007). Infants' persistence and mothers' teaching as predictors of toddlers' cognitive development. *Infant Behavior & Development, 30*(3), 479–491.

Bang, Y. (2014). Teacher-caregivers' perceptions of toddlers' adaptation to a childcare center. *Social Behavior and Personality, 42*(8), 1279–1292.

Bard, K. A., Todd, B. K., Bernier, C., Love, J., & Leavens, D. A. (2006). Self-awareness in human and chimpanzee infants: What is measured and what is meant by the mark and mirror test? *Infancy, 9*(2), 191–219.

Barone, J. G., Jasutkar, N., & Schneider, D. (2009). Later toilet training is associated with urge incontinence in children. *Journal of Pediatric Urology, 5*(6), 458–461.

Barr, R., Rovee-Collier, C., & Campanella, J. (2005). Retrieval protracts deferred imitation by 6-month-olds. *Infancy, 7*(3), 263–283.

Barrett, M. S. (2011). Musical narratives: A study of a young child's identity work in and through music-making. *Psychology of Music, 39*(4), 403–423.

Barron, I. (2011). The shadows of difference: Ethnicity and young children's friendships. *Race, Ethnicity & Education, 14*(5), 655–673.

Bartl-Pokorny, K. D., Marschik, P. B., Sachse, S., Green, V. A., Zhang, D., Van der Meer, et al. (2013). Tracking development from early speech-language acquisition to reading skills at age 13. *Developmental Neurorehabilitation, 16*(3), 188–195.

Bbaale, E. (2014). Determinants of early initiation, exclusiveness, and duration of breastfeeding in Uganda. *Journal of Health, Population & Nutrition, 32*(2), 249–260.

Beeber, L. S., Schwartz, T. A., Martinez, M. I., Holditch-Davis, D., Bledsoe, S. E., Canuso, R. et al. (2014). Depressive symptoms and compromised parenting in low-income mothers of infants and toddlers: Distal and proximal risks. *Research in Nursing & Health, 37*(4), 276–291.

Behrend, D. A., Rosengran, K. S., & Perlmutter, M. (1992). The relation between private speech and parental interactive style. In R. M. Diaz & L. E. Berk (Eds.), *Private speech: From social interaction to self-regulation* (pp. 85–100). Hillsdale, NJ: Erlbaum.

Behrens, K. Y., Hesse, E., & Main, M. (2007). Mothers' attachment status as determined by the Adult Attachment Interview predicts their 6-year-olds' reunion responses: A study conducted in Japan. *Developmental Psychology, 43*(6), 1553–1567.

Beijers, R., Riksen-Walraven, J. M., & de Weerth, C. (2013). Cortisol regulation in 12-month-old human infants: Associations with the infants' early history of breastfeeding and co-sleeping. *The International Journal on the Biology of Stress, 16*(3), 267–277.

Beilin, H. (1992). Piaget's enduring contribution to developmental psychology. *Developmental Psychology, 28*, 191–204.

Belsky, J., & Most, R. K. (1981). From exploration to play: A cross sectional study of infant free play behavior. *Developmental Psychology, 17*, 630–639.

Belsky, J., Rovine, M., & Taylor, D. G. (1984). The Pennsylvania Infant and Family Development Project, part 3. The origins of individual differences in infant-mother attachments: Maternal and infant contributions. *Child Development, 55*, 718–728.

Benton, D. (2008). The influence of children's diet on their cognition and behavior. *European Journal of Nutrition, 47*(3), 25–37.

Bera, A., Ghosh, J., Singh, A. K., Hazra, A., Mukherjee, S., & Mukherjee, R. (2014). Effect of kangaroo mother care on growth and development of low birthweight babies up to 12 months of age: A controlled clinical trial. *Acta Pædiatrica, 103*(6), 643–650.

Bergen, D., Reid, R., & Torelli, L. (2001). *Educating and caring for very young children: The infant/toddler curriculum.* New York: Teachers College Press.

Berggren, S. (2004). Massage in schools reduces stress and anxiety. *YC: Young Children, 59*(5), 67–68.

Bergin, C. C., & Bergin, D. A. (2012). *Child and adolescent development in your classroom.* Belmont, CA: Wadsworth, Cengage Learning.

Bergman, K., Sarkar, P., Glover, V., & O'Connor, T. G. (2010). Maternal prenatal cortisol and infant cognitive development: Moderation by infant-mother attachment. *Biological Psychiatry, 67*, 1026–1032.

Berk, L. E. (1994). Why children talk to themselves. *Scientific American, 271*(5), 78–83.

Berk, L. E. (2012). *Child development* (9th ed.). Upper Saddle River, NJ: Pearson.

Berk, L. E., Mann, T. D., & Ogan, A. T. (2006). Make-believe play: Wellspring for development of self-regulation. In D. G. Singer, R. M. Golinkoff, & K. Hirsh-Pasek (Eds.), *Play=learning* (pp. 74–100). New York: Oxford University Press.

Berk, L. E., & Spuhl, S. T. (1995). Maternal interaction, private speech, and task performance in preschool children. *Early Childhood Research Quarterly, 10*, 145–169.

Berk, L. E., & Winsler, A. (1995). *NAEYC research into practice series: Vol. 7. Scaffolding children's learning: Vygotsky and early childhood education.* Washington, DC: National Association for the Education of Young Children.

Berlin, L., Whiteside-Mansell, L., Roggman, L., Green, B. L., Robinson, J., & Spieker, S. (2011). Testing maternal depression and attachment style as moderators of early head start's effects on parenting. *Attachment & Human Development, 13*(1), 49–67.

Bernhardt, J. L. (2000). A primary caregiving system for infants and toddlers: Best for everyone involved. *YC: Young Children, 55*(2), 74–80.

Bernier, A., Carlson, S. M., & Whipple, N. (2010). From external regulation to self-regulation: Early parenting precursors of young children's executive functioning. *Child Development, 81*(1), 326–339.

Berry, D., Blair, C., Ursache, A., Willoughby, M., Garrett-Peters, P., Vernon-Feagans, L., et al. (2014). Child care and cortisol across early childhood: Context matters. *Developmental Psychology, 50*(2), 514–525.

Berthelsen, D., Brownlee, J., & Boulton-Lewis, G. (2002). Caregivers' epistemological beliefs in toddler programs. *Early Child Development and Care, 172*(5), 503–516.

Bibace, R. (2012). Challenges in Piaget's legacy. *Integrative Psychological & Behavioral Science, 47*, 167–175.

Bocknek, E. L., Brophy-Herb, H. E., Fitzgerald, H. E., Schiffman, R. F., & Vogel, C. (2014). Stability of biological father presence as a proxy for family stability: Cross-racial associations with the longitudinal development of emotion regulation in toddlerhood. *Infant Mental Health Journal, 35*(4), 309–321.

Bodrova, E., & Leong, D. J. (2007). *Tools of the mind: The Vygotskian approach to early childhood education* (2nd ed.). Upper Saddle River, NJ: Prentice Hall.

Boller, S. (2012). Training vs learning: What's the difference? Retrieved October 13, 2014, from http://www.bottomlineperformance.com /training-vs-learning-whats-the-difference/

Bolten, M. (2013). Infant psychiatric disorders. *European Child & Adolescent Psychiatry, 22*(Suppl.), 69–74.

Booth, A. E., & Waxman, S. R. (2008). Taking stock as theories of word learning take shape. *Developmental Science, 11*(2), 185–194.

Booth-LaForce, C., Groh, A. M., Burchinal, M. R., Roisman, G. I., Owen, M. T., & Cox, M. J. (2014). Caregiving and contextual sources of continuity and change in attachment security from infancy to late adolescence. *Monographs of the Society for Research in Child Development, 79*(3), 67–84.

Booth-LaForce, C., & Oxford, M. L. (2008). Trajectories of social withdrawal from grades 1 to 6: Prediction from early parenting, attachment, and temperament. *Developmental Psychology, 44*(5), 1298–1313.

Bornstein, M. H., Mash, C., Arterberry, M. E., & Manian, N. (2012). Object perception in 5-month-old infants of clinically depressed and nondepressed mothers. *Infant Behavior & Development, 35*(1), 150–157.

Borodachyova, O. V. (2011). Researching speech competence through psychology students' stories about themselves. *Cultural-Historical Psychology,* (4), 64–76.

Botero, H., & Sanders, C. (2014). Mother–baby relationship: A loving nest for mental health—observing 'kangaroo' infants. *Infant Observation, 17*(3), 215–232.

Bove, C. (2001). Inserimento: A strategy of delicately beginning relationships and communications. In L. Gandini & C. P. Edwards (Eds.), *Bambini: The Italian approach to infant/toddler care* (pp. 109–123). New York: Teachers College Press.

Bowlby, J. (1958). The nature of the child's tie to its mother. *International Journal of Psychoanalysis, 39,* 350–373.

Bowlby, J. (2000). *Attachment and loss: Vol. 1. Attachment.* New York: Basic Books. (Original work published 1969.)

Boyce, L. (2014). Family bookmaking: Creating links between home and early childhood programs. *YC: Young Children, 69*(4), 53–55.

Boyd, D. J., Grossman, P. L., Lankford, H., Loeb, S., & Wyckoff, J. (2009). Teacher preparation and student achievement. *Educational Evaluation and Policy Analysis, 31*(4), 416–440.

Brand, S., Marchand, J., Lilly, E., & Child, M. (2014). Home–school literacy bags for twenty-first century preschoolers. *Early Childhood Education Journal, 42*(3), 163–170.

Branscombe, N. A., Castle, K., Dorsey, A. G., Surbeck, E., & Taylor, J. B. (2003). *Early childhood curriculum: A constructivist perspective.* Boston, MA: Houghton Mifflin.

Bredekamp, S., & Copple, C. (Eds.). (1997). *Developmentally appropriate practice in early childhood programs* (Rev. ed.). Washington, DC: National Association for the Education of Young Children.

Brekken, L. (2004). Supporting children's possibilities: Infants and toddlers with disabilities and their families in Early Head Start. In J. Lombardi & M. M. Bogle (Eds.), *Beacon of hope: The promise of Early Head Start for America's youngest children* (pp. 148–167). Washington, DC: Zero to Three.

Bretherton, I. (2010). Fathers in attachment theory and research: A review. *Early Child Development and Care, 180*(1&2), 9–23.

Brewer, R. A. (2010). The Canada goose project: A first project with children under 3. *Early Childhood Research & Practice, 12*(1). Retrieved October 1, 2011, from http://ecrp.uiuc.edu/v12n1/brewer.html

Brian, J., Bryson, S. E., Garon, N., Roberts, W., Smith, I. M., Szatmari, P., et al. (2008). Clinical assessment of autism in high-risk 18-month-olds. *Autism: The International Journal of Research & Practice, 12*(5), 433–456.

Bridgett, D. J., Gartstein, M. A., Putnam, S. P., Lance, K. O., Iddins, E., Waits, R., et al. (2011). Emerging effortful control in toddlerhood: The role of infant orienting/regulation, maternal effortful control, and maternal time spent in caregiving activities. *Infant Behavior & Development, 34*(1), 189–199.

Bridgett, D. J., Gartstein, M. A., Putnam, S. P., McKay, T., Iddins, E., Robertson, C., et al. (2009). Maternal and contextual influences and the effect of temperament development during infancy on parenting in toddlerhood. *Infant Behavior & Development, 32*(1), 103–116.

Brinamen, C. F., Taranta, A. N., & Johnston, K. (2012). Expanding early childhood mental health consultation to new venues: Serving infants and young children in domestic violence and homeless shelters. *Infant Mental Health Journal, 33*(3), 283–293.

Britto, P. R., & Brooks-Gunn, J. (2001). Beyond shared book reading: Dimensions of home literacy and low-income African American preschoolers' skills. *New Directions for Child and Adolescent Development, Summer* (92), 73–89.

Bronfenbrenner, U. (1979). *The ecology of human development: Experiments by nature and design.* Cambridge, MA: Harvard University Press.

Bronfenbrenner, U. (1989). Ecological systems theory. In R. Vasta (Ed.), *Annals of child development* (Vol. 6, pp. 187–251). Greenwich, CT: JAI Press.

Bronfenbrenner, U. (1995). The bioecological model from a life course perspective: Reflections of a participant observer. In P. Moen, G. H. Elder, Jr., & K. Luscher (Eds.), *Examining lives in context* (pp. 599–618). Washington, DC: American Psychological Association.

Bronfenbrenner, U. (2001). Bioecological theory of human development. In N. J. Smelser & B. P. Baltes (Eds.), *International encyclopedia of the social and behavioral sciences,* Vol. 10 (pp. 6963–6970). New York: Elsevier.

Bronte-Tinkew, J., Carano, J., Horowitz, A., & Kinukawa, A. (2008). Involvement among resident fathers and links to infant cognitive outcomes. *Journal of Family Issues, 29*(9), 1211–1244.

Brophy-Herb, H. E., Horodynski, M., Dupuis, S. B., Bocknek, E. L., Schiffman, R., Onaga, E., et al. (2009). Early emotional development in infants and toddlers: Perspectives of Early Head Start staff and parents. *Infant Mental Health Journal, 30*(3), 203–222.

Brotherson, M. J., Summers, J. A., Naig, L. A., Kyzar, K., Friend, A., Epley, P., et al. (2010). Partnership patterns: Addressing emotional needs in early intervention. *Topics in Early Childhood Special Education, 30*(1), 32–45.

Brownell, C. A. (2013). Early development of prosocial behavior: Current perspectives. *Infancy, 18*(1), 1–9.

Brownell, C. A., Svetlova, M., Anderson, R., Nichols, S. R., & Drummond, J. (2013). Socialization of early prosocial behavior: Parents' talk about emotions is associated with sharing and helping in toddlers. *Infancy, 18*(1), 91–119.

Bruns, D. A. (2006). Promoting mother-child relationships for incarcerated women and their children. *Infants and Young Children, 19*(4), 308–322.

Buchanan, T. K., Burts, D. C., Bidner, J., White, V. F., & Charlesworth, R. (1998). Predictors of the developmental appropriateness of the beliefs and practices of first, second, and third grade teachers. *Early Childhood Research Quarterly, 13*(3), 459–483.

Bugental, D. B., Schwartz, A., & Lynch, C. (2010). Effects of an early family intervention on children's memory: The mediating effects of cortisol levels. *Mind, Brain, and Education, 4*(4), 159–170.

Butera, G., Friesen, A., Palmer, S. B., Lieber, J., Horn, E. M., Hanson, M. J., et al. (2014). Integrating mathematics problem solving and critical thinking into the curriculum. *YC: Young Children, 69*(1), 70–77.

Buyse, E., Verschueren, K., & Doumen, S. (2011). Preschoolers' attachment to mother and risk for adjustment problems in kindergarten: Can teachers make a difference? *Social Development, 20*(1) 33–50.

Bydlowski, S., Lalanne, C., Golse, B., & Vaivre-Douret, L. (2013). Postpartum blues: A marker of early neonatal organization? *Infant Mental Health Journal, 34*(6), 508–515.

Byrn, M. D., & Hourigan, R. (2010). A comparative case study of music interactions between mothers and infants. *Contributions to Music Education, 37*(1), 65–79.

Cabrera, N. J., Hofferth, S. L., & Chae, S. (2011). Patterns and predictors of father–infant engagement across race/ethnic groups. *Early Childhood Research Quarterly, 26*(3), 365–375.

Cain, C. S. (2006). *Attachment disorders: Treatment strategies for traumatized children.* Lanham, MD: Jason Aronson.

Caldera, Y. M., & Hart, S. (2004). Exposure to child care, parenting style and attachment security. *Infant & Child Development, 13*(1), 21–33.

Canale, A., Favero, E., Lacilla, M., Recchia, E., Schindler, A., Roggero, N., et al. (2006). Age at diagnosis of deaf babies: A retrospective analysis highlighting the advantage of newborn hearing screening. *International Journal of Pediatric Otorhinolaryngology, 70*(7), 1283–1289.

Cardany, A. B. (2010). Screen media and young children: Who benefits? *General Music Today, 24*(1), 50–55.

Cardon, G., De Craemer, M., De Bourdeaudhuij, I., & Verloigne, M. (2014). Plenary conference 1: More physical activity and less sitting in children: Why and how? *Science and Sports, 29*(Suppl.), S3–S5.

Carlson, E. A., Hostinar, C. E., Mliner, S. B., & Gunnar, M. R. (2014). The emergence of attachment following early social deprivation. *Development & Psychopathology, 26*(2), 479–489.

Carlson, F. M. (2011). *Big body play: Why boisterous, vigorous and very physical play is essential to children's development and learning.* Washington, DC: National Association for the Education of Young Children.

Carpendale, J. I. M., & Carpendale, A. B. (2010). The development of pointing: From personal directedness to interpersonal direction. *Human Development, 53*, 110–126.

Carpenter, M., Nagell, K., & Tomasello, M. (1998). Social cognition, joint attention, and communicative competence. *Monographs of the Society for Research in Child Development, 63*(4), 1–174.

Carranza, J. A., González-Salinas, C., & Ato, E. (2013). A longitudinal study of temperament continuity through IBQ, TBAQ, and CBQ. *Infant Behavior & Development, 36*, 749–761.

Casanueva, C., Dozier, M., Tueller, S., Dolan, M., Smith, K., Webb, M. B., et al. (2014). Caregiver instability and early life changes among infants reported to the child welfare system. *Child Abuse & Neglect, 38*(3), 498–509.

Casler, K., Hoffman, K., & Eshleman, A. (2014). Do adults make scale errors too? How function sometimes trumps size. *Journal of Experimental Psychology: General, 143*(4), 1690–1700.

Caspi, A., & Silva, P. A. (1995). Temperamental qualities at age three predict personality traits in young adulthood: Longitudinal evidence from a birth cohort. *Child Development, 66*, 486–498.

Cecchini, M., Lai, C., & Langher, V. (2007). Communication and crying in newborns. *Infant Behavior and Development, 30*(4), 655–665.

Cecchini, M., Lai, C., & Langher, V. (2010). Dysphonic newborn cries allow prediction of their perceived meaning. *Infant Behavior and Development, 33*(3), 314–320.

Center on the Developing Child at Harvard University. (2008). *InBrief: The Science of Early Childhood Development*. Retrieved February 12, 2015, from http://developingchild.harvard.edu/resources /briefs/inbrief_series/inbrief_the_science_of_ecd/

Center on the Developing Child at Harvard University. (2010). *The Foundations of Lifelong Health are built in Early Childhood*. Retrieved February 12, 2015, from http://developingchild.harvard.edu/resources /reports_and_working_papers/foundations-of -lifelong-health/

Center on the Developing Child at Harvard University. (2011). *Building the brain's "Air Traffic Control" system: How early experiences shape the development of executive function: Working paper no. 11*. Retrieved June 30, 2011, from http://developingchild .harvard.edu

Centers for Disease Control and Prevention (CDC). (nd). A journalist's guide to shaken baby syndrome: A preventable tragedy. A part of CDC's "Heads Up" Series. Retrieved October 29, 2014, from http:// www.cdc.gov/concussion/pdf/sbs_media_guide _508_optimized-a.pdf

Centers for Disease Control and Prevention (CDC). (2014a). *Autism Spectrum Disorder: Facts about ASD*. Retrieved on February 11, 2014, from http:// www.cdc.gov/ncbddd/autism/facts.html

Centers for Disease Control and Prevention (CDC). (2014b). Injury prevention and control: Division of violence prevention. Retrieved January 14, 2015, from http://www.cdc.gov/violenceprevention /acestudy/

Center for Parent Information and Resources. (2014). *Overview of early intervention*. Retrieved December 17, 2014, from http://www.parentcenterhub.org /repository/ei-overview/

Chandrasena, A. N., Mukherjee, R. A., Raja, A. S., & Turk, J. (2009). Fetal alcohol spectrum disorders: An overview of interventions for affected individuals. *Child & Adolescent Mental Health, 14*(4), 162–167.

Charles, E. P., & Rivera, S. M. (2009). Object permanence and method of disappearance: Looking measures further contradict reaching measures. *Developmental Science, 12*(6), 991–1006.

Cheatham, G. A., & Ostrosky, M. M. (2013). Goal setting during early childhood parent-teacher conferences: A comparison of three groups of parents. *Journal of Research in Childhood Education, 27*(2), 166–189.

Chen, D. (2014). Early intervention: Purpose and principles. In D. Chen (Ed.), *Essential elements in early intervention: Visual impairment and multiple disabilities* (2nd ed.), (pp. 3–33). New York: AFB Press.

Chen, J., Liu, Z., & Liu, Y. (2013). Characteristics of junior school students' victimization and its relation with parent-child attachment and peer relationship. *Chinese Journal of Clinical Psychology, 21*(5), 795–799.

Chess, S., Thomas, A., & Birch, H. G. (1976). *Your child is a person: A psychological approach to parenthood without guilt*. New York: Penguin Books.

Children's Defense Fund. (2014). *The state of America's children 2014*. Washington, DC: Author.

Chien, S. H., Palmer, J., & Teller, D. (2005). Achromatic contrast effects in infants: Adults and 4-month-old infants show similar deviations from Wallach's ratio rule. *Vision Research, 45*(22), 2854–2861.

Choi, J., Palmer, R. J., & Pyun, H. (2014). Three measures of non-resident fathers' involvement, maternal parenting and child development in low-income single-mother families. *Child and Family Social Work, 19*(3), 282–291.

Christakis, D. A., & Garrison, M. M. (2009). Preschool-aged children's television viewing in child care settings. *Pediatrics, 124*(6), 1627–1632.

Christian, K. M., Russ, S., & Short, E. J. (2011). Pretend play processes and anxiety: Considerations for the play therapist. *International Journal of Play Therapy, 20*(4), 179–192.

Christian, L. G. (2006, January). Understanding families: Applying family systems theory to early childhood practice. *Beyond the Journal: Young Children on the Web*. Retrieved December 14, 2006, from https://www.naeyc.org/files/yc/file/200601 /ChristianBTJ.pdf

Christl, B., Reilly, N., Smith, M., Sims, D., Chavasse, F., & Austin, M. (2013). The mental health of mothers of unsettled infants: Is there value in routine psychosocial assessment in this context? *Archives of Women's Mental Health, 16*(5), 391–399.

Christopher, C., Saunders, R., Jacobvitz, D., Burton, R, & Hazen, N. (2013). Maternal empathy and changes in mothers' permissiveness as predictors of toddlers' early social competence with peers: A parenting intervention study. *Journal of Child & Family Studies, 22*(6), 769–778.

Christy, T. C. (2013). Vygotsky, Cognitive Development and Language: New perspectives on the nature of grammaticalization. *Historiographia Lingüística, 40*(1/2), 199–227.

Churchill, S. L. (2003). Goodness-of-fit in early childhood settings. *Early Childhood Education Journal, 31*, 113–118.

Cipriano, E. A., & Stifter, C. A. (2010). Predicting preschool effortful control from toddler temperament and parenting behavior. *Journal of Applied Developmental Psychology, 31*, 221–230.

Clements, R., & Kuperberg, M. (2008). Viewpoint: Reaching our goals through effective communication. *Journal of Physical Education, Recreation, and Dance, 79*(3), 4–6, 11.

Cline, K. D., & Edwards, C. P. (2013). The instructional and emotional quality of parent–child book reading and early head start children's learning outcomes. *Early Education and Development, 24*(8), 1214–1231.

Colker, L. (2005). *The cooking book: Fostering young children's learning and delight.* Washington, DC: National Association for the Education of Young Children.

Collins, R., Mascia, J., Kendall, R., Golden, O., Schock, L., & Parlakian, R. (2003). Promoting mental health in child care settings: Caring for the whole child. *Zero to Three, 23*(4), 39–45.

Colombo, M. (2006). Building school partnerships with culturally and linguistically diverse families. *Phi Delta Kappan, 88*(4), 314–318.

Commodari, E. (2013). Preschool teacher attachment, school readiness and risk of learning difficulties. *Early Childhood Research Quarterly, 28*(1), 123–133.

Condon, J., Corkindale, C., Boyce, P., & Gamble, E. (2013). A longitudinal study of father-to-infant attachment: Antecedents and correlates. *Journal of Reproductive & Infant Psychology, 31*(1), 15–30.

Conway, A., McDonough, S. C., Mackenzie, M., Miller, A., Dayton, C., Rosenblum, K., et al. (2014). Maternal sensitivity and latency to positive emotion following challenge: Pathways through effortful control. *Infant Mental Health Journal, 35*(3), 274–284.

Cooney, M. H., & Buchanan, M. (2001). Documentation: Making assessment visible. *Young Exceptional Children, 4*(3), 10–16.

Coopersmith, S. (1967). *The antecedents of self-esteem.* San Francisco, CA: W. H. Freeman.

Copple, C. (2012). (Ed.) Growing minds: Building strong cognitive foundations in early childhood. Washington, DC: National Association for the Education of Young Children.

Copple, C., & Bredekamp, S. (Eds.). (2009). *Developmentally appropriate practice in early childhood programs serving children from birth through age 8* (3rd ed.). Washington, DC: National Association for the Education of Young Children.

Copple, C., Bredekamp, S., Koralek, D., & Charner, K. (Eds.). (2013). *Developmentally appropriate practices: Focus on infants and toddlers.* Washington, DC: National Association for the Education of Young Children.

Cornwell, A. C., & Feigenbaum, P. (2006). Sleep biological rhythms in normal infants and those at high risk for SIDS. *Chronobiology International: The Journal of Biological & Medical Rhythm Research, 23*(5), 935–961.

Council for Professional Recognition. (2010). *Assessment system and competency standards: Infant/toddler caregivers in center-based programs* (Rev. 3rd ed.). Washington, DC: Author.

Courage, M. L., Edison, S., & Howe, M. (2004). Variability in the early development of visual self-recognition. *Infant Behavior & Development, 27*(4), 509–532.

Courage, M. L., & Howe, M. L. (2010). To watch or not to watch: Infants and toddlers in a brave new electronic world. *Developmental Review, 30*(2), 101–115.

Cowan, P. A. (1978). *Piaget with feeling: Cognitive, social, and emotional dimensions.* New York: Holt, Rinehart and Winston.

Crockett, E. E., Holmes, B. M., Granger, D. A., & Lyons-Ruth, K. (2013). Maternal disrupted communication during face-to-face interaction at 4 months: Relation to maternal and infant cortisol among at-risk families. *Infancy, 18*(6), 1111–1134.

Cross, D. J., & Swim, T. J. (2006). A scholarly partnership for examining the pragmatics of Reggio-inspired practice in an early childhood classroom: Provocations, documentation, and time. *Scholarlypartnershipsedu, 1*(1), 47–68.

Csikszentmihalyi, M. (1990). *The psychology of optimal experience.* New York: Harper & Row.

Cunha, F., & Heckman, J. (2010). *Investing in our young people.* NBER Working Paper No. w16201. Retrieved February 2, 2015, from http://ssrn.com/abstract=1641577

Cunningham, D. D. (2014). Re-conceptualizing early childhood teacher education: Enacting a paradigm shift to bring developmentally appropriate practice to higher education. *Critical Questions in Education, 5*(1), 52–63.

Curtis, D., & Carter, M. (2015). *Designs for living and learning: Transforming early childhood environments* (2nd ed.). St. Paul, MN: Redleaf Press.

Cutler, K. (2000). Organizing the curriculum storage in a preschool/child care environment. *YC: Young Children, 55*(3), 88–92.

Dahlberg, G. (2012). Pedagogical documentation: A practice for negotiation and democracy. In C. Edwards, L. Gandini, & G. Forman (Eds.), *The hundred languages of children: The Reggio Emilia experience in transformation* (3rd ed., pp. 225–231). Santa Barbara, CA: Praeger.

Dalai Lama XIV. (2002). *The heart of compassion.* Twin Lakes, WI: Lotus Press.

Dallaire, D. H. (2007). Children with incarcerated mothers: Developmental outcomes, special challenges and recommendations. *Journal of Applied Developmental Psychology, 28,* 15–24.

Daly, L., & Beloglovsky, M. (2015). *Loose parts: Inspiring play in young children*. St. Paul, MN: Redleaf Press.

Damianova, M. K., & Sullivan, G. B. (2011). Rereading Vygotsky's theses on types of internalization and verbal mediation. *Review of General Psychology, 15*(4), 344–350.

Darbyshire, J. (2004). *Everyday learning: Vol. 2, no. 4. Everyday learning in the kitchen* (S. Wales (Series Ed.) & P. Linke (Vol. Ed.)). Watson, ACT: Early Childhood Australia, Inc.

Darling, S., & Westberg, L. (2004). Parent involvement in children's acquisition of reading. *The Reading Teacher, 57*(8), 774–776.

Da Ros-Voseles, D., & Fowler-Haughey, S. (2007). Why children's dispositions should matter to ALL teachers. *Beyond the Journal: Young Children on the Web.* Retrieved March 11, 2009, from http://journal .naeyc.org/btj/200709/pdf/DaRos-Voseles.pdf

Darwin, C. (1936). *On the origin of species by means of natural selection*. New York: Modern Library. (Original work published 1859.)

Daugherty, M., & White, C. S. (2008). Relationships among private speech and creativity in Head Start and low—socioeconomic status preschool children. *Gifted Child Quarterly, 52*(1), 30–39.

Davis, C., Godfrey, S., & Rankin, K. (2013). Unintentional injury in early childhood: Its relationship with child-care setting and provider. *Maternal & Child Health Journal, 17*(9), 1541–1549.

Davis, E., Schoppe-Sullivan, S., Mangelsdorf, S., & Brown, G. (2009). The role of infant temperament in stability and change in coparenting across the first year of life. *Parenting: Science & Practice, 9*(1/2), 143–159.

Davis, K., Desrocher, M., & Moore, T. (2011). Fetal alcohol spectrum disorder: A review of neuro developmental findings and interventions. *Journal of Developmental & Physical Disabilities, 23*(2), 143–167.

Day, M., & Parlakian, R. (2004). *How culture shapes social-emotional development: Implications for practice in infant-family programs*. Washington, DC: Zero to Three.

de Barbaro, K., Johnson, C. M., & Deák, G. O. (2013). Twelve-month "Social Revolution" emerges from mother-infant sensorimotor coordination: A longitudinal investigation. *Human Development, 56*, 223–248.

Demetriou, H., & Hay, D. F. (2004). Toddlers' reactions to the distress of familiar peers: The importance of context. *Infancy, 6*(2), 299–318.

DeMulder, E. K., Denham, S., Schmidt, M., & Mitchell, J. (2000). Q-sort assessment of attachment security during the preschool years: Links from home to school. *Developmental Psychology, 36*(2), 274–282.

Derman-Sparks, L., & Edwards, J. O. (2010). *Antibias education for young children and ourselves*. Washington, DC: National Association for the Education of Young Children.

Derman-Sparks, L., LeeKeenan, D., & Nimmo, J. (2015). *Leading anti-bias early childhood programs—A guide for change*. New York: Teachers College Press.

De Schipper, J. C., Tavecchio, L. W. C., Van IJzendoorn, M. H., & Van Zeijl, J. (2004). Goodness-of-fit in center day care: Relations of temperament, stability, and quality of care with the child's adjustment. *Early Childhood Research Quarterly, 19*, 257–272.

Dever, M. T., & Burts, D. C. (2002). An evaluation of family literacy bags as a vehicle for parent involvement. *Early Child Development and Care, 172*(4), 359–370.

DeViney, J., Duncan, S., Harris, S., Rody, M. A., & Rosenberry, L. (2010). *Inspiring spaces for young children*. Silver Spring, MD: Gryphon House, Inc.

DeVries, R. (2000). Piaget, and education: A reciprocal assimilation of theories and educational practices [electronic version]. *New Ideas in Psychology, 18*(2–3), 187–213.

DeVries, R., & Sales, C. (2011). *Ramps & pathways: A constructivist approach to physics with young children*. Washington, DC: National Association for the Education of Young Children.

DeVries, R., Zan, B., Hildebrandt, C., Edmiaston, R., & Sales, C. (2002). *Developing constructivist early childhood curriculum: Practical principles and activities*. New York: Teachers College Press.

Dewey, J. (1938). *Experience and education*. New York: Macmillan.

Deynoot-Schaub, M. J. G., & Riksen-Walraven, J. M. (2006a). Peer contacts of 15-month-olds in childcare: Links with child temperament, parent-child interaction and quality of childcare. *Social Development, 15*(4), 709–729.

Deynoot-Schaub, M. J. G., & Riksen-Walraven, J. M. (2006b). Peer interaction in child care centres at 15 and 23 months: Stability and links with children's socio-emotional adjustments. *Infant Behavior & Development, 29*, 276–288.

Diaz Soto, L., & Swadener, B. B. (2002). Towards liberatory early childhood theory, research, and praxis: Decolonizing a field. *Contemporary Issues in Early Childhood, 3*(1), 38–66.

Dodici, B. J., Draper, D. C., & Peterson, C. A. (2003). Early parent-child interactions and early literacy development. *Topics in Early Childhood Special Education, 23*(3), 124–136.

Dominey, P. F., & Dodane, C. (2004). Indeterminacy in language acquisition: The role of child directed speech and joint attention. *Journal of Neurolinguistics, 17*, 121–145.

Donaldson, M. (1978). *Children's minds.* London: Fontana.

Donate-Bartfield, E., & Passman, R. H. (2004). Relations between children's attachments to their mothers and to security blankets. *Journal of Family Psychology, 18*(3), 453–458.

Dow, C. B. (2010). Young children and movement: The power of creative dance. *YC: Young Children, 65*(2), 30–35.

Dubois, J., Dehaene-Lambertz, G., Kulikova, S., Poupon, C., Huppi, P. S., & Hertz-Pannier, L. (2014). The early development of brain white matter: A review of imaging studies in foetuses, newborns and infants. *Neuroscience, 276*, 48–71.

Duffy, R. (2004, September/October). Love, longing, l'inserimento: Waving "good-bye." *Child Care Information Exchange, 160*, 28–31.

Duncan, G. J., & Brooks-Gunn, J. (1997). *Consequences of growing up poor.* New York: Russell Sage Foundation.

Dunst, C. J., & Gorman, E. (2009). Development of infant and toddler mark making and scribbling. *CELL Reviews, 2*(2), 1–16. Retrieved February 8, 2012, from http://earlyliteracylearning.org /cellreviews/cellreviews_v2_n2.pdf

Dyer, F. J. (2004). Termination of parental rights in light of attachment theory: The case of Kaylee. *Psychology, Public Policy, & Law, 10*(1–2), 5–30.

Early Head Start National Resource Center. (2014). About Early Head Start. Retrieved February 12, 2015, from http://eclkc.ohs.acf.hhs.gov/hslc /tta-system/ehsnrc/about-ehs

Early Head Start Program Facts Sheets. (2011). *Early Head Start program facts sheet, fiscal year 2010.* Retrieved July 8, 2011, from http://www.ehsnrc.org /PDFfiles/ehsprogfactsheet.pdf

Ebbeck, M., Phoon, D. M. Y., Tan-Chong, E. C. K., Tan, M. A. B., & Goh, M. L. M. (2014). A research study on secure attachment using the primary caregiving approach. *Early Childhood Education Journal, 43*(3), 233–240.

Ebbeck, M., & Yim, H. Y. B. (2009). Rethinking attachment: Fostering positive relationships between infants, toddlers and their primary caregivers. *Early Child Development and Care, 179*(7), 899–909.

Eceiza, A., Ortiz, M. J., & Apodaca, P. (2011). Attachment security and peer relationships in infancy. *Infancia y Aprendizaje, 34*(2), 235–246.

Edwards, C. M. (2014). Maternal literacy practices and toddlers' emergent literacy skills. *Journal of Early Childhood Literacy, 14*(1), 53–79.

Edwards, C. P. (2002). Three approaches from Europe: Waldorf, Montessori, and Reggio Emilia. *Early Childhood Research and Practice, 4*(1). Retrieved March 23, 2009, from http://ecrp.uiuc.edu/v4n1 /edwards.html

Edwards, C. P., Cline, K., Gandini, L., Giacomelli, A., Giovannini, D., & Galardini, A. (2014). Books, stories, and the imagination at "The Nursery Rhyme": A qualitative case study of a preschool learning environment in Pistoia, Italy. *Journal of Research in Childhood Education, 28*(1), 18–42.

Edwards, C. P., Gandini, L., & Forman, G. (Eds.). (2012). *The hundred languages of children: The Reggio Emilia experience in transformation* (3rd ed.). Santa Barbara, CA: Praeger.

Eiden, R. D., Edwards, E. P., & Leonard, K. E. (2014). A conceptual model for the development of externalizing behavior problems among kindergarten children of alcoholic families: Role of parenting and children's self-regulation. *Developmental Psychology, 43*(5), 1187–1201.

Eisenberg, N., Edwards, A., Spinrad, T. L., Sallquist, J., Eggum, N. D., & Reiser, M. (2013). Are effortful and reactive control unique constructs in young children? *Developmental Psychology, 49*(11), 2082–2094.

Eisenberg, N., Fabes, R., & Spinrad, T. L. (2006). Prosocial development. In N. Eisenberg (Ed.), *Handbook of child psychology: Vol. 3. Social, emotional, and personality development* (6th ed., pp. 646–718). New York: Wiley.

Elicker, J., Wen, X., Kwon, K., & Sprague, J. B. (2013). Early Head Start relationships: Association with program outcomes. *Early Education & Development, 24*(4), 491–516.

Eliot, M., & Cornell, D. G. (2009). Bullying in middle school as a function of insecure attachment and aggressive attitudes. *School Psychology International, 30*(2), 201–214.

Elkind, D. (2003, Winter). Montessori and constructivism. *Montessori Life, 15*(1), 26–29.

Elkind, D. (2007). *The power of play: How spontaneous, imaginative activities lead to happier, healthier children.* Cambridge, MA: Da Capo Press.

Ellison, J. R. (2014). "I Didn't Think He Remembered": Healing the impact of domestic violence on infants and toddlers. *Zero to Three, 35*(2), 49–55.

Emery, H. T., McElwain, N. L., Groh, A. M., Haydon, K. C., & Roisman, G. I. (2014). Maternal dispositional empathy and electrodermal reactivity: Interactive contributions to maternal sensitivity with toddler-aged children. *Journal of Family Psychology, 28*(4), 505–515.

Engert, V., Efanov, S., Dedovic, K., Dagher, A., & Pruessner, J. (2011). Increased cortisol awakening response and afternoon/evening cortisol output in healthy young adults with low early life parental care. *Psychopharmacology, 214*(1), 261–268.

Epley, P., Gotto, G. S. III., Summers, J. A., Brotherson, M. J., Turnbull, A. P., & Friend, A. (2010). Supporting families of young children with disabilities: Examining the role of administrative structures. *Topics in Early Childhood Special Education, 30*(1), 20–31.

Epstein, A. S. (2007). *Essentials of active learning in preschool: Getting to know the High/Scope curriculum.* Ypsilanti, MI: High/Scope Press.

Erikson, E. H. (1950). *Childhood and society.* New York: Norton.

Erikson, E. H. (1963). *Childhood and society* (2nd ed.). New York: Norton.

Erkolahti, R., & Nyström, M. (2009). The prevalence of transitional object use in adolescence: Is there a connection between the existence of a transitional object and depressive symptoms? *European Child & Adolescent Psychiatry, 18*(7), 400–406.

Espinosa, L. (2010). *Getting it right for young children from diverse backgrounds: Applying research to improve practice.* Washington, DC: National Association for the Education of Young Children.

Essa, E., Favre, K., Thweatt, G., & Waugh, S. (1999). Continuity of care for infants and toddlers. *Early Child Development and Care, 148,* 11–19.

Estes, K. G., & Hurley, K. (2013). Infant-directed prosody helps infants map sounds to meanings. *Infancy, 18*(5), 797–824.

Evans, C. A., Nelson, L. J., Porter, C. L., Nelson, D. A., & Hart, C. H. (2012). Understanding relations among children's shy and antisocial/aggressive behaviors and mothers' parenting: The role of maternal beliefs. *Merrill-Palmer Quarterly, 58*(3), 341–374.

Faber, A. J., Willerton, E., Clymer, S. R., MacDermid, S. M., & Weiss, H. M. (2008). Ambiguous absence, ambiguous presence: A qualitative study of military reserve families in wartime. *Journal of Family Psychology, 22*(2), 222–230.

Fagan, M. K., Bergeson, T. R., & Morris, K. J. (2014). Synchrony, complexity, and directiveness in mothers' interactions with infants pre- and post-cochlear implantation. *Infant Behavior & Development, 37*(3), 249–257.

Farmer, E., Selwyn, J., & Meakings, S. (2013). "Other children say you're not normal because you don't live with your parents." Children's views of living with informal kinship carers: Social networks, stigma and attachment to careers. *Child & Family Social Work, 18*(1), 25–34.

Farrant, B. M., Devine, T. A. J., Maybery, M. T., & Fletcher, J. (2012). Empathy, perspective taking and

prosocial behaviour: The importance of parenting practices. *Infant and Child Development, 21*(2), 175–188.

Fasolo, M., Majorano, M., & D'Odorico, L. (2008). Babbling and first words in children with slow expressive development. *Clinical Linguistics & Phonetics, 22*(2), 83–94.

Feeney, B. C., Cassidy, J., & Ramos-Marcuse, F. (2008). The generalization of attachment representations to new social situations: Predicting behavior during initial interactions with strangers. *Journal of Personality and Social Psychology, 95*(6), 1481–1498.

Feinberg, M. E., & Kan, M. L. (2008). Establishing family foundations: Intervention effects on coparenting, parent/infant well-being, and parent-child relations. *Journal of Family Psychology, 22*(2), 253–263.

Feldman, R. (2006). From biological rhythms to social rhythms: Physiological precursors of mother-infant synchrony. *Developmental Psychology, 42*(1), 175–188.

Feldman, R. (2007). Parent-infant synchrony and the construction of shared timing; physiological precursors, developmental outcomes, and risk conditions. *Journal of Child Psychology and Psychiatry, 48*(3/4), 329–354.

Feldman, R., & Eidelman, A. I. (2009). Biological and environmental initial conditions shape the trajectories of cognitive and social-emotional development across the first years of life. *Developmental Science, 12*(1), 194–200.

Feldman, R., Masalha, S., & Derdikman-Eiron, R. (2010). Conflict resolution in the parent-child, marital, and peer contexts and children's aggression in the peer group: A process-oriented cultural perspective. *Developmental Psychology, 46*(2), 310–325.

Fender, J. G., Richert, R. A., Robb, M. B., & Wartella, E. (2010). Parent teaching focus and toddlers' learning from an infant DVD. *Infant & Child Development, 19*(6), 613–627.

Fidler, A. E., Zack, E., & Barr, R. (2010). Television viewing patterns in 6- to 18-month-olds: The role of caregiver-infant interactional quality. *Infancy, 15*(2), 176–196.

Figueiredo, B., Costa, R., Pacheco, A., & Pais, A. (2007). Mother-to-infant and father-to-infant initial emotional involvement. *Early Child Development & Care, 177*(5), 521–532.

Finn, C. D. (2003). *Cultural models for early caregiving.* Washington, DC: Zero to Three.

Fitzgerald, H. E., Bocknek, E. L., Hossain, Z., & Roggman, L. (2015). Reflections on fathers and infant mental health. *Infant Mental Health Journal, 36*(1), 75–77.

Flanders, J. L., Leo, V., Paquette, D., Pihl, R. O., & Séguin, J. R. (2009). Rough-and-tumble play and the regulation of aggression: An observational study of father-child play dyads. *Aggressive Behavior, 35*(4), 285–295.

Flanders, J. L., Simard, M., Paquette, D., Parent, S., Vitaro, F., Pihl, R., et al. (2010). Rough-and-tumble play and the development of physical aggression and emotion regulation: A five-year follow-up study. *Journal of Family Violence, 25*(4), 357–367.

Fleck, B. K. B., Leichtman, M. D., Pillemer, D. B., & Shanteler, L. (2013). The effects of documentation on young children's memory. *Early Childhood Research Quarterly, 28*(3), 568–577.

Fleer, M., & Hedegaard, M. (2010). Children's development as participation in everyday practices across different institutions. *Mind, Culture & Activity, 17*(2), 149–168.

Fletcher, K. L., Perez, A., Hooper, C., & Claussen, A. H. (2005). Responsiveness and attention during picture-book reading in 18-month-old to 24-month-old toddlers at risk. *Early Child Development and Care, 175*(1), 63–83.

Flykt, M., Punamäki, R., Belt, R., Biringen, Z., Salo, S., Posa, T., et al. (2012). Maternal representations and emotional availability among drug-abusing and nonusing mothers and their infants. *Infant Mental Health Journal, 33*(2), 123–138.

Forman, G., & Fyfe, B. (2012). Negotiated learning through design, documentation, and discourse. In C. Edwards, L. Gandini, & G. Forman (Eds.), *The hundred languages of children: The Reggio Emilia experience in transformation* (3rd ed., pp. 247–271). Santa Barbara, CA: Praeger.

Fornasaro-Donahue, V. M., Tovar, A., Sebelia, L., & Greene, G. W. (2014). Increasing breastfeeding in WIC participants: Cost of formula as a motivator. *Journal of Nutrition Education & Behavior, 46*(6), 560–569.

Fortuna, K., Baor, L., Israel, S., Abadi, A., Knafo, A., Gagne, J., et al. (2014). Attachment to inanimate objects and early childcare: A twin study. *Frontiers in Psychology, 5*, 1–7.

Foulkes, P., Docherty, G., & Watt, D. (2005). Phonological variation in child-directed speech. *Language, 81*(1), 177–206.

Fox, L., Hemmeter, M., Snyder, P., Binder, D. P., & Clarke, S. (2011). Coaching early childhood special educators to implement a comprehensive model for promoting young children's social competence. *Topics in Early Childhood Special Education, 31*(3), 178–192.

Fox, N. A., Henderson, H. A., Rubin, K. H., Calkins, S. D., & Schmidt, L. A. (2001). Continuity and discontinuity of behavioral inhibition and exuberance: Psychophysiological and behavioral influences across the first four years of life. *Child Development, 72*(1), 1–21.

Fox, S. E., Levitt, P., & Nelson, C. A. (2010). How the Timing and Quality of Early Experiences Influence the Development of Brain Architecture. *Child Development, 81*(1), 28–40.

Franyo, G. A., & Hyson, M. C. (1999). Temperament training for early childhood caregivers: A study of the effectiveness of training. *Child & Youth Forum, 28*, 329–349.

Franzén, K. (2014). Under-threes' mathematical learning—teachers' perspectives. *Early Years: Journal of International Research & Development, 34*(3), 241–254.

Freeman, R. (2011). Reggio Emilia, Vygotsky, and family childcare: Four American providers describe their pedagogical practice. *Child Care in Practice, 17*(3), 227–246.

Freeman, R., & Karlsson, M. (2012). Strategies for learning experiences in family child care: American and Swedish perspectives. *Childhood Education, 88*(2), 81–90.

Freeman, R., & Swim, T. J. (2009). Intellectual integrity: Examining common rituals in early childhood curriculum. *Contemporary Issues in Early Childhood, 10*(4), 366–377.

Friedman, S. (2007). Coming together for children: Six community partnerships make a big difference. *Beyond the Journal Young Children on the Web.* Retrieved October 13, 2008, from https://www.naeyc.org/files/yc/file/200703/BTJFriedman.pdf

Fuligni, A. S., Howes, C., Huang, Y., Hong, S. S., & Lara-Cinisomo, S. (2012). Activity settings and daily routines in preschool classrooms: Diverse experiences in early learning settings for low-income children. *Early Childhood Research Quarterly, 27*(2), 198–209.

Fuller, A. (2001). A blueprint for building social competencies in children and adolescents. *Australian Journal of Middle Schooling, 1*(1), 40–49.

Gabbard, C., & Kreys, R. (2012). Studying environmental influence on motor development in children. *The Physical Educator, 69*, 136–149.

Gabler, S., Bovenschen, I., Lang, K., Zimmermann, J., Nowacki, K., Kliewer, J. et al. (2014). Foster children's attachment security and behavior problems in the first six months of placement: Associations with foster parents' stress and sensitivity. *Attachment & Human Development, 16*(5), 479–498.

Gaertner, B. M., Spinrad, T. L., & Eisenberg, N. (2008). Focused attention in toddlers: Measurement, stability, and relations to negative emotion and parenting. *Infant & Child Development, 17*(4), 339–363.

Galardini, A., & Giovannini, D. (2001). Pistoia: Creating a dynamic, open system to serve children, families, and community. In L. Gandini & C. P. Edwards (Eds.), *Bambini: The Italian approach to infant/toddler care* (pp. 89–105). New York: Teachers College Press.

Galinsky, E. (2010). *Mind in the making: The seven essential life skills every child needs.* New York: HarperCollins Publisher.

Gallagher, K. C., & Mayer, K. (2008). Research in review: Enhancing development and learning through teacher-child relationships. *YC: Young Children, 63*(6), 80–87.

Gandini, L. (2001). Reggio Emilia: Experiencing life in an infant-toddler center, an interview with Cristina Bondavalli. In L. Gandini & C. P. Edwards (Eds.), *Bambini: The Italian approach to infant/toddler care* (pp. 55–66). New York: Teachers College Press.

Gandini, L. (2004). Foundations of the Reggio Emilia approach. In J. Hendrick (Ed.), *Next steps toward teaching the Reggio way: Accepting the challenge to change* (2nd ed., pp. 13–26). Upper Saddle River, NJ: Prentice Hall.

Gandini, L. (2012a). Connecting through caring and learning spaces. In C. Edwards, L. Gandini, & G. Forman (Eds.), *The hundred languages of children: The Reggio Emilia experience in transformation* (3rd ed., pp. 317–341). Santa Barbara, CA: Praeger.

Gandini, L. (2012b). History, ideas, and basic philosophy: An interview with Loris Malaguzzi. In C. Edwards, L. Gandini, & G. Forman (Eds.), *The hundred languages of children: The Reggio Emilia experience in transformation* (3rd ed., pp. 27–71). Santa Barbara, CA: Praeger.

Gandini, L., & Goldhaber, J. (2001). Two reflections about documentation. In L. Gandini & C. P. Edwards (Eds.), *Bambini: The Italian approach to infant/toddler care* (pp. 124–145). New York: Teachers College Press.

Garcia-Sanchez, I. M., Orellana, M. F., & Hopkins, M. (2011). Facilitating intercultural communication in parent-teacher conferences: Lessons from child translators. *Multicultural Perspectives, 13*(3), 148–154.

Gartstein, M. A., & Bateman, A. E. (2008). Early manifestations of childhood depression: Influences of infant temperament and parental depressive symptoms. *Infant & Child Development, 17*(3), 223–248.

Gartstein, M. A., Bridgett, D. J., Young, B. N., Panksepp, J., & Power, T. (2013). Origins of effortful control: Infant and parent contributions. *Infancy, 18*(2), 149–183.

Garvis, S., & Pendergast, D. (2011). An investigation of early childhood teacher self-efficacy beliefs in the teaching of arts education. *International Journal of Education & the Arts, 12*(8/9), 1–15.

Geangu, E., Benga, O., Stahl, D., Striano, T. (2010). Contagious crying beyond the first days of life. *Infant Behavior & Development, 33*(3), 279–288.

Geangu, E., Benga, O., Stahl, D., & Striano, T. (2011). Individual differences in infants' emotional resonance to a peer in distress: Self-other awareness and emotion regulation. *Social Development, 20*(3), 450–470.

Geddes, R., Haw, S., & Frank, J. (2010). *Interventions for Promoting Early Child Development for Health: An Environmental Scan with Special Reference to Scotland Edinburgh: Scottish Collaboration for Public Health Research and Policy.* Retrieved January 14, 2015, from http://www.scphrp.ac.uk/wp-content/uploads/2014/03/1454-scp_earlyyearsreportfinalweb.pdf

Geist, E. (2009). Infants and toddlers exploring mathematics. *YC: Young Children, 64*(3), 39–42.

George, M. R. W., Cummings, E. M., & Davies, P. T. (2010). Positive aspects of fathering and mothering, and children's attachment in kindergarten. *Early Child Development and Care, 180*(1&2), 107–119.

Georgia Department of Early Care and Learning. (2015). GELDS: Georgia Early Learning and Development Standards. Retrieved April 28, 2015, from http://gelds.decal.ga.gov/

Gerber, M., & Weaver, J. (Eds.). (1998). *Dear parent: Caring for infants with respect.* Los Angeles, CA: Resources for Infant Educarers (RIE).

Gershkoff-Stowe, L., & Thelen, E. (2004). U-shaped changes in behavior: A dynamic systems perspective. *Journal of Cognition and Development, 5*(1), 11–36.

Gesell, A. (1928). *Infancy and human growth.* New York: Macmillan.

Ghedini, P. (2001). Change in Italian national policy for children 0-3 years old and their families: Advocacy and responsibility. In L. Gandini & C. P. Edwards (Eds.), *Bambini: The Italian approach to infant/toddler care* (pp. 38–45). New York: Teachers College Press.

Ghera, M. M., Hane, A. A., Malesa, E. E., & Fox, N. A. (2006). The role of infant soothability in the relation between infant negativity and maternal sensitivity. *Infant Behavior & Development, 29*, 289–293.

Gill, K. L., & Calkins, S. D. (2003). Do aggressive/destructive toddlers lack concern for others? Behavioral and physiological indicators of empathic responding in 2-year-old children. *Developmental and Psychopathology, 15*(1), 55–71.

Glassman, M., & Whaley, K. (2000). Dynamic aims: The use of long-term projects in early childhood classrooms in light of Dewey's educational philosophy. *Early Childhood Research and Practice, 2*(1). Retrieved May 14, 2009, from http://ecrp.uiuc .edu/v2n1/glassman.html

Glaze, L. E., & Maruschak, L. M. (2009). Parents in prison and their minor children. U.S. Department of Justice, Office of Justice Programs, Bureau of Justice Statistics. Retrieved March 10, 2009, from http://www.ojp.usdoj.gov/bjs/pub/pdf/pptmc.pdf

Gliga, T., & Csibra, G. (2009). One-year-old infants appreciate the referential nature of deictic gestures and words. *Psychological Science, 20*(3), 347–353.

Gloeckler, L., & Cassell, J. (2012). Teacher practices with toddlers during social problem solving opportunities. *Early Childhood Education Journal, 40*(4), 251–257.

Goldsmith, D. (2010). The emotional dance of attachment. *Clinical Social Work Journal, 38*(1), 4–7.

Goldsmith, M., & Theilheimer, R. (2015). A powerful need for connection: When families and infants begin group care. *YC: Young Children, 70*(2), 80–85.

Goldstein, M. H., King, A. P., & West, M. J. (2003, June). Social interaction shapes babbling: Testing parallels between birdsong and speech [electronic version]. *Proceedings of the National Academy of Sciences, USA, 100*(13), 8030–8035.

Goldstein, M. H., & Schwade, J. A. (2010). From birds to words: Perception of structure in social interactions guides vocal development and language learning. In M. S. Blumberg, J. H. Freeman, & S. R. Robinson (Eds.), *The Oxford handbook of developmental behavioral neuroscience* (pp. 708–729). Oxford: Oxford University Press.

Goleman, D. (1996). *Emotional intelligence: Why it can matter more than IQ.* New York: Bantam Books.

Goleman, D. (2006). *Social intelligence: The new science of human relationships.* New York: Random House, Inc.

Gonzalez-Mena, J. (2001). *Multicultural issues in child care* (3rd ed.). Mountain View, CA: Mayfield.

Gonzalez-Mena, J. (2007). What to do for a fussy baby: A problem-solving approach. *Beyond the Journal: Young Children on the Web.* Retrieved March 14, 2009, from http://journal.naeyc.org/btj/200709/pdf /Gonzalez-Mena.pdf

Gonzalez-Mena, J., & Eyer, D. W. (2007). *Infants, toddlers, and caregivers* (7th ed.). New York: McGraw-Hill.

Goodlin-Jones, B. L., Burnham, M. M., Gaylor, E. E., & Anders, T. F. (2001). Night waking, sleep-wake organization, and self-soothing in the first year of life. *Journal of Developmental & Behavioral Pediatrics, 22*(4), 226–233.

Gore, N., Hastings, R., and Brady, S. (2014). Early intervention for children with learning disabilities: Making use of what we know. *Tizard Learning Disability Review, 19*(4), 181–189.

Gorman, G. H., Eide, M., & Hisle-Gorman, E. (2010). Wartime military deployment and increased pediatric mental and behavioral health complaints. *Pediatrics, 126*(6), 1058–1066.

Graham, S. A., & Kilbreath, C. S. (2007). It's a sign of the kind: Gestures and words guide infants' inductive inferences. *Developmental Psychology, 43*(5), 1111–1123.

Gratier, M. (2003). Expressive timing and interactional synchrony between mothers and infants: Cultural similarities, cultural differences, and the immigration experience. *Cognitive Development, 18*(4), 533–554.

Graves, S. B., & Larkin, E. (2006). Lessons from Erikson: A look at autonomy across the lifespan. *Journal of Intergenerational Relationships, 4*(2), 61–71.

Gredler, M. E. (2012). Understanding Vygotsky for the classroom: Is it too late? *Educational Psychology Review, 24*, 113–131.

Green, B. L., Ayoub, C., Bartlett, J. D., Von Ende, A., Furrer, C., Chazan-Cohen, R., et al. (2014). The effect of Early Head Start on child welfare system involvement: A first look at longitudinal child maltreatment outcomes. *Children & Youth Services Review, 42*, 127–135.

Green, E. J., Crenshaw, D. A., & Kolos, A. C. (2010). Counseling children with preverbal trauma. *International Journal of Play Therapy, 19*(2), 95–105.

Green, J. A., Whitney, P. G., & Potegal, M. (2011). Screaming, yelling, whining, and crying: Categorical and intensity differences in vocal expressions of anger and sadness in children's tantrums. *Emotion, 11*(5), 1124–1133.

Green, K. E., Groves, M. M., & Tegano, D. W. (2004). Parenting practices that limit transitional object use: An illustration. *Early Child Development and Care, 174*(5), 427–436.

Greenberg, J. R., & Mitchell, S. A. (1983). *Object relations in psychoanalytic theory.* Cambridge, MA: Harvard University Press.

Greenman, J. (2005, May). Places for childhood in the 21st century: A conceptual framework. *Beyond the Journal: Young Children on the Web.* Retrieved January 9, 2007, from https://www.naeyc.org/files /yc/file/200505/01Greenman.pdf

Greenman, J., Stonehouse, A., & Schweikert, G. (2008). *Prime times: A handbook for excellence in infant and toddler programs* (2nd ed.). St. Paul, MN: Redleaf Press.

Grusec, J. E. (1991). Socializing concerns for others in the home. *Developmental Psychology, 27*(2), 338–342.

Grusec, J. E. (1992). Social learning theory and developmental psychology: The legacies of Robert Sears and Albert Bandura. *Developmental Psychology, 28,* 776–786.

Grzegorzewska, K., & Konieczna-Blicharz, J. (2011). The lights pre-project: Implementation of the project approach with children under 3 years of age. *Early Childhood Research and Practice, 13*(1). Retrieved April 10, 2012, from http://ecrp.uiuc.edu/v13n1/grzegorzewska.html

Gunnar, M. (2006). Stress, nurture, and the young brain. In J. R. Lally, P. L. Mangione, & D. Greenwald (Eds.), *Concepts for care: 20 essays on infant/toddler development and learning* (pp. 41–44). Sausalito, CA: WestEd.

Gunnar, M. G., & Cheatham, C. L. (2003). Brain and behavior interface: Stress and the developing brain. *Infant Mental Health Journal, 24*(3), 195–211.

Gunnar, M. R. (1998). Quality of early care and buffering of neuroendocrine stress reactions: Potential effects on the developing human brain. *Preventive Medicine, 27,* 208–211.

Gunnar, M. R., Kryzer, E., Van Ryzin, M. J., & Phillips, D. A. (2010). The rise in cortisol in family day care: Associations with aspects of care quality, child behavior, and child sex. *Child Development, 81*(3), 851–869.

Guzman, C. V. (2014). School-age children of military families: Theoretical applications, skills training, considerations, and interventions. *Children & Schools, 36*(1), 9–14.

Haack, L. M., & Gerdes, A. C. (2011). Functional impairment in Latino children with ADHD: Implications for culturally appropriate conceptualization and measurement. *Clinical Child & Family Psychology Review, 14*(3), 318–328.

Hachey, A. C., & Butler, D. (2012). Creatures in the classroom: Including insects and small animals in your preschool gardening curriculum. *YC: Young Children, 67*(2), 38–42.

Hadley, F. (2014). 'It's bumpy and we understood each other at the end, I hope!': Unpacking what experiences are valued in the early childhood setting and how this impacts on parent partnerships with culturally and linguistically diverse families. *Australasian Journal of Early Childhood, 39*(2), 91–99.

Hall-Kenyon, K., Bullough, R., MacKay, K., & Marshall, E. (2014). Preschool teacher well-being: A review of the literature. *Early Childhood Education Journal, 42*(3), 153–162.

Hames, C. C., & Pedreira, D. (2003). Children with parents in prison: Disenfranchised grievers who benefit from bibliotherapy. *Illness, Crisis, & Loss, 11*(4), 377–386.

Hane, A. A., Fox, N. A., Henderson, H. A., & Marshall, P. J. (2008). Behavioral reactivity and approach-withdrawal bias in infancy. *Developmental Psychology, 44*(5), 1491–1496.

Hanline, M. F., Milton, S., & Phelps, P. C. (2010). The relationship between preschool block play and reading and math abilities in early elementary school: A longitudinal study of children with and without disabilities. *Early Child Development and Care, 180*(8), 1005–1017.

Harden, B. J., Sandstrom, H., & Chazan-Cohen, R. (2012). Early Head Start and African American families: Impacts and mechanisms of child outcomes. *Early Childhood Research Quarterly, 27,* 572–581.

Hardman, M. L., Drew, C. J., & Egan, M. W. (2006). *Human exceptionality: School, community, and family* (8th ed.). Boston, MA: Allyn and Bacon.

Hardman, M. L., Drew, C. J., & Egan, M. W. (2014). *Human exceptionality* (11th ed.). Belmont, CA: Wadsworth/Cengage Learning.

Hargreaves, A., & Fullan, M. (2012). *Professional capital: Transforming teaching in every school.* New York: Teachers College Press.

Harnett, P. H., Dawe, S., & Russell, M. (2014). An investigation of the needs of grandparents who are raising grandchildren. *Child & Family Social Work, 19*(4), 411–420.

Hatfield, B., Hestenes, L., Kintner-Duffy, V., & O'Brien, M. (2013). Classroom emotional support predicts differences in preschool children's cortisol and alpha-amylase levels. *Early Childhood Research Quarterly, 28*(2), 347–356.

Hatton, D. D., Ivy, S. E., & Boyer, C. (2013). Severe visual impairments in infants and toddlers in the United States. *Journal of Visual Impairment & Blindness, 107*(5), 325–336.

Hay, D. F., Castle, J., & Davies, L. (2000). Toddlers' use of force against familiar peers: A precursor of serious aggression? *Child Development, 71*(2), 457–467.

Hazen, N. L., McFarland, L., Jacobvitz, D., & Boyd-Soisson, E. (2010). Fathers' frightening behaviors and sensitivity with infants: Relations with fathers' attachment representations, father–infant attachment, and children's later outcomes. *Early Child Development and Care, 180*(1&2), 51–69.

Healy, J. (2004). *Your child's growing mind: A guide to learning and brain development from birth to adolescence* (3rd ed.). New York: Broadway Books.

Heath, M. A., Sheen, D., Leavy, D., Young, E., & Money, K. (2005). Bibliotherapy: A resource to facilitate emotional healing and growth. *School Psychology International, 26*(5), 563–580.

Hebbeler, K., Spiker, D., Bailey, D., Scarborough, A., Mallik, S., Simeonsson, R., et al. (2007). *Early intervention for infants and toddlers with disabilities and their families: Participants, services and outcomes—final report of the National Early Intervention Longitudinal Study (NEILS)*. Menlo Park, CA: SRI International.

Heckman, J. (2004). Invest in the very young. In R. E. Tremblay, R. G. Barr, & RDeV. Peters (eds.), *Encyclopedia on Early Childhood Development*. Montreal, Quebec: Centre of Excellence for Early Childhood Development. Retrieved February 2, 2015, from http://www.child-encyclopedia.com/Pages/PDF/HeckmanANGxp.pdf

Heisner, J. (2005). Telling stories with blocks: Encouraging language in the block center. *Early Childhood Research & Practice, 7*(2). Retrieved February 14, 2012, from http://ecrp.uiuc.edu/v7n2/heisner.html

Helm, J. H., Beneke, S., & Steinheimer, K. (2007). *Windows on learning: Documenting young children's work* (2nd ed.). New York: Teachers College Press.

Hemmeter, M., Ostrosky, M., Artman, K., & Kinder, K. (2008). Moving right along. Planning transitions to prevent challenging behavior. *YC: Young Children, 63*(3), 18–22, 24–25.

Henning, A., Striano, T., & Lieven, E. V. M. (2005). Maternal speech to infants at 1 and 3 months of age. *Infant Behavior & Development, 28*(4), 519–536.

Hepach, R., Vaish, A., & Tomasello, M. (2013). A new look at children's prosocial motivation. *Infancy, 18*(1), 67–90.

Herbert, J. S. (2011). The effect of language cues on infants' representational flexibility in a deferred imitation task. *Infant Behavior & Development, 34*(4), 632–635.

Herr, J., & Swim, T. (2002). *Creative resources for infants and toddlers* (2nd ed.). Clifton Park, NY: Thomson Delmar Learning.

Hesse, E., & Main, M. (2000). Disorganized infant, child, and adult attachment: Collapse in behavior and attachment strategies. *Journal of Psychoanalytic Association, 48*(4), 1097–1127.

Hobara, M. (2003). Prevalence of transitional objects in young children in Tokyo and New York. *Infant Mental Health Journal, 24*(2), 174–191.

Hoffman, J. L., & Paciga, K. A. (2014). Click, swipe, and read: Sharing e-books with toddlers and preschoolers. *Early Childhood Education Journal, 42*(6), 379–388.

Hogan, D. (2005). Researching "the child" in developmental psychology. In S. Greene & D. Hogan (Eds.), *Researching Children's Experiences* (pp. 22–41). London: Sage.

Holsington, C. (2002). Using photographs to support children's science inquiry. *YC: Young Children, 57*(5), 26–32.

Honda, H., Shimizu, Y., Nitto, Y., Imai, M., Ozawa, T., Iwasa, M., et al. (2009). Extraction and refinement strategy for detection of autism in 18-month-olds: A guarantee of higher sensitivity and specificity in the process of mass screening. *Journal of Child Psychology and Psychiatry, 50*(8), 972–981.

Honig, A. S. (2002). *Secure relationships: Nurturing infant/toddler attachment in early care settings*. Washington, DC: National Association for the Education of Young Children.

Honig, A. S. (2005, April). *What infants, toddlers, and preschoolers learn from play: A dozen ideas*. Paper presented at the American Montessori Society meeting, Chicago, IL.

Honig, A. S. (2015). *Experiencing nature with young children: Awakening delight, curiosity, and a sense of stewardship*. Washington, DC: National Association for the Education of Young Children.

Honig, S. B. (2014). Adopted children: The risk of interactive misattunement between the infant and adoptive mother in the child relinquished at birth. *Adoption Quarterly, 17*(3), 185–204.

Horodynski, M. A., Stommel, M., Brophy-Herb, H., & Weatherspoon, L. (2010). Mealtime television viewing and dietary quality in low-income African American and Caucasian mother-toddler dyads. *Maternal & Child Health Journal, 14*(4), 548–556.

Horst, J. S., Ellis, A. E., Samuelson, L. K., Trejo, E., Worzalla, S. L., Peltan, J. R., et al. (2009). Toddlers can adaptively change how they categorize: Same objects, same session, two different categorical distinctions. *Developmental Science, 12*(1), 96–105.

Houts, A. (2002). *Cooking around the calendar with kids: Holiday and seasonal food and fun*. Maryville, MO: Snaptail Press.

Howard, K. M., & Lipinoga, S. (2010). Closing down openings: Pretextuality and misunderstanding in parent-teacher conferences with Mexican immigrant families. *Language & Communication, 30*(1), 33–47.

Howell, S. C., & Kemp, C. R. (2010). Assessing preschool number sense: Skills demonstrated by children prior to school entry. *Educational Psychology, 30*(4), 411–429.

Huber, L. K. (2003). Knowing children and building relationships with families: A strategy for improving conferences. *Early Childhood Education Journal, 31*(1), 75–77.

Huffman, L. R., & Speer, P. W. (2000). Academic performance among at-risk children: The role of developmentally appropriate practices. *Early Childhood Research Quarterly, 15*(2), 167–184.

Humphrey, K., & Olivier, A. (2014). Investigating the impact of teenage mentors on pre-school children's development: A comparison using control groups. *Children and Youth Services Review, 44,* 20–24.

Hyson, M. (2004). *The emotional development of young children: Building an emotion-centered curriculum* (2nd ed.). New York: Teachers College Press.

Hyson, M., & Biggar Tomlinson, H. (2014). *The early years matter: Education, care, and the well-being of children, Birth to 8.* Washington, DC: National Association for the Education of Young Children.

Hyson, M., Horm, D. M., & Winton, P. J. (2012). Higher education for early childhood educators and outcomes for young children: Pathways toward greater effectiveness. In R. C. Pianta, W. S. Barnett, L. Justice, & S. M. Sheridan (Eds.), *Handbook of early childhood education* (pp. 553–583). New York: Guilford Press.

Im, J., Parlakian, R., & Sánchez, S. (2007). Understanding the influence of culture on caregiving practices . . . From the inside out. *Beyond the Journal: Young Children on the Web.* Retrieved March 2, 2009, from http://journal.naeyc.org/btj/200709/pdf/RockingRolling.pdf

Individuals with Disabilities Education Improvement Act (IDEA). (2004). Pub. L. No. 108–446, Para.632, 118 Stat. 2744.

Isabella, R. A. (1993). Origins of attachment: Maternal interactive behavior across the first year. *Child Development, 64,* 605–621.

Isabella, R. A., & Belsky, J. (1991). Interactional synchrony and the origins of infant-mother attachment: A replication study. *Child Development, 62,* 373–384.

Isbell, R., & Exelby, B. (2001). *Early learning environments that work.* Beltsville, MD: Gryphon House.

Isenberg, J. P., & Jalongo, M. R. (2001). *Creative expression and play in early childhood* (3rd ed.). Upper Saddle River, NJ: Merrill Prentice Hall.

Ishikawa, F., & Hay, D. F. (2006). Triadic interaction among newly acquainted 2-year-olds. *Social Development, 15*(1), 145–168.

Izumi-Taylor, S., Lee, Y., & Franceschini, L., III. (2011). A comparative study of childcare in Japan and the USA: Who needs to take care of our young children? *Early Child Development and Care, 181*(1), 39–54.

Jacobsen, H., Ivarsson, T., Wentzel-Larsen, T., Smith, L., & Moe, V. (2014). Attachment security in young foster children: Continuity from 2 to 3 years of age. *Attachment & Human Development, 16*(1), 42–57.

Jansen, P., Raat, H., Mackenbach, J., Jaddoe, V., Hofman, A., Verhulst, F., et al. (2009). Socioeconomic inequalities in infant temperament. *Social Psychiatry & Psychiatric Epidemiology, 44*(2), 87–95.

Jarrold, C., Mansergh, R., & Whiting, C. (2010). The representational status of pretence: Evidence from typical development and autism. *British Journal of Developmental Psychology, 28*(2), 239–254.

Jing, Y., Lin, L., Yun, Z., Guowei, H., & Wang, P. P. (2014). The association between breastfeeding and childhood obesity: A meta-analysis. *BMC Public Health, 14*(1), 467–490.

Joh, A. S., & Adolph, K. E. (2006). Learning from falling. *Child Development, 77*(1), 89–102.

Johnson, L. J., Gallagher, R. M., & LaMontagne, M. J. (eds.). (1994). *Meeting early intervention challenges: Issues from birth to three.* Baltimore, MD: Paul H. Brooks.

Johnson, M. H., & Munakata, Y. (2005). Processes of change in brain and cognitive development. *Trends in Cognitive Sciences, 9*(3), 152–158.

Johnston, M. V. (2009). Plasticity in the developing brain: Implications for rehabilitation. *Developmental Disabilities, 15*(2), 94–101.

Jones, E., & Herbert, J. S. (2006). Exploring memory in infancy: Deferred imitation and the development of declarative memory. *Infant & Child Development, 15*(2), 195–205.

Jung, S., & Stone, S. (2008). Socio demographic and programmatic moderators of Early Head Start: Evidence from the national Early Head Start research and evaluation project. *Children & Schools, 30*(3), 149–157.

Kagan, J. (2008). In defense of qualitative changes in development. *Child Development, 79*(6), 1606–1624.

Kalich, K. A., Bauer, D., & McPartlin, D. (2009). "Early Sprouts" establishing healthy food choices for young children. *YC: Young Children, 64*(4), 49–55.

Kalpidou, M. (2012). Sensory processing relates to attachment to childhood comfort objects of college students. *Early Child Development and Care, 182*(12), 1563–1574.

Kamii, C., & DeVries, R. (1978). *Physical knowledge in preschool education: Implications of Piaget's theory.* Englewood Cliffs, NJ: Prentice Hall.

Kaminsky, J. A. (2005). Reflections on inserimento, the process of welcoming children and parents into the infant-toddler center: An interview with Lella Gandini. *Innovations in Early Education: The International Reggio Exchange, 12*(2), 1–8.

Kanewischer, E. J. W. (2013). Do you ever feel that way? A story and activities about families and feelings. *Journal of Creativity in Mental Health, 8*(1), 70–80.

Kaplan, P. S., Danko, C. M., Everhart, K. D., Diaz, A., Asherin, R. M., Vogeli, J. M., et al. (2014). Maternal depression and expressive communication in one-year-old infants. *Infant Behavior & Development, 37*(3), 398–405.

Kara, B., Mukaddes, N. M., Altınkaya, I., Güntepe, D., Gökçay, G., & Özmen, M. (2014). Using the Modified Checklist for Autism in Toddlers in a well-child clinic in Turkey: Adapting the screening method based on culture and setting. *Autism: The International Journal of Research & Practice, 18*(3), 331–338.

Karoly, L. A., Kilburn, M. R., & Cannon, J. S. (2005). *Early childhood interventions: Proven results, future promise.* Retrieved January 15, 2015, from http://www.rand.org/pubs/monographs/MG341.html

Karreman, A., de Haas, S., van Tuijl, C., van Aken, M. A. G., & Deković, M. (2010). Relations among temperament, parenting and problem behavior in young children. *Infant Behavior & Development, 33*(1), 39–49.

Kärtner, J., Keller, H., & Chaudhary, N. (2010). Cognitive and social influences on early prosocial behavior in two sociocultural contexts. *Developmental Psychology, 46*(4), 905–914.

Kato, M., Onishi, K., Kanazawa, T., Hmobayashi, T., & Minami, T. (2012). Two-year-old toddlers prosocial responses to a crying peer: Social evaluation mechanisms. *Japanese Journal of Developmental Psychology, 23*(1), 12–22.

Kawakami, F., Kawakami, K., Tomonaga, M., & Takai-Kawakami, K. (2009). Can we observe spontaneous smiles in 1-year-olds? *Infant Behavior & Development, 32*(4), 416–421.

Kawakami, K., Takai-Kawakami, K., Kawakami, F., Tomonaga, M., Suzuki, M., & Shimizu, Y. (2008). Roots of smile: A preterm neonates' study. *Infant Behavior & Development, 31*(3), 518–522.

Kelly, R., & Hammond, S. (2011). The relationship between symbolic play and executive function in young children. *Australasian Journal of Early Childhood, 36*(2), 21–27.

Kennedy, M., Betts, L. R., & Underwood, J. D. M. (2014). Moving beyond the mother–child dyad: Exploring the link between maternal sensitivity and siblings' attachment styles. *The Journal of Genetic Psychology: Research and Theory on Human Development, 175*(4), 287–300.

Keyser, J. (2006). Socialization and guidance with infants and toddlers. In J. R. Lally, P. L. Mangione, & D. Greenwald (Eds.), *Concepts for care: 20 essays on infant/toddler development and learning* (pp. 101–104). Sausalito, CA: WestEd.

KidsHealth. (2014a). Growth and your 8- to 12-month old. Retrieved on November 1, 2014, from http://kidshealth.org/parent/growth/growth/grow812m.html#cat162

KidsHealth. (2014b). Abusive head trauma (shaken baby syndrome). Retrieved on October 29, 2014, from http://kidshealth.org/parent/medical/brain/shaken.html

Kiernan, K. E., & Huerta, M. C. (2008). Economic deprivation, maternal depression, parenting and children's cognitive and emotional development in early childhood. *The British Journal of Sociology, 59*(4), 783–806.

Kim, E. Y. (2010). An activating mechanism of aggressive behaviour in disorganised attachment: A moment-to-moment case analysis of a three-year-old. *Journal of Child Psychotherapy, 36*(2), 152–167.

Kim, J., & Cicchetti, D. (2010). Longitudinal pathways linking child maltreatment, emotion regulation, peer relations, and psychopathology. *Journal of Child Psychology & Psychiatry, 51*(6), 706–716.

Kim, J. (2013). Confronting invisibility: Early childhood pre-service teachers' beliefs toward homeless children. *Early Childhood Education Journal, 41*(2), 161–169.

Kim, S., Chang, M., & Kim, H. (2011). Does teacher educational training help the early math skills of English language learners in Head Start? *Children & Youth Services Review, 33*(5), 732–740.

King, A. (2001, November). *Providing culturally consistent care for infants and toddlers—strategies from the program for infant/toddler caregivers.* Paper presented at the National Association for the Education of Young Children Annual Conference, Anaheim, CA.

Kirk, E., Howlett, N., Pine, K. J., & Fletcher, B. (2013). To sign or not to sign? The impact of encouraging infants to gesture on infant language and maternal mind-mindedness. *Child Development, 84*(2), 574–590.

Kochanska, G., Aksan, N., & Carlson, J. (2005). Temperament, relationships, and young children's receptive cooperation with their parents. *Developmental Psychology, 41*(4), 648–660.

Kocovski, N. L., & Endler, N. S. (2000). Self- regulation: Social anxiety and depression. *Journal of Applied Biobehavioral Research, 5*(1), 80–91.

Kogan, Y., & Pin, J. (2009). Beginning the journey: The project approach with toddlers. *Early Childhood Research & Practice, 11*(1). Retrieved February 14, 2012, from http://ecrp.uiuc.edu/v11n1/kogan.html

Kolling, T., Óturai, G., & Knopf, M. (2014). Is selective attention the basis for selective imitation in infants? An eye-tracking study of deferred imitation with 12-month-olds. *Journal of Experimental Child Psychology, 124*, 18–35.

Koren-Karie, N., Oppenheim, D., Dolev, S., & Sher, S. (2002). Mothers' insightfulness regarding their infants' internal experience: Relations with maternal sensitivity and infant attachment. *Developmental Psychology, 38*, 534–542.

Koren-Karie, N., Oppenheim, D., Yuval-Adler, S., & Mor, H. (2013). Emotion dialogues of foster caregivers with their children: The role of the caregivers, above and beyond child characteristics, in shaping the interactions. *Attachment & Human Development, 15*(2), 175–188.

Korkmaz, I. (2007). Teachers' opinions about the responsibilities of parents, schools, and teachers in enhancing student learning. *Education, 127*(3), 389–399.

Koutra, K., Chatzi, L., Bagkeris, M., Vassilaki, M., Bitsios, P., & Kogevinas, M. (2013). Antenatal and postnatal maternal mental health as determinants of infant neurodevelopment at 18 months of age in a mother-child cohort (Rhea Study) in Crete, Greece. *Social Psychiatry & Psychiatric Epidemiology, 48*(8), 1335–1345.

Kovach, B. A., & De Ros, D. A. (1998). Respectful, individual, and responsive caregiving for infants: The key to successful care in group settings. *YC: Young Children, 53*(3), 61–64.

Kranz, A. M., Lee, J., Divaris, K., Baker, A. D., & Vann Jr., W. (2014). Access to Care. North Carolina physician-based preventive oral health services improve access and use among young Medicaid enrollees. *Health Affairs, 33*(12), 2144–2152.

Kwon, K., Jeon, H., & Elicker, J. (2013). Links among coparenting quality, parental gentle guidance, and toddlers' social emotional competencies: Testing direct, mediational, and moderational models. *Journal of Family Studies, 19*(1), 19–34.

LaBilloisa, J. M., & Lagacé-Séguin, D. G. (2009). Does a good fit matter? Exploring teaching styles, emotion regulation, and child anxiety in the classroom. *Early Child Development and Care, 179*(3), 303–315.

Lachowska, M., Surowiec, P., Morawski, K., Pierchała, K., & Niemczyk, K. (2014). Second stage of Universal Neonatal Hearing Screening: A way for diagnosis and beginning of proper treatment for infants with hearing loss. *Advances in Medical Sciences, 59*(1), 90–94.

Laible, D., Carlo, G., Murphy, T., Augustine, M., & Roesch, S. (2014). Predicting children's prosocial and co-operative behavior from their temperamental profiles: A person-centered approach. *Social Development, 23*(4), 734–752.

Lally, J. R. (2006). Metatheories of childrearing. In J. R. Lally, P. L. Mangione, & D. Greenwald (Eds.), *Concepts for care: 20 essays on infant/toddler development and learning* (pp. 47–52). Sausalito, CA: WestEd.

Lamb-Parker, F., LeBuffe, P., Powell, G., & Halpern, E. (2008). A strength-based, systemic mental health approach to support children's social and emotional development. *Infants and Young Children, 21*(1), 49–55.

Lancaster, L. (2007). Representing the ways of the world: How children under three start to use syntax in graphic signs. *Journal of Early Childhood Literacy, 7*(2), 123–154.

Lansdown, G. (1994). Children's rights. In B. Mayall (Ed.), *Children's childhoods: Observed and experienced* (pp. 33–45). London: Falmer Press.

Lavigne, H. J., Hanson, K. G., & Anderson, D. R. (2015). The influence of television coviewing on parent language directed at toddlers. *Journal of Applied Developmental Psychology, 36*, 1–10.

Lawhon, T., & Cobb, J. B. (2002). Routines that build emergent literacy skills in infants, toddlers, and preschoolers. *Early Childhood Education Journal, 30*(2), 113–118.

Lawrence, D. (2006). *Enhancing self-esteem in the classroom* (3rd ed.). London: Paul Chapman Educational Publishing.

LeBlanc, A. G., Spence, J. C., Carson, V., Connor Gorber, S., Dillman, C., Janssen, I., et al. (2012). Systematic review of sedentary behaviour and health indicators in the early years (aged 0–4 years). *Applied Physiology, Nutrition & Metabolism, 37*(4), 753–772.

Lee, K., & Johnson, A. (2007). Child Development in cultural contexts: Implications of cultural psychology for early childhood teacher education. *Early Childhood Education Journal, 35*(3), 233–243.

Lee, R., Zhai, F., Brooks-Gunn, J., Han, W., & Waldfogel, J. (2014). Head Start participation and school readiness: Evidence from the Early Childhood Longitudinal Study–Birth Cohort. *Developmental Psychology, 50*(1), 202–215.

Lee, S. M., Kaufman, R. L., & George, C. (2009). Disorganized attachment in young children: Manifestations, etiology, and implications for child custody. *Journal of Child Custody, 6*(1/2), 62–90.

Leech, E. R. B., & Cress, C. (2011). Indirect facilitation of speech in a late talking child by prompted production of picture symbols or signs. *Augmentative & Alternative Communication, 27*(1), 40–52.

Legerstee, M., & Varghese, J. (2001). The role of maternal affect mirroring on social expectancies in three-month-old infants. *Child Development, 72*(5), 1301–1313.

Lehman, E. B., Steier, A. J., Guidash, K. M., & Wanna, S. Y. (2002). Predictors of compliance in toddlers: Child temperament, maternal personality, and emotional availability. *Early Child Development and Care, 172*(3), 301–310.

Leong, D. J., & Bodrova, E. (2012). Assessing and Scaffolding Make-Believe Play. *YC: Young Children, 67*(1), 28–34.

Levine, L. E., & Conway, J. M. (2010). Self-other awareness and peer relationships in toddlers: Gender comparisons. *Infant and Child Development, 19*(5), 455–464.

Levine, S. C., Suriyakham, L. W., Rowe, M. L., Huttenlocher, J., & Gunderson, E. A. (2010). What counts in the development of young children's number knowledge? *Developmental Psychology, 46*(5), 1309–1319.

Lewin-Benham, A. (2010). *Infants and toddlers at work: Using Reggio-inspired materials to support brain development.* New York: Teachers College Press.

Lewis, C. W., Johnston, B. D., Linsenmeyar, K. A., Williams, A., & Mouradian, W. (2007). Preventive dental care for children in the United States: A national perspective. *Pediatrics, 119*(3), 544–553.

Li, I., Pawan, C., Stansbury, K. (2014). Emerging effortful control in infancy and toddlerhood and maternal support: A child driven or parent driven model? *Infant Behavior & Development, 37*(2), 216–224.

Licht, B., Simoni, H., & Perrig-Chiello, P. (2008). Conflict between peers in infancy and toddler age: What do they fight about? *Early Years, 28*(3), 235–249.

Liebel, K., Behne, T., Carpenter, M., & Tomasello, M. (2009). Infants use shared experience to interpret pointing gestures. *Developmental Science, 12*(2), 264–271.

Lieberman, A. L., & Van Horn, P. (2013). Infants and young children in military families: A conceptual model for intervention. *Clinical Child & Family Psychology Review, 16*(3), 282–293.

Lincoln, A., Swift, E., & Shorteno-Fraser, M. (2008). Psychological adjustment and treatment of children and families with parents deployed in military combat. *Journal of Clinical Psychology, 64*(8), 984–992.

Linder, S. M., Powers-Costello, B., & Stegelin, D. A. (2011). Mathematics in early childhood: Research-based rationale and practical strategies. *Early Childhood Education Journal, 39*(1), 29–37.

Lindsey, E. W. (2014). Physical activity play and preschool children's peer acceptance: Distinctions between rough-and-tumble and exercise play. *Early Education and Development, 25*(3), 277–294.

Linebarger, D. L., & Vaala, S. E. (2010). Screen media and language development in infants and toddlers: An ecological perspective. *Developmental Review, 30*(2), 176–202.

Lisonbee, J. A., Mize, J., Payne, A. L., & Granger, D. A. (2008). Children's cortisol and the quality of teacher–child relationships in child care. *Child Development, 79*(6), 1818–1832.

Locke, J. (1892). Some thoughts concerning education. In R. J. Quick (Ed.), *Locke on education* (pp. 1–236). Cambridge, London: Cambridge University Press. (Original work published 1690.)

Locke, J. L. (2006). Parental selection of vocal behavior: Crying, cooing, babbling, and the evolution of language. *Human Nature, 17*(2), 155–168.

Long, C. M., Quinonez, R. B., Rozier, R. G., Kranz, A. M., & Lee, J. Y. (2014). Barriers to pediatricians' adherence to American Academy of Pediatrics oral health referral guidelines: North Carolina general dentists' opinions. *Pediatric Dentistry, 36*(4), 309–315.

Lopez, W. D., & Seng, J. S. (2014). Posttraumatic stress disorder, smoking, and cortisol in a community sample of pregnant women. *Behaviors, 39*(10), 1408–1413.

Losonczy-Marshall, M. (2014). Stability in temperament and emotional expression in 1- to 3-year old children. *Social Behavior and Personality, 42*(9), 1421–1430.

Louie, A. D., & Cromer, L. D. (2014). Parent–child attachment during the deployment cycle: Impact on reintegration parenting stress. *Professional Psychology: Research and Practice, 45*(6), 496–503.

Louis, L. (2013). "No one's the boss of my painting": A model of the early development of artistic graphic. *International Journal of Education & the Arts, 14*(11), 1–29.

Love, J. M., Raikes, H. H., Paulsell, D., & Kisker, E. E. (2004). Early Head Start's role in promoting good-quality child care for low-income families. In J. Lombardi & M. M. Bogle (Eds.), *Beacon of hope: The promise of Early Head Start for America's youngest children* (pp. 44–62). Washington, DC: Zero to Three.

Love, J. M., Kisker, E. E., Ross, C., Raikes, H., Constantine, J., Boller, K., et al. (2005). The effectiveness of Early Head Start for 3-year-old children and their parents: Lessons for policy and programs. *Developmental Psychology, 41*(6), 885–901.

Lowe, J., Duvall, S. W., MacLean, P. C., Caprihan, A., Ohls, R., Qualls, C., et al. (2011). Comparison of structural magnetic resonance imaging and development of toddlers born very low birth weight and full-term. *Journal of Child Neurology, 26*(5), 586–592.

Luckenbill, J., & Schallock, L. (2015). Designing and using a developmentally appropriate block area for infants and toddlers. *YC: Young Children, 70*(1), 8–17.

Lyman, D. R., Njoroge, W. F. M., & Willis, D. W. (2007). Early childhood psychosocial screening in culturally diverse populations: A survey of clinical experience with the Ages and Stages Questionnaires: Social-Emotional (ASQ: SE). *Zero to Three, 27*(5), 46–54.

Lynch, E. W., & Hanson, M. J. (eds.) (2011). *Developing cross-cultural competence: A guide for working with children and families* (4th ed.). Baltimore, MD: Paul H. Brookes.

Lyons, R., O'Malley, M. P., O'Connor, P., & Monaghan, U. (2010). 'It's just so lovely to hear him talking': Exploring the early-intervention expectations and experiences of parents. *Child Language Teaching and Therapy, 26*(1), 61–76.

Mack, M., Sacks, J., Hudson, S., & Thompson, D. (2001). The impact of attenuation performance of materials under indoor equipment in child care centers. *Injury Control and Safety Promotion, 8*(1), 45–47.

Madigan, S., Moran, G., Schuengel, C., Pederson, D. R., & Otten, R. (2007). Unresolved maternal attachment representations, disrupted maternal behavior and disorganized attachment in infancy: Links to toddler behavior problems. *Journal of Child Psychology & Psychiatry, 48*(10), 1042–1050.

Maguire-Fong, M. J. (2006). Respectful teaching with infants and toddlers. In J. R. Lally, P. L. Mangione, & D. Greenwald (Eds.), *Concepts for care: 20 essays on infant/toddler development and learning* (pp. 117–122). Sausalito, CA: WestEd.

Mahler, M. S., Pine, F., & Bergman, F. (1975). *The psychological birth of the human infant: Symbiosis and individuation*. New York: Basic Books.

Main, M., & Solomon, J. (1990). Procedures for identifying infants as disorganized/disoriented during the Ainsworth Strange Situation. In M. T. Greenberg, D. Cicchetti, & E. M. Cummings (Eds.), *Attachment in the preschool years* (pp. 121–160). Chicago, IL: University of Chicago Press.

Mamedova, S., & Redford, J. (2013). Early childhood program participation, from the National Household Education Surveys Program of 2012 (NCES 2013-029), National Center for Education Statistics, Institute of Education Sciences, US Department of Education. Washington, DC. Retrieved September 22, 2014, from http://nces.ed.gov/pubsearch

Mankiw, S., & Strasser, J. (2013). Tender topics: Exploring sensitive issues with pre-K through first grade children through read-alouds. *YC: Young Children, 68*(1), 84–89.

Mann, T. L., Bogle, M. M., & Parlakian, R. (2004). Early Head Start: An overview. In J. Lombardi & M. M. Bogle (Eds.), *Beacon of hope: The promise of Early Head Start for America's youngest children* (pp. 1–19). Washington, DC: Zero to Three.

Mantovani, S. (2001). Infant-toddler centers in Italy today: Tradition and innovation. In L. Gandini & C. P. Edwards (Eds.), *Bambini: The Italian approach to infant/toddler care* (pp. 23–37). New York: Teachers College Press.

Manz, P. H., Lehtinen, J., & Bracaliello, C. (2013). A case for increasing empirical attention to Head Start's home-based program: An exploration of routine collaborative goal setting. *School Community Journal, 23*(1), 131–144.

Marcon, R. A. (2002, Spring). Moving up the grades: Relationships between preschool model and later school success. *Early Childhood Research and Practice, 4*(1). Retrieved December 12, 2006, from http://ecrp.uiuc.edu/v4n1/marcon.html

Marion, M. (2004). *Using observation in early childhood education*. Upper Saddle River, NJ: Pearson Prentice Hall.

Marion, M. (2014). *Guidance of young children* (9th ed.). Upper Saddle River, NJ: Prentice Hall.

Marion, M., & Swim, T. J. (2007). *Intentionality in child guidance: Helping ECE pre-service students understand the concept*. Paper presented at the National Association for the Education of Young Children's Professional Development Institute, Pittsburg, PA.

Markström, A. (2011). To involve parents in the assessment of the child in parent-teacher conferences: A case study. *Early Childhood Education Journal, 38*(6), 465–474.

Marotz, L. R., & Allen, K. E. (2013). *Developmental profiles: Pre-birth through adolescence*. Belmont, CA: Wadsworth.

Marriott, S. (2008). *Green baby*. New York: Dorling Kindersley.

Marschark, M. (2007). *Raising and educating a deaf child*. Oxford: Oxford University Press, Inc.

Marshall, J. (2011). Infant neurosensory development: Considerations for infant child care. *Early Childhood Education Journal, 39*(3), 175–181.

Martell, M. M., Witt, S. D., & Witt, D. D. (2013). An analysis of books for preschool children experiencing bereavement and loss. *Education & Society, 31*(1), 37–52.

Masten, A. S. (2013). Competence, risk, and resilience in military families: Conceptual commentary. *Clinical Child & Family Psychology Review, 16*, 278–281.

Matafwali, B., & Serpell, R. (2014). Design and validation of assessment tests for young children in Zambia. In R. Serpell & K. Marfo (Eds.), Child development in Africa: Views from inside (pp. 77–96). *New Directions for Child and Adolescent Development, 146*.

Mattern, J. A. (2015). A mixed-methods study of early intervention implementation in the Commonwealth of Pennsylvania: Supports, services, and policies for young children with developmental delays and disabilities. *Early Childhood Education Journal, 43*(1), 57–67.

Matusov, E., DePalma, R., & Drye, S. (2007). Whose development? Salvaging the concept of development within a sociocultural approach to education. *Educational Theory, 57*(4), 403–421.

May, N., Kantor, R., & Sanderson, M. (2004). There it is! Exploring the permanence of objects and the power of self with infants and toddlers. In J. Hendrick (Ed.), *Next steps towards teaching the Reggio way: Accepting the challenge to change* (2nd ed., pp. 164–174). Upper Saddle River, NJ: Pearson Merrill Prentice Hall.

Mayo Clinic Staff. (2011). *Relaxation techniques: Try these steps to reduce stress.* Retrieved October 11, 2011, from http://www.mayoclinic.org/healthy -lifestyle/stress-management/in-depth/relaxation -technique/art-20045368

Mayuko, K., Kenji, O., Tadahiro, K., Toshihiko, H., & Tetsuhiro, M. (2012). Two-year-old toddlers' prosocial responses to a crying peer: Social evaluation mechanisms. *Japanese Journal of Developmental Psychology, 23*(1), 12–22.

McCabe, K. M., Goehring, K., Yeh, M., & Lau, A. S. (2008). Parental locus of control and externalizing behavior problems among Mexican American preschoolers. *Journal of Emotional & Behavioral Disorders, 16*(2), 118–126.

McDevitt, T. M., & Ormrod, J. E. (2013). *Child development: Educating and working with children and adolescents* (5th ed.). Upper Saddle River, NJ: Pearson Prentice Hall.

McElroy, E. M., & Rodriguez, C. M. (2008). Mothers of children with externalizing behavior problems: Cognitive risk factors for abuse potential and discipline style and practices. *Child Abuse & Neglect, 32*(8), 774–784.

McGaha, C. G., Cummings, R., Lippard, B., & Dallas, K. (2011). Relationship building: Infants, toddlers, and 2-year-olds. *Early Childhood Research & Practice, 13*(1). Retrieved February 6, 2012, from http://ecrp .uiuc.edu/v13n1/mcgaha.html

McGee, L. M., & Richgels, D. J. (2012). *Literacy's beginnings: Supporting young readers and writers* (6th ed.). Boston, MA: Pearson.

McHenry, J. D., & Buerk, K. J. (2008). Infants and toddlers meet the natural world. *Beyond the Journal: Young Children on the Web.* Retrieved March 11, 2009, from http://journal.naeyc.org /btj/200801/pdf/BTJNatureMcHenry.pdf

McIntosh, J. E., Smyth, B. M., & Kelaher, M. (2013). Overnight care patterns following parental separation: Associations with emotion regulation in infants and young children. *Journal of Family Studies, 19*(3), 224–239.

McLaughlin, C. (2008). Emotional well-being and its relationship to schools and classrooms: A critical reflection. *British Journal of Guidance & Counselling, 36*(4), 353–366.

McLennan, D. P. (2012). Bird feeding. *YC: Young Children, 67*(5), 90–93.

McMullen, M. B. (1999). Characteristics of teachers who talk the DAP talk and walk the DAP walk. *Journal of Research in Childhood Education, 13*(2), 216–230.

McMullen, M. B., Addleman, J. M., Fulford, A. M., Moore, S. L., Mooney, S. J., Sisk, S. S., et al. (2009). Learning to be "me" while coming to understand "we": Encouraging prosocial babies in group settings. *YC: Young Children, 64*(4), 20–28.

McWilliam, R. A. (2015). Future of early intervention with infants and toddlers for whom typical experiences are not effective. *Remedial & Special Education, 36*(1), 33–38.

Meece, D., & Soderman, A. K. (2010). Children's social development and learning: Setting the stage for young children's social development. *YC: Young Children, 65*(5), 81–86.

de Mendonça, J. S., Cossette, L., Strayer, F. F., & Gravel, F. (2011). Mother-child and father-child interactional synchrony in dyadic and triadic interactions. *Sex Roles, 64*(1/2), 132–142.

Mercy, J. A., & Saul, J. (2009). Creating a healthier future through early interventions for children. *JAMA, 301*(21), 2262–2264. Retrieved August 26, 2011, from http://jama.ama-assn.org

Merz, E. C., Landry, S. H., Williams, J. M., Barnes, M. A., Eisenberg, N., Spinrad, T. L., et al. (2014). Associations among parental education, home environment quality, effortful control, and preacademic knowledge. *Journal of Applied Developmental Psychology, 35*, 304–315.

Meyer, D., Wood, S., & Stanley, B. (2013). Nurture is nature: Integrating brain development, systems theory, and attachment theory. *The Family Journal: Counseling and Therapy for Couples and Families, 21*(2) 162–169.

Miller, L. G., & Gibbs, M. J. (2002). *Making toys for infants and toddlers: Using ordinary stuff for extraordinary play.* Silver Springs, MD: Gryphon House, Inc.

Minke, K. M., Sheridan, S. M., Kim, E. M., Ryoo, J. H., & Koziol, N. A. (2014). Congruence in parent-teacher relationships: The role of shared perceptions. *The Elementary School Journal, 114*(4), 527–546.

Moehler, E., Kagan, J., Oelkers-Ax, R., Brunner, R., Poustka, L., Haffner, J., et al. (2008). Infant predictors of behavioural inhibition. *British Journal of Developmental Psychology, 26*(1), 145–150.

Mol, S. E., Neuman, S. B., & Strouse, G. A. (2014). From ABCs to DVDs: Profiles of infants' home media environments in the first two years of life. *Early Child Development & Care, 184*(8), 1250–1266.

Mollborn, S. (2009). Norms about nonmarital pregnancy and willingness to provide resources to unwed parents. *Journal of Marriage & Family, 71*(1), 122–134.

Montie, J. E., Xiang, Z., & Schweinhart, L. J. (2006). Preschool experience in 10 countries: Cognitive and language performance at age 7. *Early Childhood Research Quarterly, 21*(3), 313–331.

Moon, R. Y., Calabrese, T., & Aird, L. (2008). Reducing the risk of sudden infant death syndrome in child care and changing provider practices: Lessons learned from a demonstration project. *Pediatrics, 122*(4), 788–798.

Moore, G. A., & Calkins, S. D. (2004). Infants' vagal regulation in the still-face paradigm is related to dyadic coordination of mother-infant interaction. *Developmental Psychology, 40*(6), 1068–1080.

Morcom, V. (2014). Scaffolding social and emotional learning in an elementary classroom community: A sociocultural perspective. *International Journal of Educational Research, 67,* 18–29.

Morehouse, P. G. (2013). The importance of music making in child development. *YC: Young Children, 68*(4), 82–89.

Mortensen, E. L. (2007). Neuro-developmental effects of breastfeeding. *Acta Paediatrica, 96*(6), 796–797.

Murphy, J. L., Hatton, D., & Erickson, K. A. (2008). Exploring the early literacy practices of teachers of infants, toddlers, and preschoolers with visual impairments. *Journal of Visual Impairment & Blindness, 102*(3), 133–146.

Murray, A. D., Johnson, J., & Peters, J. (1990). Fine-tuning of utterance length to preverbal infants: Effects on later language development. *Journal of Child Language, 17,* 511–525.

Murray, A. D., & Yingling, J. L. (2000). Competence in language at 24 months: Relations with attachment security and home stimulation. *Journal of Genetic Psychology, 161*(2), 133–140.

Murrell, P. C., Diez, M. E., Feiman-Nemser, S., & Schussler, D. L. (Eds.) (2010). *Teaching as a moral practice.* Cambridge, MA: Harvard Education Press.

Nærde, A., Ogden, T., Janson, H., & Zachrisson, H. D. (2014). Normative development of physical aggression from 8 to 26 months. *Developmental Psychology, 50*(6), 1710–1720.

Nathanson, A. I., & Rasmussen, E. E. (2011). TV viewing compared to book reading and toy playing reduces responsive maternal communication with toddlers and preschoolers. *Human Communication Research, 37*(4), 465–487.

National Association for the Education of Young Children (NAEYC). (2003). *Early childhood curriculum, assessment, and program evaluation: Building an effective, accountable system in programs for children birth through age 8.* Joint position statement of NAEYC and National Association of Early Childhood Specialists in State Departments of Education (NAECS/SDE). Washington, DC: Author.

National Association for the Education of Young Children (NAEYC). (2005). Advocates in action. Building your advocacy capacity. *Young Children, 60*(3), 79.

National Association for the Education of Young Children (NAEYC). (2009). *Position statement. NAEYC standards for early childhood professional preparation programs.* Washington, DC: Author. Retrieved August 24, 2011, from http://www.naeyc .org/positionstatements/ppp

National Association for the Education of Young Children (NAEYC). (2011a). *2010 NAEYC standards for initial & advanced early childhood professional preparation programs.* Washington, DC: Author. Retrieved August 24, 2011, from http://www.naeyc .org/ncate/standards

National Association for the Education of Young Children (NAEYC). (2011b, May). *Position statement. Code of ethical conduct and statement of commitment.* Retrieved January 17, 2015, from http://www.naeyc .org/positionstatements/ethical_conduct

National Association for the Education of Young Children (NAEYC). (2014). Revised NAEYC Early Childhood Program Accreditation Criteria. Retrieved September 26, 2014, from http://www .naeyc.org/academy/files/academy/file /AllCriteriaDocument.pdf

National Center on Shaken Baby Syndrome. (nd). SBS statistics. Farmington, UT: Author. Retrieved October 29, 2014, from http://dontshake.org/sbs .php?topNavID=3&subNavID=27

National Coalition for Core Arts Standards. (2014). National core arts standards: Dance, media arts, music, theatre and visual arts. Retrieved April 28, 2015, from http://www.nationalartsstandards.org/

National Council for the Social Studies. (2010). National curriculum standards for social studies: A framework for teaching, learning, and assessment.

Retrieved April 28, 2015, from http://www
.socialstudies.org/standards

National Council of Teachers of Mathematics (NCTM).
(2000). *Principles and standards for school
mathematics.* Reston, VA: NCTM.

National Head Start Association. (2014). *Research
bites.* Retrieved September 26, 2014, from http://
www.nhsa.org/research/research_bites

National Network for Child Care. (2014). Caring for
children with special needs: HIV or AIDS. Retrieved
January 31, 2015, from http://www.ces.ncsu.edu
/depts/fcs/pdfs/NC14.pdf

National Program for Playground Safety. (2015).
S.A.F.E. Retrieved January 31, 2015, from http://
playgroundsafety.org/safe/framework

National Scientific Council on the Developing Child.
(2010). *Persistent fear and anxiety can affect young
children's learning and development: Working
paper no. 9.* Retrieved June 27, 2011, from www
.developingchild.harvard.edu

Nelemans, S., Hale, W., Branje, S., Lier, P., Jansen, L.,
Platje, E., et al. (2014). Persistent heightened cortisol awakening response and adolescent internalizing symptoms: A 3-year longitudinal community
study. *Journal of Abnormal Child Psychology, 42*(5),
767–777.

Nelson, C. A., Bos, K., Gunnar, M. R., & Sonuga-
Barke, E. J. S. (2011). The neurobiological toll
of early human deprivation. *Monographs of the
Society for Research in Child Development, 76*(4),
127–146.

Nelson, E. M. (2012). *Cultivating outdoor classrooms:
Designing and implementing child-centered
learning environments.* St. Paul, MN: Redleaf Press.

Neuman, S. B., Kaefer, T., Pinkham, A., & Strouse, G.
(2014). Can babies learn to read? A randomized trial
of baby media. *Journal of Educational Psychology,
106*(3), 815–830.

Nevanen, S., Juvonen, A., & Ruismäki, H. (2014). Does
arts education develop school readiness? Teachers'
and artists' points of view on an art education
project. *Arts Education Policy Review,
115*(3), 72–81.

New, R. (1998). Social competence in Italian early
childhood education. In D. Sharma & K. W. Fisher
(Eds.), *Socioemotional development across cultures*
(New Directions for Child Development No. 81,
pp. 87–104). San Francisco, CA: Jossey-Bass.

New, R. (2003). Reggio Emilia: New ways to think
about schooling. *Educational Leadership, 60*(7),
34–38.

Newcombe, N. S. (2013). Cognitive development:
Changing views of cognitive change. *WIREs
Cognitive Science, 4,* 479–491.

Newell, K. M., Liu, Y., & Mayer-Kress, G. (2001).
Time scales in motor learning and development.
Psychological Review, 108(1), 57–82.

Newman, R. S. (2005). The cocktail party effect in
infants revisited: Listening to one's name in noise.
Developmental Psychology, 41(2), 352–362.

Newman, R. S. (2008). The level of detail in infants'
word learning. *Current Directions in Psychological
Science: A Journal of the American Psychological
Society, 17*(3), 229–232.

NICHD Early Child Care Research Network. (1997).
The effects of infant child care on infant-mother
attachment security: Results of the NICHD study of
early child care. *Child Development, 68,* 860–879.

NICHD Early Child Care Research Network. (1998a).
*Chronicity of maternal depressive symptoms,
maternal behavior, and child functioning at
36 months: Results from the NICHD study of
early child care.* Washington, DC: Author.

NICHD Early Child Care Research Network. (1998b).
Relations between family predictors and child
outcomes: Are they weaker for children in child
care? *Developmental Psychology, 34,* 1119–1128.

NICHD Early Child Care Research Network. (1999).
Child care and mother-child interaction in the first
three years of life. *Developmental Psychology, 35,*
1399–1413.

NICHD Early Child Care Research Network. (2005).
*Child care and child development: Results from
the NICHD study of early child care and youth
development.* New York: Guilford Press.

Nichols, S. R., Svetlova, M., & Brownell, C. A. (2010).
Toddlers' understanding of peers' emotions. *The
Journal of Genetic Psychology, 171*(1), 35–53.

Nielsen, L. (2014). Parenting plans for infants,
toddlers, and preschoolers: Research and issues.
Journal of Divorce & Remarriage, 55(4), 315–333.

Nielsen, M., Suddendorf, T., & Slaughter, V. (2006).
Mirror self-recognition beyond the face. *Child
Development, 77*(1), 176–185.

Nimmo, J., & Hallet, B. (2008). Childhood in the
garden: A place to encounter natural and social
diversity. *Beyond the Journal: Young Children on the
Web.* Retrieved March 11, 2009, from http://journal
.naeyc.org/btj/200801/pdf/BTJNatureNimmo.pdf

Noddings, N. (2002). *Starting at home: Care and social
policy.* Berkeley, CA: University of California Press.

Noddings, N. (2005). *The challenge to care in schools:
An alternative approach to education* (2nd ed.).
New York: Teachers College Press.

O'Connor, E., & McCartney, K. (2006). Testing
associations between young children's relationships
with mothers and teachers. *Journal of Educational
Psychology, 98*(1), 87–98.

Oddi, K. B., Murdock, K. W., Vadnais, S., Bridgett, D. J., & Gartstein, M. A. (2013). Maternal and infant temperament characteristics as contributors to parenting stress in the first year postpartum. *Infant and Child Development, 22*, 553–579.

Odom, S. L., Teferra, T., & Kaul, S. (2004). An overview of international approaches to early intervention for young children with special needs and their families. *YC: Young Children, 59*(5), 38–43.

Ohgi, S., Arisawa, K., Takahashi, T., Kusumoto, T., Goto, Y., Akiyama, T., et al. (2003). Neonatal behavioral assessment scale as a predictor of later developmental disabilities of low birth-weight and/or premature infants. *Brain & Development, 25*(5), 313–321.

Olfman, S. (2008). What about play? In A. Pelo (Ed.), *Rethinking early childhood education* (pp. 61–64). Milwaukee, WI: Rethinking Schools Publication.

Oosterman, M., & Schuengel, C. (2008). Attachment in foster children associated with caregivers' sensitivity and behavioral problems. *Infant Mental Health Journal, 29*(6), 609–623.

Oppenheim, D., & Koren-Karie, N. (2002). Mothers' insightfulness regarding their children's internal worlds: The capacity underlying secure child-mother relationships. *Infant Mental Health Journal, 23*, 593–605.

Osofsky, J. D., & Lieberman, A. F. (2011). A call for integrating a mental health perspective into systems of care for abused and neglected infants and young children. *American Psychologist, 66*(2), 120–128.

Paley, B., Lester, P., & Mogil, C. (2013). Family Systems and Ecological Perspectives on the Impact of Deployment on Military Families. *Clinical Child & Family Psychology Review, 16*, 245–265.

Palusci, V. J. (2011). Risk factors and services for child maltreatment among infants and young children. *Children & Youth Services Review, 33*(8), 1374–1382.

Pancheri-Ambrose, B., & Tritchler-Scali, J. (2013). Beyond green: Developing social and environmental awareness in early childhood. *YC: Young Children, 68*(4), 54–61.

Pandey, J., Verbalis, A., Robins, D. L., Boorsetin, H., Klin, A., Babitz, T., et al. (2008). Screening for autism in older and younger toddlers with the modified checklist for autism in toddlers. *Autism: The International Journal of Research & Practice, 12*(5), 513–535.

Paquette, D. (2013). Is father–child rough-and-tumble play associated with attachment or activation relationships? *Early Child Development and Care, 183*(6), 760–773.

Paranjothy, S. (2009). Teenage pregnancy: Who suffers? *Archives of Disease in Childhood, 94*(3), 239–245.

Park., S., Kim, B., Kim, J., Shin, M., Yoo, H., & Cho, S. (2014). Protective effect of breastfeeding with regard to children's behavioral and cognitive problems. *Nutrition Journal, 13*(1), 84–95.

Parladé, M. V., & Iverson, J. M. (2011). The interplay between language, gesture, and affect during communicative transition: A dynamic systems approach. *Developmental Psychology, 47*(3), 820–833.

Parlakian, R., & Lerner, C. (2007). Promoting healthy eating habits right from the start. *Beyond the Journal: Young Children on the Web*. Retrieved April 11, 2009, from http://journal.naeyc.org/btj/200705/pdf/RockingandRolling.pdf

Passehl, B., McCarroll, C., Buechner, J., Gearring, C., Smith, A. E., & Trowbridge, F. (2004). Preventing childhood obesity: Establishing healthy lifestyle habits in the preschool years. *Journal of Pediatric Health Care, 18*(6), 1–4.

Patall, E. A., Cooper, H., & Robinson, J. C. (2008). The effects of choice on intrinsic motivation and related outcomes: A meta-analysis of research findings. *Psychological Bulletin, 134*(2), 270–300.

Patel, S., Gaylord, S., & Fagen, J. (2013). Generalization of deferred imitation in 6-, 9-, and 12-month-old infants using visual and auditory contexts. *Infant Behavior & Development, 36*(1), 25–31.

Patterson, J. E., & Vakili, S. (2014). Relationships, environment, and the brain: How emerging research is changing what we know about the impact of families on human development. *Family Process, 53*(1), 22–32.

Pawl, J. (2006). Being held in another's mind. In J. R. Lally, P. L. Mangione, & D. Greenwald (Eds.), *Concepts for care: 20 essays on infant/toddler development and learning* (pp. 1–4). Sausalito, CA: WestEd.

Pawl, J. (2012). Developing self-esteem in the early years. *Zero to Three, 32*(3), 22–25.

Pelo, A. (Ed.). (2008). *Rethinking early childhood education*. Milwaukee, WI: Rethinking Schools Publication.

Pentimonti, J. M., Zucker, T. A., & Justice, L. M. (2011). What are preschool teachers reading in their classrooms? *Reading Psychology, 32*(3), 197–236.

Pérez-Edgar, K., Bar-Haim, Y., McDermott, J. M., Chronis-Tuscano, A., Pine, D. S., & Fox, N. A. (2010). Attention biases to threat and behavioral inhibition in early childhood shape adolescent social withdrawal. *Emotion, 10*(3), 349–357.

Pérez-Edgar, K., Reeb-Sutherland, B. C., McDermott, J. M., White, L. K., Henderson, H. A., Degnan, K. A., et al. (2011). Attention biases to threat link behavioral inhibition to social withdrawal over time in very young children. *Journal of Abnormal Child Psychology, 39*(6), 885–895.

Pérez-Edgar, K., Schmidt, L. A., Henderson, H. A., Schulkin, J., & Fox, N. A. (2008). Salivary cortisol levels and infant temperament shape developmental trajectories in boys at risk for behavioral maladjustment. *Psychoneuroendocrinology, 33*(7), 916–925.

Perra, O., & Gattis, M. (2010). The control of social attention from 1 to 4 months. *British Journal of Developmental Psychology, 28*, 891–908.

Peterson, C. A., Mayer, L. M., Summers, J., & Luze, G. J. (2010). Meeting needs of young children at risk for or having a disability. *Early Childhood Education Journal, 37*(6), 509–517.

Peterson, C. C., & Wellman, H. M. (2009). From fancy to reason: Scaling deaf and hearing children's understanding of theory of mind and pretence. *British Journal of Developmental Psychology, 27*(2), 297–310.

Philbrook, L. E., Hozella, A. C., Kim, B., Jian, N., Shimizu, M., & Teti, D. M. (2014). Maternal emotional availability at bedtime and infant cortisol at 1 and 3 months. *Early Human Development, 90*(10), 595–605.

Phillips, R. D., Gorton, R. L., Pinciotti, P., & Sachdev, A. (2010). Promising findings on preschoolers' emergent literacy and school readiness in arts-integrated early childhood settings. *Early Childhood Education Journal, 38*(2), 111–122.

Piaget, J. (1952). *The origins of intelligence in children* (M. Cook, Trans.). New York: International University Press.

Piaget, J., & Inhelder, B. (1969). *The psychology of the child*. London: Routledge and Kegan Paul.

Pinnell, G. S., & Fountas, I. C. (2011). *Literacy beginnings: A prekindergarten handbook*. Portsmouth, NH: Heinemann.

Pintrich, P. R., Marx, R. W., & Boyle, R. A. (1993). Beyond cold conceptual change: The role of motivational beliefs and classroom contextual factors on the process of conceptual change. *Review of Educational Research, 63*(2), 167–199.

Planned Parenthood Federation of America. (2014). *Pregnancy & childbearing among US teens*. Washington, DC: Author. Retrieved January 29, 2015, from http://www.plannedparenthood.org /files/7314/0657/3708 /PregnancyChildbearing_070814.pdf

Poehlmann, J. (2003). An attachment perspective on grandparents raising their very young grandchildren: Implications for intervention and research. *Infant Mental Health Journal, 24*(2), 149–173.

Poehlmann, J. (2005a). Children's family environments and intellectual outcomes during maternal incarceration. *Journal of Marriage and Family, 67*, 1275–1285.

Poehlmann, J. (2005b). Representations of attachment relationships in children of incarcerated mothers. *Child Development, 76*(3), 679–696.

Polka, L., & Werker, J. F. (1994). Developmental changes in perception of non-native vowel contrasts. *Journal of Experimental Psychology: Human Perception and Performance, 20*, 421–435.

Ponciano, L. (2012). The influence of perception on maternal sensitivity in foster care. *Child & Youth Services, 33*(1), 70–85.

Powell, D., Dunlap, G., & Fox, L. (2006). Prevention and intervention for the challenging behaviors of toddlers and preschoolers. *Infants and Young Children, 19*(1), 25–35.

Prado, E., & Dewey, K. (2012). Nutrition and brain development in early life. *Alive & Thrive Technical Brief, 4*, 1–12.

Project Zero and Reggio Children. (2001). *Making learning visible: Children as individual and group learners*. Reggio Emilia, Italy: Reggio Children srl.

Pullen, P. C., & Justice, L. M. (2003). Enhancing phonological awareness, print awareness, and oral language skills in preschool children. *Intervention in School and Clinic, 39*(2), 87–98.

Quintanar, A. P., & Warren, S. R. (2008). Listening to the voices of Latino parent volunteers. *Kappa Delta Pi Record, 44*(3), 119–123.

Raikes, H. H., Love, J. M., Kisker, E. E., Chazan-Cohen, R., & Brooks-Gunn, J. (2004). What works: Improving the odds for infants and toddlers in low-income families. In J. Lombardi & M. M. Bogle (Eds.), *Beacon of hope: The promise of Early Head Start for America's youngest children* (pp. 20–43). Washington, DC: Zero to Three.

Raikes, H. H., Pan, B. A., Luze, G., Tamis-LeMonda, C. S., Brooks-Gunn, J., Constantine, J., et al. (2006). Mother-child bookreading in low-income families: Correlates and outcomes during the first three years of life. *Child Development, 77*(4), 924–953.

Raikes, H. H., Roggman, L. A., Peterson, C. A., Brooks-Gunn, J., Chazan-Cohen, R., Zhang, X., et al. (2014). Theories of change and outcomes in home-based Early Head Start programs. *Early Childhood Research Quarterly, 29*(4), 574–585.

Ramírez-Esparza, N., García-Sierra, A., & Kuhl, P. K. (2014). Look who's talking: Speech style and social context in language input to infants are linked to concurrent and future speech development. *Developmental Science, 17*(6), 880–891.

Rapee, R. M., Abbott, M. J., & Lyneham, H. J. (2006). Bibliotherapy for children with anxiety disorders using written materials for parents: A randomized controlled trial. *Journal of Consulting and Clinical Psychology, 74*(3), 436–444.

Rappolt-Schlichtmann, G., Willette, J. B., Ayoub, C. C., Lindsley, R., Hulette, A. C., & Fischer, K. W. (2009). Poverty, relationship conflict, and the regulation of cortisol in small and large group contexts at child care. *Mind, Brain, and Education, 3*(3), 131–142.

Recchia, S. L., & Loizou, E. (2002). Becoming an infant caregiver: Three profiles of personal and professional growth. *Journal of Research in Childhood Education, 16*(2), 133–147.

Reedy, C. K., & McGrath, W. H. (2010). Can you hear me now? Staff-parent communication in child care centres. *Early Child Development and Care, 180*(3), 347–357.

Reijntjes, A., Thomaes, S., Boelen, P., van der Schoot, M., de Castro, B. O., & Telch, M. J. (2011). Delighted when approved by others, to pieces when rejected: Children's social anxiety magnifies the linkage between self- and other-evaluations. *Journal of Child Psychology and Psychiatry, 52*(7), 774–781.

Reikerås, E., Løge, I. K., & Knivsberg, A. (2012). The mathematical competencies of toddlers expressed in their play and daily life activities in Norwegian kindergartens. *International Journal of Early Childhood, 44*(1), 91–114.

Rescorla, L. (2002, April). Language and reading outcomes to age 9 in late-talking toddlers. *Journal of Speech, Language, and Hearing Research, 45*, 360–371.

Resources and Instruction for Staff Excellence (RISE). (2000). *Winning teams: Guiding behavior for young children videoconference series*. Cincinnati, OH: Author.

Riley, D., San Juan, R. R., Klinkner, J., & Ramminger, A. (2008). *Social and emotional development: Connecting science and practice in early childhood settings*. St. Paul, MN: Redleaf Press.

Rinaldi, C. (1998). Projected curriculum constructed through documentation—Progettazione: An interview with Lella Gandini. In C. Edwards, L. Gandini, & G. Forman (Eds.), *The hundred languages of children: The Reggio Emilia approach—advanced reflections* (2nd ed., pp. 113–125). Norwood, NJ: Ablex.

Rinaldi, C. (2001a). Infant-toddler centers and preschools as places of culture. In Project Zero and Reggio Children (Eds.), *Making learning visible: Children as individual and group learners* (pp. 38–46). Reggio Emilia, Italy: Reggio Children srl.

Rinaldi, C. (2001b). Documentation and assessment: What is the relationship? In Project Zero and Reggio Children (Eds.), *Making learning visible: Children as individual and small group learners* (pp. 78–89). Reggio Emilia, Italy: Reggio Children srl.

Rinaldi, C. (2001c). Reggio Emilia: The image of the child and the child's environment as a fundamental principle. In L. Gandini & C. P. Edwards (Eds.), *Bambini: The Italian approach to infant/toddler care* (pp. 49–54). New York: Teachers College Press.

Risko, V. J., & Walker-Dalhouse, D. (2009). Parents and teachers: Talking with or past one another—or not talking at all? *The Reading Teacher, 62*(5), 442–444.

Rivkin, M. S., with Schein, D. (2014). *The great outdoors: Advocating for natural spaces for young children* (Rev. ed.). Washington, DC: National Association for the Education of Young Children.

Robb, M. B., & Lauricella, A. R. (2015). Connecting child development and technology: What we know and what it means. In C. Donahue (Ed.), *Technology and digital media in the early years: Tools for teaching and learning* (pp. 70–85). Washington, DC: National Association for the Education of Young Children.

Robinson, A., & Stark, D. R. (2005). *Advocates in action: Making a difference for young children* (Rev. ed.). Washington, DC: National Association for the Education of Young Children.

Robinson, L. E., Webster, E. K., Logan, S. W., Lucas, W. A., & Barber, L. T. (2012). Teaching practices that promote motor skills in early childhood settings. *Early Childhood Education Journal, 40*(2), 79–86.

Robinson, M., Oddy, W. H., Jianghong, L., Kendall, G. E., de Klerk, N. H., Silburn, S. R., et al. (2008). Pre- and postnatal influences on preschool mental health: A large-scale cohort study. *Journal of Child Psychology & Psychiatry, 49*(10), 1118–1128.

Rodriguez, M., McMillan, K., Crandall, L., Minter, M., Grafe, M., Poduri, A., et al. (2012). Hippocampal asymmetry and sudden unexpected death in infancy: A case report. *Forensic Science, Medicine & Pathology, 8*(4), 441–446.

Roggman, L. A., Boyce, L. K., Cook, G. A., Christiansen, K., & Jones, D. (2004). Playing with daddy: Social toy play, Early Head Start, and developmental outcomes. *Fathering, 2*(1), 83–108.

Roisman, G. I., Susman, E., Barnett-Walker, K., Booth-LaForce, C., Owen, M. T., Belsky, J., et al. (2009). Early family and child-care antecedents of awakening cortisol levels in adolescence. *Child Development, 80*, 907–920.

Rose, K., & Rose, C. (2014). Enrolling in college while in prison: Factors that promote male and female prisoners to participate. *The Journal of Correctional Education, 65*(2), 20–39.

Rosenkoetter, S., & Barton, L. R. (2002). Bridges to literacy: Early routines that promote later school success. *Zero to Three, 22*(4), 33–38.

Roth-Hanania, R., Davidov, M., & Zahn-Waxler, C. (2011). Empathy development from 8 to 16 months: Early signs of concern for others. *Infant Behavior & Development, 34*(3), 447–458.

Rothstein-Fisch, C., Trumbull, E., & Garcia, S. G. (2009). Making the implicit explicit: Supporting teachers to bridge cultures. *Early Childhood Research Quarterly 24,* 474–486.

Rousseau, J. J. (1955). *Emile.* New York: Dutton. (Original work published 1762.)

Rowe, D. W. (2008). Social contracts for writing: Negotiating shared understandings about text in the preschool years. *Reading Research Quarterly, 43*(1), 66–95.

Rubin, K. H., Bukowski, W. M., & Parker, J. G. (2006). Peer interactions, relationships, and groups. In N. Eisenberg (Ed.), *Handbook of child psychology: Vol. 3. Social, emotional, and personality development* (6th ed., pp. 571–645). New York: Wiley.

Rudasill, K. M. (2011). Child temperament, teacher-child interactions, and teacher-child relationships: A longitudinal investigation from first to third grade. *Early Childhood Research Quarterly, 26*(2), 147–156.

Rueda, M. R., Posner, M. I., & Rothbart, M. K. (2005). The development of executive attention: Contributions to the emergence of self-regulation. *Developmental Neuropsychology, 28,* 573–594.

Ruprecht, K. (2011, September 8–9). *Primary caregiving and continuity of care: Two important steps in dancing with infants and toddlers.* Paper presented at the Infant-Toddler Specialists of Indiana Annual Conference, Indianapolis, IN.

Rydell, A., Bohlin, G., & Thorell, L. B. (2005). Representations of attachment to parents and shyness as predictors of children's relationships with teachers and peer competence in preschool. *Attachment & Human Development, 7*(2), 187–204.

Saarni, C., Campos, J. J., Camras, L. A., & Witherington, D. (2006). Emotional development: Action, communication, and understanding. In N. Eisenberg (Ed.), *Handbook of child psychology: Vol. 3. Social, emotional, and personality development* (6th ed., pp. 646–718). New York: Wiley.

Sajaniemi, N., Suhonen, E., Kontu, E., Rantanen, P., Lindholm, H., Hyttinen, S., et al. (2011). Children's cortisol patterns and the quality of the early learning environment. *European Early Childhood Education Research Journal, 19*(1), 45–62.

Sakagami, H. (2010). Autonomy and emotional development in toddlerhood: Anger, guilt, and shame. *Japanese Psychological Review, 53*(1), 38–55.

Samuelsson, I. P., Carlsson, M. A., Olsson, B., Pramling, N., & Wallerstedt, C. (2009). The art of teaching children the arts: Music, dance and poetry with children aged 2–8 years old. *International Journal of Early Years Education, 17*(2), 119–135.

Sano, Y., Smith, S., & Lanigan, J. (2011). Predicting presence and level of nonresident fathers' involvement in infants' lives: Mothers' perspective. *Journal of Divorce & Remarriage, 52*(5), 350–368.

Sarkadi, A., Kristiansson, R., Oberklaid, F., & Bremberg, S. (2008). Fathers' involvement and children's developmental outcomes: A systematic review of longitudinal studies. *Acta Paediatrica, 97,* 153–158.

Sawaguchi, T., Franco, P., Kadhim, H., Groswasser, J., Sottiaux, M., Nishida, H., et al. (2004). The presence of TATA-binding protein in the brainstem, correlated with sleep apnea in SIDS victims. *Pathophysiology, 10*(3/4), 217–222.

Schmit, S., Matthews, H., Smith, S., & Robbins, T. (2013). Investing in young children: A fact sheet on early care and education participation, access, and quality. Retrieved September 23, 2014, from http://www.nccp.org/

Schoppe-Sullivan, S., Mangelsdorf, S., Brown, G., & Szewczyk Sokolowski, M. (2007). Goodness-of-fit in family context: Infant temperament, marital quality, and early coparenting behavior. *Infant Behavior & Development, 30*(1), 82–96.

Schum, T. R., Kolb, T. M., McAuliffe, T. L., Simms, M. D., Underhill, R. L., & Lewis, M. (2002). Sequential acquisition of toilet-training skills: A descriptive study of gender and age differences in normal children. *Pediatrics, 109*(3), e48.

Schwartz, T., & Luckenbill, J. (2012). Let's get messy!: Exploring sensory and art activities with infants and toddlers. *YC: Young Children, 67*(4), 26–34.

Schweinhart, L. (2004). *The High/Scope Perry preschool study through age 40: Summary, conclusions and frequently asked questions* Ypsilanti, MI: High/Scope Press.

Seldenrijk, A., Hamer, M., Lahiri, A., Penninx, B. W. J. H., & Steptoe, A. (2012). Psychological distress, cortisol stress response and subclinical coronary calcification. *Psychoneuroendocrinology, 37*(1), 48–55.

Sewell, T. (2012). Are we adequately preparing teachers to partner with families? *Early Childhood Education Journal, 40*(5), 259–263.

Shaffer, L. F., Hall, E., & Lynch, M. (2009). Toddlers' scientific explorations: Encounters with insects. *YC: Young Children, 64*(6), 18–23.

Shahtahmasebi, S., Emerson, E., Berridge, D., & Lancaster, G. (2011). Child disability and the dynamics of child poverty, hardship and financial strain: Evidence from the UK. *Journal of Social Policy, 40*, pp. 653–673.

Sheehan, E. A., Namy, L. L., & Mills, D. L. (2007). Developmental changes in neural activity to familiar words and gestures. *Brain and Language, 101*(3), 246–259.

Shi, R., & Werker, J. F. (2001). Six-month-old infants' preferences for lexical words. *Psychological Science, 12*(1), 70–75.

Shi, R., & Werker, J. F. (2003). The basis of preference for lexical words in 6-month-old infants. *Developmental Science, 6*(5), 484–488.

Shonkoff, J. P., Garner, A. S., Siegel, B. S., Dobbins, M. I., Earls, M. F., McGuinn Wood, L., et al. (2012). The lifelong effects of early childhood adversity and toxic stress. *Pediatrics, 129*(1), e232–e246.

Shonkoff, J. P., & Phillips, D. A. (Eds.). (2000). *From neurons to neighborhoods: The science of early childhood development*. Washington, DC: National Academy Press.

Shore, R. (2003). *Rethinking the brain: New insights into early development* (Rev. ed.). New York: Families and Work Institute.

Siller, M., Morgan, L., Turner-Brown, L., Baggett, K. M., Baranek, G. T., Brian, J., et al. (2013). Designing studies to evaluate parent-mediated interventions for toddlers with Autism Spectrum Disorder. *Journal of Early Intervention, 35*(4), 355–377.

Simeonova, D. I., Attalla, A. M., Nguyen, T., Stagnaro, E., Knight, B. T., Craighead, W. E., et al. (2014). Temperament and behavior in toddlers of mothers with bipolar disorder: A preliminary investigation of a population at high familial risk for psychopathology. *Journal of Child & Adolescent Psychopharmacology, 24*(10), 543–550.

Simonnet, H., Laurent-Vannier, A., Yuan, W., Hully, M., Valimahomed, S., Bourennane, M., et al. (2014). Parents' behavior in response to infant crying: Abusive head trauma education. *Child Abuse & Neglect, 38*(12), 1914–1922.

Simons, D. A., & Wurtele, S. K. (2010). Relationships between parents' use of corporal punishment and their children's endorsement of spanking and hitting other children. *Child Abuse & Neglect, 34*(9), 639–646.

Simpson, C. G., & McGuire, M. (2004). Are you ready? Supporting children in an uncertain world. *Dimensions of Early Childhood, 32*(3), 35–38.

Singh, L., Nestor, S., Parikh, C., & Yull, A. (2009). Influences of infant-directed speech on early word recognition. *Infancy, 14*(6), 654–666.

Siqveland, T. S., Haabrekke, K., Wentzel-Larsen, T., & Moe, V. (2014). Patterns of mother–infant interaction from 3 to 12 months among dyads with substance abuse and psychiatric problems. *Infant Behavior & Development, 37*(4), 772–786.

Siqveland, T. S., Olafsen, K. S., & Moe, V. (2013). The influence of maternal optimality and infant temperament on parenting stress at 12 months among mothers with substance abuse and psychiatric problems. *Scandinavian Journal of Psychology, 54*, 353–362.

Sivertsen, L., & Sivertsen, J. (2008). *Generation green: The ultimate teen guide to living an eco-friendly life.* New York: Simon Pulse.

Skinner, E. A., & Belmont, M. J. (1993). Motivation in the classroom: Reciprocal effects of teacher behavior and student engagement across the school year. *Journal of Educational Psychology, 85*, 571–581.

Smith, B. J., & Guralnick, M. J. (2007). Early intervention. In R. S. New & M. Cochran (Eds.), *Early Childhood Education: An International Encyclopedia* (pp. 329–332). Westport, CT: Praeger Publishers.

Smith, R. E., Smoll, F. L., & Cumming, S. P. (2007). Effects of a motivational climate intervention for coaches on young athletes' sport performance anxiety. *Journal of Sport & Exercise Psychology, 29*(1), 39–59.

Snider, M. H., & Fu, V. R. (1990). The effects of specialized education and job experience on early childhood teachers' knowledge of developmentally appropriate practice. *Early Childhood Research Quarterly, 5*(1), 69–78.

Solchany, J. (2007). Consequences of divorce in infancy: Three case studies of growth faltering. *Zero to Three, 27*(6), 34–41.

Soncini, I. (2012). The inclusive community. In C. Edwards, L. Gandini, & G. Forman (Eds.), *The hundred languages of children: The Reggio Emilia approach—advanced reflections* (3rd ed., pp. 187–211). Santa Barbara, CA: Praeger.

Southgate, V., van Maanen, C., & Csibra, C. (2007). Infant pointing: Communication to cooperate or communication to learn? *Child Development, 78*(3), 735–740.

Sparks, T. A., Hunter, S. K., Backman, T. L., Morgan, G. A., & Ross, R. G. (2012). Maternal parenting stress and mothers' reports of their infants' mastery motivation. *Infant Behavior & Development, 35*(1), 167–173.

Spencer, N. (2008). *Health consequences of poverty for children.* London: End Child Poverty/GMB. Retrieved January 22, 2015, from http://www .endchildpoverty.org.uk/files/Health_consequences _of_Poverty_for_children.pdf

Spinrad, T. L., Eisenberg, N., Gaertner, B., Popp, T., Smith, C. L., Kupfer, A., et al. (2007). Relations of maternal socialization and toddlers' effortful control to children's adjustment and social competence. *Developmental Psychology, 43*(5), 1170–1186.

Spinrad, T. L., & Stifter, C. A. (2006). Toddlers' empathy-related responding to distress: Predictions from negative emotionality and maternal behavior in infancy. *Infancy, 10*(2), 97–121.

Sridhar, D., & Vaughn, S. (2000). Bibliotherapy for all: Enhancing reading comprehension, self-concept, and behavior. *Teaching Exceptional Children, 33*(2), 74–82.

Stacks, A. M., Oshio, T., Gerard, J., & Roe, J. (2009). The moderating effect of parental warmth on the association between spanking and child aggression: A longitudinal approach. *Infant & Child Development, 18*(2), 178–194.

Stams, G. J., Juffer, F., & van IJzendoorn, M. H. (2002). Maternal sensitivity, infant attachment, and temperament in early childhood predict adjustment in middle childhood: The case of adopted children and their biologically unrelated parents. *Developmental Psychology, 38*, 806–821.

Stenberg, G. (2013). Do 12-month-old infants trust a competent adult? *Infancy, 18*(5), 873–904.

Stern, D. N. (1985). *The interpersonal world of the infant.* New York: Basic Books.

Stern, D. N. (2000). Putting time back into our considerations of infant experience: A microdiachronic view. *Infant Mental Health Journal, 21*(1–2), 21–28.

Stern, D. N. (2008). The clinical relevance of infancy: A progress report. *Infant Mental Health Journal, 29*(3), 177–188.

Stockall, N., Dennis, L. R., & Rueter, J. A. (2014). Developing a progress monitoring portfolio for children in early childhood special education programs. *Teaching Exceptional Children, 46*(3), 32–40.

Stoll, J., Hamilton, A., Oxley, E., Eastman, A. M., & Brent, R. (2012). Young thinkers in motion: Problem solving and physics in preschool. *YC: Young Children, 67*(2), 20–26.

Stovall-McClough, K. C., & Dozier, M. (2004). Forming attachments in foster care: Infant attachment behaviors during the first two months of placement. *Development & Psychopathology, 16*, 253–271.

Straub, S., & Dell'Antonia, K. J. (2006). *Reading with babies, toddlers, and twos: A guide to choosing, reading, and loving books together.* Naperville, IL: Sourcebooks, Inc.

Straus, M. A. (2001). New evidence for the benefits of never spanking. *Society, 38*(6), 52–60.

Strous, M. (2011). Overnights and overkill: Post-divorce contact for infants and toddlers. *South African Journal of Psychology, 41*(2), 196–206.

Sturm, J. M., Cali, K., Nelson, N. W., & Staskowski, M. (2012). The developmental writing scale: A new progress monitoring tool for beginning writers. *Topics in Language Disorders, 32*(4), 297–318.

Sturner, R., Albus, K., Thomas, J., & Howard, B. (2007). A proposed adaptation of DC: 0-3R for primary care, developmental research, and prevention of mental disorders. *Infant Mental Health Journal, 28*(1), 1–11.

Sugiura, M., Sassa, Y., Jeong, H., Horie, K., Sato, S., & Kawashima, R. (2008). Face-specific and domain-general characteristics of cortical responses during self-recognition. *NeuroImage, 42*(1), 414–422.

Sullivan, M. W., Bennett, D. S., Carpenter, K., & Lewis, M. (2008). Emotional knowledge of young neglected children. *Child Maltreatment, 13*(3), 301–306.

Summers, S. J., & Chazan-Cowen R. (2012). *Understanding early childhood mental health: A practical guide for professionals.* Baltimore, MD: Paul Brookes Publishing.

Svetlova, M., Nichols, S. R., & Brownell, C. A. (2010). Toddlers' prosocial behavior: From instrumental to empathic to altruistic helping. *Child Development, 81*(6), 1814–1827.

Swain, N., & Bodkin-Allen, S. (2014). Can't sing? Won't sing? Aotearoa/New Zealand "tone-deaf" early childhood teachers' musical beliefs. *British Journal of Music Education, 31*(3), 245–263.

Swaminathan, S., Alexander, G. R., & Boulet, S. (2006). Delivering a very low birth weight infant and the subsequent risk of divorce or separation. *Maternal Child Health Journal, 10*, 473–479.

Swim, T. J. (1998). Proper procedures: Preventing the spread of disease in infant and toddler classrooms. *Early Childhood News, 10*, 45–47.

Swim, T. J. (2003). Respecting infants and toddlers: Strategies for best practice. *Early Childhood News, 15*(5), 16–17, 20–23.

Swim, T. J. (2012). School readiness and the power of documentation: Changing the public image to see the "rich child." In T. Swim, K. Howard, & I. Kim (Eds.), *The hope for audacity: Recapturing optimism and civility in education* (pp. 63–84). New York: Peter Lang Publishing, Inc.

Swim, T. J. (2014, October). *Rough & tumble play for infants and toddlers: A necessary strategy for supporting optimal development.* Paper presented at the Indiana Infant-Toddler Institute, Indianapolis, IN.

Swim, T. J., & Isik-Ercan, Z. (2013). Dispositional development as a form of continuous professional development: Centre-based reflective practices with teachers of (very) young children. *Early Years: An International Research Journal, 33*(2), 172–185.

Swim, T. J., & Marion, M. (2006, November). *Terrific toddlers! Good relationships build autonomy, self-regulation and emotional intelligence.* Paper accepted for presentation at the National Association for the Education of Young Children Annual Conference and Expo, Atlanta, GA.

Swim, T. J., & Merz, A. H. (in press). Professional dispositions of early childhood educators. In D. Couchenour & J. K. Chrisman (Eds.), *Encyclopedia of contemporary early childhood education.* Thousand Oaks, CA: Sage Publications.

Swim, T. J., & Merz, A. H. (2011). *Deconstructing assessment practices: Are our children "needy" or "rich" in possibilities?* Manuscript submitted for publication.

Swim, T. J., & Muza, R. (1999, Spring). Planning curriculum for infants. *Texas Child Care, 22*(4), 2–7.

Symeou, L., Roussounidou, E., & Michaelides, M. (2012). "I feel much more confident now to talk with parents": An evaluation of in-service training on teacher-parent communication. *School Community Journal, 22*(1), 65–87.

Tamis-LeMonda, C. S., Kuchirko, Y., & Song, L. (2014). Why is infant language learning facilitated by parental responsiveness? *Current Directions in Psychological Science, 23*(2), 121–126.

Tanaka, K., Kon, N., Ohkawa, N., Yoshikawa, N., & Shimizu, T. (2009). Does breastfeeding in the neonatal period influence the cognitive function of very-low-birth-weight infants at 5 years of age? *Brain and Development, 31*(4), 288–293.

Tannock, M. T. (2008). Rough and tumble play: An investigation of the perceptions of educators and young children. *Early Childhood Education Journal, 35*(4), 357–361.

Taylor, N. H. (2008). *Go green: How to build an earth-friendly community.* Layton, UT: Gibbs Smith.

Thomas, A., & Chess, S. (1977). *Temperament and development.* New York: Brunner/Mazel.

Thompson, R. A. (1988). On emotion and self-regulation. In R. A. Thompson (Ed.), *Nebraska symposium on motivation: Vol. 36. Socioemotional development* (pp. 367–468). Lincoln: University of Nebraska Press.

Thompson, R. A. (1998). Early sociopersonality development. In W. Damon (Editor-in-Chief) & N. Eisenberg (Vol. Ed.), *Handbook of child psychology: Vol. 3. Social, emotional, and personality development* (5th ed., pp. 25–104). New York: Wiley.

Thompson, R. A. (2001). The legacy of early attachment. *Child Development, 71*, 145–152.

Thompson, R. A. (2006). Nurturing developing brains, minds, and hearts. In J. R. Lally, P. L. Mangione, &

D. Greenwald (Eds.), *Concepts for care: 20 essays on infant/toddler development and learning* (pp. 47–52). Sausalito, CA: WestEd.

Tomasello, M. (1999). Perceiving intentions and learning words in the second year of life. In M. Bowerman & S. Levinson (Eds.), *Language acquisition and conceptual development* (pp. 132–158). Cambridge, UK: Cambridge University Press.

Tong, L., Shinohara, R., Sugisawa, Y., Tanaka, E., Yato, Y., Yamakawa, N., et al. (2012). Early development of empathy in toddlers: Effects of daily parent–child interaction and home-rearing environment. *Journal of Applied Social Psychology, 42*(10), 2457–2478.

Topal, C. W., & Gandini, L. (1999). *Beautiful stuff: Learning with found materials.* Worcester, MA: Davis.

Trawick-Smith, J. (2010). *Early childhood development: A multicultural perspective* (5th ed.). Upper Saddle River, NJ: Merrill.

Tremblay, R. E., Nagin, D. S., Seguin, J. R., Zoccolillo, M., Zelazo, P. D., Boivin, M., et al. (2004). Physical aggression during early childhood: Trajectories and predictors. *Pediatrics, 114*(1), e43–e50.

Triebenbacher, S. L. (1997). Children's use of transitional objects: Parental attitudes and perceptions. *Child Psychiatry Human Development, 27*(4), 221–230.

Tronick, E. Z., & Cohn, J. F. (1989). Infant-mother face-to-face interaction: Age and gender differences in coordination and the occurrence of miscoordination. *Child Development, 60*, 85–92.

Turner, T., & Krechevsky, M. (2003). Who are the teachers? Who are the learners? *Educational Leadership, 60*(7), 40–43.

Tzur, R., & Lambert, M. A. (2011). Intermediate participatory stages as zone of proximal development correlate in constructing counting-on: A plausible conceptual source for children's transitory "regress" to counting-all. *Journal for Research in Mathematics Education, 42*(5), 418–450.

Uren, L. (2014). Facing austerity: The local authority response. In G. Pugh and B. Duffy (Eds.), *Contemporary issues in the early years* (6th ed., pp. 21–38). London: Sage.

US Food and Drug Administration. (2010). *Triclosan: What consumers should know.* Retrieved September 16, 2011, from http://www.fda.gov/ForConsumers /ConsumerUpdates/ucm205999.htm

Vaala, S. E. (2014). The nature and predictive value of mothers' beliefs regarding infants' and toddlers' TV/video viewing: Applying the integrative model of behavioral prediction. *Media Psychology, 17*(3), 282–310.

Vaala, S. E., Bleakley, A., & Jordan, A. B. (2013). The media environments and television-viewing diets of infants and toddlers. *Zero to Three, 33*(4), 18–24.

Vakil, S., Freeman, R., & Swim, T. J. (2003). The Reggio Emilia approach and inclusive early childhood programs. *Early Childhood Education Journal, 30*(3), 187–192.

Valentino, K., Cicchetti, D., Toth, S. L., & Rogosch, F. A. (2011). Mother–child play and maltreatment: A longitudinal analysis of emerging social behavior from infancy to toddlerhood. *Developmental Psychology, 47*(5), 1280–1294.

Vallotton, C. (2011). Babies open our minds to their minds: How "listening" to infant signs complements and extends our knowledge of infants and their development. *Infant Mental Health Journal, 32*(1), 115–133.

Vallotton, C. D., & Ayoub, C. C. (2010). Symbols build communication and thought: The role of gestures and words in the development of engagement skills and social-emotional concepts during toddlerhood. *Social Development, 19*(3), 601–626.

Vallotton, C. D., & Ayoub, C. C. (2011). Use your words: The role of language in the development of toddlers' self-regulation. *Early Childhood Research Quarterly, 26*, 169–181.

Van Aken, C., Junger, M., Verhoeven, M., Van Aken, M. A. G., & Deković, M. (2007, September). The interactive effects of temperament and maternal parenting on toddlers' externalizing behaviours. *Infant & Child Development, 16*(5), 553–572.

Van Aken, C., Junger, M., Verhoeven, M., Van Aken, M. A. G., Deković, M., & Denissen, J. J. A. (2007). Parental personality, parenting and toddlers' externalising behaviours. *European Journal of Personality, 21*(8), 993–1015.

Van Hoorn, J., Nourot, P. M., Scales, B., & Alward, K. R. (2003). *Play at the center of the curriculum* (3rd ed.). Upper Saddle River, NJ: Merrill Prentice Hall.

Van Horn, M. L., Karlin, E., & Ramey, S. L. (2012). Effects of developmentally appropriate practices on social skills and problem behaviors in 1st through 3rd grades. *Journal of Research in Childhood Education, 26*(1), 18–39.

Van Horn, M. L., Karlin, E. O., Ramey, S. L., Aldridge, J., & Snyder, S. W. (2005). Effects of developmentally appropriate practices on children's development: A review of research and discussion of methodological and analytic issues. *Elementary School Journal, 105*(4), 325–351.

Veríssimo, M., Santos, A. J., Fernandes, C., Shin, N., & Vaughn, B. E. (2014). Associations between attachment security and social competence in preschool children. *Merrill-Palmer Quarterly, 60*(1), 80–99.

Veríssimo, M., Santos, A. J., Vaughn, B. E., Torres, N., Monteiro, L., & Santos, O. (2011). Quality of attachment to father and mother and number of reciprocal friends. *Early Child Development and Care, 181*(1), 27–38.

Vogel, C. A., Bradley, R. H., Raikes, H. H., Boller, K., & Shears, J. K. (2006). Relation between father connectedness and child outcomes. *Parenting: Science and Practice, 6*(2/3), 189–209.

Volling, B. L., Herrera, C., & Poris, M. P. (2004). Situational affect and temperament: Implications for sibling caregiving. *Infant and Child Development, 13*, 173–183.

Vos, B., Lagassea, R., & Levêquea, A. (2014). Main outcomes of a newborn hearing screening program in Belgium over six years. *International Journal of Pediatric Otorhinolaryngology, 78*(9), 1496–1502.

Vukelich, C., Christie, J., & Enz, B. (2012). *Helping young children learn language and literacy: Birth through kindergarten* (3rd ed.). Boston, MA: Pearson.

Vygotsky, L. S. (1978). *Mind in society: The development of higher psychological processes* (M. Cole, V. John-Steiner, S. Scribner, & E. Souberman, Trans.). Cambridge, MA: Harvard University Press.

Vygotsky, L. S. (1986). *Thought and language* (A. Kozulin, Trans.). Cambridge, MA: MIT Press. (Original work published 1934.)

Wadsworth, B. J. (1978). *Piaget for the classroom teacher.* New York: Longman.

Waibel, R., & Misra, R. (2003). Injuries to preschool children and infection control practices in childcare programs. *Journal of School Health, 73*(5), 167–172.

Walker, C. M., & Gopnik, A. (2014). Toddlers infer higher-order relational principles in causal learning. *Psychological Science, 25*(1), 161–169.

Walsh, D. (2007). *No: Why kids-of all ages-need to hear it and ways parents can say it.* New York: Free Press.

Wang, J., Morgan, G. A., & Biringen, Z. (2014). Mother–toddler affect exchanges and children's mastery behaviours during preschool years. *Infant and Child Development, 23*(2), 139–152.

Wanless, S. B., Rosenkoetter, S. E., & McClelland, M. M. (2008). Paternal depression and infant cognitive development: Implications for research and intervention. *Infants and Young Children, 21*(2), 134–141.

Ward, K. S. (2013). Creative arts-based pedagogies in early childhood education for sustainability (EfS): Challenges and possibilities. *Australian Journal of Environmental Education, 29*(2), 165–181.

Warneken, F., & Tomasello, M. (2008). Extrinsic rewards undermine altruistic tendencies in 20-month-olds. *Developmental Psychology, 44*(6), 1785–1788.

Warren, H. K., Denham, S. A., & Bassett, H. H. (2008). The emotional foundations of social understanding. *Zero to Three, 28*(5), 32–39.

Warren, H. K., & Stifter, C. A. (2008). Maternal emotion-related socialization and preschoolers' developing emotion self-awareness. *Social Development, 17*(2), 239–258.

Washington, V. (2008). *Role, relevance, reinvention: Higher education in the field of early care and education.* Boston, MA: Wheelock College.

Watson, L. R., Baranek, G. T., & DiLavore, P. C. (2003). Toddlers with autism: Developmental perspectives. *Infants and Young Children, 16*(3), 201–214.

Weber, D. S., & Singer, D. G. (2004). The media habits of infants and toddlers: Findings from a parent survey. *Zero to Three, 25*(1), 30–36.

Weber, R. B., Grobe, D., & Davis, E. E. (2014). Does policy matter? The effect of increasing child care subsidy policy generosity on program outcomes. *Children & Youth Services Review, 44*, 135–144.

Weishaar, P. M. (2010). What's new in…. Twelve ways to incorporate strengths-based planning into the IEP process. *The Clearing House, 83*, 207–210.

Wellhousen, K., & Giles, R. M. (2005/2006). Building literacy opportunities into children's block play: What every teacher should know. *Childhood Education, 82*(2), 74–78.

Werner, N. E., Eaton, A. D., Lyle, K., Tseng, H., & Holst, B. (2014). Maternal social coaching quality interrupts the development of relational aggression during early childhood. *Social Development, 23*(3), 470–486.

Westby, C., & Wilson, D. (2007, August). *Children's play: The roots of language and literacy development.* Paper presented at the 27th World Congress of the International Association of Logopedics and Phoniatrics, Copenhagen, Denmark.

Wetherby, A. M., Brosnan-Maddox, S., Peace, V., & Newton, L. (2008). Validation of the infant—toddler checklist as a broadband screener for autism spectrum disorders from 9 to 24 months of age. *Autism: The International Journal of Research & Practice, 12*(5), 487–511.

Whalley, K. (2008). Dabbling in babbling. *Nature Reviews Neuroscience, 9*(6), 411.

Wheeler, B. L., & Stultz, S. (2008). Using typical infant development to inform music therapy with children with disabilities. *Early Childhood Education Journal, 35*, 585–591.

Wheeler, R., Ludtke, M., Helmer, J., Barna, N., Wilson, K., & Oleksiak, C. (2013). Implementation of the PICCOLO in infant mental health practice: A case study. *Infant Mental Health Journal, 34*(4), 352–358.

White, B., Swim, T. J., Freeman, R., & Norton-Smith, L. (2007). *Powerful infants and toddlers: Provocations and dialogue with preverbal children.* Paper presented at the National Association for the Education of Young Children Annual Conference, Chicago, IL.

Whiteman, J. (2013). Connecting with families: Tips for those difficult conversations. *YC: Young Children, 68*(1), 94–95.

Whitington, V., Thompson, C., & Shore, S. (2014). "Time to ponder": Professional learning in early childhood education. *Australasian Journal of Early Childhood, 39*(1), 65–72.

Wien, C. A. (2008). Toward a "Good-Enough" theory of emergent curriculum. In C.A. Wein (Ed.), *Emergent curriculum in the primary classroom: Interpreting the Reggio Emilia approach in schools* (pp. 144–161). New York: Teachers College Press.

Wien, C. A., Coates, A., Keating, B., & Bigelow, B. C. (2005, May). Designing the environment to build connection to place. *Beyond the Journal: Young Children on the Web*. Retrieved January 9, 2007, from https://www.naeyc.org/files/yc /file/200505/05Wien.pdf

Wien, C. A., Guyevskey, V., & Berdoussis, N. (2011). Learning to document in Reggio-inspired education. *Early Childhood Research and Practice, 13*(2). Retrieved January 19, 2015, from http://ecrp.uiuc .edu/v13n2/wien.html

Willerton, E., Schwarz, R. L., MacDermid Wadsworth, S. M., & Oglesby, M. S. (2011). Military fathers' perspectives on involvement. *Journal of Family Psychology, 25*(4), 521–530.

Williams, D. S., & Rose, T. (2007). I say hello; you say good-bye: When babies are born while fathers are away. *Zero to Three, 27*(6), 13–19.

Williams, M., & Rask, H. (2003). Literacy through play: How families with able children support their literacy development. *Early Child Development and Care, 173*(5), 527–533.

Williamson, R. A., Donohue, M. R., & Tully, E. C. (2013). Learning how to help others: Two-year-olds' social learning of a prosocial act. *Journal of Experimental Child Psychology, 114*(4), 543–550.

Wink, J., & Putney, L. (2002). *A vision of Vygotsky.* Boston, MA: Allyn & Bacon.

Winsler, A., Abar, B., Feder, M., Schunn, C., & Rubio, D. (2007). Private speech and executive functioning among high-functioning children with Autistic Spectrum Disorder. *Journal of Autism & Developmental Disorders, 37*(9), 1617–1635.

Winsler, A., Manfra, L., & Diaz, R. M. (2007). "Should I let them talk?": Private speech and task performance among preschool children with and without behavior problems. *Early Childhood Research Quarterly, 22*(2), 215–231.

Winsler, A., Naglieri, J., & Manfra, L. (2006). Children's search strategies and accompanying verbal and motor strategic behavior: Developmental trends and relations with task performance among children age 5 to 17. *Cognitive Development, 21*(3), 232–248.

Wittmer, D. (2012). The wonder and complexity of infant and toddler peer relationships. *YC: Young Children, 67*(4), 16–25.

World Health Organization. (2011). *World report on disability*. Retrieved January 22, 2015, from http://apps.who.int/iris/handle/10665/44575

Worley, D., Titsworth, S., Worley, D. W., & Cornett-DeVito, M. (2007). Instructional communication competence: Lessons learned from award-winning teachers. *Communication Studies, 2*(58), 207–222.

Worobey, J., & Islas-Lopez, M. (2009). Temperament measures of African-American infants: Change and convergence with age. *Early Child Development & Care, 179*(1), 107–112.

Wright, A. C., & Taylor, S. (2014). Advocacy by parents of young children with special needs: Activities, processes, and perceived effectiveness. *Journal of Social Service Research, 40*(5), 591–605.

Wurm, J. (2005). *Working in the Reggio way: A beginner's guide for American teachers*. St. Paul, MN: Redleaf Press.

Wyss, N. M., Kannass, K. N., & Haden, C. A. (2013). The effects of distraction on cognitive task performance during toddlerhood. *Infancy, 18*(4), 604–628.

Xu, F. (2013). The object concept in human infants. *Human Development, 56*(3), 167–170.

Yamazaki, J., Yoshida, M., & Mizunuma, H. (2014). Experimental analyses of the retinal and subretinal haemorrhages accompanied by shaken baby syndrome/abusive head trauma using a dummy doll. *Injury, 45*(8), 1196–1206.

Ybarra, G. Y., Passman, R. H., & Eisenberg, C. S. L. (2000). The presence of security blankets or mothers (or both) affects distress during pediatric examinations. *Journal of Consulting and Clinical Psychology, 68*(2), 322–330.

Yeary, J. (2007). Operation parenting edge: Promoting resiliency through prevention. *Zero to Three, 27*(6), 7–12.

Yeary, J., Zoll, S., & Reschke, K. (2012). When a parent is away: Promoting strong parent-child connections during parental absence. *Zero to Three, 32*(5), 5–10.

Yong, M. H., & Ruffman, T. (2014). Emotional contagion: Dogs and humans show a similar physiological response to human infant crying. *Behavioural Processes, 108*, 155–165.

Yoon, P. O., Ang, R. P., Fung, D. S. S., Wong, G., & Yiming, C. (2006). The impact of parent-child attachment on aggression, social stress and self-esteem. *School Psychology International, 27*(5), 552–566.

Youngquist, J. (2004). From medicine to microbes: A project investigation of health. *YC: Young Children, 59*(2), 28–32.

Zahner, W., & Moschkovich, J. N. (2010). Talking while computing in groups: The not-so-private functions of computational private speech in mathematical discussions. *Mind, Culture, and Activity, 17*, 265–283.

Zane, L. (2015). *Pedagogy and space: Design Inspirations for Early Childhood Classrooms*. St. Paul, MN: Redleaf Press.

Zeece, P. D., & Churchill, S. L. (2001). First stories: Emergent literacy in infants and toddlers. *Early Childhood Education Journal, 29*(2), 101–104.

Zero to Three. (2012). *Early experiences matter: Frequently asked questions*. Retrieved January 10, 2012, from http://main.zerotothree.org/site/PageServer?pagename=ter_key_brainFAQ#changes

Zmyj, N., Prinz, W., & Daum, M. M. (2013). The relation between mirror self-image reactions and imitation in 14- and 18-month-old infants. *Infant Behavior & Development, 36*(4), 809–816.

Glossary

A

accommodation Piaget's process of changing or altering skills to better fit the requirements of a task.

accreditation Process of demonstrating and validating the presence of indicators of quality as set out by national standards.

active listening The skill required to simply "feed back" the deeper felt message (not words) of the sender in the words of the receiver.

adaptation A change in behavior that helps the child survive in his or her environment; described by Piaget as a cognitive skill.

alert times Times during the day when a child is attending and attracted to the world around him or her.

ambivalent attachment A form of connection between infant and primary caregiver in which the infant simultaneously seeks and resists emotionally and physically connecting with the caregiver. The term **resistant** can be used to describe the same types of attachment behaviors.

anecdotal record A brief narrative account of one event written using descriptive language.

anti-biased curriculum An approach to curriculum development that involves directly addressing issues of identity, fairness, diversity, prejudice, and discrimination through critical thinking and taking action.

approval One of the three *A*s of child care; feedback that a person is accepted as he or she is.

assimilation Piaget's way of explaining how children refine cognitive structures into schemes.

attachment theory A theory that infants are born needing an emotional attachment to their primary caregiver.

attention One of the three *A*s of child care; focusing sensory modalities (e.g., visual, auditory) on a specific child.

attunement One of the three *A*s of child care; feedback that is *in tune with* or responsive to the behaviors or moods being currently displayed by the child.

avoidant attachment One of the types of attachment between infants and primary caregiver that is related to inconsistent and insensitive caregiver attention.

B

babble Prelanguage speech with which the baby explores the variety of sounds.

behaviorism School of psychology that studies stimuli, responses, and rewards that influence behavior.

bi-generational services When services are provided to adults and children through the same program, often at the same time.

bias A prejudgment concerning the style and forms of a specific culture.

bibliotherapy Reading books to toddlers with the goal of assisting them in solving life problems, gaining important socioemotional skills, and knowing how to behave with peers.

brain plasticity When one part of the brain is damaged, other parts take over the functions of the damaged parts.

C

calibrating Carefully observing the specific behaviors demonstrated by another during an interaction to build rapport.

caring community of learners One of the five guidelines for developmentally appropriate practice which focuses on creating a classroom context that supports the development of caring, inclusive relationships for everyone involved.

cause and effect In sensorimotor development, observation allows a child to identify the relationship between an action and its effect.

checklist A method for recording observational data that notes the presence of specific predetermined skills or behaviors.

Child Development Associate (CDA) A credential provided by the Council for Early Childhood Professional Recognition when a person has provided evidence of meeting the national standards for caregiver performance.

choke tube Plastic tube used to determine safe sizes of objects for child play.

cognitive constructivism Theory that describes learning as the active construction of knowledge.

Humans organize information about their experiences and therefore construct understanding based on their interactions with materials and people in their environment. This is also referred to as individual constructivism.

cognitive developmental theory Piaget's theory that children construct knowledge and awareness through manipulation and exploration of their environment.

consequences The natural and/or logical outcomes of actions.

continuity of care Having the same teachers work with the same group of children and families for more than one year, ideally for three years.

coo A vocalization typically produced by infants from birth to 4 months old that resembles vowel-like sounds.

crawling Strategy for mobility where the infant or toddler moves on hands and knees while using arms and legs in opposition.

creeping Strategy for moving the body through space that involves infants pulling their body with their arms or sometimes pushing with the legs to help move.

culture Values and beliefs held in common by a group of people.

curriculum Everything that occurs during the course of the day with infants and toddlers; planned learning experiences and routine care.

D

daily communication log A log for communicating with family members that covers routine care events such as eating, sleeping, toileting, and other.

daily plans An approach to curriculum in which planned learning experiences are designed daily based on specific observations of the children.

deferred imitation Imitation of another person's behavior even when that person is no longer present.

demand feeding Providing solid or liquid foods when an infant or toddler is hungry.

descriptive phrasing A technique for reporting observations that involves using words or phrases to describe observable behaviors.

development Operationally defined as general sequences and patterns of growth and maturity.

developmental delay A child who is experiencing a delay as defined by the state in which he or she resides and as measured by appropriate diagnostic instruments in one or more of the following

areas: physical development, cognitive development, communication development, social or emotional development, or adaptive development.

developmentally appropriate practice Process of making educational decisions about the well-being and education of young children based on information or knowledge about child development and learning; the needs, interests, and strengths of each individual child in the group; and the social and cultural contexts in which the individual children live.

disabled children Children who are treated differently because of an individual impairment.

disability A dynamic interaction between individual impairment and the social effects of impairment as a consequence of environmental, social, and attitudinal barriers that prevent people with impairments from maximum participation in society. Examples of disabling barriers include buildings without ramps or lifts, discriminatory attitudes, segregated education, and inadequate health care.

discipline (1) Approach to teaching appropriate behavior and setting limits on inappropriate behavior; (2) the ability to focus on an activity in the face of obstacles to reach a desired outcome.

disequilibrium An internal mental state that motivates learning because the child is uncomfortable and seeks to make sense of what he or she has observed or experienced.

disoriented attachment A form of attachment between infant and primary caregiver in which the infant has usually been traumatized by severe or prolonged abandonment.

disposition Frequent and voluntary habits of thinking and doing that represent a particular orientation to the work and responsibilities of teaching.

documentation panel A visual and written explanation of children's learning displayed to others (family members, children, colleagues, and/or community members).

dramatic play A form of play that provides opportunities to combine language with imagination.

E

early intervention Comprehensive services for infants and toddlers who have special rights or are at risk of acquiring a disability. Services may include education, health care, and/or social and psychological assistance.

ecological systems theory Bronfenbrenner's theory of nested environmental systems that influence the development and behavior of people.

emergent curriculum Devising curricular experiences based on previous observations of the children's interests, needs, and questions.

emotion-centered Children's emotions are viewed as natural, valid, and an important part of the curriculum.

emotional contagion The process through which infants and other humans "catch" emotions from those they are around.

emotional intelligence Skills learned early in life that are necessary for healthy emotional development, good relationships, and fulfillment in life experiences.

emotional regulation Learning to control and manage strong emotions in a socially and culturally acceptable manner.

emotional talk Labeling feeling states to help young children understand their emotions and how they are expressing them.

empathy Sensitivity to what others feel, need, or want; the fundamental relationship skill present at birth.

enlightened self-interest The skill of balancing awareness of one's own needs and feelings with the needs and feelings of other people.

equilibration The movement from equilibrium to disequilibrium and back to equilibrium again.

equilibrium A state of homeostasis or balance that reflects how an infant's or toddler's current cognitive schemes work to explain his or her environment.

exosystem Bronfenbrenner's term for the influences that are not a direct part of a child's experience but influence development, such as parent education.

experience-dependent Type of motor neuron pathway that waits for environmental experiences before being activated.

experience-expectant Type of motor neuron pathway that apparently expects specific stimuli at birth.

F

family capacity-building When professionals work in close collaboration with families to uncover each family members' goals and wishes for the child. Then, strategies are designed for the everyday routine and activities so that parents are able to improve their lives and the daily lives of their child.

family-caregiver conferences Periodic meetings between family members and caregiver to review documentation and interpretation of each child's developmental progress as well as to create plans for supporting development in the future.

family grouping Method for grouping children where children are of different ages.

fine motor control The ability to control small muscles such as those in the hands and fingers.

finger foods Foods that older infants and toddlers can easily feed to themselves such as crackers or dry cereal.

forebrain The portion of the brain that contains the cerebral cortex, which produces all of our complex thoughts, emotional responses, decision-making, reasoning, and communicating.

G

goodness-of-fit The temperamental match between very young children and their caregivers.

grammatical words Function words that have little meaning on their own yet affect the meaning of other words (e.g., articles, prepositions, or conjunctions).

gross motor control The control of large muscles.

H

hemiparesis Slight paralysis or weakness affecting one side of the body.

hindbrain The portion of the brain responsible for regulating automatic functions and emotional knowledge; contains the cerebellum, which controls motor movement coordination and muscle tone.

home-school journal A notebook or journal in which teachers and family members write notes about key happenings and which they send back and forth on a daily or weekly basis.

home visit A meeting in the child's home providing an opportunity for the caregiver to see how the family members and child relate to each other in the home setting.

human immunodeficiency virus (HIV) infection Immune disease that attacks white blood cells and is transmitted through open sores or other bodily fluid sources.

I

IDEA Federal law in the United States that provides rights and protections for a free and appropriate public education to all children, aged 3–21. *Part C* outlines provisions for infants, toddlers, and their families.

image of the child Beliefs about children that teachers hold; these beliefs are examined for how they impact teacher-child interactions, management of the environment, and selection of teaching strategies.

impairment A medical condition, diagnosis, or description of functioning that could be related to a difficulty with physical, sensory, cognitive/communicative, adaptive, or socioemotional functioning. Examples of impairment include cerebral palsy, deafness, learning difficulties, speech and language difficulties, and depression.

inclusive practices The act of educating and providing supports and services to disabled children in settings with their nondisabled peers.

individual constructivism Piaget's belief that each person individually creates new understandings, interpretations, and realities through interactions with materials, equipment, and people in their environment. This is also referred to as cognitive constructivism.

infant-directed speech Exaggerated intonation, reduced speech rate, and shorter utterance duration used when speaking to infants. In the past, other terms used to describe the same speech patterns were child-directed speech, motherese, or parentese.

infant mental health The capacity to regulate and express emotions, form secure attachments, and explore the environment and learn. These skills develop in the context of family and community. Infant mental health is synonymous with healthy social and emotional development from birth to age 3.

inquiry Asking and answering questions as well as solving problems that arise as the result of investigations or unexpected outcomes.

inserimento A period of gradual "settling in" or "transition and adjustment" that includes strategies for building relationships and community among adults and children when the child is first entering a Reggio Emilia–inspired child care program.

integrated project Curriculum approach where ideas are carried from one day to another as a mechanism for developing important dispositions and knowledge.

interactional synchrony A sensitively tuned "emotional dance," in which interactions are mutually rewarding to caregiver and infant.

interpretive phrasing A form of reporting that makes judgments without providing observable data to justify the conclusions.

intersubjectivity Vygotsky's term to explain how children and adults come to understand each other by adjusting perceptions to fit the other person's map of the world.

I statements Expressions about one's own thoughts and feelings without judging the other person.

J

jargon Language term that refers to the mixing of one real word with strings of babble.

L

language explosion The time during which toddlers experience a rapid growth in the size of their vocabulary and can use those words to converse.

learning The acquisition of new information through experiences, investigation, or interactions with another.

learning center A particular part of the environment where materials and equipment are organized to promote and encourage a specific type of learning, for example, music or science.

lexical words Words that have a concrete or abstract connection to objects or events (e.g., nouns, verbs, and adverbs).

licensing regulations Official rules on teacher-child ratios, safety, health, and zoning that an individual or organization must follow to be granted a license to provide care for children.

limbic system The system responsible for emotional control, emotional responses, hormonal secretions, mood, motivation, and pain/pleasure sensations.

limits Positively worded statements about desired or acceptable behavior that help children acquire appropriate behaviors for a particular setting.

locomotion The attempt to gain stability when moving forward or upwards (e.g., crawling and walking) against the force of gravity.

locus of control The extent to which a person perceives his or her life as within his or her own control.

M

macrosystem Bronfenbrenner's term for influences on development from the general culture, including laws and customs.

make-believe play Vygotsky's term for using imagination to act out internal concepts of how the world functions and how rules are formed.

manipulation Includes reaching, grasping, and releasing objects; in the first year of development, the control of objects moves from reflexive to voluntary.

mastery climate Adults create a context that focuses on self-improvement, effort, persistence, and task mastery by providing challenging tasks.

mental images Pictures in the mind with which children can carry out action sequences internally.

mesosystem Bronfenbrenner's term for the second level of influence for the child that involves interactions among microsystems, such as a teacher in a child care center and family members.

microsystem Bronfenbrenner's term for the innermost level of influence found in the immediate surroundings of the child, such as parents or an early childhood educator.

midbrain The portion of the brain that controls visual system reflexes, auditory functions, and voluntary motor functions; connects the hindbrain to the forebrain.

milestones Specific behaviors common to an entire population that are used to track development and are observed when they are first or consistently manifested.

mixed early child development intervention Intervention which includes a mix of approaches that can be center-based and home-based and/or directed at both children and parents.

motivation An internal drive that moves someone to action.

multidisciplinary Intervention teams that are comprised of professionals from two or more separate disciplines or professions working in partnership with the child and his or her family.

muscular control Gaining conscious control over muscles so that behaviors such as reaching, grabbing, and releasing can occur when the infant or toddler wants them to.

N

National Association for Family Child Care (NAFCC) An association offering professional recognition and distinction to family child care providers whose services represent high-quality child care.

National Association for the Education of Young Children (NAEYC) Professional organization that offers professional resources and development for early childhood educators, as well as recognition for programs that represent high-quality care.

natural environments Legal requirement that EI must be provided in settings that are natural or typical for a nondisabled infant or toddler to the maximum extent appropriate.

normative approach Observing large numbers of children to establish average or normal expectations of when a particular skill or ability is present.

O

object permanence The understanding that people and objects exist even if they are currently out of sight.

omnipotent The sense of being unaware of any physical limitations and feeling above physical laws.

organization A process of rearranging new sets of information (schemes) and linking them to other established schemes, resulting in an expanded cognitive system.

overgeneralize The use of one word to mean many different things.

overregularization Strategy of applying one standard grammatical rule to an irregular word, for example, "goed" for the past tense of "go."

P

pacing Matching complementary behavior to that of another person to build rapport.

parallel play Type of play in which older infants and toddlers engage with similar materials and share physical space but do not interact with one another.

partnerships Alliances with family and community members to support and enhance the well-being and learning of young children.

perspective-taking Acquiring the skills for recognizing and responding to the perspectives of others; not a skill to be expected of infants and toddlers, but the foundations for skills should be set.

philosophy Set of educational beliefs that guide behaviors and decision-making for individual teachers and groups of teachers (e.g., programs).

phonologic awareness The conscious attention to the sounds of spoken language.

phonology Understanding the basic sounds of the language and how they are combined to make words.

pincer grasp The physical skill of using the thumb and pointer finger to grasp objects.

planned experiences Curricular experiences designed to enhance and support the individual learning needs, interests, and abilities of the children in an early childhood program.

portfolio Tool for collecting, storing, and documenting what you know about a child and her development and learning.

positive attitude An aspect of self-esteem whereby children make conscious positive statements to themselves about their own value and self-worth.

positive self-talk The internalization of positive messages we hear about ourselves from others.

pragmatics An understanding of how to engage in communication with others that is socially acceptable and effective.

preconceptual The first substage of Piaget's preoperational stage of cognitive development, in which children can mentally sort some objects and actions.

preoperational stage Piaget's second stage of cognitive development, during which toddlers and preschoolers reason based on perception.

primary caregiving system Method of organizing work in which one teacher is primarily responsible for half of the children, and the other teacher is primarily responsible for the rest.

private speech Vygotsky's term for internal dialogue that children use for self-guidance and understanding.

productive communication Using actions to express messages to others. Infants progress from using noises, cries, and gestures to using babbling and words.

professional capital Assets that add to the long-term worth of each professional and the education profession; comprised of human, social, and decisional capital.

progettazione Italian term that is loosely translated as "flexible planning."

project An ongoing investigation that provokes infants, toddlers, and teachers to construct knowledge.

prosocial behavior Spontaneous communications and behaviors on the part of an infant or toddler that benefit others.

prosodic patterning Communication strategy in which toddlers learn how to use the appropriate stress and intonation to express their specific ideas.

prune The elimination of neural pathways that are not consistently used.

psychosocial theory Erikson's stage theory of development, including trust, autonomy, identity, and intimacy.

R

rapport An agreement between two people that establishes a sense of harmony.

rating scale Method of recording observational data similar to checklists, but that lists frequencies (e.g., never, seldom, always) or qualities of characteristics or activities (e.g., eats using fingers, eats using spoon, eats using fork).

reflexes Automatic responses that are present at birth.

resistant attachment A form of connection between infant and primary caregiver in which the infant simultaneously seeks and resists emotionally and physically connecting with the caregiver. The term **ambivalent** can be used to describe the same types of attachment behaviors.

respect A feeling of high regard for someone and a willingness to treat him or her accordingly.

rights of children The belief that children do not just have needs for adults to deal with but rather rights to appropriate care and education.

role playing When children represent their ideas by acting them out using props such as puppets, dolls, or other dramatic play materials.

routine care times Devoting attention to the developmental needs of children while attending to their biological needs. For example, using diapering times as opportunities for building relationships with a child and not just meeting her need to be clean.

running record A long narrative account of a significant period of time for a child, a group, or an activity written using descriptive language.

S

scaffolding A term describing incremental steps in learning and development from simple to complex.

schemes Piaget's concept to explain cognitive patterns of actions used to learn new information.

scribbling Nonsense writing marks that are a precursor to writing.

scripts A method or sequence of events to learn more about each family's cultural beliefs and values regarding the various aspects of child rearing.

secure attachment A connection between infant and primary caregiver in which the infant feels safe and responds warmly to the caregiver.

self-awareness Sensory-grounded information regarding one's existence; what a person sees, hears, and feels in the body related to self.

self-esteem Personal judgment of worthiness based on an evaluation of having, or not, particular valued characteristics or abilities.

self-recognition Conscious awareness of self as different from others and the environment; occurs first usually between 9 and 15 months of age.

self-regulation The skills necessary to direct and control one's own behavior in socially and culturally appropriate ways.

self-responsibility Taking over responsibility for fulfilling some of one's own needs.

self-soothing Comforting and making oneself at ease.

semantics The study of meaning in language, including concepts.

sensorimotor stage Piaget's first stage of cognitive development, which is focused on motor activity and coordination of movements.

separation-individuation The process of defining self as separate from others, which starts in infancy and continues throughout childhood.

separation anxiety Fear exhibited at the loss of physical or emotional connection with the primary caregiver.

seriation Ordering items in sequence based on criteria such as color, length, or size (e.g., small, medium, large).

shaken baby syndrome Damage that occurs when a baby or child is violently shaken by an adult or older child.

social learning theories A body of theory that adds social influences to behaviorism to explain development.

sociocultural theory Vygotsky's theory on development that predicts how cultural values, beliefs, and concepts are passed from one generation to the next.

solitary play Playing alone; a child may look at other children and play near them, but children do not yet interact.

special education Specifically designed instruction provided to children over the age of 3 with an impairment, disability, or developmental delay at no cost to the parents and in all settings (e.g., the classroom, physical education facilities, the home, and hospitals or institutions).

special needs A deficit model that focuses on what children are not able to do, their limitations, or what they need, oftentimes to the exclusion of their strengths or abilities.

special rights A credit or strength-based model in which all children have rights, including disabled children who have special educational rights.

specialist or specialized interventions Long-term, systematic services that are provided to children or families with acute, complex, or very high-level needs who would otherwise be at great risk.

stages Normal patterns of development that most people go through in maturation, first described by Jean-Jacques Rousseau.

stranger anxiety Fear exhibited by older toddlers around 9 months of age toward people who are

different or unknown; demonstrates their growing cognitive abilities.

symbolic play Children's symbolic representations of objects, feelings, or ideas.

synchrony See **interactional synchrony**.

syntax How words combine into understandable phrases and sentences.

T

targeted interventions Programs that target specific families or communities who are experiencing greater levels of difficulty or stress and need additional support.

telegraphic speech When infants and toddlers combine two or three words into a sentence including only key words (e.g., "go daddy").

temperament Physical, emotional, and social personality traits and characteristics.

time and event sampling techniques Strategies for quickly recording events or behaviors that you are interested in tracking.

toilet learning The developmental process for gaining control of bladder and bowels; complex process involving physical, cognitive, social, emotional, and language skills.

U

universal precautions Medical term for a series of standard procedures used to keep the patient and staff as healthy and safe as possible during physical care.

universal services Programs that are routinely available to all children and their families to promote children's healthy development.

W

weekly plans Approach to curriculum where experiences are planned on a weekly basis based on specific observations of the children.

Y

you statements Sentences that give advice to or judgment about another person, often closing off further communication.

Z

zone of proximal development Vygotsky's term for a range of tasks that a child is developmentally ready to learn.

Index

Infants and Toddlers

CAREGIVING AND RESPONSIVE CURRICULUM DEVELOPMENT Ninth Edition

Standards Correlation Chart

The following chart is intended to help students and instructors easily see the correlation between chapter content and professionally recognized standards and practices from 2010 NAEYC Standards for Initial & Advanced Early Childhood Professional Preparation Programs and NAEYC's Developmentally Appropriate Practice (DAP) guidelines adopted in 2009.

	naeyc 2010 NAEYC Standards for Initial & Advanced Early Childhood Professional Preparation Programs	DAP NAEYC's Developmentally Appropriate Practices (2009)
PART 1 Understanding the Foundations of Professional Education		
Chapter 1 Taking a Developmental Perspective	1: Promoting Child Development and Learning	1: Creating a Caring Community of Learners
Chapter 2 Physical and Cognitive/ Language Development	1: Promoting Child Development and Learning	2: Teaching to Enhance Development and Learning
Chapter 3 Social and Emotional Development	1: Promoting Child Development and Learning	2: Teaching to Enhance Development and Learning
Chapter 4 Attachment and the Three *A*s	1: Promoting Child Development and Learning 4: Using Developmentally Effective Approaches	2: Teaching to Enhance Development and Learning
Chapter 5 Professional Preparation and Tools	3: Observing, Documenting, and Assessing 6: Becoming a Professional	4: Assessing Children's Development and Learning
PART 2 Establishing a Positive Learning Environment		
Chapter 6 Building Relationships and Guiding Behaviors	1: Promoting Child Development and Learning 4: Using Developmentally Effective Approaches	1: Creating a Caring Community of Learners
Chapter 7 Supportive Communication with Families and Colleagues	2: Building Family and Community Relationships 6: Becoming a Professional	5: Establishing Reciprocal Relationships with Families

(continued)

(continued)

	naeyc 2010 NAEYC Standards for Initial & Advanced Early Childhood Professional Preparation Programs	**DAP** NAEYC's Developmentally Appropriate Practices (2009)
Chapter 8 The Indoor and Outdoor Learning Environments	1: Promoting Child Development and Learning	1: Creating a Caring Community of Learners 2: Teaching to Enhance Development and Learning
Chapter 9 Designing the Curriculum	1: Promoting Child Development and Learning	2: Teaching to Enhance Development and Learning 3: Planning Curriculum to Achieve Important Goals
PART 3 Developing Responsive Curriculum		
Chapter 10 Early Intervention	1: Promoting Child Development and Learning	2: Teaching to Enhance Development and Learning
Chapter 11 Teaching Children from Birth to Twelve Months	1: Promoting Child Development and Learning	2: Teaching to Enhance Development and Learning 3: Planning Curriculum to Achieve Important Goals
Chapter 12 Teaching Children from Twelve to Twenty-Four Months	1: Promoting Child Development and Learning 4: Using Developmentally Effective Approaches to Connect with Children and Families	2: Teaching to Enhance Development and Learning 3: Planning Curriculum to Achieve Important Goals
Chapter 13 Teaching Children from Twenty-Four to Thirty-Six Months	1: Promoting Child Development and Learning	2: Teaching to Enhance Development and Learning 3: Planning Curriculum to Achieve Important Goals
Chapter 14 Developmentally Appropriate Content	5: Using Content Knowledge	2: Teaching to Enhance Development and Learning 3: Planning Curriculum to Achieve Important Goals

Sources: National Association for the Education of Young Children (NAEYC). (2011). *2010 NAEYC standards for initial & advanced early childhood professional preparation programs*. Washington, DC: Author. Retrieved August 24, 2011, from http://www.naeyc.org/ncate/standards.

Copple, C., & Bredekamp, S. (Eds.) (2009). Developmentally Appropriate Practice in Early Childhood Programs Serving Children From Birth Through Age 8 (3rd ed.) Washington, DC: National Association for the Education of Young Children.